Christian Czarnecki, Peter Fettke (Eds.)
Robotic Process Automation

Also of Interest

Machine Learning and Visual Perception
Baochang Zhang, 2020
ISBN 978-3-11-059553-6, e-ISBN (PDF) 978-3-11-059556-7
e-ISBN (EPUB) 978-3-11-059322-8

Personalized Human-Computer Interaction
Edited by: Mirjam Augstein, Eelco Herder, Wolfgang Wörndl, 2019
ISBN 978-3-11-055247-8, e-ISBN (PDF) 978-3-11-055248-5
e-ISBN (EPUB) 978-3-11-055261-4

De Gruyter Series on the Applications of Mathematics in Engineering and Information Sciences
Edited by: Mangey Ram
ISSN 2626-5427, e-ISSN 2626-5435

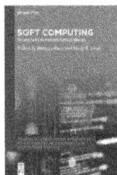

Soft Computing
Techniques in Engineering Sciences
Edited by: Mangey Ram, Suraj B. Singh, 2020
ISBN 978-3-11-062560-8, e-ISBN (PDF) 978-3-11-062861-6
e-ISBN (EPUB) 978-3-11-062571-4

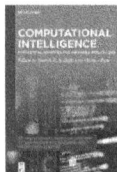

Computational Intelligence
Theoretical Advances and Advanced Applications
Edited by: Dinesh C.S. Bisht, Mangey Ram, 2020
ISBN 978-3-11-065524-7, e-ISBN (PDF) 978-3-11-067135-3
e-ISBN (EPUB) 978-3-11-066833-9

Robotic Process Automation

Management, Technology, Applications

Edited by
Christian Czarnecki and Peter Fettke

DE GRUYTER
OLDENBOURG

Editors

Prof. Dr.-Ing. Christian Czarnecki
Hamm-Lippstadt University of
Applied Sciences
Marker Allee 76-78
59063 Hamm
Germany
christian.czarnecki@hshl.de

Prof. Dr. Peter Fettke
Saarland University
German Research Center
for Artificial Intelligence (DFKI)
Campus D3 2
66123 Saarbrücken
Germany
peter.fettke@dfki.de

ISBN 978-3-11-067668-6
e-ISBN (PDF) 978-3-11-067669-3
e-ISBN (EPUB) 978-3-11-067677-8

Library of Congress Control Number: 2021930950

Bibliographic information published by the Deutsche Nationalbibliothek
The Deutsche Nationalbibliothek lists this publication in the Deutsche Nationalbibliografie;
detailed bibliographic data are available on the Internet at http://dnb.dnb.de.

© 2021 Walter de Gruyter GmbH, Berlin/Boston
Cover image: Scientific American Volume 80 Number 03 (January 1899), scanned by Jason Scott
Typesetting: VTeX UAB, Lithuania
Printing and binding: CPI books GmbH, Leck

www.degruyter.com

Preface

For decades, business processes have been understood as a necessary but complex conglomeration of boxes and arrows. Their design, optimization, and management were and are undoubtedly an interesting field of activity for researchers and practitioners. We both have a long passion for processes. Christian traveled the Middle East for more than 10 years helping companies in managing their processes before he started teaching this topic. Peter firmly believes that processes must be understood as first-class citizens when designing computer-integrated systems. However, the valid but unpleasant question of whether processes are just paper work with – at best – only limited impact on reality was somehow the metaphoric Sword of Damocles hanging over our processes.

Therefore, the imagination of tiny robots running through these processes was fascinating from the first moment. It closes the gap between the conceptual work and its implementation. Additionally, it gives a flavor of innovation to a topic that already became a little outmoded in times of digitalization, artificial intelligence, and Industry 4.0. In the end, it comes as no surprise that robotic process automation (RPA) is today a widely discussed and recognized topic in practice and academia.

The idea to combine the results and insights of researchers and practitioners in one book was born at the end of 2019. We both believe that RPA is a broad topic with interesting and promising opportunities as well as developments in various content areas. Our aim with this book is to bring these different viewpoints together and to offer an understanding of RPA that goes beyond a simple automation of routine tasks. In addition, the publication of application-oriented results as well as the knowledge transfer between research and practice were our major goal. Now, we are happy to present 19 chapters written by 51 authors coming from 7 countries. The topics range from management over technology to applications.

When we launched the call for chapters in January 2020, at that point we did not expect that writing this book would coincide with one of the worst pandemic situations of this century. We sincerely appreciate the commitment of all authors in these difficult times. They all did a great job! Each chapter offers interesting insights, new developments, and/or inspiring viewpoints. All chapters have been subject to various reviews, and all authors have worked hard to make this book a reality.

Looking back, we both have enjoyed editing this book. We have met new and old friends, were in contact with widely recognized experts in their field, have visited – at least virtually – relevant conferences, and learned new perspectives on RPA. We hope that our readers feel our passion for their topics. Enjoy reading!

February 2021

Christian Czarnecki, Düsseldorf
Peter Fettke, Saarbrücken

https://doi.org/10.1515/9783110676693-201

Contents

Part I: Introduction

Christian Czarnecki and Peter Fettke

Part II: RPA management

Lukas-Valentin Herm, Christian Janiesch, Theresa Steinbach, and Daniel Wüllner

Frank Bensberg, Gunnar Auth, and Christian Czarnecki

Adrian Hofmann, Tobias Prätori, Franz Seubert, Jonas Wanner, Marcus Fischer, and Axel Winkelmann

Stefan Rechberger and Stefan Oppl

Corinna Rutschi and Jens Dibbern

Editors

Prof. Dr. Christian Czarnecki

Professor of Information Systems, Hamm-Lippstadt University of Applied Sciences, Germany

Dr. Christian Czarnecki is a professor of information systems at the Hamm-Lippstadt University of Applied Sciences. After studying business informatics at the University of Münster, he gained more than 10 years practical experience in various consultancies and managed a large number of transformation projects in Europe, Africa and the Middle East. He received his doctorate in engineering from the University of Magdeburg in 2013. His main research interests are Digital Transformation, Process Management, Robotic Process Automation, Internet of Things and Enterprise Architectures. His work has been published in leading academic journals, at international conferences and in various books.

Prof. Dr. Peter Fettke

Professor of Business Informatics, German Research Center for Artificial Intelligence (DFKI) and Saarland University, Germany

Dr. Peter Fettke is a professor of business informatics at Saarland University and principal researcher, research fellow and group leader at the German Research Center for Artificial Intelligence (DFKI), Saarbrücken. Peter, with his group of about 30 people, is interested in concepts, methods, and techniques at the intersection between business informatics and artificial intelligence, namely the modeling of computer-integrated systems, automated planning, and deep learning. Peter is the author of more than 150 peer-reviewed publications. His work is among the most cited articles in leading international journals on business informatics and he is one of the top 5 most cited scientists at DFKI. He is also a sought-after reviewer for renowned conferences, journals, and research organizations.

https://doi.org/10.1515/9783110676693-202

Authors

Dr. Simone Agostinelli
PhD Student in Engineering in Computer Science, Sapienza Università di Roma, Italy

Dr. Simone Agostinelli received the B. S. and M. S. degrees in engineering in computer science from Sapienza Università di Roma. He is currently pursuing the Ph. D. degree in engineering in computer Science with the Sapienza Università di Roma. His research interests include synthesizing strategies for robotic process automation via process mining and automated planning techniques. In 2019, he received the Forum Award at the 31st International Conference on Advanced Information Systems Engineering (CAiSE).

Prof. Dr. Gunnar Auth
Professor of Information Systems and e-Government, Meissen University of Applied Sciences (HSF), Germany

Dr. Gunnar Auth is professor of information systems and e-government at Meissen University of Applied Sciences (HSF), Germany. He completed his diploma degree in business information systems at the University of Bamberg, Germany, and received a PhD degree in economics from the University of St Gallen (HSG), Switzerland. He started his professional career as an internal consultant at DaimlerChrysler where he later worked in several management positions in logistics, operations and quality management. Before he became a professor in 2012, he acted as IT director and representative of the CIO board at Leipzig University. His research focuses on IT project management, IT service management and information management.

Prof. Dr. Frank Bensberg
Professor of Information Systems, Osnabrück University of Applied Sciences, Germany

Frank Bensberg is Professor of Information Systems at the Faculty of Economic and Social Sciences at Osnabrück University of Applied Sciences. After receiving the doctoral degree and the qualification to lecture in Information Systems from the University of Münster, he worked at the Hochschule für Telekommunikation Leipzig, Germany. Focal research areas are digitization, big data, data mining, job mining and text analytics.

Dr. Tathagata Chakraborti
IBM Research, Cambridge, USA

Dr. Tathagata Chakraborti is with IBM Research. His research focuses on human-AI interaction and explainable AI. He received his Ph. D. from Arizona State University in 2018 with a CIDSE Graduate Student of the Year Award and an honorable mention for the Best Dissertation Award from ICAPS, the premier conference on automated planning and scheduling. He became one of IEEE's AI's 10 to Watch in 2020.

Prof. Dr. Alina Chircu
Professor of Information and Process Management and Senior Associate Dean of Business for Graduate Programs, Bentley University, USA

Dr. Alina Chircu is a Professor and Senior Associate Dean at Bentley University, USA. She holds a Ph. D. degree in Management Information Systems and bachelor's and master's degrees in Com-

https://doi.org/10.1515/9783110676693-203

puter Science. Her research interests include the business value, design, adoption and implementation of digital transformation initiatives and business process management. Her work has been published in many academic journals, at international conferences and in various books. Dr. Chircu has served as senior editor for the Electronic Commerce Research and Applications journal, associate editor for journals and conferences, and chair, moderator and presenter in academic and practitioner panels and workshops.

Philipp Croon
Lawyer, Kanzlei am Burgberg, Heinsberg, Germany

Philipp Croon is a lawyer in a small sized law firm in Germany and specializes in intellectual property law and commercial and corporate law. Besides his main practice, he lectures students of cultural education at the University of Applied Sciences Niederrhein.

Prof. Dr. Jens Dibbern
Professor of Information Systems, University of Bern, Switzerland

Dr. Jens Dibbern is professor of information systems at the University of Bern, Department of Business Administration in Switzerland. His research focuses on IT sourcing, platform ecosystems, system implementation/use, and distributed collaboration. His publications appeared in Information Systems Research (ISR), Management Information Systems Quarterly (MISQ), Journal of Management Information Systems (JMIS), Journal of the Association of Information Systems (JAIS), and others. He currently serves as department editor of Business & Information Systems Engineering (BISE).

Dr. José González Enríquez
Assistant Professor of Information Systems, Department of Languages and Information Systems, University of Sevilla, Spain.

José González Enríquez received the PhD degree in computer science, in 2017. He is currently a Lecturer with the Department of Computing Languages and Systems, University of Seville. He has been a part of the organizing committee of different international conferences. He has collaborated with many universities in several countries such as Southampton, Berkeley, or Poland, among others. In 2015, he received the Innovation Award for its innovative activity by Fujitsu Laboratories of Europe. His research interests focus on robotic process automation, early testing, model-driven engineering and systematic reviews methods.

Dr. Marcus Fischer
Researcher, Chair of Business Administration and Business Informatics, University of Würzburg, Germany

Marcus Fischer holds a Ph. D. in Business Information System as well as a Bachelor's and Master's degree in Business & Administration from the Julius-Maximilians-Universität Würzburg. He focuses his research on business process management and business software. His work has been published in Information & Management and Electronic Markets and has been presented at multiple international conferences, including the International Conference on Information Systems (ICIS), the European Conference on Information Systems (ECIS), the Human Computer Interaction International (HCII), and the Americas Conference on Information Systems (AMCIS).

Daniel Friedmann
Capgemini, Nuremberg, Germany

Daniel Friedmann completed his B. Sc. in Computer Science and Media at the Nuremberg Institute of Technology in 2019. He is currently studying for a master's degree in Computer Science and working at Capgemini as part of his master's thesis. His areas of interest are cloud and container technology as well as microservices and machine learning.

Oliver Gutermuth
Institute for Information Systems (IWi) at the German Research Center for Artificial Intelligence (DFKI) and Saarland University, Germany

Oliver Gutermuth started researching at the Institute for Information Systems (IWi) at the German Research Center for Artificial Intelligence (DFKI) in 2018. In the course of his doctoral studies, he is working on intelligent technologies for the digital transformation of administrations. Strategies to support and automate business processes in this domain are an important focus. His main tasks include the management and execution of industrial and research projects as well as consulting for the public sector. In these projects, he investigates, among other things, the potential of Robotic Process Automation, mobile technologies as well as Process Mining. Furthermore, he develops application concepts using artificial intelligence.

Lukas-Valentin Herm, M. Sc.
Research Assistant, University of Würzburg, Germany

Lukas-Valentin Herm is a research assistant and PhD student at the Julius-Maximilians-Universität Würzburg. His research is focusing on the fields of explainable artificial intelligence as well as robotic process automation. Research topics include the application and impact of XAI-based systems, enabling RPA in practice as well as the intersection of both topics. He has authored scholarly publications in various conferences proceedings including ICIS, ECIS, HICSS and BPM.

Adrian Hofmann
Research Assistant, Chair of Business Administration and Business Informatics, University of Würzburg, Germany

Adrian Hofmann is a Research and Teaching Assistant at the Julius-Maximilians-Universität in Würzburg, Germany. He holds a master's degree in Mathematics with Economics from the Technical University Darmstadt. Currently, his research focuses on applying data-driven approaches in various fields of information systems such as standardization, blockchain and BPM. His work appeared in various international journals and conferences, including ISJ, Electronic Markets, ICIS, ECIS and AMCIS.

Dr. Constantin Houy
Institute for Information Systems (IWi) at the German Research Center for Artificial Intelligence (DFKI) and Saarland University, Germany

Dr. Constantin Houy works at the Institute for Information Systems (IWi) at the German Research Center for Artificial Intelligence (DFKI) as Chief Engineer. His research interests comprise business process management, conceptual modeling, and theory development in information systems. He has published 70 scientific contributions and his doctoral dissertation on process model understandability was awarded the Dr.-Eduard-Martin award of Saarland University in 2019 as well as the 2020 dissertation award of the Institute for Empirical Economic Research (IfeW). In addition to accompanying research and development projects with partners from the private sector and academia, Constantin also conducted organizational studies in public administration. He is currently investigating the potential of innovative technologies for the design of administrative processes.

Dr. Vatche Isahagian
IBM Research, Cambridge, USA

Dr. Vatche Isahagian's research spans a broad set of disciplines across distributed systems, AI, and business processes. As a research staff member at IBM Research, he worked on several projects including business process insight and service composition, OpenWhisk large scale Serverless Computing framework, and the IBM Deep Learning as a Service. He currently co-leads a team of researchers focused on improving business processes using AI capabilities such as planning and conversational interfaces. Vatche has published in top-tier conferences such as CACM, BPM, AAAI, KDD, VLDB, SDM, and INFOCOM. His first-authored work at the Middleware 2012 Conference received the Best Paper award. He co-organized several workshops, and served as a program committee member, demo co-chair, and publicity chair on several conferences.

Prof. Dr. Christian Janiesch
Assistant Professor for Information Management, University of Würzburg, Germany

Christian Janiesch is assistant professor at the Julius-Maximilians-Universität Würzburg. Before, Christian worked full-time at the Westfälische Wilhelms-Universität in Münster, at the SAP Research Center Brisbane at SAP Australia Pty. Ltd., and at the Karlsruhe Institute of Technology. His research is at the intersection of business process management and business analytics with frequent applications in the Industrial Internet of Things. He is on the Department Editorial Board for BISE and has authored over 150 scholarly publications. His work has appeared journals such as the Journal of the Association for Information Systems, Decision Support Systems, Information & Management, Business & Information Systems Engineering, Future Generation Computer Systems, Information Systems as well as various major conferences and has been registered as U.S. patents.

Dr. Yasaman Khazaeni
IBM Research, Cambridge, USA

Dr. Yasaman Khazaeni is a Research Staff Member and manager at IBM Research where she focuses on application of conversational multi-agent systems in various applications like business process automation and customer care. She holds an undergraduate degree in both electrical engineering and petroleum engineering from Sharif University of Technology in Iran. In 2009, she continued her graduate studies in petroleum engineering at West Virginia University where she earned her master's degree in reservoir engineering. She received her PhD in Systems Engineering from Boston University where she focused on multi-agent systems control and optimization with a specific interest in event-driven systems. Her research interests are in the area of multi-agent systems, mathematical modeling, optimization, operations research, machine learning and statistics.

Dr. Julia Kokina
Associate Professor of Accounting, Babson College, USA

Dr. Julia Kokina is an Associate Professor of Accounting at Babson College. She teaches accounting analytics and undergraduate and graduate managerial accounting courses. Dr. Kokina's research has been published in various highly-ranked academic accounting journals. She has presented her work at national and international conferences. Notably, in 2018, she was invited to speak at the PCAOB International Audit Institute and in 2017 she was invited by the American Accounting Association to give a TED-like presentation on cognitive technologies in accounting at the Accounting is Big Data Conference. Her current research work focuses on the implementation of Robotic Process Automation in accounting and finance tasks and her teaching innovation centers around the incorporation of Alteryx and Tableau in accounting curriculum.

Dr. Andreas Kronz
Head of BPM Consulting, Scheer GmbH, Saarbrücken, Germany

Dr. Andreas Kronz is Head of Process and Management Consulting at Scheer GmbH. His focus is on consulting around the topic of business process management from strategic introduction and organization to benefit-oriented implementation of BPM solutions. He has led many projects in different industries such as telecommunications, manufacturing, financial services, automotive or utilities and published numerous articles and scientific papers. In the course of these activities, he deals with current trends such as digitalization, S/4HANA, process mining and robotic process automation. Andreas earned his PhD in business informatics under the professorship of Prof. Dr. Dr. h.c. mult. August-Wilhelm Scheer and can now look back on almost 30 years of professional experience.

Prof. Dr. Christian Langmann
Professor of Accounting, Munich University of Applied Sciences, Germany

Dr. Christian Langmann is Professor of Accounting at the Munich University of Applied Sciences. He teaches a variety of managerial accounting courses (including the digital transformation of managerial accounting) in undergraduate, graduate and advanced education. His research focus is the application of modern digitalization technologies and statistical methods in the (managerial) accounting. He published a variety of articles and books in this field of research. He also advises companies how to digitally transform their (managerial) accounting. Before becoming Professor, he served as Chief Financial Officer (CFO) and finance director for software and telecommunication companies. His career started as a project manager at the international management consultancy Horváth & Partners.

Prof. Dr. Henrik Leopold
Associate Professor for Data Science and Business Intelligence, Kühne Logistics University, Germany

Dr. Henrik Leopold is associate professor for data science and business intelligence at the Kühne Logistics University (KLU) and adjunct professor at the Hasso Plattner Institute (HPI), University of Potsdam. He obtained his PhD degree in information systems from the Humboldt-Universität zu Berlin, Germany. Before joining KLU and HPI, he held positions at the Vrije Universiteit Amsterdam as well as WU Vienna. His research is mainly concerned with leveraging artificial intelligence to analyze and improve business processes. He has published over 80 scientific contributions, among others, in

IEEE Transactions on Software Engineering, IEEE Transactions on Knowledge and Data Engineering, Decision Support Systems, and Information Systems.

Prof. Dr. Andrea Marrella
Assistant Professor at Sapienza Università di Roma, Italy

Prof. Andrea Marrella is currently an assistant Professor with the Sapienza Università di Roma. His research interest includes how to integrate artificial intelligence with business process management solutions, to untangle complex challenges from the fields of process mining and robotic process automation. He has coauthored more than 70 peer-reviewed publications in renowned international conferences and top journals. Since 2017, he has been the Information Director of the ACM Journal of Data and Information Quality.

Prof. Dr. Massimo Mecella
Full Professor at Sapienza Università di Roma, Italy

Prof. Massimo Mecella is a full Professor at Sapienza Università di Roma. His research focuses on service oriented computing, business process management, cyber-physical systems and Internet-of-Things, advanced interfaces and human-computer interaction. He published more than 150 research papers and chaired different conferences in the above areas. In 2021 he acts as General Chair of BPM 2021 and as Program Chair of IE 2021 and ICSOC 2021.

Tim Merscheid
Cybersecurity Management Consultant, Capgemini, Cologne, Germany

Tim Merscheid completed his B. Sc. in Business Information Systems at the University of Cologne in July 2016 and his M. Sc., also in Business Information Systems, at the University of Duisburg-Essen in May 2019. In 2018, he specialized in cybersecurity at California State University, San Marcos, USA. After his M. Sc. graduation, he joined Capgemini as a Cybersecurity Management Consultant in the Cologne office. His focus is to provide strategic advice on the use of cybersecurity that is consistent with the long-term business goals of his clients. The use of machine learning and artificial intelligence will play a significant role in this field in the future and is his current area of research.

Prof. Dr. Stefan Oppl
Professor of Technology-enhanced Learning, Danube-University Krems,
Austria

Stefan Oppl is a professor of technology-enhanced learning and heads the department for continuing education research and educational technology at Danube University Krems, Austria. He has graduated in computer science and applied knowledge management at the Kepler University of Linz and has earned his PhD in computer science from the Technical University of Vienna in 2010. His research in the field of business informatics focuses on collaborative learning support systems, formative learning analytics and articulation of work knowledge. Stefan has coordinated several national and EU-founded research projects on these topics and has published over 80 papers on both, design-oriented and empirical research in these fields.

Prof. Dr. Ralf Jürgen Ostendorf
Professor of Finance and Business Management, Hochschule Niederrhein University of Applied Sciences, Germany

Dr. Ralf Jürgen Ostendorf is a professor of finance, accounting, controlling and cost analysis at the Niederrhein University of Applied Sciences. After studying Controlling at the University of Duisburg, he worked for the University of Witten. He received his doctorate in strategic management from the University of Duisburg in 2000. More than eight years Ralf Jürgen was responsible Controller in several Banks. In 2010 he became Professor in Düsseldorf and in 2012 in Krefeld. His main research interests are Banking and Finance, developments on the Stock Exchange and competitive strategies. His work has been published in around 100 books and articles.

Peter Pfeiffer
German Research Center for Artificial Intelligence (DFIKI) and Saarland University, Germany

Peter Pfeiffer is a researcher at the Institute for Information Systems (IWi) at the German Research Center for Artificial Intelligence (DFKI) since 2019. In 2020 he pursued his master's in business informatics as a participant of the Software Campus where he was working on a project to retrieve CAD models from 2D images. He is currently working on the application of Artificial Intelligence in Business Processes, e. g. in manufacturing or health care. His research interest also cover Machine Learning methods on Business Process Data and Cognitive Robotic Process Automation.

René Plath
Mobility Services Consultant, MHP – A Porsche Company, Berlin, Germany

René Plath is an IT- and Management Consultant at MHP – A Porsche Company and holds a master's degree in Business Informatics. With 6+ years of experience, he continually expands his range of perspectives on product development covering business and technology aspects. His profession includes identifying and creating digital services for branch leading companies along with scouting cooperating startups and technologies to optimize and extend the service offerings of multinational corporates. Driven by the overall question of how to shape mobility more sustainable with new technologies, he is working in digital units of Germany's premium car manufacturers in the role of a System Architect and Product Owner Support as defined in the Scaled Agile Framework SAFe.

Tobias Prätori
Research Assistant, Chair of Business Administration and Business Informatics, University of Würzburg, Germany

Tobias Prätori is a research assistant at the Chair of Business Administration and Information at the Julias-Maximilians-Universität Würzburg. He holds a master's degree in Business Information Systems. He is fascinated by the groundbreaking opportunities that data science and machine learning offer to society. Furthermore, he is interested in the circular economy. His current research is about how information systems can support product designers to improve plastic products' recyclability.

Dr. Andrés Jiménez Ramírez
Assistant Professor of Information Systems, Department of Languages and Information Systems, University of Sevilla, Spain

Andrés Jiménez Ramírez is a lecturer and researcher at the University of Seville, Spain. He started his career as a software engineer in the R&D department of a Spanish consultancy firm. In 2014, Andrés obtained his PhD degree in Computer Science at the University of Sevilla where he is member of the Web Engineering and Early Testing (IWT2) group. His research focuses on intelligent techniques for BPM, flexible business processes and process automation, hereby combining different disciplines like constraint programming and declarative business process modelling. Andres has published his research at international journals and conferences like Data and Knowledge Engineering, Information and Software Technology, Knowledge and Information Systems or CAiSE.

Stefan Rechberger, BSc
RPA Developer, Raiffeisen Software GmbH, Linz, Austria

Stefan Rechberger is an RPA developer at Raiffeisen Software GmbH in Linz and implements RPA processes with Blue Prism. He has been working in the financial services sector for over 10 years and has supervised a large number of projects in the areas of Treasury, Settlements, Accounting, Bank Harmonization and Robotic Process Automation at the Raiffeisenlandesbank Oberösterreich AG. In addition to his practical experience, he completed his bachelor's degree in business informatics at the Johannes Kepler University in Linz with distinction and is currently writing his master's thesis "Forecasting of sales quantities – A comparison of methods for increasing the forecast quality with volatile and limited data".

Prof. Dr. Ir. Hajo A. Reijers
Professor of Business Informatics, Department of Information and Computing Sciences, Utrecht University, The Netherlands/Professor of Computer Science, Department of Mathematics and Computer Science, Eindhoven University of Technology, The Netherlands

Hajo Reijers is a full professor in the Department of Information and Computing Sciences of Utrecht University, where he leads the Business Process (BPM) Management & Analytics group. He is also a part-time, full professor in the Department of Mathematics and Computer Science of Eindhoven University of Technology. Previously, he worked for various management consultancy companies and led the BPM research group at Lexmark. Hajo's research and teaching focus on BPM, data analytics, and information systems engineering. On these and other topics, he published over 200 scientific papers, chapters in edited books, as well as articles in professional journals.

Konstantin Ritschel
Management Consultant, Detecon International GmbH, Cologne, Germany

Konstantin Ritschel is a consultant for Robotic Process Automation and Process Management with focus on the telecommunication industry at the technology management consultancy Detecon International GmbH in Cologne, Germany. After working in the telecommunication industry during his dual studies in Business Information Technology at the Hochschule für Telekommunikation in Leipzig, he joined Detecon full time. He successfully implemented RPA in different projects within Germany, working as a project lead, solution designer and developer. He aims to achieve optimization of business processes and to drive a sustainable optimization of business process for his clients.

Dr. Yara Rizk
IBM Research, Cambridge, USA

Dr. Yara Rizk is a researcher at IBM Research. She received her doctorate in Electrical and Computer Engineering from the American University of Beirut (AUB) in 2018. Prior, she obtained a Bachelor of Engineering in Computer and Communication Engineering from AUB, Lebanon, in 2012. Her research interests span, artificial intelligence, machine learning, multi-agent systems, business automation, and robotic process automation. Her work has led to multiple peer-reviewed publications in leading academic journals and international conferences.

Prof. Dr. Peter Gordon Rötzel, LL. M.
Professor of Accounting and Information Systems, University of Applied Sciences Aschaffenburg and University of Stuttgart, Germany

Dr. Peter Gordon Roetzel is professor for accounting and information systems at University of Applied Sciences Aschaffenburg and University of Stuttgart. He is head of the Behavioral Accounting & Finance Lab. His research focus is on how information overload affects managerial decision making and how new instruments of management and leadership (e. g., enterprise social media, AI-based decision aid, explainable AI) affects manager's behavior. He is interested in mixed-method interdisciplinary information systems research and published his work in leading academic journals and at international conferences.

Corinna Rutschi
PhD Candidate of Information Systems, University of Bern, Switzerland

Corinna Rutschi is a Ph. D. candidate of information systems at the Institute of Information Systems at the University of Bern, Switzerland. Prior to starting her doctorate, she completed her master's degree in information systems at the University of Bern and gained practical experience in IT consulting in the pharma and life sciences sector. Her research focuses on technologies that help automate processes previously performed by humans. Here, she is looking at technologies that perform processes human-like and are intelligent in some way, with the aim of better understanding their development and implementation. She has published in The DATA BASE for Advances in Information Systems and in conference proceedings of the Hawaii International Conference on System Science.

Franz Seubert
Research Assistant, Chair of Business Administration and Business Informatics, University of Würzburg, Germany

Franz Seubert is a Research and Teaching Assistant at the Julius-Maximilians-Universität in Würzburg, Germany. He holds a master's degree in Business Information Systems. He runs the chairs ERP-lab with more than 30 different ERP-Systems. He is currently researching how already in ERP-Systems, existing data can be leveraged with artificial intelligence to improve automated ordering systems for perishable goods.

Kalpesh Sharma
Director, Principal Enterprise Architect, Capgemini, USA

Kalpesh Sharma is a Director and Account Chief Architect at Capgemini. He holds bachelor's degree in Electrical Engineering and has 19+ years of IT experience. He is a successful and recognized thought leader with experience in architecting and implementing enterprise-level business solutions covering strategy definition, blueprint creation and laying out roadmap to implement short-term, medium-term and long-term goals. His research area includes artificial intelligence, machine learning and its implementation for the benefits of solving critical business challenges. Kalpesh has authored several technical articles, served as a speaker in technology conferences, and is a certified IT Architecture trainer.

Mario Richard Smeets, M. Sc., MBA
Senior Manager of DCP Deutsche Consulting Partner and Managing Director of the RPA-Consultancy "Weisskopf 21", Germany

Mario Richard Smeets is a management consultant for banks, insurance companies and financial service providers and co-founder and managing director of a process automation and software manufactory. One of his consulting focuses lies in process management and automation. After studying business administration and economics in Hagen, Bonn and Cambridge, MA, Mario is now researching on Artificial Intelligence in managerial decision making at TH Aschaffenburg. He published different books and articles, mainly on the topic of process automation.

Theresa Steinbach, B. Sc.
Student, University of Würzburg, Germany

Theresa Steinbach received her bachelor's degree in 2018 and is now doing her master's degree at the Julius-Maximilians-Universität Würzburg. Her research interests are robotic process automation and explainable artificial intelligence. Since 2019, she is working as student assistant at the chair of Prof. Janiesch.

Adina Stenzel
Management Consultant, Detecon International GmbH, Berlin, Germany

Adina Stenzel is an expert for Robotic Process Automation and Artificial Intelligence at the technology management consultancy Detecon International GmbH in Berlin, Germany. After studying Cognitive Science & Artificial Intelligence at Tilburg University in the Netherlands and living and working internationally, she gained years of practical experience in various digitalization and automation projects across Germany. She is particularly interested in new technologies and its impact on an individual and social level. She helps enterprises to optimize and automate business processes and support their employees, with a passionate focus on ethical technology.

Christoph Stummer
Management Consultant, Detecon International GmbH, Cologne, Germany

Christoph Stummer is a management consultant for process automation, process transformation, change management and team building at the Management & IT Consultancy Detecon International

GmbH. After studying business management in Stuttgart, he gained more than 20 years of professional experience in various industries, in particular the telecommunications industry. He supported companies in convert and optimize their processes into leading edge processes with a holistic end-to-end view. The focus of his work lies on the customer perspective, thus on customer satisfaction and value streams. He applied agile IT requirement management and implemented RPA to realize automation in a short time. He published his expertise and recommendations in various papers.

Dr. Eldar Sultanow
Capgemini, Nuremberg, Germany

Eldar Sultanow is an Enterprise Architect at Capgemini. In 2015, he completed his doctoral studies at the Chair of Business Information Systems and Electronic Government at the University of Potsdam. His areas of interest are AI, modern software architecture and Computer Science. After completing his Studies at Hasso Plattner Institute, University of Potsdam, Eldar worked for many years in the area of E-Commerce as a JEE developer and architect at Europe's leading consumer information portal. Afterwards he was CIO in a medium-sized pharmaceutical wholesale for 5 years. Eldar is an author of books, a series of conference papers and numerous journal articles.

Thomas Thiel, MBA
Head of Competence Center RPA, Scheer GmbH, Saarbrücken, Germany

During the implementation of the project addressed in the case study co-authored by him, Thomas Thiel was Head of Competence Center RPA at Scheer GmbH. He earned his MBA from Frankfurt School of Finance and Management. Fascinated by the trade-off between business and IT, it is his passion to provide consulting services in the field of intelligent business process automation. Besides Robotic Process Automation, which is Thomas' main field of expertise, his technological focus lies on the usage of Optical Character Recognition technologies for the sake of Smart Data Extraction as well as on Workflow Management Systems. Thomas has led numerous digitization projects in various industries, including Logistics, Banking, Automotive and Electronics.

Prof. Dr. Han van der Aa
Junior Professor in Artificial Intelligence Methods, University of Mannheim, Germany

Dr. Han van der Aa is a junior professor in the Data and Web Science Group at the University of Mannheim. Before that, he was an Alexander von Humboldt Fellow at the Humboldt-Universität zu Berlin. In 2018, he obtained a PhD from the Department of Computer Science of the Vrije Universiteit Amsterdam, the Netherlands. His research targets the development of automated methods for process analysis, with a particular focus on the consideration of natural language and data uncertainty in this regard. His work has been published in leading academic journals, such as IEEE Transactions on Knowledge and Data Engineering, Decision Support Systems, and Information Systems.

Prof. Dr. Ir. Wil van der Aalst
Professor of Process and Data Science, RWTH Aachen University, Germany and Fraunhofer FIT, Sankt Augustin, Germany

Wil van der Aalst is a full professor at RWTH Aachen University leading the Process and Data Science group. He is also part-time affiliated with the Fraunhofer-Institut für Angewandte Informationstechnik (FIT) and is a member of the Board of Governors of Tilburg University. Van der Aalst is an IFIP Fellow, IEEE Fellow, ACM Fellow, and received honorary degrees from the Moscow Higher School of Economics (Prof. h. c.), Tsinghua University, and Hasselt University (Dr. h. c.). He is also an elected member of the Royal Netherlands Academy of Arts and Sciences, the Royal Holland Society of Sciences and Humanities, the Academy of Europe, and the North Rhine-Westphalian Academy of Sciences, Humanities and the Arts. In 2018, he was awarded an Alexander-von-Humboldt Professorship.

Jonas Wanner
Research Assistant, Assisstant Professor for Information Management, University of Würzburg, Germany

Jonas Wanner is a research associate and lecturer at Julius Maximilian University in Würzburg, Germany. He holds a Bachelor's degree in Business Information Systems from DHBW Stuttgart and a Master's degree in Business Management from the University of Würzburg, Germany. His research focuses on explainable artificial intelligence and real-time analysis of processes. His work has appeared in several international journals and conferences, including Business Research, EMISJ, ICIS, and ECIS.

Prof. Dr. Axel Winkelmann
Professor of Information Systems, University of Würzburg, Germany

Prof. Dr. Axel Winkelmann holds the Chair of Business Administration and Information Systems at the University of Würzburg and has the largest laboratory for enterprise software in Germany. His research and teaching focus on integrating enterprise software and the potential applications of modern technologies such as AI, blockchain or BPM.

Daniel Wüllner, B. Sc.
Working student, SYSTHEMIS AG, Würzburg, Germany

Daniel Wüllner received his bachelor's degree and is now doing his master's degree in information systems at Julius-Maximilians-Universität Würzburg. His research interest is focusing on the field of robotic process automation, as well as Business Process Management. Since 2017, he is working at SYSTHEMIS AG in the field of RPA, BPM and Software development.

Part I: **Introduction**

Christian Czarnecki and Peter Fettke

1 Robotic process automation

Positioning, structuring, and framing the work

Abstract: Robotic process automation (RPA) has attracted increasing attention in research and practice. This chapter positions, structures, and frames the topic as an introduction to this book. RPA is understood as a broad concept that comprises a variety of concrete solutions. From a management perspective RPA offers an innovative approach for realizing automation potentials, whereas from a technical perspective the implementation based on software products and the impact of artificial intelligence (AI) and machine learning (ML) are relevant. RPA is industry-independent and can be used, for example, in finance, telecommunications, and the public sector. With respect to RPA this chapter discusses definitions, related approaches, a structuring framework, a research framework, and an inside as well as outside architectural view. Furthermore, it provides an overview of the book combined with short summaries of each chapter.

Keywords: Robotic process automation, management, technology, applications, research framework, enterprise architecture

1.1 Introduction

In practice, a broad variety of robotic process automation (RPA) cases have been documented, such as the automation of core processes at Telefonica O2 (Lacity et al., 2015), the RPA usage at the University Hospitals Birmingham as well as at Gazprom Energy (Willcocks et al., 2015), the virtual assistance in financial processes at Opus-Capita (Asatiani and Penttinen, 2016), automated data extraction and processing at a public administration (Houy et al., 2019), and the automation of field service as well as problem solving processes at Deutsche Telekom (Schmitz et al., 2018). In fact, RPA has attracted increasing attention in research and practice, and the term is used for a broad variety of automation techniques (e. g., Agostinelli et al., 2019; Chakraborti et al., 2020; Enriquez et al., 2020; Herm et al., 2020; van der Aalst et al., 2018).

RPA is an innovative approach to transform the process execution without changing the underlying application systems (e. g., Houy et al., 2019; Smeets et al., 2019; Langmann and Turi, 2020). The initial idea of RPA is that software robots perform formerly human work (e. g., Willcocks et al., 2015). In contrast to robotics in production processes (e. g., Groover, 2008), RPA does not use tangible robots but autonomous acting software systems – so-called software robots. They learn and adopt human ac-

https://doi.org/10.1515/9783110676693-001

tivities, and handle application systems through user interfaces. The software robots use the existing input forms of the underlying application systems. Hence, changes of the existing application landscape are not required, which is one of the major benefits of RPA in practice (Willcocks et al., 2017).

This book follows a broad understanding of RPA, as an umbrella term for different automation approaches (e. g., Asatiani et al., 2020; Leopold et al., 2018; Rutschi and Dibbern, 2020). This chapter positions, structures, and frames the general topic. We start in Section 1.2 with an explanation of the automatic duck, illustrated on the front cover, and discuss how it might be related to modern software robots. Section 1.3 provides an application example that serves as a starting point for the topic. The positioning is discussed based on related approaches (cf. Section 1.4) and on an understanding of the basic terms (cf. Section 1.5). An overall structure for RPA is proposed in Section 1.6. From an architectural perspective, Section 1.7 frames the topic from an outside and inside view. Current research is discussed in Section 1.8, and the structure of this book is explained in Section 1.9.

1.2 The automatic duck – a *gedankenexperiment*

On January 21, 1899, Scientific American overviewed "Some Curious Automata." One of them was the automatic duck created by the French inventor Jacques de Vaucanson in the eighteenth century shown in Figure 1. This automatic duck "waddled off in search of food, and picked up and swallowed the seeds that it met with. These seeds [...] passed into the stomach through a series of triturations that facilitated the introduction of them into the intestines and caused them to accomplish all the phases of digestion. It was impossible to distinguish this duck from a living one. It splashed about in the water and quacked at pleasure" (Scientific American, 1899).

Note that there is debate whether the (graphical) description of the automatic duck given above is historically correct. From our research background, we do not feel competent to contribute to this episode of the history of automation. However, we like to use this background as a setting for the following *gedankenexperiment* (thought experiment). For the sake of our argument, we do like to focus on the following thesis, which was already stated above in a slightly different form:

It is impossible to distinguish the automatic duck from a real, living one.

Hence, we like to ask the following question:

What are the necessary prerequisites that this statement – impossible to distinguish the automatic duck from a real, living one – is true?

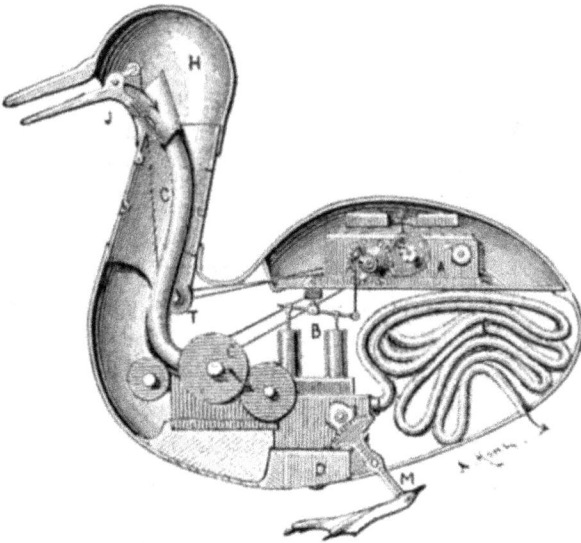

INTERIOR OF VAUCANSON'S AUTOMATIC DUCK.

A, clockwork; *B*, pump; *C*, mill for grinding grain; *F*, intestinal tube;
J, bill; *H*, head; *M*, feet.

Figure 1: Blueprint of an automatic duck (Scientific American, 1899, p. 43).

Imagine an automatic duck in our time. What would be required to confirm the above statement? At least, the following assumptions have to be made:

1. *Sensors*: Our automatic duck needs to have some mechanical or digital sensors to realize the world around it. With respect to today's state-of-the-art technology, this might be, for example, a digital camera, to search for and identify seeds. Presumably, our automatic duck is equipped with further sensors like radar sensors, some GPS antenna or light detection, and ranging sensor (lidar).
2. *Actuators*: Our automatic duck has to have some mechanical beak, legs, and wings, which enable the duck to pick, to move, and to fly around. Those actuators are required to interact with the real world.
3. *Functions*: Our automatic duck must be able to perform some typical actions, which a real duck can perform, for instance, waddling, quaking, and splashing in the water.

To be sure, these are at least some minimal requirements to make this imagination of an automatic duck true. If this illusion will be perfect, then it is clear that the automatic duck is still a thing, a piece of human engineering art, but not a real, living duck. However, by definition, an ideal, automatic duck cannot be distinguished from a real duck. Therefore, we can call such an automatic duck functionally equivalent to a real duck.

A very interesting question is now, what is meant by "functionally equivalent"? In which contexts does it make sense to distinguish between a real and an automatic duck? For example, on the one hand, it can be argued that the automatic duck must be fed the same way as a real duck when it is "hungry." On the other hand, it might be countered that it is not necessary, because the automatic duck is just a machine.

As long as we keep the postulation that our automatic duck should be an equivalent to a real duck, there should be no discussion about copying all aspects. However, this approach comes to a point where some aspects might be questionable or even inadequate. For example, would it really be advisable that our automatic duck has a lifetime comparable to that of a real duck? Even if this point is confirmed, how should the aging for an automatic duck be realized technically? In addition, from an environmental perspective, is it really reasonable to produce a machine that has a predetermined, man-made end of life? Obviously, there are other aspects of a real duck (e. g., reproduction) that would – at least – require intense discussions that go beyond the scope of this book. In conclusion, the equivalent between our automatic duck and a real duck would only be valid for a set of aspects.

Excluding the postulation of a full equivalent between real and automatic duck, the required functionalities can only be judged based on the usage context. For example, for an automatic duck that is used in an educational context for agricultural students, simulating an adequate duck housing, feeding is an essential functionality, whereas an automatic duck used in a surveillance context to deter potential housebreakers, quacking is the core functionality, while feeding might even be hindering in this case.

Furthermore, while developing an automatic duck further questions arise: Would it be a good idea to construct a duck which does not consume so many seeds? Or to construct a duck that is capable to fly much faster and higher than a real duck? Is such a duck still functionally equivalent to a real duck? Of course not; however, changing or optimizing functionalities could be recommendable, and might lead to an advantage of our automatic duck compared to a real duck. For example, in the usage scenario of the agricultural education the possibility of reusing seeds due to an intentionally omitted digestion function is clearly beneficial. Further developments could include useful functionalities for this context (e. g., evaluation of students' performance) which have never been a part of a real duck.

In summary, our *gedankenexperiment* demonstrates three facets:
1. Although it might be interesting to have a full functionally equivalent duck, in most practical cases the functional scope is limited to a specific set of aspects, and does not imply copying all functions of a real duck.
2. Assuming that a full equivalent is not intended, it is unclear when it is acceptable to understand our automatic duck as a real duck. It depends on the context if the automatic duck can be seen as an adequate functionally equivalent of a real duck.
3. In practical cases, extending or changing functionalities could be advisable, which would improve our automatic duck compared to a real duck.

What can we learn from these thoughts about RPA? The initial idea of RPA is developing an automation that is functionally equivalent to a human, acting in a specific business process. Learning and emulating human behavior, for example, entering data in an input mask, is seen as a key aspect of an RPA system. Even though it is obvious that a full functional equivalent with respect to all human aspects is not intended, defining the functionality of an RPA system is not trivial. The following analogies to our automatic duck can be stated:

1. By selecting and describing the processes to be automated, the functional scope of an RPA system is defined, which might range from simple emulation of routine tasks to autonomously reaching complex decisions.
2. A proper automation of a manual process does not necessarily mean that all tasks are performed in an equivalent manner, which makes it difficult to understand and manage the transformation from manual to automated processes.
3. It might be useful to extend RPA by further functionalities that could help improving existing processes or even develop completely new processes.

Building machines that copy their behavior from reality is not new, and as a sole idea not a guarantee for success. The idea of RPA goes beyond a simple automation and emulation of human activities. **Selection and improving** the relevant processes, **extending** RPA by further technologies, and **managing the transformation** from manual to automated are important topics to gain the full potential of RPA.

1.3 Application example

As the RPA concept was motivated by a range of successful automation projects in practice (e. g., Houy et al., 2019; Lacity et al., 2015; Schmitz et al., 2018), understanding those application cases seems to be a good starting point for this book. Administrative processes with a combination of manual activities and automated tasks in existing application systems are typical candidates for RPA. A common example is the invoice verification process, that can be found in almost every enterprise. Dependent on the level of integration along the supply chain, the invoice verification still includes manual steps.

Figure 2 shows an example of a common process in practice. An accountant has to handle paper invoices manually, which includes scanning and uploading of the invoice as well as extraction and booking of consumption values. Even though the process is supported by an existing enterprise resource planning (ERP) system, it contains various manual steps. Assuming an average monthly amount of 1,800 invoices for this specific use case with a manual effort of 5 minutes per invoice the overall saving potential per year would result in 225 working days, which are comparable to one full-time

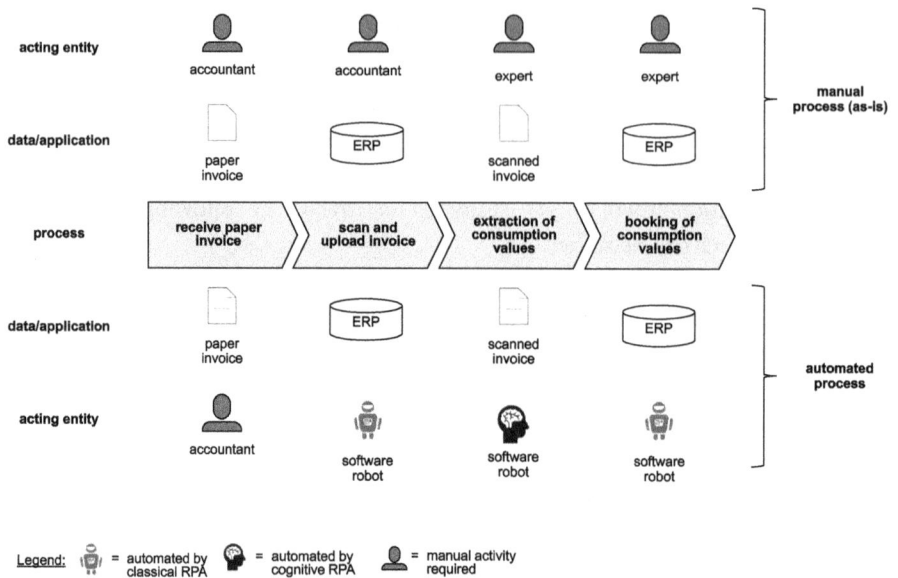

Figure 2: Application example: invoice verification process.

equivalent (FTE). These savings could as well be realized through optimizing the existing ERP systems. In contrast, the RPA approach keeps the ERP system unchanged and automates the existing process through new RPA software systems. In the example, both manual activities are then performed by software robots. The scanning and uploading of invoices are routine activities that can easily be performed by a simple RPA system, whereas extracting consumption values from unstructured data requires further cognitive capabilities. For both functionalities standard RPA software systems are available on the market.

This example illustrates **typical aspects of the RPA usage in practice**:

1. RPA systems are often used as a workaround to fix deficiencies of existing application landscapes. In the above example, the same result could have been realized by an integration of the ERP systems between the enterprise and its suppliers combined with an electronic exchange of invoices.

2. The expected benefits are often related to time savings. The monetary potential can be easily estimated using well-known methods, for example, the *Time Savings Time Salary* (TSTS) method (Sassone, 1987). The monetary benefit potential is usually in a range that would not allow a substantial reengineering project. As in the above example, savings of 1 FTE would not be sufficient for a complex ERP project.

3. The realization is related to concrete and detailed knowledge of the specific process, and hence is in most cases initiated by business units. The essential step in the RPA implementation is "teaching" the specific process to the software robot.

In practice, RPA implementations are often related to a broad variety of different processes with hundreds of software robots.

4. The RPA system is constantly adapted to new requirements and extended to further processes. The idea of a software robot implies a flexible and agile entity. These different software robots form a highly dynamic and complex system.

5. The RPA implementation is typically not a single application system but a combination of different standard software systems. For example, complex processes – such as the extraction of consumption values from unstructured data – require further cognitive capabilities. Hence, RPA implementations are often subject to a continuous refinement and extension.

In summary, **RPA implementations have some specifics that differ from common information systems projects**. This book discusses management, technical, and application aspects of RPA projects. Furthermore, it provides insights to real-life implementation cases.

1.4 Process automation – related approaches

Increasing the automation of processes through technological progress is not a new idea, but a core topic of various business, informatics, and engineering disciplines, that has been discussed for decades (e. g., Hammer and Champy, 1994; Porter, 2004). While the process defines the operational provision of services through activities, an application system describes the handling of information, and can either (1) take over the process execution or (2) support people in its execution (e. g., Alpar et al., 2019; Laudon and Laudon, 2012). The first case represents an automation of the complete process, whereas in the second case individual sub-processes are automated. The basic benefit aspects of automation are cost savings, higher availability, shorter throughput times, and higher reliability as well as transparency. Furthermore, certain processes are only made possible by new technologies. This innovation potential resulting from the interaction of processes and technology was already discussed in the 1990s in the context of business process reengineering (e. g., Davenport, 1993; Hammer and Champy, 1994).

Basically, two approaches are possible for the automation of processes that will be referred to as **traditional approaches to process automation** in the following:

– The *implementation of processes through application systems*, such as systems for ERP or customer relationship management (CRM): Since there is usually a difference between the existing processes and the available functionalities of the used application systems (e. g., Fischer et al., 2017), these application systems often need to be adapted to process requirements, or process adaptations to existing functionalities are required. Based on traditional approaches of business process management (BPM), comprehensive models of the actual situation and target concepts are created in this context (Becker, 2011; vom Brocke et al., 2014; Dumas et al., 2018), which are then implemented both technically and organizationally.

– *Automation through business process management systems (BPMS)* proposes a dedicated system to automatically orchestrate the process execution. A distinction is made between ad hoc workflow systems, production workflow systems, and case handling systems (Dumas et al., 2018). The process models are executed step by step, whereby the integration of additional business logic is possible through interfaces to other application systems (Dumas et al., 2018). The basis is usually a process model, and related application systems (such as ERP, CRM) are integrated by the BPMS.

The core focus of those traditional process automation approaches is an execution of process flows according to mainly static requirements that are either hard-coded in an application system or defined in a BPMS. Decisions are realized through pre-defined conditions, so-called business rules. New or changed requirements result in programming or customization efforts. The next evolution of this concept was the combination with intelligent techniques that allow automatic changes in a process flow based on learning and experiences. In this context, the terms *intelligent process automation* and *smart process automation* were proposed (Langmann and Turi, 2020). The idea is the combination of process automation with *artificial intelligence* (AI), in particular *machine learning* (ML), which could be either integrated in application systems or BPMS or realized through a new system. For example, today system vendors combine their existing ERP systems with AI functionalities (Langmann and Turi, 2020).

RPA can be linked to **related approaches** in BPM, BPMS, process automation, and application systems implementation. However, in contrast to **traditional process automation**, RPA does not require changes of existing applications, which might result in a faster and easier implementation. In addition, today's RPA concepts include approaches of AI, in particular ML, to enable an automatic adaption to process changes.

1.5 Defining RPA

Initially RPA was used in practice as a term for a variety of software tools that allow a fast and simple automation of processes. First authors have characterized those systems by the ease of implementation – no or only minimal programming effort – and the simple integration in existing application landscapes through user interfaces (Lacity et al., 2015; Willcocks et al., 2015). The starting point for this development was the observation that despite the use of application systems (such as ERP and CRM), additional manual activities are still necessary (Scheer, 2017). In the RPA approach, those manual activities are learned and automated by so-called software robots. In doing

Table 1: Exemplary definitions of RPA in scientific literature.

Definitions of RPA	Author(s)
"Although the term 'Robotic Process Automation' suggests physical robots wandering around offices performing human tasks, RPA is a software-based solution. In RPA parlance, a 'robot' is equivalent to one software license. [...] That's what Robotic Process Automation (RPA) does—interacts with other computers systems just like a human would."	Willcocks et al. (2015)
"Robotic Process Automation (RPA) emerges as software-based solution to automate rules-based business processes that involve routine tasks, structured data and deterministic outcomes."	Aguirre and Rodriguez (2017)
RPA is a "preconfigured software instance that uses business rules and predefined activity choreography to complete the autonomous execution of a combination of processes, activities, transactions, and tasks in one or more unrelated software systems to deliver a result or service with human exception management."	IEEE (2017)
In RPA "manual activities are learned and automated by so-called software robots. Thereby, the inputs are emulated on the existing presentation layer, so that no changes to existing application systems are necessary."[1]	Czarnecki (2018)
"RPA is mostly associated with the task level. The application areas include finance and accounting, IT infrastructure maintenance, and front-office processing. The so-called robots are software programs that interact with systems, such as enterprise resource planning and customer relationship management systems."	Mendling et al. (2018)
"RPA is an umbrella term for tools that operate on the user interface of other computer systems in the way a human would do. RPA aims to replace people by automation done in an 'outside-in' manner."	van der Aalst et al. (2018)
"For business processes, the term RPA means the technological extrapolation of a human worker, whose objective is to tackle structured and repetitive tasks (very common in ERP systems or productivity tools), quickly and profitably."	Enriquez et al. (2020)

[1]Translated.

so, the inputs are emulated on the existing presentation layer, so that no changes to existing application systems are necessary. This idea has interrelations with prior approaches, such as desktop automation, screen scraping, and macros, and can be seen as a combination and further development of those approaches. In this context, Willcocks et al. (2015) have used the term "swivel chair processes" to illustrate the initial concept of a software robot that replaces simple human activities of handling different application systems. Hence, the term RPA goes back to the metaphoric idea of a robot using a computer for administrative tasks, such as filling input masks, extracting and combining data, creating reports, executing transactions in ERP systems, or opening and processing e-mails (Scheer, 2017; Czarnecki, 2018).

Defining the term RPA is not that easy, as it is more an idea inspired by practice, instead of a carefully developed concept. Fettke and Loos (2019) have summarized the goal of RPA as follows: "Similar to the substitution of physical work in manufacturing processes with physical robots (*blue-collar automation*), RPA tries to substitute intellectual work in office and administration processes with software robots (*white-collar automation*)."

The simplicity of this idea – software robots just do what humans have done before – combined with existing standard software products, promising easy implementation – ideally no or minimal programming efforts – and significant benefit potentials, especially for routine tasks with many repetitions (e. g., Lacity et al., 2015; Schmitz et al., 2018), has attracted much attention in practice. Once could say that RPA was more a marketing term, used by software vendors to sell their automation solutions. Hence, RPA stands for a variety of different concepts that are refined constantly. Since then, various researchers have analyzed the term RPA and proposed definitions. For example, Hofmann et al. (2020) have performed a systematic literature review and found that software robots automate processes by following a choreography and using established applications. Table 1 shows further exemplary definitions of RPA.

This book follows a broad understanding of RPA, as a range of approaches and technical concepts that support the automation of processes in organizations by using software robots that perform tasks.

Robotic process automation (RPA) is an umbrella term for a broad range of concepts that enable processes to be executed automatically using software robots that handle existing application systems.

Typically, companies implementing RPA combine different RPA standard software programs to an RPA system that run hundreds of software robots working in their processes (e. g., Schmitz et al., 2018).

The core of an **RPA system** consists of input sensors, an intelligence center, and output actuators. It can be realized by one or more RPA software systems. This core part is supported by management functionalities, such as administration and monitoring, which are either realized by each software system or in an overall RPA management system.

A **software robot** – also called bot – is a single instance of the RPA system that automates a concrete process instance. A software robot is the equivalent to a single employee. Each software robot requires a separate login on existing application systems.

1.6 Structuring the concept of RPA

As RPA can be seen as an umbrella term for various different concepts that are constantly refined based on new developments, structuring this concept is a complex endeavor. Based on an extensive analysis, Enriquez et al. (2020) came up with 48 different functionalities to classify RPA systems, which shows the complexity of the topic.

Therefore, we argue for a broad understanding of RPA and propose structuring the topic according to the following dimensions:
1. The *business view* is the starting point. It contains the objective, which is strongly related to the benefits expected, as well as the complexity of the processes to be automated.
2. The *RPA capabilities* contain the functional requirements. This dimension is hardly influenced by the ongoing refinements.
3. The *realization view* contains the concrete technical realization, for example, based on standard software products.
4. The *usage view* shows how the RPA system is used to select and automate processes.

For those dimensions detailed sub-dimensions and characteristics are proposed in Table 2 based on ongoing research activities as well as the results presented in this book. Neither completeness nor rigidity are objectives of this table. It should be understood as a first starting point for discussing and structuring the relevant topics related to RPA.

From the **business view** the implementation of RPA could be related to different strategic objectives (Czarnecki et al., 2019). A software robot might completely take over manual tasks formerly performed by humans such as entering an order in a sales system. Hence, it will replace a human task. A software robot might support humans' tasks by executing smaller routine tasks. This relieves employees and enables them to use their working hours for meaningful duties. Furthermore, the RPA system might enable completely new tasks that could become a part of new business models.

The starting point of RPA are the processes to be automated. Based on their complexity the following categories can be differentiated (Czarnecki and Auth, 2018):
– *routine tasks*, in which data from different application systems are copied or combined;
– *structured tasks* with rule-based decisions, in which data from different application systems are used and evaluated using a set of rules;
– *unstructured tasks and decisions*, in which, in addition to existing data and rules, experience and cognition are necessary.

The **RPA capabilities** vary according to the used software systems and are subject to a continuous progress. The typical interaction of today's RPA standard software systems are existing applications and structured data, while – based on cognitive functionalities – also unstructured data can be handled. Further possibilities are inter-

Table 2: Structuring the concept of RPA.

		replace human task	support human task	innovate new task
Business view	Objective	replace human task	support human task	innovate new task
	Process complexity	routine task	structured task	unstructured task
RPA capabilities	Interaction capabilities	user interface / application	structured data / unstructured data	other (ro)bots / real world
	Decision capabilities	no decision	rule-based decision	intelligent decision
	Learning capabilities	no learning	learning based on observation of human actions	learning based on own experience
	Governance structure	independent software robots without governance	vendor-specific governance for selected software robots	centralized governance for all software robots
	Software type	standard software product(s)	standard software product(s) with own extension(s)	own development
Realization view	System complexity	single system / different systems without integration	different systems, partially integrated	different systems, fully integrated
	System operations	cloud	hybrid	on-premise
Usage view	Process selection	decentralized selection by process users	centralized selection / manual selection	automated selection
	Process execution	decentralized process execution by process users	centralized process execution / process execution by business units only	process execution involving IT department

faces to human users, for example, by combining RPA with chatbots, or the real word, for example, by using advanced sensor technologies. Also, the interaction with other robots might become relevant if the diffusion of RPA further increases. The decision and learning capabilities vary from simple systems with no decision functionalities to advanced systems with intelligent decision and learning capabilities. Whereas the former can be used for the automation of simple routine tasks, the latter are required for complex unstructured tasks. Assuming that an RPA implementation might consist of a multitude of independent acting software robots, the governance structure goes from no governance to a centralized governance structure for all software robots, which could be referred to as an *RPA management system*.

The **realization** aspects of RPA are comparable to other information systems. They might vary from standard software products to own developments, and from single systems to fully integrated sub-systems, which could be operated on-premise, in a cloud, or with a hybrid approach. However, as the ease of implementation is a major aspect of RPA usage in practice, so far, RPA implementations are typically realized by standard software systems.

The **usage** of RPA is related to the process selection and its automated execution. The selection can be centralized or decentralized, and manual or automated. In an automated process selection RPA would be related to *process mining* concepts. A centralized selection would speak for a standardized RPA implementation method and governance. Also, the process execution varies in the level of centralization as well as the involvement of the IT department. A major difference of RPA to traditional information systems' projects is the possibility of an autonomous realization by business units. However, it can be expected that more complex RPA implementations would require an involvement of IT departments.

> **Following a broad understanding of RPA,** the topic is related to various different aspects. A first structuring of those aspects is proposed in Table 2. Most of these topics are covered and discussed in greater detail in this book.

1.7 RPA architecture

Existing concepts of enterprise architectures (EAs) (e. g., Winter and Fischer, 2007) can be used to structure RPA systems. Typically, EA follows a layered architecture that includes processes, application systems, and data. The RPA system is linked to the process execution. For specific activities the software robot takes over the execution, which contains the handling of involved application systems through the existing presentation layer. Hence, neither processes nor application systems are changed, and data are only handled via existing applications (cf. Figure 3). This simplicity of the architecture is a major advantage of the RPA concept, and can be seen as a primary reason for its success in practice.

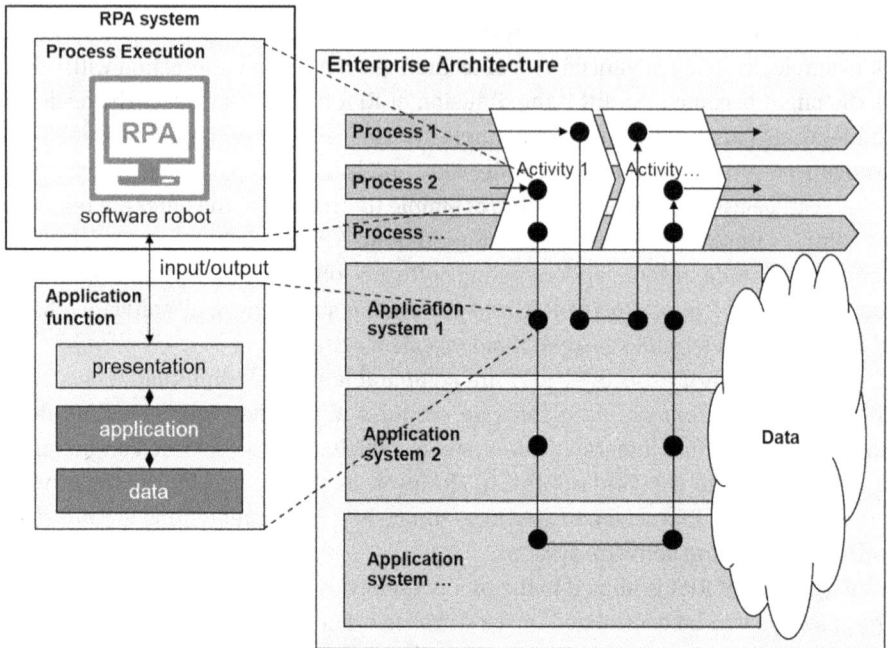

Figure 3: Integration of RPA in an overall EA (according to Auth et al., 2019).

This architectural concept leads to the following implications:

1. The *RPA system is a lightweight implementation* that is realized beside the existing application landscape executing existing processes.
2. Understanding the *as-is situation and selecting the right processes* are essential aspects.
3. The RPA system has *multiple instances* – so-called software robots or bots – that independently act as users of the existing application systems.

Comparable to tangible robots, the high-level structure of a software robot can be understood as an intelligent machine consisting of three typical components (Fettke and Loos, 2019): (1) software robots can grasp their environment by *sensors*, which generate data about the environment, and manipulate their environment by (2) *actuators*, which allow the software robot to communicate with the environment and to generate output data as input for other systems. (3) The *intelligence center* of a software robot handles the input data of the sensors and generates the output data.

Hence, the core part of an RPA system can be structured into input sensors, an intelligence center, and output actuators (Fettke and Loos, 2019) (cf. Figure 4). The intelligence center can vary from simple rule-based decisions to cognitive robots using advanced concepts such as AI (Czarnecki and Auth, 2018; Houy et al., 2019;

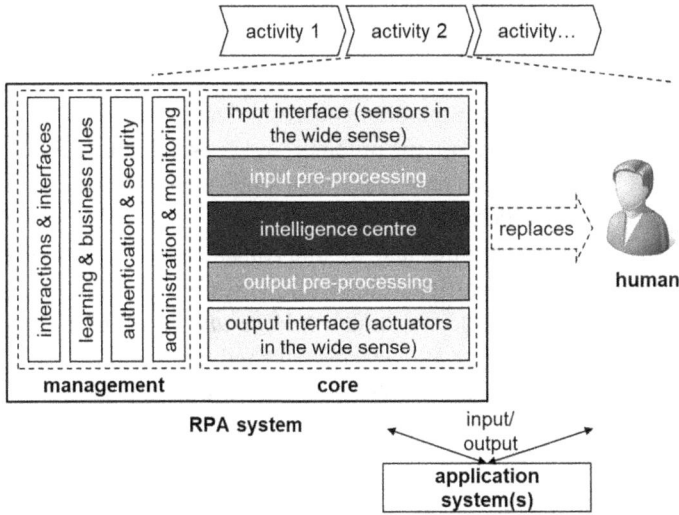

Figure 4: RPA architecture (according to Czarnecki, 2018; Fettke and Loos, 2019).

Enriquez et al., 2020). Whereas the initial idea of RPA was the automation of so-called swivel chair processes (Willcocks et al., 2015), today's RPA usage in practice develops towards more complex processes. In this context, broadening the initial scope of RPA towards *cognitive RPA* has been proposed in literature (e. g., Hofmann et al., 2020; Houy et al., 2019). Cognitive RPA uses AI, in particular ML, capabilities in the intelligence center in order to automate complex processes that require cognitive abilities.

In addition, RPA systems require management functionalities that become more important according to the complexity of the overall RPA implementation. The management part might include (1) administration and monitoring of the RPA system, (2) authentication and security that also covers the login data for each software robot and application system, (3) functionalities for learning processes or defining business rules dependent on the intelligence center, and (4) interactions and interfaces to, for example, other RPA systems or the real world.

- From an outside view, RPA systems are lightweight implementations beside existing EAs that deal with as-is processes by creating multiple software robots working in the execution of process instances.
- From an inside view, RPA systems can be structured in a core and management part. The core part consists of input sensors, an intelligence center, and output actuators.

1.8 RPA research

In science and engineering, a term is often simultaneously used to denote a problem, a class of solution methods that work well on the problem, and the scientific field that studies this problem as well as its solution methods. In the following, we focus on the scientific field of the solution RPA which is emerging.

Currently, several scientific communities take up and consolidate the main idea of RPA. Two research communities are particularly worthy to mention:

1. *Business process management* (BPM) community: *RPA Forum* with the *International Conference on Business Process Management* pitched the idea for RPA in 2020. Ten contributions were presented at this conference (Asatiani et al., 2020). Again, in 2021, a second RPA Forum is planned.
2. *Artificial Intelligence* community: *Association for the Advancement of Artificial Intelligence* (AAAI) workshop on RPA in 2020. Sixteen contributions (including keynotes, invited talks, and posters) were presented at this conference (Zhang et al., 2020).

In addition, RPA has interrelations with other research communities, for example:

- *Business informatics*: Business informatics focus on the development of RPA applications. Particularly from that perspective, RPA applications in different business processes have to be designed, the system development perspective is of major importance.
- *Management science*: Which managerial implications do the application and use of RPA have on management practice and organization development?
- *Social/behavioral sciences*: Which social implications does the use of robots have?
- *Information systems*: When are RPA systems accepted? What are organizational implications of using RPA?
- *Computer science*: Several subfields of computer science, for instance, software engineering, ML, process mining, and workflow management have relevant questions on this topic.
- *Application fields*: Various application fields started to study the use of RPA in their research practice, for instance, finance, accounting, and health.
- *Law*: Legal aspects, for instance, liability and contractual agreements, are of interest. Actual discussions are mainly in the broader context of robotics or AI.

Against this background, it is difficult to draw some sharp boundaries around the field of RPA. It is unclear how the field will develop in the next years. As a first proposal to structure the most important research questions which have to be addressed, we propose to distinguish this emergent field from the following perspectives:

1. *RPA management:* Substituting manual work practice with machines is not new. However, currently there are various particular questions, such as how to start an RPA project, how to select appropriate application cases and processes, how

to structure a center of excellence for RPA, and many others. These are mainly managerial questions regarding the application of RPA.

2. *RPA technology:* The field of RPA research is strongly fueled by the availability of RPA systems which offer particular functions for the automation of tasks. The technology behind these systems has to be developed and new ideas for developing the technology are needed. For instance, how will techniques from the field of AI, in particular ML and natural language processing (NLP), be fruitfully integrated in RPA systems? These are mainly technical questions on developing RPA systems.

3. *RPA applications:* Last, but not least, RPA applications are of major importance. Some industries, for instance, banking, insurance, and the public sectors, are more impacted by RPA than other sectors, for instance, manufacturing or the creativity/art sector. Furthermore, not all actions of a business system are homogeneously automated, for instance, accounting is a good candidate for further automation, while strategic planning still requires manual tasks. To get a better understanding which practice is changed by RPA, a deeper understanding of the application of RPA in these particular fields is needed.

Figure 5 overviews our proposal for understanding RPA research. Since we strongly believe that RPA research as many other fields of informatics and engineering disciplines is strongly related to RPA practice, we explicitly state that the starting point of RPA research is RPA practice, namely, the RPA problems which are faced in practice. These problems can be researched from three perspectives:

1. RPA management;
2. RPA technology, and
3. RPA applications.

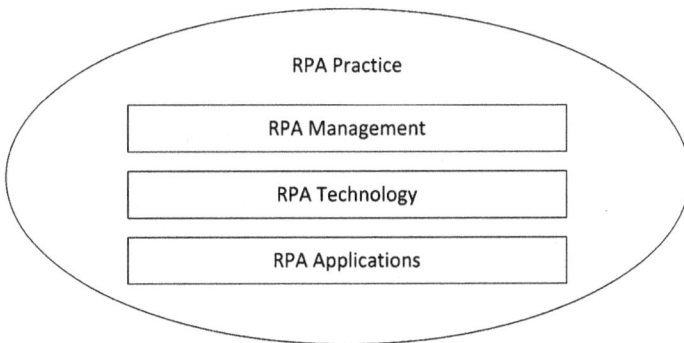

Figure 5: RPA research framework.

RPA is an emerging and interdisciplinary research field. Motivated by practical problems future research questions can be structured in **RPA practice, management, technology, and applications**.

1.9 Outline of this book

The book is structured in five parts.

Part I introduces the topic of RPA and contains one – i. e., this – chapter.

1. "Robotic process automation – Positioning, structuring, and framing the work" by Christian Czarnecki and Peter Fettke: This chapter sets the stage for the rest of the book.

Part II deals with *RPA management*. It consists of six chapters.

2. "Managing RPA implementation projects – A framework applied at SYSTHEMIS AG" by Lukas-Valentin Herm, Christian Janiesch, Theresa Steinbach, and Daniel Wüllner: This chapter presents a framework for initiating RPA projects. The presented framework comprises variable stages that offer guidelines applicable under complex and heterogeneous business environments. The suitability of the framework is demonstrated with a case study from a software development and IT consulting company.

3. "Finding the perfect RPA match – A criteria-based selection method for RPA solutions" by Frank Bensberg, Gunnar Auth, and Christian Czarnecki: The systematic selection of an adequate RPA solution is described and demonstrated in this chapter. Therefore, the authors used theoretically sound methods from the field of dynamic investment planning.

4. "Process selection for RPA projects – A data-driven approach" by Adrian Hofmann, Tobias Prätori, Franz Seubert, Marcus Fischer, and Axel Winkelmann: The right selection of relevant processes which can be automated is demonstrated in this chapter. Therefore, the authors propose the idea of a data-driven approach in which desktop activity and process mining are used to identify important process steps which can be automated by RPA.

5. "Selecting processes for RPA – A study of relevant key process indicators in the finance industry" by Stefan Rechberger and Stefan Oppl: This chapter addresses the problem of selecting the right processes for RPA from the perspective of key process indicators. The idea and approach are illustrated by an example from the finance industry.

6. "Transforming and recombining routines to scale the implementation of software robots" by Corinna Rutschi and Jens Dibbern: From the perspective of management and organizational science, processes can be understood as organizational routines. Based on this theoretical lens, the authors explain how RPA can be used in different organizational settings and provide guidelines for performing an RPA project.

7. "Liability for loss or damages caused by RPA" by Philipp Croon and Christian Czarnecki: Similar to humans, also software robots may fail in performing their work and may cause damage. Possible first answers to this question are elaborated in this chapter.

Part III focuses on *RPA technology*. It consists of five chapters.

8. "Towards end-to-end business process automation: RPA composition and orchestration" by Yara Rizk, Tathagata Chakraborti, Vatche Isahagian, and Yasaman Khazaeni: Composition and orchestration are well-known concepts in software engineering. How these concepts can be understood in the context of RPA is discussed in this chapter.
9. "Human–computer interaction analysis for RPA support – Framework and new horizons" by Andrés Jiménez Ramírez, Hajo A. Reijers, and José González Enríquez: RPA solutions can analyze the interaction between humans and machines to understand and learn how software is operated by users. This chapter presents a general framework for such an analysis and some particular techniques.
10. "Supporting RPA through natural language processing" by Han van der Aa and Henrik Leopold: Natural language processing (NLP) is a well-known field from AI concerned with the analysis and generation of natural language from a computational perspective. How NLP techniques can be used in the context of RPA is discussed in this chapter.
11. "Automated segmentation of user interface logs" by Simone Agostinelli, Andrea Marrella, and Massimo Mecella: A user interface log typically consists of actions belonging to different organizational routines. The issue to automatically understand which user actions contribute to a particular routine is the focus of this chapter.
12. "Process mining and RPA – How to pick your automation battles?" by Wil van der Aalst: This chapter draws some parallels between RPA and workflow management. In the latter field, process mining has led to some important improvements leading to the main question of this chapter: How might process mining also be beneficial for RPA?

Part IV deals with *RPA applications*. It consists of four chapters.

13. "RPA in accounting" by Christian Langmann and Julia Kokina: Accounting is one of the major application fields of RPA and is discussed from different perspectives in this chapters.
14. "RPA for the financial industry – Particular challenges and outstanding suitability combined" by Mario Richard Smeets, Ralf Jürgen Ostendorf, and Peter Gordon Rötzel: This chapters presents several ideas and potentials for using RPA in the financial industry.
15. "RPA for public administration enhancement" by Oliver Gutermuth, Constantin Houy, and Peter Fettke: Public administrations often consist of a huge amount of different, not well-integrated software systems. Typical applications in this field are presented in this chapter.

16. "Application of RPA in industrial manufacturing" by Peter Pfeiffer and Peter Fettke: Industrial manufacturing is not a typical application domain for RPA. However, this chapter demonstrates that this application field has some interesting potentials for RPA.

Part V concludes the book with three chapters presenting *practical insights* from the application of RPA.

17. "AI evolves IA – A practitioner view on artificial intelligence information architecture" by Eldar Sultanow, Alina Chircu, René Plath, Daniel Friedmann, Tim Merscheid, and Kalpesh Sharma: This chapters overviews several application cases in different industries and business functions based on practical experiences made by a consulting company. Particularly the use of AI is stressed in different RPA scenarios.
18. "The broad use of RPA based on three practical cases" by Adina Stenzel, Konstantin Ritschel, and Christoph Stummer: This chapter presents experiences from implementing RPA in three different cases within different industries. These experiences are consolidated from the view of a consulting company offering RPA services.
19. "Digitization applied to automate freight paper processing" by Andreas Kronz and Thomas Thiel: This project description describes the experiences made by implementing RPA for freight paper processing. Again, the experiences are reported from a consulting firm that was in charge of this project.

In summary, **19 chapters written by 51 authors** provide new insights, results, and viewpoints on RPA.

Bibliography

Agostinelli S, Marrella A, Mecella M (2019) Research challenges for intelligent robotic process automation. In: Di Francescomarino C, Dijkman R, Zdun U (eds) Business process management workshops. Springer, Cham, pp 12–18

Aguirre S, Rodriguez A (2017) Automation of a business process using robotic process automation (RPA): a case study. In: Figueroa-García JC, López-Santana ER, Villa-Ramírez JL, Ferro-Escobar R (eds) Applied computer sciences in engineering. Springer, Cham, pp 65–71

Alpar P, Alt R, Bensberg F, Weimann P (2019) Anwendungsorientierte Wirtschaftsinformatik: strategische Planung, Entwicklung und Nutzung von Informationssystemen, 9., überarbeitete Auflage. Springer, Wiesbaden

Asatiani A, García JM, Helander N et al (2020) Business process management. In: Proceedings, blockchain and robotic process automation forum: BPM 2020 blockchain and RPA forum, Seville, Spain, September 13–18, 2020

Asatiani A, Penttinen E (2016) Turning robotic process automation into commercial success – case OpusCapita. J Inf Technol Teaching Cases 6:67–74. https://doi.org/10.1057/jittc.2016.5

Auth G, Czarnecki C, Bensberg F (2019) Impact of robotic process automation on enterprise architectures. In: 50 Jahre Gesellschaft für Informatik – Informatik für Gesellschaft (Workshop-Beiträge). Gesellschaft für Informatik e.V, Bonn, pp 59–65

Becker J (ed) (2011) Process management: a guide for the design of business processes 2nd edn. Springer, Berlin

Chakraborti T, Isahagian V, Khalaf R et al (2020) From robotic process automation to intelligent process automation: – emerging trends. In: Asatiani A, García JM, Helander N et al (eds) Business process management: blockchain and robotic process automation forum. Springer, Cham, pp 215–228

Czarnecki C (2018) Robotergesteuerte Prozessautomatisierung. In: Gronau N, Becker J, Kliewer N et al (eds) Enzyklopädie der Wirtschaftsinformatik – Online-Lexikon, 10th edn. GITO Verlag, Berlin

Czarnecki C, Auth G (2018) Prozessdigitalisierung durch robotic process automation. In: Barton T, Müller C, Seel C (eds) Digitalisierung in Unternehmen. Springer Fachmedien Wiesbaden, Wiesbaden, pp 113–131

Czarnecki C, Bensberg F, Auth G (2019) Die Rolle von Softwarerobotern für die zukünftige Arbeitswelt. HMD, Prax Wirtschinform 56:795–808. https://doi.org/10.1365/s40702-019-00548-z

Davenport TH (1993) Process innovation: reengineering work through information technology. Harvard Business School Press, Boston

Dumas M, La Rosa M, Mendling J, Reijers HA (2018) Fundamentals of business process management. Springer Berlin Heidelberg, Berlin, Heidelberg

Enriquez JG, Jimenez-Ramirez A, Dominguez-Mayo FJ, Garcia-Garcia JA (2020) Robotic process automation: a scientific and industrial systematic mapping study. IEEE Access 8:39113–39129. https://doi.org/10.1109/ACCESS.2020.2974934

Fettke P, Loos P (2019) "Strukturieren, Strukturieren, Strukturieren" in the era of robotic process automation. In: Bergener K, Räckers M, Stein A (eds) The art of structuring. Springer, Cham, pp 191–201

Fischer M, Heim D, Janiesch C, Winkelmann A (2017) Assessing process fit in ERP implementation projects: a methodological approach. In: Maedche A, vom Brocke J, Hevner A (eds) Designing the digital transformation. Springer, Cham, pp 3–20

Groover MP (2008) Automation, production systems, and computer-integrated manufacturing, 3rd edn. Prentice Hall, Upper Saddle River, N.J

Hammer M, Champy J (1994) Reengineering the corporation: a manifesto for business revolution. HarperBusiness, New York, NY

Herm L-V, Janiesch C, Helm A et al (2020) A consolidated framework for implementing robotic process automation projects. In: Proceedings of the 18th international conference on business process management. Lecture Notes in Computer Science. Springer, Sevilla, pp 471–488

Hofmann P, Samp C, Urbach N (2020) Robotic process automation. EM 30:99–106. https://doi.org/10.1007/s12525-019-00365-8

Houy C, Hamberg M, Fettke P (2019) Robotic process automation in public administrations. In: Räckers M, Halsbenning S, Rätz D et al (eds) Digitalisierung von staat und verwaltung. Gesellschaft für Informatik e.V, Bonn, pp 62–74

IEEE (2017) IEEE guide for terms and concepts in intelligent process automation. IEEE

Lacity M, Willcocks LP, Craig A (2015) Robotic process automation at Telefonica O2. The London School of Economics and Political Science, London, UK

Langmann C, Turi D (2020) Robotic Process Automation (RPA) – Digitalisierung und Automatisierung von Prozessen: Voraussetzungen, Funktionsweise und Implementierung am Beispiel des Controllings und Rechnungswesens. Springer Fachmedien Wiesbaden, Wiesbaden

Laudon KC, Laudon JP (2012) Management information systems: managing the digital firm, 12th edn. Prentice Hall, Boston

Leopold H, van der Aa H, Reijers HA (2018) Identifying candidate tasks for robotic process automation in textual process descriptions. In: Gulden J, Reinhartz-Berger I, Schmidt R et al (eds) Enterprise, business-process and information systems modeling. Springer, Cham, pp 67–81

Mendling J, Decker G, Hull R et al (2018) How do machine learning, robotic process automation, and blockchains affect the human factor in business process management? In: CAIS, pp 297–320. https://doi.org/10.17705/1CAIS.04319

Porter ME (2004) Competitive advantage. Free, New York, London

Rutschi C, Dibbern J (2020) Towards a framework of implementing software robots: transforming human-executed routines into machines. SIGMIS Database 51:104–128. https://doi.org/10.1145/3380799.3380808

Sassone PG (1987) Cost-benefit methodology for office systems. ACM Trans Inf Syst 5:273–289. https://doi.org/10.1145/27641.28059

Scheer A-W (2017) Performancesteigerung durch Automatisierung von Geschäftsprozessen. AWS-Institut für digitale Produkte und Prozesse, Saarbrücken

Schmitz M, Dietze C, Czarnecki C (2018) Enabling digital transformation through robotic process automation at Deutsche Telekom. In: Urbach N, Röglinger M (eds) Digitalization cases. Springer, Berlin

Scientific American (1899) Some curious automata. Scientific American 80:43

Smeets M, Erhard R, Kaußler T (2019) Robotic Process Automation (RPA). In: der Finanzwirtschaft: Technologie – Implementierung – Erfolgsfaktoren für Entscheider und Anwender. Springer Wiesbaden, Wiesbaden

van der Aalst WMP, Bichler M, Heinzl A (2018) Robotic process automation. Bus Inf Syst Eng 60:269–272. https://doi.org/10.1007/s12599-018-0542-4

vom Brocke J, Schmiedel T, Recker J et al (2014) Ten principles of good business process management. Bus Process Manag J 20:530–548. https://doi.org/10.1108/BPMJ-06-2013-0074

Willcocks L, Lacity M, Craig A (2015) The IT function and robotic process automation. The London School of Economics and Political Science

Willcocks L, Lacity M, Craig A (2017) Robotic process automation: strategic transformation lever for global business services? J Inf Technol Teaching Cases 7:17–28. https://doi.org/10.1057/s41266-016-0016-9

Winter R, Fischer R (2007) Essential layers, artifacts, and dependencies of enterprise architecture. J Enterp Archit 2:7–18

Zhang D, Freitas A, Tao D, Song D (2020) In: Proceedings of the AAAI-20 workshop on intelligent process automation (IPA-20)

Part II: **RPA management**

Lukas-Valentin Herm, Christian Janiesch, Theresa Steinbach, and
Daniel Wüllner

2 Managing RPA implementation projects

A framework applied at SYSTHEMIS AG

Abstract: While much of our daily working life has been digitized, it is by no means
fully automated. Several issues such as programming cost, lack of skill, or project complexity hinder the implementation of fully automated integrated solutions using enterprise software or business process management systems. Hence, many tasks, sub-
processes, or even whole processes are still performed manually despite obvious automation potential. Robotic process automation (RPA) is a fairly new technology to
automate these digital yet manual tasks by only accessing the presentation layer of
IT systems and imitating human behavior. Due to the novelty of this approach and
the associated lack of knowledge about the execution of RPA projects, up to 50 % of
RPA projects fail. In response, we present and illustrate a framework for the initiation
of RPA projects based on published RPA case studies and expert interviews. The consolidated framework comprises variable stages that offer guidelines applicable under
complex and heterogeneous business environments. We illustrate the framework using a settlement process of SYSTHEMIS AG, a software development and IT consulting
company.

Keywords: Robotic process automation, implementation, framework, use case

2.1 Introduction

Due to the transformative capabilities of the digital age, the nature of business and the
way companies work change sustainably (Matt et al., 2015). Being competitive and agile in international markets is getting increasingly important (Syed et al., 2020). A key
driver for creating new advantages in this highly volatile environment is to work efficiently and change flexibly. Since many processes within companies are already performed in a digital manner, this offers many potentials for further optimization (Imgrund et al., 2018). In order to benefit from these potentials, a process-oriented organization is required that focuses on the values of agility and collaboration as well as
promotes activities that are knowledge-intense and value creating for the company
(Fischer et al., 2020).

   A discipline that deals with the management of business processes in a holistic
manner is business process management (BPM). It encompasses several methods and
techniques to adapt and improve processes in a continuous plan-do-check-act cycle
(Dumas et al., 2018). Contrary to the widespread use of technological innovations that

https://doi.org/10.1515/9783110676693-002

favor a process-oriented view, resource-intense processes weaving through different applications are still prevalent in many companies (van der Aalst et al., 2018). Resource constraints are the reason why many companies only focus on the improvement of a few main processes, while neglecting most of their low-value but in sum economically crucial processes. The theory of the long tail of business processes conceptualizes this observation (Imgrund et al., 2017). To effectively manage the low-value processes of this long tail, there is a high demand for economically feasible solutions. The lean automation of these processes could be a viable answer. However, established enterprise or BPM software lack the flexibility for agile lightweight automation projects (Syed et al., 2020).

Robotic process automation (RPA) could address this gap. RPA is a technology that enables the automation of processes or parts thereof such as manual routine tasks (Lacity et al., 2016; van der Aalst et al., 2018). As many of these repetitive tasks are demanding high administrative effort, RPA can be a valuable tool for many companies to automate and manage structured tasks in a straightforward and cost-efficient manner (Mendling et al., 2018). The advantages of using RPA in terms of increased quality, compliance, productivity, or economic efficiency are shown in manifold studies (Schmitz et al., 2019; Aguirre and Rodriguez, 2017). Moreover, the adoption of RPA was reported to lead to higher organizational success compared to traditional methods since its lightweight approach shortens the time to a return on investment (van der Aalst et al., 2018).

Nevertheless, inflated expectations, according to the Gartner hype cycle, lead to a misunderstanding of the full potential (Kenneth et al., 2019). Therefore, current RPA projects face several challenges. One major concern is the selection of appropriate, that is, reliable and scalable, processes as it requires in-depth knowledge of the business processes as well as of the special characteristics of the organization's process architecture (Geyer-Klingeberg et al., 2018; van der Aalst et al., 2018). Moreover, between 30 % and 50 % of all RPA initiatives fail today because of misapplication (Ravn et al., 2016). Hence the overall success of an initial RPA implementation crucially depends on a cautious selection practice based on a systematic implementation approach (Herm et al., 2020; Wanner et al., 2019; Asatiani and Penttinen, 2016).

Aiming to provide guidance for companies, Herm et al. (2020) introduce a consolidated framework for RPA implementation projects. In this chapter, we report on its application in a real-world use case with a German company, SYSTHEMIS AG (SYSTHEMIS), to demonstrate and evaluate the framework's utility in practice. The case company, SYSTHEMIS, is a software development and IT consulting company with 20 employees that is part of the Prof. Thome Gruppe with more than 200 employees.

The remainder of this chapter is structured as follows: We introduce the framework and present the use case in Sections 2.2 and 2.3. In the final section, we summarize the results and provide an outlook.

2.2 Framework for RPA project implementation

In this section we present the methodology used for the developed RPA framework as well as a brief description of the framework.

2.2.1 Applied methodology

The consolidated framework for implementing RPA projects was compiled and validated following a design research approach (DSR) by Peffers et al. (2007). First, we defined the problem and how to address this issue. Second, we extended the data collection through a theory building procedure according to a structured literature review as well as grounded theory research (Webster and Watson, 2002; Strauss and Corbin, 1994). According to this procedure, we were able to build a framework for the implementation of RPA projects. Lastly, we evaluated our framework through an additional expert survey. This procedure is also shown in Figure 1.

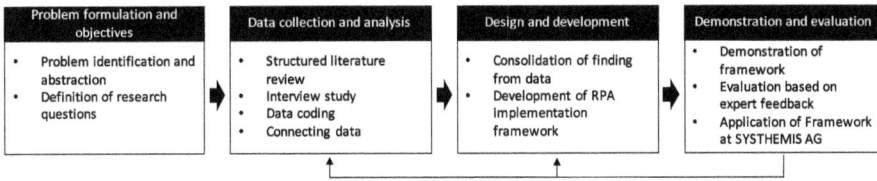

Figure 1: Research methodology according to Peffers et al. (2007).

2.2.2 Data collection, analysis, and application

Literature review

For data collection, we conducted a systematic literature review as recommended by Webster and Watson (2002). We searched common databases in the field of information systems for RPA use cases, leading to a final set of 23 studies. The analysis of the implementation stages mentioned within these case studies resulted in a first prototype of the framework. An overview of the review is shown in Figure 2.

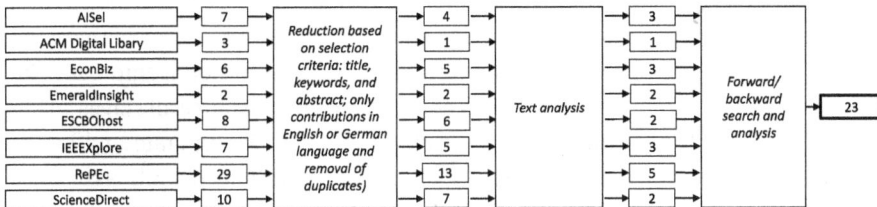

Figure 2: Overview of literature review (cf. Herm et al. 2020).

Expert interviews

In a second iteration semi-structured expert interviews were conducted to verify and evaluate the findings of the literature analysis. Therefore eight experts, contacted via an RPA practitioner network on XING, have been interviewed about the identified stages. The practitioners work primarily as internal or external consultants in small- to medium-sized companies. One of the eight practitioners works as an RPA provider. Overall, the audio recordings of the telephone interviews have a total length of 583 minutes, which is equivalent to 150 pages of transcriptions. The analysis of the interviews was based on the grounded theory research and led to the final framework. More details on the research process and framework development can be obtained in Helm et al. (2020) and Herm et al. (2020).

Application at SYSTHEMIS

Since the daily business of SYSTHEMIS is almost exclusively project-based, a regular task is the generation of invoices including performance records for their projects. Data from the enterprise system SAP Business ByDesign (ByD) as well as from other heterogeneous preceding systems serve as a basis for this task. The timestamps are currently exported manually from these preceding systems and are imported into ByD. Further, performance records have to be converted into a suitable format. This situation gives rise to various problems. Execution is digital yet manual and very repetitive involving multiple systems. The process must be executed regularly, on schedule, and without mistakes to meet customer demands and ensure seamless invoice processing. Therefore, SYSTHEMIS recognizes the opportunity to automate this process to make their project management more efficient. However, SYSTHEMIS finds that a full-blown integration project is too costly and instead, they decided to trial RPA software. Thus, they constitute a suitable demonstration use case for our framework.

2.2.3 Consolidated framework

In Figure 3, we present a brief overview of the framework resulting from the data collection and analysis as developed in Herm et al. (2020). It comprises the three phases of *initialization*, *implementation*, and *scaling* with several stages.

The framework comprises all tasks necessary for RPA project implementation without any preparatory work necessary. As indicated in Figure 3, some of the stages can be performed with or by external consultants if necessary for example for skill reasons or time constraints. However, it is not advisable to outsource all stages as RPA projects should still be aligned with the company's goals, incorporate and benefit from internal knowledge, and eventually be managed without outside assistance. Hence, typical involvement of external consultants is centered around the implementation stages of software robots. It is conceivable to involve them at earlier stages from

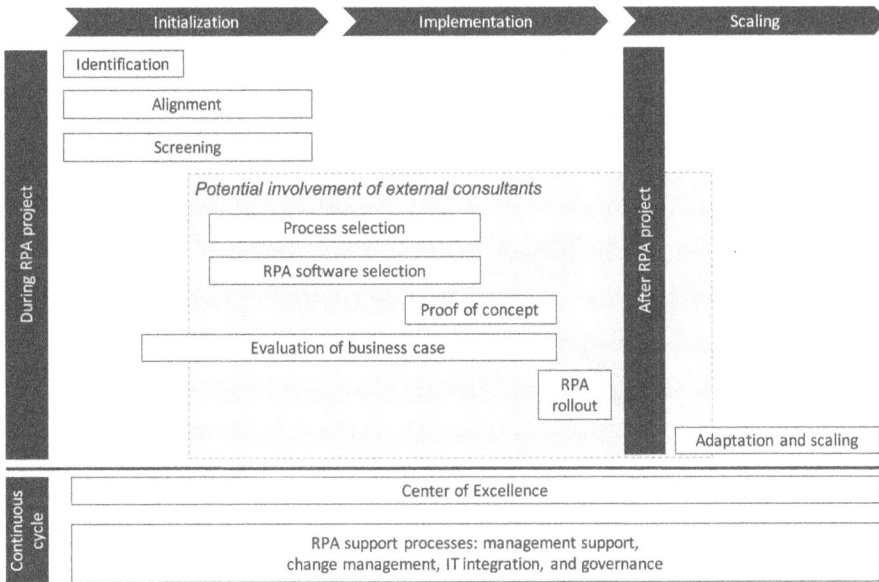

Figure 3: Consolidated framework for RPA project implementation (cf. Herm et al. 2020).

the beginning of a project if no prior RPA knowledge exists and cannot be established internally.

In Table 1, we describe the framework's stages as well as their primary outputs to provide an initial overview. These outputs are typically a key input for the next stage, which requires further information provided for example by system analysis, interviews, workshops, or document analysis, to name a few.

In the following section, we provide a more detailed description linked to the use case at SYSTHEMIS. For a detailed description of the framework only, please refer to Herm et al. (2020).

2.3 Use case based on the RPA framework at SYSTHEMIS

As a German software development and IT consulting company, SYSTHEMIS's daily business is centered on project work. Due to the high competition in IT consulting and software development, SYSTHEMIS must work as efficiently as possible. Thus, they continuously try to improve their processes within and for those projects. RPA caught their eye, as RPA projects promise short implementation cycles without any required adaptations to software back-ends due to the robot's exclusive interaction with the user interface. In order to do so, they looked for guidance on RPA projects and applied

Table 1: Description of the stages of the framework.

Stage	Description	Output
Identification of automation need	Identification of potential for automation through various observation and examination techniques	Process automation needs and opportunities
Alignment with business strategy	Alignment of RPA and business strategy in order to use aspects of RPA for improving the strategic management	RPA success factors
Screening of different technologies	Search and evaluation for alternative automation approaches for specific needs	Feasibility study
Process selection	Selection on suitable processes for automation	Prioritized list of processes
RPA software selection	Evaluation of different RPA platforms	Prioritized list of RPA software
Proof of concept (PoC)	Examination of technical and financial feasibility in the specific company context	Live functional prototype
Evaluation of business case	Derived from PoC in order to gain management support for wide rollout	Evaluated metrics
RPA rollout	Spread software robot for company-wide use	Live functional robots
Adaption and scaling of RPA services	Extend current RPA portfolio of a company and ensure scaling of results to further RPA initiatives	Libraries, templates, user studies, etc.
Center of Excellence (CoE)	Central responsibility for roles and skills regarding to RPA projects as well as maintaining and monitoring tasks	Governance body for RPA robots
RPA support processes	Holistic management support for change management, IT integration and Governance to ensure long-term success	Management briefings, change management plans, etc.

our RPA framework to their company processes. We explain the steps taken below. All implementation was performed internally at SYSTHEMIS, the Julius-Maximilians-Universität Würzburg only provided supervision and analysis.

2.3.1 Identification of automation need

The initialization phase starts with the identification of unexploited opportunities within the company and the process automation need. No requisites are necessary for the identification of automation needs. Therefore, for example, a suggestion made by an employee can lead to a focused analysis. This can be accomplished through various direct and indirect observation techniques like workshops, surveys, or document analysis as well as through the usage of information technology or even process mining in more digitalized companies (Asatiani and Penttinen, 2016; Geyer-Klingeberg et al., 2018). Also, informal discussions with responsible departments and daily business units can reveal a need for automation (Lacity et al., 2016).

The daily business at SYSTHEMIS is almost exclusively conducted in projects. Thus, invoices are created regularly including a detailed proof of performance for the rendered services. The basis for this is data stemming from ByD as well as from heterogeneous further systems. Examples are ActiveCollab for project management, common Microsoft Office applications, or ZEP for time recording. To this point, there is no automated data connection between the systems in part because this software resides in secure networks with user interface access only. This implied for instance that working hours first had to be exported manually from these systems and secondly be reimported into ByD. Additionally, the adjustment of data formats is often mandatory for further processing in ByD.

As exposed in conversations with employees from the business department as well as the business manager, the traditional invoice creation was a very time consuming and resource-intense task. Furthermore, processes with manual transformation of data between different interfaces in general are highly vulnerable to errors. The accurate and timely generation of project invoices is however critical for SYSTHEMIS. Consequently, there was a high need for automation regarding this daily business task.

2.3.2 Alignment with business strategy

The early alignment of an RPA project with the business strategy is a crucial step in RPA initiatives. Companies need to set up success factors for their organization as well as assess the utility and the added value that comes along with the implementation of RPA. On the one hand, benefits of this step include the ability to identify organizational problems and solve them right at the beginning of the project. On the other hand, a misalignment between the initiative and the business strategy is a strong indication to force project termination.

The alignment of an RPA project and the business strategy at SYSTHEMIS was evaluated during semi-structured interviews with employees of different organizational levels. So far, there was no widespread use of RPA or other automation techniques in the company. However, the interviews showed that initiatives for the implementation of automation technologies in several processes were being planned and SYSTHEMIS is largely positive about such technology. Thus, there was no general rejection of automation techniques straight from the start.

To assess the utility and the added value of the automation, the participants were asked to formulate specific business requirements regarding a successful RPA project and to discuss the impact of the automation on the company. Major requirements and success factors are aspects to increase the process quality, reducing the manual failure rate and using human resources for higher-value tasks through supporting as well as establishing data processing standards and control mechanisms.

2.3.3 Screening of different (RPA) technologies

Besides the numerous offers for RPA, various alternative technologies exist on the market. RPA is not a one-size-fits-all solution. In fact, the examination of the practicability and efficiency of the technology at this stage could reveal that different methods such as rapid process reengineering or traditional BPM may be more appropriate in a specific context (van der Aalst et al., 2018; DeBrusk, 2017). Therefore, companies need to screen the wide range of automation possibilities to choose the most suitable one (Hallikainen et al., 2018). This can be done proactively or exploratorily.

SYSTHEMIS had assessed several alternatives to RPA, but they decided to use RPA due to its advantages such as quick return on investment and using the user interface rather than implementing application programming interfaces (if available at all). Furthermore, SYSTHEMIS has preferred to use RPA due to the short development time of such projects.

2.3.4 Process selection

Once RPA is set as a technology for process automation, suitable process candidates must be selected and prioritized. In order to do so, involved users, stakeholders, and the departments of boundary spanning processes need to be engaged. Typical indicators for the suitability are a low process complexity to reduce the initial implementation and testing effort or a high degree of process maturity to ensure a sound process documentation. Besides, the execution frequency and volume of the processes could be indicators (Lacity et al., 2016). A mandatory prerequisite to automate processes with RPA is, however, their digitalization (Wanner et al., 2019).

At SYSTHEMIS, conversations with different stakeholders already revealed within the first stage of *identification of automation need* that tasks connected to the process "invoice creation" have a high automation potential. Based on this finding, the suitability of the process for the specific RPA project was assessed. For a better insight into the indicators, which led to the selection of this process, a brief description of the process follows.

The process "invoice creation" consists of several activities and sub-processes during which numerous documents are used as input and output. It is executed monthly and starts time-dependently until the 4th of each month. First, an availability check of invoiceable services in the internal ByD system takes place. If all services are already booked internally the invoicing follows directly. Otherwise the relevant data for generating a proof of performance (e. g., service number, task number, task description, date, duration) is extracted from the external systems ZEP and ActiveCollab. In a second step, the employees edit the data extract in Microsoft Excel for further processing. Afterwards, they import the Excel file into ByD. As soon as the import is successful and the times have been approved, the invoice can be created from a CSV export. One artifact of this is the "proof of performance" document. To bring this document into an easily readable format, again a processing step in Microsoft Excel takes place before the sending to the customer. See Figure 4 for a simplified overview in BPMN. It is not intended to contain exceptions or loops, which explicate fine-grained behavior, but to visualize the order of the necessary tasks.

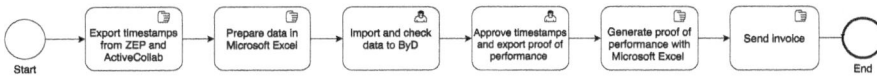

Figure 4: Invoice creation in BPMN.

Indicators to select this process as ideal candidate for the RPA project have been the execution frequency, the variance within the process, and therefore the susceptibility to errors, as well as the relevance of the process.

2.3.5 Software selection

The RPA software selection stage comprises the evaluation of the available software for automation and subsequently their selection. This is often executed based on classic criteria such as costs, skill requirements, availability of external skills, vendor reliability, or data protection and security features.

To select a suitable RPA software for the implementation project, SYSTHEMIS conducted a multi-stage selection process. As some of the systems (like ZEP) involved in the process are conducted on a secure net on the client side, a user interface-based automation solution was needed. First, a comparison of five different RPA software providers, namely, UiPath, Automation Anywhere, BluePrism, NICE, and Kryon, was carried out. This pre-selection was based on the Top 5 of the Forrester Wave Report, which evaluated 15 RPA software providers regarding 30 criteria (Le Clair et al., 2018).

The relevant comparison criteria at SYSTHEMIS can be divided into the categories "scope of offer" and "strategy." Thereby, the category "scope of offer" evaluates the utility from the system side. This includes the robot development and the support of developers as well as management of existing robots. The category "strategy" focuses on aspects of the embedding and fitting of the system in broader networks such as collaboration ecosystems.

UiPath met most criteria, followed by Automation Anywhere as well as BluePrism and NICE. Kryon did not meet the requirements. Hence, SYSTHEMIS decided to only review UiPath and Automation Anywhere in more detail.

In both systems, the creation of supervised as well as unsupervised software robots is possible. Besides, both systems include recorders, to save a sequence of the human process execution. Subsequently, options are available for the automatic generation of the program sequence. A difference between both offers lies in the attached visual process designer. While the process presentation within Automation Anywhere is script-based, UiPath is more diagram-oriented. As the "invoice creation" process at SYSTHEMIS is recorded and designed using diagrams of the Business Process Model & Notation (BPMN), UiPath offers advantages in this criterion.

Another advantage of UiPath is, in contrast to Automation Anywhere, that the freely accessible test version is not time-limited. Thus, a prototypical implementation can be realized without time constraints. Further, after the registration on the web site of the provider, the use of the community edition of UiPath is free and unlimited. Although there is no support for the free version, blogs, forums, and community discussions provide help for the most common questions, especially for "real-world" problems.

Regarding training and further education, both RPA software alternatives offer free access to basic training courses. Automation Anywhere also provides free access to some expert courses. However, as UiPath provides users the opportunity to become certified for free, it is preferred from SYSTHEMIS.

Overall, both products are comparable at a high technical level. Nevertheless, UiPath had some minor additional advantages in the case of SYSTHEMIS compared to Automation Anywhere. Thus, SYSTHEMIS selected UiPath Studio as software for their RPA project.

2.3.6 Proof of concept implementation

A proof of concept (PoC) implementation on a small scale helps to verify whether the introduction of an RPA technology is functional and feasible for a company in the given case. To gather meaningful insights on a well-funded foundation, a preferably simple process executed over several months should be chosen for the PoC. Subsequently, the reasonability of RPA can be assessed through indicators such as the process quality or the return on investment (Asatiani and Penttinen, 2016; Lacity et al., 2016).

At SYSTHEMIS, the prototypical PoC was implemented in the several sub-processes of the "invoice creation" process. Since checking for billable services, which has traditionally marked the beginning of the process, is not easily predictable, the automation begins with the extraction of data from external systems. The following sub-processes are the formatting of the data, the import of the data into the SAP system, the workflow for the time approval that leads to the invoice creation, the formatting of the invoice, and ultimately the sending of the invoice to the customer. An overview of the high-level process is presented below (see Figure 5).

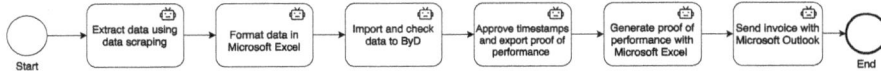

Figure 5: RPA process of proof of concept.

Extract data using data scraping

The first task of the automated process opens a browser. Variables that are attached to this activity are the type of the browser as well as an option for starting a new session. To ensure the execution of the correct web site the second step checks the elements by comparing them with sample pictures of the respective web sites. Subsequently, the robot continues with the automated login and the navigation to the time sheets on the web sites. This is conducted by a browser record of a human process execution. To extract the required project data, the system uses the function "data scraping" of the UiPath Studio. This method extracts and reads structured data and loads them into the cache in a data-table-variable format. Finally, the RPA system saves the data extract in a Microsoft Excel table for further processing and closes the browser again.

Format data in Microsoft Excel

The import into ByD requires some mandatory information as well as a special data format. As cloud systems store data differently (e. g., service times), some information must first be linked via a separate table. The software robot performs four distinct steps to prepare the table: read data, cleanse data, format decimal places, and format delimiters.

Import into ByD

For importing the formatted data into ByD, the robot uses a Microsoft Excel add-in. By clicking the import button by a browser record, this add-in sets up a connection with ByD and imports the data. As a result, a message box shows the success or the failure of the import. The string variables of the message box are read, saved, and transmitted to a decision element. Finally, the system closes Microsoft Excel based on an indicator of the application window.

Approve timestamps and export proof of performance

All steps are performed within ByD accessible via a browser. Therefore, the robot checks whether the user is already logged into the system. A browser record then conducts the ByD logon. As the browser saves the specific user login data directly, they do not have to be provided to or be processed by the software robot itself. Following, again a browser record navigates to the respective sites and automatically clicks on the approval button. As soon as all times are approved, the system creates the invoice and the proof of performance documents. However, this requires the selection of the project, the selection of the accounting period, and the assignment to invoice positions, which as well conducts a browser record. Variable steps of the last activities (e. g., the import of project numbers) are implemented using a writing activity. ByD returns the proof of performance document as a CSV file.

Generate proof of performance with Microsoft Excel

To transform the CSV file into an easily readable document, first the robot imports the file again into Microsoft Excel. Subsequently, it opens a suitable template, copies the data of the CSV file, and inserts them into the respective columns. As the format of the template is pre-defined, the columns can be specified in an absolute manner. After that the RPA system closes Microsoft Excel again.

Send invoice with Microsoft Outlook

The last automated sequence contains the sending of the invoice via e-mail. In order to do so, the software robot loads the Excel data of the previous step into an array and hands it over to a Microsoft Outlook mail message as an attachment. As soon as the sender account is specified and the array containing the invoice data is attached the robot sends the mail to the customer.

2.3.7 Evaluation of business case

The definition and evaluation of a business case serves as intermediate step between the small-scale PoC and the organization-wide rollout of the RPA technology. It helps to detect deficiencies and to weigh the costs and the benefits of a project. Besides, the consideration of indicators such as processing time, IT costs, or infrastructure significantly contributes to gathering an enduring management support (Willcocks et al., 2015).

The underlying business case of the RPA project at SYSTHEMIS was the automation of its process "invoice creation." On the one hand the analysis of the traditional process execution revealed several deficiencies such as the potential for a high error rate, a significant time consumption, and an intense resource demand. On the other hand, the delivery of project-based invoices is a crucial part of the daily business at SYSTHEMIS. Thus, the company selected this process for the automation project and implemented it in the small-scale PoC.

Performance measurement

SYSTHEMIS evaluated the business case based on the execution time of the software robot compared to the time an experienced user needed to conduct the process. According to the six distinct sub-sequences defined in the PoC, the execution time of each sub-sequence was measured separately. Therefore, the evaluation started with data extraction from the external system and finished with sending the e-mail. The system clock measured the execution time of the human user, whereas the output data of UiPath indicated the time of the software robot. To compensate inaccuracies within the measurements, SYSTHEMIS executed three separate runs on a test environment as shown in Table 2.

Table 2: Performance comparison of a user and a RPA robot.

Steps of process	Evaluation test 1		Evaluation test 2		Evaluation test 3		Rounded average	
	User	RPA robot	User	RPA robot	User	RPA robot	User	RPA robot
Export timestamps	58	23	62	27	58	25	59	25
Prepare data	218	20	204	19	219	22	214	20
Import and check data	38	12	41	10	41	13	40	12
Approve timestamps and generate invoice	242	34	240	36	239	40	240	37
Generate proof of performance	205	40	206	38	198	37	203	38
Send Invoice	38	8	41	12	45	10	41	10
Cycle time (secs.)	799	137	794	142	800	142	798	142

The performance measurement clearly demonstrated the software robot to be significantly faster in all steps and over all runs (on average 2 minutes 37 seconds vs. 13 minutes and 29 seconds). Especially at formatting steps and when it came to changing interfaces, the software robot was significantly faster due to underlying clear instructions and its processing speed. When the process step only consisted of minor tasks, which do not require logical reflection, the execution times of the experienced user and the robot were closer. However, as it was an experienced user in the trial, the differences in the execution times between the robot and the user are assumed to be greater if a new user conducts the process.

Furthermore, as humans are often exposed to distractions, the execution times varied strongly compared to the stable times of the robot. Taken together, the performance measurement showed that using a software robot in this data-driven process can lower its time consumption significantly.

Organizational benefit

To assess the organizational benefit of the RPA project, the impact was compared to the business requirements defined earlier in the "business alignment" stage. Beyond the reduction of the process execution time, the implementation of RPA also released employees to higher-value tasks and, thus, improved the quality of work. It led to an increase in the overall productivity and enhanced the organizational development. Due to the robot always performing the process consistently, a high process quality could be ensured. Also, the automation avoids execution errors and consequently prevents follow-up costs due to corrections and rework.

Economic efficiency

The business case was also evaluated in terms of its economic efficiency. Therefore, the costs of an employee conducting the process were compared to the costs that arise when the robot is implemented, which is a simplified measure common for assessing RPA projects. The internal hourly rate of the employee was the base for the employee costs. The costs of the robot were set as the hourly rate of the developer that developed the robot. As UiPath Studio is a free version, there were no further costs for the development of the prototype. All other costs are contemplated equally for both execution types. Thus, SYSTHEMIS did not consider them in the following.

Taking an average value of 13 minutes and 29 seconds (0.22 hours) for the execution time and the internal rate of 62.50 € per hour, the costs of a human process execution per year are 167.43 €. The development of the prototype on the other hand would require a unique investment of 750 €, as the development of the prototype takes around 12 hours and the internal rate is 62.50 € per hour. As shown in Figure 6, the comparison of both values reveals that the investment in the robot development amortizes within four and a half years.

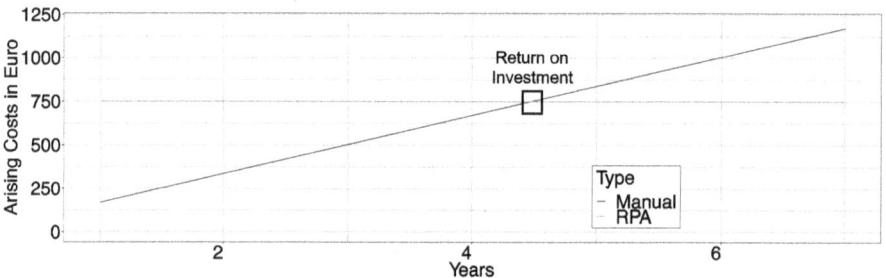

Figure 6: Break-even of the RPA robot at SYSTHEMIS.

While the results indicate that the RPA implementation takes a long time to amortize and one may question its value, it rather becomes clear that the common measure that we used for this use case does not tell the whole story. In this calculation, the benefit obtained from the automation as well as the (negligible) costs for running and maintaining these bots is not included. Neither is the search and rectification time for human errors in the invoices. Further, this calculation does not incorporate skill acquisition cost. Hence, we assume the amortization time to be significantly shorter as is the satisfaction with the process. Even more so, scaling from one robot to many will provide further benefits that are not reflected in this calculation model. Research has yet to provide a more comprehensive schema to monetize the benefits of RPA robots in contrast to human labor.

2.3.8 RPA rollout

The RPA rollout is the stage where the implemented software robot is activated and made available throughout the whole organization. Thus, it comprises all activities and effort leading to the company-wide deployment of RPA in the production process flow (Syed et al., 2020). SYSTHEMIS spread the implemented software robot for the automation of the process "invoice creation" throughout the company and thus replaced the traditional human task while not replacing the human worker but enabling him or her to attend to other tasks.

2.3.9 Adaption and scaling of RPA services

After the implementation phase has finished in a successful RPA rollout, the subsequent scaling phase comprises several activities to ensure the adaption and scaling of the results to further RPA initiatives. The prospective extension of the RPA portfolio could for example be facilitated by the creation of RPA libraries along with associated templates (Schmitz et al., 2019). Besides, this could be eased by setting up approaches for the early involvement and motivation of employees and by a step-wise extension of the software licenses (Lacity et al., 2016). To increase the understanding of the RPA and the automation feasibility by the RPA team, the complexity of the processes should rise continually. Also, external consultants should be included to support in complex processes.

So far, no continuous cycle for RPA projects has been established at SYSTHEMIS and the presented project is the only use case. Nevertheless, ambitions for further implementation projects are ongoing. Additionally, intelligent process automation could extend the automated process to automatically decide, based on artificial intelligence, which projects are yet invoiceable. Lastly, the acquisition of excellence by scaling and adapting RPA projects along with getting certified in the field of RPA is a promising extension of the corporate purpose in the future.

2.3.10 Center of excellence

The establishment of a center of excellence (CoE) complements the RPA project. As its main tasks are the definition of roles, skills, or performance indicators, the CoE acts as central organizational unit for monitoring the implementation project (Anagnoste, 2018). Further, the CoE coordinates the maintenance of the software robots. It identifies opportunities for process innovation and future automation potential and continuously improves the project under efficiency aspects (Aguirre and Rodriguez, 2017). However, especially for small- and medium-sized businesses a large CoE is often not feasible. Nevertheless, it is also recommended for them to set up a CoE that at least consists of one full-time employee.

2.3.11 RPA support processes

RPA support processes are essential to ensure the long-term success of RPA implementations. Previous governance principles may occasionally need to be adapted. In terms of financial and strategic aspects, a high-level support from management side is favorable. IT integration and change management assist in dealing with integration issues and promote the human–machine interaction. Overall, these support processes help to raise the awareness within the company for the capabilities and limitations of software robots (Anagnoste, 2018). SYSTHEMIS has not yet entered the continuous cycle of RPA improvement.

2.4 Discussion, conclusion, and outlook

In our work, we outlined a structured RPA implementation project at the German IT consulting company SYSTHEMIS following the consolidated framework of Herm et al. (2020). By linking the stages of the framework to the corresponding implementation stages in the real-world scenario and describing them in a step-by-step manner, we applied the framework in practice, where it served as a template for the RPA implementation project of the presented use case at SYSTHEMIS. The application showed that the automation of the process "invoice creation" generated several organizational and economic benefits in the reported case. First, it liberated tied up resources from a repetitive task and, thus, led to a higher quality of work for the employees. Also, the use of RPA reduced the execution time significantly and led to a lower error rate.

Another benefit was the ensuring of a constantly high process quality. Economic efficiency of the automation was shown by a cost comparison with the traditional execution costs. The results of this comparison were only indicative to some respect due to the simplified measurement.

Lastly, the framework as well as its application in the case study face some limitations. SYSTHEMIS has not yet applied a continuous RPA cycle as mandated by the framework. So far, the presented use case is unique within the company. Thus, the long-term success and the company-wide adoption of the technology remain open to further inquiry. However, the implementation of a continuous cycle as well as further RPA projects are a pursued objective of the company. Besides, there are still several possibilities to improve the effectiveness of the process as such. Extending the process with intelligent process automation could for example facilitate execution efforts. Consequently, process improvement does not end with the implementation of RPA and complementary technologies may need to be considered.

As stated in the work of Herm et al. (2020), numerous promising concepts for the implementation of RPA have already been developed in theory but have not yet been addressed by companies in practice. Given the fact that 30 % to 50 % of all implementation projects fail today because of an RPA misapplication there is a large need for a structured approach (Asatiani and Penttinen, 2016). The presented framework provides this structure and thus can narrow the gap between theory and practice.

Overall, the evaluation of the framework in practice showed that the framework proved to be beneficial for conducting a structured RPA project. It successfully guided the implementation of a software robot within a company. To verify its general usefulness, we must apply it in further scenarios and in different organizational settings. Furthermore, as additional learning, more focus should be placed on the stage of process selection to achieve a faster and/or higher return on investment. Likewise, through the use case, the need for guidance within our framework for small- and medium-sized companies manifested. Addressing this should enable those companies with more restrictions on budget and time to use our framework.

Bibliography

Aguirre S, Rodriguez A (2017) Automation of a business process using robotic process automation (RPA): a case study. In: Proceedings of the 4th workshop on engineering applications (WEA). Springer, Berlin, pp 65–71

Anagnoste S (2018) Setting up a robotic process automation center of excellence. Manag Dyn Knowl Econ 6(2):307–332

Asatiani A, Penttinen E (2016) Get ready for robots: why planning makes the difference between success and disappointment. J Inf Technol Teaching Cases 6(2):67–74

Asatiani A, Penttinen E (2016) Turning robotic process automation into commercial success–case OpusCapita. J Inf Technol Teaching Cases 6(2):67–74

DeBrusk C (2017) Five robotic process automation risks to avoid. MIT Sloan Manag Rev Oct.(1)

Dumas M, Rosa ML, Mendling J, Reijers HA (2018) Fundamentals of business process management. Springer, Berlin

Fischer M, Imgrund F, Janiesch C, Winkelmann A (2020) Strategy archetypes for digital transformation: defining meta objectives using business process management. Inf Manag, online first

Geyer-Klingeberg J, Nakladal J, Baldauf F, Veit F (2018) Process mining and robotic process automation: a perfect match. In: Proceedings of the 16th international conference on business process management (BPM). CEUR workshop proceedings, Sydney, vol 2196, pp 124–131

Hallikainen P, Bekkhus R, Pan SL (2018) How opuscapita used internal rpa capabilities to offer services to clients. MIS Q Exec 17(1):41–52

Helm A, Herm L-V, Imgrund F, Janiesch C (2020) Interview guideline, transcriptions, and coding for "A Consolidated Framework for Implementing Robotic Process Automation Project. EUDAT B2SHARE." https://doi.org/10.23728/b2share.402d2d1544124d24902182652d1bc77a. Accessed: 2020-06-15

Herm L-V, Janiesch C, Helm A, Imgrund F, Fuchs K, Hofmann A, Winkelmann A (2020) A consolidated framework for implementing robotic process automation projects. In: Proceedings of the 18th international conference on business process management. Lecture Notes in Computer Science, vol 12168. Springer, Sevilla, pp 471–488

Imgrund F, Fischer M, Janiesch C, Winkelmann A (2017) Managing the long tail of business processes. In: Proceedings of the 25th European conference on information systems (ECIS), Guimarães, pp 595–610

Imgrund F, Fischer M, Janiesch C, Winkelmann A (2018) Conceptualizing a framework to manage the short head and long tail of business processes. In: 16th international conference business process management (BPM), Sydney. Lecture Notes in Computer Science, vol 11080. Springer, pp 392–408

Kenneth B, Jim H, Svetlana S (2019) Hype cycle for artificial intelligence. https://www.gartner.com/en/documents/3953603/hype-cycle-for-artificial-intelligence-2019. Accessed: 2020-05-30

Lacity M, Willcocks L, Craig A (2016) Robotizing global financial shared services at Royal DSM. Paper Series in Financial Service, vol 46(1), pp 62–76

Le Clair C, UiPath AA, Prism B (2018) The forrester wave®: robotic process automation, q2 2018. Forrester Res

Matt C, Hess T, Benlian A (2015) Digital transformation strategies. Bus Inf Syst Eng 57(5):339–343

Mendling J, Decker G, Hull R, Reijers HA, Weber I (2018) How do machine learning, robotic process automation, and blockchains affect the human factor in business process management? Commun Assoc Inf Syst 43(1):297–320

Peffers K, Tuunanen T, Rothenberger MA, Chatterjee S (2007) A design science research methodology for information systems research. J Manag Inf Syst 24(3):45–77

Ravn R, Halberg P, Gustafsson J, Groes J (2016) Get ready for robots: why planning makes the difference between success and disappointment. http://eyfinancialservicesthoughtgallery.ie/wp-content/uploads/2016/11/ey-get-ready-for-robots.pdf. Accessed: 2020-08-20

Schmitz M, Dietze C, Czarnecki C (2019) Enabling digital transformation through robotic process automation at Deutsche Telekom. In: Digitalization cases. Springer, Berlin, pp 15–33

Strauss A, Corbin J (1994) Grounded theory methodology. In: Handbook of qualitative research, vol 17, pp 273–285

Syed R, Suriadi S, Adams M, Bandara W, Leemans SJ, Ouyang C, ter Hofstede AH, van de Weerd I, Wynn MT, Reijers HA (2020) Robotic process automation: contemporary themes and challenges. Comput Ind 115:1–15

van der Aalst WM, Bichler M, Heinzl A (2018) Robotic process automation. Bus Inf Syst Eng 60(4):269–272

Wanner J, Hofmann A, Fischer M, Imgrund F, Janiesch C, Geyer-Klingeberg J (2019) Process selection in rpa projects: towards a quantifiable method of decision making. In: Proceedings of the 40th international conference on information systems (ICIS), München, pp 1–17

Webster J, Watson RT (2002) Analyzing the past to prepare for the future: writing a literature review. MIS Q 26(2):xiii–xxiii

Willcocks LP, Lacity M, Craig A (2015) The IT function and robotic process automation. The Outsourcing Unit Working Research Paper Series, vol 15(5)

Frank Bensberg, Gunnar Auth, and Christian Czarnecki

3 Finding the perfect RPA match

A criteria-based selection method for RPA solutions

Abstract: The benefits of robotic process automation (RPA) are highly related to the usage of commercial off-the-shelf (COTS) software products that can be easily implemented and customized by business units. But, how to find the best fitting RPA product for a specific situation that creates the expected benefits? This question is related to the general area of software evaluation and selection. In the face of more than 75 RPA products currently on the market, guidance considering those specifics is required. Therefore, this chapter proposes a criteria-based selection method specifically for RPA. The method includes a quantitative evaluation of costs and benefits as well as a qualitative utility analysis based on functional criteria. By using the visualization of financial implications (VOFI) method, an application-oriented structure is provided that opposes the total cost of ownership to the time savings times salary (TSTS). For the utility analysis a detailed list of functional criteria for RPA is offered. The whole method is based on a multi-vocal review of scientific and non-scholarly literature including publications by business practitioners, consultants, and vendors. The application of the method is illustrated by a concrete RPA example. The illustrated structures, templates, and criteria can be directly utilized by practitioners in their real-life RPA implementations. In addition, a normative decision process for selecting RPA alternatives is proposed before the chapter closes with a discussion and outlook.

Keywords: Robotic process automation, business process automation, commercial off-the-shelf solutions, software evaluation, software selection, time savings times salary, visualization of financial implications

3.1 Introduction

Over recent years, robotic process automation (RPA) has emerged as a new software-based approach for automating business processes across application systems and data collections that lack comprehensive integration on the process, function, and/or data level (van der Aalst et al., 2018; Ivančić et al., 2019; Hofmann et al., 2020; Scheppler and Weber, 2020). An organization that plans the implementation of RPA for automating its business processes faces a broad supply of RPA software products including commercial off-the-shelf (COTS) solutions as well as several open source (OS) packages. A popular online software catalog lists 76 products under the category RPA (both COTS and OS) at present (Capterra, 2020). In this situation, the process of finding the

https://doi.org/10.1515/9783110676693-003

best-fit RPA solution can be difficult and time consuming, and bears the risk of sunk costs due to investments for an inapplicable software product. As for other business software categories, market analysts like Gartner and Forrester offer guidance, such as Magic Quadrant and Wave reports (Miers et al., 2019; Le Clair, 2019). Although these reports can provide a rough market overview, they are not meant to offer a systematic selection method. Most of those reports are targeted at the executive level, and therefore use only few aggregated comparison criteria.

Since software product evaluation and selection is a well-known problem in information systems research, there is a sound theoretical foundation for constructing selection methods as well as a rich choice of literature on applied selection methods for several business software categories, e. g., enterprise resource planning (ERP) software. Nevertheless, to our best knowledge there is no published criteria-based selection method for RPA software yet. To close this gap, we formulated our research question as follows: *How can organizations find the most appropriate RPA software product for automating its business processes with a selection method built on criteria-based evaluation?*

The structure of the chapter reflects our constructive research approach. In the related work section the basic concept of RPA and its current role for business process automation are briefly described. The dominance of COTS-type solutions for RPA is illustrated with examples for both COTS and OS solutions, followed by a review of approaches for software evaluation and selection in the RPA context. In the third section we present our design of a criteria-based selection method for RPA based on a reference framework with respect to both efficiency and effectivity. As guidance for conducting an RPA selection project in a real-world scenario we reference a normative management process consisting of six steps. The chapter closes with a discussion of the presented method and a short outlook on future developments of RPA solutions.

3.2 Related work

In practice, a broad variety of RPA cases has been documented (Devarajan, 2018), such as the automation of core processes at Telefonica O2 (Lacity et al., 2015), the RPA usage at the University Hospitals Birmingham as well as at Gazprom Energy (Willcocks et al., 2015), the virtual assistance in financial processes at OpusCapita (Asatiani and Penttinen, 2016), automated data extraction and processing at a public administration (Houy et al., 2019), and the automation of field service as well as problem solving processes at Deutsche Telekom (Schmitz et al., 2019). In fact, RPA has attracted increasing attention in practice, and some researchers even see RPA as a "popular topic in the corporate world" with a lack in scientific analysis (Hofmann et al., 2020, p. 99). However, the simplicity of the general idea that software robots perform formerly human work without changing the underlying application systems (Willcocks et al., 2015) might be one of the major success factors of RPA. A fast implementation, based on standard software products (also referred to as "solutions") that only requires little or even no programming capabilities is seen as an important aspect (Willcocks et al., 2015; All-weyer, 2016; Czarnecki et al., 2019). Some RPA solutions can be implemented by end users with no or only minor support of IT units, e. g., (Schmitz et al., 2019). Therefore, the usage of standard software products can be seen as an integral part of RPA.

In this context, the RPA implementation has two important selection aspects (cf. Figure 1): (1) selecting the right process to be implemented by the RPA solution (e. g., Wanner et al., 2019) and (2) selecting the right RPA solution (e. g., Enriquez et al., 2020). The first aspect, selecting the right process, is discussed by various researchers (e. g., Wanner et al., 2019; Beetz and Riedl, 2019; Bosco et al., 2019). In this chapter, we focus on the second aspect in order to propose a grounded and practicable method for selecting an RPA solution in a business context.

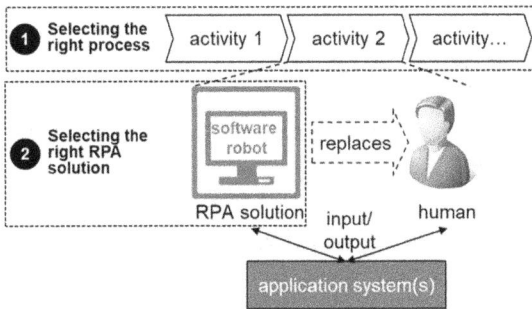

Figure 1: Selection aspects of RPA implementation.

3.2.1 RPA solutions

From a practical perspective, selecting the right RPA solution is critical, especially if the implementation is mainly driven by the business units. Furthermore, the benefits related to RPA, namely, fast and easy implementation as well as less effort, are based on the usage of a standard software product. Czarnecki and Auth (2018) have identified ten leading RPA software products based on an analysis of commercial market studies. Enriquez et al. (2020) performed a comprehensive review of scientific literature and industry studies. They have identified 14 RPA software products and combined them with a list of features supported by each product. Table 1 combines both lists of RPA solutions that can be used as a starting point.

Although the RPA solution landscape clearly is dominated by closed source (CS) products, we also found a growing number of open source tools. Some of them are still in project status and do not offer a stable release yet could be included into a sincere

Table 1: Selected RPA solutions.

Vendor	Product	Web site	Source
Advanced Systems Concepts	ActiveBatch	www.advsyscon.com/en-us/activebatch	2
Automation Anywhere	Automation Anywhere Enterprise	www.automationanywhere.com/products/enterprise	1, 2
Blue Prism	Blue Prism	www.blueprism.com/product	1, 2
SAP	SAP Intelligent Robotic Process Automation	www.sap.com/products/robotic-process-automation.html	2
EdgeVerve Systems	AssistEdge	www.edgeverve.com/assistedge	2
Kofax	Kofax Kapow	www.kofax.com/Products/rpa/overview	1, 2
Kryon Systems	Leo	www.kryonsystems.com	1, 2
NICE	NICE Robotic Automation	www.nice.com/rpa/robotic-automation/	1, 2
Pegasystems	Pega platform	www.pega.com/products/pega-platform	1, 2
Redwood Robotics	Redwood Robotics	www.redwood.com/	1, 2
Softomotive	ProcessRobot	www.softomotive.com/processrobot/	1, 2
UiPath	UiPath	www.uipath.com/product/platform	1, 2
WorkFusion	Smart Process Automation	www.workfusion.com/platform/	1, 2

1 = Czarnecki and Auth (2018) 2 = Enriquez et al. (2020).

selection process for professional use (e. g., Robocode, Telligro Opal). Others are designed to be used primarily by software developers and require decent programming skills (e. g., TagUI, RPA for Python, Robot Framework). The short list of OS RPA solutions presented in Table 2 only includes products that are also targeted to business users and therefore offer functionality like task recording and/or graphical process modeling.

In the RPA literature, the open source option is barely considered. Taulli (2020) covers the topic in a small chapter, explaining the basic OS concept, discussing pro and con arguments, and briefly describing selected OS solutions. The arguments are in line with the general arguments and criteria for deciding between CS and OS (e. g., Benlian and Hess, 2011). Hence, we do not further distinguish between OS and CS solutions for RPA in this article. Nevertheless, our criteria-based selection method allows for adding OS-related criteria, when required (e. g., to implement a strict OS strategy).

Table 2: Selected OS RPA solutions.

Vendor	Product	Web site
Automagica Software Inc.	Automagica	automagica.com
A. Zimmermann	Open RPA	openrpa.openrpa.dk
J. Bayldon	Taskt	www.taskt.net
a9t9 software GmbH	UI.Vision RPA	ui.vision/rpa

3.2.2 Software evaluation and selection in the RPA context

Different approaches and techniques for the evaluation of software systems have been developed in order to support different tasks in the software lifecycle. For instance, *ex ante* evaluation is vital in order to provide a valid information basis for investment decision making in software solutions, whereas *ex post* evaluation deals with the realized effects and consequences caused by the software adoption within institutional working activities (Walter and Spitta, 2004). As a common evaluation framework for software systems, the cost–benefit analysis (CBA) evolved, which relies on monetary quantification of costs and benefits (Sassone and Schaffer, 1978). The broad acceptance of the CBA can be traced back to its diffusion within public institutions for purposes of decision making. It carries the notion of a formal-rational, consequentialistic perspective, which is deeply rooted in management science and economic theory (Makowsky and Wagner, 2009). Furthermore, in order to process and aggregate the financial consequences of software decisions, methodologies from the domain of investment calculation have been used, e. g., cost comparison methods, net present value, internal rate of return, or return on investment (ROI) (Kütz, 2013). Besides, also interpretive approaches appeared, which focus on social context and political factors of software adoption, but their practical impact has been rather limited.

Despite widespread use of the CBA framework, this approach still has deficits. In particular, it lacks established methods to adequately consider and monetarize the intangible effects of software systems, which are also labeled as soft benefits (Oesterreich and Teuteberg, 2018). In order to override this shortcoming, complementary techniques from decision analysis (e. g., multi-criteria decision making techniques) or strategic management (e. g., balanced scorecard) have found acceptance (Alpar et al., 2019).

With regard to the RPA domain, software evaluation is predominantly focused on potential performance improvements and human resource cost reductions, which can be achieved by applying RPA to structured and repetitive tasks in business processes. In particular, a number of case studies is available, which document impressive cost savings effects for business processes in different functional and sectoral domains (Osman, 2019). From a methodological point of view, this body of research is in line with prior approaches to evaluate the economic impacts of workflow management systems (WfMSs), which – different from RPA – try to plan, control, and execute operational procedures (business processes) enforcing the collaboration of people and information systems (Gruber and Huemer, 2009). With regard to the core components of the CBA framework, current research faces challenges to give a clear guidance on how to calculate costs and quantify monetary benefits of RPA software, which are both required to provide an adequate basis for rational investment decisions. Despite this, current research provides conceptualizations of RPA that focus on purpose, structure, characteristics, and capabilities of RPA. For instance, Hofmann et al. (2020) describe a conceptual framework, meant to characterize RPA in a holistic and structured way. While the authors recommend the framework for evaluating the corporate relevance of implementing RPA, it lacks appropriate elements to evaluate efficiency and effectivity of RPA solutions. Enriquez et al., 2020 perform a systematic mapping study to identify a set of 57 criteria for RPA software evaluation, which are structured by an RPA lifecycle model. While the extensive set of features and functions can be used as input for multi-criteria decision making techniques, the focus is rather on characterizing RPA for implementation than on evaluating and selecting RPA software products. Taulli (2020) also stresses the RPA vendor as object of evaluation, which indicates that an RPA software decision is coined by specific investments and imposes severe switching costs. Issac et al. (2018) delineate nine criteria for analyzing and comparing RPA products, but do not intend to deliver a selection method.

Eventually, the character of RPA solutions as COTS software products provides guidance for identifying appropriate evaluation criteria. COTS software, which is also known as standard software or sometimes "ready to use software product" (RUSP, e. g., Kato and Ishikawa, 2016), is developed by its vendor as a commercial product for a preferably large number of buyers. Therefore, the product functionality is designed to fulfill common requirements of many users. Implementing specific requirements of individual users would lead to higher development and support costs and thus is not included in a standard product strategy. With a growing number of available alternatives for a certain type of standard software, selecting the best-fitting one becomes a relevant decision problem. Accordingly, the adoption of the aforementioned evaluation methods on software products has been object to research for decades. Especially for the case of ERP systems several research contributions are available (Salazar et al., 2013; Ranjan et al., 2016). Besides, software product quality and evaluation are also covered by the well-established international standards series ISO 25000 – Systems and software Quality Requirements and Evaluation (SQuaRE).

In order to overcome the identified shortcomings of evaluation methodologies applied in the RPA domain, we propose a criteria-based selection method, which is in line with the CBA framework and therefore follows a cumulative tradition.

3.3 Design of a criteria-based selection method for RPA

In this section we describe our criteria-based selection method specifically for RPA. The method includes a quantitative evaluation of costs and benefits as well as a qualitative utility analysis based on functional criteria. By using the visualization of financial implications (VOFI) method, an application-oriented structure is provided that opposes the total cost of ownership to the time savings times salary. For the utility analysis a detailed list of functional criteria for RPA is offered. Finally, a normative decision process for guiding RPA selection projects is presented.

3.3.1 Reference framework for RPA software evaluation

From a CBA perspective, software products like RPA tools are to be evaluated according to the dimension of economic profitability. In general, profitability is understood to be an evaluation standard for an investment object that expresses the relationship between the output (benefit) and the input (costs) both evaluated in monetary terms (Grob and Bensberg, 2005). In this way, the connection between the use of scarce resources and the resulting benefits is established so that an evaluation of the net benefits is possible under consideration of operational facts.

The evaluation of RPA tools according to the scale of economic profitability therefore requires the operationalization and determination of system-related effects (RPA output) as well as the system-related use of resources (RPA input). The recording of the output effects must be oriented to the objectives that are linked to the use and generally consist in the achievement of factual objectives (effectiveness objectives) or formal objectives (efficiency objectives). In contrast, the use of resources includes all input factors that are necessary for the design of a productive RPA solution. In addition to human resources, software and hardware resources are of central importance. By combining these resources, the RPA solution is established as a sociotechnical system (human, task, technology), which can unfold its target-related effects in various work processes. To systematize these interrelations, the reference framework depicted in Figure 2 is proposed as a conceptual basis, which identifies the components of the economic evaluation of RPA solutions. Within this context, RPA solutions are to be conceptualized as work systems (Zangemeister, 2000), which are able to exert an impact on different organizational levels (Schumann, 1992).

In order to record and evaluate the use of resources, it is necessary to collect all cost-relevant facts for the design of the RPA solution and to allocate them according to their cause. Although the primary objective of software robots is replacing human labor in routine tasks, their design requires new non-routine tasks, which, in accordance with the software lifecycle, concentrate on the development, introduction, and

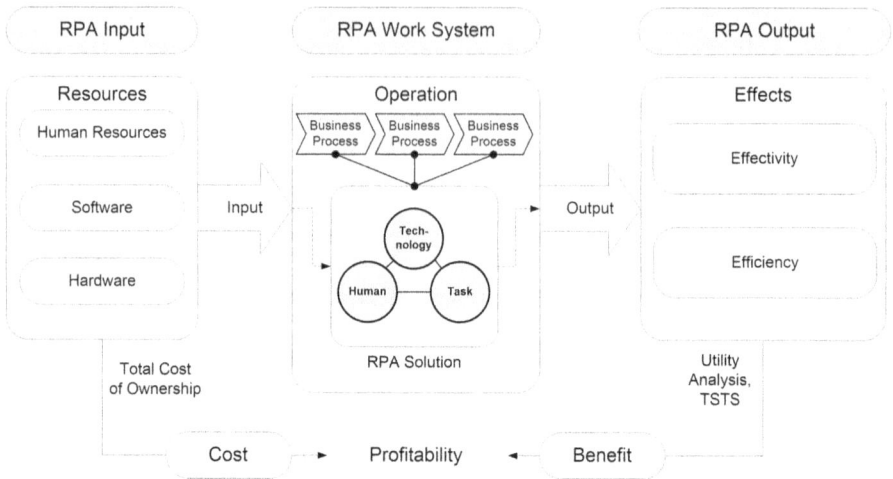

Figure 2: Reference framework for RPA software evaluation.

subsequent productive operation of the RPA solution, and which require human labor. The total cost of ownership (TCO) approach, for example, is an established methodology for condensing the monetary consequences for the input factors (Ellram, 1993). This approach records all costs incurred during the lifecycle of a procurement object in a way that the long-term time horizon of an RPA solution as an investment object is met.

With regard to the level model shown in Figure 2, the challenge of recording and evaluating the effects of RPA solutions on the effectiveness and efficiency of work processes arises in order to determine and assess the benefits (RPA output). With regard to *effectiveness*, the objectives linked to the work process must be focused. The focus is usually on the work process result (output or outcome), which must meet certain requirements (e. g., in terms of quality of results, availability, correctness, or customer satisfaction). The objectives of the use of an RPA solution must be recorded and evaluated in a differentiated manner depending on the respective business process. Thus, software robots can be used not only with the objective of automating human actions, but also to achieve better and faster work results than human actors. Since a monetary evaluation of such effects is often problematic in practice, the application of non-monetary evaluation methods like *utility analysis* discussed in the domain of multiple-criteria decision making (MCDM) (Ramesh and Zionts, 2013) is reasonable.

From an *efficiency* perspective, the question must be answered to which extent an RPA solution leads to a rationalization of the resource usage for the execution of a business process. This is done primarily by automating individual actions or chains of action of the work process, so that personnel costs and other complementary cost elements can be saved. To quantify these savings, the time savings times salary (TSTS) methodology can be used, which is oriented towards different employee groups and task classes. In addition, from an efficiency perspective the question may arise to what degree employees extend their value adding activities by RPA, such that the whole job profile has to be evaluated. This approach is covered by hedonic wage models, which focus on the intrinsic value of working activities of white-collar employees (Sassone, 1987).

In view of the reference framework outlined above, it is clear that the economic evaluation of RPA solutions requires the processing of monetary data that primarily relate to the use of resources and the achievable hard benefits (hard savings). On the other hand, the effects on the work result must also be taken into account, which are often non-monetary, intangible benefits. As a result, a differentiated approach to evaluating the profitability of RPA solutions offers itself, which processes monetary and non-monetary consequences separately. However, the aggregation of non-monetary consequences for effectivity can be based on a multi-criteria, non-monetary evaluation procedure, such as the utility value analysis (Zangemeister, 2000) or the analytical hierarchy process (AHP, Saaty, 2010).

Since the monetary consequences of RPA solutions must be made transparent in the course of rational investment decisions, for example, for the purpose of cost comparison calculations for different system alternatives (see Table 2), the TCO approach will be methodically deepened in the following subsection.

3.3.2 Evaluation of RPA resource usage – total cost of ownership

In the TCO calculation, all costs resulting from the decision to introduce and use an RPA solution must be determined. At the center of TCO models is a durable investment object which allocates all costs. However, in long-term economic considerations, it is not costs but payments that are relevant, since these lead to a change in the capital lockup and thus influence the required interest payments (Grob and Lahme 2004). Consequently, methods from the field of capital budgeting are necessary, which consider the interest of the internal funds and the outside capital rate of interest. A suitable method is the *visualization of financial implications* (VOFI), which allows a long-term perspective and is also able to make the tax implications of the investment transparent (Grob 2006).

Figure 3 demonstrates the basic structure of the TCO model using an exemplary valuation case. The monetary consequences of an RPA solution are determined here for a calculation horizon of four years, whereby the solution is created in the first year and then used productively. In this VOFI, the development and operating costs (1) for the RPA solution are first determined over the four periods and condensed into a series of payment (2). The structure of the cost categories in Figure 3 is strongly inspired by requirements of the German federal government on economic evaluation of IT investments (Sydow, 2014). This approach strictly differentiates between development

TCO VOFI RPA Solution				
Time	0	1	2	3
① Development Costs				
Planning Costs	10,000	0	0	0
Investment Costs	100,000	0	0	0
System Implementation Costs	25,000	0	0	0
Operating Costs				
Ongoing Software Costs		25,000	26,000	27,000
Ongoing Personnel Costs		80,000	82,400	84,872
∑Payout	135,000	105,000	108,400	111,872
② **Series of Payments**	-135,000	-105,000	-108,400	-111,872	460,272
③ **Internal Funds**	50,000	50,000	50,000	50,000
④ **Standard Loan**				
+ Credit Intake	74,500	16,108	19,051	22,148
- Redemption	0	0	0	0
- Debt Interest	0	3,725	4,530	5,483	13,738
⑤ **Tax Payments**				
- Payout		0	0	0
+ Refund	10,500	42,618	43,879	45,206	142,203
Credit Status	74,500	90,608	109,659	131,807

all values in euro

Figure 3: VOFI to evaluate the resource usage for an RPA solution.

costs and operating costs for an IT investment and is popular in business practice, since development and operating activities are frequently performed by different organizational units acting as cost centers. Other categorization schemes can also be used for cost classification (Kütz, 2013), e. g., by referencing the established chart of accounts of the company under consideration.

For the financing of the resulting payments, available own financial resources from the internal funds (3) as well as a required standard loan (4) with the corresponding monetary consequences such as redemption and debit interest are recorded. Although a constant annual amount of internal funds is available in this case, it is not sufficient to finance the RPA solution. The standard loan is therefore taken out to cover the financing requirement, for which debit interest has to be paid in the following periods (5 % annual interest rate). In segment (5) of the VOFI the tax effect of the investment is recorded. Since only disbursements are listed in the model, tax refunds result purely arithmetically and are determined using an income tax rate of 30 %. These have a *positive effect* on the TCO. When attributing a tax refund, it is assumed that the attributable loss can be compensated with surpluses from the rest of the company and therefore has a tax debt reducing effect. In order to calculate the tax refunds, an auxiliary calculation also considers the depreciations for the investment costs covering an operating life of three years.

The VOFI provides the essential information for determining the aggregated TCO, which is summarized in Figure 4. The basis is first of all the lifecycle costs, to which the external capital costs (interest) are added. This results in the pagatorial TCO, which is extended by the internal capital costs, namely, the opportunity costs for the lost credit

TCO for RPA Solution	
Total cost of ownership for the lifecycle of the RPA Solution	460,272
+ Cost of debt capital (interest)	13,738
= Pagatorial TCO	474,010
+ Cost of internal funds (interest)	15,391
= Calculated TCO before taxes	489,401
- Income tax refund	142,203
= **TCO (calculatory, after tax)**	347,198

all values in euro

Figure 4: Calculation of the TCO for an RPA solution.

interest of the internal funds. The value shown in Figure 4 results from a secondary calculation, assuming an opportunity cost rate of 5 %. The interim result, the TCO before taxes, is finally reduced by the tax refunds.

As the model calculation shows, a long-term TCO analysis opens up the possibility of making the financial and tax consequences of investing in an RPA solution transparent. It provides a methodically sound planning basis that allows a comparison with the monetary consequences of decision alternatives. By this, the monetary implications of different RPA solutions (see Table 1) can also be determined by TCO calculations, so that a contribution can be made to support a rational decision between competing alternatives. In this case, the specific conditions attached to different RPA vendors and platforms have to be considered. For instance, pricing models for RPA may depend on the required number of attended or unattended bots. Attended bots involve automation of processes that still require human collaboration, whereas unattended bots completely automate a process or task. Additionally, the RPA usage by other software systems (e. g., ERP systems) and their transactions may be a relevant cost driver (Taulli, 2020).

In order to determine the monetary benefits of RPA solutions, the rationalization of work activities has to be focused in a subsequent step by use of the TSTS methodology described in the following subsection.

3.3.3 Evaluation of RPA efficiency – time savings

In order to evaluate the efficiency of an RPA solution, it is reasonable to use the TSTS approach, since this methodology leads to conservative estimations of savings and is widely accepted in business practice (Gruber and Huemer, 2009). In general, it estimates the working hours a specific IT investment (e. g., a new application) will save, and then multiplies this volume of hours with the salaries of the affected employees (Mutschler et al., 2007). This methodology clarifies the approach commonly used in practice to calculate staff savings for IT investments, typically measured in full-time equivalents (FTEs). Originally, the TSTS methodology does not intend to recommend strict cost displacement by job reductions. Rather, it assumes that an employee's value to the organization equals his cost to the organization (Sassone, 1987). Consequently, the technically induced increase of time savings is considered as a means to lever the productivity of the workforce.

In order to quantify the time savings-related efficiency impacts of RPA solutions, it is necessary to use a long-term model which considers the potential monetary savings achievable by RPA solutions and to integrate this with the TCO model presented in the preceding subsection. In order to achieve this, we propose a method which starts with a defined set of business processes and applies quantitative flow analysis (Dumas et al., 2018). Flow analysis assumes that the performance of a business process can be made transparent if knowledge about the performance of its single activities is given on a granular level. Typically, branching probabilities for the activities and timing or cost data on each activity are collected and aggregated. In order to evaluate the achievable savings for a set of n business processes by adoption of an RPA solution, it is necessary to derive the operational process models for the RPA process portfolio and to enrich it for the following attributes explicated in Figure 5:

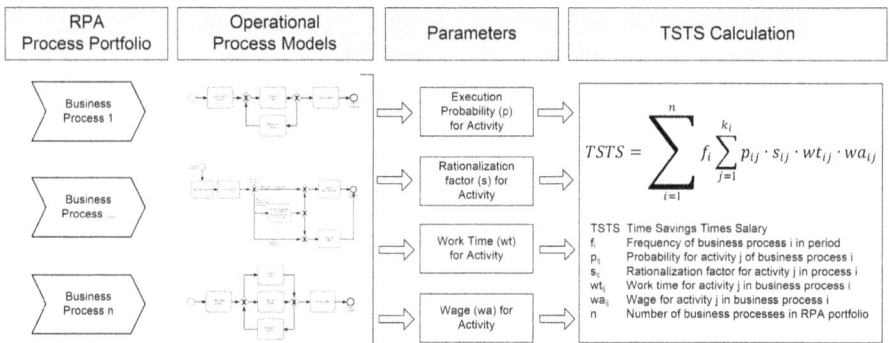

Figure 5: TSTS calculation model for an RPA process portfolio.

- The execution probabilities p for all work activities in all n business processes of the portfolio have to be determined. These probabilities may be determined by interviewing relevant stakeholders, observing the process during a period of time, or collecting process-related logs from relevant information systems in the IT landscape (Dumas et al., 2018). Flow analysis typically uses local branching probabilities, which denote the frequency with which a given branch of a decision gateway is taken, to determine the overall execution probability of an activity within an instance of a business process.
- In addition, it is necessary to estimate the rationalization factor s for each activity. This rate specifies the expected proportional reduction in work by introduction of an RPA solution. This approach is in general used for calculating the profitability

of substitutional application systems which try to replace human work by mechanical work (Alpar et al., 2016). Typically, a high rationalization factor can be achieved for manual and repetitive activities within the RPA process portfolio, are deal with the digital input and output of data, e. g., the creation of spreadsheets with customer data from one system that needs to be entered into another application (Kirchmer and Franz, 2019).

- The work time wt for the individual activities is necessary in order to provide the quantitative structure for the amount of work necessary to reach the objectives of the business process(es). With reference to flow analysis, the work time – measured in hours – may be considered as the cycle time of an activity, which is the average time it takes between the moment the activity starts and the moment it completes (Dumas et al., 2018).
- In order to derive a monetary valuation standard, the cost for all activities in the process portfolio have to be gathered. In order to achieve this, established cost accounting methods like activity-based costing (ABC) and advanced analytical techniques for process intelligence can be used (Grob et al., 2004). This cost of each activity can be split into the labor cost and other costs. The labor cost is the cost of the human resource that performs the activity. Other costs correspond to costs that are caused by an execution of a task, but are not related to the time spent by human resources on the activity, like expenditures for research, machinery, or office furniture (Mutschler et al., 2007). For the purpose of substituting human work by mechanical work, we use the wage wa as an average hourly rate, which has to be allocated for employees carrying out an activity.

In order to integrate the proposed model with the TCO model presented in the preceding subsection, the TSTS calculation has to be transformed into a dynamic model which is compatible with the requirements of capital budgeting. In order to demonstrate the basic approach, Figure 6 contains the TSTS calculation for a sample business process consisting of five activities. For these activities, the relevant parameters of the model are fixed. As the rationalization factor shows, activities may be fully automatable (activity A5) or remain unaffected by introduction of an RPA solution (activity A1). By multiplication of the parameters, the savings on the activity and process level can be determined (RPA Savings per Process Instance). Section C of Figure 6 uses these data to develop a TSTS VOFI, which considers the process frequencies for all periods in the calculation horizon after introduction of the RPA solution in period 0. For the sake of simplicity, this example assumes constant RPA savings over the complete planning period, such that inflationary effects (e. g., salary increases) are neglected. Within the VOFI, the cost reductions are modeled as inpayments, which – following a strict cost displacement strategy – can be realized by job reductions. From a less rigid point of view, the inpayments result from a reduction in the payout level for the company, such that new degrees of freedom for the investment policy are created. As can be derived from Figure 6C, this reduction in the payout level on the one hand leads to

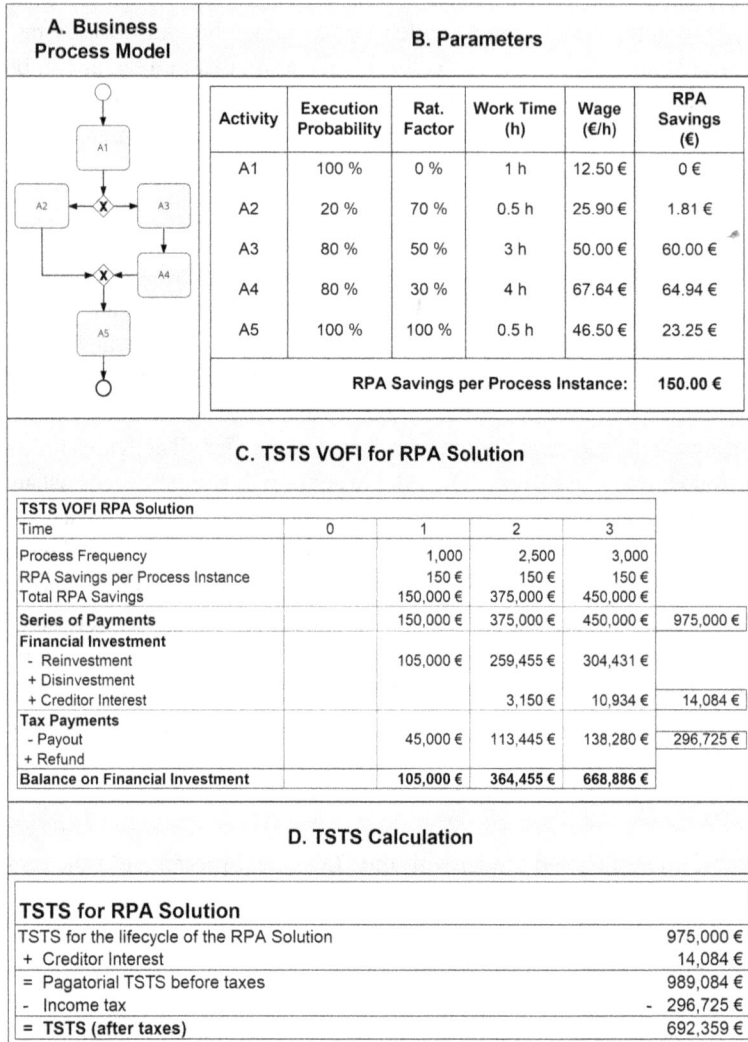

Figure 6: TSTS calculation for a sample business process.

the possibility to realize financial investments generating credit interest payments. On the other hand, the reduction in the payout level raises the taxable income, resulting in additional tax payments. Finally, the TSTS after taxes are calculated in Figure 6D, such that a comparison with the RPA TCO (see Figure 4) is possible.

In any case, the TSTS determined above represent the core of a more comprehensive investment calculation for RPA investments. It should be noted that the proposed TSTS methodology focuses on the application of RPA as a substitutional technology for precisely defined processes. In the case that RPA adoption targets the implementation of new business activities, this approach is not applicable. Instead, a business case based on the new business model is required which covers all monetary consequences caused by the new business activities (inpayments) and the required RPA technology base (payouts).

In order to ensure rationality of decision making, it is necessary to complement the monetary benefits calculated by use of the TSTS methodology with a systematic analysis of the non-monetary effects.

3.3.4 Evaluation of RPA effectivity – utility analysis

From an effectivity perspective, the benefit effects of information systems result from user satisfaction together with actual use of the system as it was intended (DeLone and McLean, 2003). Both of these factors depend on information, service, and system quality. Especially when evaluating COTS solutions, vendor quality is often drawn on as relevant factor, e. g., (Wei et al., 2005; Taulli, 2020), which also is related to service quality. In this context, service refers to support in using the system, i. e., selection and procurement, installation, configuration, user support, etc. Both the internal IT organization and the COTS vendor usually are involved. Because in the case of RPA solutions, information quality in terms of completeness or timeliness is strongly influenced by the connected application systems, we focus on system and vendor quality as a starting point for evaluating RPA effectivity.

With regard to system quality, the product quality model described by the international standard ISO/IEC 25010 (ISO, 2011) is a widely recognized conceptualization consisting of eight main characteristics: (1) functional suitability, (2) performance efficiency, (3) compatibility, (4) usability, (5) reliability, (6) security, (7) maintainability, and (8) portability. With respect to our focus on RPA solutions and our research question, the first characteristic, functional suitability (FS), is most relevant. The remaining characteristics are not specific for RPA solutions but can be applied for evaluating COTS solutions in general. Besides the according sub-characteristics and measures described by ISO 25010, 25023 (ISO, 2016), and 25051 (ISO, 2014), numerous studies on general COTS selection criteria are available (e. g., Kontio et al., 1995; Jadhav and Sonar, 2009; Krcmar, 2015).

ISO 25010 defines FS as the "degree to which a product or system provides functions that meet stated and implied needs when used under specified conditions" (ISO, 2011, p. 10). In the ISO 25010 product quality model FS is further detailed into three sub-characteristics: (1) functional completeness, (2) correctness, and (3) appropriateness. To evaluate the product quality of different RPA solutions, we operationalized FS into appropriate evaluation criteria. For this purpose, we identified specific functions of RPA solutions that support the general purpose of automating business tasks and processes based on existing application systems. This was achieved by conducting a narrative literature review based on findings of our previous research on RPA (Auth et al., 2019) following the recommendations of vom Brocke et al. (2015). Starting with the keyword "robotic process automation," we used Google Scholar, Springer Link, IEEE Xplorer, and the ACM Digital Library, including forward and backward search. According to our review objectives, we concentrated on studies analyzing RPA from a conceptual, functional, and/or architectural view. Although aware of quality risks, we decided for a multi-vocal review (Ogawa and Malen, 1991) and included non-scholarly literature by business practitioners, consultants, and even vendors. Nevertheless, the focus was on extracting common available functions in existing RPA products. Therefore, functions described in product roadmaps or discussed in outlook sections were excluded.

As expected, we found a broad set of functional descriptions on different detail levels. Through generalization/specialization and composition/decomposition we created a three-level hierarchy for structuring criteria for FS of RPA: level 1 – function group, level 2 – main function, and level 3 – function. Level 1 comprises three function groups: (1) process development, (2) robot capabilities, and (3) enterprise management. The function groups together with their main functions, functions, and according references are listed and briefly described in Table 3. The references in the table are encoded following the Lecture Notes in Informatics (LNI) citation style (GI, 2020) and can all be found in the references section of this chapter. For instance, (Fettke and Loos, 2018) was encoded into [FL18]. It should be noted that the listed criteria are selected to cover only RPA-specific functionality. There might be other common evaluation criteria for COTS software that should be added for a comprehensive evaluation, e. g., support of creating individual reports. For applying the criteria model to an individual business context with specific use cases, it might be necessary to add further specific functions or further increase the detail level of the described RPA functions. Eventually, for a comprehensive software product evaluation, also the remaining main characteristics of the ISO product quality model should be included. For instance, several studies explicitly state security as an important criterion (Everest Group, 2019; Miers et al., 2019; Schmitz et al., 2019; Tornbohm and Dunie, 2017) which is also covered as main characteristic by ISO 25010.

Another evaluation method element for including individual preferences determined by the business context are criterion weights. Weights are determined by the relative importance of criteria in a particular evaluation situation (Heinrich et al., 2014). A simple way to determine weights is to assign a relative value to each criterion in percent where all weights sum up to 100 %. Alternatively, pairwise comparison of criteria could be used for a more sophisticated weighting, as included in the AHP (Saaty, 2010; Wei et al., 2005). A special type of weights can be used for defining decisive factors (Heinrich et al., 2014). These factors represent indispensable requirements. An alternative which fails to fulfill the according criterion will be eliminated from the evaluation. With decisive factors at the beginning of the evaluation process, a large choice of available alternatives can be transformed into a short list. After this pre-selection,

Table 3: Functional criteria for evaluating RPA solutions.

Id.	Det. lvl.	Functionality	Description/occurrences	References
F1.0.0	1	Process development	Functional support for designing processes intended for robot automation	
F1.1.0	2	Process definition	Functional support for defining processes as sequence of activities	[HSU20], [Mi19], [SDC19]
F1.1.1	3	Graphical modeling	Means to create process diagrams	[Ev19], [En20], [IMD18], [Iv19]
F1.1.2	3	Recording	Means to create activity sequences by tracing manual process execution	[Ev19], [En20], [HSU20], [Iv19], [IMD18], [SW20]
F1.1.3	3	Scripting	Means to manipulate process details using programming languages, e. g., Visual Basic	[Ev19], [HHF19], [IMD18], [Iv19], [Mi19], [TD17], [SW20]
F1.1.4	3	Testing/ debugging	Means to test process definitions and retrace/fix automation defects	[Ev19], [En20], [SW20]
F1.1.5	3	Low code support	Functional support for defining processes (completely) without coding, targeted at business users	[Iv19], [Le19], [SW20], [TD17]
F1.2.0	2	Process flow control	Functional support for controlling the activity flow of a process	[HHF19], [HSU20], [Iv19], [SW20]
F1.2.1	3	Control structures	Means to control the activity flow through business rules, e. g., sequence, choice, loop, exception	[En20], [HSU20], [HHF19], [Iv19]
F1.2.2	3	Logical operators and expressions	Means to define process logic through Boolean operators, e. g., AND, OR, NOT	[HSU20], [Iv19]
F1.2.3	3	Event triggers	Means to wait for specified events to initiate further activities, e. g., detect new file	[Ev19], [HSU20], [HHF19]
F2.0.0	1	Robot capabilities	Capabilities of a robot for executing predefined processes	
F2.1.0	2	Application control	Capabilities for controlling and utilizing application systems	[De18], [En20], [HHF19], [HSU20], [Iv19], [Mi19], [SDC19], [SW20]
F2.1.1	3	Web applications	Support of browsers, standards (e. g., XAML), frameworks, etc.	[En20], [Mi19], [SW20], [TD17]

Table 3: (continued)

Id.	Det. lvl.	Functionality	Description/occurrences	References
F2.1.2	3	Office applications	Support of certain office applications (e. g., text, spreadsheet, presentation)	[En20], [HSU20], [Mi19], [SW20]
F2.1.3	3	Enterprise applications	Support of certain enterprise applications (e. g., ERP, CRM, BPM, ECM)	[De18], [HSU20], [HHF19], [Mi19]
F2.1.4	3	Collaboration applications	E-mail, calendar, messenger, etc.	[HSU20], [HHF19], [Mi19]
F2.1.5	3	Legacy/other applications	Support of individually developed or other process-related applications	[De18], [En20], [HHF19], [Mi19], [TD17], [SW20]
F2.2.0	2	UI control	Capabilities for controlling and utilizing (graphical) user interfaces	[De18], [Ev19], [FL18], [Iv19], [Mi19], [SW20], [TD17], [vBH18]
F2.2.1	3	UI element recognition	Recognizing and identifying a UI element on the screen, e. g., a certain button and its position	[FL18], [Mi19], [vBH18]
F2.2.2	3	UI element operation	Means to perform an operation on a selected UI element, e. g., click, select from list, enter text	[FL18], [Mi19], [HHF19]
F2.3.0	2	Data control	Capabilities for processing and manipulating data via different interfaces	[De18], [En20], [FL18], [HHF19], [HSU20], [Iv19], [Mi19], [SDC19]
F2.3.1	3	Data input	Available methods for data input, e. g., read/extract data from file, database, screen/UI elements	[De18], [En20], [FL18], [HHF19], [HSU20], [Mi19]
F2.3.2	3	Data manipulation	Available methods for data manipulation, e. g., calculation, sort/filter, string manipulation, formatting	[De18], [En20], [FL18], [HHF19], [HSU20], [Mi19]
F2.3.3	3	Data output	Available methods for data output, e. g., write/send data to file, database, screen/UI elements, devices	[De18], [En20], [FL18], [HHF19], [HSU20], [Mi19]
F2.4.0	2	AI capabilities	Cognitive computing capabilities for executing complex processes (also termed "cognitive RPA" or "intelligent process automation" [IPA])	[De18], [En20], [FL18], [HHF19], [Iv19], [Le19], [Mi19], [SDC19], [SW20]
F2.4.1	3	Feature extraction and identification	Extracting/identifying specific objects from data, e. g., optical character recognition (OCR)	[De18], [HHF19], [Iv19], [Mi19], [SDC19]

Table 3: (continued)

Id.	Det. lvl.	Functionality	Description/occurrences	References
F2.4.2	3	Predicting	Estimating future events or conditions	[Ev19], [FL18], [Mi19]
F2.4.3	3	Decision making	Selecting from alternatives based on data	[Ev19], [FL18], [HHF19], [Le19], [SW20]
F2.4.4	3	Generating	Producing or creating artefacts, e. g., natural language for chatbot integration	[De18], [Ev19], [FL18], [Iv19], [Mi19]
F2.4.5	3	Learning	Memorizing new problem solutions	[De18], [HSU20], [HHF19], [Iv19], [Le19], [Mi19], [SDC19], [SW20]
F3.0.0	1	Enterprise management	Functional support for implementing large-scale RPA use on enterprise level	
F3.1.0	2	Roboforce management & orchestration	Functional support for operating and controlling large numbers of robots	[Ev19], [Le19], [SW20], [TD17]
F3.1.1	3	Execution modes	Attended/unattended/hybrid	[IMD18], [Iv19], [Mi19], [SW20], [TD17]
F3.1.2	3	Planning	Means to plan and set up unattended robot operations in advance	[Ev19], [SW20]
F3.1.3	3	Monitoring & controlling	Means to view information on and control the execution of robots	[De18], [En20], [Ev19], [HHF19], [SDC19], [TD17]
F3.1.4	3	Exception handling	Means to hand over process execution to a human agent in case of failure/problem	[De18], [En20], [Mi19]
F3.1.5	3	Audit/compliance support	Means to support audits and follow compliance rules, e. g., logging an audit trail	[De18], [HSU20], [Mi19], [TD17]
F3.2.0	2	Large-scale support	Functional support for implementing RPA in large organizations	[De18], [Le19], [SDC19]
F3.2.1	3	Process candidate discovery	Advanced support for identifying candidates suitable for RPA, e. g., process analytics/mining, crowdsourcing	[Ev19], [En20], [Iv19], [Le19], [Mi19]
F3.2.2	3	Team development	Means to support team development, e. g., source control, automated documentation, knowledge management	[Ev19], [SDC19]

Table 3: (continued)

Id.	Det. lvl.	Functionality	Description/occurrences	References
F3.2.3	3	Design for reuse	Means to support reuse of automated processes, e. g., repository, libraries, templates	[Ev19], [HSU20], [Mi19], [SW20]
F3.2.4	3	User community	Means to share knowledge with other users/developers	[Ev19], [IMD18], [Le19]
F3.2.5	3	Third-party integration	Means to find and integrate RPA product extensions or robots from third-party vendors, e. g., online marketplace	[Ev19], [HSU20], [Le19], [Mi19], [SW20]

only the remaining alternatives on the short list go through the full evaluation process. Pre-selection can help to reduce time and resource consumption for the overall evaluation. Since there is a risk that with decisive factors alternatives are eliminated too early, their definition and use should be well thought out.

The vendor of a standard software product controls the design and development of the product. Therefore, his or her role for adapting the standard product to individual requirements, fixing product errors, or adding new features is essential. The vendor's role for successfully implementing and using standard software has been recognized for long, e. g., for ERP systems (Haines and Goodhue 2000). Accordingly, well-proven evaluation criteria for vendor quality are available. For ERP systems, Wei et al. (2005) proposed (1) reputation (including financial condition), (2) technical capability, and (3) ongoing service, underpinned by another ten more detailed sub-criteria. Since the term RPA is still relatively new in the IT solution market and draws a lot of attention and expectations, several new vendors and solution providers have appeared recently in the market (van der Aalst et al., 2018). Not all of these newcomers will turn out to be competitive in the long term. In this respect, evaluating RPA vendor quality is even more important to avoid the trouble of being forced to rapidly migrate to another product/vendor because the old one has vanished from the market.

3.3.5 Selection method within a normative decision process

In order to structure the activities required for a rational decision process for RPA software alternatives, we reference a normative management process, which is depicted in Figure 7. In general, decision problems resulting from discrepancies between given and desired operational facts should be understood as formative objects of management processes in companies. The decision problem to decide between different RPA software alternatives may originate from different internal or external factors. With

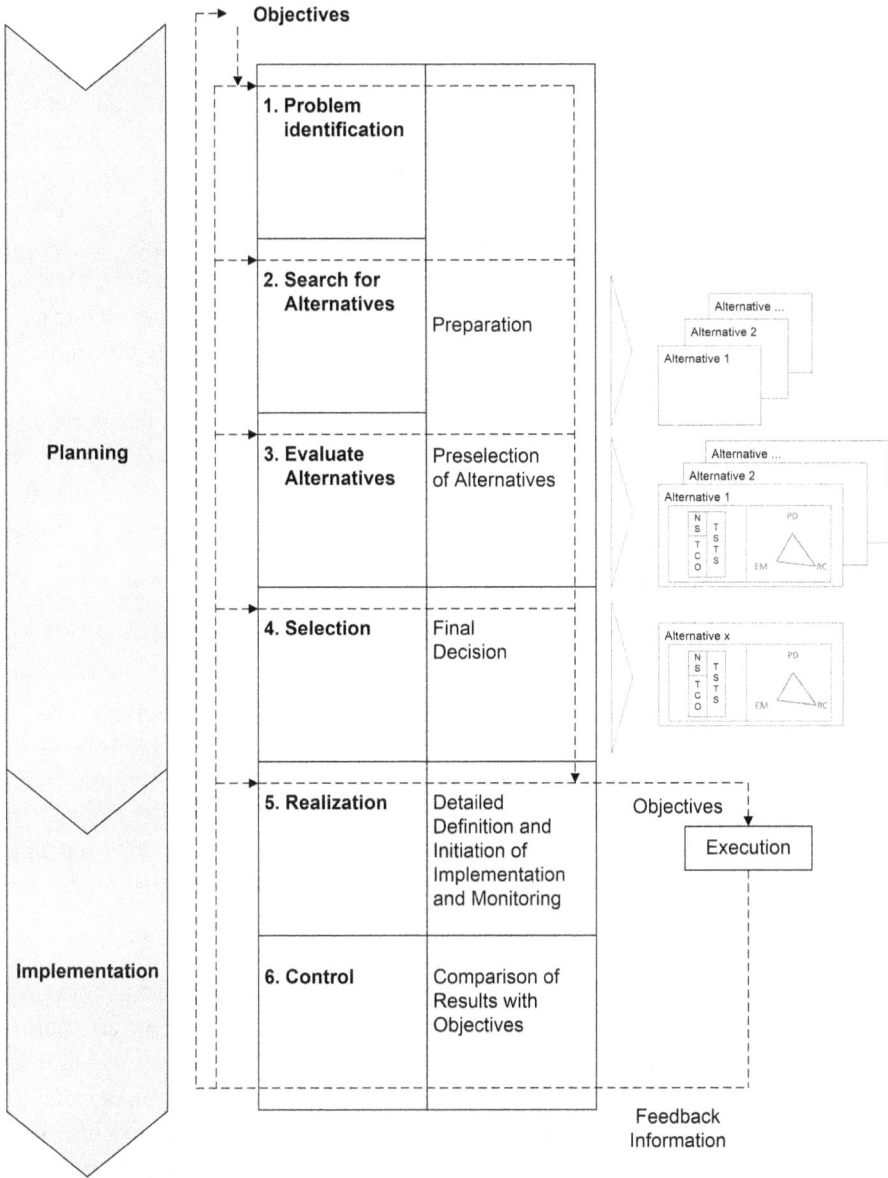

Figure 7: Normative decision process for RPA alternatives (Grob and Bensberg, 2009).

regard to internal factors, the need to introduce RPA technology may be driven by as-is process costs relative to the competition, while on the external perspective lacking supply in competent workforce due to demographic change may be a strategic driving factor. These factors stimulate the first phase in the decision making process, which identifies a deviation between an objective (e. g., targeted values for process costs or fluctuation rates) and the actual or the predicted value of these indicators. In order to achieve the desired target state, in a normative decision process it is necessary to search for feasible alternatives. This is done in the second phase, which identifies different alternatives to solve the decision problem. This phase has to collect the necessary information on RPA alternatives and should rely on available RPA market information (e. g., see Table 1).

After the definition of the set of alternatives, it is necessary to evaluate all relevant alternatives with regard to their monetary and non-monetary consequences. With regard to the proposed evaluation methodology (Sections 3.3.2, 3.3.3), it is therefore necessary to carry out the following calculations to make the monetary implications of RPA transparent:

- The *TCO calculation* for all RPA alternatives is required, which implies that the financial parameters (e. g., internal funds, capital rate, tax rate) are determined and a calculation horizon for the RPA decision problem is fixed. Additionally, the licensing models of the different RPA alternatives have to be surveyed, such that the cost data can be completed.
- The *TSTS calculation* requires the initial definition of an RPA process portfolio that contains operational process models as a structural database to derive the time savings. In this evaluation activity, the correct estimation of the rationalization factor is crucial. In the case that no internal data are available, e. g., by carrying out prototypical RPA implementations for representative process candidates, external data can be gained by reference to the increasing amount of documented RPA use cases in the literature. Furthermore, the TSTS VOFI calculation demands the specification of wages and work time data, such that data from multiple sources within the company (e. g., human resources, cost accounting) are collected and aggregated.

As depicted in Figure 7, the derived monetary key figures for each decision alternative have to be compared. If the TSTS dominate the TCO of an alternative the alternative should be pre-selected, since from a pure monetary perspective it is rational to realize positive *net savings* (NS). However, this decision is based on a differential calculus ignoring uncertainty. Therefore, more sophisticated models may make use of a total comparative calculation for the RPA investment decision, using established methods like Monte Carlo simulation to anticipate uncertainty, for instance with regard to the model's core parameters like the rationalization factor, interest rates, and process frequencies.

Pre-selected RPA alternatives should be subsequently evaluated according to their non-monetary consequences by use of the criteria contained in the attribute hierarchy introduced in Section 3.3.4. This results in evaluations for the three categories process development (PD), robot capabilities (RC), and enterprise management (EM), which are indicated in Figure 7. By using established methods like utility value analysis, the resulting evaluation data can be aggregated to rank the RPA alternatives according to their overall utility value.

In the subsequent step of the normative decision process, the value maximizing alternative has to be selected. This can be prepared by ranking the pre-selected alternatives according their *net savings* and their *utility value*. In this situation, the ranking sequences of pre-selected alternatives according to both criteria may differ. In this case, the decision maker has to weigh the monetary and non-monetary evaluations, for instance by explicit formulation of a higher-level utility function which synthesizes both kinds of evaluation (Grob and Bensberg, 2009).

The last two steps within the decision process deal with the implementation and control of the selected RPA alternative. The realization requires the definition of the implementation plan by using established instruments of IT project management and the monitoring of the results. The monitoring of the results has to deliver the data required to calculate the realized effects of the RPA solution. Finally, the control activity in Figure 7 has to compare the realized effects to the effects intended. In particular, the TCO VOFI and TSTS VOFI have to be populated with the as-is data, such that deviations from the planning calculations can be identified and traced back to the causing parameters, e. g., process frequencies and rationalization factors. This creates a valuable database, which opens up the chance to learn for future implementation projects dealing with process automation.

Altogether, the described decision process is based on normative decision theory and imposes a high effort to create the required informational basis of decision making. Consequently, for business practice it may be reasonable to tailor the proposed decision process to practical requirements. This can be achieved with regard to the monetary evaluation models (TCO VOFI, TSTS VOFI) by using estimation techniques to derive the required parameters. In the context of the non-monetary evaluation by use of the proposed attribute hierarchy, a reduction of the criteria set can be realized with regard to the objectives attached to the introduction of an RPA software solution.

3.4 Discussion and outlook

The implementation of RPA in practice requires two selection tasks: (1) selection of the processes to be automated and (2) selection of the RPA software. Looking at the documented RPA cases, most of the benefits are related to the usage of a standard software product. A broad variety of RPA software products including COTS solutions as well as several OS packages is offered. For example, an online software catalog lists 76 products (both COTS and OS) at present (Capterra, 2020). Hence, companies and organizations require guidance, how to select the proper RPA software meeting their requirements.

This chapter proposes a criteria-based selection method for RPA solutions that is structured into (1) resource usage based on TCO, (2) efficiency potentials based on time savings, and (3) functional suitability. The first two aspects are combined in a *visualization of financial implications* (VOFI), which offers a transparent method to structure the quantitative aspects of the investment decision. From a qualitative perspective the functional suitability is structured according to a set of specific functionalities for RPA solutions. With this combination of qualitative and quantitative aspects, a comprehensive method for the selection of RPA solutions is provided. The application of this method is illustrated based on concrete examples. Those examples are derived from real-life implementation cases, which provide a first validation of the proposed method.

In practice, the presented results can be used as guidance for companies and organizations during the planning and design of RPA implementations. Exemplary structures and templates are provided for the quantitative evaluation that can be easily applied. The detailed list of specific functionalities can be used as a starting point to define the concrete requirements, for example, as part of a request-for-proposal document. Both the qualitative and quantitative aspects can be customized according to a specific implementation scenario, and different existing tools (e. g., VOFI template, WiBe calculator, SuperDecisions) are available for their operationalization. As a contribution to research, the chapter provides a balanced structure of the different relevant aspects of the RPA selection that can be easily extended by future research results, e. g., further functional details of RPA software. Furthermore, the results can be used for an *ex ante* evaluation of new RPA capabilities as well as for an *ex post* evaluation of existing RPA cases.

The presented results are based on extensive literature references and market studies. The selection method is exemplified using real-life examples that can be seen as a first verification. The method itself is based on well-recognized existing approaches and standards in the field of software selection and investment evaluation, such as VOFI and ISO 25010. However, experiences with the application of the proposed RPA selection method should be used for further evaluations. So far, the functional aspects are defined on a high level according to existing RPA software products. Currently RPA is a fast-changing topic with a broad variety of innovative developments in practice and research. Therefore, especially the defined functionalities require further detailing as well as a continuous adaptation to future innovations (e. g., cognitive functionalities).

A possible risk of RPA, although not yet addressed in scientific research, often is technical debt. Technical debt is a metaphor used in software development to explain the mostly invisible problems caused by decisions that value time and cost over quality. These problems can affect both code and architecture. In the long run, they lead to significant reductions of maintainability and evolvability (Kruchten et al., 2012). Similar to financial debt, which is growing over time through interest, technical debt is piling up through more and more dependencies. According to (Kruchten et al., 2012), the main reasons for accumulating technical debt are carelessness, lack of education, poor processes, non-systematic verification of quality, or basic incompetence. At first, poor processes lead the way to causing technical debt through RPA. Since the use of RPA often aims for quick wins that require little investment (van der Aalst et al., 2018), there is a risk that implementing RPA does not include process improvement prior to process automation (Scheppler and Weber, 2020). Thus, ineffective processes remain ineffective after automation, although they may run more efficient now. If a process also produces defects, RPA could produce defects even faster, leading to significant rework (Kirchmer, 2017). Another type of technical debt by RPA relates to architecture. Since RPA solutions mainly use graphical user interfaces to automate applications, they should be able to adapt to changes of the user interface design, e. g., a new position of a button. Furthermore, to avoid growing technical debt, solutions should be able to predict the impact of such changes in advance (Miers et al., 2019). While general approaches to measure technical debt and include it into decision making exist, e. g., (Seaman et al., 2012), their applicability and adaptation to RPA selection requires further research.

Regarding the future development of RPA solutions, it will be interesting how the market will react to the maturing process of RPA technology. Besides the increase of dedicated RPA vendors, it can be observed that also vendors of traditional enterprise systems have realized the potential of RPA technology and start to integrate it into their product portfolios. SAP, for instance, has acquired the French RPA vendor Contextor in 2018 (Wheatley, 2018) and has integrated its products into a solution now called SAP Intelligent Robotic Process Automation. Even more relevant for the further development of RPA might be the recent acquisition of the UK-based RPA vendor Softomotive by Microsoft "to accelerate and expand its Robotic Process Automation capabilities" (Softomotive, 2020). With its dominant market power, Microsoft might be able to transform the RPA market into a near-monopoly, similar to the market for office software.

Bibliography

Allweyer T (2016) Robotic Process Automation – Neue Perspektiven für die Prozessautomatisierung. https://www.kurze-prozesse.de/blog/wp-content/uploads/2016/11/Neue-Perspektiven-durch-Robotic-Process-Automation.pdf (accessed 06/07/2020)

Alpar P, Alt R, Bensberg F, Lothar Grob H, Weimann P, Winter R (2016) Anwendungsorientierte Wirtschaftsinformatik Springer Fachmedien Wiesbaden, Wiesbaden. https://doi.org/10.1007/978-3-658-14146-2

Alpar P, Alt R, Bensberg F, Weimann P (2019) Anwendungsorientierte Wirtschaftsinformatik: Strategische Planung, Entwicklung und Nutzung von Informationssystemen. Springer Fachmedien Wiesbaden, Wiesbaden. https://doi.org/10.1007/978-3-658-25581-7

Asatiani A, Penttinen E (2016) Turning robotic process automation into commercial success – case OpusCapita. J Inf Technol Teaching Cases 6(2):67–74. https://doi.org/10.1057/jittc.2016.5

Auth G, Czarnecki C, Bensberg F (2019) Impact of robotic process automation on enterprise architectures. Gesellschaft für Informatik e. V. https://doi.org/10.18420/INF2019_WS05

Beetz R, Riedl Y (2019) Robotic process automation: developing a multi-criteria evaluation model for the selection of automatable business processes. In: AMCIS

Benlian A, Hess T (2011) Comparing the relative importance of evaluation criteria in proprietary and open-source enterprise application software selection – a conjoint study of ERP and Office systems. Inf Syst J 21(6):503–525. https://doi.org/10.1111/j.1365-2575.2010.00357.x

Bosco A, Augusto A, Dumas M, La Rosa M, Fortino G (2019) Discovering automatable routines from user interaction logs. In: Hildebrandt T, van Dongen BF, Röglinger M, Mendling J (eds) Business process management forum. Lecture Notes in Business Information Processing, vol 360. Springer, Cham, Switzerland, pp 144–162. https://doi.org/10.1007/978-3-030-26643-1_9

Capterra (2020) Robotic process automation software. https://www.capterra.com/robotic-process-automation-software/ (accessed 02/25/2020)

Czarnecki C, Auth G (2018) Prozessdigitalisierung durch Robotic Process Automation. In: Barton T, et al (eds) Digitalisierung in Unternehmen, Angewandte Wirtschaftsinformatik. SpringerVieweg, Wiesbaden, Germany, pp 113–131. https://doi.org/10.1007/978-3-658-22773-9_7

Czarnecki C, Bensberg F, Auth G (2019) Die Rolle von Softwarerobotern für die zukünftige Arbeitswelt. HMD, Prax Wirtschinform 56(4):795–808. https://doi.org/10.1365/s40702-019-00548-z

del Rosario Pérez Salazar M, Rivera I, Cristóbal Vázquez IM (2013) ERP selection: a literature review. Int J Ind Syst Eng 13(3):309–324. https://doi.org/10.1504/IJISE.2013.052279

DeLone WH, McLean
ER (2003) The DeLone and McLean model of information systems success: a ten-year update. J Manag Inf Syst 19(4):9–30. https://doi.org/10.1080/07421222.2003.11045748

Devarajan Y (2018) A study of robotic process automation use cases today for tomorrow's business. Int J Comput Tech 5(6):12–18

Dumas M, La Rosa M,
Mendling J, Reijers HA (2018) In: Fundamentals of business process management. Springer Berlin Heidelberg, Berlin, Heidelberg. https://doi.org/10.1007/978-3-662-56509-4

Ellram L (1993) Total cost of ownership: elements and implementation. Int J Purch Mater Manag 29(3):2–11. https://doi.org/10.1111/j.1745-493X.1993.tb00013.x

Enriquez JG, Jimenez-Ramirez A, Dominguez-Mayo FJ, Garcia-Garcia JA (2020) Robotic process automation: a scientific and industrial systematic mapping study. IEEE Access 8:39113–39129. https://doi.org/10.1109/ACCESS.2020.2974934

Everest Group (2019) Everest Group PEAK Matrix™ for robotic process automation (RPA) technology vendors 2019. https://www2.everestgrp.com/reportaction/EGR-2019-38-R-3217/toc (accessed 05/31/2020)

Fettke P, Loos P (2018) Structuring information systems in the era of robotic process automation. https://doi.org/10.13140/RG.2.2.18811.36648

GI (2020) LNI Authors Instructions. https://gi.de/fileadmin/GI/Hauptseite/Service/Publikationen/LNI/LNI-authorsinstructions-english.doc (accessed 06/04/2020)

Grob HL (2006) Einführung in die Investitionsrechnung: eine Fallstudiengeschichte. 5., vollst. überarb. und erw. Aufl. Vahlen, München, Germany

Grob HL, Bensberg F (2005) Kosten- und Leistungsrechnung: Theorie und SAP-Praxis. Vahlen, München

Grob HL, Bensberg F (2009) Controllingsysteme: entscheidungstheoretische und informationstechnische Grundlagen. Vahlen, München

Grob HL, Lahme N (2004) Total Cost of Ownership-Analyse mit vollständigen Finanzplänen. Controlling 16(11):157–164

Grob HL, Bensberg F, Coners A (2004) Analytisches time-driven activity-based costing. Controlling 16(11):603–611

Gruber H, Huemer C (2009) Profitability analysis of workflow management systems. In: 2009 IEEE conference on commerce and enterprise computing. IEEE, Vienna, Austria, pp 233–238. https://doi.org/10.1109/CEC.2009.34

Haines MN, Goodhue D (2000) ERP implementations: the role of implementation partners. In: Challenges of Information Technology Management in the 21st Century, International Conference, Anchorage, Alaska, USA, May 21–24, 2000, pp 34–38

Heinrich LJ, Riedl R, Stelzer D (2014) Informationsmanagement: Grundlagen, Aufgaben, Methoden 11, vollst überarb Aufl. De Gruyter Oldenbourg, Berlin [u. a.]

Hofmann P, Samp C, Urbach N (2020) Robotic process automation. EM 30(1):99–106. https://doi.org/10.1007/s12525-019-00365-8

Houy C, Hamberg M, Fettke P (2019) Robotic Process Automation in Public Administrations. Digitalisierung von Staat und Verwaltung Gesellschaft für Informatik e. V., Bonn, Germany, pp 62–74

ISO (2011) ISO/IEC 25010:2011 – systems and software engineering – systems and software Quality Requirements and Evaluation (SQuaRE) – system and software quality models

ISO (2014) ISO/IEC 25051:2014 – software engineering – systems and Software Quality Requirements and Evaluation (SQuaRE) – requirements for quality of Ready to Use Software Product (RUSP) and instructions for testing

ISO (2016) ISO/IEC 25023:2016 – systems and software engineering – systems and software Quality Requirements and Evaluation (SQuaRE) – measurement of system and software product quality

Issac R, Riya M, Desai K (2018) Delineated analysis of robotic process automation tools. In: 2018 second international conference on advances in electronics, computers and communications (ICAECC). IEEE, Bangalore, pp 1–5. https://doi.org/10.1109/ICAECC.2018.8479511

Ivančić L, Suša Vugec D, Bosilj Vukšić V (2019) Robotic process automation: systematic literature review. In: Di Ciccio C, Gabryelczyk R, García-Bañuelos L, Hernaus T, Hull R, Indihar Štemberger M, Kő A, Staples M (eds) Business process management: blockchain and central and eastern Europe forum (lecture notes in business information processing), vol 361. Springer, Cham, Switzerland, pp 280–295. https://doi.org/10.1007/978-3-030-30429-4_19

Jadhav AS, Sonar RM (2009) Evaluating and selecting software packages: a review. Inf Softw Technol 51(3):555–563. https://doi.org/10.1016/j.infsof.2008.09.003

Kato D, Ishikawa H (2016) Develop quality characteristics based quality evaluation process for ready to use software products. In: Computer Science & Information Technology (CS & IT). Academy & Industry Research Collaboration Center (AIRCC), pp 09–21. https://doi.org/10.5121/csit.2016.60302

Kirchmer M (2017) Robotic process automation – pragmatic solution or dangerous illusion? https://insights.btoes.com/risks-robotic-process-automation-pragmatic-solution-or-dangerous-illusion (accessed 06/07/2020)

Kirchmer M, Franz P (2019) Value-driven robotic process automation (RPA): a process-led approach to fast results at minimal risk. In: Shishkov B (ed) Business modeling and software design (lecture notes in business information processing), vol 356. Springer, Cham, pp 31–46. https://doi.org/10.1007/978-3-030-24854-3_3

Kontio J, Chen S-F, Limperos K, Tesoriero R, Caldiera G, Deutsch M (1995) A COTS selection method and experiences of its use. 16. Maryland

Krcmar H (2015) Informationsmanagement. 6., überarbeitete Auflage. Springer Gabler, Berlin Heidelberg

Kruchten P, Nord RL, Ozkaya I (2012) Technical debt: from metaphor to theory and practice. IEEE Softw 29(6):18–21. https://doi.org/10.1109/MS.2012.167

Kütz M (2013) IT-Controlling für die Praxis: Konzeption und Methoden. 2., überarbeitete und erweiterte Auflage. dpunkt.verlag, Heidelberg

Lacity M, Willcocks L, Craig A (2015) Robotic process automation at Telefónica O2. The Outsourcing Unit Working Research Paper Series. Paper 15/02

Le Clair C (2019) The Forrester Wave™: robotic process automation, Q4 2019. https://www.forrester.com/report/The+Forrester+Wave+Robotic+Process+Automation+Q4+2019/-/E-RES147757 (accessed 05/31/2020)

Makowsky MD, Wagner RE (2009) From scholarly idea to budgetary institution: the emergence of cost-benefit analysis. Const Polit Econ 20(1):57–70. https://doi.org/10.1007/s10602-008-9051-7

Miers D, Kerremans M, Ray S, Tornbohm C (2019) Magic quadrant for robotic process automation software. https://www.gartner.com/en/documents/3947184/magic-quadrant-for-robotic-process-automation-software (accessed 05/31/2020)

Mutschler BB, Zarvic N, Reichert MU (2007) A survey on economic-driven evaluations of information technology. http://dbis.eprints.uni-ulm.de/416/1/TR-CTIT-07-21(Bela).pdf (accessed 05/23/2020)

Oesterreich TD, Teuteberg F (2018) Why one big picture is worth a thousand numbers: measuring intangible benefits of investments in augmented reality based assistive technology using utility effect chains and system dynamics. Inf Syst E-Bus Manag 16(2):407–441. https://doi.org/10.1007/s10257-017-0367-6

Ogawa RT, Malen B (1991) Towards rigor in reviews of multivocal literatures: applying the exploratory case study method. Rev Educ Res 61(3):265–286. https://doi.org/10.3102/00346543061003265

Osman C-C (2019) Robotic process automation: lessons learned from case studies. Inf Econ 23(4/2019):66–71. https://doi.org/10.12948/issn14531305/23.4.2019.06

Ramesh R, Zionts S (2013) Multiple criteria decision making. In: Gass SI, Fu MC (eds) Encyclopedia of operations research and management science. Springer, Boston, pp 1007–1013. https://doi.org/10.1007/978-1-4419-1153-7_653

Ranjan S, Kumar Jha V, Pal P (2016) Literature review on ERP implementation challenges. Int J Bus Inf Syst 21(3):388–402. https://doi.org/10.1504/IJBIS.2016.074766

Saaty TL (2010) Principia mathematica decernendi =: mathematical principles of decision making: generalization of the analytic network process to neural firing and synthesis. RWS Publications, Pittsburgh, Pa

Sassone PG (1987) Cost-benefit methodology for office systems. ACM Trans Inf Syst 5(3):273–289. https://doi.org/10.1145/27641.28059

Sassone PG, Schaffer WA (1978) Cost-benefit analysis: a handbook. Operations Research and Industrial Engineering Series. Academic Press, New York

Scheppler B, Weber C (2020) Robotic process automation. Inform-Spektrum 43(2):152–156. https://doi.org/10.1007/s00287-020-01263-6

Schmitz M, Dietze C, Czarnecki C (2019) Enabling Digital Transformation Through Robotic Process Automation at Deutsche Telekom. In: Urbach N, Röglinger M (eds) Digitalization cases (management for professionals). Springer, Cham, Switzerland, pp 15–33. https://doi.org/10.1007/978-3-319-95273-4_2

Schumann M (1992) Beurteilung der Wirtschaftlichkeit von IV-Investitionen. In: Betriebliche Nutzeffekte und Strategiebeiträge der großintegrierten Informationsverarbeitung (Betriebs- Und Wirtschaftsinformatik), vol 52. Springer, Berlin, pp 148–234. https://doi.org/10.1007/978-3-642-77036-4_4

Seaman C, Guo Y, Zazworka N, Shull F, Izurieta C, Cai Y, Vetro A (2012) Using technical debt data in decision making: potential decision approaches. In: 2012 third international workshop on managing technical debt (MTD). IEEE, Zurich, Switzerland, pp 45–48. https://doi.org/10.1109/MTD.2012.6225999

Softomotive (2020) Microsoft acquires Softomotive to accelerate and expand its Robotic Process Automation capabilities. Softomotive https://www.softomotive.com/microsoft-acquires-softomotive/ (accessed 06/07/2020)

Sydow D (2014) Wirtschaftlichkeitsbetrachtungen zur Investitionsrechnung in der IT - Erfahrungen und kritische Betrachtung im Kontext der öffentlichen Verwaltung. AV Akademikerverlag, Saarbrücken

Taulli T (2020) The robotic process automation handbook: a guide to implementing RPA systems. Apress, Berkeley

Tornbohm C, Dunie R (2017) Market guide for robotic process automation software. https://www.gartner.com/en/documents/3835771/market-guide-for-robotic-process-automation-software (accessed 05/31/2020)

van der Aalst WMP, Bichler M, Heinzl A (2018) Robotic process automation. Bus Inf Syst Eng 60(4):269–272. https://doi.org/10.1007/s12599-018-0542-4

vom Brocke J, Simons A, Riemer K, Niehaves B, Plattfaut R, Cleven A (2015) Standing on the shoulders of giants: challenges and recommendations of literature search in information systems research. Commun Assoc Inf Syst 37. https://doi.org/10.17705/1CAIS.03709

Walter SG, Spitta T (2004) Approaches to the ex-ante evaluation of investments into information systems. WIRTSCHAFTSINFORMATIK 46(3):171–180. https://doi.org/10.1007/BF03250934

Wanner J, Hofmann A, Fischer M, Imgrund F, Janiesch C, Geyer-Klingeberg J (2019) Process selection in RPA projects -towards a quantifiable method of decision making. In: International conference on information systems 2019 (ICIS)

Wei C-C, Chien C-F, Wang M-JJ (2005) An AHP-based approach to ERP system selection. Int J Prod Econ 96(1):47–62. https://doi.org/10.1016/j.ijpe.2004.03.004

Wheatley M (2018) With Contextor acquisition, SAP jumps into hot robotic process automation market. SiliconANGLE. https://siliconangle.com/2018/11/19/sap-jumps-robotic-process-automation-contextor-acquisition/ (accessed 06/07/2020)

Willcocks L, Lacity M, Craig A (2015) The IT function and robotic process automation. The outsourcing. Unit Working Research Paper Series. Paper 15/05

Zangemeister C (2000) Erweiterte Wirtschaftlichkeitsanalyse (EWA): Grundlagen, Leitfaden und PC-gestützte Arbeitshilfen für ein "3-Stufen-Verfahren" zur Arbeitssystembewertung (Schriftenreihe der Bundesanstalt für Arbeitsschutz und Arbeitsmedizin Forschung, Fb 879). 2. aktualisierte Überarb. Bremerhaven: Wirtschaftsverl. NW, Verl. für Neue Wiss

Adrian Hofmann, Tobias Prätori, Franz Seubert, Jonas Wanner,
Marcus Fischer, and Axel Winkelmann

4 Process selection for RPA projects

A holistic approach

Abstract: The identification and selection of suitable processes are an essential success factor for robotic process automation (RPA) projects. Numerous studies show that 80 % of RPA projects fail due to wrong decisions in this phase. Insufficient decision quality often results from inaccurate qualitative analysis methods based on interviews, observations, and estimates. Several research frameworks have recently been developed to address this problem. They postulate to use process mining to collect accurate and robust information that can be used for decision support. However, process mining is based on analyzing event logs, which are only available in sufficient quality and information width and depth in process-oriented information systems. Activities performed in these systems are typically not suitable for RPA, as they can be automated directly via system-specific workflows. To address this shortcoming, we introduce a novel approach that combines desktop activity mining and process mining techniques in the present chapter. We use desktop activity mining to record and analyze all user interactions during the process execution, such as clicks and keystrokes. To comply with privacy regulations, we limit recording to a short period of time. Furthermore, we extract process execution data from ERP systems, merge it with our data set, and extrapolate previous findings to obtain a more holistic understanding of a process's suitability for RPA. We conceptualize our approach in a five-step iterative framework and demonstrate its practical implications by applying it to experimental data.

Keywords: Process mining, desktop activity mining, robotic process automation, framework

4.1 The need for a holistic process selection

An increasing number of companies heavily rely on optimizing and automating their business processes to remain competitive in a more global and interconnected economy (Antomarioni et al., 2019). However, most processes and tasks are still performed manually, despite their often rule-based and repetitive nature (van der Aalst, 2016). Hence, they are often error-prone and lack efficiency and effectiveness. Automation can solve many of these problems.

https://doi.org/10.1515/9783110676693-004

Automating manual activities is often associated with significant complexity. Due to the involvement of multiple systems and tools, new approaches, such as robotic process automation (RPA) (Kenneth and Svetlana, 2020), promise a more lightweight and convenient solution. RPA is the generic term for automation technologies that mimic human behavior in computer systems. As RPA exclusively applies to the user interface, it does not require adaptations to the underlying systems, which frequently lead to errors due to unforeseen interdependencies (van der Aalst et al., 2018). Hence, RPA provides the means to automate processes effectively and at low costs, thus eliminating repetitive tasks that hardly contribute to the value creation (Aguirre and Rodriguez, 2017).

In practice, these promises yield high expectations, which often remain unfulfilled (Lamberton et al., 2016). Notably, many companies highlight that the success of RPA depends heavily on identifying and selecting the right processes. Additionally, available methods are hardly capable of supporting these tasks (Wanner et al., 2019). More specifically, they use qualitative methods, such as interviews, observations, and estimations, to obtain a rough yet subjective and inaccurate understanding of a process's structure and characteristics.

Today, most business processes are supported by software systems and leave digital footprints in database operations or document flows. Process mining (PM) uses these footprints to reconstruct a process's structure and generate vast insights into its performance, efficiency, and potential areas of improvement (Wang et al., 2014). Due to its various benefits and application scenarios, more and more companies have adopted the technology over the last decade (Park et al., 2015).

In research, some articles have advocated using PM to identify suitable processes for RPA (Geyer-Klingeberg et al., 2018; Wanner et al., 2019). However, most business processes involve multiple software systems, limiting PM's applicability, which is mainly used to extract and analyze data from process-oriented information systems, not to track activities in essential tools like Microsoft Excel or PowerPoint. In contrast, desktop activity mining (DAM) focuses on user interactions at the workstation level (Dev and Liu, 2017). It records all activities, such as mouse clicks or keystrokes, without being restricted to the boundaries of a single system (Suriadi et al., 2017). Due to privacy regulations, DAM cannot be run continuously but is often limited to a short period of time. Additionally, the DAM logs lack a case ID, and hence the recordings of a workstation can not easily be assigned to singular process executions. Consequently, it does not provide sufficient data to fully grasp the automation potential of a process, especially regarding its financial feasibility.

To address these shortcomings, we present an integrated five-step framework that combines the best of both worlds. Thereby, we use DAM to obtain a detailed understanding of a process's systems and user interactions. At the same time, PM provides long-term insights into more general aspects, such as its execution frequency and variants.

4.2 Conceptual foundations

4.2.1 Robotic process automation

RPA comprises tools that interact with the user interface of a computer and mimic human behavior (van der Aalst et al., 2018). Technically, a virtual robot carries out tasks by simulating inputs via mouse and keyboard (Asatiani and Penttinen, 2016). As RPA is a "front-end" automation, no modifications of the software systems are needed with which the robot interacts. This makes it possible to automate tasks involving different environments and systems without the need for application programming interfaces (APIs). RPA is particularly suitable for a "swivel chair work." This refers to rule-based activities in which employees manually enter data into one system, process it, and manually enter the output into another system (Willcocks et al., 2015). Several studies have mentioned improvements in financial performance, transparency, efficiency, effectiveness, service quality, or productivity as possible positive effects of RPA (Schmitz et al., 2019; Willcocks et al., 2015; Lacity and Willcocks, 2015; Aguirre and Rodriguez, 2017).

4.2.2 Process mining

PM is a data-driven technique that allows business processes to be reconstructed, analyzed, and improved (Geyer-Klingeberg et al., 2018). Therefore, PM is based on recorded data from software systems, defined as process-aware information systems (PAISs). PAISs manage and execute operational processes involving people, applications, and information sources based on process models (van der Aalst, 2009). Typical PAISs are, e. g., enterprise resource planning (ERP) systems and other office applications. The activity recordings of these systems can be transformed into *event logs* with a timestamp, activity name, and case ID (van der Aalst et al., 2004). These event log data are extracted, analyzed, and visualized (van der Aalst et al., 2011). This allows companies to achieve various goals, such as obtaining a better understanding and control of processes or discovering weaknesses in process flows (Li et al., 2008).

4.2.3 Desktop activity mining

DAM helps companies to capture and analyze digital user interactions at individual workstations (Dev and Liu, 2017). Thus, it becomes possible to understand how employees perform tasks and to highlight related potential improvements. User interaction data are information that arises whenever a user is interacting with his or her computer system (Accorsi et al., 2012). This allows companies to complete the overview of process flows without being limited to PAISs. Technically, an employee's activities are recorded by using special tools that collect user interactions such as clicks and keystrokes within an application or even on web sites (Dev and Liu, 2017). Therefore, the tracking of user activities provides the data basis for an entire process analysis (Suriadi et al., 2017). However, these recordings contain all processes that the user is involved in, as well as other completely unrelated activities, and, therefore, contains more noise than PM logs.

4.3 Problem identification

Options for a fast and low-complexity front-end automation by innovative technologies around RPA expand corporate digitization opportunities. In addition to the technical realization, innovations often require a corresponding understanding of and around practical implementation. From a business process management perspective, it is valid to challenge preliminary work and knowledge to better understand best practices of (successful) RPA initiatives.

We first analyze existing case studies to understand the challenges faced in today's RPA projects (Aguirre and Rodriguez, 2017; Schmitz et al., 2019; Asatiani and Penttinen, 2016). We found that implementing RPA bots' primary goals are to reduce the number of full-time equivalents (FTE) or shift resources from repetitive tasks to more complex and value adding activities. We further noticed the lack of a standardized approach to select the right processes for RPA. While our results suggest that this forces many companies into developing individual methods, we found that those with objective measures tend to achieve better results.

Furthermore, we found that RPA requires a thorough cost–benefit analysis before the start of a project. However, most companies skip this critical step and analyze their business case only after the completed project. This often yields situations in which expected benefits regarding process performance or cost savings could not be met, and RPA is perceived as over-promising. We also recognized that the automation potential of a process could change over time, making it pivotal to review a process over time-based and standardized procedures.

To address the open issues and to validate the findings of today's scientific knowledge, we have conducted an expert study. Thus, we interviewed a total of 15 experts from major RPA software vendors (AutomationAnywhere, UiPath, and BluePrism), consulting firms (Ernst&Young, Brightcape, and Capgemini), process mining companies (Celonis), and companies from a wide range of industries that have implemented RPA in the past.

First, all experts confirmed that there is a lack of suitable process selection methods. They stated that this is one of the main reasons why RPA projects often fail. Thus, the need has already been recognized in practice. They further highlighted a particular interest in an objective approach to understanding process automation potential as most RPA providers today draw upon customer surveys. This is highly subjective and might lead to wrong conclusions. Further, most experts advocated the importance of performing a cost–benefit analysis before starting an RPA project and agreed that a process's automation potential could change over time.

4.4 A standardized framework for process selection

As the identification of suitable processes is a critical success factor for RPA projects, we now introduce a standardized framework to overcome this hurdle. Thus, we seek to support decision makers with practical guidelines to identify, prioritize, and select processes iteratively and based on objective criteria. With the insights gained from the expert survey and the combination of data-driven approaches, we define an approach that allows processes to be evaluated based on quantitative measures to increase decision making quality.

Various process mining frameworks have been developed to collect accurate and robust information from PAISs in the past. However, several issues occur in the context of process mining (Suriadi et al., 2017; Dev and Liu, 2017). So-called hidden tasks are, for example, process tasks that have been performed outside PAISs. This can be answering e-mails or entering data into a web interface. We pursue a combined approach that uses PM and DAM techniques, enabling us to get a holistic view of processes. Altogether, the framework consists of five steps explained in each sub-section and forms an iterative procedure (see Figure 1).

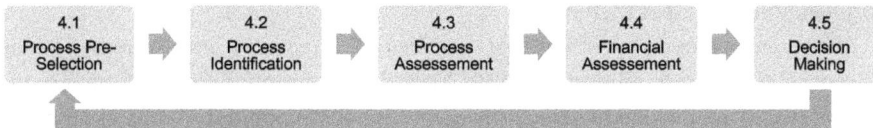

Figure 1: Framework for process selection in RPA projects.

4.4.1 Process pre-selection

Every business optimization or reorganization pursues a specific goal. This is also evident in the area of RPA. To ensure that the selection of the right processes is target-oriented and aligned with the overall objective behind the RPA initiative, such as an improved service quality, processes are first pre-selected internally by relevant departments. A good and straightforward method of the internal pre-selection is the classification of business processes into three types (see Figure 2).

Value-added processes are generally mapped via PAISs and should be automated within the software system's back-end. Such automation would not be suitable for a

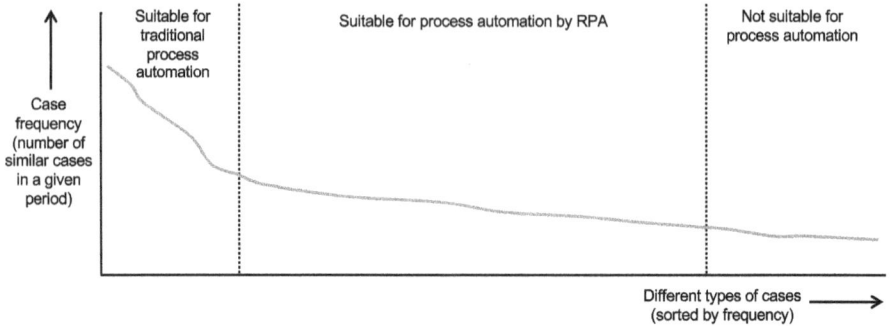

Figure 2: Process types by automation potential (van der Aalst et al., 2018).

large number of processes in the extensive middle section. However, it is precisely here that automation can now also be realized economically thanks to the new possibilities of RPA. Processes or activities in the third section, the right part, are not suitable for automation due to their low frequency.

Thus, the processes should first be separated by the schema provided in Figure 2. To do so, responsible persons in companies are interviewed.

4.4.2 Process identification

At first glance, process identification consists of assessing the automation potential for the processes or process steps pre-selected in the previous step and choosing the most valuable processes therein.

However, as proven by former best practices (cf. Chapter 3), such a method is not existent yet (Jimenez-Ramirez et al., 2019). Therefore, appropriate key performance indicators (KPIs) are needed to objectively determine RPA potentials of processes since implementing RPA robots in a productive environment faces high risks (Jimenez-Ramirez et al., 2019). Today, the selection process is mainly based on interviews and detailed observation of the dedicated staff (Leno et al., 2020).

To change this, we asked our experts in the second part of our expert study which KPIs should be used best to determine the RPA potential of a process (Wanner et al., 2019). As an example, execution frequency is named by almost all experts, along with the cost to execute the process. However, as additional data are needed to precisely calculate the cost and other relevant KPIs, this is a time consuming and, therefore, expensive task (Leno et al., 2020). Besides, today it is usually rather an estimation than an objective calculation. Domain experts would prefer an automated data-driven approach instead (Herm et al., 2020). Furthermore, existing process documentation is often incomplete, inaccurate, or outdated. Therefore, RPA process selection based on this documentation is not reliable (Jimenez-Ramirez et al., 2019).

As shown in Figure 3, we use PM to reconstruct the business processes from the process log generated by a PAIS. To track the outside activities, we use a DAM. Based on the process log, we can precisely determine when the process is continued outside the PAIS, and when it returns to the PAIS. Therefore, we can focus the DAM at specific time intervals and tasks. With this combination, we can reconstruct the whole process.

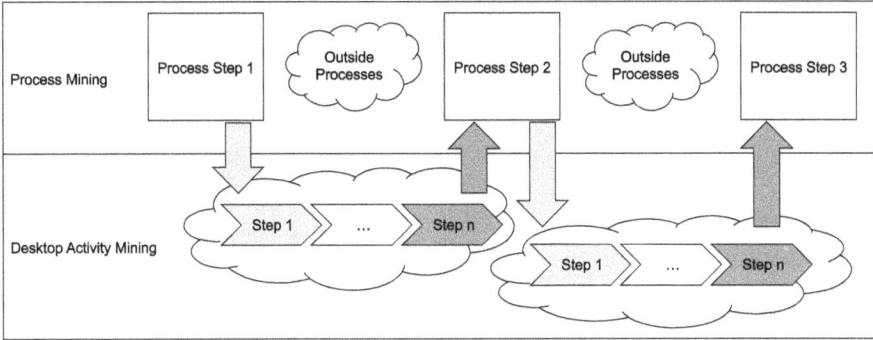

Figure 3: Combining PM with DAM to all sub-processes and tasks.

By combining PM and DAM, we are not just able to capture the full process. We can also easily extrapolate the DAM observation period based on the process logs over an extended period.

4.4.2.1 Setup

To test our approach, we created a realistic test setup. Thus, we used Microsoft Business Central 365 (MBC) as a PAIS ERP system and Microsoft Outlook as a peripheral system to receive e-mails. For DAM, we used a customized task logger. The logger records every user action like clicks and keystrokes. Every event is saved in a database with a unique ID, program name, and timestamp. Furthermore, we log the machine name and user name, as well as the absolute and relative X and Y positions of windows and user clicks. We constructed a standard order to cash end-to-end processes with three different employees involved.

As shown in Figure 4, the process involves ARP Ltd. and a customer. The customer starts the process with an order request via e-mail. To simulate different possible process flows, we created a total of 400 unique customer orders, each with one to five different order positions. Out of the 400 order requests, 300 came from already known customers (including customer ID) and 100 from new customers.

The sales employee opens the incoming mail in Outlook. If the customer is already in the database, she directly creates a sales quote in MBC. Otherwise, the customer is

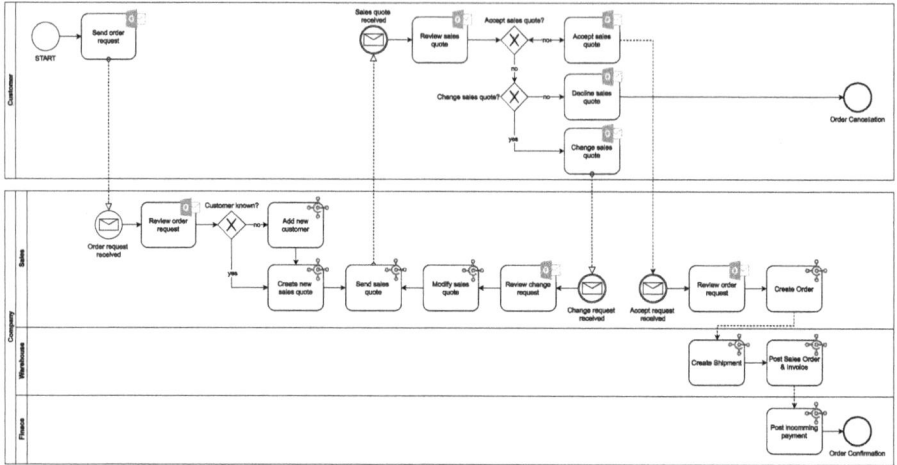

Figure 4: Combining PM with DAM for all sub-processes and tasks.

first added to the database. In the next step, she sends the customer the sales quote via MBC for approval. Possible change requests from the customer are made in MBC. If the customer sends the final approval, the sales employee creates an order and sends an order confirmation via e-mail.

In the next step, the process is handed over to the warehouse department, where the shipping is created within MBC. After shipping is confirmed, the order and invoice are posted. The final step is posting the incoming payment by another employee in the finance department. A detailed analysis of the created log is provided in the following section.

4.4.2.2 Data extraction

Process logs from PAIS can be recorded for an extended period. There are several reasons why DAM logs can and should only be recorded for a limited time. On the one hand, there are legal reasons and privacy concerns for the involved employees. On the other hand, DAM logs tend to include more granular data and quickly become too large to analyze with conventional software. Hence, we recommend limiting the DAM logging to two weeks. The PAIS logs can be recorded as long as the underlying core process does not change substantially. The data are then extracted from the PAIS and transformed with a data model to a complete process log. This transformation process differs for each process and is well documented in the process mining literature (Andrews et al., 2020). Figure 5 shows how data from the PAIS log are transformed by linking events with a case ID.

DAM logs require a different form of pre-processing. The logs contain a lot of data unrelated to the process. The data are very noisy since they include unintentional ac-

Table	Primary Key	Field	Old Val	New Val	Timestamp
Sales Req	0123	Req Nr		0123	2020-03-12 09:15:00
Sales Req	0123	Offer Nr		1234	2020-03-12 16:10:00
Sales Offers	1234	Offer Nr		1234	2020-03-12 16:10:00
Sales Offers	1234	Price		99,00	2020-03-12 16:10:00
Sales Offers	1234	Price	99,00	95,00	2020-03-17 10:30:00
Dispatch Advise	9923	Adv Nr		9923	2020-03-17 18:00:00
Dispatch Advise	9923	Offer Nr		1234	2020-03-17 18:00:00
Invoices	2342	Invoic Nr		2342	2020-03-18 10:00:00
Invoices	2342	Offer Nr		1234	2020-03-18 10:00:00
Sales Req	0124	Req Nr		0124	2020-03-13 17:30:00
Sales Req	0124	Offer Nr		1235	2020-03-13 17:30:00

ERP Log

Case ID	Timestamp	Activity
1234	2020-03-12 09:15:00	Sales offer created
1234	2020-03-12 16:10:00	Sales offer created
1234	2020-03-17 10:30:00	Sales offer updated
1234	2020-03-17 18:00:00	Shipping notification created
1234	2020-03-18 10:00:00	Invoice issued
1235	2020-03-13 17:30:00	Sales offer created
1235	...	...
1235	...	...
1235	...	...

Process Log

Figure 5: ERP and process logs.

tions of the users, such as misclicks and programs that pop up alerts and interrupt the process. We recommend cleaning up the log by including only those programs into the log that are involved in the process in some way. This can be done in an exploratory manner by examining software that is used directly before and after software directly involved in the process.

4.4.2.3 Data merging

By merging the PM and DAM logs, the insights gained over the short period of DAM recording can be extrapolated to a longer period. The events of both logs overlap in the PAIS. Since both logs are timestamped, activities of the PM log and the DAM log can be matched when the users interact with the PAIS. The two logs can, therefore, be joined on the attributes *user* and *timestamp* (see Figure 6). The DAM logs enable determining the exact execution time of each activity. Additionally, the complexity of all activities can be assessed by examining the click structure and keyboard inputs.

Application	Window Title	Start Time	End Time	User
Outlook	0123	2020-03-12 09:10:00	2020-03-12 09:12:00	1
Excel	0123	2020-03-12 09:12:00	2020-03-12 09:13:00	1
ERP	1234	2020-03-12 09:13:00	2020-03-12 09:14:00	1
Excel	1234	2020-03-12 09:14:00	2020-03-12 09:15:00	1
ERP	**1234**	**2020-03-12 09:15:00**	**2020-03-12 09:20:00**	**1**
Chrome	9923	2020-03-12 09:20:00	2020-03-12 09:30:00	1

Task Mining Log

Case ID	Timestamp	Activity	User
1234	**2020-03-12 09:15:00**	**Sales offer created**	1
1234	2020-03-12 16:10:00	Sales offer created	1
1234	2020-03-17 10:30:00	Sales offer updated	1
1234	2020-03-17 18:00:00	Shipping notification created	2
1234	2020-03-18 10:00:00	Invoice issued	3
1235	2020-03-13 17:30:00	Sales offer created	1
1235	.	.	
1235	.	.	
1235	.	.	

Process Log

Figure 6: Joining PM and DAM data by user and timestamp.

4.4.3 Process assessment

After a pre-selection has been made and the data have been recoded and extracted, the actual quantitative process selection can be carried out. To find characteristics and to identify different categories of processes, we rely on findings from academic literature, case studies, and the expert interviews. From this, we were able to derive six process characteristics that are best suited as indicators for process selection and were the most commonly named KPIs by the experts (see Table 1) (Wanner et al., 2019).

Table 1: Indicators for process assessment.

Process characteristics	Description	Direction
Execution frequency (EF)	Repetitive process tasks with a high volume of transactions, sub-tasks, and frequent interactions between different systems or interfaces	+
Execution time (ET)	Average execution time of a process task	+
Standardization (SD)	Streamlined process tasks with a priori knowledge of possible events and outcomes	+
Stability (ST)	Process tasks with a low probability of exception and a high predictability of outcomes	+
Failure rate (FR)	Throwbacks ratio of process tasks, i. e., unusual and repetitive (partial) tasks until completion	+
Automation rate (AR)	Process tasks with a small number of steps that are already automated and offer less significant economic benefits	−
Systemic heterogeneity (SH)	The number of multiple applications involved within a process	+

The direction column indicates whether a higher value of an indicator increases or decreases the automation potential. Processes that are executed very often (EF) or take a long time to be completed (ET) are particularly suitable for RPA. However, if processes are highly automated (AR), their potential for automation by RPA decreases. In addition to these PM-specific indicators, we have identified the number of different applications used during the process (SH) as an additional RPA suitability indicator. Frequent human interaction with multiple systems is particularly prone to errors and inefficient performance (Fung, 2014). Hence, such processes are particularly suitable for RPA. To ensure practical feasibility, we have ensured that all indicators are calculated from the properties of the data structures recorded by PM and DAM.

4.4.4 Financial assessment

After the indicators for evaluating the automation potential have been presented, it is explained below how a standardized financial assessment can be performed. Here, we once again used our expert survey to shed light on the necessary measures relevant to determine the financial cost–benefit calculation method (Wanner et al., 2019).

First, a profitability analysis must be carried out. We reduce this step to the comparison of the two components: benefits and costs. For simplicity, benefits are the cost savings achieved by replacing human labor by robots. On the other hand, costs are represented by the investment costs and the costs to set up, configure, and maintain RPA bots. In both cases, a distinction between variable and fixed costs can be made (see Table 2).

Table 2: Indicators for financial assessment.

Financial indicator	Description
Fixed cost of human labor (FLC)	Fixed cost rate for each process with execution-independent costs such as rent or equipment
Variable cost of human labor (VLC)	Variable cost rate for each process execution with a certain degree of human interaction based on the relative amount of salary payments
Fixed cost of RPA (FRC)	Fixed of rate to configure and maintain robots, depending on process's stability and degree of standardization as well as the cost of writing code
Variable cost of RPA (VRC)	Variable cost rate for each process step execution based on cost agreement(s) with RPA service(s)

Using these four cost variables, it is possible to calculate the time of amortization per process task. To do so, the cost functions of both executing the task by manual work (human) and completing the task automatically (bot) are compared. The RPA bot usually starts with a higher fixed cost rate, due to the high project and implementation costs of RPA initiatives. However, it is usually characterized by lower variable costs per task execution compared to manual work by a human. The intersection of the two cost functions, if one exists, indicates the point in time where the investment becomes profitable.

4.4.5 Decision making

Besides a simple cost–benefit analysis, it is crucial to maximize the economic return of an RPA project. Based on a previous interview study's findings, two practical constraints can be derived: budget and amortization time (Wanner et al., 2019). Thus, like in other projects, RPA projects are restricted by budget constraints (BCs). This includes financial resources for implementation, configuration, and maintenance of the bots. On the other hand, the amortization time constraint (ATC) implies that the RPA project should become profitable after a specific time period. In practice, this is usually between 6 and 36 months.

This leads to an optimization problem of maximizing the economic profitability of the RPA initiative, under given constraints. These constraints are BCs, ATC, and completeness, as the need to decide whether to fully automate a single process task or not to automate it. To calculate the optimization problem, the results of the cost–benefit analysis per process task are used. This comparison allows for a list of prioritization regarding the task saving potentials. It indicates which process tasks an RPA bot should automate and which it should not, on the basis of the constraints given.

4.5 Management summary

RPA offers various benefits, such as increasing process transparency, efficiency, effectiveness, quality, and productivity. However, many projects fail because companies do not understand those characteristics of a process that ultimately determine their automation potential. This chapter presented an approach that supports companies in making more informed decisions based on objective criteria to address this shortcoming. Based on a literature review and an extensive interview study, we identified four requirements for successful RPA projects.

First, decision makers require metrics to support them in assessing a process's automation potential objectively. Hence, we introduced seven indicators that operationalize data from PM and DAM. Second, as PM is only applicable to PAISs, such as ERP or CRM systems, companies rely on DAM to obtain a holistic picture of their processes that also account for activities performed in essential tools, such as Microsoft Excel or Outlook. Third, it is crucial to conduct a profitability analysis before implementing an RPA project. Hence, we presented an integrated approach that compares cost saving generated by eliminating human labor with the costs of implementing, maintaining, and running RPA. Ultimately, our findings suggest that a process's automation potential varies over time. Thus, we argue that companies must run the previously described steps iteratively.

The resulting framework consists of four steps.

Step 1: Process pre-selection. As any optimization project pursues a specific goal to improve service quality, it is necessary to identify the most promising processes by internal interviewing of stakeholders and consulting external experts.

Step 2: Process identification. We use PM and DAM to assess each candidate's automation potential. First, companies choose an appropriate setup for data collection. For example, this entails identifying relevant software systems for DAM. Due to privacy regulation, companies can only use DAM for a short period, during which they have to capture sub-processes and tasks in the form of user interactions. Companies rely on PM and thus must extract process execution data from relevant PAIS to understand a process's characteristics over time. Subsequently, they can merge both data sets. Thereby, insight from DAM is extrapolated with those from PM.

Step 3: Process assessment. Based on the complete data set, companies can assess relevant indicators and thus quantify their processes' automation potential. These metrics are execution frequency, execution time, standardization, stability, failure rate, automation rate, and systemic heterogeneity.

Step 4: Financial assessment. The fixed and variable costs imposed by human labor and the use of software robots are compared. Besides, we incorporate a budget as well as an amortization constraint into the financial assessment.

Step 5: Decision making. By combining all insights, companies can make a well-informed decision. Because a process's automation potential can vary over time, companies should repeat steps 1 to 4 in reasonable time intervals.

In summary, this chapter proposed a data-driven framework that enables companies to assess their processes' automation potential objectively. Therefore, we combined techniques from the fields of PM and DAM to build a holistic understanding of a process's structure and characteristics. Our approach significantly improves the quality of decisions during process selection in RPA projects.

Bibliography

Accorsi R, Ullrich M, van der Aalst W (2012) Aktuelles schlagwort: process mining. Inform-Spektrum 35(5):354–359

Aguirre S, Rodriguez A (2017) Automation of a business process using robotic process automation (rpa): a case study. In: Workshop on engineering applications. Springer, Berlin, pp 65–71

Andrews R, van Dun CG, Wynn MT, Kratsch W, Röglinger M, ter Hofstede AH (2020) Quality-informed semi-automated event log generation for process mining. Decis Support Syst 113265

Antomarioni S, Bevilacqua M, Potena D, Diamantini C (2019) Defining a data-driven maintenance policy: an application to an oil refinery plant. Int J Qual Reliab Manag

Asatiani A, Penttinen E (2016) Turning robotic process automation into commercial success–case opuscapita. J Inf Technol Teaching Cases 6(2):67–74

Dev H, Liu Z (2017) Identifying frequent user tasks from application logs. In: Proceedings of the 22nd international conference on intelligent user interfaces, pp 263–273

Fung HP (2014) Criteria, use cases and effects of information technology process automation (itpa). In: Advances in robotics & automation, vol 3

Geyer-Klingeberg J, Nakladal J, Baldauf F, Veit F (2018) Process mining and robotic process automation: a perfect match. In: 16th international conference on business process management, Sydney, pp 124–131

Herm L-V, Fuchs K, Helm A, Hofmann A, Imgrund F, Janiesch C, Winkelmann A (2020) A consolidated framework for implementing robotic process automation projects. In: Proceedings of the 18th international conference on business process management. Springer, Sevilla. Accepted for publication

Jimenez-Ramirez A, Reijers HA, Barba I, Del Valle C (2019) A method to improve the early stages of the robotic process automation lifecycle. In: Giorgini P, Weber B (eds) Advanced information systems engineering. Lecture Notes in Computer Science, vol 11483. Springer, Cham, pp 446–461

Kenneth B, Svetlana S Hype cycle for artificial intelligence. https://www.gartner.com/en/documents/3883863/hype-cycle-for-artificial-intelligence-2018. Accessed: 2020-03-03

Lacity M, Willcocks L (2015) Robotic process automation: Mature capabilities in the energy sector (the outsourcing unit research paper series paper 15/06), Hentet fra, https://irpaai.com/robotic-process-automation-mature-capabilities-in-the-energysector

Lamberton C, Gillard A, Kaczmarskyj G (2016) Get ready for robots-why planning makes the difference between success and disappointment. EYGM Limited, United Kingdom

Leno V, Polyvyanyy A, Dumas M, La Rosa M, Maggi FM (2020) Robotic process mining: vision and challenges. Bus Inf Syst Eng

Li C, Reichert M, Wombacher A (2008) Mining process variants: goals and issues. In: 2008 IEEE international conference on services computing, vol 2. IEEE, pp 573–576

Park M, Song M, Baek TH, Son S, Ha SJ, Cho SW (2015) Workload and delay analysis in manufacturing process using process mining. In: Asia-Pacific conference on business process management. Springer, Berlin, pp 138–151

Schmitz M, Dietze C, Czarnecki C (2019) Enabling digital transformation through robotic process automation at Deutsche Telekom. In: Digitalization cases. Springer, Berlin, pp 15–33

Suriadi S, Andrews R, ter Hofstede AH, Wynn MT (2017) Event log imperfection patterns for process mining: towards a systematic approach to cleaning event logs. Inf Sci 64:132–150

van der Aalst WM (2009) Process-aware information systems: lessons to be learned from process mining. In: Transactions on petri nets and other models of concurrency II. Springer, Berlin, pp 1–26

van der Aalst W (2016) Data science in action. In: Process mining. Springer, Berlin, pp 3–23

van der Aalst W, Weijters T, Maruster L (2004) Workflow mining: discovering process models from event logs. IEEE Trans Knowl Data Eng 16(9):1128–1142

van der Aalst W, Adriansyah A, De Medeiros AKA, Arcieri F, Baier T, Blickle T, Bose JC, Van Den Brand P, Brandtjen R, Buijs J et al (2011) Process mining manifesto. In: International conference on business process management. Springer, Berlin, pp 169–194

van der Aalst WM, Bichler M, Heinzl A (2018) Robotic process automation. Bus Inf Syst Eng 60(4):269–272

Wang Y, Caron F, Vanthienen J, Huang L, Guo Y (2014) Acquiring logistics process intelligence: methodology and an application for a Chinese bulk port. Expert Syst Appl 41(1):195–209

Wanner J, Hofmann A, Fischer M, Imgrund F, Janiesch C, Geyer-Klingeberg J (2019) Process selection in rpa projects: towards a quantifiable method of decision making. In: Proceedings of the 40th international conference on information systems (ICIS), München. AIS, pp 1–17

Willcocks LP, Lacity M, Craig A (2015) The it function and robotic process automation

Stefan Rechberger and Stefan Oppl

5 Selecting processes for RPA

A study of relevant key process indicators in the finance industry

Abstract: Robotic process automation (RPA) is an enabler for the implementation of business process automation and is becoming increasingly important in the services sector. The use of software robots is promising because of its short project implementation time and cost efficiency, which can hardly be achieved in the context of traditional process automation. However, not all processes are equally suitable for RPA support. Consequently, the selection of suitable business processes is a decisive success factor in large-scale RPA projects. Due to the usually large number of processes, companies face the challenge of applying meaningful criteria for process selection. The aim of this chapter is to propose a method to select processes that are suitable for process automation using RPA in the services industry following a design science approach. To these ends, benefit analysis as an established selection method is extended to include relevant process indicators, which suggest suitability for an RPA implementation. These process indicators are validated by RPA experts from the finance industry for their relevance with respect to RPA, and supplemented by other process indicators that are proposed by the experts, based on their expertise and experience. The overall collection is evaluated by the experts, using a benefit analysis scheme, in order to be able to highlight the key process indicators and rank them according to their importance. The result of the presented study provides a basis for organizations to develop a company-specific variant of the method.

Keywords: RPA, process indicators, process key figures, finance industry

5.1 Introduction

In the context of business and information systems engineering (BISE), the question repeatedly arises as to which processes in an organization are suitable for automation. Robotic process automation (RPA) is a form of technology that enables the implementation of process automation in BISE (van der Aalst et al., 2018). The use of RPA is nowadays increasingly important in process management and has become a core component of process automation options (Kirchmer, 2017; Willcocks et al., 2015). A large number of organizations active in service industries have already implemented pro-

Acknowledgement: The authors would like to thank the experts for their openness when participating in the study and the anonymous reviewers for their constructive feedback on the initial version of this chapter.

https://doi.org/10.1515/9783110676693-005

cess automation, in particular in the area of financial and accounting services (Fernandez and Aman, 2018; Anagnoste, 2017). The importance of RPA is also backed by a study showing that it could play an essential role in the financial services industry in the future (Waidelich and Schmidt, 2018). The participating institutions see an increased potential of RPA, primarily in the areas of settlement, back office, sales, insurance business, and compliance areas (Waidelich and Schmidt, 2018). Fernandez and Aman (2018) report on the potential of RPA in the services sector in general and also stress its potential for tasks such as accounting and back office management.

In order to gain a practical perspective of which typical tasks can be performed by RPA, informal interviews were held in advance with the regional provider of financial and banking services (Raiffeisenlandesbank Oberösterreich AG, RLB). RLB explained its pilot process (see Section 5.2 for details), which has already been implemented prototypically with RPA. In the context of the interviews with RLB, however, the opportunity of rolling out process automation using RPA is associated with the challenge of process selection. According to RLB, after completion of the first pilot process, around 1000 processes were submitted for automation by various operative departments. The company therefore faces the challenge of selecting and prioritizing suitable processes for RPA development. This selection problem is not only evident in the individual case of RLB, but can also be found in the respective literature. Van der Aalst et al. (2018) recently referred to this issue as an open research area and asked the following question: "What characteristics make processes suitable to be supported by RPA?" Organizations have countless business processes and it is almost impossible to automate all processes through software development projects (van der Aalst et al., 2018). It is therefore crucial to identify those processes which are most suitable for process automation. In an average organization there are a multitude of processes that occur at different frequencies in relation to their case variations (Fleischmann et al., 2020). The higher is the process frequency with a correspondingly low number of case variations, the higher can the potential cost savings through process automation be (van der Aalst et al., 2018). Automation software development techniques, however, would not pay off in many processes. Such processes are suitable candidates for RPA (van der Aalst et al., 2018). It is, however, currently still unclear which concrete process characteristics these candidates should have in order to be suitable for RPA (van der Aalst et al., 2018). In addition, there is no corresponding transfer of the characteristics into measurable process indicators (van der Aalst et al., 2018). This results in a key question in connection with RPA, as to which characteristics and key figures a process should have, in order to be suitable for an RPA implementation (van der Aalst et al., 2018). The relevance of this question is also supported by Wanner et al. (2019), who underpin that companies need decision support for the selection of processes. The decision problem of selecting processes for automation is basically not a novelty. There are many different methods and approaches for process selection for software development processes in the relevant literature. For example, process mining could be an approach to identify and evaluate processes (van der Aalst, 2011). Established methods for process selection, however, do not take sufficient account of the special features of RPA (van der Aalst et al., 2018).

The present chapter contributes to address this challenge and aims to develop and provide a practically applicable method to systematically approach the decision problem in RPA process selection in service industries. Methodologically, the study described here follows a design science process (Peffers et al., 2007; Johannesson and Perjons, 2014), which provides a framework for developing theoretically grounded and empirically validated artifacts that support the resolution of practical problems. The iterative nature of the process is particularly suitable for challenges that are not yet fully examined or driven by rapidly changing technological developments, both of which are the case for the problem at hand. In the present chapter, we present the initial design iterations and thus provide a basis for future research in increasing both depth and breath of the applicability of the proposed method.

5.1.1 Methodology

The research presented in this chapter is based on a design science approach as described by Johannesson and Perjons (2014). Its output is an artifact that is developed step by step in several phases. A design approach referred to as "development- and evaluation-focused design science research" is applied (see Figure 1), which focuses on the development and evaluation of the artifact (Johannesson and Perjons, 2014). In Section 5.1, the problem of process selection for automation with RPA is derived and explained, based on practical experience and backed by results from existing literature. The knowledge gained is illustrated using a running example of a simplified scenario from RLB. The purpose of the problem definition is to achieve an assessment of the requirements for the artifact. Based on the defined requirements for the artifact, we adapt an existing selection method in Section 5.2, which enables existing business processes to be evaluated on the basis of specific process criteria. The design of the artifact is divided into two consecutive iterations. In the first iteration, an artifact is developed based on a literature search to identify existing relevant process indicators. In a second iteration, these identified indicators are refined and expanded by practical experience in the form of expert interviews. After completion of the development, the artifact is evaluated in Section 5.3 by experts from the financial industry through structured interviews. A benefit analysis (BA) is applied to obtain a weighted assessment. Finally, the "artifact knowledge" (Johannesson and Perjons, 2014), i. e., the resulting criteria which are embedded in an existing selection method, is communicated to practitioners and researchers in the form of a discussion (Section 5.4) and a final conclusion (Section 5.5).

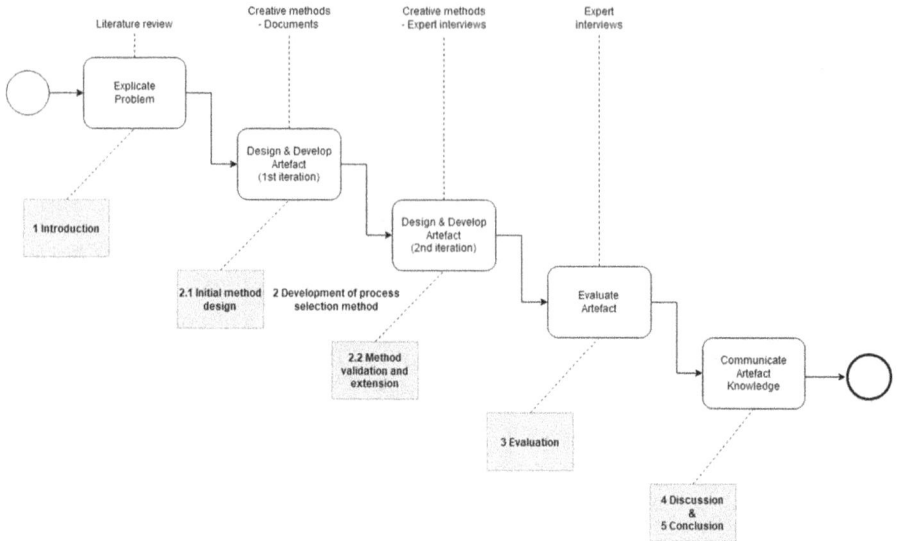

Figure 1: Development- and evaluation-focused design science research.

5.2 Development of a process selection method

In the current section, we develop an artifact by applying a design science approach as proposed by Johannesson and Perjons (2014). As explained in Section 5.1, a method is to be developed as an artifact in this study, which offers a solution to the decision problem of process selection in the context of RPA.

A literature research is used as the research strategy, in which a literature-based theory is developed first and then verified by empirical findings in the financial industry. Based on the recommendations of Johannesson and Perjons (2014), the design and development of the method are carried out in two successive iterations. In the first iteration (see Section 5.2.1), the scientific research status is determined as the starting point by means of literature research. The literature-based findings serve to develop an initial version of the RPA-specific selection method. In the second iteration (see Section 5.2.2), the specific method variant is to be expanded to include practical experience. Expert interviews are carried out in order to achieve a method that can be used in practice. Since companies are actually faced with a decision problem here, care is taken in the context of this chapter to use practical application scenarios. The artifact is developed alongside a practical scenario by RLB and offers a generally applicable method. Experts from the financial industry will later be consulted to validate the method. The following business process of RLB should serve as a case study to form a better understanding:

"Customer data are processed and sent to managers by e-mail. Basically three different applications are involved in this process. The business process is started every

Friday at 8 am by an employee. This process is carried out repeatedly for each individual customer. First, the customer appointments from the past week are exported from the CRM system. Second, the relevant customer data are exported from the core banking system, based on the customer appointments. After successful export from the two applications, these data are linked with each other via the customer number and combined to form a report. For the completion of the report, calculations on customer limits and margin results and economic classification are carried out in parallel. As soon as all calculations have been completed, the data in the report are checked for completeness. The result of the decision can provide three states: 'complete': the report is complete and ready for dispatch; 'known incompleteness': individual data records are incomplete and can be corrected in a standardized manner; and 'undefined data structure': the report contains irreparable error and the process must be terminated. Depending on the state, either the process is terminated or the report is prepared accordingly for dispatch. The final process step is to send the customer report by e-mail. Here again, depending on the economic classification, it is decided whether the report should be sent to the managers. If the report is to be sent, a decision is also made as to which management level should receive the report."

The outlined business process is also presented as a process model (cf. Figure 2) using BPMN (White and Miers, 2008) for better understanding.

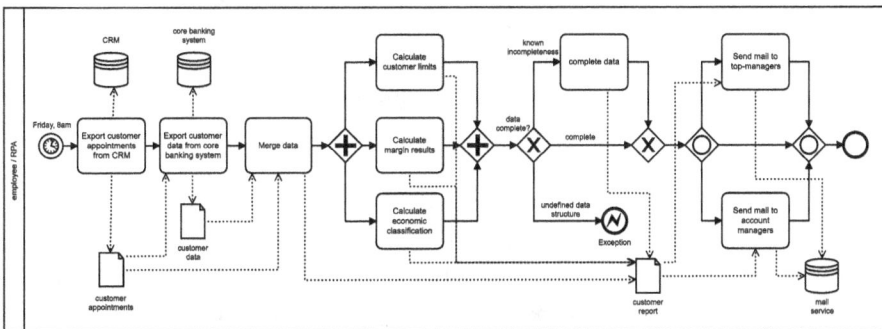

Figure 2: BPMN process of running example.

5.2.1 Initial method design

Academic papers have been examined to collect data for the development of an initial method, in the form of a literature review. Three search strategies are essentially required for this. Firstly, it is necessary to find an established method for comparing business processes. Secondly, this method requires RPA-specific characteristics on the basis of which processes can be selected. Thirdly, literature is required in order to be able to metrically represent the process characteristics found. First of all, an existing method is needed that is suitable for comparing business processes. To search for a suitable basic method for the approach, the following search phrase was used in the search engines Science Direct and Springer Link: (ALL("method decision problem business process criteria") OR ALL(title=process+selection) OR ALL("process selection method")).

A total of 183 records (including duplicates) were observed. The records were selected manually, based on the abstract. A contribution by Riedl (2006) was found, which contrasts established methods for selecting decision problems. According to Riedl (2006), BA and the analytical hierarchy process (AHP) are available as multi-attributive selection procedures to evaluate criteria. Comparing the two methods, Riedl (2006) explain that the traceability and comprehensibility of BA are higher than those of the AHP. Due to the restriction-free possibility to add criteria later, a transparent traceability, and no existing hierarchy of criteria, it was decided to use BA as the basis for the RPA-specific method development. The procedures of applying BA are not altered here; the contribution of this chapter is rooted in the identification and validation of the RPA-specific selection criteria to be used when implementing the method.

The Kühnapfel (2014) pair comparison method is used to create the RPA-specific method variant. For this purpose, selected decision alternatives are evaluated on the basis of decision criteria and then the individual evaluation results (scale [0; 5]) are summed up and presented as benefit values (the higher the benefit value, the better a decision alternative) (Kühnapfel, 2014). The collection of decision criteria is a process of finding the essential criteria for solving the decision problem. When selecting criteria, it is essential to define suitable criteria for problem solving. The catalog of the selected criteria should fulfill the characteristics of reproducibility, accessibility, relevance, and completeness (Kühnapfel, 2014). The decision alternatives in our case are the business processes to be evaluated. The decision criteria will be derived from a literature review in the context of RPA. The construction of a matrix supporting the decision process is depicted in Figure 3. Each decision alternative is listed as a separate row in the table. All the decision criteria for determining the benefit value are listed the columns on the table. As a basis for calculating the benefit value for each business process, each process is evaluated on the basis of each individual criterion. In Figure 3 a range of 0 to 5 points is defined for the evaluation. For example, Process 1 fulfills criterion 1 only very marginally and is therefore only rated with 1 point. After the evaluation of all processes on the basis of all criteria, the evaluation results for each decision alternative are summed up to a total benefit value. A total of five individual evaluations were carried out for Process 1 in Figure 3, which have a total benefit value of 10 points (1 + 1 + 4 + 4 + 0). Finally, the calculated benefit values are compared between the processes and a prioritization for the selection can be determined. The higher the benefit value, the more appropriate a process is for RPA. In the example

Criterion \\ Process	Criterion 1	Criterion 2	⋮	⋮	Criterion N	Σ
Process 1	1 +	1 +	4 +	4 +	0 =	**10**
Process 2	2	2	4	5	1	**14**
...	...	...	...	...	...	...
...	...	...	...	...	...	...
Process N	3	1	2	1	4	**11**

benefit values

Figure 3: Benefit analysis – example for pair comparison matrix.

in Figure 3, according to the definition, Process 2 is more suitable for automation than Process 1.

As already mentioned, decision criteria are required for the method development. Therefore, a literature review was carried out in order to gain insight into the state-of-the-art on which process characteristics are decisive for assessing the suitability of a business process for implementation with RPA. The search engines Science Direct and Springer Link were scanned with the following entire query: (ALL(title="robotic process automation") OR ALL(title=RPA)).

Overall 79 results could be achieved with this query. The results were inspected manually based on the abstract for their relevance in the context of process characteristics. Four of the 79 contributions provided insight into process characteristics and were examined in more detail. Alexander et al. (2018) underpins the decision problem in the context of process characteristics and points out that extensive analysis and planning of tasks (which are too complex and cannot be standardized sufficiently) is necessary in order to select suitable processes for RPA. In summary, the following criteria could be found in the literature and are recommended for the process selection:

- tasks that make low cognitive demands and leave no room for an interpretation of decisions, as well as tasks that do not require a subjective assessment (Aguirre and Rodriguez, 2017; Allweyer, 2016; Smeets et al., 2019; Willcocks et al., 2017);
- processes with a high frequency (number of process instances in a certain period) (Aguirre and Rodriguez, 2017; Allweyer, 2016);
- business processes that use a large number of software components or applications (Willcocks et al., 2017);
- processes that contain no, or a limited number of, exceptional cases (Aguirre and Rodriguez, 2017; Smeets et al., 2019; Willcocks et al., 2017);
- activities that are very prone to error when carried out by a human (Aguirre and Rodriguez, 2017; Allweyer, 2016; Smeets et al., 2019).

In addition to the process properties listed above, back office processes are particularly suitable for automation using RPA, since they are usually much more standardized and do not have as many exceptions as front office processes (Aguirre and Rodriguez, 2017). Characteristics already exist that should be suitable for RPA-compatible processes, but there is still no transition to measurable process characteristics and process indicators. As a result, a key question remains open in the BISE company in connection with RPA, as to which properties and key figures business processes should have in order to be suitable for an RPA implementation (van der Aalst et al., 2018). Since these process characteristics are often not tangible and cannot be measured, we here attempt to transfer these characteristics into measurable process indicators. For this purpose, a further literature search is carried out. The aim of the literature search is to obtain an overview of potential key performance indicators (KPIs) and measurable process indicators, in order to be able to map the described process characteristics. The search term "(title=process key performance indicators)" was queried in the search engine Springer Link. With this search strategy, 95 academic papers were found. When reviewing the results, an ISO-Standard 22400-2:2014 (2014) for KPIs and several instructions to be able to design own process key figures according to Van Looy and Shafagatova (2016), Keeble et al. (2003), and Wetzstein et al. (2008) were found. In addition, a contribution by Cardoso (2005) was found to calculate the complexity of a business process. In the following subsections we assign relevant KPIs to the process characteristics and demonstrate the respective calculation, using the running example. For process characteristics that cannot be matched with KPIs mentioned in literature, separate key figures are suggested.

Process complexity: For RPA, processes that have low cognitive requirements are suitable, together with those which have no room for interpretation when making decisions and do not require a subjective evaluation of the process results and interim process results (Aguirre and Rodriguez, 2017; Allweyer, 2016; Smeets et al., 2019; Willcocks et al., 2017). The mapping of cognitive requirements as process metrics is fundamentally difficult, but an approach is made to at least partially measure this requirement, based on the complexity of a process. Cardoso (2005) derived a metric from the McCabe metric to convert process complexity into a measurable indicator, using a business process model. To determine the metric, simply add the number of outgoing control flows for each decision node. The key figure is calculated using the following types of decision nodes:

- **AND-split:** All paths are executed in parallel (addition of the value 1 per AND-split).
- **XOR-split:** Only one path of the possible selection options is chosen (addition of the value n or the number of possible paths).
- **OR-split:** At least one path and a maximum of all selection options are executed (addition of 2 to the maximum number minus 1 or addition of $2^n - 1$).

The total sum of the values of the individual decision nodes gives the measurable process complexity. The process complexity (Table 1) of the running example (Figure 2)

Table 1: Process complexity of running example.

Split type	Paths	Formula	Complexity
XOR-split	3	number of paths	3
OR-split	3	$2^n - 1$	7
AND-split	3	value 1 per split	1
Total sum			11

can be calculated using the decision nodes. In the current example, a total of three different gateways are included, i. e., one gateway for an AND-split, one XOR-split, and one OR-split. Table 1 demonstrates an example calculation of process complexity.

Process frequency: Business processes that have a high number of instances are qualified for process automation using RPA (Aguirre and Rodriguez, 2017; Allweyer, 2016). The KPI process frequency of the ISO-Standard 22400-2:2014 (2014) is used to compare process instances between processes. The process frequency indicates how many process instances occur in a certain period of time (for example, instances per month or per annum). As a result, the process frequency measure could be the number of process instances per month. For the demonstration in our running example, RLB OOE AG was asked how many customer reports are created approximately per month. According to RLB's records, around 860 customer reports are created each month.

Multiple software components: In the field of RPA software, processes that use a higher number of software components have proven to be suitable (Willcocks et al., 2017). No KPI for mapping dependencies to applications could be found in the literature. Therefore, an own indicator is defined according to Van Looy and Shafagatova (2016). The indicator only measures the number of applications involved in the process. In the running example, the CRM system and the core banking system are used as the source system, and the mail service for sending the entire customer reports to the managers. Accordingly, the key figure of the applications involved in the process is 3 (see Figure 2).

Exception handling: According to Aguirre and Rodriguez (2017), Smeets et al. (2019), and Willcocks et al. (2017), processes that only contain a small number or no exceptional cases are particularly recommended for an RPA implementation. No KPI for mapping dependencies to applications could be found in the literature. Therefore, an own indicator is defined according to Van Looy and Shafagatova (2016). The number of exceptional cases within a business process is defined as the process indicator. In the running example, a path with an exception is shown for the XOR-gateway. Accordingly, the number of exceptional cases is 1 (see Figure 2).

Error rate: Business processes that are prone to human error are predestined for automation through RPA (Aguirre and Rodriguez, 2017; Allweyer, 2016; Smeets et al., 2019). The KPI error rate of the ISO-Standard 22400-2:2014 (2014) is used. It is calculated as a ratio of the process instances with occurred errors and the total process instances (ISO-Standard 22400-2:2014, 2014). For our running example, RLB asked how many customer reports were incorrectly created on average during manual processing. According to RLB, around 40 reports per month are incorrect. This corresponds to an error rate of 5 % (40/860).

The literature review enabled process characteristics to be found that are essential prerequisites for the implementation of RPA. For this purpose, an attempt was made to assign the process characteristics to measurable key figures, or own indicators were defined for missing key figures. Based on these results, an initial matrix for selecting business processes that are suitable for RPA using BA was developed (see Figure 4 for a better understanding of the matrix).

Criterion / Process	Process complexity	Process frequency	Involved applications	Exceptional cases	Error rate	Σ
Process 1	...	...	...	...	...	...
Process 2	...	...	...	...	...	...
...	...	...	...	...	...	...
...	...	...	...	...	...	...
Process N	...	...	...	...	...	...

Figure 4: Initial selection matrix.

5.2.2 Method validation and extension

The developed initial method variant is to be validated and potentially expanded by practical experience in a second design iteration. A semi-structured interview with experts is carried out as a data collection method. The aim of these expert interviews is to validate the existing criteria and find additional criteria that expand the initial method and supplement the literature-based criteria. As RPA is still a quite new technology, it is particularly important to select experts for the evaluation of the process criteria who have plenty of practical experience in the RPA area. As stated in Section 5.1, the validation is carried out in the context of the financial industry. For the specific selection of RPA experts, Austrian banks with the highest turnover were asked whether they already had experience in the RPA area. From the banks asked, two experts who already have automated business processes in their organizations using RPA, and are running them productively, agreed to participate in the study. In addition to the two bank employees, two consultants in the field of RPA also agreed to participate in the study. The interviews with the experts were carried out in one-to-one settings. The initial method and its decision criteria were presented to the experts in advance. The experts were asked which additional process measurements and indicators are used in practice. The process indicators mentioned by the experts were discussed more intensively during the interviews. In the course of this, they also elaborated on the respective calculation methods for the individual criteria. These are now described and exemplified in more detail in the following subsections.

Process stability: Experts A, B, and D cited the level of maturity of a business process as an indicator. According to Expert A, the degree of maturity can be read from the process stability. The process stability could be defined as the number of potential adaptations to a business process. In other words, the more often a business process changes in a certain period of time, the more unstable the process is. The number of process adaptations per annum is defined as a measure. For our running example, RLB was asked how often the customer report process was adjusted in the last year. Two process adaptations were specified last year.

Application stability: All the experts listed the application stability. In summary, the experts emphasized that the applications involved play an important role in the context. Existing applications are integrated in the course of an RPA implementation. Depending on the availability and stability of the applications integrated in the process, a business process is to a greater or lesser extent suitable for RPA. The number of application failures per annum is used to calculate the application stability and serves as a measurable indicator. As part of the running example, one of the three applications (CRM system, core banking system, mail service) is according to RLB usually not available to the user twice a month. Converted on an annual basis, this corresponds to a number of 12 application failures per year.

Running process costs: Experts A and C explained that the automation of a process is usually related to an economic benefit. Expert A defined the indicator for taking economic advantage into account as running process costs and explained it as follows: "The indicator of whether a process is suitable for RPA or not is the amount of running process costs such as personnel costs, license costs, performance peaks, etc., or the amount of costs that can be saved by process automation." The running process costs, in the example used, amount to around 500 euros per month (according to RLB). Converted on an annual basis, the total costs amount to 6000 euros.

Processing time: Expert B explained that the processing time (or throughput time) of a process instance can determine whether the business process is suitable for RPA. If, for example, an instance needs several days for one run, this can be critical with regard to the availability of applications or also trigger problems in rollback scenarios. Expert B defined the average throughput time per process instance as an indicator. According to RLB, processing a customer report in our running example, i. e., a process instance, takes around 5 minutes.

In summary, four additional measurable process indicators could be identified by interviewing the experts. The initial selection matrix can therefore be expanded to include these decision criteria. The resulting selection matrix is depicted in Figure 5. A total of nine relevant process indicators were identified in the course of the

Criterion / Process	Process complexity	Process frequency	Involved applications	Exceptional cases	Error rate	Process stability	Application stability	Running process costs	Processing time	Σ
Process 1	...	...	...	...	...	...	...	...	...	...
Process 2	...	...	...	...	...	...	...	...	...	...
...	...	...	...	...	...	...	...	...	...	...
...	...	...	...	...	...	...	...	...	...	...
Process N	...	...	...	...	...	...	...	...	...	...

Figure 5: Extended selection matrix.

approach, which together form an extended method. This extended selection matrix will be evaluated in Section 5.3.

5.3 Evaluation

The same experts as interviewed during the development of the extended method were consulted for validation again. Focus was put on assessing the relevance of the identified process indicators for process selection in RPA. This step should ensure that the developed artifact comprises practically relevant indicators and also allows to assess their relative importance with respect to RPA suitability of the process.

5.3.1 Methodology

The process indicators are compared with each other to evaluate the individual decision criteria. For this purpose, as described in Section 5.2.1 for the initial method development, a BA is used for the evaluation. Due to the larger number of criteria, the pair comparison method according to Kühnapfel (2014) is applied as an auxiliary instrument for the evaluation of the criteria. First, all criteria to be evaluated are shown in a cross table (cf. Figure 6). Each expert evaluates the individual criteria in pairs, independently of the other participants (e. g., criterion C1 with criterion C2). A total of 10 points are awarded for each comparison of two criteria. By assigning 10 points, the distances can be represented better in terms of relevance. For example, criterion C1 is more important than criterion C2, so 6 points are entered in row C1 and column C2 and only 4 points in row C2 and column C1. If two criteria are equally insignificant, the point system would assign 5 points to be entered in both crossing points. In order to subsequently nullify criteria that have no significance regarding the decision problem, an exception is defined when comparing two insignificant criteria. If both criteria are

Criterion	C1	C2	C3	C4	C5	C6	C7	C8	C9	Σ	Weight
C1	■	6	4	7	2	2	3	6	7	37	10.3 %
C2	4	■	4	7	2	2	1	3	9	32	8.9 %
C3	6	6	■	9	6	3	3	4	8	45	12.5 %
C4	3	3	1	■	2	2	2	3	6	22	6.1 %
C5	8	8	4	8	■	4	3	6	8	49	13.6 %
C6	8	8	7	8	6	■	5	7	8	57	15.8 %
C7	7	9	7	8	7	5	■	8	10	61	16.9 %
C8	4	7	6	7	4	3	2	■	8	41	11.4 %
C9	3	1	2	4	2	2	0	2	■	16	4.4 %
Total sum										360	100.0 %

Figure 6: Example cross table of expert A.

not significant, 0 points may be entered in both crossing points. Finally, the individual evaluations of the pair comparisons can be used to calculate point totals that represent a weighting of the criteria or a prioritization. The weighting of the individual criteria results from the total points of the criterion divided by the total sum of all criteria.

5.3.2 Results

The following criteria were defined in the previous section for the evaluation by the experts: process complexity, number of process instances per month, number of applications involved in the process, number of exceptions, error rate, number of process adaptations per annum, number of application failures per annum, running process costs per annum, and processing time. The experts were interviewed individually and independently of one another. A separate cross table was created for each expert and filled in separately by the experts. The individual evaluations of the experts were evaluated and are summarized, summed up, and weighted in the following table (cf. Figure 7). Generally, each expert awarded points for all the decision criteria, meaning that according to the experts, none of the evaluated criteria is fundamentally irrelevant with regard to the identification of suitable business processes.

Rank	Process indicator	A	B	C	D	Σ	Weight
1.	Number of application failures p.a.	61	42	51	64	218	15.1 %
2.	Number of process adaptations p.a.	57	38	54	64	213	14.8 %
3.	Running process costs p.a.	41	47	40	50	178	12.4 %
4.	Error rate	49	34	44	28	155	10.8 %
5.	Number of process instances per month	32	47	36	35	150	10.4 %
6.	Processing time	16	62	45	25	148	10.3 %
7.	Process complexity	37	34	25	43	139	9.7 %
8.	Number of applications involved in the process	45	30	23	32	130	9.0 %
9.	Number of exceptions	22	26	42	19	109	7.6 %

Figure 7: Summarized results of expert interviews.

If one looks at the average number of points (cf. Figure 8) awarded per expert and per key figure, it can be said that three out of four experts rank the number of application failures and the number of process adaptations as most informative. The number of exceptional cases, on the other hand, is classified by three out of four experts as a key figure with little informative value. All other process indicators are quite homogeneously considered to play an important role in the identification of the RPA suitability. The only criterion with significantly diverging opinions is the processing time, which one expert rated as a key figure with high informative value, whereas two others considered it of limited value.

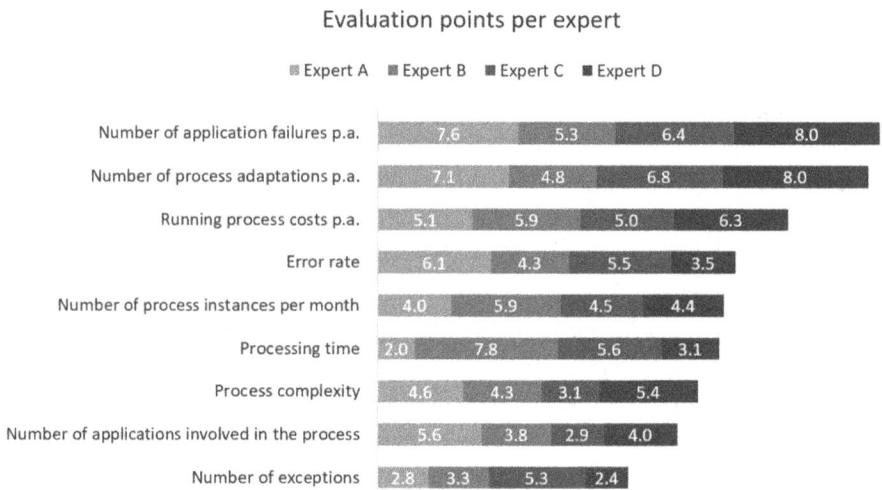

Evaluation points per expert

▨ Expert A   ▪ Expert B   ▪ Expert C   ▪ Expert D

Number of application failures p.a.	7.6	5.3	6.4	8.0
Number of process adaptations p.a.	7.1	4.8	6.8	8.0
Running process costs p.a.	5.1	5.9	5.0	6.3
Error rate	6.1	4.3	5.5	3.5
Number of process instances per month	4.0	5.9	4.5	4.4
Processing time	2.0	7.8	5.6	3.1
Process complexity	4.6	4.3	3.1	5.4
Number of applications involved in the process	5.6	3.8	2.9	4.0
Number of exceptions	2.8	3.3	5.3	2.4

Figure 8: Evaluation points per expert, sorted by overall importance.

5.4 Discussion

The aim of this study was to develop a method that should make it easier for organizations to select suitable processes for RPA implementations. However, the weighting numbers and the average evaluation points underline the difficulty in identifying business processes that are suitable for RPA, meaning that it is difficult to determine the suitability based on a single key figure. Consequently, the result of the expert interviews confirms the need for identification to apply a number of decision criteria or process indicators. The experts particularly emphasize the number of application failures and the number of process adaptations as very significant with regard to their suitability for RPA. The stability of the application, integrated in the process, is repeatedly mentioned in the discussions with the experts as a decisive factor in order to be able to guarantee faultless operation. If there is no application stability, operational implementation leads to error handling measures, which in turn have a negative impact on the economy of process automation. The process stability is also regarded as the basic building block for RPA. However, the crucial importance of process stability is not really a new finding, since even in conventional process automation, a reduced number of change management tasks has an economically positive effect on maintenance and repair costs. The third place in the expert evaluation are the running process costs. In terms of economy, personnel and license costs quantify the potential savings through RPA process automation. The application of RPA does not necessarily have to have an economic cause but can also be used to achieve quality goals. Because of this, the process costs are not mentioned as the most important criterion.

The evaluation results of the experts show that the key figures error rate, number of process instances, processing time, process complexity, and number of applications involved in the process are significant and approximately considered equally important. The error rate contains both a qualitative and an economic component. The business process suffers in both the cost-effectiveness and the quality of the task management from human error (e. g., damage to the image). The number of process instances primarily quantifies the profitability of an RPA implementation, i. e., an increased process frequency leads to the goal of process automation. As a result, a large number of process instances have a positive impact on RPA suitability. The process throughput time is to be considered from the perspective of the required hardware resources. The longer a process instance needs for complete processing, the longer the required resource for process processing is blocked. The longer a process run takes, the less a business process is suitable for RPA. The process complexity is ranked further down the line, since RPA basically has no restrictions regarding the complexity. However, the process complexity has to be considered in the context of the initial implementation costs and running maintenance costs, since these costs increase with higher process complexity. As a result, high process complexity has a negative impact on RPA suitability. An essential added value of RPA in business processes is that it includes several applications, resulting in no interfaces between the applications. RPA is therefore particularly suitable for processes whose applications cannot be implemented through interfaces. With a large number of process-related applications, RPA is therefore more suitable than conventional process automation, and has a positive effect on RPA suitability. The number of exceptional cases in a process is of little significance with regard to RPA suitability, due to the possible solutions of the RPA software providers for exception handling. From the experts' point of view, this key figure is of little significance, since artificial intelligence and machine learning will offer further options for handling exceptional cases in the future.

If one compares the developed method variant with other process selection models, such as process mining, this approach provides a simple, practical solution. Companies can use this method without specific knowledge and IT skills for their decision problems in the context of RPA. However, the developed artifact is based on some assumptions that can only be temporarily confirmed by the rapid development of RPA technology. Other procedures, such as process mining, may take superior process selection decisions based on data-based objective calculations (van der Aalst, 2011). The conducted evaluation is based on the practical experience of the experts and, in contrast to process mining, is based on a subjective awareness. If one looks at the results of the evaluation in comparison to the related work, there are some additions regarding the process criteria, which can be determined and are not covered by the developed artifact. In the research literature, the characteristics rule-based structure, degree of standardization, digitality, and structure of the data are mentioned as essential basic requirements for the application of RPA (Aguirre and Rodriguez, 2017; Allweyer, 2016; Willcocks et al., 2017). The most important criterion Smeets et al. (2019) mention is the digitizability of the data, since RPA cannot provide support for process automation, due to the lack of digitization. In addition, related work mentions that the data types used in the process can be taken into account as a criterion (Allweyer, 2016). As an example of differentiation of data types, it is stated that text and numbers can be automated better by RPA than pictures and handwritten data (Allweyer, 2016). Smeets et al. (2019) explain that several process selection criteria can be used and that individual criteria can also be weighted. When selecting a process, it should be noted that priority should not only be given according to the defined criteria, since in practice it often turns out that at least parts of the process under consideration can be easily automated, despite failure to meet the criteria considered (Smeets et al., 2019). Furthermore, practice shows that organizations that already have more experience with RPA tend to automate more complex business processes using RPA (Smeets et al., 2019). The more experience an organization has with RPA implementation, the lower the importance of process complexity becomes (Smeets et al., 2019).

5.5 Conclusion

In summary, the potential of RPA looks promising, especially in processes with a high number of monotonous and repetitive tasks. The basic requirement for RPA is that the data to be processed must be structured. In addition, RPA offers a suitable option for process automation for business processes. As a result of the descriptive characteristics, measurable process indicators were derived, which can be used in a method for the selection of RPA-suitable business processes. This study is motivated by a decision problem at RLB, which is faced with the challenge of selecting suitable processes for RPA implementation. A real business process from RLB was used for illustration in this study. In the course of the design phase, process indicators for the development of the method variant were identified in two iterations. In the first iteration, a literature search was used to find a suitable method and relevant selection criteria for the decision problem. Due to the possibility to add new criteria during the procedure and a realistic representation of the decision problem, BA was chosen as a suitable basic method for the development of the method. After selecting the method, process characteristics were derived using the existing literature and assigned to common KPIs. The initial literature-based method variant was extended in a second iteration by additional process indicators from experts through semi-structured interviews. Four experts from Austrian organizations in the finance industry, who already have experience with RPA, were consulted for the development of the extended selection matrix to be used in the method. In order to ensure the significance of the respective individually defined process indicators with regard to the RPA suitability, the indicators were evaluated and weighted by the four RPA specialists, applying structured interviews, using a BA. In summary, all criteria that have been defined have a certain degree of informative value regarding the RPA suitability of a business process. The results of the expert interviews show that two key figures (the number of application failures and the number of process adaptations) are particularly significant with regard to their suitability for RPA. The key figures processing time, error rate, running process costs, number of process instances, process complexity, and number of process-related applications play an important role in the process selection. According to experts, only the number of exceptional cases is of little significance regarding the suitability for RPA.

The result of this research study is addressed to practitioners and scientific researchers, providing a method for the selection of business processes that are suitable for RPA, but so far it remains unclear to what extent the process key figures are available in the respective organization, when comparing specific business processes. In order to be able to check the applicability of the developed method, it would be necessary to carry out further studies that validate specific processes for their RPA suitability, based on the process indicators developed. This study is subject to some limitations and challenges and thus opens up potential research areas for future work, to consolidate the knowledge gained. The derived process indicators and the process metrics, supplemented by the experts, do not represent the absolute entirety or completeness of all conceivable criteria. In the process of BA, the collection of decision criteria is provided as a creative method and therefore does not impose any restriction with regard to the selection of the criteria. In order to obtain a more extensive assessment of potential criteria, an alternative procedure could be chosen, other industries examined, or a larger number of experts involved. It would also be interesting to see how the identification of RPA-compatible processes in other industries takes place, on the one hand, the extent to which further process indicators have to be added in other industries and, on the other hand, how the weighting of the evaluated process indicators in other industries compare to the finance industry. However, the developed artifact is generic and offers an easily understandable RPA-specific alternative to existing process selection methods for practice.

Bibliography

Aguirre S, Rodriguez A (2017) Automation of a business process using robotic process automation (RPA): a case study. In: Figueroa-García JC, López-Santana ER, Villa-Ramírez JL, Ferro-Escobar R (eds) Applied computer sciences in engineering. Communications in Computer and Information Science. Springer, Berlin, pp 65–71

Alexander S, Haisermann A, Schabicki T, Frank S (2018) Robotic Process Automation (RPA) im Rechnungswesen und Controlling – welche Chancen ergeben sich? Controlling 30(3):11–19

Allweyer T (2016) Robotic Process Automation – Neue Perspektiven für die Prozessautomatisierung. Fachbereich Informatik und Mikrosystemtechnik Hochschule Kaiserslautern

Anagnoste S (2017) Robotic automation process – the next major revolution in terms of back office operations improvement. Proc Int Conf Bus Exc 11(1):676–686

Cardoso J (2005) How to measure the control-flow complexity of web processes and workflows. In: Workflow handbook, vol 2005, pp 199–212

Fernandez D, Aman A (2018) Impacts of robotic process automation on global accounting services. Asian J Account Govern 9(0)

Fleischmann A, Oppl S, Schmidt W, Stary C (2020) Contextual process digitalization: changing perspectives – design thinking – value-led design. Springer International Publishing

ISO-Standard 22400-2:2014 (2014) Automation systems and integration — key performance indicators (kpis) for manufacturing operations management — part 2: Definitions and descriptions. Library Catalog: www.iso.org

Johannesson P, Perjons E (2014) An introduction to design science. Springer, Berlin

Keeble JJ, Topiol S, Berkeley S (2003) Using indicators to measure sustainability performance at a corporate and project level. J Bus Ethics 44(2):149–158

Kirchmer M (2017) Robotic process automation-pragmatic solution or dangerous illusion. BTOES Insights, June

Kühnapfel J (2014) Nutzwertanalysen in Marketing und Vertrieb. Essentials, Management & HR. Gabler Verlag.

Peffers K, Tuunanen T, Rothenberger MA, Chatterjee S (2007) A design science research methodology for information systems research. J Manag Inf Syst 24(3):45–77

Riedl R (2006) Analytischer Hierarchieprozess vs. Nutzwertanalyse: Eine vergleichende Gegenüberstellung zweier multiattributiver Auswahlverfahren am Beispiel Application Service Providing. In: Wirtschaftsinformatik als Schlüssel zum Unternehmenserfolg. DUV, Wiesbaden, pp 99–127

Smeets M, Erhard R, Kaußler T (2019) Anwendungsbereiche von RPA. In: Smeets M, Erhard R, Kaußler T (eds) Robotic Process Automation (RPA) in der Finanzwirtschaft: Technologie – Implementierung – Erfolgsfaktoren für Entscheider und Anwender. Springer, Wiesbaden, pp 37–46

van der Aalst WMP (2011) Process discovery: an introduction. In: van der Aalst WMP (ed) Process mining: discovery, conformance and enhancement of business processes. Springer, Berlin, pp 125–156

van der Aalst WMP, Bichler M, Heinzl A (2018) Robotic process automation. Bus Inf Syst Eng 1–4

Van Looy A, Shafagatova A (2016) Business process performance measurement: a structured literature review of indicators, measures and metrics. SpringerPlus 5(1):1797

Waidelich M, Schmidt D (2018) Zukünftige Entwicklungen im Bankenwesen. In: Dimler N, Peter J, Karcher B (eds) Unternehmensfinanzierung im Mittelstand: Lösungsansätze für eine maßgeschneiderte Finanzierung. Springer Fachmedien Wiesbaden, Wiesbaden, pp 57–74

Wanner J, Hofmann FM, Imgrund F, Janiesch C, Geyer-Klingeberg J (2019) Process selection in RPA projects – towards a quantifiable method of decision making. In: ICIS 2019 proceedings

Wetzstein B, Ma Z, Leymann F (2008) Towards measuring key performance indicators of semantic business processes. In: Abramowicz W, Fensel D (eds) Business information systems. Lecture Notes in Business Information Processing. Springer, Berlin, pp 227–238

White SA, Miers D (2008) BPMN modeling and reference guide: understanding and using BPMN. J Strateg Inf Syst 3

Willcocks LP, Lacity M, Craig A (2015) The IT function and robotic process automation. The Outsourcing Unit Working Research Paper Series, London School of Economics and Political Science

Willcocks L, Lacity M, Craig A (2017) Robotic process automation: strategic transformation lever for global business services? J Inf Technol Teaching Cases 7(1):17–28

Corinna Rutschi and Jens Dibbern

6 Transforming and recombining routines to scale the implementation of software robots

Abstract: With the increasing potential to automate business processes using software robots, companies face the challenge of scaling the implementation of such robotic systems in order to enable their efficient evolution. The implementation of software robots is based on the often time consuming work carried out by the project team, which often leads to higher than expected costs and time delays. This can be made more efficient by scaling the extension of the robot's functionalities. However, scaling can only take place once one has understood what can be scaled, how it can be scaled, and to what extent. Routine theoretical concepts help us better understand the extent to which processes previously carried out by humans can be transformed and transferred to robots. We build on literature on routine dynamics as well as digital scaling to understand the mechanisms required to scale the implementation of software robots. Therefore, based on an empirically illustrated theoretical conceptualization of scaling the software robot implementation, we elaborate in this chapter how routines evolve and dynamically influence each other in order to explain how scaling can be approached when implementing software robots. In doing so, we rely on data from two case studies. In one case study a chatbot was contextually expanded over time. In the second case study a series of robotic process automation (RPA) robots were implemented.

Keywords: Software robots, robotic process automation, chatbot, software implementation, digital scaling, routine theory

6.1 Introduction

Companies are increasingly introducing software robots to automate some of their business processes. They often start with implementing software robots in a specific area or department, such as customer support (Willcocks and Lacity, 2016). Based on such initial experiences, they may identify additional departments or contexts in which they could implement additional robots. However, if they start from scratch for each new robot to be programmed this results in high costs and time expenditure. Accordingly, companies may ask themselves how they could speed up the robot implementation process. Ideally, robots are implemented with the intention of extending their scope and reach, which simultaneously poses the challenge of scaling their implementation. While the initial development and programming of robots often mirrors an innovative process, which requires exploration and experimentation, their further development can be made more efficient by drawing from scaling mechanisms. Such

https://doi.org/10.1515/9783110676693-006

scaling should allow for a more efficient implementation of software robots since it allows for extending functionality of current robots or developing additional robots in novel contexts, without significant additional costs. As a result, the conditions for scaling the implementation of software robots are an important area of inquiry.

Prior research on software robot implementations has mainly focused on the above-mentioned one-time implementation process. Thereby, drawing on routine theory, the implementation of software robots has been viewed as the transfer of routines from humans to robots (D'Adderio, 2011; Rutschi and Dibbern, 2019, 2020). This has led to initial insights into the steps to be taken and the underlying conditions for automating particular (business) processes (Rutschi and Dibbern, 2019, 2020). It was shown that the basis of automation requires an understanding of the structure of both, existing business processes to be automated and the operating principle of a robot, i. e., one needs to think like a robot.

In this study, we seek to develop a better understanding of the robot implementation process to consider how it changes when companies already implemented software robots that can be taken as a basis to develop additional robots. Thereby, we seek to close the gap in understanding the dynamic evolution of software robots by developing some foundational knowledge on the scaling of the implementation of software robots. The notion of scaling has recently been gaining increased interest in the IS literature, when it comes to understanding the exponential growth of digital startups and entrepreneurs. Such digital growth often rests on the creation and recombination of digital resources, which has also been referred to as the scaling of digital infrastructures (Henfridsson and Bygstad, 2013). In a like vein, an existing software robot may also be viewed as a digital resource that serves as the basis for scaling the process of software robot implementations. However, little is known about what this process of scaling actually looks like in the context of software robots. Accordingly, we aim at investigating how the implementation of software robots can be accelerated. In order to gain insights into how such acceleration or scaling can be achieved, we need to understand what can be scaled (i. e., scaling resources), how it can be scaled (i. e., scaling mechanisms), and to what extent it can be scaled (conditions for contextual growth). In line with existing research on software robot implementations (Rutschi and Dibbern, 2019, 2020), we draw on routine theory (D'Adderio, 2011; Leonardi, 2011) as a basis for understanding how human-executed business processes can be transformed into robot-automated processes. Specifically, we draw on recent advances in routine theory that explain how the performance of routines to achieve particular ends leads to the generation of means that can be reused to achieve new ends (Dittrich and Seidl, 2018; Howard-Grenville, 2005). By reusing generated means, the overall pace of achieving a specific end can be accelerated. A similar dynamic can be observed in the implementation of software robots, where certain components can be created that can subsequently be reused, which may result in scaling the implementation process. Such digital scaling may be described as a dynamic reinforcing process by which the reach of a software robot is extended either through expanding its functionalities or by transferring its functionalities to additional software robots that may reuse part of its components (Henfridsson and Bygstad, 2013). In order to better understand digital scaling in the context of software robot implementations, we formulate the following research question: How can the implementation of software robots be accelerated and thus the transfer of routines to software robots be scaled?

We seek to address this research question by taking a dynamic perspective and by exploring the generative mechanisms that help in scaling the transfer of routines to robots, i. e., the robot implementation process. Our overarching objective is to explain what digital scaling means in relation to transferring routines to robots. Routine theoretical concepts help us better understand the extent to which processes previously carried out by humans can be transformed and transferred to robots not only once, but concurrently. We build on literature on routine dynamics as well as digital scaling to understand the conditions for scaling the implementation of software robots. Therefore, based on an empirically illustrated theoretical conceptualization of scaling the software robot implementation, we elaborate how routines evolve and dynamically influence each other in order to explain how scaling can be approached when implementing software robots. In doing so, we rely on data from two case studies that we use for an illustrative purpose in this chapter. In one case study a chatbot was implemented. In the second case study RPA robots were implemented.

6.2 Scaling as a process of routine emergence

For a successful evolution of software robots, the process of enlarging its reach and functionalities over time must be understood. In an information systems (IS) perspective, scaling means extending an IS in size and/or scope within the same or a new environment. In relation to software robots, an environment could describe the setting (or context) in which a software robot acts involving all surrounding actors. Thus, scaling describes practices that allow a technology to be "spread, enhanced, scoped, and enlarged" (Sahay and Walsham, 2006, p. 43). In contrast, the term scale refers to the size and scope of an IS that can be achieved by scaling (Sahay and Walsham, 2006). Up to now, scaling has mainly been used to achieve economies of scale through standardization (Chandler, 1990). Scaling may thereby lead to different outcomes, such as an increased user base (Huang et al., 2017) or a successfully evolved digital infrastructure (Henfridsson and Bygstad, 2013). The implementation of software robots essentially describes the transformation of human-executed processes to such carried out by a robot (D'Adderio, 2011; Rutschi and Dibbern, 2019, 2020). Such processes could be associated with routines. A routine can thereby be described as a series of interdependent actions performed on a pattern basis whereby various actors can be involved (Feldman and Pentland, 2003; Feldman et al., 2016). Routines are composed of ostensive and performative aspects. The ostensive aspect refers to formal rules and procedures that can be described as the "guidelines" of how to perform the routine. The performative aspect refers to the actual performance of these rules and procedures. Both the performative and ostensive aspects of a routine influence each other if the routine is performed by a human (D'Adderio, 2011; Feldman et al., 2016; Pentland and Feldman, 2005). To illustrate this using an example, consider an employee A who must prepare a monthly report. Since employee A must prepare the report in the same way every month following certain guidelines, we can characterize this process as a routine. The guidelines describe the ostensive aspect of the routine. The actual preparation of the report describes the performative aspect of the routine. Each time employee A prepares the report, he or she could potentially identify means to prepare the report in a better way or more efficiently next time. This would cause the performative aspect of the routine (i. e., the way of preparing the report) to change. Over time, employee A could thus deviate from the original guidelines. This would also cause the ostensive aspect to change. Thus, employee A has an influence on both the ostensive and the performative aspects of the routine of preparing the monthly report. Suppose employee A hands over the task of preparing the report to another employee B. Employee A would have to explain to employee B how to prepare the report (i. e., ostensive aspect) before employee B could actually prepare the report (i. e., performative aspect). Eventually, employee B will bring in his or her own way of doing things and thus change the performative aspect of the routine, which may lead to a change in the ostensive aspect as well.

Humans do not always perform routines in the same way. They can change routines due to changing contexts or circumstances (Dittrich and Seidl, 2018; Howard-Grenville, 2005). Thus, humans can influence and change the performative as well as the ostensive aspect of a routine. Routine theory helps to unlock the black box of how humans perform routines (Leonardi, 2011). Before routines can be transferred to robots at all, an understanding of how the routine is composed and the extent to which it has previously been performed by humans must first be gained. An understanding must be gained of both the ostensive and performative aspects of the routine as it is performed by a human.

Once such an understanding has been established, one must comprehend the dynamics of software robots and the extent to which robots are capable of performing routines. One must think like a robot to understand how a routine previously performed by a human can be adequately translated so that the robot can later understand and perform it (D'Adderio, 2011; Rutschi and Dibbern, 2019, 2020). Our focus here lays on software robots that execute rule-based processes and are not able to learn autonomously. Such robots are developed by humans (for example the developers) by means of programming within a given software environment. The software robot then determines how a certain routine must look for the robot to perform it. Thus, the robot can initially influence the ostensive aspect of the routine. Once implemented, however, the robot cannot influence the routine itself anymore but executes it according to the implemented guidelines (i. e., the ostensive aspect). Unlike humans, software robots execute routines by strictly following the given guidelines. Consequently, when a robot executes a routine, no reciprocity between the ostensive and the performative aspect can be observed, rather the ostensive aspect corresponds with the performative aspect.

Rutschi and Dibbern (2020) explain the phenomenon of automating processes by means of software robots and introduce an iterative framework of routine automation, which they use to explain to what extent routines can be transferred from humans to robots. They explored the extent to which an individual process or routine can be transferred from a human to a robot (Rutschi and Dibbern, 2020). In case a company wants to automate numerous processes and thus transfer them to robots, it can lead to enormous costs and time expenditures if the company must approach the automation of each process or the programming of each robot individually. This could be made more efficient if one could draw on prior automation approaches and thus accelerate the whole automation process. In order to ensure a successful evolution of software robots, it is essential to understand what scaling means in this context. This requires an understanding of what is scalable, i. e., of what can be scaled, how it can be scaled, and to what extent it can be scaled (Sahay and Walsham, 2006).

6.2.1 What to scale

Robots are designed to perform certain tasks by following certain behavior patterns or rules. In addition, robots include features such as "adaptivity, robustness, versatility and agility" (Pfeifer et al., 2007, p. 1088). Generally, a robotic system or a software robot can be any machine replacing work performed by humans (Willcocks and Lacity, 2016) while gathering information and following instructions to execute tasks (Tirgul and Naik, 2016). Examples for robotic systems are robotic process automation (RPA) (Willcocks and Lacity, 2016) and chatbots (Sengupta and Lakshman, 2017). Implementing RPA robots allows companies to automate back office business processes (Slaby, 2012; Willcocks and Lacity, 2016).

RPA robots execute processes like humans while interacting with IT systems through their user interface (Asatiani and Penttinen, 2016; Willcocks and Lacity, 2016). In doing so, RPA robots log in (and out) of systems like humans do (Willcocks and Lacity, 2016).

Implementing a chatbot allows companies to automate conversational business processes (Heller et al., 2005; Shawar and Atwell, 2007). After releasing a chatbot into the live system, the human user can interact with it via a user interface, such as a pop-up window integrated on a web site (Sengupta and Lakshman, 2017), Facebook Messenger, Skype, or Slack (Patil et al., 2017).

By introducing software robots, companies can benefit from improved performance in terms of quality and efficiency, as robots outperform humans in executing certain tasks and processes (Fung, 2014; Guzman and Pathania, 2016; Sengupta and Lakshman, 2017; Sharma et al., 2016; Slaby, 2012). Scaling in the sense of implementing robots might be described as engineering robots "capable of performing a large variety of tasks" (Pfeifer et al., 2007, p. 1091). However, scaling does not refer to the extent to which a system can be configured, customized, parameterized (Sahay and Walsham, 2006), or adapted. Adaptation may be necessary in the case of environmental changes so that a system can perform processes exactly as it did before the change. However, this does not mean that its functionalities are extended and therefore cannot be called scaling. What can be described as scaling is the step-by-step process in which technology changes into a more complex form (Henfridsson and Bygstad, 2013).

Routine theory describes the dynamic evolution of routines through the performance of preceding routines. As outlined above, humans do not always perform routines in the same way, which implies that routines change over time or new routines emerge. Humans play a central role in changing existing and generating new routines (Feldman, 2000; Howard-Grenville, 2005). Performing routines thus causes routines to change or new routines to emerge (Pentland et al., 2012). Dittrich and Seidl (2018) argue that means can be created while performing routines. These means can be reused to define and achieve current and new ends. Reusing means in any subsequent performance of a routine results in the routine to change over time (Dittrich and Seidl, 2018). To draw the analogy to the implementation of software robots, one could argue that in the course of programming software robots means are generated that can subsequentially be reused in the further programming of software robots. Such means could be described as components that can be used to build and implement a software robot.

Today, standard robotic implementation solutions are available that provide a kind of toolbox, whereby the robot can be built with the help of the elements contained therein. An example of this is Blue Prism,[1] which allows one to build RPA robots by modeling business processes in processes and objects. A process describes the logic of how an RPA robot should perform a specific task. An object describes the RPA robot's interaction with specific systems on their user interface.

Another example is IBM Watson Conversation Services,[2] which make it possible to create a chatbot by modeling conversations in decision trees and introducing variations and synonyms. A decision tree refers to the structure of a specific dialogue. Variations refer to different semantic structures of questions and answers within the decision tree. Synonyms refer to different terms for the same elements within specific questions and answers.

With regard to RPA robots, means or components that can be reused could be process structures and objects. With regard to chatbots, means or components that can

---

[1] https://www.blueprism.com/
[2] https://www.ibm.com/watson/ph-en/conversational-ai/

be reused could be decision trees, variations, and synonyms. Reusing components allows the transfer of routines from humans to robots to be performed more efficiently. In other words, the robot implementation process can be scaled. This essentially implies that the process of transferring routines from humans to robots may have been very complex in the past but certain components have been created that can now be reused. By reusing these same components, the further transfer of routines to robots can be made more efficient and thus scaled.

Thus, scaling can be described as a generative process, which requires actions taken by actors such as the developer. Such actions can be associated with reuse. Reuse enables the development and implementation of IT systems in a more efficient way. Thus, scaling requires that certain components can be reused. Hence, what to scale refers to the components that can be reused in the further implementation of software robots.

6.2.2 How to scale

Reuse of already created components can be considered as a mechanism that triggers scaling by enabling the addition or transfer of functionality (Banker and Kauffman, 1992; Basili et al., 1996). The flexibility of technology can thereby be innovatively exploited by extending functionality within the same or a new environment or context. Thus, the addition of new functionalities (mutation) to an IS can describe one mode of scaling. Another mode of scaling describes the transfer of functionalities (inheritance) to a new IS (Huang et al., 2017; Svahn et al., 2017; Yoo et al., 2012). In regard of the implementation of software robots this means that components may be reused in the same or a new environment or context. Hence, how to scale refers to whether components are reused to transfer functionality into a different or new context or to extend functionality in a current context.

6.2.3 To what extent to scale

However, not everything can be reused directly but certain components may first have to be modified so that they can then be reused to transfer or extend functionality. The reuse mechanism can therefore not always be applied directly but depends on contextual factors (see Adler et al., 1999). It is important to understand what the contextual factors are that prevent direct reuse and how components can be adapted in order to be reused (see Adler et al., 1999).

If components can be reused directly, it can also be said that they can be reproduced into an existing context. If means cannot be directly reused, it can also be said that they must be recreated into a different or new context. Reproduction indicates that means can be directly reused regardless of contextual factors. Recreation indicates that means must be adapted depending on contextual factors in order to be reused (Dittrich and Seidl, 2018).

Hence, to what extent to scale refers to whether components need to be adapted or not in order to be reused within a certain context and, if so, how components need to be adapted.

6.3 Conceptualization of scaling the implementation of software robots

Thus, in order to better understand the scaling of implementing software robots, it is necessary to analyze which components can be reused (what), how, and to what extent (Henfridsson and Bygstad, 2013; Huang et al., 2017; Svahn et al., 2017; Yoo et al., 2012). Implementing software robots by transforming human-executed processes (i. e. routines) into robot-automated processes can be done more efficiently as the implementation process scales. Based on theoretical concepts of routine theory, as well as digital scaling literature and our preliminary data, we have developed an initial model of scaling the implementation of software robots (see Figure 1). Routine theory and digital scaling literature allow us to theoretically open the black box of a successful evolution of software robots and how the associated scaling can be approached.

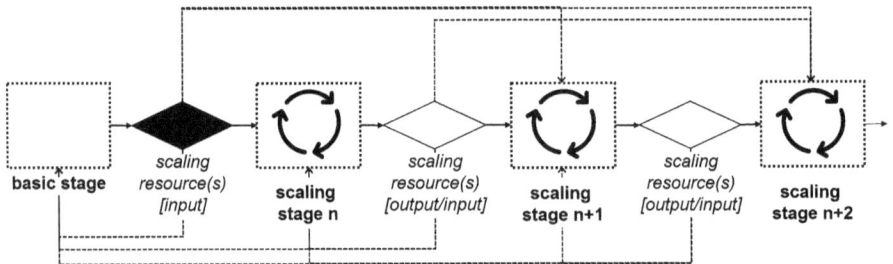

Figure 1: Phase of scaling.

The model is composed of multiple elements (see Table 1). Here, scaling the implementation of software robots is described as a circular process in the context of which scaling resources are created that can be reused in the further course of scaling. Thus, scaling resources refer to components that can be created in the course of implementing or programming software robots. Once created, scaling resources can be reused to accelerate or scale the implementation of software robots.

The whole scaling process can be divided into different stages of scaling, which can take place sequentially or in parallel. Scaling can be initiated once a basic stage

Table 1: Description of scaling elements.

	Description
Basic stage	The basic stage describes a first phase of the development of a software robot, based on which the robot implementation can be scaled subsequently
Scaling resource(s)	Scaling resources describe components that were created in the course of the previous development of a software robot and can be reused in further development. They can result as output from a scaling stage and they can be used as input to continue in a current scaling stage or to initiate a new scaling stage
Scaling stage	A scaling stage describes a phase of scaling in the implementation of software robots

has been completed. The basic stage refers to a first phase of the development of a software robot. Thus, the initial development or programming of the software robot can not yet be scaled but a software robot must already have been developed to a certain degree so that its further development can be scaled. Scaling resources can result from the basic stage and from each subsequent scaling stage. They can be considered as necessary input to enable scaling in each scaling stage and as potential output that can result from the basic stage and each subsequent scaling stage. As a resulting output, scaling resources can be reused in any past, current, or subsequent scaling stage. Thus, scaling resources can be reused not only prospectively but also retroactively either in the scaling stage from which they resulted or in any preceding scaling stage.

6.4 Illustration through case data

To better understand scaling in the context of implementing software robots, we have made first steps towards a theoretical understanding and empirical illustration of the scaling of the implementation of software robots. We have chosen a reciprocal approach that has enabled us to conceptualize a model, in which we have derived theoretical elements of routine theory and digital scaling literature deductively and inductively from empirical data of two case studies. However, the model developed in this chapter represents a first draft and needs to be further refined and substantiated with additional data. With the help of theoretical sampling, we identified two cases that seemed to contribute to an empirical illustration of our conceptualized model. Case 1 describes a chatbot project at a Swiss bank. Case 2 describes an RPA project at another Swiss bank. The aim is not to test the model but to illustrate it and to show how our model can be instantiated while some aspects of the model have also been derived from the case data (see, e. g., Leonardi, 2011). We conducted nine semi-structured interviews with people in different roles within the project team of case 1 between October and November 2017, in a second round in September 2018, and in a third round in March and April 2020. For case 2, we conducted three semi-structured interviews in October and November 2017. This helped us to obtain a holistic picture of both cases (Miles and Huberman, 1994; Yin, 2003). In addition, we also analyzed other data such as robot software suit manuals. Given that our key objective is to build theory, the research thrust is exploratory in nature (Benbasat et al., 1987). Qualitative research methods are suitable for "generating novel theory" (Eisenhardt, 1989, p. 546) – in particular theory that aims at answering "how" and "why" questions (Yin, 2003). This is true for our study as the key objective is to understand how to scale the robot implementation process.

6.4.1 Case narrative 1

The case describes a bank that wanted to optimize its contact center (CC) in terms of efficiency and in terms of improving performance and reducing costs. Therefore, chatbots were deemed suitable to automate processes. The project regarded was initiated in October 2016.

The team consisted of a product owner, a scrum master, an external partner, an application manager, and the content team. The product owner and the scrum master were primarily responsible for managing the project. The product owner focused mainly on the business aspects and the scrum master on the IT aspects of the project. The external partner helped the bank to acquire the necessary know-how to implement the chatbot. Since it was the first chatbot project of the bank, this was essential. The application manager was responsible for maintaining the chatbot application and integrating it into the existing system architecture. The role of the content team was to generate the content, based on which the chatbot should conduct dialogues. By content, topics and corresponding dialogues are meant. The content team therefore had to identify such topics on the one hand and then define and implement corresponding dialogues. An example of such a topic would be the query of the current account balance by a customer.

The chatbot software used by the bank was relatively simple. Decision trees could be modeled graphically. Thus, the content team mostly modeled dialogues directly in the chatbot framework itself. The chatbot framework describes the chatbot software used by the bank and its functionalities, which the project team used to build the chatbot.

In the course of the project, the chatbot was not only continuously developed but the project team was able to benefit from already created components to the extent that it was able to scale the entire implementation process of the chatbot. Thus, by evaluating the project, different scaling stages could be identified. In summary, three different incidents, which each reflect one stage of scaling could be identified that together

represent an evolutionary path that the chatbot went through during its implementation. These are the scaling from the German to the French chatbot, the scaling to the
e-banking chatbot, and the scaling to the voicebot. In each of the three scaling stages
certain components could be reused and thus functionalities could be transferred. It
was, however, only possible to digitally scale after the chatbot had been developed
and implemented to a certain extent, i. e., the German bot had been created.

6.4.1.1 Basic stage – German bot

The basic prerequisite for scaling the implementation of the bank's chatbot was therefore the previous development and implementation process of the basic stage of the
chatbot, i. e., the German version of the chatbot. The development of the basic stage
basically meant to model German conversational processes within decision trees and
to implement variations and synonyms. Decision trees were modeled around one main
question, which constituted the root, while possible direct answers and follow-up
questions formed the branches of each decision tree. One main question then required
about 100 variations, so that the chatbot was able to answer accurately. "Still, if there
is a 101st question and the syntax is wrong, we are pretty sure the chatbot is going to
map the question to the right main question" (external partner). Decision trees refer
to a dialogue's structure, while the main questions refer to dialogue topics.

Initially, the chatbot could answer simple questions in German that contained
general information; occurred in high volumes; contained self-service components or
aspects that the end user could handle him or herself; and referred to a non-value
adding process. Thus, in this basic stage the chatbot was able to conduct simple conversations in German, which did not require any kind of system integration. Users
could access the chatbot through the bank's website without being logged in.

As long as decision trees were extended and new variations and synonyms were
added that allowed the chatbot to run processes more accurately in the same domain,
i. e., around the same topic, no scaling was performed. Thus, the initial development
and implementation phase of the chatbot cannot be referred to as scaling. The German
version of the chatbot was officially released in November 2017.

6.4.1.2 Scaling stage 1 – French bot

After completion of the basic stage, in which the German chatbot was developed, the
first scaling stage of the development of the French chatbot could be initiated. Based
on the basic stage the project team could further develop the chatbot so that it could
conduct conversations not merely in German but also in French. This can be referred to
as the first scaling stage. The basic idea of this stage was to build on the conversations
or dialogue topics that had previously been built up in German. These conversations

should be translated into French. As the decision trees of the German dialogues already contained a considerable amount of questions and corresponding answers, the project team assumed that this stage could be completed relatively quickly. In principle, the project team assumed that the dialogues previously set up in German could now be translated directly into French. However, the complete reuse of dialogue topics and dialogue structures was not possible as only some components could indeed be reused. Reuse was prevented by the users who were supposed to use the chatbot in French. The reason for this was that the French speaking users expressed themselves and structured dialogues differently than the German speaking users.

During the development of the German version of the chatbot, the project team acquired considerable knowledge about the extent to which a chatbot needs to be developed at all, and which topics the users want to address via the chatbot. The project team could build on this knowledge to develop the French version of the chatbot faster. In addition, however, they had to analyze and better understand their French speaking users as well as their behaviors in order to set up and structure the French dialogues accordingly. To accomplish this, the content team has been expanded to include a native French speaker.

Thus, in the first scaling stage, some components could be directly reused, while for the reuse of other components, these first had to be made compatible with the corresponding context. Concretely, this meant that the knowledge acquired for the development of the chatbot and the dialogue topics previously established for the German bot could be directly reused for the French bot. The reuse of the knowledge enabled the project team to design the dialogs for the French bot more efficiently and faster. The German dialogue structures, on the other hand, could not be directly reused, although their structure had to be revised to suit the French speaking users. The French chatbot was released in October 2018.

6.4.1.3 Scaling stage 2 – e-banking bot

The second scaling stage then describes the evolution from the development of the German and French dialogues to the integration of the chatbot into the e-banking system. This should allow the users of the chatbot not only to have general conversations but also to ask user-specific questions while being logged into the bank's e-banking system. Until then, the chatbot was dependent on the information the user provided in a chat. With the integration into the e-banking system, the chatbot could now directly retrieve information about a specific user from the system. However, this not only meant that the conversations needed to be tailored to a specific user but it also meant that sensitive user-specific data should become part of the dialogues.

The chatbot software used by the bank was based on cloud servers located abroad. However, the Swiss data protection law stipulated that sensitive user data may only be processed on cloud servers located in Switzerland. Consequently, for the bank this meant that the dialogues processed on the cloud servers of the chatbot software provider could not contain any sensitive data. The project team was confronted with the problem that with the integration into the e-banking system, sensitive data would become part of the conversations but that these sensitive data cannot be sent via the chat, because otherwise it would be stored in the chatlog on the cloud abroad.

The project team solved this problem with so-called deep links. In doing so, the user could for example ask, "What is my account balance?" Rather than the chatbot answering the user's account balance in the chat field, the chatbot would reply "You can find your account balance in the red marked field on your screen." If it was sensitive data that the chatbot was supposed to give out, it was not displayed in the chat field but highlighted directly on the bank's website. The sensitive data entered by users were encrypted in order to ensure compliance with data protection laws.

For the integration of the chatbot into the e-banking system, the project team was once again able to draw on the knowledge they had already gained in developing the German and French bots. In addition, the previously modeled dialogue topics in German and French could be reused. These dialogue topics were previously modeled in a very general and not user-specific manner. The integration into the e-banking system, however, should now focus on the chatbot being able to conduct user-specific dialogues. The previous dialogue topics could thus be used as a basis, which now had to be tailored specifically to the user.

In addition to the already existing dialogue topics, new topics had to be covered by new dialogues. When modeling these new dialogue topics, certain dialogue structures of the previous dialogues could be reused.

In the second scaling stage, most components could be directly reused. The reuse of these components enabled the project team to design the dialogues for the e-banking bot more efficiently and faster. The integration into the e-banking system was initiated in summer 2018 and a first version got released in early 2019.

6.4.1.4 Scaling stage 3 – voicebot

Finally, the third scaling stage describes the evolution from the integration into the e-banking system to the extension of the chatbot to a voicebot. This third stage was initiated shortly after the start of the second stage of the integration into the e-banking system. The voicebot should allow users to interact with the bot not merely by text input but also by voice input. The users were to reach the voicebot by phone, just as they had reached CC employees before. In a first phase, no integration of the voicebot into the web site or the mobile application was planned. The project team still left this possibility open.

The project team again assumed that a considerable part of the dialogue topics and structures already created for the chatbot could be reused for the development of the voicebot. This was again not as easy as one had hoped for. The project team had to realize that not only the German and French speaking users expressed themselves differently, but all users spoke differently than they wrote. "For example, the syntax is completely different when the customer asks, 'Can I check my account balance, please?' Then he writes on the text channel: 'Account balance please'. Maybe two words. [...] But when he enters it in the voice channel, it's more of a dialogue and he says, 'Yes, I think I got my paycheck yesterday and I need to know what my balance is and check if I can pay my bills.' [...] And you just can't compare how the customers write and how they talk to the assistant [voicebot]" (product owner).

Thus, it turned out to be much more difficult to reuse already modeled dialogues for the voicebot. The project team therefore had to rethink its approach. They did this by adopting a voice-first approach and trained all team members accordingly. Voice-first meant that the project team would create all newly generated dialogues for the voice channel first, in a form in which they could potentially be used for the text channel in a second step.

The project team also reworked some of the existing dialogue topics and structures so that they were compatible for the voice channel. "We will not be able to make 100 % of the content we have modeled suitable for voice. That would lead to too much effort at the moment" (product owner).

As with the integration into the e-banking system, the transition to voice posed the challenge of sensitive data. However, this time it was not possible to use deep links and show the sensitive aspects of a conversation to the respective user on the visual user interface. Once conversations are conducted via voice channel, there is no visible user interface. As mentioned above, the bank was not allowed to process sensitive data on a foreign cloud due to applicable regulations. The provider of the chatbot software used until then was neither willing to install a cloud in Switzerland, nor to offer the software on-premise. The bank was thus forced to look for another solution.

They found what they were looking for in another provider who delivered their chatbot software on-premise. The text-based chatbots should run on the old chatbot software for the time being. The voicebot should be based on the new chatbot software. However, the long-term goal was to completely replace the old chatbot software with the new one.

For the development of the voicebot the project team was not able to directly reuse the dialogue topics and structures that have been created in previous stages. Instead, the dialogue structures had to be made compatible with the voice channel. Accordingly, the project team translated some of the text dialogues into voice dialogues. However, some of the text dialogues hardly seemed suitable for the voice channel. Here the project team had to reverse the approach and henceforth model voice-first dialogues, which could then be reused for the text channel and thus the further extension of the text-based bots.

In the third scaling stage, most components could not be directly reused but they had to be revised to suit the voicebot. Reuse was reversed here in that the dialogue structures created for the voicebot were to be reused retroactively for the text-based bots. The transition from the text to the voicebot is still in progress. A first version of the voicebot was released in June 2020.

6.4.2 Case narrative 2

The case describes another bank that also wanted to optimize its CC in terms of efficiency, improved performance, and reduced costs. Therefore, multiple RPA robots should allow the automation of business processes. The project was initiated in July 2017. The project team consisted of different roles. As this was the bank's first RPA project, the project was implemented in collaboration with an external consultancy firm.

Similarly to the case previously outlined, certain scaling dynamics could be identified in this case as well. Unlike in the chatbot case, however, no multiple scaling stages could be identified but scaling was instead applied step by step within one single stage of scaling. In this scaling stage, various business processes were to be automated with the help of several RPA robots.

6.4.2.1 Basic stage

The basic prerequisite for scaling the implementation of the bank's RPA robots was an initial phase where the project team had to understand the RPA robot design. This was critical, because it determined how business processes could be introduced to the RPA software so that an RPA robot could execute them.

The RPA software used allowed the programming of RPA robots that could perform a sequence of process steps and mimicking what the human user normally does. The automation of business processes through the development of RPA robots was thereby done in the software's Studio, which was divided into Process Studio and Object Studio. Process Studio enabled the configuration of the process logic and the business rules (i. e., the process structure). Object Studio enabled the creation of reusable objects. A process described the logic of how a specific RPA robot executed tasks. An object described the RPA robot's interaction with specific systems on their user interface.

The developers did not actually have to program the automation of business processes but could graphically model them with the help of various flowchart elements. In Process Studio, one could either entirely model business processes or split them into multiple process steps. Each process step could be modeled in a separate page. Throughout all the pages, the main process could be kept slim on the main process page; frequently used process steps within a particular process could be reused.

In Object Studio objects could be created, which allowed integrating external systems into the RPA software framework. With the "spying mode" of Object Studio, every system button could be tracked and added to the corresponding object. Once a system and its entire corresponding buttons had been integrated, actions linked to the usage of a specific system could be modeled. Unlike in Process Studio, pages were hereby used to model individual actions related to a specific object. For example, in one of the business processes to be automated, the RPA robot had to send a confirmation letter to a customer who had opened a new account. For this purpose, the RPA robot had to know the respective system button "print" and execute the action "print confirmation letter." To then add an action to a process in Process Studio, one could access the corresponding action from Object Studio. To do this, the flowchart element "action" had to be inserted into the main process or a process step page in Process Studio.

In summary, Object Studio enabled the integration of specific systems needed so that the RPA robots could execute the business processes modeled in Process Studio. Once the project team had gained an understanding of the design of the RPA software, the actual process automation could be initiated.

Business processes suitable for automation had to be executed in high volume and on a computer; they had to be rule-based and should entail limited exceptions; they should implicate structured data, and each business process to be automated should replace 0.3 full-time equivalents (FTE) in order to achieve the break-even point after one year. It was only worthwhile to develop a robot in case it could undertake the work of 0.3 FTE. Based on these criteria and a list of all processes executed in the CC, the project team identified four business processes with automation potential. Those four processes should be automated first while potential additional processes should follow later.

The development of the first four RPA robots was initiated with the modeling of the respective business processes. This was done within Process Studio and Object Studio. Each RPA robot was hereby set up through one process containing various objects that described the actions an RPA robot had to take in various process steps. However, some of the developers initially created RPA robots within objects instead of forming processes by using objects. "The object is something that you can reuse. The process is something you are only using for the current robotic process. So... you should not create a process inside an object. But many times, they did it" (supplier chief developer). If done so, objects could only be used for one specific process, while reuse was not possible. However, the idea of using objects to build processes was to be able to reuse the objects for several processes involving the same systems and thus to scale the RPA robot implementation process. Even though this approach required more effort in the beginning, it allowed a more efficient and faster implementation of subsequent RPA robots accessing the same systems. "Because the first robots are always the hardest. How so? Because... you develop that in objects. These are objects that can be reused in other robots. This automatically means that subsequent robots can be developed faster" (supplier project manager 2). Once the chief developer discovered that the other developers defined processes within objects instead of using various objects to define one process, he drew their attention to it, and they changed their approach from object-based to process-based development.

The initial development and implementation phase of the RPA robots cannot be referred to as scaling but allowed the creation of objects that could be reused later on.

6.4.2.2 Scaling stage 1

After completion of the basic stage, in which initial objects were created, scaling could be initiated. The automation of the four processes originally identified took place in parallel. The basic stage was not completed with the completion of the implementation of the four corresponding RPA robots. Rather, it was possible to move from the basic stage to scaling stage 1 after some initial objects were created that could be reused continuously and thus contributed to implement RPA robots more efficient. Thus, the previously created objects could be reused in the further implementation of the RPA robots. This helped to speed up the overall implementation process of the robots.

In the course of the development of multiple RPA robots some components, i. e., objects and process structures, could be reused. This enabled a more efficient implementation of the RPA robots and thus scaling. However, not only were existing objects and process structures reused but also new ones were created even after the completion of the basic stage. Scaling was thus achieved through the creation of objects and process structures. After a period of five months, the first out of the initial four RPA robots was released in November 2017.

6.5 Discussion

Implementing software robots essentially describes an approach of automating business processes. In this chapter we associate such business processes with routines. The performance of routines often implies that certain means are used to achieve certain ends. It has been argued in previous literature that the ends determine which means should be used in achieving ends (Feldman et al., 2016). Dittrich and Seidl (2018) add to this that certain means originate in the performance of routines and can be used to define and achieve new ends. A similar dynamic can be observed in the implementation of software robots.

One could describe the implementation of software robots as automating processes by means of programming software robots (Rutschi and Dibbern, 2019, 2020). While implementing software robots, components or resources can be created that can be reused for the further programming of past, current, or new robots. This allows for a more efficient and faster programming of software robots and thus to accelerate or scale the software robot implementation process (Dittrich and Seidl, 2018).

By scaling the implementation of software robots, functionality of a current robot can be extended or transferred to a different robot or context. As a result, the evolution of software robots can be accelerated. Such acceleration or scaling can be achieved when certain resources are created during the initial programming of software robots. These same resources can then be reused.

To better understand how to scale the implementation of software robots, it is essential to understand which resources can be reused, how they can be reused (in the same or a different context), and to what extent they can be reused (through reproduction or recreation) (Henfridsson and Bygstad, 2013; Huang et al., 2017; Svahn et al., 2017; Yoo et al., 2012). In this chapter we provide insights into all three of these aspects: (1) what to scale (i. e., which means or resources), (2) how to scale (i. e., through which type of reuse), and (3) to what extent to scale (i. e., the type of contextual extension). In the following, we will again discuss and elaborate on all three aspects and show how they apply in the two cases analyzed.

6.5.1 What to scale

In order to scale at all, certain resources or means must be created, which can be reused subsequently. Hereafter we will go into more detail about what such resources could look like, and which concrete resources were created in the two cases. As outlined above, a routine consists of an ostensive and a performative aspect (D'Adderio, 2011; Feldman et al., 2016; Pentland and Feldman, 2005). If we now want to transfer a routine from a human to a robot, we need to comprehend both the ostensive aspect and the performative aspect of the human-executed routine. Only then can we transfer the human-executed routine into a robot-automated routine. Therefore, we need to translate the ostensive and performative aspects of the human-executed routine into ostensive and performative aspects of the robot-automated routine.

The ostensive and performative aspects differ from each other when a routine is performed by a human, since the human can continuously influence both aspects. This is different for software robots. The robot has an initial influence on the ostensive aspect of the routine by specifying the extent to which it can and cannot perform a routine. The rules and procedures (i. e., the ostensive aspect) according to which a human has executed the routine in the past must therefore be translated to correspond to the robot design.

Once a routine has been implemented as a software robot, it does not change anymore. The robot performs the routine by strictly following the given rules and procedures (i. e., the ostensive aspect). Different from when a human performs a routine, the ostensive and performative aspects are the same when a routine is executed by a software robot.

When a company decides to implement software robots to automate certain business processes, there are several ways to approach this. The company can automate each process individually, starting from scratch each time. Alternatively, the company can combine the automation of several processes and build on already created resources or means. In fact, these resources can be referred to as the ostensive aspect of the routine or a part of it, which is implemented as a robot.

For each automation of a process Pn+1, which is preceded by another automation of a similar process Pn, it must be examined to what extent the ostensive aspect On of process Pn corresponds to the ostensive aspect On+1 of process Pn+1. The difference or delta between On and On+1 must be evaluated (see Figure 2). The more the two overlap and the larger the delta, the more resources can be reused. Therefore, the delta describes what can be reused or scaled. If the delta is positive, scaling resources can be reused in any current or subsequent scaling stage. If the delta is negative, scaling resources can be reused retroactively.

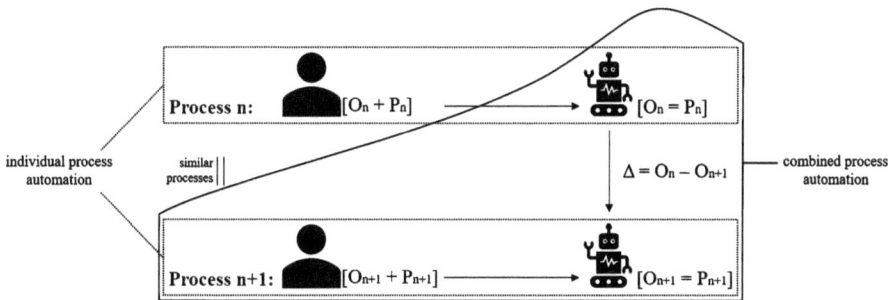

Figure 2: Individual and combined process automation.

In case 1, the implementation of the German, French, and e-banking bots and the voicebot led to the generation of scaling resources (i. e., means) such as dialogue topics (in German and French) and dialogue structures (in German and French, and of general as well as of user-specifically tailored text- and voice-based nature). Reusing these scaling resources resulted in an acceleration of the implementation of the chatbot (see Table 2).

In case 2, the implementation of the first RPA robots led to the generation of scaling resources (i. e., means) such as process structures and objects. Reusing these scaling resources resulted in an acceleration of the implementation of the RPA robots. However, the project team did not initially create scaling resources but some of the developers created RPA robots within objects instead of forming processes by using objects. As a result, every new development of an RPA robot had to be started from scratch and could not be based on already existing components or scaling resources. When they realized this, they adapted their implementation approach and created components (i. e., scaling resources) that could be reused (see Table 3).

Table 2: Scaling process in case 1.

Basic stage	Scaling resource(s) (input)	Scaling stage 1	Scaling resource(s) (output/input)	Scaling stage 2	Scaling resource(s) (output/input)	Scaling stage 3	Scaling resource(s) (output/input)
Development of German bot	Dialogue structures and dialogue topics in German	Development of French bot	Dialogue structures and dialogue topics in French	Development of e-banking bot	Dialogue structures, additional dialogue topics, and deep link integrations	Development of voicebot	Voice-first dialogue structures and additional dialogue topics

Table 3: Scaling process in case 2.

Basic stage	Scaling resource(s) (input)	Scaling stage 1	Scaling resource(s) (output/input)
Initial development of RPA robots	Process structures and objects	Further development of RPA robots	Additional process structures and objects

6.5.2 How to scale

Once it has been defined what (i. e., what scaling resources) can be scaled, one must evaluate how to scale. Scaling resources can be reused to accelerate the implementation of a current, a subsequent, or a previous software robot. Scaling resources can be reused to extend functionality of a robot or to transfer functionality from one robot to another. This results in two types of reuse (i. e., how to scale). Expanding functionality can be referred to as *mutation*. Transferring functionality can be referred to as *inheritance* (Henfridsson and Bygstad, 2013).

In case 1, scaling resources were reused for extending as well as transferring functionality. Scaling resources that resulted from the basic stage (i. e., implementing the German bot) were reused to accelerate the further development of the German bot (first context) as well as the initial developments of the French bot (second context), the e-banking bot (third context), and the voicebot (fourth context). Scaling resources that resulted from scaling stage 1 (i. e., implementing the French bot) were reused to accelerate the further developments of the German (first context) and French bots (second context) as well as the initial developments of the e-banking bot (third context) and the voicebot (fourth context). Scaling resources that resulted from scaling stage 2 (i. e., implementing the e-banking bot) were reused to accelerate the further development of the e-banking bot (third context) as well as the initial development of the voicebot (fourth context). Scaling resources that resulted from scaling stage 3 (i. e., implementing the voicebot) were reused to accelerate the further development of the voicebot (fourth context) as well as the further development of the German (first context), French (second context), and e-banking bots (third context).

In case 2, scaling resources were reused in order to extend functionality of current RPA robots as well as to transfer functionality to other RPA robots.

6.5.3 To what extent to scale

Finally, one must understand in what context scaling takes place (i. e., the type of contextual extension). Direct reuse may be hampered whereas scaling resources may not always be reproduced but need to be recreated if they are to be reused in a different context. *Reproduction* indicates that means or scaling resources were directly reused independent of the context. *Recreation* indicates that means or scaling resources were adapted according to a new context in order to be reused.

In case 1, some scaling resources (i. e., dialogue topics) could be reused directly while others (i. e., dialogue structures) had to be adapted to different contexts in order to be reused. Overall, scaling dynamics could be observed in multiple (i. e., three) scaling stages within case 1.

In case 2, all RPA robots should be implemented in the same department. Thus, scaling resources (i. e., process structures and objects) could be reused directly without any need for context-specific adaptations in case 2. Unlike in case 1, in case 2 scaling dynamics could merely be observed in one stage of scaling.

6.6 Conclusion and outlook

Software robots are expected to dramatically improve the efficiency of companies and disrupt the way humans and machines work and collaborate (Willcocks and Lacity, 2016). It is crucial for companies to understand how business processes can be automated successfully by implementing software robots and how such robot implementations can be scaled. Implementing software robots by transforming human-executed routines into robot-automated processes can be done more efficiently by scaling the implementation process.

Despite the automation through software robots, the human factor plays an important role here. This may change as technology advances and robots are able to learn how to take over and perform certain processes autonomously without any need for human intervention. Given the type of software robots (i. e., chatbots and RPA robots) we are looking at here, this is not the case. Such software robots can take over and perform processes only after a human (i. e., the developer) has programmed the robot accordingly.

For this to be done more efficiently, the human must understand the delta and thus the degree of scaling. In other words, the developer must understand the extent to which the ostensive aspect of two similar processes or routines to be automated overlap. Depending on whether the delta between two ostensive aspects is positive or negative, scaling resources can be reused for current and subsequent robot implementations or retroactively for preceding robot implementations.

We contribute to routine theory and literature on digital scaling by examining how the implementation of software robots can be scaled. Specifically, we found that (1) for scaling the implementation of software robots, one can build on what already exists (scaling resources), (2) scaling resources can be reused for functionality extension or transfer (mutation vs. inheritance), and (3) scaling resources can be reused in different contexts, in which they can be reused directly or through adaptations (reproduction vs. recreation).

In this regard, we have conceptualized a model for scaling the implementation of software robots based on existing constructs from routine theory and digital scaling literature. Some aspects of the model have also been derived from the data.

Besides the implications of our research, we also must acknowledge its limitations. The model developed in this chapter describes an initial model and needs to be further refined and substantiated with additional data.

We have shown exemplarily how scaling was approached in two cases. It was shown that digital scaling can be divided into different scaling stages, within which scaling resources (i. e., means) are created and can be reused. The reuse of scaling resources can be considered as a mechanism that triggers scaling by enabling the extension (i. e., mutation) or transfer (i. e., inheritance) of functionality (Banker and Kauffman, 1992; Basili et al., 1996). The implementation of software robots is associated with high costs and time expenditure. These can be reduced by scaling and therefore the implementation of software robots can be made more efficient. However, in order to be able to scale at all, it must be understood what can be scaled (i. e., what scaling resources or means), how it can be scaled (i. e., in what contexts), and to what extent it can be scaled (i. e., through reproduction or recreation).

An understanding of how to scale the software robot implementation process is of great interest to both research and practice. We make first steps in conceptualizing and theorizing the three aspects (i. e., what, how, and to what extent) of scaling the implementation of software robots. Future research could seek to better understand which contextual factors could impede direct reuse of scaling resources and why reuse is performed this or that way.

Bibliography

Adler PS, Goldoftas B, Levine DI (1999) Flexibility versus efficiency? A case study of model changeovers in the toyota production system. Organ Sci 10(1):43–68

Asatiani A, Penttinen E (2016) Turning robotic process automation into commercial success – case OpusCapita. J Inf Technol Teaching Cases 6(2):67–74

Banker RD, Kauffman RJ (1992) Reuse and productivity in integrated computer-aided software engineering: an empirical study. MIS Q 14(3):374–401

Basili VR, Briand LC, Melo WL (1996) How reuse influences productivity in object-oriented systems. Commun ACM 39(10):104–116

Benbasat I, Goldstein DK, Mead M (1987) The case research strategy in studies of information systems. MIS Q 11(3):369–386

Chandler AD (1990) Strategy and structure: chapters in the history of the industrial enterprise, vol 461. MIT press

D'Adderio L (2011) Artifacts at the centre of routines: performing the material turn in routines theory. J Inst Econ 7(2):197–230

Dittrich K, Seidl D (2018) Emerging intentionality in routine dynamics: a pragmatist view. Acad Manag J 61(1):111–138

Eisenhardt KM (1989) Building theories from case study research. Acad Manag Rev 14(4):532–550

Feldman MS (2000) Organizational routines as a source of continuous change. Organ Sci 11(6):611–629

Feldman MS, Pentland BT (2003) Reconceptualizing organizational routines as a source of flexibility and change. Adm Sci Q 48(1):94–118

Feldman MS, Pentland BT, D'Adderio L, Lazaric N (2016) Beyond routines as things: introduction to the special issue on routine dynamics. Organ Sci 27(3):505–513

Fung HP (2014) Criteria, use cases and effects of information technology process automation (ITPA). In: Advances in robotics & automation, vol 3

Guzman I, Pathania A (2016). Chatbots in customer service. Retrieved 25 Oct, 2017, from https://www.accenture.com/t00010101T000000__w__/br-pt/_acnmedia/PDF45/Accenture-Chatbots-Customer-Service.pdf

Heller B, Proctor M, Mah D, Jewell L, Cheung B (2005) Freudbot: an investigation of chatbot technology in distance education. Paper presented at the EdMedia: World Conference on Educational Media and Technology

Henfridsson O, Bygstad B (2013) The generative mechanisms of digital infrastructure evolution. MIS Q 907–931

Howard-Grenville JA (2005) The persistence of flexible organizational routines: the role of agency and organizational context. Organ Sci 16(6):618–636

Huang J, Henfridsson O, Liu MJ, Newell S (2017) Growing on steroids: rapidly scaling the user base of digital ventures through digital innovation. MIS Q 41(1)

Leonardi PM (2011) When flexible routines meet flexible technologies: affordance, constraint, and the imbrication of human and material agencies. MIS Q 35(1):147–167

Miles MB, Huberman AM (1994) Qualitative data analysis: an expanded sourcebook. Sage Publications, Thousand Oaks, CA, USA

Patil A, Marimuthu K, Niranchana R (2017) Comparative study of cloud platforms to develop a chatbot. Int J Eng Technol 6(3):57–61

Pentland BT, Feldman MS (2005) Organizational routines as a unit of analysis. Ind Corp Change 14(5):793–815

Pentland BT, Feldman MS, Becker MC, Liu P (2012) Dynamics of organizational routines: a generative model. J Manag Stud 49(8):1484–1508

Pfeifer R, Lungarella M, Iida F (2007) Self-organization, embodiment, and biologically inspired robotics. Science 318(5853):1088–1093

Rutschi C, Dibbern J (2019) Mastering software robot development projects: understanding the association between system attributes & design practices. In: Paper presented at the proceedings of the 52nd Hawaii international conference on system sciences, Hawaii, USA

Rutschi C, Dibbern J (2020) Towards a framework of implementing software robots: transforming human-executed routines into machines. ACM SIGMIS Database 51(1):104–128

Sahay S, Walsham G (2006) Scaling of health information systems in India: challenges and approaches. Inf Technol Dev 12(3):185–200

Sengupta R, Lakshman S (2017) Conversational chatbots – let's chat. Retrieved 25 Oct, 2017 from https://www2.deloitte.com/content/dam/Deloitte/in/Documents/strategy/instrategy-innovation-conversational-chatbots-lets-chat-final-report-noexp.pdf

Sharma P, Southern R, Dalton D (2016) The discruptive chat bots – sizing up real opportunities for business. Retrieved from https://www2.deloitte.com/content/dam/Deloitte/ie/Documents/ie-dispruptivechat-bots.pdf

Shawar BA, Atwell E (2007) Different measurements metrics to evaluate a chatbot system. In: Paper presented at the proceedings of the workshop on bridging the gap: academic and industrial research in dialog technologies, Rochester, NY, USA

Slaby JR (2012) Robotic automation emerges as a threat to traditional low-cost outsourcing. HfS Research Ltd.

Svahn F, Mathiassen L, Lindgren R (2017) Embracing digital innovation in incumbent firms: how volvo cars managed competing concerns. MIS Q 41(1)

Tirgul CS, Naik MR (2016) Artificial intelligence and robotics. Int J Adv Res Comput Eng Technol 5(6):1787–1793

Willcocks L, Lacity MC (2016) Service automation: robots and the future of work. Steve Brookes Publishing

Yin RK (2003) Case study research. In: Applied social research methods series, vol 5. Sage Publications, Beverly Hills, CA, USA

Yoo Y, Boland RJ Jr, Lyytinen K, Majchrzak A (2012) Organizing for innovation in the digitized world. Organ Sci 23(5):1398–1408

Philipp Croon and Christian Czarnecki

7 Liability for loss or damages caused by RPA

Abstract: Intelligent autonomous software robots replacing human activities and performing administrative processes are reality in today's corporate world. This includes, for example, decisions about invoice payments, identification of customers for a marketing campaign, and answering customer complaints. What happens if such a software robot causes a damage? Due to the complete absence of human activities, the question is not trivial. It could even happen that no one is liable for a damage towards a third party, which could create an uncalculatable legal risk for business partners. Furthermore, the implementation and operation of those software robots involves various stakeholders, which result in the unsolvable endeavor of identifying the originator of a damage. Overall it is advisable to all involved parties to carefully consider the legal situation. This chapter discusses the liability of software robots from an interdisciplinary perspective. Based on different technical scenarios the legal aspects of liability are discussed.

Keywords: Robotic process automation, artificial intelligence, liability, culpability

7.1 Introduction

Can *Alexa* – the virtual assistant offered by Amazon – be liable for damages? The question is not as absurd as it sounds. Since Amazon's product was introduced in 2017, the German police reported several cases of rogue *Alexas*, partying loud at night, causing annoyed neighbors to call the police. One case, in Pinneberg (a small town in Germany), had *Alexa* blasting music at night after being remotely activated by a music streaming service that also turned the volume to the maximum. It seems that no direct human action led to this nightly disturbance. The police mission tallied at about 3,000 €, which – in the end – was paid by Amazon out of goodwill. The question remains though: Who is really liable when an autonomously acting software system causes a damage?

Also in a corporate environment an increasing number of processes is automated by software programs, so-called software robots (e. g., Schmitz et al., 2018; Willcocks et al., 2017). In this chapter the term *robotic process automation* (RPA) is used for a range of approaches and technical concepts that support the automation of business processes by using software robots. Those systems can be structured into input sensors, an intelligence center, and output actuators (Fettke and Loos, 2019). The intelligence center can vary from simple rule-based decisions to cognitive robots using advanced concepts, such as artificial intelligence (AI) (Enriquez et al., 2020; Houy et al., 2019). In this context, a typical, exemplary use case is the automation of the invoice

https://doi.org/10.1515/9783110676693-007

verification, which is an administrative process that can be found in almost every organization. This process requires different checks (e. g., consistency of ordered amount, delivered amount, and invoiced amount), and due to possible exceptions (e. g., handwritten correction), it often contains manual activities. Therefore, the automation by RPA requires a cognitive intelligence center that transfers the unstructured paper invoice into structured data. These structured data are then verified, and – if correct – automatically paid. Based on this typical use case the following two errors of the RPA system are possible: (1) a correct invoice is not paid, or (2) an unjustified invoice is paid. The first error might incur a financial damage to a third party caused by default. The second error could cause a financial damage for the company itself, for example, if the unjustified invoice is a fraud case. In both cases the question arises if someone can be held liable for the incurred damage.

Even though the question of liability is one of the oldest well-discussed questions of legal practice, judging the liability in the above described scenario is a complex issue. First, the legal treatment of robots offers from a juridical perspective open scientific questions, such as the self-responsibility of robots and the sufficiency of existing laws (e. g., Bertolini, 2013; Gless et al., 2016; Hubbard, 2015). Second, from an application-oriented perspective the current development of RPA systems requires legal guidance which is an interdisciplinary topic composed of computer science and law. This second perspective is the focus of this chapter. In Section 7.2 basic concepts of liability in robotics are explained. Then, in Section 7.3 concrete liability scenarios of RPA are proposed, and their legal impact is discussed based on their technical realization. While, in general, liability can be differentiated in the civil and criminal liability side, this chapter focuses on the civil liability. As legislation and jurisdiction varies in different countries, an application-oriented discussion can only be exemplary based on concrete laws. This chapter mainly focuses on European legal traditions, most of the time stemming from German legal traditions, so the concepts discussed can be transferred to European legal systems and similar legal traditions. The basic thought process behind liability for RPA systems also can be applied to different legal systems, for example, the Anglo-American common law. The transfer to other legal systems is discussed as part of the outlook in Section 7.4. As this chapter is not an exhausting legal examination, a comparative discussion of different legal systems and their liability solutions for RPA is not discussed in depth here.

7.2 Basic concepts of liability in RPA

While from a technical perspective RPA is different from physical robots, from a legal perspective both topics are quite similar. At the end, a machine consisting of software and hardware components causes a loss or damage. The essential points are the degree of autonomy and automation, which are typical questions of robotics. Hence, the liability of RPA can, from a legal perspective, be traced back to the broader context of robotics. The possible types of the loss or damage depend on the concrete technical realization, for example, a physical robot with a strong arm could create a physical damage, which is obviously impossible for a software robot that only uses application systems. The general types of liability – independent from involved machines – are discussed in Section 7.2.1. Related work about the general question of liability in robotics is explained in Section 7.2.2. Its transfer to RPA is discussed in Section 7.2.3.

7.2.1 Types of liability

Typically, law knows several kinds of civil legal liability, but the liability can basically be divided into two kinds of civil liability: contractual liability and tortious liability. *Contractual liability* is liability based on a contract or quasi-contract while *tortious liability* is based on the behavior of a person. Each of these two broad categories is further divided into several "sub-categories" of liability. In the scope of this chapter the *product liability*, a tortious liability based on the placing of a product on the market, is especially relevant.

7.2.2 General questions of liability in robotics

Due to the increased diffusion of robotics and their usage in private as well as commercial circumstances, legal questions of robotics have been discussed by various authors (e. g., Bertolini, 2013; Gless et al., 2016; Hubbard, 2015), and are a broad and complex field. Some discussions are inspired by the idea of a humanoid machine as described in science fiction literature. In such a scenario the question arises if robots are self-responsible for their actions, and if existing law systems are capable to deal with this situation.

From a technical perspective, there is a consensus that the development of robots should consider certain standards of ethics and safety (Murphy and Woods, 2009). However, robots may act autonomously, and therefore developers should be able to foresee or influence future actions of their robots. According to Bertolini (2013) autonomy is discussed around the aspects of (1) self-awareness or self-consciousness, (2) intelligent interaction in operating environments, and (3) the ability of learn. By applying AI concepts, robots can become autonomous machines that learn from past experience, act independently, and make individual decisions. Hence, a robot might act differently in the same situation depending on his past learning experience (Čerka et al., 2015). Therefore, some authors argue that it is in principle not possible to predict the robot's behavior, which leads to a responsibility and liability gap (Matthias, 2004), and propose a regulation of robots by law (e. g., Leenes and Lucivero, 2014; Palmerini et al., 2016). In fact, it is a relevant question if lawmakers have to adapt existing laws, or even develop completely new laws in order to consider innovative technologies such as AI and robots. Palmerini et al. (2016) argue that many legislative domains are affected by robotics, and some of them might require new rules; however, for many fields existing laws are sufficient.

With respect to liability, the level of autonomy is important (Bertolini, 2013). If a robot would act and decide completely autonomously, which would require self-awareness or self-consciousness, this robot must be liable for its actions as a legal person (Čerka et al., 2015). However, in all – or at least almost all – practical cases to-day's and in the near future expected robots, such as driverless vehicles and intelligent personal assistants, are weak autonomous systems producing functional states still under a human supervision (Bertolini, 2013). Hence, as long as robots do not achieve self-consciousness there is no legal foundation to consider them as independent le-gal subjects, but they are artifacts designed by humans for an intended purpose, also known as products (Bertolini, 2013). As a consequence, most liability cases of robots can be solved by existing liability laws for product safety (Hubbard, 2015; Palmerini et al., 2016). In this context, the concrete implementation scenario as well as the agree-ments of the involved parties is important.

7.2.3 Legal practice in RPA – autonomy vs. automatic

The known legal practice for damage caused by RPA systems is lacking in decided cases. There are, however, in the theoretical discussion, several ideas for a solution to the liability problems (e. g., Foerster, 2019). Some voices in literature have discussed problems arising from the use of automated systems and their autonomous decisions (Beck, 2009; Foerster, 2019; Gless and Janal, 2016) for the protection of "victims" of malfunctions.

The first legal question is if the RPA system is truly autonomous or simply auto-mated. An example for an automated system is that of a vending machine. The vend-ing machine simply checks if the coin put into it is genuine, and then, following its instructions, dispenses its product (Kirn and Müller-Hengstenberg, 2015; Sosnitza, 2016). The true autonomous system is described as a system where the exact result cannot be prognosticated (Kirn and Müller-Hengstenberg, 2015; Sosnitza, 2016). An example given is that of the autonomous algorithms of online retailers.

While that distinction may be of interest for certain legal aspects, even the true autonomous system is not autonomous in the sense of a true "free will." Even the most sophisticated automated system will only be able to "decide" on the parame-ters programmed into it by a developer. Only if a system would be truly free in every parameter, even in the parameter if it acts at all, it could be considered autonomous (Foerster, 2019).

The legal consequence of a truly autonomous system would be far reaching, but as a true AI remains science fiction, these problems will not be discussed here. At the moment, it can be assumed that any liability for a malfunctioning RPA system lies with the humans that have developed or are operating the system, and not with the software robot itself. Hence, with respect to legal practice the liability of an RPA system can be traced back to known questions of product liability. However, in a real-life case the liability would be highly dependent on the technical realization. Those concrete liability scenarios are explained and discussed in the next section.

7.3 Liability scenarios in RPA

7.3.1 Technical realization scenarios

From a technical perspective the implementation of an RPA system might involve the following roles:

1. **The RPA software developer** has programmed the software that is used for the RPA application system.
2. **The RPA product vendor** has sold the software product as an RPA standard software system.
3. **The RPA system integrator** has implemented the RPA application system within its operating environment.
4. **The RPA application operator** is the entity that operates the RPA application system.
5. **The software robot trainer** is the entity that has trained the intelligence center within the RPA application system.
6. **The RPA consultant** has supported the selection and implementation of the RPA application system.
7. **The business owner** is the entity that uses the RPA application system to automate his business processes.

In a real-life realization scenario, not necessarily all roles are involved. At the end, the specific arrangement of those roles, their mapping to legal entities, and the contractual arrangements between those legal entities are essential for the legal assessment of a concrete liability situation. It can be assumed that in all scenarios the business owner is an independent legal entity. The simplest – and also most unlikely – scenario would be that the business owner programs his own RPA system from scratch, implements and operates this system on his own technical infrastructure, and trains the software robots by his own. In the most sophisticated scenario all roles are linked to different legal entities that interact in an ecosystem based on a complex structure of bilateral agreements. For example, company A is a vendor of RPA standard software products that were programmed by company B. The RPA software was bought by company C, which is a cloud service operator and now operates the RPA software as part of a service offering. Implementation and training were realized by further companies (D and E). The business owner, company F, buys this RPA service from company C.

In practice, typical implementation scenarios are between those two extrema. For the further legal assessment, the following exemplary technical scenarios are defined (cf. Figure 1):

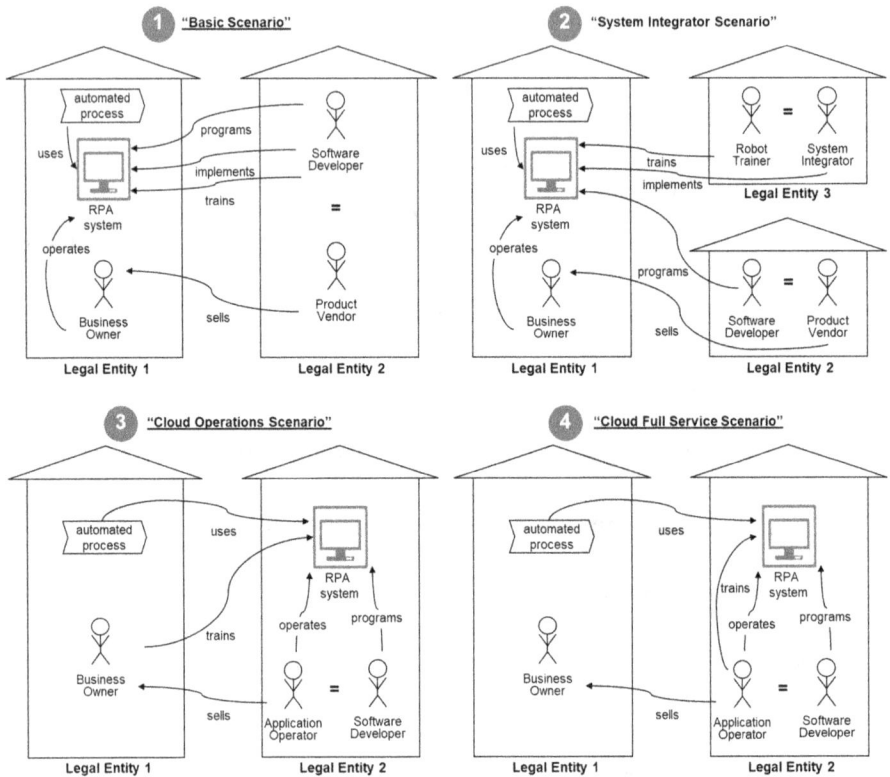

Figure 1: Technical scenarios of RPA implementation.

- **Technical scenario 1 – "basic scenario":** The business owner buys RPA standard software from a software vendor who is also the developer. The software vendor helps the business owner in the initial implementation and training of the system, which is afterwards handed over to the business owner. The system is operated by the business owner on his own infrastructure.
- **Technical scenario 2 – "system integrator scenario":** Same as scenario 1, but the business owner is supported by a system integrator who implements and trains the RPA system that is still operated on the business owner's own infrastructure.
- **Technical scenario 3 – "cloud operations scenario":** The RPA application is operated in a cloud by a service provider who has programmed the RPA software. The agreement between business owner and service provider covers the operation

of the RPA application. The business owner is responsible for the training of the
software robots.
- **Technical scenario 4 – "cloud full service scenario"**: This scenario is the same
as scenario 3, but the business owner has a full-service agreement with the service
provider. This agreement includes the training of the software robots.

All four scenarios are theoretical concepts and might vary in a real-life implementation. At present, the technical scenarios 1 and 2 are more likely. However, first offers of
RPA as a cloud solution are available at the market which could lead to the technical
scenarios 3 and 4. The role of the RPA consultant could be included in all scenarios
either as an in-house consultant belonging to the business owner, or a consulting
service offered by the system vendor, or an independent consultant as an additional
legal entity.

Assuming the RPA system has caused a damage that can be traced back to a defect
in the broader context of the RPA system, identifying the originator of the defect is not
easy. Possible reasons for a defect could be (1) a programming error caused by the RPA
software developer, (2) a wrong customization of the intelligence center caused by the
software robot trainer, (3) an inadequate technical infrastructure caused by the RPA
system integrator, or (4) an incomplete conceptual design caused by the RPA consultant. In computer sciences, proving the total correctness of a software is a difficult endeavor that is in most cases irresolvable. In practice, different standards (e. g., ISO/IEC
9126) are used to define software quality based on functional and non-functional aspects. From a contractual perspective, the inspection and approval of a software program is typically based on a defined set of requirements and test cases. With respect
to the initial example of invoice verification, different errors causing the non-payment
of an invoice are possible. A wrong memory management, i. e., a programming error,
could lead to lost invoice data sets. Non-considering invoices in a foreign language,
i. e., a training error, could cause a wrong invoice rejection. An inadequate network
bandwidth, i. e., an architectural error, could be the reason for lost connections causing data inconsistency. Non-considering a concept for a proper controlling and monitoring of the software robots, i. e., a conceptual design error, could be the root cause
for not detecting the wrongdoing of the software robot. In a real-life case a defect of a
software could possibly be linked to a mixture of different reasons. Hence, finding the
originator of a defect is a critical question that is not easy to answer.

7.3.2 Legal assessment

Answering the question of liability first of all requires the differentiation between the
following two legal scenarios (cf. Figure 2), which can be mapped to each of the technical scenarios (cf. Section 7.3.1):

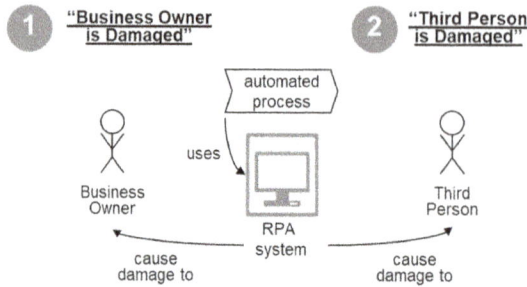

Figure 2: Legal scenarios of RPA liability.

- **Legal scenario 1 – the business owner is damaged**: This would usually mean that the business owner using the RPA system is damaged by his own system. Possible damage could be an automatic fulfilment of a fraudulent invoice, leading to a financial loss as the money cannot be recuperated.
- **Legal scenario 2 – a third person is damaged**: Under this scenario, a third party is damaged by the RPA system. For example, a valid invoice is rejected, leading to interest and legal costs to a third party.

7.3.2.1 Contractual liability

7.3.2.1.1 To the business owner – legal scenario 1

Contractual liability has typically several criterions that need to be fulfilled to hold someone liable for a damage.

The first characteristic is the existence of a legal obligation itself, usually a contract. In none of the above-mentioned technical scenarios (cf. Section 7.3.1) this will be of any problem. In technical scenario 1, the business owner has closed a sales contract for the RPA system with the software vendor. In technical scenario 2, the business owner has closed a contract with a software vendor and another contract with a system integrator. In technical scenario 3, the business owner has a contract with the cloud operator as in technical scenario 4.

The second criterion is the breach of contractual duty. That breach of contractual duty is constituted for example under German law by the tenet that one has to respect other people's rights, found in §241 of the civil code, but other European law systems have similar stipulations. A faulty product or service is usually a breach of contractual duty. That criterion is legally trivial but can (and will) in practice of course be argued. In technical scenario 1, the business owner has only one contract partner, so it is safe to assume that a faulty RPA system violates the contractional duty of the seller, but it is entirely plausible that the seller argues that the product is not faulty but exactly what was ordered. A complex system, like an RPA system, can be tailored to various specifications and even in the basic scenario evidence has to be produced that a contractional duty was really breached. Going over to technical scenario 2 this problem becomes even more evident – with two possible liable entities it has to be proven exactly to whose contractional duty the faulty RPA system can be linked. There is also the possibility that the causality for the problem with the RPA system is shared by the vendor of the system and the system integrator. It could even be assumed that the fault is cumulative between vendor and system integrator (e. g., the faulty RPA software in itself is not a problem, but in combination with the wrong training of the software robots, the fault becomes damaging).

The third criterion is actual damage. A faulty RPA system in itself is certainly subject to warranty – but a liability for damages require actual damage, so no claim can be made if nothing gets damaged. In all described scenarios a damage – either to the business owner or a third person – was caused. It can be assumed that evidence for this damage can be produced undoubtedly.

The fourth and last criterion is the culpability. Culpability is the subjective, personal fault of the culprit. In legal scenario 1, the culpability is not problematic, as the culpability is usually given if a vendor sells faulty software or a system integrator does something wrong, for example, while training software robots.

If those criteria are all met, the business owner has a damage claim against his contractual partner – at least in theory. In practice, the question of breach of contractual duty and culpability will have to be established very carefully. The problem for the business owner will be, in most cases, to actually find out what exactly went wrong with the RPA system, as he has to prove every criterion in a court case. This will most often lead to high obstacles to actually assert a claim, especially in cases where the business owner knows *that* something went wrong, but not exactly *what*. There is also the possibility that the business owner ordered – with respect to his actual requirements – an insufficient RPA system, for example, due to a lack of knowledge or an incomplete requirements engineering. It could be established that his contractual partners have an obligation to inform him in case they would realize that their customer (i. e., the business owner) is doing something wrong while ordering. However, widening the scope of contractual duties like that should only be done sparingly, as usually additional liability will lead to a higher compensation (e. g., the RPA system will be more expensive) – therefore, widening the scope of contractual duties after the fact will lead to an unfair advantage to the business owner. The business owner will have to decide if he wishes to take the risk of ordering something without appropriate prior consultation. In this context, the business owner should think about the option to hire someone, for example an RPA consultant, to provide him with the expert knowledge needed to order the RPA system tailored to his requirements, a wise move as he gets an additional contractual party to push a claim against if a damage claim against other parties seems hard to realize.

7.3.2.1.2 To a third party – legal scenario 2

Liability of the business owner

If a third party is damaged by the business owner, the perspective changes. First, the following key question has to be answered: When is the business owner liable for damages caused by his own RPA system? In this context, the technical scenarios are of secondary concern. However, if the culpability of the business owner is established, the claim he has to settle can possibly cause a damage to the business owner that can be traced back to legal scenario 1 (cf. Section 7.3.2.1.1).

Under legal scenario 2 – i. e., a damage to a third party – the obligation will usually not be a problem. In most cases, the RPA system damages a business partner of the business owner. The scenario that an RPA system damages a third party without a contractual relation to the business owner is certainly viable, but will be discussed at a later point. There is also the additional legal problem that the RPA system could be used to close a contract with a third party, and the RPA system declines to close the contract due to a faulty function. That scenario has extensive legal problems of its own (e. g., the question if the customer has the right to close a contract) which are not discussed in the scope of this chapter.

The breach of contractual duty will also usually not pose a problem. If the RPA application leads to any harm of the financial assets of a third party, the contractional duty of the business owner is breached. This breach of contract may be, for example, a denied payment which leads to a damage in interest. This breach has to lead to a damage which in the most cases should also be no further problem. Damage is an involuntary setback to the protected legal assets. It is possible that this damage is the denial of a contract, as discussed briefly earlier, which would lead to problems outside the scope of this chapter; however, – in most cases – this criterion is fairly straightforward. The customer will, in most cases, be able to declare a straightforward damage, for example, interest damage after receiving money too late or legal fees after having to take legal action against the business owner for not paying.

The last criterion is the culpability, which is the real problem of legal scenario 2. Culpability is the subjective, personal fault of the culprit. Under legal scenario 2, the culprit is the business owner. The RPA system itself cannot, as has been established earlier (cf. Section 7.2.3), be truly free in its decisions, and is therefore – based on the technical and legal situation at present – not culpable and cannot be held responsible for its actions. The RPA system is legally seen a non-entity, simply the tool used by the business owner, so any culpability has to be in the person of the business owner.

From a general perspective, there are two categories of culpability: (1) *intent* and (2) *negligence*. Intent is acting with the knowledge and the will to cause harm to another one's assets, negligence is the lack of due diligence and care. If the business owner had acted himself, culpability would not pose any serious problem. But in all above defined scenarios the business owner does not act directly, but the RPA system is the acting party, without any necessary involvement by the business owner him- or herself. It is however possible to find an act by the business owner, prior to the act of the RPA system, which directly causes a loss to the third party.

First, this act could be the acquiring and training of the RPA system. In the simplest scenario the business owner has at least programmed and trained the RPA himself. It would be possible to ascertain, if he made any mistakes while programming and training out of negligence (or even intentional), which would be enough to establish culpability. But, as discussed previously, this simplest scenario is highly fictional. In technical scenarios 1 to 4, the business owner has acquired the RPA system from a third party, and only in scenario 3 he or she has trained the system by himself. Only in extreme cases it could be assumed that the business owner acquires a faulty working RPA system intentionally or even out of negligence. The business owner would have to have any inclination that his RPA is not working right. This may, certainly, be only established after the first fault of the RPA system and even then, the fault that led to the damage in this case has to be the same fault that led to a damage beforehand.

If the business owner has an indication that his or her RPA system is acting faulty in any way, the follow-up question would be: Did he or she have any reason to suspect a fault with his RPA system? A general suspicion regarding RPA would go too far and certainly be not valid from a technical standpoint. So, in practice, the business owner would basically only have to state that he has bought an RPA software that he had no suspicions about (assuming a bare minimum of the business owner's diligence).

The other question is: Did the business owner perform enough to control the RPA system while it was working? From a technical perspective, controlling an RPA system is possible, and should be part of a professional systems design. Beside technical monitoring capabilities (e. g., lost connections, error logs), also the process itself should consider the handling of exceptions. With respect to the above invoice verification case, for example, an insufficient scanned invoice should not lead to an automatic refusion of the payment, but to a manual check and correction.

In practice, quite a serious problem will be to prove to the business owner that he did not control his RPA system properly, and – more importantly – that he could have been able to prevent the damage caused by the RPA system. If the damage would have occurred even while the business owner was supervising the RPA system, a lack of supervision will not lead to liability. That means in essence that the business owner only has to claim that his RPA system was chosen carefully and supervised correctly to escape any culpability for the RPA system.

There is of course the question if a user of an RPA system is legally required to read up on any technical developments regarding RPA systems, as the law requires of certain professions, like lawyers and medical experts. That question is undecided as of yet. A compelling argument can be made that requiring this of a business owner may lead to a widening of liability that would lead to an unfair situation, giving a business owner additional duties, in most cases outside the scope of his education; for example, requiring a baker to read up on RPA technology just for using an RPA system would make those systems probably highly unattractive to the baker. On the other hand, the argument could be made that an RPA system is an inherently dangerous application, as it takes away the element of human control, so requiring the user to stay on top of the technical state of the art may be a sensible precaution – after all, we require a driver's license from someone wishing to drive a car as well.

Liability of the business owner for other people

If the business owner is not liable for his own actions it could on the other hand be possible that he is liable for the actions of other people, such as under the provisions of §278 of the German civil code – other legal systems have similar institutions. Being held liable for a third party requires that someone uses a third party to fulfill contractional obligations which under the discussed legal scenarios will be the case.

The first question is if the business owner can be held liable for a failure of the RPA system under his provisions. As discussed earlier, the RPA system is no legal entity in itself, but rather a tool, so no liability for the RPA system can be grounded on these provisions.

The follow-up question is if another party in technical scenarios 1 to 4 might be held liable. In technical scenario 1, the third party is the vendor of the system. The vendor of the system is usually not employed to fulfill legal obligations by the buyer, but rather acting in his own self-interest, so the vendor cannot be the third party the business owner is liable for.

In technical scenario 2, the business owner employs a service provider in the form of the system integrator who trains the RPA system bought from the vendor. The system integrator is closer to being employed to fulfill a legal obligation and in certain cases it may be argued that the system integrator is close enough to the business owner, to be considered an agent of the business owner in regard to his or her business partners. This certainly depends on the specifics of the contract between those two parties.

In technical scenario 3, the business owner employs a cloud service provider to operate the RPA system. In this case, similar as in technical scenario 2, a lot will depend on the contracts between the cloud operator and the business owner. It is quite possible to see the cloud service operator as an agent of the business owner.

In technical scenario 4, the business owner employs a full-service operator who will likely be considered an agent of the business owner in regards to his business partner, as the full-service operator extensively acts in the interest of the business owner and provides him or her with all means to close and fulfill contracts with his or her business partners. At least in this technical scenario, the third party will likely be considered an agent of the business owner.

If the third party is an agent of the business owner, used to fulfill contractional obligations, the business owner will be held liable for any wrongdoings of that third party within the scope of the contract. If, for example, in technical scenario 4, the RPA system works faulty because of a lack of proper service by the full-service operator and this lack of proper care leads to a damage with a business partner of the business owner, the business owner will be liable to his or her business partner. The business owner will, of course, be then able to redress his or her damage, as explained in the legal scenario 1, with the full-service provider.

7.3.2.1.3 Tortious liability

Tortious liability for an action is different from contractual liability most notably by the lack of a contractual obligation. That means in effect that the scope of liability is far broader and more incalculable. Therefore, tortious liability is constricted to a damage of only certain legal values. For example, protected through tortious liability under §823 of the German civil code are life, body, health, freedom, possessions, or a comparable right. Not protected is the estate of a third party, meaning that certain damages that accrue from faulty RPA systems are simply not protected under the law.

Culpable liability

The first variant of tortious liability is culpable liability. Necessary for a culpable liability is the damage to one of aforementioned legal values by an action while acting intentionally or out of negligence. Insofar, much of the earlier established legal reasoning is valid here. The real difference is that there is no liability for a third party under tortious liability, so any liability by the business owner will usually not be applicable at this point.

There is, however – quite special to the German legal tradition – §831 of the German civil code, which stipulates a liability for a third party employed by someone. It has been discussed to use these rules for automated processes (e. g., Riehm, 2014; Hacker, 2018; Zech, 2019). Under these rules, the business owner would be liable for the deeds of his or her employee (or, if applicable, his or her RPA system), but could exculpate him- or herself by stating that he or she has selected the RPA system with due diligence and supervised his or her system correctly.

Strict liability

The other possible liability could be strict liability, a liability without any need of personal culpability. Strict liability is, as should be obvious, a legal tool that is only used very restrictively, as the strict liability enforces a liability without any kind of real wrongdoing. Strict liability is reserved for cases where someone uses something prone to danger, and can therefore be held liable for that reason alone. Strict liability is enumerative in European legal tradition and similar other legal codes. Certain objects, like cars, airplanes, trains, and animals, are subject to strict liability. An analogue is only permitted in extreme circumstances.

An argument can certainly be that an RPA system should be subject to a strict liability, but so far only RPA systems used in any kind of equipment are subject to strict liability (e. g., a car with an integrated RPA system). Foerster (2019) certainly makes the claim that any automation whose behavior cannot be predicted exactly cannot be controlled completely, and therefore should be subject to strict liability. His argument is compelling, especially as under the current set of legal rules, an injured party will in certain cases have severe problems of pushing a claim, while the business owner can claim a correct due diligence, and is therefore out of any obligations.

Product liability

A possible liability for a faulty RPA system could be the product liability rules, for example, harmonized in the European Union. The product liability lies with the producer or importer of certain goods which would also include software like the RPA system. Necessary for product liability is first of all an injury of life, body, or health, or the possessions of someone.

Product liability does not require any culpability, just the offering of a product on the market as a producer or importer, while also falling on those entities who print their trademark on a product – for example when selling OEM products. The product liability is excluded if the product was not brought onto the market voluntarily (in the case of an RPA system an illegal copy, for example), if the product was not already faulty when it was brought into the market, if the product followed required legal stipulations when it was brought into the markets, if the production or selling was not to make a profit, or if the fault could not be identified under the state of science when the product was brought into the market (i. e., a fault that no one could have found). Also, the producer will escape product liability if a mistake by the injured party led to the injury (for example, a wrong use of the product). Finally, the product liability has a deductible of 500 € for the injured party.

These criteria will, in the discussed legal scenarios, usually preclude any claim by the injured party. Only in very special cases will the RPA system damage something different than the estate of the injured party. If that is truly the case, then the producer will usually be able to state that the RPA system was not faulty when brought into the market, or that the fault could not be identified under state of science.

7.3.3 Obligation to inform

Lastly, the question arises if the business owner might be obligated to inform his or her business partner about his or her usage of an RPA system. Such an obligation might arise from contractional duties to respect the interests and needs of a business partner and to provide him or her any information he or she can expect to get from his or her business partner. The use of an RPA system might, at times, be obvious to the business partner, but if this is not the case, a special obligation can certainly arise to inform, if that would be a good business practice. As the RPA system has distinctly different legal consequences and may, at times, even lead to a difficult situation to press claims in court, such an obligation could be argued in court. With the distinct lack of decisions regarding RPA systems, a final answer cannot be made, although an obligation to inform would certainly compensate for several of the problems outlined in this chapter.

7.4 Conclusion, limitations, and outlook

Independently acting software robots are no science fiction, but reality in today's organizations. Cost pressure leads to new forms of automation with the objective of replacing administrative human activities by RPA systems. Already today RPA is available as standard software systems, and can easily be implemented in practice. However, what happens if such a software robot makes a fault, for example, takes a wrong decision, that leads to a damage? Considering the growing interest towards RPA combined with the fast development of intelligent (cognitive) software robots, it can be assumed that liability of RPA systems will become an increasingly relevant topic. However, whom to held liable for a damage caused by a software robot is not easy to answer. Even though, based on the current technical capabilities, the software robot cannot be understood as a legal entity, applying existing laws shows some insufficiencies, especially when it comes to culpability.

From a legal perspective two different scenarios can be differentiated: (1) the business owner using the RPA system is damaged, or (2) a third party is damaged. Assuming a faulty RPA system, the first scenario is from a legal perspective quite trivial; however, from a practical perspective it might be difficult to establish a fault to the responsible originator, especially if the implementation of the RPA system involves different stakeholders. The second scenario is more difficult from a legal perspective and might, in most cases, lead to the result that no one can be held liable for the damage caused by the RPA system to a third party. Certainly, it can be discussed if this is a truly fair situation, and it might be advisable for lawmakers to consider strict liability for the use of RPA systems.

In general, the legal discussion of robotics and AI is a broad and complex topic. The purpose of this chapter is an interdisciplinary discussion of exemplary questions of liability of software robots from a legal as well as a technical perspective. This discussion shows the importance of considering legal aspects already during the planning, design, and implementation of RPA systems. It is critical to understand that the entire elimination of human interactions – which is the fundamental objective of RPA – leads to a completely new legal situation. Assuming that the ecosystem offering and using RPA is comparable with the ecosystem offering other information systems, the legal impact is not comparable. For example, a fault in the semi-automated invoice verification process can in most cases be easily traced back to the human employee. Hence, the stakeholders, such as, business consultants, software vendors, or system integrators, are now confronted with a new legal situation, and it is most likely that their existing contracts and processes are not sufficient any more. Also, the business owner using an RPA system should carefully consider the legal implications. At present, acting as a business partner with someone who uses RPA systems could lead to a new and unpredictable legal risk. In most cases the business partner does not know that he or she has a transaction with an entity using RPA which could end up in an unpleasant surprise, when it comes to a liability case. Considering that some of today's organizations already use hundreds or even thousands of software robots in their daily business, an evaluation of legal risks as well as contractual countermeasures is advisable to all involved parties.

This chapter only focuses on the question of liability inspired by the simple use case of invoice verification. This question is exemplarily answered by applying European legal traditions. Therefore, the proposed argumentations and solutions can be applied to the legal systems of countries in the European Union. The basic arguments are also not fixed to a certain legal system – even though the common law, used, for example, by the UK and the US, follows different concepts, the arguments for liability and product safety remain similar. In an ever-widening legal world, legal ideas and concepts will have to be solved internationally.

Transferring the results to other law systems or discussing cases in a combination of parties from different countries could be a starting point for future research. The results presented here are mainly based on a theoretical deduction with reference to existing laws and research studies. Further evaluation of real-life cases, for example, with respect to their contractual agreements, as well as the analysis of first concrete judgments could lead to new insights. Beside the question of liability also further legal questions could be assessed. For example, what happens if a software robot closes a contract? What happens if a software robot has a business transaction with another software robot? Also, RPA in combination with cognitive approaches is currently an innovative and fast-changing topic. Hence, the interdisciplinary discussion of further RPA uses cases with respect to their legal implications could generate new interesting questions for future research.

Bibliography

Beck S (2009) Grundlegende Fragen zum rechtlichen Umgang mit der Robotik. Jurist Rundsch 2009(6). https://doi.org/10.1515/JURU.2009.225

Bertolini A (2013) Robots as products: the case for a realistic analysis of robotic applications and liability rules. Law Innov Technol 5(2):214–247. https://doi.org/10.5235/17579961.5.2.214

Čerka P, Grigienė J, Sirbikytė G (2015) Liability for damages caused by artificial intelligence. Comput Law Secur Rev 31(3):376–389. https://doi.org/10.1016/j.clsr.2015.03.008

Enriquez JG, Jimenez-Ramirez A, Dominguez-Mayo FJ, Garcia-Garcia JA (2020) Robotic process automation: a scientific and industrial systematic mapping study. IEEE Access 8:39113–39129. https://doi.org/10.1109/ACCESS.2020.2974934

Fettke P, Loos P (2019) "Strukturieren, Strukturieren, Strukturieren" in the era of robotic process automation. In: Bergener K, Räckers M, Stein A (eds) The art of structuring. Springer, Cham, pp 191–201. https://doi.org/10.1007/978-3-030-06234-7_18

Foerster M (2019) Automatisierung und Verantwortung im Zivilrecht. ZfPW 418–435

Gless S, Janal R (2016) Hochautomatisiertes und autonomes Autofahren – Risiko und rechtliche Verantwortung. Jurist Rundsch 2016(10). https://doi.org/10.1515/juru-2016-0072

Gless S, Silverman E, Weigend T (2016) If robots cause harm, who is to blame? Self-driving cars and criminal liability. SSRN Electron J. https://doi.org/10.2139/ssrn.2724592

Hacker P (2018) Verhaltens- und Wissenszurechnung beim Einsatz von Künstlicher Intelligenz. Rechtswissenschaft 9(3):243–288. https://doi.org/10.5771/1868-8098-2018-3-243

Houy C, Hamberg M, Fettke P (2019) Robotic process automation in public administrations. In: Räckers M, Halsbenning S, Rätz D, Richter D, Schweighofer E (eds) Digitalisierung von Staat und Verwaltung. Gesellschaft für Informatik e. V., Bonn, pp 62–74

Hubbard FP (2015) "Sophisticated Robots": balancing liability, regulation, and innovation. Florida Law Rev 66(5)

Kirn S, Müller-Hengstenberg CD (2015) Technische und rechtliche Betrachtungen zur Autonomie kooperativ-intelligenter Softwareagenten. Künstl Intell 29(1):59–74. https://doi.org/10.1007/s13218-014-0334-z

Leenes R, Lucivero F
(2014) Laws on robots, laws by robots, laws in robots: regulating robot behaviour by design. Law Innov Technol 6(2):193–220. https://doi.org/10.5235/17579961.6.2.193

Matthias A (2004) The responsibility gap: ascribing responsibility for the actions of learning automata. Ethics Inf Technol 6(3):175–183. https://doi.org/10.1007/s10676-004-3422-1

Murphy R, Woods DD (2009) Beyond Asimov: the three laws of responsible robotics. IEEE Intell Syst 24(4):14–20. https://doi.org/10.1109/MIS.2009.69

Palmerini E, Bertolini A, Battaglia F, Koops B-J, Carnevale A, Salvini P (2016) RoboLaw: towards a European framework for robotics regulation. Robot Auton Syst 86:78–85. https://doi.org/10.1016/j.robot.2016.08.026

Riehm T (2014) Von Drohnen, Google-Cars und Software-Agenten – Rechtliche Herausforderungen autonomer Systeme. IT-Rechts-Berater 2014:113–115

Schmitz M, Dietze C, Czarnecki C (2018) Enabling digital transformation through robotic process automation at deutsche telekom. In: Urbach N, Röglinger M (eds) Digitalization cases. Springer, Berlin

Sosnitza O (2016) Das Internet der Dinge – Herausforderung oder gewohntes Terrain für das Zivilrecht? Computerrecht 32(11). https://doi.org/10.9785/cr-2016-1124

Willcocks L, Lacity M, Craig A (2017) Robotic process automation: strategic transformation lever for global business services? J Inf Technol Teaching Cases 7(1):17–28. https://doi.org/10.1057/s41266-016-0016-9

Zech H (2019) Künstliche Intelligenz und Haftungsfragen. ZfPW 198–219

Part III: **RPA technology**

Yara Rizk, Tathagata Chakraborti, Vatche Isahagian, and
Yasaman Khazaeni

8 Towards end-to-end business process automation

RPA composition and orchestration

Abstract: In recent years, robotic process automation (RPA) emerged as a vehicle to digital transformation in enterprises. However, RPA still possesses many shortcomings that have prevented it from generalizing well to new domains while minimizing coding overhead and approaching end-to-end business process automation. Recent work has looked to utilize artificial intelligence technology to address RPA's limitations. In this work, we discuss the different approaches to RPA collaboration which is essential to achieving end-to-end automation. From rule-based composition to offline composition using automated planning and online composition using multi-agent orchestration, we present existing approaches in the literature, analyze remaining challenges, and propose insights into future research directions.

Keywords: Robotic process automation, composition, orchestration

8.1 Introduction

In the digital transformation era, robotic process automation (RPA) has been one of its main drivers (Hartley and Sawaya, 2019; Siderska, 2020). Targeting enterprises reluctant to adopt automation due to the significant cost of upgrading ubiquitous legacy software (Agrawal et al., 2019), RPA presented a low-cost approach that did not require any software overhauls (Lamberton et al., 2017). It automated the mouse click in user interfaces of highly repetitive simple tasks by learning from user logs or natural language descriptions of tasks (van der Aalst et al., 2018).

The success of RPAs fueled the digital transformation and motivated further research to achieve low-cost, end-to-end business process automation (Chakraborti et al., 2020b). The first step towards that goal was developing unassisted RPAs, also called RPA 2.0 (Gupta et al., 2019), based on machine learning algorithms to reduce the dependence on humans to train RPAs and to improve their generalization capabilities. While not mature enough for widespread adoption, machine learning-based RPA is a promising research direction (Syed et al., 2020; Chakraborti et al., 2020b). Furthermore, most RPAs focused on automating tasks related to data entry and management; automating more complex tasks that involve decision making and execution are another focus area for business process automation (Mohapatra, 2009). How can RPAs contribute to these more complex tasks while maintaining their low deploy-

https://doi.org/10.1515/9783110676693-008

ment overhead? Composing RPAs into more powerful bots that can collaborate on such tasks may be the solution.

Composition is a prevalent methodology in computer science that has allowed the creation of complex constructs from simpler ones. It is the act of combining objects to construct more complex entities that behave as one within an environment. From object composition in object-oriented programming (creating complex object types from simpler variable data types) to function composition (combining simpler functions into more complex ones) and autonomous agent composition (creating a unified autonomous agent from several agents), composition provided a modular approach that simplified programming, debugging, and maintaining the composed entities throughout their lifecycles. Extending this methodology to RPAs would allow us to address some of RPAs limitations, namely, their generalization and collaboration difficulties. In short, composition enforces modular RPA designs that are easier to debug, maintain, and reuse.

In this work, we consider three types of composition: the prevalent but cumbersome rule-based composition, automated offline composition, and automated online composition, which we also refer to as orchestration. Defined as the dynamic coordination of actions across multiple services under the supervision of a central entity in the web services domain (Dragoni et al., 2017), this concept can be extended to RPAs that collaborate on tasks as opposed to acting in silos. Automated composition and orchestration help us achieve numerous goals from better generalization capabilities for RPAs to low coding overhead and successful complex task execution. However, many challenges remain, including scalability, agent lifecycle, and others, before effective automated composition (especially on-the-fly composition) realizes its full potential.

The main contribution of this work is surveying existing composition techniques, especially planning-based and orchestration algorithms, while identifying their limitations and possible future solutions. Next, Section 8.2 introduces key terminology, concepts, and application domains that are relevant to our discussion. Section 8.3 briefly presents the state of the art in RPAs. Section 8.4 delves into the three composition techniques by defining their scope and presenting relevant works in the literature. Finally, Section 8.5 discusses remaining challenges that face RPA composition and presents some insights into research directions that could address these challenges, and Section 8.6 concludes with final remarks.

8.2 Background

8.2.1 Business processes

A business process is a collection of tasks that are executed in a specific sequence to achieve some business goal, such as producing a service or product for customers (Weske, 2019). Tasks within a business process are generally assigned to specific personas and can range in complexity from novice to expert. Processes are generally expressed in a graphical notation called business process model notation (BPMN) (Grosskopf et al., 2009). Events and activities are represented by circles and rounded-corner rectangles, respectively, whereas gateways are represented by diamonds that allow paths to conditionally merge or diverge.

Business process management (BPM) is a multi-disciplinary field that facilities the management of business processes, especially as they become larger and more complex. Such tools involve modeling, execution, management, and performance measurement of workflows (the flow among activities), in addition to the human workforce and stakeholders. Implementing a process in BPM software facilitates the exchange of information among personas, minimizing the risk of failure due to lack of communication. In workflow management, processes are modeled in a very rigid manner that requires strict ordering of activities, control flows, and information tunneling (Leymann and Roller, 1999). In case management, more flexible modeling is allowed where cases consist of people, documents, and tasks that can be performed without explicit ordering (Weske, 2019).

Seeking to leverage technological advancements in the field of computer programming, business process automation looks to inject into processes autonomous bots capable of performing specific tasks or sub-tasks. This allows businesses to improve efficiency and reduce the cost and time of processes. Process automation looked to artificial intelligence to automate business process tasks. RPA was one component of business process automation that created bots to perform manual repetitive tasks such as data entry.

8.2.2 Artificial intelligence

Next, we define a few concepts commonly adopted in the fields of computer science, and artificial intelligence specifically, that will appear in this chapter. Functions are atomic units of automation that require a set of input parameters and return a set of outputs. For example, a function that automatically retrieves a customer's credit score may require as inputs the customer's name and account number and produce as output the credit score or an error if the retrieval fails.

Agents are entities that interact with their environment by observing it (through sensors) and acting on it (using actuators) to achieve their goal (Stuart and Norvig, 2020). Agents can be non-learning or learning; learning agents rely on machine learning approaches to develop evolving models of the world so they can accomplish their goals. Learning models may rely on feedback from the environment or other agents. Agents can be either embodied or virtual (i. e., physical or software robots). In this work, we use the terms agents and bots interchangeable.

A multi-agent system is a collection of agents that operate and interact in the same environment (Ferber and Weiss, 1999). Agents' interactions can be classified as positive or negative. In negative interaction, agents actively hinder each other from achieving their goals. Positive interaction implies that agents help each other achieve their individual goals. In this work, we focus on positive interaction and specifically collaborative interaction. In such interactions, agents actively assist each other in accomplishing their shared goals, i. e., the agents' goals cannot be accomplished unless they collaborate. This type of interaction is especially relevant to RPAs performing tasks within a business process: unless they collaborate, accomplishing the business process's goal would not be feasible.

8.2.3 Applications

Business processes have been adopted in many service enterprises from banking and finance to retail and airline companies including in many of their departments (customer care, human resources). We will rely on a simplified loan application use case to illustrate the various composition techniques discussed hereafter.

Figure 1 (denoted in BPMN) depicts the tasks that are performed when a bank customer applies for a loan which includes their requested loan amount and loan period along with personal financial details such as their credit score, employment status, yearly income, etc. This specific business process includes the tasks of verifying the submitted information by accessing reliable information sources such as requesting a credit report. Once the application's information is verified, the loan request is reviewed, and a decision is made on whether to grant the loan or not. Additional information can be returned along with the decision, such as the terms of the loan (amount and duration) or reasons for rejection. Decision making in this process is not constrained to information in the application under consideration but can also use information from previous applications, the economic situation, government regulations, etc. The process considers two main personas: the loan applicant and the loan officer (or reviewer).

Figure 1: Simplified loan application process.

8.3 RPA state of the art

Two main types of automation strategies can be adopted: front-end vs. back-end automation. RPAs belong to the former by operating on the user interface to automatically perform repetitive, manual tasks which makes RPAs low-cost solutions for legacy software. RPAs fall into two main subsets based on how they are trained: assisted vs. unassisted. The former implies that RPAs rely on humans to learn while the latter takes the human out of the training loop.

In assisted training, RPAs learn from demonstrations or from natural language documents describing the tasks. For example, Gao et al. deduced if-then-else rules from behavior logs (by extracting input–output patterns) to create RPA scripts (Gao et al., 2019). Le and Gulwani (2014) provided the input–output patterns directly the program that extracted the underlying rules using inductive program synthesis. Miltner et al. (2019) used behavior logs to find repetitive edits and proposed rules to automate these edits. When natural language instructions exist, RPAs can be trained to perform the described tasks by processing these instructions using natural language understanding models. Leopold et al. (2018) used a quadratic optimization algorithm trained on natural language features extracted from the text by semantic models. Similarly, Han et al. (2020) processed natural language documents using deep learning language models to derive relationships between process activities. Human-in-the-loop RPA training is very common, but it generates RPAs that do not generalize well because they learn in highly specific environments.

In unassisted training, RPAs leverage feedback from the environment to learn the proper actions to take when performing tasks (Gupta et al., 2019). Using the reinforcement learning paradigm in artificial intelligence, it is the least mature of all RPA training approaches but it will lead to the most generalizable solutions.

We refer readers to three recent surveys for more details on state-of-the-art RPAs (Ivančić et al., 2019), remaining challenges to achieve intelligent process automation (Chakraborti et al., 2020b), and existing RPA platforms in industry (Agostinelli et al., 2020).

8.4 RPA composition

RPAs have mainly focused on automating specific tasks; however, any process consists of multiple tasks and successfully completing a process hinges on the coordination of multiple personas executing these tasks (Mendling et al., 2018). Therefore, enabling RPA cooperation is crucial to achieving end-to-end business process automation. One approach is composing RPAs into more powerful agents.

8.4.1 Rule-based composition

Rule-based agent composition requires developers to write scripts of code that pipeline functions together, in a specific order of execution, and deploy these pipelined functions as a new agent that can be invoked as a single unified entity. In the loan use case, a static RPA composition could be a loan RPA that is invoked when a bank customer submits a loan. The RPA would process the loan application, verifying the information and making a decision, all wrapped as a single RPA. In essence, this implies automating the entire workflow using a single RPA.

Rule-based composition has been adopted in many domains from software development to process automation. Static RPA composition is one of the most popular approaches in the literature. One such approach divided automation into multiple stages and statically connected these stages, with each stage containing multiple tasks of a business process (Heo et al., 2018). The resulting RPA was connected to a chatbot and handled a pizza delivery process and a product purchase process. In Madakam et al. (2019), multiple RPAs were deployed to assist the Airtel company in customer care applications; each RPA handled one task in a process. The business process served as the static composition of the RPAs into a single more powerful RPA.

While static, labor-intensive, and time consuming, this approach is the most reliable and deterministic. The composed agent behaves as the developer intended it to with little chance of failure. However, this approach does not maximize code reuse and creates rigid agents that perform well on tasks they were designed for but do not generalize well to other tasks.

8.4.2 Offline composition

Instead of relying on manual composition of RPAs, automated composition takes out the human from the equation. In offline composition, agents are composed from functions before they are deployed and would not change after that. Such an approach reduces the manual overhead of creating more powerful automation solutions. However, it does require some initial overhead, such as variable alignment, to ensure that RPAs can be successfully composed.

Multiple domains have implemented automated offline composition of software bots to perform more complex tasks. From program synthesis to web services, these domains have adopted diverse solutions including planning (Bertoli et al., 2010), genetic algorithms (Rodriguez-Mier et al., 2010), and other optimization techniques. Automated planning techniques have been one of the main approaches adopted in web service composition (Dong et al., 2004; Araghi, 2012) since they inherently attempt to create a sequence of actions that achieves an end goal. We refer readers to Rao and Su (2004) for a summary of planning in web service composition and Srivastava and Koehler (2003), Sohrabi (2010) for a discussion of challenges in this domain.

Focusing on process composition and RPAs, Mendes et al. proposed an offline Petri Nets model based on composition logic (Marco Mendes et al., 2010). Furthermore, planning algorithms composed workflows and corresponding RPAs that were created to automate specific tasks within these workflows in Chakraborti and Khazaeni (2020), Chakraborti et al. (2020a). However, this approach requires a unified variable vocabulary among all RPAs which implies an additional overhead before successful composition is possible.

To better grasp what an automated planning-based solution for RPA offline composition looks like, we dive deeper into the approach proposed in Chakraborti et al. (2020a). First, a function, such as an RPA, should be defined as shown in Figure 2 with the inputs and outputs of the function (e. g., given a bank account ID, the RPA can retrieve the name, date of birth, and credit score of the loan applicant). To compose multiple of these functions into a single agent, the functions should share the same vocabulary of inputs and outputs. Using planning-based algorithms (LaValle, 2006), the functions can be composed into a tree that includes multiple paths to reach the agent's goal. At run-time, depending on the execution of the functions, different paths in the tree could be traversed until the goal is achieved.

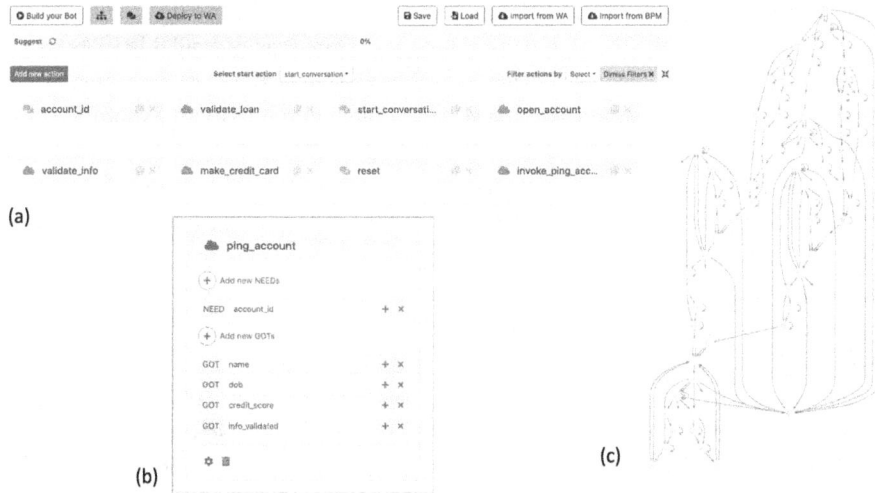

Figure 2: (a) Set of functions. (b) Sample function. (c) Composed tree (adapted from Chakraborti et al., 2020a).

8.4.3 Online composition: orchestration

Online composition, or orchestration, is defined as the composition of agents at run-time that act as a single entity for a limited time and under some conditions. This approach is the most dynamic and flexible but the most error-prone, susceptible to noise, and unpredictable. Tasks within a business process are automated individually and independently. At run-time, depending on the outcomes of the tasks, the orchestrator determines which task to run next. In a sense, it converts the embodiment of a business process from a workflow model to a case model and the orchestrator rebuilds the workflow model by sequencing the tasks.

Orchestration has been adopted for microservices (Kiss et al., 2019), web services (Daniel and Pernici, 2006), containers (Casalicchio, 2019), and Internet of Things (Wen et al., 2017), among others. The most common approach is formulating the orchestration problem as a constrained optimization problem (de Sousa et al., 2019; Upadhyay et al., 2019) solved using traditional optimization solvers like mixed-integer programming solvers (Alvizu et al., 2018). More sophisticated machine learning algorithms have been developed in certain domains as well, such as reinforcement learning (Natalino et al., 2018; Upadhyay et al., 2019), regression prediction (Natalino et al., 2018), genetic algorithm (Wen et al., 2017), and others.

Some work has investigated the orchestration of RPAs. Marco Mendes et al. (2010) proposed an online workflow composition approach that relies on a service-oriented architecture to allow the flow of information between multiple Petri Nets models. However, the success of this approach hinges on describing transitions between models beforehand. Rizk et al. (2020a) relied on humans to determine the next task and invoke the appropriate RPA through natural language from a set of available RPAs using posterior orchestration techniques, whereas Sreedharan et al. (2020) investigated an online planning algorithm to solve the same problem and obtain an explainable orchestration.

To understand what an RPA orchestration solution looks like, let us dive deeper into the approach from Rizk et al. (2020b). The authors proposed a multi-agent framework that allowed RPA bots, viewed as agents within the system, to share context and interact with business users through natural language. The orchestrator is triggered by a natural language event (or non-natural language event from agents within the system) and processes the event by broadcasting it to the agents within the system, as shown in Figure 3. Based on the agents' responses and other features, the orchestrator scores the responses, selects the agent(s) with the best response (maximum score), orders the execution of agents (if more than one is selected), and returns a human-consumable response if needed. Throughout the conversation turns, multiple agents can execute and share the context among themselves, which allows them to cooperate on complex tasks.

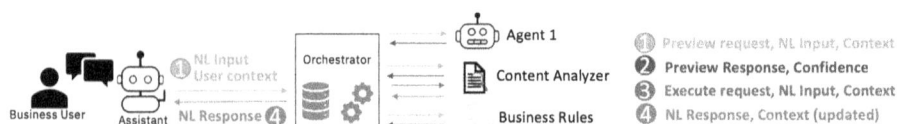

Figure 3: Multi-RPA orchestration (adapted from Rizk et al., 2020b).

In the loan business process, the framework invoked an RPA agent (called *content analyzer* in Figure 3) to process a loan application submitted as a PDF and extract the necessary information through natural language (a human typed in a chat interface "process this loan application" with an attached PDF), as shown in Figure 4. Then, the *business rules* RPA bot was invoked to analyze the information and determine whether to approve or reject the loan request (again through natural language). RPAs were wrapped with natural language understanding and generation layers to achieve this type of RPA orchestration. While this approach still keeps a human in the loop to reduce the risk of catastrophic failures, some RPA invocations may still fail. This approach fits the orchestration of RPAs definition because it dynamically coordinates the actions of agents.

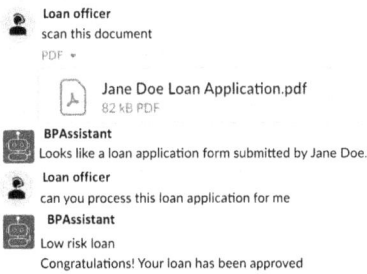

Loan officer
scan this document
PDF ▾

Jane Doe Loan Application.pdf
82 kB PDF

BPAssistant
Looks like a loan application form submitted by Jane Doe.

Loan officer
can you process this loan application for me

BPAssistant
Low risk loan
Congratulations! Your loan has been approved

Figure 4: Sample RPA orchestration using natural language (from Rizk et al., 2020b).

8.5 Remaining challenges

The composition approaches discussed above could significantly increase the scope of RPAs and their applicability to more complex tasks, as observed in other domains like web services (Portchelvi et al., 2012). However, challenges unique to the process automation domain imply that special considerations must be made for RPA composition. Specifically, RPA solutions tend to be deployed in domains where the end user is not tech-savvy. Also, highly regulated domains are much slower at adopting automation solutions due to liability issues.

8.5.1 Conversational interactions

Composing RPAs into more powerful agents allows them to perform complex tasks. However, automated composition and execution of these agents may not always produce predictable behavior. Hence, highly regulated industries may be reluctant to adopt it. The end users in these industries do not have the programming background to understand and analyze the behavior of the composed agents. Building conversational interaction into the composed agents could make this technology accessible to non-tech-savvy users, as in Rizk et al. (2020a,b). However, many RPAs have not been designed to be conversational. How can we compose conversational agents with minimal additional coding overhead? Addressing this and many more research questions to deploy interactive RPA, especially through natural language, could determine the success of RPA composition technology.

8.5.2 Scalability and generalizability

As the number of RPAs increases, so does the number of possible compositions and the possibility of overlap in RPA functionality. Composition techniques, especially orchestration, should take this into account to efficiently produce the most optimal compositions. Furthermore, these approaches should be domain-agnostic, or they should have good generalizability across multiple domains. Some RPAs will be inherently domain-agnostic, while others operate in one (or more) domains. Before composing RPAs, how can we identify their domains, if not immediately known, and ensure that compositions are compatible? Enforcing a unified vocabulary is one solution (Chakraborti et al., 2020a), but its overhead may discourage adoption.

8.5.3 Lifecycle

Like all software products, RPAs have a lifecycle (Jimenez-Ramirez et al., 2019). Newer versions are released to improve performance, resolve bugs or vulnerabilities, and ensure compatibility with the evolving tasks. What will the lifecycle of composed RPAs look like? With some of these RPAs relying on machine learning-based models, their lifetime may be even shorter due to frequent retraining of these models. The lifecycle of the composed agents would be some combination of the individual RPAs' lifecycles. Should the composition algorithm optimize for overall agent lifecycle in addition to performance and compatibility? These questions and others should be addressed to successfully operate in real-world scenarios.

8.5.4 Unified language

Composing RPAs into unified agents requires the individual RPAs to speak the same language. The variables that one RPA uses must map to those that another expects, to achieve composition and collaboration among RPAs. Ensuring a unified language is challenging, especially considering the fact that RPAs would be independently developed for different applications. Even within the same domain, different RPAs may use slightly different terminology. Registering RPAs within a catalog and enforcing a unified vocabulary may be one approach to resolve this issue (Chakraborti et al., 2020a). Another would be to leverage semantic knowledge from natural language understanding domains to create data adaptors that resolve variable mappings, at least in a fuzzy way, while requesting humans to verify or approve the mapping.

8.5.5 Explainability

An important aspect of encouraging adoption of RPA composition algorithms is making them explainable. This allows business users to understand why certain RPAs were composed into an agent and not others. Explainable compositions would provide some transparency into the inner workings of the algorithms that produce these more complex RPA agents, as in Sreedharan et al. (2020). Hence, some trust would be instilled in these agents by the business users and leads to more adoption of such technology, especially in highly regulated industries where liability is an issue.

Another interpretation of explainability in this context is ensuring that the composition of individual explainable RPAs would result in an explainable composed RPA. In other words, if individual RPAs can explain their actions, after composing them into a unified agent, that agent should maintain the explainability property. While this property may not be linear for many compositions, considering post hoc approaches to generating explanations of the composed agent could be crucial to the successful deployment of such agents.

8.6 Conclusion

RPAs have allowed enterprises to make progress in their digit transformation journey. Even though they provide a lightweight approach to inject automation into prevalent legacy software, they can only handle a certain class of tasks, namely, simple repetitive tasks such as data entry. While the research community's efforts to leverage machine learning will improve RPAs, we argued in this work that enabling collaborative RPAs is also crucial for end-to-end process automation.

We discussed three types of composition: rule-based composition, automated offline composition, and automated online composition. We focused on two approaches that used planning-based offline composition that combined multiple RPA bots into business workflows and a conversational multi-agent system that orchestrated multiple RPAs when automating tasks. Both made significant assumptions that should be relaxed before widespread adoption can be realized. The first required a unified variable vocabulary to compose more complex agents which may not be realistic in real-world applications, whereas the second assumed that RPA bots have conversational capabilities (either intrinsic or added by developers).

Future work includes addressing the aforementioned challenges such as composing bots that do not use the same variable naming, addressing questions about RPA lifecycle and governance, enabling conversational interactions, and others. Leveraging artificial intelligence advancements will be central to realizing end-to-end automation of business processes. Therefore, a synergy between both artificial intelligence and business process communities will be necessary; signs of this synergy are already emerging through the latest works in the literature.

Bibliography

Agostinelli S, Marrella A, Mecella M (2020) Towards intelligent robotic process automation for bpmers. In: AAAI workshop on intelligent process automation

Agrawal P, Narain R, Ullah I (2019) Analysis of barriers in implementation of digital transformation of supply chain using interpretive structural modelling approach. J Model Manag

Alvizu R, Troia S, Maier G, Pattavina A (2018) Machine-learning-based prediction and optimization of mobile metro-core networks. In: IEEE photonics society summer topical meeting series, pp 155–156

Araghi SS (2012) Customizing the composition of web services and beyond. PhD thesis, U Toronto

Bertoli P, Pistore M, Traverso P (2010) Automated composition of web services via planning in asynchronous domains. Artif Intell 174(3–4):316–361

Casalicchio E (2019) Container orchestration: a survey. In: Systems modeling: methodologies and tools. Springer, Berlin, pp 221–235

Chakraborti T, Khazaeni Y (2020) D3BA: a tool for optimizing business processes using non-deterministic planning. In: AAAI workshop on intelligent process automation

Chakraborti T, Agarwal S, Isahagian V, Khazaeni Y, Rizk Y (2020a) An multi-agent composition and orchestration framework for financial business process automation. In: International conference on business process management workshop on AI4BPM

Chakraborti T, Isahagian V, Khalaf R, Khazaeni Y, Muthusamy V, Rizk Y, Unuvar M (2020b) From robotic process automation to intelligent process automation: emerging trends. In: Business process management: blockchain and robotic process automation forum: BPM 2020 blockchain and RPA forum, proceedings 18, Seville, Spain, September 13–18, 2020, pp 215–225

Daniel F, Pernici B (2006) Insights into web service orchestration and choreography. Int J E-Bus Res 2(1):58–77

de Sousa NFS, Perez DAL, Rosa RV, Santos MAS, Rothenberg CE (2019) Network service orchestration: A survey. Comput Commun

Dong X, Halevy A, Madhavan J, Nemes E, Zhang J (2004) Similarity search for web services. In: VLDB

Dragoni N, Giallorenzo S, Lafuente AL, Mazzara M, Montesi F, Mustafin R, Safina L (2017) Microservices: yesterday, today, and tomorrow. In: Present and ulterior software engineering. Springer, Berlin, pp 195–216

Ferber J, Weiss G (1999) Multi-agent systems: an introduction to distributed artificial intelligence, vol 1. Addison-Wesley, Reading

Gao J, van Zelst SJ, Lu X, van der Aalst WMP (2019) Automated robotic process automation: a self-learning approach. In: OTM confederated international conferences

Grosskopf A, Decker G, Weske M (2009) The process: business process modeling using BPMN. Meghan Kiffer Press

Gupta S, Rani S, Dixit A (2019) Recent trends in automation: a study of rpa development tools. In: 3rd IEEE international conference on recent developments in control, automation & power engineering, pp 159–163

Han X, Hu L, Dang Y, Agarwal S, Mei L, Li S, Zhou X (2020) Automatic business process structure discovery using ordered neurons lstm: a preliminary study. In: AAAI IPA

Hartley JL, Sawaya WJ (2019) Tortoise, not the hare: digital transformation of supply chain business processes. Bus Horiz 62(6):707–715

Heo M et al (2018) Chatbot as a new business communication tool: the case of naver talktalk. Bus Commun Res Practice 1(1):41–45

Ivančić L, Vugec DS, Vukšić VB (2019) Robotic process automation: systematic literature review. In: International conference on business process management. Springer, Berlin, pp 280–295

Jimenez-Ramirez A, Reijers HA, Barba I, Del Valle C (2019) A method to improve the early stages of the robotic process automation lifecycle. In: Int conf advanced information systems engineering, pp 446–461

Kiss T, Kacsuk P, Kovács J, Rakoczi B, Hajnal A, Farkas A, Gesmier G, Terstyanszky G (2019) Micado—microservice-based cloud application-level dynamic orchestrator. Future Gener Comput Syst 94:937–946

Lamberton C, Brigo D, Hoy D (2017) Impact of robotics, rpa and ai on the insurance industry: challenges and opportunities. J Fin Perspect 4(1)

LaValle SM (2006) Planning algorithms. Cambridge University Press

Le V, Gulwani S (2014) Flashextract: a framework for data extraction by examples. In: Proceedings of the 35th ACM SIGPLAN PLDI

Leopold H, van der Aa H, Reijers HA (2018) Identifying candidate tasks for robotic process automation in textual process descriptions. In: Enterprise, business-process and information systems modeling

Leymann F, Roller D (1999) Production workflow: concepts and techniques. Prentice Hall PTR, USA

Madakam S, Holmukhe RM, Kumar Jaiswal D (2019) The future digital work force: robotic process automation (rpa). J Inf Syst Technol Manag 16

Marco Mendes J, Leitão P, Restivo F, Colombo AW (2010) Composition of petri nets models in service-oriented industrial automation. In: 8th IEEE int conf industrial informatics, pp 578–583

Mendling J, Decker G, Hull R, Reijers HA, Weber I (2018) How do machine learning, robotic process automation, and blockchains affect the human factor in business process management? Commun Assoc Inf Syst 43(1):19

Miltner A, Gulwani S, Le V, Leung A, Radhakrishna A, Soares G, Tiwari A, Udupa A (2019) On the fly synthesis of edit suggestions. In: OOPSLA

Mohapatra S (2009) Business process automation. PHI Learning Pvt Ltd.

Natalino C, Rehan Raza M, Rostami A, Öhlen P, Wosinska L, Monti P (2018) Machine learning aided orchestration in multi-tenant networks. In: IEEE photonics society summer topical meeting series, pp 125–126

Portchelvi V, Prasanna Venkatesan V, Shanmugasundaram G (2012) Achieving web services composition—a survey. Softw Eng 2(5):195–202

Rao J, Su X (2004) A survey of automated web service composition methods. In: ICWS workshop on semantic web services and web process composition

Rizk Y, Bhandwalder A, Boag S, Chakraborti T, Isahagian V, Khazaeni Y, Pollok F, Unuvar M (2020a) A unified conversational assistant framework for business process automation. In: AAAI workshop on intelligent process automation

Rizk Y, Isahagian V, Boag S, Khazaeni Y, Unuvar M, Muthusamy V, Khalaf R (2020b) A conversational digital assistant for intelligent process automation. In: Business process management: blockchain and robotic process automation forum, proceedings 18, Seville, Spain, September 13–18, 2020, pp 85–100

Rodriguez-Mier P, Mucientes M, Lama M, Couto MI (2010) Composition of web services through genetic programming. Evol Intell 3(3–4):171–186

Siderska J (2020) Robotic process automation: a driver of digital transformation? Eng Manag Prod Serv 12(2):21–31

Sohrabi S (2010) Customizing the composition of actions, programs, and web services with user preferences. In: ISWC

Sreedharan S, Chakraborti T, Rizk Y, Khazaeni Y (2020) Explainable composition of aggregated assistants. In: ICAPS workshop on explainable AI planners

Srivastava B, Koehler J (2003) Web service composition – current solutions and open problems. In: ICAPS workshop on planning for web services

Stuart JR, Norvig P (2020) Artificial intelligence: a modern approach. Prentice Hall, New York

Syed R, Suriadi S, Adams M, Bandara W, Leemans S, Ouyang C, ter Hofstede A, van de Weerd I, Wynn MT, Reijers HA (2020) Robotic process automation: Contemporary themes and challenges. Computers in Industry 115:103162

Upadhyay S, Agarwal M, Bounneffouf D, Khazaeni Y (2019) A bandit approach to posterior dialog orchestration under a budget. arXiv preprint arXiv:1906.09384

van der Aalst WMP, Bichler M, Heinzl A (2018) Robotic process automation

Wen Z, Yang R, Garraghan P, Lin T, Xu J, Rovatsos M (2017) Fog orchestration for Internet of things services. IEEE Internet Comput 21(2):16–24

Weske M (2019) Business process management: concepts, languages, architectures. Springer, Berlin

Andrés Jiménez Ramírez, Hajo A. Reijers, and
José González Enríquez

9 Human–computer interaction analysis for RPA support

Framework and new horizons

Abstract: In the last decade, industry has wholeheartedly embraced RPA. A large number of RPA projects have been conducted, which all involve the mimicking of human behavior by software. Although vendor-specific frameworks exist to support all aspects of RPA solutions – from the analysis of the system until the enactment and control of the developed robots – most of them base their solution on workflow diagrams (e. g., BluePrism or UIPath). This chapter explores the benefits of a conceptual RPA framework that is based on log information related to the exact human–computer interaction. While the observation of employees' computers (i. e., clicks and keystrokes) may lead to the desired data, it is by no means trivial to convert such events into a meaningful log. Our approach shows how to create a so-called user interface (UI) log based on image similarity techniques. This UI log can then be used to provide support for all stages of the RPA lifecycle. Specifically, we will describe a use case in which the UI log is used (1) to support the analysis of the underlying process and (2) to generate a test platform which checks whether or not the developed robots behave in accordance with the analyzed process. We will also discuss how other stages of the RPA lifecycle can leverage the existence of such a UI log, which leads to the identification of new research lines.

Keywords: Robotic process automation, process mining, image processing

9.1 Introduction

Conducting an RPA project requires following a lifecycle similar to any other software project. Variations of this lifecycle can be observed in the literature (Flechsig et al., 2019; Enríquez et al., 2020) but, in general, they have the following activities: *analysis*, *design*, *development*, *deployment*, *control and operation*, and *evaluation*.

Nowadays, industry has come up with RPA platforms, like UiPath, that are intended to cover the complete lifecycle of RPA. However, these platforms provide polished solutions mainly for the development and later stages but neglect mature sup-

Acknowledgement: Research supported by the NICO project (PID2019-105455GB-C31) of the Spanish Ministry of Science, Innovation and Universities, the Trop@ project (CEI-12-TIC021) of the Junta de Andalucía, and the AIRPA (P011-19/E09) project of Spain's CDTI.

https://doi.org/10.1515/9783110676693-009

port for the early stage of analysis and design (Enríquez et al., 2020). Therefore, RPA projects still rely on analyzing process documentation – which may be of poor quality – or manual inspections of the information systems (ISs) – which require substantial effort – to create a basic understanding of the processes to robotize. That situation potentially leads to an inaccurate analysis, which is fatal since robots are typically deployed in production environments accessing real ISs.

To prevent this scenario from happening, a common practice in RPA adoption is to keep both people and robots working in the same processes simultaneously. More precisely, human workers are the first ones who deal with the ISs and the processes. They will experience the exceptions, undocumented cases, etc., and learn how to solve such situations, i. e., *on-the-job training*. The generated knowledge during these experiences is key to increase the probability of success when conducting the RPA project. Only later the digital workforce is created, which will carry out the most repetitive and mundane tasks of the processes. Nonetheless, due to the lack of proper support within commercial RPA platforms, this accumulated knowledge is typically transferred informally, e. g., through interviews or manually created reports.

Against this backdrop, approaches that formally analyze the human–computer interaction (HCI) are now beginning to appear. Such approaches are referred to with the brand new term of task mining (Reinkemeyer, 2020), an adaptation of the process mining paradigm (van der Aalst, 2016). Characteristic for task mining is that the computers of the human workers need to be monitored by recording the screen, mouse, and keyboard events while the humans are interacting with the user interfaces (UIs) of the related ISs. Next, these events are processed to obtain a meaningful log, the so-called UI log. This log can then be used to discover the underlying process by using process discovery algorithms (Geyer-klingeberg and Nakladal, 2018; van der Aalst et al., 2018; Leno et al., 2018; Jimenez-Ramirez et al., 2019; Leno et al., 2020). Although the processing of the UI log is non-trivial, the benefits of using this automated discovery over a manual approach have been clearly recognized in recent literature (Jimenez-Ramirez et al., 2019).

Different steps in the RPA lifecycle may leverage the results of the task mining methods. First, it becomes (1) straightforward to analyze the *as-is* processes and (2) easier to detect the candidate processes to robotize being able to provide a *to-be* design for them. In addition, logged data consist of valuable information for developing robots and testing them before deployment. Moreover, the continuous monitoring of the deployed bots may generate useful metrics for controlling their performance. Also, this may generate recommendations of operational actions in the case of failures or unexpected behaviors, which supports the governance of the digital workforce. What is more, process redesign actions can be recommended in the case of changes or optimizations being detected within the processes.

The objective of this chapter is twofold. First of all, it aims to describe a conceptual framework for HCI analysis and how it can be applied in an industrial environment in the domain of business process outsourcing (BPO), i. e., a company that executes processes which belong to a different company. Although not limited to the BPO context, the back-office departments of BPO companies are identified as optimal candidates for RPA projects (Geyer-klingeberg and Nakladal, 2018) and, besides, they provide particularly challenging settings when strict security policies are in force. Secondly, this chapter goes through the phases of the RPA project lifecycle to discuss the application horizon of this task mining paradigm. In doing so, research lines that still need to be explored are identified.

The rest of the chapter is structured as follows. Section 9.2 shows an RPA context where the HCI analysis is applicable. Section 9.3 describes the HCI approach. Section 9.4 details an application of this approach in the test phase. Section 9.5 discusses the applicability and limitations of the HCI approach in the other phases of the lifecycle. Finally, Section 9.6 concludes the chapter.

9.2 Human-first context

Scenarios like the back-office of a BPO company historically employ only human workers to accomplish their processes. Nowadays, back-offices are becoming hybrids, i. e., some of these processes – or parts of them – are being shifted to digital workers (cf. Figure 1a and b) thanks to rapid market penetration of the RPA technology (Biscotti, 2018). Regardless of the kind of workers, the documentation of the prescribed process is a crucial ingredient. However, each kind of worker – human or digital – behaves differently in the case of non-documented cases, exceptions, or deviations.

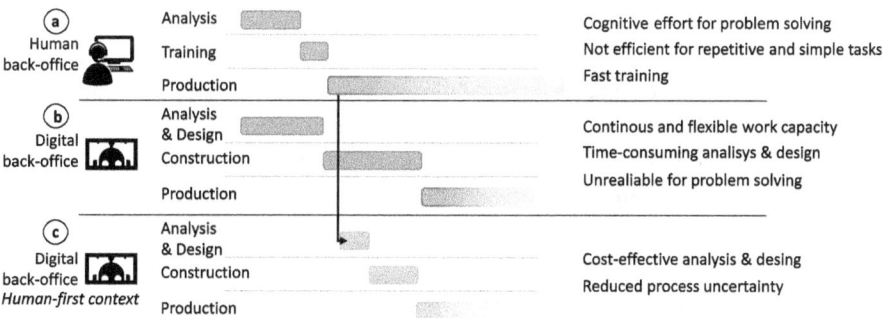

Figure 1: Early stages in back-office.

On the one hand, the human workers are trained according to the documentation of the prescribed process before the real ISs are faced. Since humans are expected to perform flexibly, they can make decisions when some unexpected situation arises by applying a cognitive effort – probably just by using common sense (i. e., *on-the-job training). Effective improvisations might later on be shared among the rest of the team.* Nonetheless, although human workers generally perform well, as already identified in the literature (Aguirre and Rodriguez, 2017), they behave poorly on repetitive, high-volume, and simple tasks.

On the other hand, regarding the digital workers, constructing them requires conducting the RPA lifecycle similarly for any other software product. Analyzing and designing the desired robot implies a significant effort. The reason for this is that ambiguity and uncertainty of the prescribed process should be minimized and the selected parts to robotized need to be formalized. Once constructed, multiple instances of the same robots are deployed gradually while their behavior is controlled and tested. In the case that something occurs that is not covered by the robot's design, the robot gets stuck and suffers the following maintenance process. First, a human operator takes control of the robot and tries to repair it either by completing the running instance or by bringing the robot to a controlled situation. Second, the robot behavior is analyzed to disclose the root cause of the error. Finally, a new RPA lifecycle starts either to include or to explicitly exclude the new behavior in the robot design – leaving it for the human workers. Whatever happens next, the new version of the robot will not get stuck again in a similar situation. As the reader may understand, this process is considerably more time consuming than the *on-the-job training* of human workers. Still, the digital workforce provides more work flexibility and predictability since they can work continuously and the size of the team can be altered on demand.

Interestingly, companies have acknowledged that there is an efficient way to obtain their hybrid back-office: the so-called human-first context, i. e., the human back-office works first and, when the knowledge of the process is more mature, the digital back-office is created (cf. Figure 1c). In this context, three periods can be identified regarding the workload shifting between humans and robots (cf. Figure 2). After the "human-first period," where the human workforce is in charge of the entire process, the first versions of robots are deployed gradually to handle those first identified candidates. It is in the "first version of robots" period in which the largest and most robust shift of workload occurs. The "maintenance and adjustments period" aims to achieve the highest level of digitization. It must be acknowledged that there is an asymptotic limit that the current state of technology cannot exceed. Eventually, only the most unstable and judgment-based parts of the process remain handled by humans. The sooner this eventual situation is reached, the more profitable the RPA project is. However, this is not an entirely stable situation since there might be changes in processes, UIs, and systems. If these changes are produced but not notified to the robots manager, they can potentially produce misbehavior of the robots, which implies that humans have to take care of the affected processes until the new version of the robots is deployed. Therefore, the human workload increases temporally.

This human-first context still presents some inefficiencies regarding the duplication of duties. For example, the training of humans requires analyzing the same documentation that is required for the construction of the first version of the robots. In

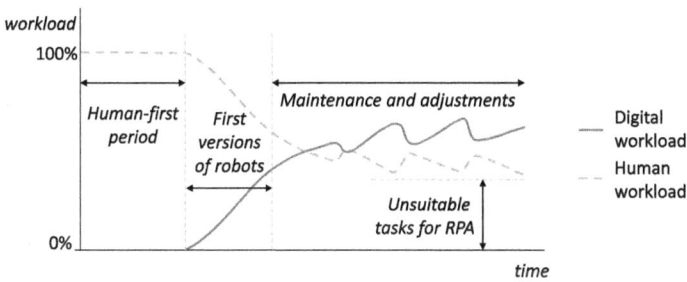

Figure 2: Workload shift from humans to robots.

addition, when humans do *on-the-job training* they perform a similar analysis as the one which is needed when misbehavior is detected in a robot. Therefore, the identified challenge and the focus of this chapter is to leverage the knowledge of the human team to be used by the different phases of the RPA lifecycle.

9.3 Learning from humans

This section describes how the analysis of the HCI can be used to leverage the human knowledge in the context of an RPA project. This analysis is conducted from a human-first viewpoint. Although different approaches can be found in the literature (Leno et al., 2018; Himel and Liu, 2017; Leno et al., 2020), the basic pipeline that they follow is described here (cf. Figure 3).

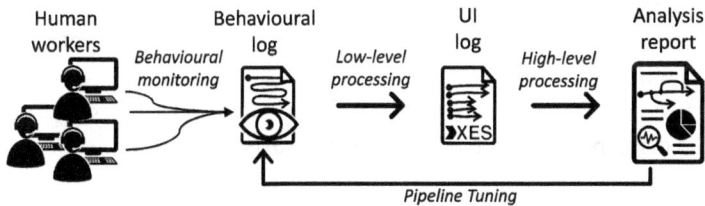

Figure 3: Basic pipeline for learning from HCI.

9.3.1 Behavioral monitoring

This step pursues capturing as much information as possible from the computers of the human workforce during working hours. Some HCI approaches include sophisticated sensors (e. g., eye trackers or vision-based gesture recognition) (Sharma et al., 1998) to capture the broadest number of events from the physical world in a digital log. However, such sensing is uncommon in a back-office workplace and thus, the behavior that can be feasibly monitored is tightened to mouse clicks, keystrokes, and screen captures, i. e., the one produced by the most common peripheral devices.

The event streams of these peripherals need to be recorded through non-intrusive monitoring software (i. e., its existence is transparent for the user) on each back-office computer and, thereafter, put all together in the same behavioral log.[1] The basic information that each behavioral event may include is:

- computer: it identifies the physical machine where the event is registered;
- timestamp: when this event occurs;
- image: a screen capture taken in this computer at this timestamp;
- keystrokes: the sequence (possibly empty) of keystrokes which are pushed at this timestamp;
- clicktype: the type of mouse click (i. e., left, right, middle, or none) which is done at this timestamp;
- clickcoords: the coordinates of the mouse at this timestamp.

Every time the human performs a mouse click or a sequence of keystrokes, an event is recorded. The resulting log consists of a single long trace which may be related to more than one instance of the processes that the back-office has performed.

9.3.2 Low-level processing

In the low-level processing step, the single-trace log is processed to become a more meaningful log from a process analysis perspective, i. e., a UI log (Jimenez-Ramirez et al., 2019) that can be expressed in the standard XES format (XES, 2016). For this, each behavioral event is enriched with two new attributes:

- UI event: identifies the atomic process activity which is associated with each behavioral event (e. g., login into the system, or submitting a form);
- trace: identifies the single execution/instance of the process that a sorted sequence of events corresponds to – also knows as the *case*.

First, this low-level processing includes the identification of repeated UI events. Some approaches like *robotic process mining* (Leno et al., 2020) or *desktop activity mining* (Linn et al., 2018) accomplish this step relying on UI information like window names or web page frames, which, in turn, disables its application in contexts where the humans interact with the ISs through secured connections. A more general approach (Jimenez-Ramirez et al., 2019) is based on image similarity techniques. More precisely, an efficient bit-wise comparison (Gusfield, 1999) between images fingerprints (i. e.,

---

1 Since the human workers have received similar training, they are expected to behave similarly and so their individual logs.

short hashes which are obtained from each image in a deterministic way) (Wong et al., 2002) is used to state that two screen captures (i. e., events) are related to the same activity (i. e., UI event) according to some pre-fixed similarity threshold.

Second, the one-trace log is split in different traces. For this, one UI event is selected as the starting event of each trace which uses to be the most repeated one (Jimenez-Ramirez et al., 2019) or one which is manually selected (Leno et al., 2018).

Besides calculating these two new attributes, this low-level processing might be used to wipe out some unnecessary events. Since not all the activities of the human workers are relevant for the RPA development (e. g., social networking or some web surfing), some of them can be detected at the image level. Techniques like optical character recognition – that looks for a text within an image – or template matching – that detects if a small image is part of a bigger image – are useful candidates to clean the behavioral log which may result in a cleaner UI log. In addition, the process mining community recognizes that the presence of these unnecessary events – noise – leads to the discovery of complex and inaccurate process models (Suriadi et al., 2017). To remedy this, they provide numerous techniques (Cheng and Kumar, 2015; Măruşter et al., 2006) to reduce such noise and enhance the quality of logs. Thus, they can be adapted to be included in this low-level processing.

9.3.3 High-level processing

The high-level processing step leverages the mature technology of process mining (van der Aalst, 2016) to analyze the UI log and discover the underlying process that the human workers perform. This discovered process is the result of high-level processing that produces a graphical process model where the considered traces and events are represented and where the variation points can be identified. At this level, a new attribute, called a *variant*, is included in the log to identify the process variant that each trace belongs to.

In addition, several statistical properties can be extracted from each variant, trace, and event (e. g., frequency, duration, or size) which are crucial to determine which parts are relevant enough for the RPA project. Furthermore, this high-level processing enables additional mechanisms to wipe out the previous log. At this point, marginal variants or variants that contain undesired process patterns are taken out of the process (e. g., variants which present long delays between two activities may be due to the existence of some physical activity, the whole variant thus being irrelevant for RPA).

As the reader may have seen, decisions which are taken in the previous step (e. g., choosing a similarity threshold or removing some events) have a clear impact on the resulting analysis. Therefore, this pipeline may require some iterations and manual fine-tuning before obtaining the desired result. Eventually, such a result represents the *as-is* process model that serves as the input of an RPA project.

9.3.4 Preliminary evaluation

The positive impact that the HCI analysis contributes to the RPA lifecycle has been established in a preliminary evaluation (Jimenez-Ramirez et al., 2019). This evaluation compared the outcomes obtained by the current approach with those that resulted from the conventional analysis and design activities.

Four steps were conducted during the evaluation (cf. Figure 4). First, one back-office computer was monitored to obtain the behavioral log for a period of one week, which comprises 200 complete cases approximately. Second, the obtained behavioral log was processed by the pipeline (cf. Figure 3) to generate an initial *as-is* process model. Third, the analyst repeated the pipeline several times applying some cognitive effort to obtain a final *as-is* process model. Lastly, the two obtained process models were compared with the one obtained conventionally, i. e., based on traditional, document-oriented analysis and design phases.

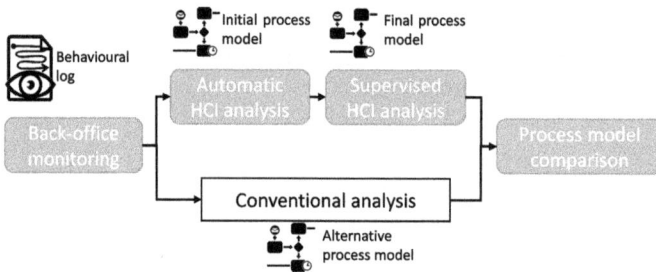

Figure 4: Steps in the preliminary evaluation.

This evaluation was applied to two outsourced processes of a Spanish company, which is active in the BPO domain. Different measures were used to compare the performance of each analysis: (1) the number of process variants that were included in each model (i. e., # Var conven, # Var auto, # Var super), (2) the percentage of new variants that the supervised analysis detects where the conventional analysis missed (i. e., % New), and (3) the percentage of variants that were included in the conventional analysis but not in the supervised one (i. e., % Missed).

The following conclusions can be drawn after analyzing the results of the evaluation (cf. Table 1):

Table 1: Result of the preliminary evaluation.

Process	#Var conven	#Var auto	#Var super	%New	%Missed
#1	5	46	12	7/12 (58 %)	0/5 (0 %)
#2	9	60	13	5/13 (38 %)	1/9 (11 %)

- Regarding the columns # Var conven and # Var super, the supervised HCI analysis discovers a greater variety of paths than the conventional way. As observed in the column % New, this increment is above 38 % in both processes. This implies that employees had to deal with variants which were not included in the conventional analysis yet existed in the behavior of the IS.
- Regarding the % Missed variants, it is relevant to note that only one was missed in the second process. This can be interpreted as follows: (1) the behavioral log was too small and did not contain all the relevant paths or (2) the path was actually not relevant for the analyst.
- Finally, regarding the # Var auto, it clearly shows that the cognitive labor of the analyst is much required to tune the pipeline, since many variants were included. Nonetheless, most of them were considered noise and irrelevant to the analysis, e. g., interrupted cases or errors.

9.4 Application example: the test phase

As mentioned above, testing the robots before they are deployed into production is of paramount importance to ensure the integrity of the ISs. Although proposals exist to improve the RPA test phase (Hannonen, 2020; Cewe et al., 2017), these all involve some manual work. The example application described in this section allows to do testing automatically, based on the results of the HCI analysis (Jiménez-Ramírez et al., 2020). This is done by including a testing cycle in the traditional RPA lifecycle (cf. Figure 5).

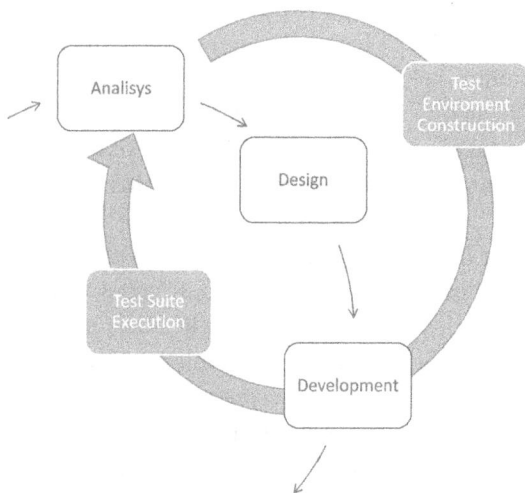

Figure 5: Including automatic testing in the RPA lifecycle.

More precisely, the HCI analysis is leveraged to simulate the behavior of a real IS, which may include its own databases and complex interactions with external ISs (cf. Figure 6). The behavior which is stored in the UI log can then be reproduced on a "fake" IS, i. e., the testing environment. This may seem identical to the real IS, but its behavior is limited to the one contained in the UI log. Once the development phase is finished, robots are tested against this test environment to ensure the proper execution of the robots in a minimally intrusive way.

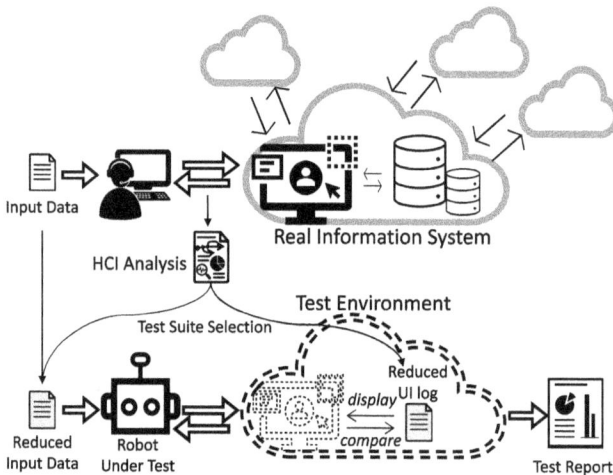

Figure 6: Automatic testing process.

In addition to the UI log, the described approach requires that input data of each process instance are recorded as well. Since the UI log might be rather lengthy for an efficient test cycle, a minimum test suite is selected. That is, on the basis of HCI analysis, the input data and the UI log related to one process instance for each process variant of the discovered process model are extracted. This results in two elements: (1) the reduced input data and (2) the reduced UI log, which only contains the traces of the selected process instances.

The test environment (i. e., the fake IS) consists of an IS that receives the reduced UI log and offers two main functionalities: (1) to display views, i. e., full-screen images, in a sequential way, simulating the behavior of the real application; and (2) to capture the interaction with the fake IS, i. e., it just waits for every interaction and then it captures the event information: mouse, keystrokes, and screen. The purpose of the test environment is to compare the events stored in the reduced UI log with the events performed by the robot in the test condition, which, in its turn, has also received the reduced input data. In the case that the events are similar, the test environment will show the next screen capture of the UI log and then wait for an interaction. Else, a failure test report is generated including (1) the events performed by the robot being tested and (2) the last event that was expected but was not similar to the received one.

In summary, this test environment is suitable for automatically designing and running functional tests for developed robots before they are being deployed. This approach guarantees that test data do not influence the system after the test has finished, which simplifies its incorporation into a continuous integration DevOps practice (Pinto et al., 2017). The test reports that are being generated identify errors at the workflow level, which provide a reasonably good starting point for debugging.

Example 1. Figure 7 shows a test suite obtained from a complete UI log (Jiménez-Ramírez et al., 2020). Here, *img_12* is shown first in the automatic testing since it is the image of the first event. In addition, the first expected event is a text action containing "Tari Tavarez." Assuming correct behavior of the robot, the test environment will show the image of the subsequent event (i. e., *img_13*) and wait for an event of the robot. In the case the robot does something different than clicking on a screen zone close to "120,205" – the expected event – the test case will be completed by producing the failure test report.

Reduced Input data

name	grade
Tari Tavarez	4.0
Burton Bertram	8.7

Reduced UI Log

timestamp	trace	keystrokes	clicktype	clickcoords	image
2020/09/10-0:4:32	1	"Tari Tavarez"			img_12
2020/09/10-0:4:35	1		Left	120,205	img_13
2020/09/10-0:4:50	1	"4.0"			img_14
2020/09/10-0:4:54	1		Left	10,240	img_15
2020/09/10-0:5:05	2	"Burton Bertram"			img_16
2020/09/10-0:5:09	2		Left	115,206	img_17

Figure 7: Example of a test suite.

9.5 Application horizons

Besides its application to the test phase, the HCI analysis report has potential impacts on further phases of the RPA lifecycle, as described in this section.

9.5.1 Analysis

The obtained analysis report represents a key element for the analysis phase since it includes: (1) on-the-field information about the real process, which is generally more accurate than the documentation of the process, (2) statistical estimates on the frequency of the variants, which are needed to identify the candidate variants to robotize, and (3) the human effort that is being used to execute the process, which is crucial to evaluate the return on investment and the potential performance of the RPA deployment.

In addition, as shown in Figure 8, the time required to acquire the process knowledge is drastically reduced by following the proposed approach. This is due to the fact that the HCI analysis can include the entire, unbiased interactions of several human workers at the same time.

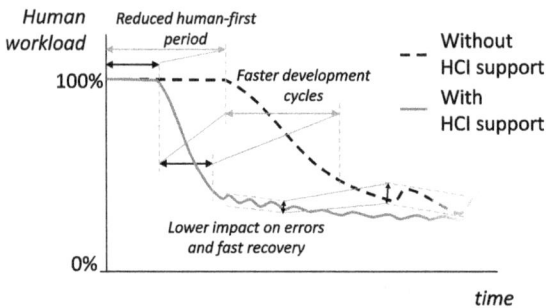

Figure 8: Temporal improvements due to HCI analysis and continuous monitoring.

The semi-automatic HCI approach that is explained in this chapter will require an analyst to make some decisions when fine-tuning the pipeline. State-of-the-art artificial intelligence (AI) technology is likely to be capable to support such professionals by learning from them, using appropriate parameters, to reduce the number of iterations that are needed. The HCI analysis is also based on the behavioral events that are captured. It is not always trivial to distinguish between the behavior that is and is not relevant to the process. Again, it can be expected that advanced algorithms can be developed that learn from the analysts to automate the first level of noise cleaning. This will require further investigation.

9.5.2 Design

Designing the robot according to the approach that is described in this chapter is greatly supported by the output of the HCI analysis. After all, the workflow of the obtained process models is intended to be similar in the designed *to-be* process model. In addition, each process activity can be traced back to its different behavioral events which may disclose valuable information for the designers. Therefore, as seen in Figure 8, the development cycles – starting with the design – can be greatly reduced.

Despite these advantages, two different challenges remain open to include such information into the design. The first one relates to design the events which move a robot from one to the next activity, i. e., a click or keystrokes. For this, once all the behavioral events which are logged for a given activity are grouped, it is possible to obtain the abstract event which governs all of them. Two different situations might be faced. The simplest one is that all the required information is within the logged information of these events. For example, given a set of click events in different-but-close screen positions, the abstract event would be clicking in the centroid of the point cloud. The more complex one requires information from other parts of the log (Leno et al., 2018). In this case, it would be required to, first, find the relation between the event and some instance data in the log, e. g., given a set of different keystrokes, it could be inferred from the log that these keystrokes correspond to the input data "student name." Thereafter, the abstract event will be parameterized with the found relation. What is more, this information could be depicted in the screen, so computer vision techniques would be needed to process all the screen captures to extract text data from them to enable this relation analysis.

The second challenge relates to the decision logic that may exist in a variation point to differentiate one process branch from the others. This logic may still need to be generated. Decision trees or any other data mining technique based on the characterization of the instances are good candidates to address this challenge. For this to work, it is required to have as much information as possible to characterize each branch at such a variation point. As before, this information may come from the behavioral log, the input information of the traces, or even information that is displayed in the screen captures.

9.5.3 Development

In this phase, the construction of the robot is carried out based on the results obtained from the execution of the analysis and design phases. Relying on the process design obtained from the HCI analysis, robot development can be boosted by model-based engineering methods (Staron, 2006). As proposed in (Leno et al., 2020) – where the RPA script is the last point of the pipeline – the robot code can be generated, tailored to a specific target platform, e. g., UiPath. To this end, the robot design must contain extended attributes that enable the implementation of actions and decision rules, as is being provided for in the approach described in this chapter.

However, the robot design may include advanced actions which are beyond the basic workflow behavior (e. g., computer vision). Moreover, each RPA platform has its custom set of components, which evolve in different ways. Considering that a deep understanding of a platform is necessary for RPA development (ABBYY, 2020), trying to cover all of them when generating the robot code results seems infeasible. Nonetheless, to address this issue, a platform-independent classification of RPA components could be investigated to map between the components of different RPA platforms.

9.5.4 Control and operation

The main objective of this phase of the lifecycle is to check the performance and to monitor the robots for detecting errors. In this sense, the HCI approach can be used to monitor the robotic workforce when the robots are deployed. This continuous monitoring would support the accomplishment of different tasks.

There are different directions to further support this monitoring phase. First, conformance checking techniques (van der Aalst et al., 2018) can be applied to quickly detect when a monitored robot is not behaving as designed. As a follow-up, these can be reported to the development team. In this way, the implication that this failure may affect the complete workforce is reduced to a minimum.

In addition, the robots which display misbehavior must be *repaired* by an RPA operator, e. g., when the UI of an IS changes. As stated before, this repair action consists of (1) driving the instance to a place where the robot can continue and (2) analyzing this robot instance to design and develop changes in the software as a new robot version. During this repair period, human workers should carry out more work to substitute for the robots being repaired. In the context of continuous HCI monitoring, each time a robot fails and the human operator takes control to repair it, the interaction would be logged as a new case. When finished, the pipeline would be automatically applied – with the same pipeline parameters – to discover the new process variant to be included in the process design, which would be delivered to development. In this way, as seen in Figure 8, human efforts required during the maintenance period are minimized since developing and propagating these new changes will go faster.

An interesting responsibility of the RPA manager is to decide the minimum size of the workforce to deploy for fulfilling some service-level agreements. Based on statistical data of the different process variants, the mean of the previous duration can be estimated to guess the required size. However, deviations may occur during the execution of the robots, which invalidate previous estimations. In such a situation, the manager would require additional support to make a decision. The HCI report that our approach generates can provide a detailed distribution of the different variants that have been dealt with so far, along with the real duration of each case. This information would serve the manager well for making workforce estimates and, what is more, can be used to define auto-scaling rules to keep an efficient workforce size.

9.5.5 Evaluation

In a way that is similar to how the described approach supports the control and operation phase, continuous HCI monitoring can provide a basis to support the process evaluation. Since RPA projects may evolve over time, variants that were once highly repetitive may become marginal at some point, or vice versa. Because of this dynamism, both the robots and the human workforce need to be continuously monitored. A set of key performance indicators could be generated in an unattended way by executing the HCI pipeline periodically. By doing so, a manager could be provided with an extended governance dashboard, which displays crucial information like new process candidates to robotize, relevant changes in the performance of the robotized variants, and those variants which are facing more problems and required a redesign.

Another evaluation task relates to understanding *why* humans performed a specific task in a particular way. Although RPA is said to be auditable (Criteria, 2014), it mainly allows auditors to know *what* has been done by looking at the audit trails. However, this may not suffice when the root cause of a problem needs to be understood. In the proposed approach, the HCI analysis keeps track of all the individual human actions that motivated the robot design, as well as its consequent development. Moreover, in the continuous HCI monitoring context, the precise information that the robot receives through the graphical UI is also captured and ready to be audited. Therefore, besides seeing just what has been done, auditors may rely on more quality information to know the *why*.

9.6 Conclusion

In this chapter, the benefits of a conceptual RPA framework based on the information retrieved from the HCI have been described. This conceptual framework is proposed in a *human-first context*, where the key to boost the development of the RPA project is to rely on the study of the behavior of humans carrying out a certain process. To enable this approach, the basic pipeline for learning from HCI was presented.

From the perspective of the RPA project lifecycle, the HCI proposal may contribute to bring benefits all its phases. Regarding the *analysis* phase, this proposal delivers an enriched report that helps to understand the underlying process and offers crucial information for the correct design of the robot in the design phase. The *development* phase could be systematized and partially automated by applying techniques based on the model-based engineering paradigm. Moreover, a non-intrusive automatic *testing* process has been thoroughly described to help to detect errors early in the development. This would help to lower the cost of robot development and to prevent fatal errors in the companies' production environments. The proposal is useful too as a continuous *monitoring* of robots that would help in the fast detection of misbehavior in the behavior in the *control and operation* phase. Finally, in the *evaluation* phase, it becomes easier to create indicators that enable observing the performance of the robots.

Many lines of future work can be considered for emerging technology such as RPA. First, due to the amount of rich data that the HCI provides, the combination with AI in this context can support a range of decision making activities. In addition, deciding on the minimum number of robots that need to be spawned to fulfill a company's service-level agreement is also amenable to be automated by using AI techniques. Regarding the development of robots, it would be valuable to work on new solutions that help to systematize and automate their development. Finally, scaling this HCI approach to a big-company level requires great computing capabilities for executing artificial vision algorithms and other image processing. Therefore, efficient techniques are in demand to detect and reduce unnecessary computations.

Bibliography

ABBYY (2020) State of process mining and robotic process automation 2020. Available at: www.abbyy.com/en-us/solutions/process-intelligence/research-report-2020. Last accessed: May 2020

Aguirre S, Rodriguez A (2017) Automation of a business process using robotic process automation (RPA): a case study. In: Proceedings – applied computer sciences in engineering: 4th workshop on engineering applications, WEA 2017, pp 65–71. ISBN 978-3-319-66963-2. https://doi.org/10.1007/978-3-319-66963-2_7

Biscotti F (2018) In: Gartner market share analysis: robotic process automation, Worldwide

Cewe C, Koch D, Mertens R (2017) Minimal effort requirements engineering for robotic process automation with test driven development and screen recording. In: International conference on business process management. Springer, Berlin, pp 642–648

Cheng H-J, Kumar A (2015) Process mining on noisy logs – can log sanitization help to improve performance? Decis Support Syst 79:138–149

Criteria HPF (2014) Use cases and effects of information technology process automation (ITPA). Adv Robot Autom 3(3):1–11. ISSN 21689695. 10.4172/2168-9695.1000124

Enríquez JG, Jiménez-Ramírez A, Domínguez-Mayo FJ, García-García JA (2020) Robotic process automation: a scientific and industrial systematic mapping study. IEEE Access 8:39113–39129

eXtensible Event Stream (XES) for achieving interoperability in event logs and event streams (2016) IEEE Std 1849-2016, pp 1–50

Flechsig C, Lohmer J, Lasch R (2019) Realizing the full potential of robotic process automation through a combination with bpm. In: Logistics management. Springer, Berlin, pp 104–119

Geyer-klingeberg J, Nakladal J (2018) Process mining and robotic process automation: a perfect match. In: 16th international conference on business process management, industry track session, number July, pp 1–8

Gusfield D (1999) Algorithms on strings, trees, and sequences: computer science and computational biology. Cambridge University Press, Cambridge

Hannonen A (2020) Automated testing for software process automation. Master's thesis, School of Technology and Innovations, University of Vaasa

Himel D, Liu Z (2017) Identifying frequent user tasks from application logs. In: Proceedings of the 22nd international conference on intelligent user interfaces, pp 263–273

Jimenez-Ramirez A, Reijers HA, Barba I, Del Valle C (2019) A method to improve the early stages of the robotic process automation lifecycle. In: International conference on advanced information systems engineering. Springer, Berlin, pp 446–461

Jiménez-Ramírez A, Chacón-Montero J, Wojdynsky T, González Enríquez J (2020) Automated testing in robotic process automation projects. J Softw Evol Process e2259. https://doi.org/10.1002/smr.2259

Leno V, Dumas M, Maggi FM, La Rosa M (2018) Multi-perspective process model discovery for robotic process automation. In: CEUR workshop proceedings, vol 2114, pp 37–45

Leno V, Polyvyanyy A, Dumas M, La Rosa M, Maggi FM (2020) Robotic process mining: vision and challenges. Bus Inf Syst Eng. ISSN 1867-0202. https://doi.org/10.1007/s12599-020-00641-4

Linn C, Zimmermann P, Werth D (2018) Desktop activity mining – a new level of detail in mining business processes. In: Workshops der INFORMATIK 2018 – Architekturen, Prozesse, Sicherheit und Nachhaltigkeit, pp 245–258

Mărușter L, Ton Weijters AJMM, van Der Aalst WMP, van Den Bosch A (2006) A rule-based approach for process discovery: dealing with noise and imbalance in process logs. Data Min Knowl Discov 13(1):67–87

Pinto G, Reboucas M, Castor F (2017) Inadequate testing, time pressure, and (over) confidence: a tale of continuous integration users. In: 2017 IEEE/ACM 10th international workshop on cooperative and human aspects of software engineering (CHASE), pp 74–77

Reinkemeyer L (2020) Process mining in action. Principles, use cases and outlook. Springer, Berlin. ISBN 978-3-030-40172-6

Sharma R, Pavlovic VI, Huang TS (1998) Toward multimodal human-computer interface. Proc IEEE 86(5):853–869

Staron M (2006) Adopting model driven software development in industry – a case study at two companies. In: Nierstrasz O, Whittle J, Harel D, Reggio G (eds) Model driven engineering languages and systems, Berlin, Heidelberg. Springer, Berlin, pp 57–72

Suriadi S, Andrews R, ter Hofstede AHM, Wynn MT (2017) Event log imperfection patterns for process mining: towards a systematic approach to cleaning event logs. Inf Syst 64:132–150

van der Aalst WMP (2016) Process mining: data science in action. Springer, Heidelberg

van der Aalst WMP, Bichler M, Heinzl A (2018) Robotic process automation. Bus Inf Syst Eng 60(4):269–272. ISSN 1867-0202. 10.1007/s12599-018-0542-4

Wong C, Bern MW, Goldberg D (2002) An image signature for any kind of image. In: International conference on image processing, pp 409–412

Han van der Aa and Henrik Leopold

10 Supporting RPA through natural language processing

Abstract: Natural language processing (NLP) is a field concerned with the analysis of natural language from a computational perspective. NLP techniques cover a wide range of tasks, such as information extraction, classification, and semantic analysis. As such, NLP has considerable potential to support robotic process automation (RPA) efforts. In particular, we use this chapter to highlight selected opportunities where a successful application of NLP techniques can support various stages of the RPA lifecycle. Therefore, we consider the potential of NLP for the identification of RPA opportunities and the design of RPA routines, as well as their actual execution. We discuss how these opportunities can be supported through the application of existing techniques and, furthermore, highlight open research challenges.

Keywords: Robotic process automation, natural language processing

10.1 Introduction

Many organizations currently face the challenge of keeping up with increasing digitization. Among others, it requires them to adapt existing business models and to respectively improve the automation of their business processes (Leyh et al., 2016). While the former is a rather strategic task, the latter calls for specific operational solutions. One of the most recent developments to increase the level of automation is referred to as robotic process automation (RPA). In essence, RPA emerges in the form of software-based solutions that automatically execute repetitive and routine tasks (Aguirre and Rodriguez, 2017). In this way, knowledge workers can dedicate their time and effort to more complex and value adding tasks.

Natural language processing (NLP) is a field concerned with the analysis of natural language from a computational perspective (Dan, 2000). NLP techniques cover a wide range of tasks, such as information extraction, classification, and semantic analysis. In the last decade, the maturity achieved by NLP technology, together with the explosion of big data and deep learning techniques, have turned the spotlight to the possibilities offered by NLP approaches for a variety of novel applications. Specifically, the potential of NLP to synthesize information from unstructured and semi-structured sources, such as textual documentation and free-text comments, makes it a prime candidate to support tedious, time consuming tasks in organizational settings (van der Aa et al., 2018a).

As such, we believe that NLP has a lot to offer in the context of RPA. Therefore, we use this chapter to outline various opportunities that NLP provides for different tasks

https://doi.org/10.1515/9783110676693-010

in an RPA lifecycle. In particular, we discuss the application of NLP for the following purposes:

1. *Identifying RPA opportunities*: NLP techniques can be leveraged to identify potential automation candidates through, e. g., semantic analysis of process documentation and the identification of reoccurring patterns.

2. *Designing RPA routines*: To implement RPA routines, tasks in an organizational process need to be transformed into a formalized, automatically executable representation format. NLP techniques can support this endeavor through, e. g., the automated extraction of formal specifications from textual resources, such as work instructions.

3. *Executing RPA routines*: Finally, NLP techniques can be used during the actual execution of implemented RPA routines. In this manner, RPA can become *smarter* and go beyond the automation of simple tasks (van der Aalst et al., 2018). For instance, by automating process steps involving the actual interpretation of unstructured input, such as e-mails from clients.

The remainder of this chapter is structured as follows. Section 10.2 discusses how NLP techniques are already applied in the closely related area of business process management (BPM). Then, Section 10.3 shows how these and other NLP-based techniques can be lifted to the context of RPA. Finally, Section 10.4 concludes the chapter and highlights open research directions.

10.2 Background

In this section, we reflect on NLP-based approaches developed to target several use cases in the context of BPM. BPM is a research area concerned with the analysis of how work is performed in an organization. The overall aim is to ensure consistent process outcomes and to take advantage of improvement opportunities (Dumas et al., 2013). As such, there is a clear relation between the goals and methods of BPM and RPA (van der Aalst et al., 2018).

In this section, we discuss various use cases of applying NLP to BPM, which can be lifted to RPA settings as well. We divide this discussion into the analysis of text inside of process models (Section 10.2.1) and the analysis of text outside of process models, i. e., in supplementary resources (Section 10.2.2).

10.2.1 Analyzing text within process models

In this section, we first introduce the notion of process models. Then, we illustrate the analysis of text within process models through label parsing and the use cases that parsing opens up.

Process models

Process models are the de facto standard to capture organizational processes in a structured manner. As such, they form the central artifact for the vast majority of process analysis techniques, including those described in this chapter.

Various notations are used to define process models, of which Petri Nets represent the most common formal model, whereas event-driven process chains (EPCs) (Scheer et al., 2005) and business process model and notation (BPMN) (Chinosi and Bpmn, 2012) represent the most commonly adopted methods in practice. Figure 1 depicts an exemplary BPMN model. The rounded rectangles denote the four *activities* in the process, whereas the circles are used to, respectively, depict the start and end *events* of the process. Finally, the diamond shapes with a plus sign indicate that the two activities in between them can be executed *concurrently*.

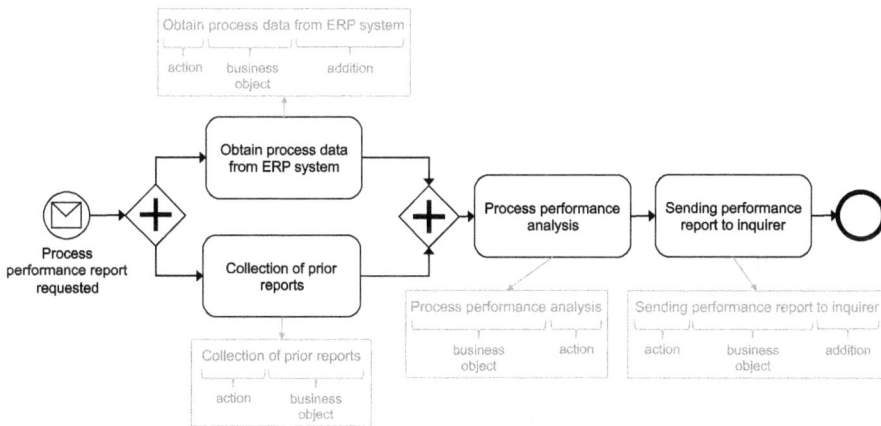

Figure 1: BPMN model example with annotated activity labels (from Leopold et al., 2019a).

The gray nodes are semantic annotations of the activity labels in the model. They are not part of BPMN models but result from the NLP-based analysis technique discussed next.

Label parsing

The parsing of process model activity labels focuses on the recognition of several semantic components in the labels. In particular, parsers generally aim to extract the *action*, e. g., "*obtain,*" the *business object* to which this action relates, e. g., "*process data,*" and some *additional* information fragment, e. g., "*from the ERP system.*" Such semantic annotations are depicted for the activities in Figure 1. Automatically obtaining these annotations is a challenging task, however. The two activities "*process performance analysis*" and "*sending performance report to inquirer*" illustrate this vividly.

Both activity labels are short, do not represent proper sentences (they do not contain a verb), and the underlying syntactical patterns differ. In the former case, the action is provided as a noun at the end of the label (*"analysis"*); in the latter case, the action is provided as a noun in the beginning (*"sending"*). Because of these factors, standard NLP tools, such as the Stanford Parser, are not applicable (Leopold, 2013). However, there are dedicated label annotation techniques available. Among others, there is a heuristics-based technique exploiting the label context (Leopold et al., 2012) and a technique building on hidden Markov models (Leopold et al., 2019a).

Label-based analysis
The availability of activity label annotations opens the door for several advanced analyses. For example, the annotations allow to automatically check different quality criteria of process models, such as naming conventions (Leopold et al., 2013) and linguistic consistency (Pittke et al., 2013). They also provide the basis for the identification of recurring patterns in process model collections (Leopold et al., 2015) and for the detection of commonalities and differences between process models (Weidlich et al., 2010).

10.2.2 Analyzing process-related information in textual documents

On top of the analysis of text within process models, a range of existing works targets the analysis of process-related information contained in different kinds of textual resources. A majority of these focus on the extraction of process models from such textual documents, whereas others target situations in which textual documents exist alongside of process models themselves.

Extracting process models from texts
Given their potential as a basis for various analysis techniques, the benefits of documenting organizational processes using process models are clear. However, in practice, process information is often spread over informational artifacts beyond these models (van der Aa et al., 2017b). Realizing that some stakeholders struggle to read and interpret process models, organizations have recognized the value of maintaining text-based process descriptions in place of or alongside model-based ones (Leopold et al., 2014). While such textual descriptions may not be suitable to represent complex aspects of a process in a precise manner, they can be created, maintained, and understood by virtually everyone.

In order to make the information contained in textual documentation suitable for process analysis techniques, various approaches have been developed that elicit process models from different kinds of texts, so-called *text-to-model* transformation ap-

proaches. Some approaches target specific kinds of documents, such as the generation of models from use cases (Sinha and Paradkar, 2010), group stories (de Gonçalves
et al., 2009), or methodological descriptions (Viorica Epure et al., 2015), while others
take general imperative (Ghose et al., 2007; Friedrich et al., 2011) and declarative (van
der Aa et al., 2019) process descriptions as input. These techniques combine extensive
use of general-purpose NLP tools with specifically tailored analysis techniques in order to extract process-related information from natural language texts. Nevertheless,
due to the complexity of the overall challenge and the inherent ambiguity of natural
language (van der Aa et al., 2018b), the process models obtained in this manner typically require manual verification (Selway et al., 2015).

Analyzing supplementary materials

Recognizing that textual documents often exist alongside of process models, various
techniques have been developed that target both model and text at the same time. For
instance, different approaches (Sànchez-Ferreres et al., 2017; van der Aa et al., 2017a)
have been established that align and compare process models against textual descriptions in order to ensure consistency across representations. Other works exploit the
additional execution details provided by *work instructions* that are associated with
process models. This information is, for instance, employed to improve the alignment
of process models to recorded process executions (Baier et al., 2014) and to increase
the recall in process querying (Leopold et al., 2019b).

10.3 Scenarios for NLP in RPA

In this section, we will illustrate how NLP can contribute to the identification of RPA
opportunities (Section 10.3.1), the design of RPA routines (Section 10.3.2), and the execution of routines themselves (Section 10.3.3).

10.3.1 NLP for RPA opportunity identification

With RPA opportunity identification we refer to the identification of routines (either
processes or parts thereof) that are good candidates to be automated through RPA
bots. Existing RPA tools provide limited support for this challenge. As a result, this
task often requires a considerable amount of manual effort, by means of interviews,
observation, and analysis of documentation (Agostinelli et al., 2020).

   Several recent research directions aim to support this task through the analysis of
event logs. For instance, Jimenez-Ramirez et al. (2019) propose a method that incor-
porates process mining techniques into the early stages (including opportunity identification) of the RPA lifecycle, whereas Bosco et al. (2019) present a concrete method

to detect deterministic routines in user interaction logs. Complimentary to such approaches, NLP techniques can be used in various manners to support the identification of RPA opportunities. Specifically, existing work can primarily support opportunity identification through the automatic detection of user tasks and the recognition of recurring process patterns:

Automatically detecting automation candidates

Prime candidates for RPA are so-called *user tasks*, which are defined as process steps in which a user interacts with an information system (Dumas et al., 2013). Such user tasks are likely to be good automation candidates because the fact that a user interacts with an information system makes it more likely that the associated manual effort can actually be emulated by an RPA bot.

In earlier work, we developed an approach (Leopold et al., 2018) to automatically identify these user tasks in process repositories. This approach employs NLP techniques to first extract activities (i. e., process steps) from various available resources, such as process models and textual work instructions. Afterwards, the approach classifies the activities according to their degree of automation, i. e., recognizing whether an activity is manual, a user task, or automated. While not all user tasks identified in this manner may necessarily be suitable for automation, the approach represents a valuable filtering technique that can serve as a starting point for the identification of opportunities, even in the presence of vast process repositories.

Similarly, we have developed an approach that allows users to query process repositories, covering both process models and textual documents, for specific behavioral patterns. In the context of RPA opportunity identification, this can be employed to easily retrieve all cases in which a specific activity routine occurs. For instance, users can query all cases in which a user fills in an electronic form based on information retrieved from a customer order, which is a typical target for automation efforts. While this requires some input based on domain knowledge as opposed to the previous fully automated classification approach, it has the benefit that the obtained results are more specific and, therefore, more accurate.

A primary benefit shared by these two approaches is that their incorporation of NLP techniques allows them to identify RPA opportunities in textual documentation associated with (parts of) processes. As shown in Leopold et al. (2019b), the number of relevant results that can be obtained by also querying these documents can increase considerably, because process models typically provide a relatively high-level view on a process. By contrast, information relevant to the identification of RPA opportunities, such as how exactly a process step is currently performed, is typically stored in more detailed work instructions. For instance, in Figure 2, only by considering the work instruction associated with the *"opening of a new bank account for customer"* activity, it becomes clear that this activity involves the entering of information into a form and forwarding it in a mail. By analyzing this instruction using NLP techniques, it would

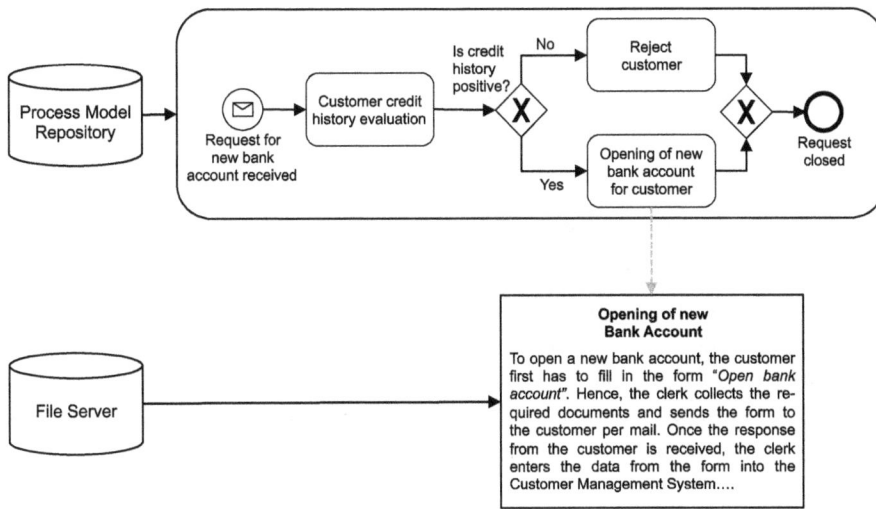

Figure 2: Process model and associated work instruction (from Leopold et al., 2019b).

thus be possible to recognize that this process step provides a promising candidate for automation. This opportunity would be missed without employing natural language analysis.

Detecting recurring patterns

In organizations with dozens or hundreds of processes, efforts to automate process steps using RPA are, arguably, best invested into commonly occurring routines, because the return on investment tends to be bigger when automating routines that recur in various processes throughout an organization.

Such recurring patterns can be recognized by detecting commonly occurring behavioral patterns in process repositories. Without employing NLP techniques, one could detect these when there are fully identical fragments present in multiple process models. To illustrate this, consider the process model fragment in Figure 3a, which depicts a part of a process model concerned with receiving and responding to meeting requests. It is well imaginable that this procedure is relevant to a variety of processes in an organization. For example, it may be part of any process in which a third party, such as a customer, supplier, or another department, needs to schedule a meeting. If this exact fragment is used in all these processes, it would be straightforward to recognize this recurring pattern.

However, the potential of such pattern detection can be greatly improved by employing NLP techniques. Consider the model fragment depicted in Figure 3b, which describes an equivalent process fragment, though with very different terminology from Figure 3a. By employing NLP techniques, one would be able to automatically

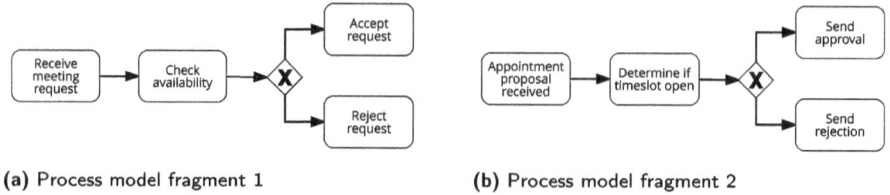

(a) Process model fragment 1   (b) Process model fragment 2

Figure 3: Semantically similar process model fragments.

recognize that these fragments are closely related, for instance, by recognizing the *semantic similarity* between terms such as *"meeting"* and *"appointment"* and *"accept"* and *"approval."* So-called *process model matchers* (Weidlich et al., 2010) address this task by considering a variety of factors that may indicate similarity between parts of processes, including syntactic similarity, synonyms, and hypernyms. In this manner, NLP techniques make the detection of reoccurring patterns much more robust to terminological differences that are commonly part of real-world process model collections. By employing label parsing techniques, as discussed in Section 10.2.1, pattern detection may even be used to recognize reoccurring patterns involving different business objects (Smirnov et al., 2012).

Overall, the two general use cases discussed in this section should be regarded as complementary. The former use case targets the detection of specific process model activities or fragments that are relatively easy to automate, whereas the latter use case focuses on the detection of reoccurring patterns that make the investment required for automation more worthwhile.

10.3.2 NLP for RPA routine design

Once a suitable opportunity for automation has been identified, the next step is to design the RPA routine that can emulate the currently manual actions. This involves the formalization of the procedure, which typically is achieved by a human designer who establishes a flowchart. This flowchart captures the actions to be performed by an RPA bot on a specific system (Agostinelli et al., 2020).

NLP techniques, in particular the text-to-model transformation techniques discussed in Section 10.2.2, can provide valuable support to human designers in this regard. The transformation techniques can be applied to textual documents capturing an entire process, but may also be applied on work instructions, which provide detailed explanations of how specific steps of a process should be executed. The latter is particularly promising, since these work instructions are much more likely to provide the details necessary for the automation of a certain step than process models (van der Aa et al., 2017b).

The choice for a particular technique to be employed for this purpose depends on the characteristics of the textual document(s) used as input. Documents that provide a chronological description of a process (or process step) can best be handled by techniques that extract imperative process models from text, such as the state-of-the-art technique by Friedrich et al. (2011). However, for documents that are closer to a requirement or regulatory specification, techniques to extract declarative process models (van der Aa et al., 2019) or business rules (Winter and Rinderle-Ma, 2018) may be more suitable.

In any case, the process models extracted by these NLP-based techniques should be regarded as a helpful starting point for the formal definition of automation routines. On the one hand, manual analysis is required to ensure that the obtained models are correct and to resolve any ambiguity (Selway et al., 2015; van der Aa et al., 2018b). On the other hand, this step only covers the extraction of the as-is state of the process, including the steps that are currently performed manually. How to automate the interaction with an information system will most likely still require manual input or a combination with other techniques.

10.3.3 NLP in routine execution

Finally, we consider the actual execution of RPA routines. The value of NLP to enhance this task is already widely recognized and part of what both scholars and tool vendors refer to as *cognitive RPA* (Lacity and Willcocks, 2018). While cognitive RPA is not limited to the application of NLP in routine execution, NLP plays a major role due to the general prevalence of textual content in organizational processes. This is also reflected by specialized RPA tool vendors, such as Lexalytics,[1] Expert System,[2] or RoboRana,[3] which do not only use but also advertize building on NLP techniques.

The use cases for NLP in the context of routine execution can be divided into two main categories. The first relates to the automated analysis of *semi-structured content*, which can be, among others, found in invoices, insurance claims, and contracts. While such documents contain free natural language text, the documents adhere to an overall structure and typically have a number of specific data items (e. g., the final amount on an invoice) that provide a certain degree of structure and orientation. The second category relates to analysis of *unstructured content*, which can be typically encountered in customer e-mails, phone calls, chats, and social media posts. These sources need to be expected to be free of any regular structure. In the following, we discuss three major NLP use cases in more detail: the first relating to the analysis of semi-structured content and the latter two to the analysis of unstructured content.

---

[1] https://www.lexalytics.com/
[2] https://expertsystem.com/
[3] https://roborana.be/en/

Invoice processing

A relevant use case relating to the analysis of *semi-structured content* is the automated processing of invoices. Based on semi-structured document parsers, a routine could provide the possibility to automatically (1) extract relevant data (such as the invoicing company, products, services, amounts, and dates), (2) store the extracted data in a database or a file, and (3) trigger an automated payment. In the case an invoice is not available as a document that can be parsed (e. g., consider PDFs created from scans), optical character recognition (OCR) techniques can be used in the pre-processing phase. It is interesting to point out that the technology required for extracting data from semi-structured text documents is not new. Many techniques and patents date back to the early and mid 2000s (see e. g. Lemon et al., 2005; Chieu and Ng, 2002). However, the combination with existing RPA capabilities provides a new context for their use.

Ticket classification

A frequently discussed use case relating to the analysis of *unstructured content* is the automated classification of tickets. Since many organizations face hundreds or even thousands of support tickets every day, automated support can be expected to come with considerable time savings. Such automated support may be as simple as using document classification techniques to determine what a ticket is about and what problems the person is having. As a result, organizations can benefit from faster triage and faster allocation to the right expert. While document classification techniques have been around for some time, particularly the automated classification of tickets is a rather recent and active area of research (Maksai et al., 2014; Altintas and Cuneyd Tantug, 2014).

Automated customer service

A use case that is taking ticket classification a step further is automated customer service. The main observation behind this use case is that many customer requests relate to rather trivial matters. If it is possible to set up an RPA routine for some of these trivial matters (e. g., for changing an address or changing the seat on an aircraft), it would be possible to build a system that either (1) matches a request to an existing routine or (2) decides that human intervention is required. From a technological perspective, such a system is challenging because it needs to interact with the customer automatically (e. g., to obtain further information or validate the customer's ID). An example for such a system is the chat bot system of the Dutch airline KLM called *DigitalGenius*.[4] DigitalGenius was set up to deal with customer inquiries that would be typically found in tickets. According to KLM, DigitalGenius supports up to 50 % of all

---

4 https://www.digitalgenius.com/

customer inquires, leading to a significant reduction in both the human effort required and response time for the client.

The three use cases described above illustrate that existing NLP techniques provide interesting opportunities to enhance traditional RPA capabilities. The key challenge for the successful application in practice is to properly address the problem of accuracy: NLP-based techniques simply cannot be expected to always deliver perfect results. This means that NLP-based RPA routines need to be able to decide when they are unable to accurately process a certain task and need to include a human in the loop.

10.4 Conclusion

In this chapter, we highlighted the potential of employing NLP techniques to support various tasks in the RPA lifecycle. In particular, we first showed how NLP techniques can help to identify suitable candidates for automation through the identification of so-called user tasks and by identifying reoccurring process patterns. Second, we illustrated how text-to-model transformation approaches can be used as a first step in the formalization of RPA routines by automatically extracting structured process information from textual documentation. Finally, we considered how NLP can contribute to the actual execution of RPA routines themselves. We discussed use cases that involve the automation of routines dealing with both semi-structured and unstructured content. Here, we specifically illustrated how NLP techniques can enable the automation of tasks related to invoice processing, ticket classification, and automated customer service.

Maturity
The maturity of state-of-the-art approaches for all three tasks leaves considerable opportunities for further improvement:
1. The use of NLP for the identification of RPA opportunities is still relatively new. Out of the various techniques developed to support the identification of RPA opportunities, only the few approaches discussed in Section 10.3.1 incorporate considerations of natural language. As such, there are still substantial opportunities for further work in this direction, e. g., through the development of new NLP-driven identification approaches or by combining NLP-driven approaches with approaches targeting other process perspectives, such as control flow and data transformations.
2. The use of NLP to support routine design, as discussed in Section 10.3.2, is driven by existing work on the transformation of textual descriptions into formal process specifications. These current approaches are primarily heuristics-based, which results in problems when dealing with highly flexible textual documents from

practice. However, recent advances in NLP, such as deep bidirectional transformers (Devlin et al., 2018), provide a promising endeavor for future development in order to move away from heuristics-based transformation and to, therefore, overcome limitations of the current state of the art.

3. Finally, NLP has been applied to support the execution of RPA routines in various manners, though the potential for further development is considerable. Such development can focus on both the design of more advanced techniques to provide better solutions in existing scenarios and the usage of NLP to enable novel scenarios in which RPA can be employed.

Outlook

Although the benefits of applying NLP in all three discussed tasks are apparent, we believe that the main potential for future work lies in the application of NLP to routine execution itself. While the application of NLP for the first two tasks, opportunity identification and routine formalization, reduces the manual effort required for these tasks, the application of NLP for routine execution can truly expand the task's potential and, thus, broaden the potential of RPA as a whole. By employing NLP techniques for this purpose, RPA can thus be transformed from a rudimentary to an intelligent automation tool.

Bibliography

Agostinelli S, Marrella A, Mecella M (2020) Towards intelligent robotic process automation for bpmers. arXiv preprint arXiv:2001.00804

Aguirre S, Rodriguez A (2017) Automation of a business process using robotic process automation (RPA): a case study. In: Workshop on engineering applications. Springer, Berlin, pp 65–71

Altintas M, Cuneyd Tantug A (2014) Machine learning based ticket classification in issue tracking systems. In: Proceedings of international conference on artificial intelligence and computer science (AICS 2014)

Baier T, Mendling J, Weske M (2014) Bridging abstraction layers in process mining. Inf Syst 46:123–139

Bosco A, Augusto A, Dumas M, La Rosa M, Fortino G (2019) Discovering automatable routines from user interaction logs. In: International conference on business process management. Springer, Berlin, pp 144–162

Chieu HL, Ng HT (2002) A maximum entropy approach to information extraction from semi-structured and free text. In: AAAI 2002, pp 786–791

Chinosi M, Bpmn AT (2012) An introduction to the standard. Comput Stand Interfaces 34(1):124–134

Dan J (2000) Speech & language processing. Pearson Education India

de Gonçalves JC, Santoro FM, Baiao FA (2009) Business process mining from group stories. In: 13th international conference on computer supported cooperative work in design, 2009. CSCWD 2009. IEEE, pp 161–166

Devlin J, Chang M-W, Lee K, Toutanova K (2018) BERT: pre-training of deep bidirectional transformers for language understanding. arXiv preprint arXiv:1810.04805

Dumas M, La Rosa M, Mendling J, Reijers HA et al (2013) Fundamentals of business process management, vol 1. Springer, Berlin

Friedrich F, Mendling J, Puhlmann F (2011) Process model generation from natural language text. In: International conference on advanced information systems engineering. Springer, Berlin, pp 482–496

Ghose A, Koliadis G, Chueng A (2007) Process discovery from model and text artefacts. In: 2007 IEEE congress on services. IEEE, pp 167–174

Jimenez-Ramirez A, Reijers HA, Barba I, Del Valle C (2019) A method to improve the early stages of the robotic process automation lifecycle. In: International conference on advanced information systems engineering. Springer, Berlin, pp 446–461

Lacity M, Willcocks LP (2018) Robotic process and cognitive automation: the next phase. SB Publishing

Lemon MJ, Castellanos M, Stinger JR (2005) Method for content mining of semi-structured documents, June 28 2005. US Patent 6,912,555

Leopold H (2013) Natural language in business process models. PhD thesis, Springer

Leopold H, Smirnov S, Mendling J (2012) On the refactoring of activity labels in business process models. Inf Syst 37(5):443–459

Leopold H, Eid-Sabbagh R-H, Mendling J, Azevedo LG, Baião FA (2013) Detection of naming convention violations in process models for different languages. Decis Support Syst 56:310–325

Leopold H, Mendling J, Polyvyanyy A (2014) Supporting process model validation through natural language generation. IEEE Trans Softw Eng 40(8):818–840

Leopold H, Pittke F, Mendling J (2015) Automatic service derivation from business process model repositories via semantic technology. J Syst Softw 108:134–147

Leopold H, van der Aa H, Reijers HA (2018) Identifying candidate tasks for robotic process automation in textual process descriptions. In: Enterprise, business-process and information systems modeling. Springer, Berlin, pp 67–81

Leopold H, van der Aa H, Offenberg J, Reijers HA (2019a) Using hidden Markov models for the accurate linguistic analysis of process model activity labels. Inf Syst 83:30–39

Leopold H, van der Aa H, Pittke F, Raffel M, Mendling J, Reijers HA (2019b) Searching textual and model-based process descriptions based on a unified data format. Softw Syst Model 18(2):1179–1194

Leyh C, Bley K, Seek S (2016) Elicitation of processes in business process management in the era of digitization–the same techniques as decades ago? In: International conference on enterprise resource planning systems. Springer, Berlin, pp 42–56

Maksai A, Bogojeska J, Wiesmann D (2014) Hierarchical incident ticket classification with minimal supervision. In: 2014 IEEE international conference on data mining. IEEE, pp 923–928

Pittke F, Leopold H, Mendling J (2013) Spotting terminology deficiencies in process model repositories. In: Enterprise, business-process and information systems modeling. Springer, Berlin, pp 292–307

Sánchez-Ferreres J, Carmona J, Padró L (2017) Aligning textual and graphical descriptions of processes through ilp techniques. In: International conference on advanced information systems engineering. Springer, Berlin, pp 413–427

Scheer A-W, Thomas O, Adam O (2005) Process modeling using event-driven process chains. In: Process-aware information systems, vol 119

Selway M, Grossmann G, Mayer W, Stumptner M (2015) Formalising natural language specifications using a cognitive linguistic/configuration based approach. Inf Syst 54:191–208

Sinha A, Paradkar A (2010) Use cases to process specifications in business process modeling notation. In: IEEE international conference on web services, pp 473–480

Smirnov S, Weidlich M, Mendling J, Weske M (2012) Action patterns in business process model repositories. Comput Ind 63(2):98–111

van der Aa H, Leopold H, Reijers HA (2017a) Comparing textual descriptions to process models–the automatic detection of inconsistencies. Inf Syst 64:447–460

van der Aa H, Leopold H, van de Weerd I, Reijers HA (2017b) Causes and consequences of fragmented process information: Insights from a case study. In: AMCIS

van der Aa H, Carmona Vargas J, Leopold H, Mendling J, Padró L (2018a) Challenges and opportunities of applying natural language processing in business process management. In: COLING. Association for Computational Linguistics, pp 2791–2801

van der Aa H, Leopold H, Reijers HA (2018b) Checking process compliance against natural language specifications using behavioral spaces. Inf Syst 78:83–95

van der Aa H, Di Ciccio C, Leopold H, Reijers HA (2019) Extracting declarative process models from natural language. In: International conference on advanced information systems engineering. Springer, Berlin, pp 365–382

van der Aalst WMP, Bichler M, Heinzl A (2018) Robotic process automation

Viorica Epure E, Martín-Rodilla P, Hug C, Deneckère R, Salinesi C (2015) Automatic process model discovery from textual methodologies. In: 9th international conference on research challenges in information science (RCIS), 2015 IEEE. IEEE, pp 19–30

Weidlich M, Dijkman R, Mendling J (2010) The icop framework: identification of correspondences between process models. In: International conference on advanced information systems engineering. Springer, Berlin, pp 483–498

Winter K, Rinderle-Ma S (2018) Detecting constraints and their relations from regulatory documents using nlp techniques. In: OTM confederated international conferences"on the move to meaningful Internet systems". Springer, Berlin, pp 261–278

Simone Agostinelli, Andrea Marrella, and Massimo Mecella

11 Automated segmentation of user interface logs

Abstract: Robotic process automation (RPA) tools are able to capture in dedicated user interface (UI) logs the execution of high-volume routines previously performed by a human user on the interface of a computer system, and then emulate their enactment in place of the user by means of a software robot. A UI log can record information about several routines, whose actions and events are mixed in some order that reflects the particular order of their execution by the user. In addition, the same user action may belong to different routines, making its automated identification far from trivial. The issue to automatically understand which user actions contribute to a specific routine inside the UI log is also known as *segmentation*. In this contribution, after discussing in detail the issue of segmentation and all its potential variants, we present a novel segmentation technique that leverages trace alignment in process mining for automatically deriving the boundaries of a routine by analyzing the UI logs that keep track of its execution, in order to cluster all user actions associated with the routine itself in well-bounded routine traces.

Keywords: Robotic process automation, segmentation of user interface logs, trace alignment in process mining

11.1 Introduction

Robotic process automation (RPA) uses *software robots* (or simply *SW robots*) to mimic and replicate the execution of highly routine tasks (in the following, called *routines*) performed by humans in their application's user interface (UI). SW robots encode, by means of executable scripts, sequences of fine-grained interactions with a computer system, such as opening a file, selecting a field in a form or a cell in a spreadsheet, copy and paste data across cells of a spreadsheet, extract semi-structured data from documents, read and write from/to databases, open e-mails and attachments, make calculations, etc. (Willcocks, 2016). A typical routine that can be automated by a SW robot using a RPA tool is transferring data from one system to another via their respective UIs, e. g., copying records from a spreadsheet application into a web-based enterprise information system (Leno et al., 2020b).

Commercial RPA tools allow SW robots to automate a wide range of routines in a record-and-replay fashion. The current practice for identifying the single steps of a routine is by means of interviews, walk-throughs, and detailed observation of workers conducting their daily work (Jimenez-Ramirez et al., 2019). A recent approach pro-

https://doi.org/10.1515/9783110676693-011

posed by Bosco et al. (2019) makes this identification less time consuming and error-prone, as it enables to automatically extract from a UI log, which records the UI inter-actions during a routine enactment, those routine steps to be automated with a SW robot. While this approach is effective in the case of UI logs that keep track of single routine executions, i. e., there is an exact 1:1 mapping among a recorded user action and the specific routine it belongs to, it becomes inadequate when the UI log records information about several routines whose actions are mixed in some order that re-flects the particular order of their execution by the user. In addition, since the same user action may belong to different routines, the automated identification of those user actions that belong to a specific routine is far from trivial. The challenge to automat-ically understand which user actions contribute to which routines inside a UI log is also known as *segmentation* (Agostinelli et al., 2019; Leno et al., 2020b).

In this chapter, after discussing in detail the issue of segmentation and all its po-tential variants, we present a technique for automatically deriving the boundaries of a routine by analyzing the UI log that keeps track of its execution, in order to clus-ter all user actions associated with the routine itself in well-bounded *routine traces*. A routine trace represents an execution instance of a routine within a UI log. To be more precise, as shown in Figure 1, starting from a UI log previously recorded by a RPA tool and an *interaction model* representing the expected behavior of a routine per-formed during an interaction session with the UI, we propose a supervised algorithm that leverages *trace alignment* in process mining (Adriansyah et al., 2011; de Leoni and Marrella, 2017; de Leoni et al., 2018) to automatically identify and extract the routine traces by the UI log. Such traces are finally stored in a dedicated *routine-based log*, which captures exactly all the user actions which happened during many different ex-ecutions of the routine, thus achieving the segmentation task. By identifying the rou-tine traces, we are also able to filter out those actions in the UI log that are not part of the routine under observation and hence are redundant or represent noise. It is worth noticing that a routine-based log obtained in this way can eventually be employed by the commercial RPA tools to synthesize executable scripts in form of SW robots that will emulate the routine behavior.

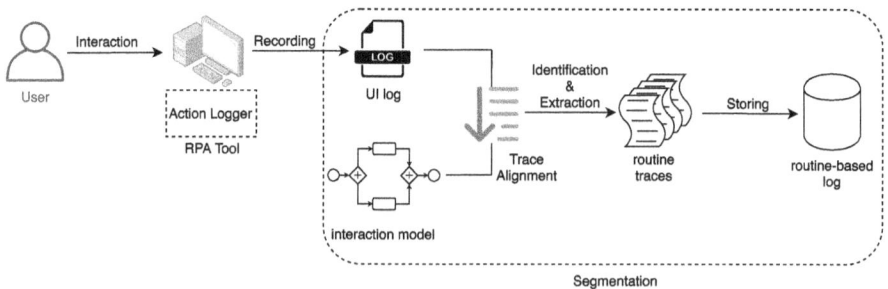

Figure 1: Overview of the proposed segmentation technique.

The rest of the chapter is organized as follows. Section 11.2 introduces a running example that will be used to explain our technique. Section 11.3 describes the relevant background on interaction models and UI logs. Section 11.4 illustrates the concept of segmentation and all its peculiarities. Section 11.5 presents the details of our technique to the automated segmentation of UI logs. Finally, Section 11.6 discusses the related work, while Section 11.7 draws conclusions and outlines future works.

11.2 Running example

Below, we describe a RPA use case inspired by a real-life scenario at the Department of Computer, Control and Management Engineering (DIAG) of Sapienza Universitá di Roma. The scenario concerns the filling of the travel authorization request form made by professors, researchers, and PhD students of DIAG for travel requiring prior approval. The request applicant must fill a well-structured Excel spreadsheet (cf. Figure 2a) providing some personal information, such as his or her bio-data and the e-mail address, together with further information related to the travel, including the destination, the starting/ending date/time, the means of transport to be used, the travel purpose, and the envisioned amount of travel expenses, associated with the possibility to request an anticipation of the expenses already incurred (e. g., to request in advance a visa). When ready, the spreadsheet is sent via e-mail to an employee of the Administration Office of DIAG, which is in charge of approving and (only in this case) elaborating the request. Concretely, for each row in the spreadsheet, the employee manually copies every cell in that row and pastes that into the corresponding text field in a dedicated Google form (cf. Figure 2b), accessible just by the administration staff. Once the data transfer for a given travel authorization request has been completed, the employee presses the "Submit" button to submit the data into an internal database.

In addition, if the request applicant declares that he or she would like to use his or her personal car as one of the means of transport for the travel, then he or she has to fill a dedicated (simple) web form required for activating a special insurance for the part of the travel that will be performed with the car. This further request will be delivered to the administration staff via e-mail, and the employee in charge of processing it can either approve or reject such request. At the end, the applicant will be automatically notified via e-mail of the approval/rejection of the request.

The above procedure, which involves two main routines (in the following, we will denote them as R1 and R2), is performed manually by an employee of the Administration Office of DIAG, and it should be repeated for any new travel request. Routines such as these ones are good candidates to be encoded with executable scripts and enacted by means of a SW robot within a commercial RPA tool. However, unless there

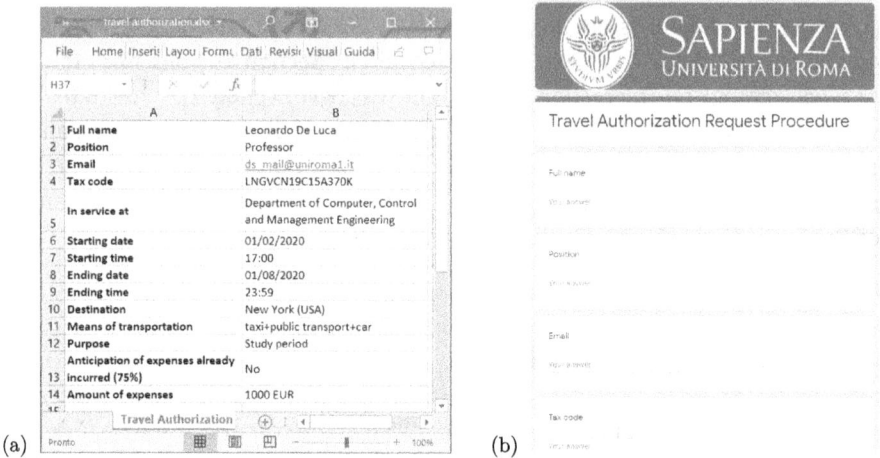

Figure 2: UIs involved in the running example.

is complete a priori knowledge of the specific routines that are enacted on the UI and of their concrete composition (this may happen only if the exact sequence of user actions required to achieve the routines' targets on the UI is recorded in the context of controlled training sessions), their automated identification from a UI log is challenging, since the associated user actions may be scattered across the log, interleaved with other actions that are not part of the routine under analysis, and potentially shared by many routines.

11.3 Preliminaries

In this section, we present some preliminary concepts used throughout the chapter. In Section 11.3.1, we describe the Petri Net modeling language, which will be used to formally specify the interaction models required to represent the structure of the routines of interest, while in Section 11.3.2 we introduce the notion of UI log.

11.3.1 Interaction models as Petri Nets

The research literature is rich of notations for expressing human–computer dialogs as interaction models that allow to see at a glance the structure of a user interaction with a UI (Paternò, 1999; Dix et al., 2004). Existing notations can be categorized in two main classes: *diagrammatic* and *textual*. Diagrammatic notations include (among others) various forms of state transition networks (STNs) (Wasserman, 1985), Petri nets (Sy et al., 2000), Harel state charts (Statecharts, 1987), flow charts (Dix et al., 2004), JSD diagrams (Sutcliffe and Wang, 1991), and ConcurTaskTrees (CTT) (Mori et al., 2002). Textual notations include regular expressions (van Den Bos et al., 1983), Linear Temporal Logic (LTL) (Pnueli, 1977), Communicating Sequential Processes (CSPs) (Dignum, 2004), GOMS (John and Kieras, 1996), modal action logic (Campos et al., 2016), and BNF and production rules (Feary, 2010).

While there are major differences in expressive power between different notations, an increased expressive power is not always desirable as it may suggest a harder to understand description, i. e., the dialog of a UI can become unmanageable (Dix et al., 2004). To guarantee a good trade-off between expressive power and understandability of the models, we decided to use *Petri Nets* for their specification. Petri Nets have proven to be adequate for defining interaction models (Dix et al., 2004; Palanque and Petri, 1995; Marrella and Catarci, 2018). They may contain exclusive choices, parallel branches, and loops, allowing the representation of extremely complex behaviors in a very compact way. Last but not least, Petri Nets provide a formal semantics, which allows to interpret the meaning of an interaction model unambiguously.

From a formal point of view, a Petri Net $W = (P, T, S)$ is a directed graph with a set P of nodes called *places* and a set T of *transitions*. The nodes are connected via directed arcs $S \subseteq (P \times T) \cup (T \times P)$. Connections between two nodes of the same type are not allowed. Places are represented by circles and transitions by rectangles. Figures 3 and 4 illustrate the Petri Nets used to represent the interaction models of R1 and R2. Transitions are associated with *labels* reflecting the user actions (e. g., system commands executed, buttons clicked, etc.) required to accomplish a routine on the UI.

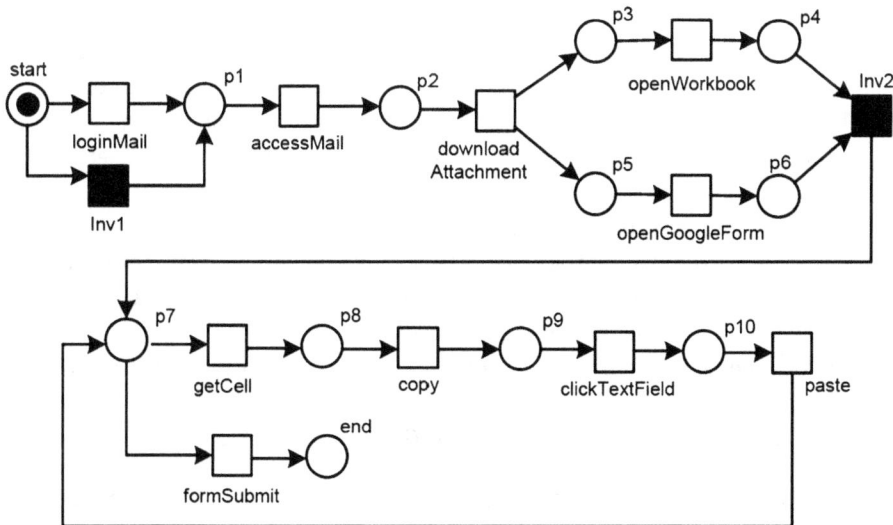

Figure 3: Interaction model for R1.

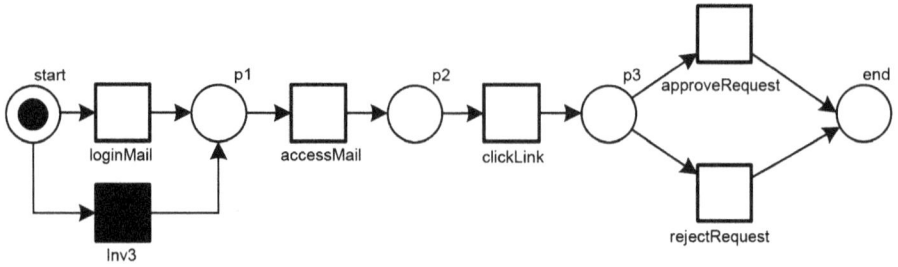

Figure 4: Interaction model for R2.

For example, a proper execution of R1 requires a path on the UI made by the following user actions:
- loginMail, to access the client e-mail;
- accessMail, to access the specific e-mail with the travel request;
- downloadAttachment, to download the Excel file including the travel request;
- openWorkbook, to open the Excel spreadsheet;
- openGoogleForm, to access the Google Form to be filled;
- getCell, to select the cell in the i-th row of the Excel spreadsheet;
- copy, to copy the content of the selected cell;
- clickTextField, to select the specific text field of the Google form where the content of the cell should be pasted;
- paste, to paste the content of the cell into the corresponding text field of the Google form;
- formSubmit, to press the button to finally submit the Google form to the internal database.

Note that, as shown in Figure 3, the user actions openWorkbook and openGoogleForm can be performed in any order. Moreover, the sequence of actions ⟨getCell, copy, clickTextField, paste⟩ will be repeated for any travel information to be moved from the Excel spreadsheet to the Google form. On the other hand, the path of user actions in the UI to properly enact R2 is as follows:
- loginMail, to access the client e-mail;
- accessMail, to access the specific e-mail with the request for travel insurance;
- clickLink, to click the link included in the e-mail that opens the Google form with the request to activate the travel insurance on a web browser;
- approveRequest, to press the button on the Google form that approves the request;
- rejectRequest, to press the button on the Google form that rejects the request.

Note that the execution of approveRequest and rejectRequest is exclusive. Then, in the interaction models of R1 and R2, there are transitions that do not represent user actions but are needed to correctly represent the structure of such models. These transitions, drawn with a black-filled rectangle, are said to be "invisible," and are not recorded in the UI logs (cf. Inv1, Inv2, and Inv3).

To understand our segmentation technique based on trace alignment in process mining, we also need to briefly illustrate the dynamic behavior of a Petri Net, i. e., its operational semantics. Given a transition $t \in T$, $^{\bullet}t$ is used to indicate the set of *input places* of t, which are the places p with a directed arc from p to t (i. e., such that $(p,t) \in S$). Similarly, $t^{\bullet}$ indicates the set of *output places*, namely, the places p with a direct arc from t to p. At any time, a place can contain zero or more *tokens*, drawn as black dots. The state of a Petri Net, i. e., its *marking*, is determined by the number of tokens in places. Therefore, a marking m is a function $m : P \rightarrow \mathbb{N}$. In any run of a Petri net, the number of tokens in places may change, i. e., the Petri Net marking. A transition t is *enabled* at a marking m iff each input place contains at least one token, i. e., $\forall p \in {}^{\bullet}t, m(p) > 0$. A transition t can *fire* at a marking m if and only if it is enabled. As a result of firing a transition t, one token is "consumed" from each input place and one is "produced" in each output place. This is denoted as $m \xrightarrow{t} m'$. In the remainder, given a sequence of transition firing $\sigma = \langle t_1, \ldots, t_n \rangle \in T^*$, $m_0 \xrightarrow{\sigma} m_n$ is used to indicate $m_0 \xrightarrow{t_1} m_1 \xrightarrow{t_2} \ldots \xrightarrow{t_n} m_n$, i. e., m_n is *reachable* from m_0.

Since the executions of a routine have a start and a end, the interaction models represented through Petri Nets need to be associated with an initial and final marking. For example, in both routines of Figures 3 and 4, the markings with respectively one token in place *start* or in place *end* are the initial and final marking (and no tokens in any other place). In the remainder of this paper, we assume all Petri Nets to be 1-bounded. A Petri Net is 1-bounded if in any reachable marking from the initial marking, no place ever contains more than 1 token. One-boundedness is not a large limitation as the behavior allowed by interaction models can be represented as 1-bounded Petri Nets (Dix et al., 2004; Marrella and Catarci, 2018).

11.3.2 UI logs

A single UI log in its raw form consists of a long sequence of user actions recorded during one user session.[1] Such actions include all the steps required to accomplish one or more relevant routines using the UI of one or many SW applications. For instance, in Figure 5, we show a snapshot of a UI log captured using a dedicated action logger[2] during the execution of R1 and R2. The employed action logger enables to record the *events* that happened on the UI, enriched with several data fields describing their "anatomy." For a given event, such fields are useful to keep track of the name and the

---

[1] We interpret a user session as a group of interactions that a single user takes within a given time frame on the UI of a specific computer system.

[2] The working of the action logger is described in Agostinelli et al. (2020). The tool is available at https://github.com/bpm-diag/smartRPA

	A	B	C	D	E	F	G	H	I	J	
1	timestamp	user	category	application	event type	event src path	clipboard content	workbook	worksheet	cell content	
2	2020-04-06 13:47	Simone	Mail	Outlook	loginMail						R2
3	2020-04-06 13:47	Simone	Mail	Outlook	accessMail						
4	2020-04-06 13:47	Simone	Mail	Outlook	downloadAttachment						R1
5	2020-04-06 13:47	Simone	MicrosoftOffice	Microsoft Excel	openWorkbook	C:\Users\Simone\Desktop\richiesta missione ac	richiesta missione.xlsx	Foglio1		
6	2020-04-06 13:47	Simone	MicrosoftOffice	Microsoft Excel	openWindow	C:\Users\Simone\Desktop		richiesta missione.xlsx	Foglio1		
7	2020-04-06 13:47	Simone	MicrosoftOffice	Microsoft Excel	afterCalculate						
8	2020-04-06 13:47	Simone	MicrosoftOffice	Microsoft Excel	resizeWindow	C:\Users\Simone\Desktop		richiesta missione.xlsx	Foglio1		
9	2020-04-06 13:47	Simone	Browser	Chrome	openGoogleForm						
10	2020-04-06 13:47	Simone	MicrosoftOffice	Microsoft Excel	getCell			richiesta missione.xlsx	Foglio1	Simone Agostinelli	R1
11	2020-04-06 13:47	Simone	Clipboard	Clipboard	copy		Simone Agostinelli				
12	2020-04-06 13:47	Simone	Browser	Chrome	clickTextField						
13	2020-04-06 13:48	Simone	Mail	Outlook	clickLink						R2
14	2020-04-06 13:48	Simone	Browser	Chrome	paste		Simone Agostinelli				R1
15	2020-04-06 13:48	Simone	Browser	Chrome	changeField						
16	2020-04-06 13:48	Simone	Browser	Chrome	approveRequest						R2
17	2020-04-06 13:48	Simone	MicrosoftOffice	Microsoft Excel	getCell			richiesta missione.xlsx	Foglio1	Dottorando	R1
18	2020-04-06 13:48	Simone	Clipboard	Clipboard	copy		Dottorando				
19	2020-04-06 13:48	Simone	MicrosoftOffice	Microsoft Excel	resizeWindow	C:\Users\Simone\Desktop		richiesta missione.xlsx	Foglio1		
20	2020-04-06 13:48	Simone	Browser	Chrome	clickTextField						R1
21	2020-04-06 13:48	Simone	Browser	Chrome	paste		Dottorando				

Figure 5: Snapshot of a UI log captured during the executions of R1 and R2.

timestamp of the user action performed on the UI, the involved SW application, the human/SW resource that performed the action, etc.

For the sake of understandability, we assume here that any user action associated to each event recorded in the UI log is mapped at most with one (and only one) Petri Net transition, and that the collection of labels associated to the Petri Net transitions is defined over the same alphabet as the user actions in the UI log,[3] i. e., the alphabet of user actions in the UI log is a *superset* of that used for defining the labels of Petri Net transitions. In the running example, we can recognize in R1 and R2 a universe of user actions of interest $Z = \{A, B, C, D, E, F, G, H, I, L, M, N, O\}$, such that $A = \mathsf{loginMail}$, $B = \mathsf{accessMail}$, $C = \mathsf{downloadAttachment}$, $D = \mathsf{openWorkbook}$, $E = \mathsf{openGoogleForm}$, $F = \mathsf{getCell}$, $G = \mathsf{copy}$, $H = \mathsf{clickTextField}$, $I = \mathsf{paste}$, $L = \mathsf{formSubmit}$, $M = \mathsf{clickLink}$, $N = \mathsf{approveRequest}$, and $O = \mathsf{rejectRequest}$.

As shown in Figure 5, a UI log is not specifically recorded to capture pre-identified routines. A UI log may contain multiple and interleaved executions of one or many routines (cf. in Figure 5 the blue/red boxes that group the user actions belonging to R1 and R2, respectively), as well as redundant behavior and noise. We consider as *redundant* any user action that is unnecessarily repeated during the execution of a routine, e. g., a text value that is first pasted in a wrong field by mistake and then is moved in the right place through a corrective action on the UI. On the other hand, we consider as *noise* all those user actions that do not contribute to the achievement of any routine target, e. g., a window that is resized. In Figure 5, the sequences of user actions that are not surrounded by a blue/red box can be safely labeled as noise.

Based on the foregoing, our segmentation technique aims at extracting from the UI log all those user actions that match a distinguishable pattern as represented by the interaction model of a generic routine R, filtering out redundant actions and noise. To be more specific, any sequence of user actions in the UI log that can be replayed from

---

3 In de Leoni and Marrella (2017), it is shown how these assumptions can be removed.

the initial to the final marking of the Petri Net-based interaction model of R is said to be a *routine trace* of R, i. e., a complete execution instance of R within the UI log. For example, a valid routine trace of R1 is $\langle A, B, C, D, E, F, G, H, I, L \rangle$. The interaction model of R1 suggests that valid routine traces are also those ones where (1) A is skipped (if the user is already logged in the client e-mail); (2) the pair of actions $\langle D, E \rangle$ is performed in reverse order; (3) the sequence of actions $\langle F, G, H, I \rangle$ is executed several times before submitting the Google form. On the other hand, two main routine traces can be extracted from R2: $\langle A, B, M, N \rangle$ and $\langle A, B, M, O \rangle$, again with the possibility to skip A, i. e., the access to the client e-mail. Note that within a routine trace, the concept of time is usually defined in a way that user actions in a trace are sorted according to the timestamp of their occurrence.

We conclude this section by introducing the concept of *routine-based* log as a special container that stores all the routine traces extracted by a UI log and associated to a generic routine R. Thus, the final outcome of our segmentation technique will be a collection of as many routine-based logs as are the interaction models of the routines of interest.

11.4 Segmentation

Given a UI log consisting of events including user actions having the same granularity[4] and potentially belonging to different routines, in the RPA domain *segmentation* is the task of clustering parts of the log together which belong to the same routine. In a nutshell, the challenge is to automatically understand which user actions contribute to which routines, and organize such user actions in well-bounded routine traces Agostinelli et al. (2019), Leno et al. (2020b).

As shown in Section 11.3.2, in general a UI log stores information about several routines enacted in an interleaved fashion, with the possibility that a specific user action is shared by different routines. Furthermore, actions providing redundant behavior or not belonging to any of the routine under observation may be recorded in the log, generating noise that should be filtered out by a segmentation technique. We can distinguish among three main forms of UI logs, which can be categorized according to the fact that (1) any user action in the log exclusively belongs to a specific routine; (2) the log records the execution of many routines that do not have any user action in common; (3) the log records the execution of many routines, and the possibility exists that some performed user actions are shared by many routines at the same time. In the following, we analyze in detail case by case.

---

4 The UI logs created by generic action loggers usually consist of low-level events associated one-by-one to a recorded user action on the UI (e. g., mouse clicks, etc.). We will discuss the abstraction issue in Section 11.6, where state-of-the-art techniques are shown that enable to flatten the content of a log to a same granularity level.

– **Case 1:** This is the case when a UI log captures many executions of the same routine. Of course, in this scenario it is not possible to distinguish between shared and non-shared user actions by different routines, since the UI log keeps track only of executions associated to a single routine.

Starting from our running example in Section 11.2, let us consider the simplest case of a UI log U that records a sequence of user actions resulting from many non-interleaved executions of R1: $U = \{A_{11}, B_{11}, C_{11}, D_{11}, E_{11}, F_{11}, G_{11}, H_{11}, I_{11}, L_{11}, \ldots, A_{12}, B_{12}, C_{12}, D_{12}, E_{12}, F_{12}, G_{12}, H_{12}, I_{12}, L_{12}\}$. For the sake of understandability, we use a numerical subscript ij associated to any user action to indicate that it belongs to the j-th execution of the i-th routine under study. Of course, this information is not recorded in the UI log, and discovering it (i. e., the identification of the subscripts) is one of the "implicit" effects of segmentation when routine traces are built. Applying a segmentation technique to the above UI log would trivially produce a routine-based log U_{R1} where the (already well-bounded) executions of R1 are organized as different routine traces: $U_{R1} = \{\langle A_{11}, B_{11}, C_{11}, D_{11}, E_{11}, F_{11}, G_{11}, H_{11}, I_{11}, L_{11}, \rangle, \ldots, \langle A_{12}, B_{12}, C_{12}, D_{12}, E_{12}, F_{12}, G_{12}, H_{12}, I_{12}, L_{12}\rangle\}$.

The same routine-based log U_{R1} would be obtained when the executions of R1 are recorded in an interleaved fashion in the UI log, e. g., $U = \{A, B_{11}, B_{12}, C_{11}, D_{11}, C_{12}, D_{12}, E_{12}, F_{12}, G_{12}, H_{12}, I_{12}, L_{12}, E_{11}, F_{11}, G_{11}, H_{11}, I_{11}, L_{11}, \ldots\}$. Here, the segmentation task becomes more challenging, not only because the user actions of different executions of a same routine are interleaved among each others, and it is not known a priori to which execution they belong, but also for the presence of some user actions that potentially belong *at the same time* to many executions of the routine itself. This is the case of A (that corresponds to loginMail), which can be performed exactly once at the beginning of a user session and can be "shared" by many executions of the same routine.

Another variant is when the execution of a routine is affected by *noise* or *redundant* actions. For example, let us consider the following UI log recorded after many executions of R1: $U = \{A_{11}, B_{11}, C_{11}, \boldsymbol{Y_1}, D_{11}, E_{11}, F_{11}, G_{11}, G_{11}, G_{11}, H_{11}, I_{11}, L_{11}, \ldots, A_{12}, \boldsymbol{Y_{n-1}}, B_{12}, C_{12}, D_{12}, E_{12}, \boldsymbol{Y_n}, F_{12}, G_{12}, H_{12}, I_{12}, I_{12}, I_{12}, L_{12}\}$. This log contains elements of noise, i. e., user actions $\boldsymbol{Y_{k \in \{1,n\}}} \in Z$ (recall that Z is the universe of user actions allowed by a UI log, as introduced in Section 11.3.2) that are not allowed by R1, and redundant actions like G_{11} (copy action) and I_{12} (paste action) that are unnecessarily repeated multiple times. Noise and redundant actions need to be filtered out during the segmentation task because they do not contribute to the achievement of the routine's target.

– **Case 2:** In this case, a UI log captures many executions of different routines, with the assumption that the interaction models of such routines include only transitions associated to user actions that are exclusive for those routines. For example, let us suppose that in both interaction models of R1 and R2 the transitions $\boldsymbol{A}$ and $\boldsymbol{B}$

are not required, and the UI log is as follows: $U = \{C_{11}, D_{11}, E_{11}, F_{11}, G_{11}, H_{11}, I_{11}, L_{11},$ $M_{21}, N_{21}, \ldots, C_{12}, D_{12}, E_{12}, F_{12}, G_{12}, H_{12}, I_{12}, L_{12}, M_{22}, O_{22}\}$. The output of the segmentation task would consist of two routine-based logs, one per routine, which include the following routine traces:

- $U_{R1} = \{\langle C_{11}, D_{11}, E_{11}, F_{11}, G_{11}, H_{11}, I_{11}, L_{11}\rangle, \ldots, \langle C_{12}, D_{12}, E_{12}, F_{12}, G_{12}, H_{12}, I_{12}, L_{12}\rangle\}$;
- $U_{R2} = \{\langle M_{21}, N_{21}\rangle, \ldots, \langle M_{22}, O_{22}\rangle\}$.

Similarly to what was already seen in Case 1, it may happen that many executions of the same routine (and, in this case, also of many different routines) are interleaved among each other, and that noise and redundant actions are also recorded in the log. Since we are assuming that there are no shared actions among different routines, the complexity of the segmentation task in the presence of interleaved actions, noise, and redundancy can be reduced to the case of a single routine; cf. Case 1.

- **Case 3**: In this case, a UI log captures many executions of different routines, and there exist user actions that are shared by such routines. This case perfectly reflects what happens in the running example of Section 11.2. Let us consider the following UI log: $U = \{A, B, C_{11}, D_{11}, E_{11}, F_{11}, G_{11}, H_{11}, I_{11}, L_{11}, B, M_{21}, N_{21}, \ldots, B, C_{12}, D_{12}, E_{12}, F_{12}, G_{12}, H_{12}, I_{12}, L_{12}, B, M_{22}, O_{22}\}$, where A and B are shared by R1 and R2, as they are included in the interaction models of both routines. By analyzing the log, it can be noted that A is *potentially involved* in the enactment of any execution of R1 and R2, while B is *required by all* executions of R1 and R2, but the association between the single executions of B and the routine executions they belong to is not clear. The complexity of the segmentation task here lies in understanding to which routine traces the execution of A and B belong. The outcome of the segmentation task will be a pair of routine-based logs generated as follows:
  - $U_{R1} = \{\langle A, B_{11}, C_{11}, D_{11}, E_{11}, F_{11}, G_{11}, H_{11}, I_{11}, L_{11}\rangle, \ldots, \langle A, B_{12}, C_{12}, D_{12}, E_{12}, F_{12}, G_{12}, H_{12}, I_{12}, L_{12}\rangle\}$;
  - $U_{R2} = \{\langle A, B_{21}, M_{21}, N_{21}\rangle, \ldots, \langle A, B_{22}, M_{22}, O_{22}\rangle\}$.

  Consider that while A can belong to some routine executions and not to others, making it impossible to understand to which exact routine execution it can be associated, in the case of B it is important to identify the association between its i-th execution and the specific routine execution it belongs to.

The above cases have in common that all the user actions are stored within a single UI log. It may happen that the same routine is spread across multiple UI logs, in particular when there are multiple users that are involved in the execution of the routine on different computer systems. This case can be tackled by "merging" the UI logs where the routine execution is distributed into a single UI log, reducing the segmentation issue to one of the already analyzed cases.

11.5 Segmentation technique

In this section, we present our technique to tackle the segmentation issue of UI logs that leverages trace alignment in process mining for deriving the boundaries of a routine by analyzing the UI log that keeps track of its execution, in order to cluster all user actions associated with the routine itself in well-bounded routine traces. Specifically, in Section 11.5.1, we first provide the relevant background on trace alignment. Then, in Section 11.5.2, we present an overview of the general approach underlying our segmentation technique depicting its main steps, and we describe the technical details of the algorithm that implements the technique.

11.5.1 Alignment between UI logs and interaction models as Petri Nets

Trace alignment (Adriansyah et al., 2011; de Leoni and Marrella, 2017; de Leoni et al., 2018) is a conformance checking technique within process mining that is employed to replay the content of any trace of an event log against a process model represented as a Petri Net, one event at a time. For each trace in the log, the technique identifies the closest corresponding trace that can be parsed by the model, i. e., an *alignment*, together with a *fitness* value, which quantifies how much the trace adheres to the process model. The fitness value can vary from 0 to 1. A fitness value equal to 1 means a perfect matching between the trace and the model.

We perform trace alignment by constructing an alignment of a UI log U (note that we can consider the entire content of the UI log as a single trace) and an interaction model W as a Petri Net, which allows us to exactly pinpoint where deviations occur. To this aim, the events in U need to be related to transitions in the model, and vice versa. Building this alignment is far from trivial, since the log may deviate from the model at an arbitrary number of places. To be more specific, we need to relate "moves" in the log to "moves" in the model in order to establish an alignment between an interaction model and a UI log. However, it may be that some of the moves in the log cannot be mimicked by the model and vice versa. We explicitly denote such "no moves" by $\gg$.

Definition 11.5.1 (Alignment moves). Let $W = (P, T, S)$ be a Petri Net and let U be a UI log. A legal *alignment move* for W and U is represented by a pair $(q_U, q_W) \in (T \cup \{\gg\} \times T \cup \{\gg\}) \setminus \{(\gg, \gg)\}$ such that:

- (q_U, q_W) is a *move in log* if $q_U \neq \gg$ and $q_W = \gg$;
- (q_U, q_W) is a *move in model* if $q_U = \gg$ and $q_W \in T$;
- (q_U, q_W) is a *synchronous move* if $q_U = q_W$.

An alignment is a sequence of alignment moves.

Definition 11.5.2 (Alignment). Let $W = (P, T, S)$ be a Petri Net with an initial marking and final marking denoted with m_i and m_f. Let also U be a UI log. Let Γ_W be the universe of all alignment moves for W and U. Sequence $y \in \Gamma_W^*$ is an *alignment* of W and U if, ignoring all occurrences of $\gg$, the projection on the first element yields U and the projection on the second yields a sequence $\sigma'' \in T^*$ such that $m_i \xrightarrow{\sigma''} m_f$.

A move in log for a transition t indicates that t occurred when not allowed; a move in model for a visible transition t indicates that t did not occur when, conversely, expected. Many alignments are possible for the same UI log and a Petri Net. For example, Figure 6 shows two possible alignments for a UI log consisting of the following sequence of user actions $\langle A, B, M, N \rangle$ and the Petri Net in Figure 4, representing the interaction model of R2. Note how moves are represented vertically. For example, as shown in Figure 6, the first move of y_1 is (A, A), i. e., a *synchronous move* of A, while the first and second moves of y_2 are a move in log and model, respectively. We aim at finding a complete alignment of U and W with minimal number of deviations (i. e., of moves in log/model) for visible transitions, also known in the literature as *optimal alignments*. With reference to the alignments in Figure 6, y_1 has four synchronous moves and y_2 has one move in log for visible transitions and one move in model for the invisible transition *Inv3* (that does not count for the computation of the fitness value). As a consequence, y_1 is an optimal alignment and can be returned. Note that its fitness value is exactly equal to 1, since it consists only of synchronous moves enabling U to be completely replayed from the initial to the final marking of W. For the sake of simplicity, we are assuming here that all the deviations have the same severity. However, the severity of a deviation can be customized on an ad hoc basis (de Leoni and Marrella, 2017).

$$y_1 = \frac{\begin{array}{|c|c|c|c|} A & B & M & N \end{array}}{\begin{array}{|c|c|c|c|} A & B & M & N \end{array}}$$

$$y_2 = \frac{\begin{array}{|c|c|c|c|c|} A & \gg & B & M & N \end{array}}{\begin{array}{|c|c|c|c|c|} \gg & Inv3 & B & M & N \end{array}}$$

Figure 6: Alignments of $\langle A, B, M, N \rangle$ and the Petri Net in Figure 4.

11.5.2 The general approach and the segmentation algorithm

The general approach underlying our segmentation techniques consists of two methodological phases, *filtering* and *trace alignment*, to be applied in sequence, as shown in Figure 7. Algorithm 1 shows the technical details of the algorithm that concretely implements such phases.

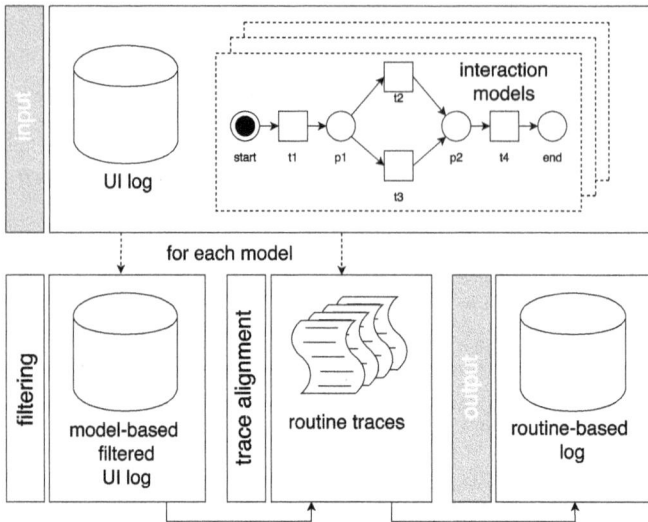

Figure 7: Overview of the general approach underlying the proposed segmentation technique.

The algorithm takes as input a UI log U and a set of interaction models W_{set} and returns a set of routine-based logs U_{set}. For each interaction model $w \in W_{set}$ (one for each routine of interest) represented as Petri Nets, the algorithm performs the following steps:

1. **Filtering**: The filtering phase is used to filter out noisy actions from the UI log. Specifically, for each interaction model $w \in W_{set}$, a local copy of the UI log U^w is created (line 3). Then, all user actions that appear in U^w but that cannot be replayed by any transition of w are removed from U^w. The output of this step is a *model-based filtered UI log* U_ϕ^w (line 4). Working with U_ϕ^w rather than with U^w will allow us to apply the trace alignment technique neglecting all the potential moves in the log with user actions that could never be replayed by w. As a consequence, this will drastically reduce the number of alignment steps required to find optimal alignments, and at the same time optimize the performance of the algorithm. Before moving to the next step, a new routine-based log U_R^w is initialized (line 5).

2. **Trace alignment**: The second step consists of applying the trace alignment technique discussed in Section 11.5.1 for any interaction model $w \in W_{set}$ and its associated model-based filtered UI log U_ϕ^w. This enables to extract from U_ϕ^w all those user actions that match a distinguishable pattern with w in the form of an optimal alignment γ^{opt} (line 7). Trace alignment allows to pinpoint the *synchronous moves* between U_ϕ^w and w. If they exist, the user actions involved in synchronous moves are extracted and stored into γ_{sm}^{opt} (line 8). Note that focusing just on syn-

---

Algorithm 1: Algorithm implementing our segmentation technique.

Parameters: a UI log U, a set of interaction models W_{set}

Result: A set U_{set} of routine-based logs

1   $U_{set} \leftarrow \emptyset$;

2   **forall** $w \in W_{set}$ **do**

3      $U^w \leftarrow duplicate(U)$;

4      $U^w_\phi \leftarrow filter(U^w)$;

5      $U^w_R \leftarrow \emptyset$;

6   **repeat**

7          $\gamma^{opt} \leftarrow$ *trace alignment* (U^w_ϕ, w);

8          $\gamma^{opt}_{sm} \leftarrow extract(\gamma^{opt})$;

9   **if** γ^{opt}_{sm} *is not empty* **then**

10   create a trace τ_{sm} from γ^{opt}_{sm};

11   create a temporary UI log U^w_{sm} from τ_{sm};

12             $fitness \leftarrow$ compute fitness from *trace alignment* (U^w_{sm}, w);

13   **if** $fitness$ *is 1* **then**

14   add τ_{sm} to U^w_R;

15   **else**

16   discard τ_{sm};

17   **end**

18   remove the events associated to τ_{sm} from U^w_ϕ;

19   **end**

20   **until** γ^{opt}_{sm} *is not empty*;

21   add U^w_R to U_{set};

22 **end**

23 **return** U_{set}

---

chronous moves allows us to exclude all redundant user actions from the analysis. Then, the algorithm:

(a) creates a trace τ_{sm} consisting of the user actions associated with the synchronous moves stored in γ^{opt}_{sm} (line 10);

(b) creates a (temporary) UI log U^w_{sm} containing only the trace τ_{sm} (line 11), which is required to properly run (again) trace alignment;

(c) performs a new alignment between U^w_{sm} and w with the goal to compute the fitness value (line 12).

In the case the fitness value is equal to 1, this means that U^w_{sm} (and, consequently, τ_{sm}) can be replayed from the start to the final marking of w, making τ_{sm} a valid routine trace of w. In such a case, τ_{sm} is stored into U^w_R (line 14) and all the events associated to the synchronous moves in τ_{sm} are removed by U^w_ϕ (line 18). On the contrary, a fitness value lower than 1 indicates the presence of at least one move in the model in τ_{sm} with respect to w, i. e., τ_{sm} cannot be completely replayed by w and is not a valid routine trace, meaning that we can discard it (line 16).

The above two steps can be repeated until y_{sm}^{opt} is not empty (line 20), i. e., until there are synchronous moves in the computed alignment. At the end of the iteration, the routine-based log U_R^w is stored into U_{set} (line 21), and the algorithm starts to analyze the next interaction model into W_{set}. In conclusion, the algorithm computes a number of routine-based logs equal to the number of interaction models under study.

It is worth to notice that: (i) for the computation of the trace alignment, the algorithm relies on the highly scalable planning-based alignment technique implemented in our previous work (de Leoni and Marrella, 2017), which we have properly customized for our purposes; and (ii) the algorithm is able to achieve cases 1, 2, and 3 discussed in Section 11.4, except when there are interleaved executions of shared user actions by different routines. In that case, the risk exists that a shared user action is associated to a wrong routine execution, i. e., clustered in a wrong routine trace.

11.5.2.1 An execution instance of the segmentation algorithm

We show now an execution instance of Algorithm 1 applied to the following UI log: $U = \{A, B, C, Y_1, D, E, F, G, G, G, H, I, L, B, M, N, \ldots, B, Y_{n-1}, C, D, E, Y_n, F, G, H, I, I, I, L, B, M, O\}$. The log contains elements of noise, i. e., user actions $Y_{k \in \{1,n\}}$ that are not allowed by R1 and R2, and redundant actions like G and I that are unnecessarily repeated multiple times. In addition, A and B are shared by R1 and R2, as they are included in the interaction models of both routines. In particular, A is potentially involved in the enactment of any execution of R1 and R2, while B is required by all executions of R1 and R2.

The algorithm takes as input (1) the UI log U and (2) the interaction models of R1 and R2, and computes a set of routine-based logs U_{set} by executing the following steps:
- (line 1): initializes the set of interaction models U_{set};
- (line 2): iterates on the interaction models of R1 and R2; for the sake of space, we focus only on the steps computed in the case of R1;
- (line 3): creates a local copy of U, namely U^w;
- (line 4): filters U^w from noise, so $U_\phi^w = \{A, B, C, D, E, F, G, G, G, H, I, L, B, \ldots, B, C, D, E, F, G, H, I, I, I, L, B\}$; in this step, the user actions $Y_{k \in \{1,n\}}$ and M, N, M (being exclusively related to R2) are filtered out by the log; on the other hand, redundant actions still remain in the log;
- (line 5): initializes the routine-based log U_R^w;

- (line 7): computes the trace alignment between U_ϕ^w and the interaction model of R1, namely, w;

$$\gamma^{\mathrm{opt}} = \frac{A|B|C|D|E|F|G|G|G|H|I|L|B|\ldots|B}{A|B|C|D|E|F|G|\gg|\gg|H|I|L|\gg|\ldots|\gg}$$

- (line 8): extracts the synchronous moves from γ^{opt} into $\gamma_{\mathrm{sm}}^{\mathrm{opt}}$;
- (line 9): evaluates to True, as $\gamma_{\mathrm{sm}}^{\mathrm{opt}}$ is not empty;
- (line 10): computes the trace τ_{sm} starting from $\gamma_{\mathrm{sm}}^{\mathrm{opt}}$, so $\tau_{\mathrm{sm}} = \langle A, B, C, D, E, F, G, H, I, L\rangle$;
- (line 11): adds the trace τ_{sm} in U_{sm}^w;
- (line 12): computes trace alignment between U_{sm}^w and w;

$$\frac{A|B|C|D|E|F|G|H|I|L}{A|B|C|D|E|F|G|H|I|L}$$

U_{sm}^w can be replayed without deviations from the start to the final marking of w, meaning a perfect fitness between the log and the interaction model;
- (line 13): evaluates to True, as the fitness of the alignment (cf. line 12) is equal to 1;
- (line 14): adds τ_{sm} in U_R^w, i. e., τ_{sm} is recognized as a valid routine trace;
- (line 18): removes all the events associated with the synchronous moves in τ_{sm} from U_ϕ^w; thus, $U_\phi^w = \{G, G, B, \ldots, B, C, D, E, F, G, H, I, I, I, L, B\}$;
- (line 20): since $\gamma_{\mathrm{sm}}^{\mathrm{opt}}$ is not empty, the algorithm comes back to line 6.
  After repeating the above steps from line 7 to line 14, the algorithm discovers a second routine trace $\tau_{\mathrm{sm}} = \langle B, C, D, E, F, G, H, I, L\rangle$ and adds it to U_R^w. Like before, all the events associated with the synchronous moves in τ_{sm} are removed from U_ϕ^w. Thus, $U_\phi^w = \{G, G, B, \ldots, I, I, B\}$.
  The subsequent iterations of the algorithm do not discover new routine traces for R1, since the only synchronous moves extracted in the various alignment steps between w and U_ϕ^w are the Bs, Gs, and Is that are discarded (due to the fitness value of $\gamma_{\mathrm{sm}}^{\mathrm{opt}}$ that is < 1). It is worth to notice that redundant user actions G and I are removed from U_ϕ^w during these iterations. The algorithm ends to iterate when $\gamma_{\mathrm{sm}}^{\mathrm{opt}}$ is empty, that is, when there are no more synchronous moves to extract;
- (line 21): after the last iteration ends, the routine-based log U_R^w is stored into U_{set}, and the algorithm starts to analyze the interaction model of R2.

The outcome of the segmentation task will be a set of routine-based logs (in this case two, since the number of interaction models under study is two) generated as follows:
$U_{\mathrm{set}} = \{\{\langle A, B_{11}, C_{11}, D_{11}, E_{11}, F_{11}, G_{11}, H_{11}, I_{11}, L_{11}\rangle, \ldots, \langle B_{12}, C_{12}, D_{12}, E_{12}, F_{12}, G_{12}, H_{12}, I_{12}, L_{12}\rangle\}, \{\langle A, B_{21}, M_{21}, N_{21}\rangle, \ldots, \langle B_{22}, M_{22}, O_{22}\rangle\}\}$.

11.6 Related work

In the field of RPA, segmentation is an issue still not so much explored, since the current practice adopted by commercial RPA tools for identifying the routine steps often consists of detailed observations of workers conducting their daily work. Such observations are then "converted" in explicit flowchart diagrams (Jimenez-Ramirez et al., 2019), which are manually modeled by expert RPA analysts to depict all the potential behaviors (i. e., the traces) of a specific routine. In this setting, as the routine traces have been already (implicitly) identified, segmentation can be neglected.

On the other hand, following a similar trend that has been occurring in the business process management (BPM) domain (Marrella et al., 2018; Marrella, 2019), the research on RPA is moving towards the application of intelligent techniques to automate all the steps of a RPA project, as proven by many recent works in this direction (see below). In this context, segmentation can be considered as one of the "hot" key research topics to investigate (Agostinelli et al., 2019; Leno et al., 2020b).

With regard to previous works, even if more focused on traditional business processes in BPM rather than on RPA routines, Fazzinga et al. (2018) comes closest to our technique. This work proposes a probabilistic interpretation approach that employs predefined behavioral models to establish which process activities (generated by an arbitrary number of process instances) belong to which process model. Similarly to Fazzinga et al. (2018), our segmentation technique falls in the supervised category, as it can be applied only in the presence of pre-defined interaction models in input. On the other hand, differently from Fazzinga et al. (2018), our approach is not probabilistic, but is thoroughly quantitative, based on the computation of fitness values.

In Bosco et al. (2019), the authors provide a method to analyze UI logs in order to discover routines that are fully deterministic and thus amenable for automation. The method combines a technique for compressing a set of sequences of user actions into an acyclic automaton using rule mining techniques and data transformations. However, this approach is effective in the case of UI logs that keep track of well-bounded routine executions, and becomes inadequate when the UI log records information about several routines whose actions are potentially interleaved.

In Leno et al. (2020a), the authors propose a technique to identify candidate routines to be automated starting from an unsegmented UI log. The technique is able to discover the execution traces of a specific routine relying on the automated synthesis of a control-flow graph that describes the observed directly follow relations between the user actions. The technique in Leno et al. (2020a) is effective to tackle some simple variants of Case 1 and Case 2 (cf. Section 11.4), while it loses accuracy in the presence of recurrent noise and interleaved routine executions.

In Gao et al. (2019), the authors propose a self-learning approach to automatically detect high-level RPA rules from captured historical low-level behavior logs. An if-then-else deduction logic is used to infer rules from behavior logs by learning relations between the different routines performed in the past. Then, such rules are employed to facilitate the SW robots instantiation. A similar approach is adopted in Le and Gulwani (2014), where the *FlashExtract* framework is presented. FlashExtract allows to extract relevant data from semi-structured documents using input–output examples, from which one can derive some relations underlying the working of a routine. Differently from our segmentation technique, which is able to extract the routine traces, i. e., the concrete behaviors of a routine, the above works allow to discover partial views of the working of a routine.

There exist other approaches that focus on learning the anatomy of routines not analyzing UI logs but from natural language descriptions of the procedures underlying such routines. In this direction, the work (Ito et al., 2020) defines a new grammar for complex workflows with chaining machine-executable meaning representations for semantic parsing. In Leopold et al. (2018), the authors provide an approach to learn activities from text documents employing supervised machine learning techniques such as feature extraction and support vector machine training. Similarly, in Han et al. (2020) the authors adopt a deep learning approach based on long short-term memory (LSTM) recurrent neural networks to learn the relationship between user actions.

Moreover, even if the target is not to resolve the segmentation issue, many research works exist that analyze UI logs at different levels of abstraction and that can be potentially useful to realize segmentation techniques. With the term *"abstraction"* we mean that groups of user actions are to be interpreted as executions of high-level activities. In Baier et al. (2014), the authors present a semi-automated approach for finding a set of candidate mappings between the user actions stored in a UI log and instances of high-level activities. This scenario requires a human-in-the-loop to be involved in the filtering phase to resolve the ambiguities on the mapping between user actions and activities. The work (Baier et al., 2015) proposes a method to find a global one-to-one mapping between the user actions that appear in the UI log and the high-level activities of a given interaction model. This method leverages constraint satisfaction techniques to reduce the set of candidate mappings. Similarly, in Ferreira et al. (2014), starting from a state machine model describing the routine of interest in terms of high-level activities, the authors employ heuristic techniques to find a mapping from a "micro-sequence" of user actions to the "macro-sequence" of activities in the state machine model. Finally, in Mannhardt et al. (2018), a technique is presented that maps low-level event types to multiple high-level activities (while the event instances, i. e., with a specific timestamp in the log, can be coupled with a single high-level activity). However, segmentation techniques in RPA must enable to associate low-level event instances (corresponding to our UI actions) to multiple routines.

In addition to the above supervised techniques, there are unsupervised techniques (Günther et al., 2009; Bose and van der Aalst, 2009; Folino et al., 2014, 2015) that try to convert each sequence of user actions into a sequence of higher-level activities without any background knowledge on the structure of the routines whose execution generates the UI log. Starting from the UI log, such works exploit clustering techniques to aggregate user actions into clusters, where any cluster represents a high-level activity associated to a well-defined sequence of user actions. The final outcome is an abstracted view of the UI log, obtained by replacing each user action with a label identifying the cluster containing it.

11.7 Conclusion

To tackle the *segmentation* challenge, in this chapter we have presented a technique, coupled with a supervised algorithm, leveraging trace alignment in process mining to identify sequences of user actions in a UI log that belong to specific routine executions, clustering them in well-bounded routine traces. Our work is based on a supervised assumption since we know a priori the structure of the routines, namely, the interaction models. Despite this limitation, we consider this contribution as an important first step towards the development of a more complete and unsupervised technique to the segmentation of UI logs.

In this direction, as a future work, we are going to perform a robust evaluation of the algorithm on synthetic and real-world case studies with heterogeneous UI logs. In addition, we aim at relaxing the supervised assumption in different ways: (1) by employing declarative rules (Pesic et al., 2007) rather than Petri Nets to represent interaction models, allowing us to reason over a partial knowledge of the working of the routines; (2) by investigating *sequential pattern mining* techniques (Dong, 2009) to examine frequent sequences of user actions having common data attributes; (3) by analyzing *web log mining* techniques (Mobasher and Nasraoui, 2011), whose input is a set of clickstreams and the goal is to extract sessions where a user engages with a web application to fulfill a goal; (4) by employing *machine learning* techniques to automatically identify sequences of user actions associated with a routine execution without any previous knowledge of the routines' structure.

Bibliography

Adriansyah A, Sidorova N, van Dongen BF (2011) Cost-based fitness in conformance checking. In: Int conf on application of concurrency to system design. IEEE, pp 57–66

Agostinelli S, Marrella A, Mecella M (2019) Research challenges for intelligent robotic process automation. In: Business process management workshops – BPM 2019 int workshops, pp 12–18

Agostinelli S, Lupia M, Marrella A, Mecella M (2020) Automated generation of executable RPA scripts from user interface logs. In: Business process management: blockchain and robotic process automation forum – BPM 2020 blockchain and RPA forum

Baier T, Mendling J, Weske M (2014) Bridging abstraction layers in process mining. Inf Sci 46:123–139

Baier T, Rogge-Solti A, Mendling J, Weske M (2015) Matching of events and activities: an approach based on behavioral constraint satisfaction. In: ACM symp on applied computing, pp 1225–1230

Bosco A, Augusto A, Dumas M, La Rosa M, Fortino G (2019) Discovering automatable routines from user interaction logs. In: Int conf on business process management (BPM'19), forum track, Vienna, Austria. Springer, pp 144–162

Bose RJC, van der Aalst WMP (2009) Abstractions in process mining: a taxonomy of patterns. In: Int conf on business process management. Springer, Berlin, pp 159–175

Campos JC, Sousa M, Alves MCB, Harrison MD (2016) Formal verification of a space system's user interface with the IVY workbench. IEEE SMC 46(2)

de Leoni M, Marrella A (2017) Aligning real process executions and prescriptive process models through automated planning. Expert Syst Appl 82:162–183

de Leoni M, Lanciano G, Marrella A (2018) Aligning partially-ordered process-execution traces and models using automated planning. In: Proc of the twenty-eight int conf on automated planning and scheduling (ICAPS 2018), pp 321–329

Dignum MV (2004) A model for organizational interaction: based on agents, founded in logic. In: SIKS

Dix A, Finlay J, Abowd G, Beale R (2004) Human-computer interaction. Pearson

Dong G (2009) Sequence data mining. Springer, Berlin. ISBN 1441943528, 9781441943521

Fazzinga B, Flesca S, Furfaro F, Masciari E, Pontieri L (2018) Efficiently interpreting traces of low level events in business process logs. Inf Syst 73:1–24

Feary MS (2010) A toolset for supporting iterative human automation: Interaction in design. NASA Ames Research Center

Ferreira DR, Szimanski F, Ralha CG (2014) Improving process models by mining mappings of low-level events to high-level activities. Intell Inf Syst 43(2):379–407

Folino F, Guarascio M, Pontieri L (2014) Mining predictive process models out of low-level multidimensional logs. In: Int conf on advanced information systems engineering. Springer, Berlin, pp 533–547

Folino F, Guarascio M, Pontieri L (2015) Mining multi-variant process models from low-level logs. In: Int conf on business information systems. Springer, Berlin, pp 165–177

Gao J, van Zelst SJ, Lu X, van der Aalst WMP (2019) Automated robotic process automation: a self-learning approach. In: On the move to meaningful Internet systems: OTM 2019 conf. Springer, Berlin, pp 95–112. ISBN 978-3-030-33246-4

Günther CW, Rozinat A, van Der Aalst WMP (2009) Activity mining by global trace segmentation. In: Int conf on business process management. Springer, Berlin, pp 128–139

Han X, Hu L, Dang Y, Agarwal S, Mei L, Li S, Zhou X (2020) Automatic business process structure discovery using ordered neurons LSTM: a preliminary study. arXiv CoRR abs/2001.01243. https://arxiv.org/abs/2001.01243

Ito N, Suzuki Y, Aizawa A (2020) From Natural Language Instructions to Complex Processes: Issues in Chaining Trigger Action Rules. arXiv CoRR abs/2001.02462. https://arxiv.org/abs/2001.02462

Jimenez-Ramirez A, Reijers HA, Barba I, Del Valle C (2019) A method to improve the early stages of the robotic process automation lifecycle. In: 31st int conf on advanced information systems engineering (CAiSE'19), pp 446–461. ISBN 978-3-030-21290-2

John BE, Kieras DE (1996) The GOMS family of user interface analysis techniques: comparison and contrast. In: ACM TOCHI, vol 3(4)

Le V, Gulwani S (2014) FlashExtract: a framework for data extraction by examples. In: ACM SIGPLAN PLDI '14, pp 542–553

Leno V, Augusto A, Dumas M, La Rosa M, Maggi FM, Polyvyanyy A (2020a) Identifying candidate routines for robotic process automation from unsegmented UI logs. In: 2nd international conference on process mining, ICPM'20, pp 153–160

Leno V, Polyvyanyy A, Dumas M, La Rosa M, Maggi FM (2020b) Robotic process mining: vision and challenges. Bus Inf Syst Eng

Leopold H, van der Aa H, Reijers HA (2018) Identifying candidate tasks for robotic process automation in textual process descriptions. In: Int conf on bus proc mod, dev and supp (BPMDS'18)

Mannhardt F, de Leoni M, Reijers HA, van der Aalst WMP, Toussaint PJ (2018) Guided process discovery – a pattern-based approach. Inf Syst 76:1–18

Marrella A (2019) Automated planning for business process management. J Data Semant 8(2):79–98

Marrella A, Catarci T (2018) Measuring the learnability of interactive systems using a petri net based approach. In: 2018 designing interactive systems conf, DIS '18. ACM, New York, pp 1309–1319. ISBN 978-1-4503-5198-0

Marrella A, Mecella M, Sardiña S (2018) Supporting adaptiveness of cyber-physical processes through action-based formalisms. AI Commun 31(1):47–74

Mobasher B, Nasraoui O (2011) Web Usage Mining, Web Data Mining. Exploring Hyperlinks, Contents, and Usage Data, B. Liu

Mori G, Paternò F, Santoro C (2002) CTTE: support for developing and analyzing task models for interactive system design. IEEE Trans Softw Eng 28(8)

Palanque PA, Petri RB (1995) Net based design of user-driven interfaces using the interactive cooperative objects formalism. In: Interactive systems: design, specification, and verification. Springer, Berlin

Paternò F (1999) Model-based design and evaluation of interactive applications, 1st edn. Springer, Berlin. ISBN 1852331550

Pesic M, Schonenberg H, van der Aalst WMP (2007) DECLARE: full support for loosely-structured processes. In: IEEE int enterprise distributed object computing conf (EDOC 2007), pp 287–300

Pnueli A (1977) The temporal logic of programs. In: F. of Comp. Sc

Statecharts DH (1987) A visual formalism for complex systems. Sci Comput Program 8(3):231–274

Sutcliffe AG, Wang I (1991) Integrating human computer interaction with Jackson system development. Comput J 34(2)

Sy O, Bastide R, Palanque P, Le D, Navarre D (2000) PetShop: a CASE tool for the petri net based specification and prototyping of CORBA systems. In: Petri nets, vol 2000

van Den Bos J, Plasmeijer MJ, Hartel PH (1983) Input–output tools: a language facility for interactive and real-time systems. IEEE Trans Softw Eng 3

Wasserman AI (1985) Extending state transition diagrams for the specification of human-computer interaction. IEEE Trans Softw Eng 8:699–713

Willcocks L (2016) Service automation: robots and the future of work. Steve Brookes Publishing, Warwickshire, United Kingdom. ISBN 0956414567

Wil M. P. van der Aalst

12 Process mining and RPA

How to pick your automation battles?

Abstract: Robotic process automation (RPA) has lowered the threshold for process automation. Repetitive tasks done by people are handed over to software robots. For RPA, there is no need to change or replace the pre-existing information systems. Instead, software robots replace users by interacting directly with the user interfaces normally operated by humans. Actually, RPA can be seen as "the poor man's workflow management solution" because it is cheaper than traditional automation. Therefore, it can be used to automate routine work that would normally not be cost-effective. Process mining plays a key role in deciding what to automate and how. Therefore, RPA is closely related to process mining. Before introducing RPA, one needs to analyze the processes to be automated. Process mining can help to identify promising candidates. Moreover, after RPA has been implemented, process mining can be used to monitor processes and systems even if these use a mixture of RPA, workers, and traditional automation.

Keywords: Robotic process automation (RPA), process mining, workflow management, business process management

12.1 Introduction

This chapter aims to relate *robotic process automation* (RPA) and *process mining* and put both in a historical context. *Workflow management* (WFM) has been around for several decades (van der Aalst and van Hee, 2004). In the mid 1990s, the term *straight through processing* (STP) was used to describe the ultimate goal of WFM: making operational processes cheaper, faster, and better by avoiding manual intervention. This turned out to be challenging and many WFM projects failed. WFM was subsequently replaced by *business process management* (BPM), which had a broader scope and put more emphasis on management aspects (van der Aalst, 2013; Dumas et al., 2013; Weske, 2007). However, traditional BPM often relied on modeling, leading to a "disconnect" with reality. We have all seen the idealized process models expressed in languages like BPMN that completely failed to capture the real problems. Moreover, the goal should not be to model, but to improve the process at hand. This often did not happen because it would be too expensive to change the information systems or the actual inefficiencies and compliance problems remained invisible.

Some will argue that RPA is not new at all, thereby referring to "screen scraping" (capturing data by reading text from a computer display and transferring it to a new

Acknowledgement: We thank the Alexander von Humboldt (AvH) Stiftung for supporting our research.

https://doi.org/10.1515/9783110676693-012

application) and "Taylorism" (i. e., analyzing and improving work processes systematically). However, the combination of process mining and RPA provides new ways of
learning and automating routine processes.

The goal of this chapter is not to discuss specific RPA or process mining techniques. Instead, we focus on the relations between both worlds and possible interfaces. Therefore, we elaborate on the specifics of event data used in an RPA context.
Moreover, we discuss possible use cases for this combination. These show that process mining and RPA complement each other: the former learns about processes and
the latter automates them.

In this chapter, we first sketch the history of process automation (Section 12.2). In
this context, we position RPA as "the poor man's WFM" in Section 12.3. Then we introduce process mining as a way to exploit event data (Section 12.4). Section 12.5 connects
process mining and RPA by discussing the specifics of RPA-based event data. This section shows that many design choices are needed to bridge the gap between both. Section 12.6 elaborates on the interplay between both worlds. Section 12.7 concludes the
chapter.

12.2 A brief history of WFM and BPM

Since the industrial revolution, productivity has been increasing because of technical
innovations, improvements in the organization of work, and the use of information
technology (van der Aalst, 2013). Adam Smith (1723–1790) showed the advantages of
the division of labor. Frederick Taylor (1856–1915) introduced the initial principles of
scientific management. In the 1970s, people like Skip Ellis and Michael Zisman already
worked on so-called office information systems, which were driven by explicit process
models (van der Aalst, 2013). Skip Ellis developed the Officetalk system at Xerox PARC
in the late 1970s using information control nets (ICN), a variant of Petri Nets, to model
processes (Ellis, 1979). Also, the office automation system System for Computerizing
of Office Processes (SCOOP) developed by Michael Zisman used Petri Nets to represent business processes. These systems can be seen as early *workflow management
(WFM) systems*. However, it took another 15 years until WFM technology was ready
to be applied at a large scale. In the mid 1990s, many commercial WFM systems were
available and there was the expectation that WFM systems would be an integral part
of any information system (van der Aalst and van Hee, 2004).

Figure 1 shows the development of information systems over time, explaining the
initial great optimism related to WFM technology. Initially, information systems were
developed from scratch, i. e., everything had to be programmed, even storing and retrieving data. Soon people realized that many information systems had similar requirements with respect to data management. Therefore, this generic functionality
was sub-contracted to a database system. Later, generic functionality related to user

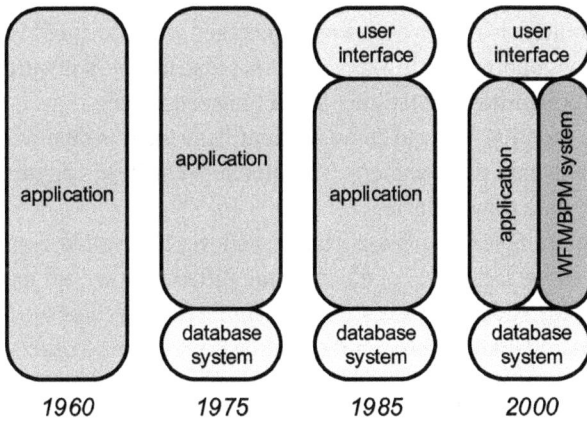

Figure 1: Positioning of WFM/BPM systems in a historical context (based on van der Aalst, 1998, 2013).

interaction (forms, buttons, graphs, etc.) was subcontracted to tools that can automatically generate user interfaces. The trend to subcontract recurring functionality to generic tools continued in different areas. Workflow management (WFM) systems are similar to database management (DBM) systems but focus on processes rather than data. In the mid 1990s, many WFM systems became available. These systems focused on automating workflows with little support for process analysis, process flexibility, and process management. Nevertheless, many expected that WFM systems would be as common as DBM systems. However, this did not happen. WFM systems were succeeded by *business process management (BPM) systems* that were broader in scope. The BPM discipline combines knowledge from information technology and knowledge from management sciences and applies this to operational business processes (van der Aalst, 2013; Dumas et al., 2013; Weske, 2007). BPM systems are generic software systems that are driven by explicit process designs to enact and manage operational business processes. Examples of BPM systems include the software products from Pegasystems, Appian, IBM, Bizagi, Oracle, Software AG, TIBCO Software, Bonitasoft, Kofax, and Signavio. However, despite the availability of WFM/BPM systems, process management is not subcontracted to such systems at a scale comparable to DBM systems. The application of "pure" WFM/BPM systems is still limited to specific industries such as banking and insurance. However, WFM/BPM technology is often hidden inside other systems. For example, ERP systems like SAP and Oracle provide workflow engines. Therefore, the landscape is not so clear. Organizations such as Gartner also invent new terms such as "intelligent business process management suites" (iBPMSs), yet the actual usage of such systems remains limited.

There seem to be three main reasons why the adoption of WFM/BPM technology is low.

- Applying WFM/BPM technology is rather *expensive*. Processes are hardcoded in application software or not supported at all. Many processes also involve software from different vendors, making integration difficult and time consuming.
- Although the "M" in WFM and BPM refers to "management," the focus is on modeling and automation rather than management. Traditional WFM/BPM systems fail to learn from the event data they collect.
- Real-life processes are more *complex* than people like to believe. The well-known 80/20 rule applies to processes, i. e., 80 % of all cases are rather simple, but explain only 20 % of the complexity of the process. The remaining 20 % of cases tend to be neglected by software and management, but consume 80 % of the resources of an organization.

The above three obstacles for WFM/BPM explain the current interest in RPA and process mining.

12.3 RPA: the poor man's WFM

Robotic process automation (RPA) is a form of automation using software robots (bots) replacing humans. The three main RPA vendors are UiPath (founded in 2005), Automation Anywhere (founded in 2003), and Blue Prism (founded in 2001). Other vendors include Workfusion, Kryon Systems, Softomotive, Contextor, EdgeVerve, Nice, and Redwood Software. The key difference between RPA and traditional WFM/BPM is that RPA does not aim to replace existing (back-end) information systems. Instead, software robots interact with the existing information systems in the same way as humans do. In traditional WFM/BPM systems, the process is specified precisely and the WFM/BPM system orchestrates the modeled process by implementing simple activities and calling pre-existing applications through application programming interfaces (APIs). In contrast, RPA software interacts with the pre-existing applications through (graphical) user interfaces directly replacing humans, i. e., automation is realized by taking over tasks from workers directly through the user interface. A typical RPA scenario is a sequence of copy-and-paste actions normally performed by a human. *Since there is no need to replace the existing information systems, RPA can be seen as "the poor man's WFM."* Figure 2 shows the situation before (left) and after (right) introducing RPA.

To understand RPA, it is important to realize that workers and information are "dancing" together. An information system may trigger its users and provide information. Similarly, people start applications and enter information. Consider, for example, the usage of forms. Most forms are partly pre-filled with information and users complete the missing information, thereby possibly triggering new actions. Sometimes the user takes the initiative and sometimes the system. When there are

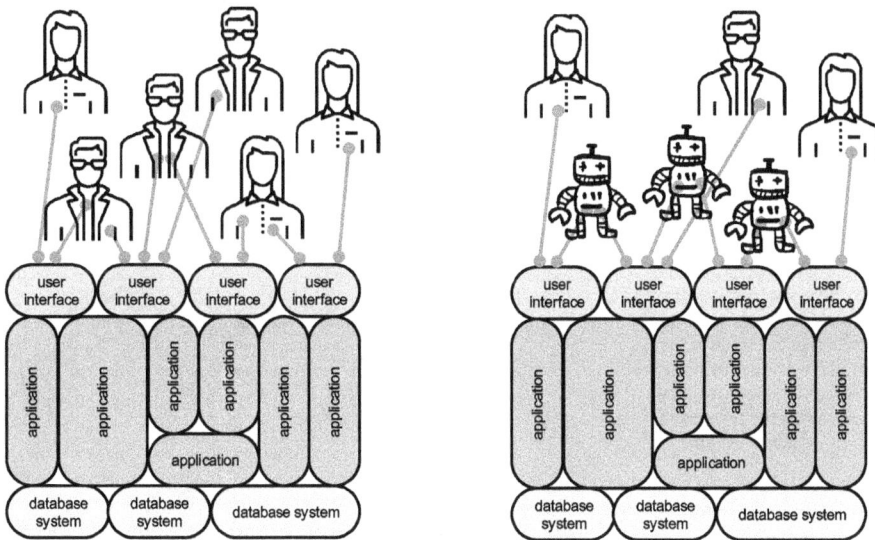

Figure 2: People tend to be the glue between different applications (left). RPA does not change the "back-end" like in traditional automation (compare with Figure 1). Robots interact with the information systems as if they are people (right).

multiple information systems, people are often the "glue" between the different parts (cf. Figure 2). See, for example, the scenario where a user copies address information from one information system to another one.

Figure 3 further illustrates the positioning of RPA with respect to the traditional setting and the situation where WFM/BPM software is used. Both RPA and WFM/BPM automate simple tasks and provide the glue between existing information systems. WFM/BPM connects to these systems via the "back-end" using APIs. RPA connects to these systems via the "front-end" using (graphical) user interfaces. In van der Aalst et al. (2018), the terms "inside-out" and "outside-in" are used for respectively the back-end WFM/BPM approach and the front-end RPA approach. RPA can be much more cost-effective than traditional automation because the information systems do not need to be changed or replaced. RPA can automate various mundane and routine tasks in the workplace. At the same time, there are some risks. RPA can handle processes and tasks that are repetitive and deterministic. However, these should require little to no judgment and have few exceptions. Technical glitches, exceptions, changing user interfaces, or changing contextual factors provide problems for software robots. There are also obvious security risks, and the lack of communication may conceal important issues (e. g., recurring problems are detected too late). Therefore, sometimes it is better to only use RPA as an "auto-completion tool" where a human still needs to confirm the suggested solution. In Auth et al. (2019) the relation between RPA and enterprise architecture (EA) is discussed in more detail.

Traditional setting not using WFM, BPM, and RPA software. Processes are supported by people and partly hard-coded in the information systems.

Situation using WFM/BPM software supporting processes and partly automating the work done by workers. The system itself needs to be changed and the WFM/BPM system interacts via APIs with the pre-existing information systems.

Situation using RPA. The pre-existing information systems remain unchanged. Workers are (partly) replaced by software robots that interact via GUIs with existing information systems. Software robots perform simple tasks and provide the "glue" between different systems.

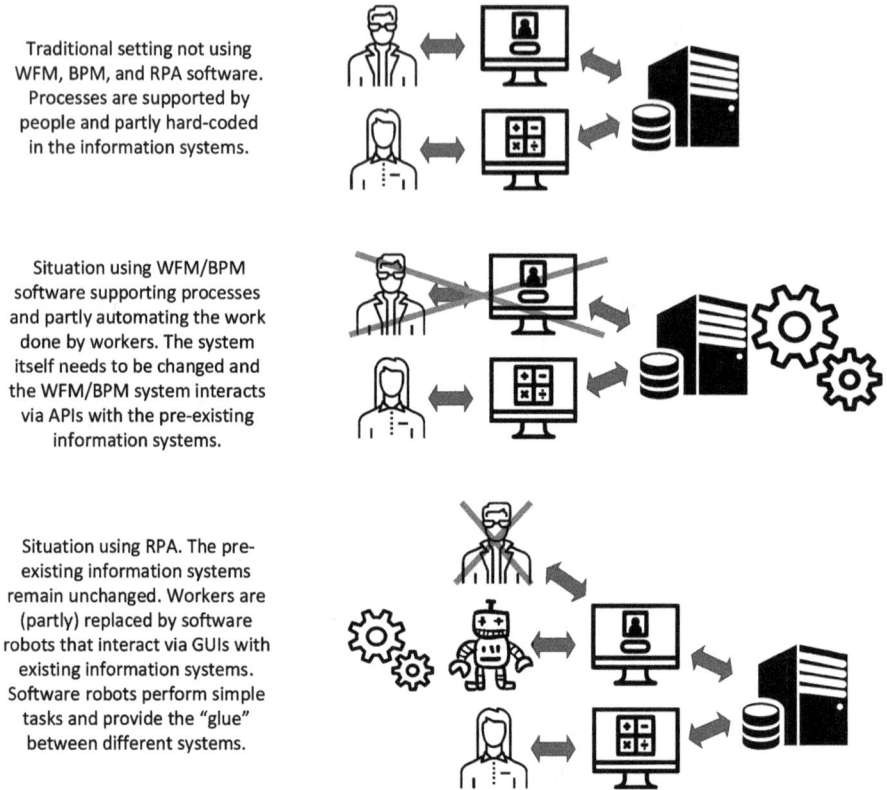

Figure 3: Three situations. (a) Traditional setting. (b) WFM/BPM setting. (c) RPA setting.

Most of the RPA vendors emphasize the link between RPA and *artificial intelligence* (AI) and *machine learning* (ML). Classical RPA applications are rule-based and are basically programmed by people. More innovative RPA approaches, sometimes called *cognitive RPA*, aim to learn from humans by observing repetitive tasks (Houy et al., 2019). For example, natural language processing (NLP) techniques are used to classify text and routed to the right resource. Image recognition can be used to recognize a button or an edit field, and optical character recognition (OCR) can retrieve handwritten text. However, the examples reported are typically focusing on a single well-defined task (like classification). Note that it is relatively easy to recognize buttons, etc., and program actions like clicking such a button and entering a username and password. However, all of this is done without understanding the semantics of the actions. Moreover, AI and ML are rarely used for learning dynamic behavior.

In Leopold et al. (2018a), the authors propose an NLP-based approach that automatically identifies and classifies tasks from textual process descriptions as manual, user, or automated. The goal of the approach is to reduce the effort that is required to identify suitable candidates for RPA. However, the work highly depends on the presence of such descriptions. Often such information is missing, over-simplified, or out-dated. Therefore, we focus on the actual behavior observed.

12.4 Using process mining to pick your automation battles

Process mining techniques use event data to show what people, machines, and organizations are really doing. Process mining provides novel insights that can be used to identify and address performance and compliance problems (van der Aalst, 2016). Just like spreadsheets can do anything with numbers, process mining can do anything with event data, i. e., it is a generic, domain-independent technology to improve processes. The application of process mining is much broader than that of RPA. However, let us first relate both using Figure 4. The diagram sketches the typical Pareto distribution found in event logs. Often, a small percentage of activities account for most of the events and a small percentage of trace variants account for most of the traces (van der Aalst et al., 2018). For example, 20 % of the activities may account for 80 % of the events. Similarly, the 20 % most frequent process variants may explain 80 % of the cases. Traditional process automation focuses on the most frequent activities and process variants. Only for highly frequent activities and process variants, it may be cost-effective to automate tasks and introduce WFM/BPM. Less frequent activities and process variants need to be handled by workers that exploit human flexibility and creativity. RPA focuses on the middle part, i. e., routine work that is not frequent enough to be automated in the traditional sense. *Process mining is a key technology to identify routine work that can be supported using RPA.* Therefore, we claim that process mining can be used to pick the "automation battles" that are cost-effective and feasible.

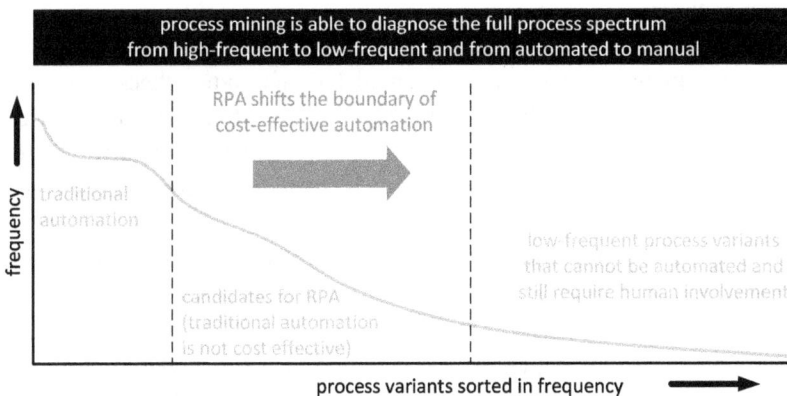

Figure 4: Relating RPA and process mining (based on van der Aalst et al., 2018).

Process mining starts from *event data*, typically stored in an *event log* (see Section 12.5). An event log views a process from a particular angle. Each event in the log refers to at least (1) a particular process instance (called a *case*), (2) an *activity*, and (3) a *timestamp*. There may be additional event attributes referring to resources, people, costs, etc., but these are optional. With some effort, such data can be extracted from the information systems used by the organization. For example, an SAP system may hold thousands of tables with information about hundreds of processes. In real-life information systems, there may be many possible case identifiers. Therefore, it is often better to use an intermediate logging format where events may refer to any number of objects (cf. Definition 3).

Process mining uses such event data to answer a variety of process-related questions. Process mining techniques such as process discovery, conformance checking, model enhancement, and operational support can be used to improve performance and compliance (van der Aalst, 2016). Currently, there are over 30 commercial offerings of process mining software (e. g., Celonis, Disco, ProcessGold, myInvenio, PAFnow, Minit, QPR, Mehrwerk, Puzzledata, LanaLabs, StereoLogic, Everflow, TimelinePI, Signavio, and Logpickr). They all can discover so-called *directly follows graphs* (DFGs) showing frequencies and bottlenecks. DFGs can be seamlessly simplified by removing nodes and edges based on frequency thresholds. DFGs are simple and provide interesting insights, but only provide a starting point. More advanced discovery algorithms like the inductive miner discover better process models, also showing concurrency (e. g., Petri Nets, BPMN diagrams, and UML activity diagrams) (van der Aalst, 2016). Typically, four types of process mining are identified (van der Aalst, 2016).

–   *Process discovery*: learning process models from event data. A discovery technique takes an event log and produces a process model without using additional information. An example is the well-known Alpha algorithm, which takes an event log and produces a Petri Net explaining the behavior recorded in the log. Most of the commercial process mining tools first discover DFGs before conducting further analysis.
–   *Conformance checking*: detecting and diagnosing both differences and commonalities between an event log and a process model. Conformance checking can be used to check if reality, as recorded in the log, conforms to the model and vice versa. The process model used as input may be descriptive or normative. Moreover, the process model may have been made by hand or learned using process discovery.
–   *Process reengineering*: improving or extending the model based on event data. Like for conformance checking, both an event log and a process model are used as input. However, now, the goal is not to diagnose differences. The goal is to change the process model. For example, it is possible to repair the model to better reflect reality. It is also possible to enrich an existing process model with additional perspectives. For example, replay techniques can be used to show bottlenecks or

resource usage. Process reengineering yields updated models. These models can be used to improve the actual processes.

- *Operational support*: directly influencing the process by providing warnings, predictions, or recommendations. Conformance checking can be done "on-the-fly," allowing people to act the moment things deviate. Based on the model and event data related to running process instances, one can predict the remaining flow time, the likelihood of meeting the legal deadline, the associated costs, the probability that a case will be rejected, etc. The process is not improved by changing the model, but by directly providing data-driven support in the form of warnings, predictions, and/or recommendations.

All techniques start from the so-called control-flow perspective, which focuses on the ordering of activities. Then the time perspective (bottlenecks, delays, and frequencies), the data perspective (understanding decisions), and the resource and organization perspective (social networks, roles, and authorizations) are added.

12.5 Formalizing the input

To be able to learn from people performing activities that should be taken over by software robots, we need to record the interactions between users and the interfaces they use. Figure 5 provides a simplistic illustration where every low-level interaction is represented by a black dot. Such a dot may refer to a mouse click, closing a window, typing an address, selecting a name from a pull-down menu, etc. Existing RPA solutions are able to capture such events. For example, UiPath Studio provides several types of recording (e. g., basic, desktop, web, image). The so-called "Universal Recorder" of Automation Anywhere also supports getting events from various applications (e. g., SAP, Office, and Oracle), web browsers, and operating systems (e. g., windows desktop). Such recordings are mostly used for manual analysis and scenario building. Often screenshots can be recorded to better contextualize events. This helps to understand why users perform certain actions in exceptional situations (e. g., in case of a system failure). Skan CPX is an example of software that is focusing on capturing events using computer vision. Collecting events from the user interface is relatively easy, but it is much more difficult to attach semantics automatically.

The low-level interactions recorded by RPA software can be viewed as events, but cannot be directly used for process mining. The data recorded by RPA software are ad hoc and highly system-dependent. Low-level interactions need to be *aggregated* and *correlated* to create event logs that can be used for process mining. To discuss this in a meaningful way, we first need to formalize the elements of an event log.

In its simplest form, an event log can be seen as a multi-set of traces where each trace is a sequence of activities, e. g., $L = [\langle a, b, c, e \rangle^{45}, \langle a, c, b, e \rangle^{38}, \langle a, d, e \rangle^{27}]$. This

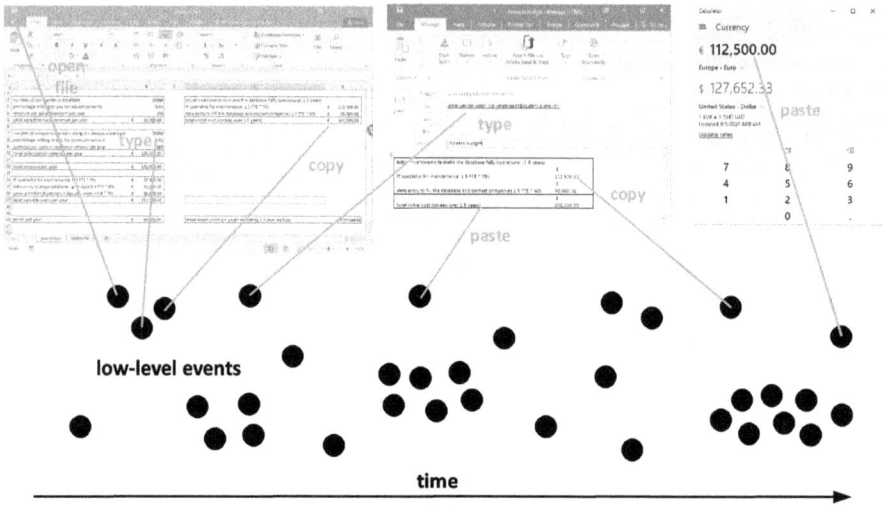

Figure 5: To learn processes in an RPA context, we need to record all relevant user interactions. Actions performed by users (typing, clicking, etc.) can be seen as low-level events.

view may be adequate for control-flow discovery, but is too simple for RPA applications that lack a clear case notion. Therefore, we introduce so-called *object-centric event logs* (van der Aalst, 2019). An event in such a log may refer to any number of objects and attribute values.

Definition 1 (Universes and events). To define events, we introduce the following universes:

- $\mathbb{U}_{ei}$ is the universe of event identifiers;
- $\mathbb{U}_{act}$ is the universe of activity names;
- $\mathbb{U}_{time}$ is the universe of timestamps;
- $\mathbb{U}_{ot}$ is the universe of object types (also called classes);
- $\mathbb{U}_{oi}$ is the universe of object identifiers (also called entities);
- $type \in \mathbb{U}_{oi} \to \mathbb{U}_{ot}$ assigns precisely one type to each object identifier;
- $\mathbb{U}_{omap} = \{omap \in \mathbb{U}_{ot} \nrightarrow \mathcal{P}(\mathbb{U}_{oi}) \mid \forall_{ot \in dom(omap)} \forall_{oi \in omap(ot)} type(oi) = ot\}$ is the universe of all object mappings indicating which object identifiers are included per type;[1]
- $\mathbb{U}_{att}$ is the universe of attribute names;
- $\mathbb{U}_{val}$ is the universe of attribute values;

---

1 $\mathcal{P}(\mathbb{U}_{oi})$ is the powerset of the universe of object identifiers, i. e., objects types are mapped onto sets of object identifiers. $omap \in \mathbb{U}_{ot} \nrightarrow \mathcal{P}(\mathbb{U}_{oi})$ is a partial function. If $ot \notin dom(omap)$, then we assume that $omap(ot) = \emptyset$.

- $\mathbb{U}_{vmap} = \mathbb{U}_{att} \nrightarrow \mathbb{U}_{val}$ is the universe of value assignments,[2] and
- $\mathbb{U}_{event} = \mathbb{U}_{ei} \times \mathbb{U}_{act} \times \mathbb{U}_{time} \times \mathbb{U}_{omap} \times \mathbb{U}_{vmap}$ is the universe of events.

An event $e = (ei, act, time, omap, vmap) \in \mathbb{U}_{event}$ is characterized by a unique event identifier ei, the corresponding activity act, the event's timestamp time, and two mappings omap and vmap for object references and attribute values, respectively.

Definition 2 (Event projection). Given $e = (ei, act, time, omap, vmap) \in \mathbb{U}_{event}$, $\pi_{ei}(e) = ei$, $\pi_{act}(e) = act$, $\pi_{time}(e) = time$, $\pi_{omap}(e) = omap$, and $\pi_{vmap}(e) = vmap$.

Consider a event e with $\pi_{act}(e) = $ "place order" and $\pi_{time}(e) = $ "2020-10-07 08:23:19"; $\pi_{omap}(e) \in \mathbb{U}_{ot} \nrightarrow \mathcal{P}(\mathbb{U}_{oi})$ maps a subset of object types onto sets of object identifiers for an event e. For example, $\pi_{omap}(e)(\text{Order}) = \{o_{4567}\}$, $\pi_{omap}(e)(\text{Item}) = \{i_{786}, i_{888}, i_{923}\}$, and $\pi_{omap}(e)(\text{Payments}) = \emptyset$ (i.e., the place order event e refers to one order, three items, and no payments). And $\pi_{vmap}(e) \in \mathbb{U}_{att} \nrightarrow \mathbb{U}_{val}$ maps a subset of attribute names onto attribute values. For example, $\pi_{vmap}(e)(\text{cost}) = 75$ and $\pi_{vmap}(e)(\text{location}) = $ "Berlin".

An *object-centric event log* is a collection of *partially ordered events* (van der Aalst, 2019). Event identifiers are unique, i.e., two events cannot have the same event identifier.

Definition 3 (Object-centric event log). Consider the event log $L = (E, \preceq_E)$ with $E \subseteq \mathbb{U}_{event}$ and $\preceq_E \subseteq E \times E$ such that:
- $\preceq_E$ defines a partial order (reflexive, antisymmetric, and transitive);
- $\forall_{e_1, e_2 \in E} \pi_{ei}(e_1) = \pi_{ei}(e_2) \Rightarrow e_1 = e_2$, and
- $\forall_{e_1, e_2 \in E} e_1 \preceq_E e_2 \Rightarrow \pi_{time}(e_1) \leq \pi_{time}(e_2)$.

Object-centric event logs generalize the traditional event log notion where each event has precisely one case identifier. We can mimic such logs using a special object type Case $\in \mathbb{U}_{ot}$ such that $|\pi_{omap}(e)(\text{Case})| = 1$ for any event $e \in E$. Since traditional process mining techniques assume this, it is common practice to convert event data with events referring to a variable number of objects to classical event logs by "flattening" the event data. Assume that we take a specific object type as a case identifier. If an event has multiple objects of that type, then we can simply create one event for each object. If an event has no objects of that type, then we simply omit the event. If an event has precisely one object of the selected type, then we keep that event. Hence, by selecting an object type as the case identifier, we can "flatten" the log and apply standard process discovery and conformance checking techniques.

Let us assume that we want an event log $L = (E, \preceq_E)$ in order to apply various process mining techniques in an RPA setting as described before. *How can we get such*

---

2 $\mathbb{U}_{att} \nrightarrow \mathbb{U}_{val}$ is the set of all partial functions mapping a subset of attribute names onto the corresponding values.

an event log in the context of RPA? As illustrated in Figure 6 we cannot directly use the low-level events and need to aggregate and correlate user interactions.

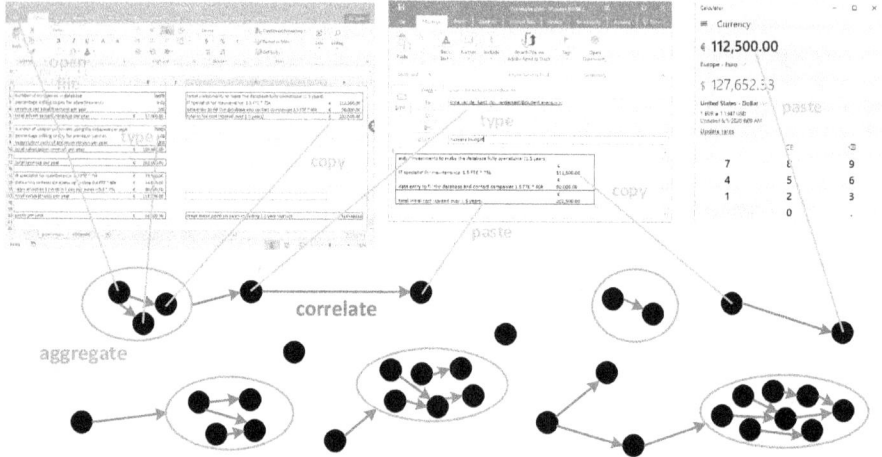

Figure 6: Low-level user interactions need to be aggregated and correlated to build event logs.

Aggregation

First, we need to decide at what level we would like to record user activities. Examples of *low-level activities* include click, double click, select item, type text, copy, paste, close window, etc. It is possible to see each of these as individual events or they can be grouped into *higher-level events* such as filling out a form. It is also possible to think of hierarchical recordings having multiple levels. Only low-level events can be seen as atomic. For example, it may take a few minutes to fill out a form in one system while gathering information from other systems. How to segment low-level events and create such a hierarchy is situation dependent.

Correlation

Related to aggregation is the topic of correlation. A user may use different systems at the same time and work on multiple cases. Copying an address from SAP and pasting the address in a web form are clearly related. However, the user may also simply type the address in the web form manually (while looking at the SAP screen). Correlation is often based on comparing values, e. g., the zip code "D-52074" or URL "pads.rwth-aachen.de" appearing in two different windows. In object-centric event logs, events can have multiple object identifiers without picking a specific case notion. This provides the required flexibility. However, the mapping from values and identifiers in the user interface to event attributes and objects remains something that is application-

and situation-dependent. This is unavoidable given the ad hoc nature of low-level user interaction recordings.

The process sketched in Figure 6 is far from trivial. Earlier, we defined events to be of the form $e = (ei, act, time, omap, vmap) \in \mathbb{U}_{event}$. The correlation between events (aggregated or not) needs to take place via omap (i. e., the objects the event is referring to). For example, events e_{356} and e_{412} are related because $\pi_{omap}(e_{356})(Zip) = \{\text{"D-52074"}\}$ and $\pi_{omap}(e_{412})(Zip) = \{\text{"D-52074"}\}$. Events may have standard attributes and object types, e. g., vmap and omap may contain mandatory information on user name, computer name, window ID, session ID, etc. When aggregating events, it makes sense to have two times ($time_{start}$ and $time_{end}$) for each event. Similarly, it may make sense to split omap and vmap into input and output, i. e., $omap_{in}$, $vmap_{in}$, $omap_{out}$, and $vmap_{out}$. This way one can infer create, read, update, and delete actions in forms. For example, if $omap_{in}(Price) = 500$ and $omap_{out}(Price) = 600$, then we know that the price was increased by 100. Hence, high-level events could be of the form $e = (ei, act, time_{start}, time_{end}, omap_{in}, vmap_{in}, omap_{out}, vmap_{out})$ to better capture the duration, input, and output. However, the resulting log can still be viewed as an object-centric event log that can be used to generate different flattened event logs depending on the questions that need to be answered.

The above discussion shows that it is far from trivial to create meaningful event logs from low-level user interactions. However, this step is essential when deciding on what to automate.

12.6 On the interplay between process mining and RPA

The connection between process mining and RPA was first discussed in van der Aalst et al. (2018). In Geyer-Klingeberg et al. (2018) it is shown how a commercial process mining system like Celonis can be used to support the whole lifecycle of RPA initiatives. In Leno et al. (2020) the term robotic process mining (RPM) is introduced to refer to "a class of techniques and tools to analyze data collected during the execution of user-driven tasks in order to support the identification and assessment of candidate routines for automation and the discovery of routine specifications that can be executed by RPA bots." The authors propose a framework and RPM pipeline combining RPA and process mining, and identify challenges related to recording, filtering, segmentation, simplification, identification, discovery, and compilation. In Gao et al. (2019) an RPA rule deduction approach is presented combining process mining and captured user behavior in the form of input–output logs.

As mentioned earlier, *the scope of process mining extends far beyond RPA* since it also covers process steps fully handled by humans or automated in the traditional way. However, RPA is not just related to process mining and influences the broader

BPM discipline. The role of RPA in BPM architectures was already elaborated in Houy et al. (2019). The paper focuses on the use of RPA in public administration (e. g., automatically classifying documents). In Syeda et al. (2020) a review of the state of the art in RPA and 15 challenges are given. Both papers identify a gap between the inflated expectations and the actual tool support provided. RPA vendors tend to present general-purpose artificial intelligence and machine learning techniques as breakthroughs in process automation. However, process mining shows that even structured processes like Purchase-To-Pay (P2P) and Order-To-Cash (O2C) tend to be much more complex than anticipated. Such reality checks are essential to make proper RPA decisions.

To conclude the chapter, we discuss the *relationship between process mining and RPA* in more detail using Figure 7. In Figure 7a, the traditional usage of process mining is described. In this scenario, event data are extracted from the information systems supporting the process. Workers are not observed directly. In Figure 7b, process mining is applied to event data collected directly from the (graphical) user interfaces, i. e., the interactions between workers and information systems are directly recorded. This scenario is particularly useful in the phase before RPA is introduced. Process mining can be used to detect routine work that can be automated by mimicking the behavior of workers. Rather than manually programming robots, process discovery can be used to configure the robots correctly. In Figure 7c, process mining is used after introducing RPA. Part of the work formerly done by workers is now done by software robots. In this scenario, process mining is used to check whether the processes run as planned. If a software robot malfunctions due to technical glitches, exceptions, changing user interfaces, or changing contextual factors, then this can be detected using conformance checking techniques. Note that a lack of human oversight of the work produced by robots constitutes a real risk of catastrophic outcomes. Figure 7d describes the most advanced scenario. In this scenario, the work is flexibly distributed over workers and software robots. For example, tasks are initially performed by robots and are escalated to workers the moment there is a complication of exception. Similarly, workers can hand off work to robots using an "auto-complete" option. Moreover, the RPA solution may adapt due to changes in the underlying process (e. g., concept drift).

12.7 Conclusion

Process automation has a long history. WFM and BPM systems have been around for decades, but their application is limited to high-volume structured processes. RPA has lowered the threshold for automation. The phrase "RPA is the poor man's WFM" (coined in the paper on which this chapter is based) illustrates this. Due to RPA, it is possible to automate many mundane repetitive routines in an economically viable manner. Process mining helps to identify process fragments that can be supported using RPA. This is the reason that process mining and RPA vendors have joined forces.

(a) Traditional process mining using event data extracted from the information systems supporting the process.

(b) Process mining using event data obtained by observing the workers using the information systems.

(c) Process mining after introducing RPA. Event data are obtained by observing workers and robots.

(d) Process mining after introducing RPA using an adaptive distribution of work over workers and robots.

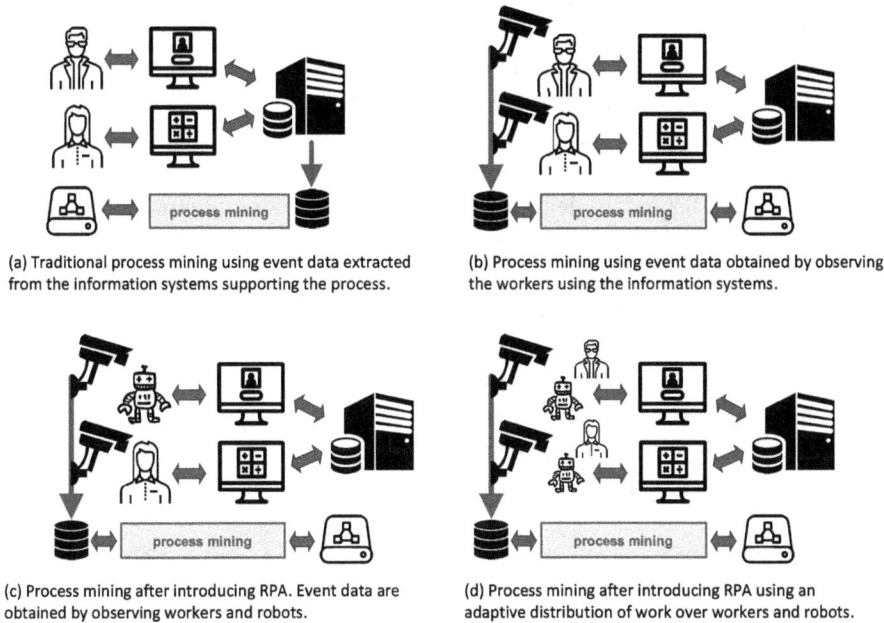

Figure 7: Process mining can be used before and after the introduction of RPA. Robots and workers use the same (graphical) user interfaces and the role distribution may be flexible and change over time. Fortunately, process mining provides a holistic view of the processes at hand and the interplay between robots and workers.

For example, in October 2019, process mining vendor ProcessGold was acquired by RPA vendor UiPath. Similarly, vendors like Celonis started to support "task mining" and "action automation" (using the action engine) to boost RPA-related capabilities. Skan is combining computer vision and machine learning capabilities with process mining.

According to Deloitte and EY, up to 30 % to 50 % of RPA projects fail, and most are more expensive and time consuming than planned (Dutta et al., 2016; Wright et al., 2017). Process mining can be used to avoid such failures. As Figure 4 shows, the scope of process mining includes everything from routine activities and processes automated using WFM, BPM, and RPA to one-of-a-kind activities and processes that require human interventions and creativity. Moreover, process mining helps to support the different phases of RPA as highlighted in Figure 7.

Hence, there is huge potential. However, many challenges need to be addressed. Actually, the uptake of RPA triggers many interesting research questions.

– *What event data to store and how to structure these?* Computer vision, image recognition, OCR, and NLP can be used to capture events. However, how to add semantics and how to decide that event are relevant for the process.

- *What characteristics make processes suitable to be supported by RPA?* Many RPA projects fail because automation turns out to be infeasible or they try to automate processes that are too infrequent or changing too fast. RPA needs to be approached more systematically using data-driven cost–benefit analyses.
- *How to control software robots and avoid security, compliance, and economic risks?* The ISO 10218-1 standard defines safety requirements for industrial robots. Such standards are missing for software robots. However, malfunctioning robots (e. g., due to changing circumstances) may have devastating effects for an organization (e. g., leaking sensitive information or making costly decisions).
- *How can software robots and people seamlessly work together?* The border between tasks best done by humans and tasks best done by machines will continue to shift. Intelligence amplification (also referred to as machine-augmented intelligence or enhanced intelligence) aims to enhance the human worker using AI. This results in processes where robots and people seamlessly work together.

Process mining plays a key role in answering these questions and can be placed in a larger context where work is distributed among machines and people.

The frontier between the tasks performed by humans and those performed by machines and algorithms is continuously moving and changing global labor markets. In Hawksworth et al. (2018) three waves of automation (algorithmic, augmentation, and autonomous) are predicted to replace much of the work previously done by people. In Frey and Osborne (2017), Frey and Osborne predict the degree of computerization for 702 occupations. They estimate that 47 % of jobs in the US will be replaced by (software) robots. In Leopold et al. (2018b) three types of roles are identified: stable roles (work that remains), new roles (new types of work that did not exist before), and redundant roles (work that is taken over by, e. g., robots). These broader trends highlight the economic and social impact of RPA and process mining.

Bibliography

Auth G, Czarnecki C, Bensberg F (2019) Impact of robotic process automation on enterprise architectures. In: Draude C, Lange M, Sick B (eds) INFORMATIK 2019. Lecture Notes in Informatics, vol 295. GI, pp 59–65

Dumas M, La Rosa M, Mendling J, Reijers H (2013) Fundamentals of business process management. Springer, Berlin

Dutta D, Gillard A, Kaczmarskyj G (2016) Get ready for robots: why planning makes the difference between success and disappointment. Ernst and Young. https:// eyfinancialservicesthoughtgallery.ie/wp-content/uploads/2016/11/ey-get-ready-for-robots. pdf

Ellis CA (1979) Information control nets: a mathematical model of office information flow. In: Proceedings of the conference on simulation, measurement and modeling of computer systems. ACM Press, Boulder, Colorado, pp 225–240

Frey CB, Osborne MA (2017) The future of employment: how susceptible are jobs to computerisation? Technol Forecast Soc Change 114(C):254–280

Gao J, van Zelst SJ, Lu X, van der Aalst WMP (2019) Automated robotic process automation: a self-learning approach. In: Panetto H, Debruyne C, Hepp M, Lewis D, Ardagna CA, Meersman R (eds) On the move to meaningful Internet systems, international conference on cooperative information systems (CoopIS 2019). Lecture Notes in Computer Science, vol 11877. Springer, Berlin, pp 95–112

Geyer-Klingeberg J, Nakladal J, Baldauf F, Veit F (2018) Process mining and robotic process automation: a perfect match. In: Proceedings of the industrial track at the 16th international conference on business process management (BPM 2018), pp 124–131

Hawksworth J, Berriman R, Goel S (2018) Will robots really steal our jobs? An international analysis of the potential long term impact of automation. Technical report, PricewaterhouseCoopers

Houy C, Hamberg M, Fettke P (2019) Robotic process automation in public administrations. In: Michael R, Sebastian H, Ratz D, Richter D, Schweighofer E (eds) Digitalisierung von Staat und Verwaltung. Lecture Notes in Informatics, vol 291. GI, pp 62–74

Leno V, Polyvyanyy A, Dumas M, La Rosa M, Maggi FM (2020) Robotic process mining: vision and challenges. Bus Inf Syst Eng

Leopold TA, Ratcheva V, Zahidi S (2018b) The future of jobs report. Technical report, Centre for the New Economy and Society, World Economic Forum

Leopold H, van der Aa H, Reijers HA (2018a) Identifying candidate tasks for robotic process automation in textual process descriptions. In: Gulden J, Reinhartz-Berger I, Schmidt R, Guerreiro S, Guédria W, Bera P (eds) Enterprise, business-process and information systems modeling. Springer, Berlin, pp 67–81

Syeda R, Suriadia S, Adamsa M, Bandaraa W, Leemans S, Ouyang C, ter Hofstede A, van de Weerd I, Wynn M, Reijers H (2020) Robotic process automation: contemporary themes and challenges. Comput Ind 115(1):103162

van der Aalst WMP (1998) The application of Petri nets to workflow management. J Circuits Syst Comput 8(1):21–66

van der Aalst WMP (2013) Business process management: a comprehensive survey. ISRN Softw Eng 1–37. https://doi.org/10.1155/2013/507984

van der Aalst WMP (2016) Process mining: data science in action. Springer, Berlin

van der Aalst WMP (2019) Object-centric process mining: dealing with divergence and convergence in event data. In: Ölveczky PC, Salaün G (eds) Software engineering and formal methods (SEFM 2019). Lecture Notes in Computer Science, vol 11724. Springer, Berlin, pp 3–25

van der Aalst WMP, van Hee KM (2004) Workflow management: models, methods, and systems. MIT Press, Cambridge, MA

van der Aalst WMP, Bichler M, Heinzl A (2018) Robotic process automation. Bus Inf Syst Eng 60(4):269–272

Weske M (2007) Business process management: concepts, languages, architectures. Springer, Berlin

Wright D, Witherick D, Gordeeva M (2017) The robots are ready. Are you? Untapped advantage in your digital workforce. Deloitte. https://www2.deloitte.com/uk/en/pages/consulting/articles/the-robots-are-ready-are-you.html

Part IV: **RPA applications**

Christian Langmann and Julia Kokina
13 RPA in accounting

Abstract: Finance and accounting are the leading areas for the implementation of robotic process automation (RPA). Next to other technologies RPA is a core driver of the digitalization of accounting. However, academic research in this area is still limited, especially on the adoption of RPA in corporate accounting settings. Therefore, this chapter reviews existing academic research on RPA in accounting settings and provides insights into the suitability of the various processes in accounting and management accounting for RPA. Finally, we look at the future impact that RPA will likely have on the role of corporate accountants.

Keywords: Robotic process automation, robotics, accounting, finance, management accounting

13.1 Digitalization technologies in the field of accounting

Accounting is undergoing vast digital transformations in many organizations today, and robotic process automation (RPA) is at the heart of those efforts. Along with other digitalization tools at accountants' disposal, such as tools for data extraction, transformation, and loading (ETL) and data analytics and visualization, RPA is viewed as a foundation for future use of more advanced cognitive computing. While classical RPA intends to use applications on existing interfaces in the same way as humans use the application, intelligent process automation (IPA) makes additional use of digitalization technologies from the field of artificial intelligence. As a result, IPA mimics the processes carried out by humans and after some time learns to do them even better (Berruti et al., 2017; Houy et al., 2019; Taulli, 2020). RPA combined with an intelligent optical character recognition engine (backed by machine learning) to scan, read, and learn to correctly interpret data from invoice documents to generate an automated booking is just one example (e. g., Anagnoste, 2018).

Concerning the adoption of RPA, a survey of the top 25 global RPA service providers drawing upon 5800 customer deployments revealed that finance and accounting were the leading areas of RPA implementation constituting 36 % of all RPA use cases (Forrester, 2019). Furthermore, a recent PwC study reported that within accounting areas processes most suitable for RPA are those in accounts receivable (72 %), accounts payable (51 %), and monthly closing (28 %) (PwC, 2020).

Motivated by the widespread adoption of RPA in finance and accounting, in this chapter we focus on various important aspects of RPA implementation integrating di-

https://doi.org/10.1515/9783110676693-013

verse insights from literature targeting accounting practitioner and academic audiences. Our chapter is structured as follows:

- Section 13.2: In this section, we first analyze publications in academic journals focused on the various aspects of RPA implementation. We highlight that much of the published work on the topic has been in the area of auditing and public accounting in the US context, with a slight focus on RPA implementation in corporate settings.
- Section 13.3: Based on the identified shortcomings from the literature review, we identify broad characteristics of accounting processes that make them good candidates for RPA. Further, we discuss the differences between financial and managerial accounting and position these areas alongside two dimensions of task analyzability and exception quantities using Perrow's framework. Finally, we provide some examples of specific accounting tasks that organizations have automated with RPA.
- Section 13.4: In this section, we present RPA process suitability via visualizations using heatmaps that was discussed on a broad theoretical basis in Section 13.3. We highlight a separate heatmap for processes within financial and managerial accounting. We underscore that process suitability for RPA is determined at a more granular sub-process level as opposed to automating a process in its entirety.
- Section 13.5: We discuss the RPA-enabled changing roles of accountants that involve a shift from being a scorekeeper mainly focusing on transaction processing and compliance to becoming a valued strategic advisor and business partner. To provide a real-world example, we describe future management accounting roles at BASF. In addition, we address the need for accountants' digital upskilling in order to successfully work with the new technologies.
- Section 13.6: We conclude with providing key takeaways from our chapter and a future outlook on RPA in accounting. The impact of RPA on the role and skills of future accountants provides further research opportunities, especially when looking at the combination of RPA with other cognitive advanced digitalization technologies.

13.2 Literature review on the use of RPA in accounting

The use of RPA in accounting has become an area of interest explored in several recent studies published in academic journals as well as working papers. While the majority of papers focus on examining RPA in public accounting (Cooper et al., 2019a, 2019b), especially auditing (Moffitt et al., 2018; Huang and Vasarhelyi, 2019; Zhang, 2019; Tiberius and Hirth, 2019; Manita et al., 2020), other papers address topics such as RPA implementation for accounting tasks in industry (Kokina and Blanchette, 2019), roles and competencies of accountants and controllers as integral RPA implementation players (Kokina et al., 2019; Oesterreich et al., 2019), and ethical implications associated with the use of artificial intelligence in auditing (Munoko et al., 2019).

Ongoing RPA work explores the use of bots in the internal audit function (Eulerich and Pawlowski, 2020; Eulerich and Masli, 2020), issues related to auditing an RPA-enabled accounting system (Appelbaum and Kozlowski, 2020), the adoption of bots in public accounting (Bakarich and O'Brien, 2020), and the role intelligent agents play in diffusing managers' responsibility for earnings management (Kipp et al., 2020). As RPA implementation in accounting becomes more mature and widespread, we anticipate that this area of research will grow both in the depth and breadth of RPA-related issues examined and the diversity of methodologies employed. For example, there is a notable lack of literature addressing RPA implementation in the area of taxation even though Cooper et al. (2019a, 2019b) highlight that the tax function in public accounting reports the greatest RPA adoption levels.

13.2.1 Review of literature on RPA in auditing

Audit automation has been a subject of academic inquiry for several decades. Early examples of audit automation were computer-assisted audit tools and techniques that were later integrated into various decision support tools which have now become embedded in the business processes themselves (Vasarhelyi, 2013). The goal of automation has been the reduction of latency occurring throughout business process performance. Vasarhelyi et al. (2010) conceptualized audit automation to consist of four areas aimed at latency reduction: automation of labor-intensive tasks, automation of staged data collection and data delivery, automation of decision making, and automation of decision implementation. Unstructured decision making and decision implementation, however, could not be easily automated given the technology at the time. Instead, in order to automate decision making, "...substantive formalization..." as well as "...classification structures like taxonomies and hierarchies must be expanded to harden 'soft' knowledge into computable structures..." (Vasarhelyi, 2013, 9). Further, to automate decision implementation, an auditor, for example, could consider "progressive automation" accomplished by increasing the sample or type of transactions selected for confirmations. Subsequent publications provide a more detailed overview and examples of the use of automation in auditing. It is worth noting that even though opportunities for automation in audit are vast, it is "...a still somewhat artisanal process dominated by anachronistic standards and *ad hoc* judgment..." (Moffitt et al., 2018, 1).

Kokina and Davenport (2017) present a set of tasks performed by cognitive technologies and their intelligence level emphasizing that repetitive task automation is ongoing in large accounting firms. They state that RPA is particularly useful for automating structured audit processes and point out that almost 40 % of all audit tasks can be classified as structured which makes them good candidates for automation. Moffitt et al. (2018) report that repetitive audit tasks in areas such as reconciliations, testing of internal controls, and substantive testing can be automated. Furthermore, the role of the auditor would shift from mainly performing data collection, processing, and analysis to evaluating the audit procedures (Moffitt et al., 2018). As it relates to RPA implementation in audit, they emphasize the importance of the validity of both RPA tools and the data, ensuring proper validity checks and segregation of duties, the need to automate the processing of notable items generated by RPA tools, and the need for privacy and security considerations in order to manage digital audit evidence.

Huang and Vasarhelyi (2019) introduce a four-stage framework for RPA implementation in audit practice and present the outcomes of a pilot project that automates the confirmation process. The RPA-enabled confirmation process occurs by first logging into the electronic confirmation platform, sending confirmation requests, extracting account balances, and downloading the final confirmation (Huang and Vasarhelyi, 2019). The results are then compared to the same confirmation process performed manually to ensure a complete match for accuracy. This paper showcases the feasibility of RPA implementation for certain audit tasks without introducing additional detection or audit risks while decreasing the number of hours spent on the process.

By introducing artificial intelligence (AI) to RPA, Zhang (2019) presents a framework for intelligent process automation (IPA) for audits. IPA encompasses a suite of technologies that can be found on the continuum between RPA and cognitive automation, technologies that can automate tasks using structured data as well as unstructured data for inference involving processes (Lacity and Willcocks, 2017). As it relates to auditing, Zhang (2019) describes potential opportunities for IPA use in the audits of pensions (by using natural language processing [NLP] or computer vision to organize digital pension plans) and inventory (by using drones to scan RFID tags and an AI tool to analyze images). Further evidence is needed to ascertain whether IPA can or should be implemented in actual audit engagements.

Moving beyond conceptual work, Tiberius and Hirth (2019) conduct an exploratory survey of experts in a two-round Delphi study in Germany to generate the most likely scenario with regard to a broad array of technological trends in auditing for 5–10 years into the future. In terms of RPA-related predictions, the study reports that 93 % of respondents agreed that routine audit tasks will be automated, thus relieving auditors to focus more on more challenging judgment encompassing work. Interestingly, the overall expert impression is that they do not foresee significant disruptive changes caused by the advancements in technology influencing auditing practice in the near future.

Highlighting the importance of engaging with professionals, Manita et al. (2020) report results of interviews with experienced auditors of the five largest firms in France. They suggest that digitalization will make audit more relevant and improve its value proposition by removing the need to manually perform repetitive tasks, thus allowing the auditors to focus on evaluation of estimates, judgments, and unusual transactions.

Munoko et al. (2019) uniquely focus on exploring the ethical implications of AI in auditing. They emphasize the importance of ethical AI governance and practical guidance related to AI use for individual auditors, audit firms, and the profession and society as a whole.

13.2.2 Review of literature on RPA in public accounting

In addition to exploring RPA tool implementation in auditing, there are two studies that expand to other areas of RPA implementation in public accounting. Cooper et al. (2019a) interview RPA leaders at Big Four accounting firms in the US and find that RPA has reached the greatest levels of adoption in tax services, with slower adoptions in advisory and audit services. They also report that lower-level employees often drive RPA implementation and that it has resulted in measurable and significant cost savings and efficiency improvements (Cooper et al., 2019a). Subsequently, Cooper et al. (2019b) compare RPA-related perceptions of top- and bottom-level employees in public accounting and report general agreement of the positive influence of RPA on the work of accountants.

13.2.3 Review of literature on RPA for accounting tasks in industry

Another stream of literature employs qualitative methods to investigate the use of RPA tools for accounting and finance tasks in companies from various industries. Kokina and Blanchette (2019) interview experienced accounting professionals who have had firsthand exposure to RPA implementation. Through the lens of Task–Technology Fit and Technology-to-Performance Chain, they document task suitability for RPA, motivation to implement the tools, challenges encountered in early RPA implementation, changes in risk and control environment, as well as organizational governance structures necessary for successful RPA deployment. They also document quantitative and qualitative performance indicators specific to RPA. They find that organizations are challenged by the need to understand a process at a keystroke level and the need to build in error handling which requires documentation of the failures that could occur at each step of the process that is being automated.

To address the uncertainty surrounding the roles that the human accountants need to fill to successfully work alongside bots and the competencies that need to be developed, Kokina et al. (2019) conduct interviews with professionals to document and categorize the skills required in order for accountants to actively engage in RPA implementations in their organizations. Adapting the categories of AI-driven business and technology roles, they thematically organize the skills and competencies specific to RPA implementation alongside the following five roles: Identifier, Explainer, Trainer, Sustainer, and Analyzer. They find that the work of accountants is transitioning from "doing" to "reviewing" and that accountants are uniquely positioned to serve as subject matter experts or Explainers who can communicate to bot developers in great detail the steps and internal controls of a particular process or task. In addition, accountants can successfully fulfill the Sustainer role, in which they manage bots and monitor the environment for changes and determine whether the IT organization needs to be notified in order to make those changes in bot code.

Oesterreich et al. (2019) also look within organizations to determine how the role of a controller has changed as a result of automation. They report that controllers' roles have become more data-driven and that data science and IT skills are central to their role in addition to being able to fulfill the role of a strategic business partner.

In sum, the literature review shows that much of the published work on RPA has been in the area of auditing and public accounting in the US context, but only few studies have looked at RPA in corporate accounting settings. As a result, we analyze the characteristics of (corporate) accounting processes that make them good candidates for RPA in the next section.

13.3 RPA and the nature of accounting processes

Generally, companies regard RPA to be well suited for the automation of processes that are mature and rules-based, have high volume and are repetitive, and operate in digital form with multiple systems (e. g., Lacity et al., 2015; Kokina and Blanchette, 2019). Hence, in order to analyze the applicability of RPA for accounting processes, we must first take a look at the nature of accounting tasks.

While there are many structured frameworks to characterize tasks, Perrow's (1970) framework characterizes tasks by their degree of routineness which in return reflects the uncertainty of the task. Brownell and Dunk (1991) constitute that "[...] the underpinnings of virtually all conceptualizations of task uncertainty in the literature related to the work of Perrow" (Brownell and Dunk, 1991, 694). Perrow's framework has been widely adopted in the academic literature (e. g., Brownell and Dunk, 1991; Sicotte and Langley, 2000; Fry and Slocum, 1984; Williams and Seaman, 2002; Ylinen and Gullkvist, 2011).

According to Perrow (1970), tasks can be described as "non-routine," when established techniques for handling tasks do not exist (low analyzability) or when substantial variety or novelty in the tasks is encountered (high number of exceptions). Conversely, when tasks are analyzable with few exceptions, they are described as "routine." Figure 1 shows the relationships between the two dimensions (Abernethy and Brownell, 1997).

Task Analyzability

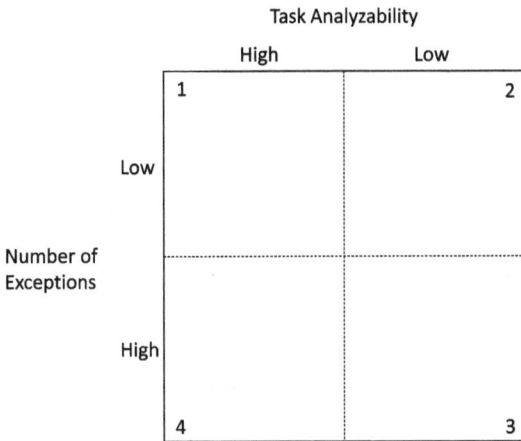

Figure 1: Perrow's framework for task routines (Perrow, 1970).

In order to apply Perrow's framework to accounting processes, a closer look at the accounting discipline itself is recommended. The accounting discipline is made up of various branches, not just one. The two major branches are management accounting and financial accounting, further branches are tax accounting and auditing. Management accounting and financial accounting are comprised of different processes and tasks that fulfill the information needs of different stakeholders. Financial accounting has the primary responsibility of preparing financial statements through bookkeeping processes in accordance with law, rules, standards, and regulations to communicate this information to parties outside the organization. Instead, management accounting is not governed by any statue and covers key processes such as strategic and operational planning (budgeting), forecasting, and management reporting, with the primary focus on the information needs of the internal decision makers like the management (Libby et al., 2020).

As a result, the nature of management accounting tasks differs from financial accounting tasks. While the two disciplines contain both routine and non-routine tasks, research implies that financial accounting tasks are generally to a greater extent structured with fewer exceptions, and therefore tend to experience higher routineness than management accounting tasks. For example, Alix et al. (1996) note that bookkeeping as central part of financial accounting "[...] is a highly structured, repetitive part of accounting" (Alix et al., 1996, 375) and Moffitt et al. (2018) point out that "[...] tasks associated with payroll, accounts payable, and accounts receivable are often mundane and recurring [...]" (Moffitt et al., 2018, 3).

Further support for this view can be drawn from the shared service center (SSC) literature. SSCs are regarded as ideal for tasks that are structured, standardized, and repetitive and are in a transaction processing environment (e. g., Lacity et al., 2011). A survey in Germany, Austria, and Switzerland conducted by the University of St.

Gallen together with KPMG indicates that financial accounting tasks like bookkeeping are regarded as highly suitable for SSCs due to their repetitive and transactional nature, whereas management accounting tasks were seen with less prevalence (Reimann and Möller, 2013). Correspondingly, other research shows that companies primarily transfer financial accounting tasks such as accounts payable to SSCs whereas management accountings tasks such as planning and budgeting are rarely transferred out (PWC, 2013; Stewart et al., 2004).

Based on the argumentation above on the nature of their tasks, financial accounting and management accounting processes can be depicted in Perrow's framework as illustrated in Figure 2. Hence, financial accounting processes as a whole tend to have a higher degree of routineness, whereas management accounting processes have a higher number of exceptions and a lower analyzability which leads to lower degree of routineness. Undoubtedly, this conceptual view provides opportunities for further empirical research.

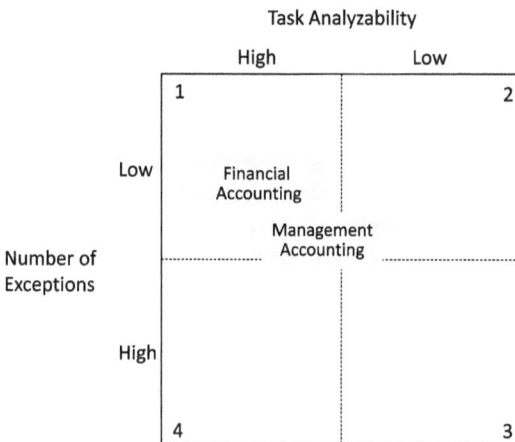

Figure 2: Nature of financial and management accounting tasks.

To provide some examples of specific accounting tasks that organizations have automated with RPA, Kokina and Blanchette (2019) summarize early RPA implementation and find that RPA is widely used to automate processes in the following financial accounting areas:

Order-to-cash

- Customer master file: new customer record creation, customer data maintenance, customer credit limit approval, loans, and bank account applications.
- Invoicing: customer order entry, invoice preparation, invoice exception handling, and reinvoicing.
- Cash receipts: identification of duplicate payments and cash application.

– Resolution process: customer follow-up, issue identification and support, and client communication.

Procure-to-pay
– Vendor master file information: vendor creation.
– Purchase order activity: purchase order creation and modification, and open purchase order management.
– Invoice processing: incomplete invoice information identification, audit and review of travel invoices, preparation of procure-to-pay reports, and unpaid invoice issue resolution.
– Cash disbursements: payment processing and requesting payment date for invoices.

Record-to-report
– Journal entries: data entry and account classification, journal entry preparation and entry.
– Reconciliation and analysis: extraction of account activity from bank web site, uploading and validation of bank statement activity.
– Account analysis: accruals creation, calculation of warranties, commissions, and rebates.
– Closing process: export and data consolidation, reconciliation process.

In these automations, RPA was most often used to open, read, and create e-mails, log in to enterprise apps, copy/paste and fill in forms, read or write to database, follow decision rules, extract data from documents, and obtain human input via e-mails/workflow. RPA functionality such as moving files and folders, collecting statistics, making calculations, and pulling data from the internet were used less frequently.

Transferring this line of argumentation to the applicability of RPA for accounting, financial accounting in general seems to be more suitable for RPA than management accounting processes. Indeed, empirical studies (see Section 13.2) and publicly available reports of companies like Merck (Pellegrino and Mega, 2020), Daimler (PWC, 2018), KION Group, or ProSieben Media (Beisswenger et al., 2020) indicate that the introduction of RPA in the accounting field is mainly driven by financial accounting processes. Reports on the introduction of RPA in the field of management accounting, instead, are far more seldom or limited to the use of RPA for automating management reports (Hermann et al., 2018).

13.4 RPA heatmaps for accounting processes

Financial and management accounting are dominated by a number of processes. Central processes in management accounting include, for example, management reporting, operational planning (budgeting), forecasting, or cost and performance accounting (e. g., International Group of Controlling, 2012). Instead, key processes in financial accounting are, for example, payroll, accounts receivable, accounts payable, cash management, or fixed asset accounting.

For each of the described processes in accounting the question arises, how well suited they are for the use of RPA. Of course, not all processes are equally suitable. To graphically present the suitability of accounting processes and sub-processes, process heatmaps are an established instrument in practice. Regarding the suitability of RPA for accounting processes, there are various heatmaps available, mainly driven by consulting companies (e. g., Deloitte, 2018; Langmann and Turi, 2020; Wenning and Przytulla, 2020). Although such heatmaps are typically generated by practical project experience rather than scientific rigorous approaches, they give first indications of which processes in accounting might be more suitable for RPA and provide further opportunity for research. In other words, they show how strong the individual processes are affected by the introduction of RPA. Figure 3 shows an RPA process heatmap for management accounting processes while Figure 4 shows an RPA process heatmap for financial accounting processes. Conceptually, such RPA heatmaps are based on the extent to which the respective process fulfills the evaluation criteria such as being rules-based, high-volume, or repetitive (e. g., Lacity et al., 2015). A look at Deloitte's (2018) RPA heatmap of financial accounting shows that sub-processes of accounts receivable, accounts payable, accounts payable, general accounting, and management reporting are are particularly suitable for robotization (see Figure 3). In management accounting, the sub-processes of cost and profit accounting and management reporting stand out as good candidates for automation (see Figure 4).

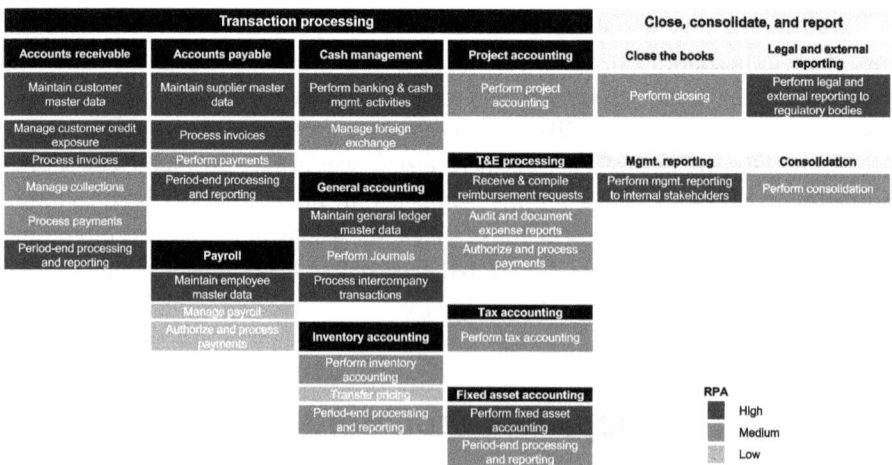

Figure 3: RPA – heatmap of financial accounting processes (Deloitte, 2018).

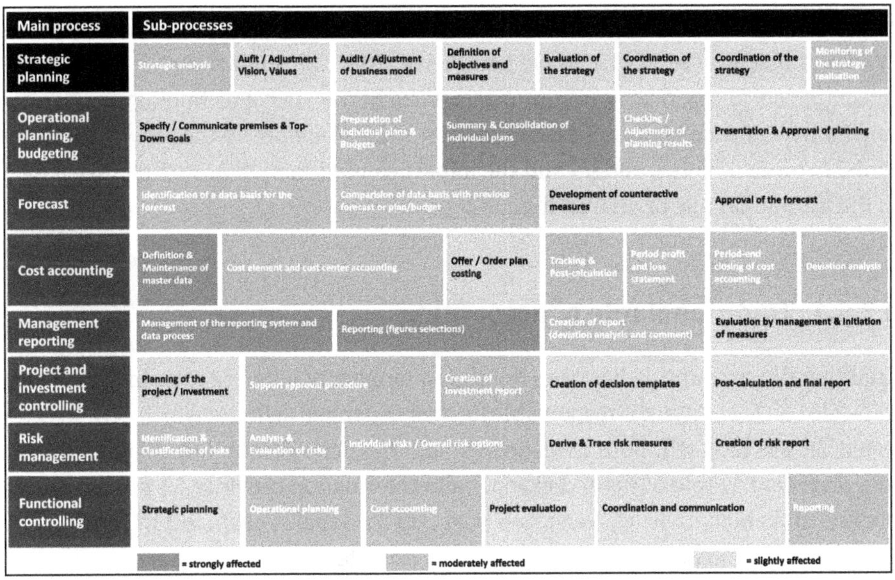

Main process	Sub-processes							
Strategic planning	Strategic analysis	Audit / Adjustment Vision, Values	Audit / Adjustment of business model	Definition of objectives and measures	Evaluation of the strategy	Coordination of the strategy	Coordination of the strategy	Monitoring of the strategy realization
Operational planning, budgeting	Specify / Communicate premises & Top-Down Goals	Preparation of individual plans & Budgets	Summary & Consolidation of individual plans	Checking / Adjustment of planning results	Presentation & Approval of planning			
Forecast	Identification of a data basis for the forecast	Comparison of data basis with previous forecast or plan/budget	Development of counteractive measures	Approval of the forecast				
Cost accounting	Definition & Maintenance of master data	Cost element and cost center accounting	Offer / Order plan costing	Tracking & Post-calculation	Period profit and loss statement	Period-end closing of cost accounting	Deviation analysis	
Management reporting	Management of the reporting system and data process	Reporting (figures selections)	Creation of report (deviation analysis and comment)	Evaluation by management & initiation of measures				
Project and investment controlling	Planning of the project / Investment	Support approval procedure	Creation of investment report	Creation of decision templates	Post-calculation and final report			
Risk management	Identification & Classification of risks	Analysis & Evaluation of risks	Individual risks / Overall risk options	Derive & Trace risk measures	Creation of risk report			
Functional controlling	Strategic planning	Operational planning	Cost accounting	Project evaluation	Coordination and communication	Reporting		

= strongly affected   = moderately affected   = slightly affected

Figure 4: RPA – heatmap of management accounting processes (Wenning and Przytulla, 2020).

Both heatmaps highlight that rather than an entire accounting process (e. g., fixed asset accounting or management reporting) being suited for RPA, sub-processes are the right level of detail for selection. For example, not the entire management reporting process is well suited for RPA, but rather the sub-process steps of "report generation" and "management reporting system and data process." These sub-process steps typically are highly repetitive, rule-based, and standardized, and are mostly carried out frequently (daily, monthly). Other sub-process steps such as the "management evaluation and initiation of measures" are highly individual and unstructured, and normally require an individual discussion which makes them unsuitable for RPA.

Although the heatmaps' indications seem logical and convincing, in practice processes may vary completely from company to company. As a result, a sub-process like "report generation" might be conceptually convincing to be supported by RPA, in reality however, the process could have such small volumes (e. g., only one small report once a month), not making it a good case for introducing RPA into that process.

13.5 RPA as a driver for new roles in accounting

Advances in information technologies often serve as a driver for reducing the traditional role of the accountant which has been transaction processing and financial report preparation, while supporting a shift towards the role of a business partner (El-Sayed and Youssef, 2015; Byrne and Pierce, 2007; Järvenpää, 2007). By partially or completely taking over accounting processes, RPA is such a technology with direct and indirect effect on tasks and competencies – and therefore on the role – of accountants. In order to better understand the impact coming from RPA, we first take a look at the traditional role of accounting.

13.5.1 Traditional role of accounting

Traditionally, accounting has been fulfilling a number of different roles in a company. Typically, an accountant is responsible for a set of defined tasks for which certain competencies are required. Both management and financial accountants have traditionally played a key role of the scorekeeper and information provider for decision makers and stakeholders (e. g., Verstegen et al., 2007; Needles et al., 2013). In this role, both management and financial accountants execute standard (transactional) activities – financial accountants, for example, perform invoice processing and bookkeeping; management accountants, for example, undertake cost allocations and performance measurement – and generate the resulting information (e. g., management reports and accounting statements).

However, the performance of transactional activities and the simple provision of numbers and standard reports generate only limited added value in many companies today. Due to the ongoing adoption of ERP systems and business intelligence systems which began more than two decades ago, transactional activities have been continuously automated and decision makers either automatically receive current financial performance information from a system or can create such reports via self-service at any time (e. g., Peters et al., 2016; Sánchez–Rodríguez and Spraakman, 2012). For this reason, accountants are expected to shift their focus towards enriched tasks such as those focused on being business partners, hence acting as a proactive source of ideas and as consultants (e. g., Bhimani and Willcocks, 2014; Oesterreich et al., 2019, Schäfer and Weber, 2018). As a *business partner*, financial and management accountants should, for example, actively advice on balance sheet policy and tax optimization, independently keep an eye on the achievement of the objectives, while monitoring and coordinating countermeasures that have been initiated.

13.5.2 RPA-related changes in accountants' roles

The increasing spread of digitalization technologies such as big data, analytics, and RPA change tasks, skills, and competencies of financial and management accounting professionals (e. g., Bhimani and Willcocks, 2014; Oesterreich et al., 2019, Kokina et al., 2019). As an automation technology, RPA aims at efficiency gains by performing transactional activities with standardized and repetitive patterns. As a result, the traditional role of the accountant as scorekeeper and information provider performing mainly transactional tasks will probably be largely or even completely replaced in the future by robots. At the same time, the importance of the accountant's role as business partner will increase. Supporting this view, El-Sayed and Youssef (2015) conclude their literature review stating that the change of "[...] the role of accountants from a traditional bookkeeper to more of a business partner..." is likely to occur in the near future (El-Sayed and Youssef, 2015, 206). Lawson (2019) similarly notes that the new role of finance and accounting professionals will include "[...] providing business insight and serving as strategically oriented business partners" (Lawson, 2019, 18). To serve as business partners, accountants will need a solid understanding of the business model and communicative and analytical strength, as well as a problem solving-oriented and critical mindset paired with coordination skills (Burns and Baldvinsdottir, 2005; Siegel et al., 2003). These are all skills and competencies in which an accountant, rather than an accounting robot, has his or her strengths.

In corporate practice, however, research also shows that accountants still focus on traditional tasks today. Pietrzak and Wnuk-Pel (2015) conclude their research study on management accountants that accountants "[...] still focus on traditional areas of costing and financial analysis, like performance measurement, operational budgeting and cost control" (Pietrzak and Wnuk-Pel, 2015, 285). Also, Rieg (2018) summarizes his study's results on management accounting tasks by stating: "[...] yet the emphasis of MA work still seems to lie in the operational area" (Rieg, 2018, 203). Other current studies on the role of management accounting show similar results (e. g., Schäffer and Weber, 2018; Oesterreich et al., 2019).

In recent years new roles for financial and management accounting have emerged in corporate practice and research next to the traditional roles discussed above (e. g., Schäffer and Brückner, 2019). Two roles that are particularly interesting with respect to the impact of RPA as an automation technology can be found in Figure 5, which displays a model for future roles in management accounting at BASF. These roles are *guardian* (focused on governance) and *pathfinder* (focused on innovation) (Seufert and Kruk, 2016).

In the *guardian* role, an accountant should ensure the establishment of and compliance with company-wide guidelines and standards in the area of compliance, e. g., travel expenses, account assignment guidelines, or defining key figures. With the introduction of RPA and other digitalization technologies, this is likely to become more important in the future. The use of RPA in accounting requires regulations that are not only IT-technical in nature. Questions such as "which accounting data can be used by robots?" or "what are the specifics for governance in the accounting field to mitigate risks arising from the use of RPA?" must be clarified. A role such as the *pathfinder* has the task of continuously screening for new trends, digitalization technologies, and processes and methods for accounting, such as analytics or RPA. The accountant fill-

Business Partner	Pathfinder
▪ Acting entrepreneurially	▪ Sourcing trends and technologies
▪ Giving financial business advice	▪ Bridging business with data scientists
▪ Supporting and driving change	▪ Driving Controlling transformation

**Analyzing business
Challenging constructively
Communicating concisely**

Guardian	Service Expert
▪ Managing risks	▪ Managing effective and efficient processes
▪ Giving guidance in governance processes	▪ Continously improving workflows
▪ Performing internal process controls	▪ Providing Controlling trainings and support

All Controlling roles equally important in moving towards „Controlling 2025"

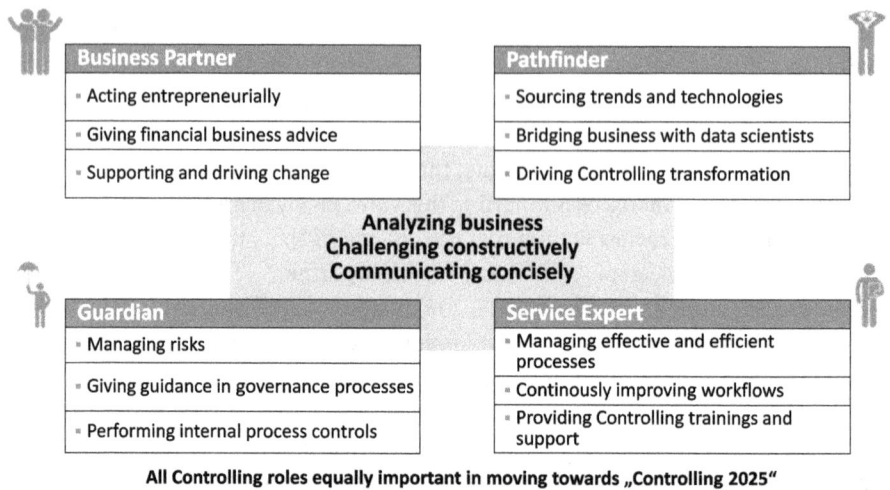

Figure 5: Management accounting roles at BASF (Seufert and Kruk, 2016).

ing this role screens, for example, RPA tools concerning their portability and applicability for particular accounting processes (Seufert and Kruk, 2016).

While the *pathfinder* seems a rather broad role concerning digitalization technologies, some companies develop roles in the accounting organization specifically for RPA as a technology. Deutsche Post DHL, one of the world's leading logistics companies, for example, introduced two new roles in accounting, each focusing on different aspects of RPA. In the role of a *process champion* an accountant is responsible for monitoring and controlling an automated end-to-end process. Accordingly, this role ensures the actual process is carried out as defined by the target process, both operationally by employees and system-wise by the automated technologies. The rationale is that even if RPA is a rule-based technology that basically works successfully with careful implementation, failures can still occur again and again such as unexpected, new pop-ups which the technology does not know how to handle. Instead, the *automation design expert* at Deutsche Post DHL is also an employee of the accounting department (e. g., accounts payable or central accounting) with a focus on technically maintaining established RPA solutions, i. e., performing first-level maintenance activities. Next to maintenance, this role also technically implements desired extensions and improvements in robots (Wenzel, 2020). Next to these new roles within accounting departments specifically linked to RPA, Kokina et al. (2019) identified further roles such as the *identifier*, who spots opportunities for RPA, and *analyzer*, who uses the output of RPA tools to provide future-oriented insight.

In summary, RPA as an automation technology acts as an enabler that further shifts the emphasis of accounting away from the traditional role as information provider towards a *business partner* and roles like a *pathfinder* or *automation design expert*.

13.5.3 Role shifting requires new skills and competencies

The new roles connected to the introduction of RPA presented above require skills and competencies that go far beyond those of traditional accountants (e. g., Kokina et al., 2019). To assess their applicability and to support the implementation in the field of accounting, she is required to have knowledge of RPA as an automation technology. As a result, today's accountants who step into new roles handling technologies such as RPA should build corresponding skills and competencies. In Deutsche Post DHL, for example, accountants accompanying the new role of *automation design expert* build up their skills in the organization's own automation academy.

Even if not every accountant is supposed to jump into more technically oriented new roles such as the *automation design expert*, he or she must have a solid basic understanding of RPA, including its application possibilities and limits, in order to effectively use and work with the technology, or to serve as respected interface to technical RPA units. The Institute for Management Accountants (IMA, 2019) supports this argumentation by stating in their current framework that accountants should demonstrate an understanding of the potential applications of emerging technologies such as RPA. The shift in roles accompanied by the shift in skills and competencies is also reflected in the training and education offered by leading universities and accounting associations for future accounting experts (e. g., AICPA, 2020; University of Washington, 2019).

However, using the example of management accountants in particular, research shows that the shift of the role of accountants as discussed above cannot be found in the broad market of job postings or skill profiles of accountants in professional social networks (Oesterreich et al., 2019). Hence, it seems like the digital transformation resulting from RPA adoption is not yet widespread in accounting departments.

13.6 Summary and outlook

RPA is driving the digital transformation of accounting in many organizations today. Looking at the nature of accounting processes, especially financial accounting processes with their routine nature such as accounts receivable, accounts payable, or monthly closing are highly suitable for RPA. Within management accounting especially the core processes management reporting and cost accounting are highly suitable for the use of RPA. As a result, the role and competences of accountants will shift from the traditional role as information provider towards more digital and communicative roles like the *business partner* or new digitalization roles like the *pathfinder* or *automation design expert*.

In the coming years, the ongoing expansion of RPA towards IPA with other digitalization technologies from the field of artificial intelligence such as NLP, sentiment analysis, or machine learning algorithms will make robots more intelligent and suitable for more complex tasks. IPA has the power to grasp even more process activities in accounting and therefore speed up the shift of roles and competencies outlined above.

Although there is a body of literature, individual reports from corporates, and first empirical studies on the use of RPA within accounting, further research is required in a number of fields. First, while there are a number of conceptual papers and studies on the suitability of RPA in public accounting and auditing, only very few empirical studies have looked at the implementation of RPA in financial accounting, tax, or even management accounting at all. Hence, empirical research on the suitability of RPA for management accounting processes provides a research opportunity. Second, further empirical research could explore the ways in which RPA is changing the role of accountants and their skills and competencies. Finally, future research could look at the long-term effects of RPA on the accounting function itself. The shift of processes towards RPA in an organization might change the entire organizational setup, including accounting departments. Today's responsibilities and resources of departments in the corporate landscape might fundamentally change with a broad introduction of RPA.

Bibliography

Abernethy MA, Brownell P (1997) Management control systems in research and development organizations: the role of accounting, behavior and personnel controls. Account Organ Soc 22(3–4):233–248

Alix J, Rock RJ, Stenger T (1996) Financial handbook for bankruptcy professionals: a financial and accounting guide for bankruptcy judges, attorneys, and accountants. West, Saint-Paul, USA

American Institute of Certified Public Accountants (AICPA) (2020) Robotic process automation fundamentals for accounting and finance professionals certificate. Available at: https://www.aicpastore.com/ConsultingServices/PRD~PC-188710/PC-188710.jsp

Anagnoste S (2018) Robotic automation process – the operating system for the digital enterprise. In: Proceedings of the international conference on business excellence, vol 12(1), pp 54–69

Appelbaum DA, Kozlowski S (2020) Auditing an RPA-enabled accounting information system. Working paper presented at the 2020 Joint Midyear Meeting of the AIS, SET, and International Sections. American Accounting Association

Bakarich KM, O'Brien P (2020) The robots are coming... but aren't here yet: the use of artificial intelligence technologies in the public accounting profession. Working paper presented at the 2020 Joint Midyear Meeting of the AIS, SET, and International Sections. American Accounting Association

Beisswenger A, Schlott A, von Hirschhausen G, Küster T, Hamann K, Leser C (2020) Robotic process automation im accounting – Beispiele von ProSiebenSat. 1, KION und PwC. ReThinking Finance 3:17–26

Berruti A, Nixon G, Taglioni G, Whiteman R (2017) Intelligent process automation: the engine at the core of the next–generation operating model. Digital McKinsey, March 14

Bhimani A, Willcocks LP (2014) Digitisation, 'big data' and the transformation of accounting information. Account Bus Res 44(4):469–490

Brownell P, Dunk AS (1991) Task uncertainty and its interaction with budgetary participation and budget emphasis: some methodological issues and empirical investigation. Account Organ Soc 16(8):693–703

Burns J, Baldvinsdottir G (2005) An institutional perspective of accountants' new roles – the interplay of contradictions and praxis. Eur Account Rev 14(4):725–757

Byrne S, Pierce B (2007) Towards a more comprehensive understanding of the roles of management accountants. Eur Account Rev 16(3):469–498

Cooper L, Holderness DK, Sorensen T, Wood DA (2019a) Robotic process automation in public accounting. Account Horiz 33(4):15–35

Cooper L, Holderness DK, Sorensen T, Wood DA (2019b) Perceptions of robotic process automation in public accounting. Working paper. Available at: https://papers.ssrn.com/sol3/papers.cfm?abstract_id=3445005&download=yes

Deloitte (2018) Internal controls over financial reporting considerations for developing and implementing bots. Available at: https://www2.deloitte.com/content/dam/Deloitte/us/Documents/audit/us-audit-internal-controls-over-financial-reporting-considerations-for-developing-and-implementing-bots.pdf

El-Sayed H, Youssef MAE-A (2015) "Modes of mediation" for conceptualizing how different roles for accountants are made present. Qual Res Account Manag 12(3):202–229

Eulerich M, Masli A (2020) The use of technology based audit techniques in the internal audit function—is there an improvement in efficiency and effectiveness? Working paper presented at the 2020 Joint Midyear Meeting of the AIS, SET, and International Sections. American Accounting Association

Eulerich M, Pawlowski J (2020) Using robotic process automation (RPA) in the internal audit function: use cases and a potential framework. Working paper presented at the 2020 joint midyear meeting of the AIS, SET, and international sections. American Accounting Association

Forrester (2019) The RPA services market will grow to reach $12 billion by 2023. July 10

Fry LW, Slocum JW (1984) Technology, structure, and workgroup effectiveness: a test of a contingency model. Acad Manag J 27(2):221–224

Hermann K, Stoi R, Wolf B (2018) Robotic process automation im finance & controlling der Mann+Hummel Gruppe. Controlling 30(3):28–34

Houy C, Hamberg M, Fettke P (2019) Robotic process automation in public administration. In: Räckers M, Halsbenning S, Rätz D, Richter D, Schweighofer E (eds) Digitalisierung von Staat und Verwaltung 2019. Gesellschaft für Informatik e. V., Bonn, Germany, pp 62–74

Huang F, Vasarhelyi MA (2019) Applying robotic process automation (RPA) in auditing: a framework. Int J Account Inf Syst 35

IMA – Institute for Management Accountants (2019) IMA management accounting competency framework. Available at: https://www.imanet.org/-/media/590889ef44ad401bb94d83cd43e584b8.ashx?la=en

International Group of Controlling (2012) Controlling process model. Available at: https://www.igc-controlling.org/fileadmin/downloads/Standards/Controlling_Process_Model.pdf

Järvenpää M (2007) Making business partners: a case study on how management accounting culture was changed. Eur Account Rev 16(1):99–142

Kipp P, Curtis MB, Li Z (2020) The attenuating effect of intelligent agents and agent autonomy on managers' ability to diffuse responsibility for and engage in earnings management. Working paper presented at the 2020 joint midyear meeting of the AIS, SET, and international sections. American Accounting Association

Kokina J, Blanchette S (2019) Early evidence of digital labor in accounting: innovation with robotic process automation. Int J Account Inf Syst 35

Kokina J, Davenport TH (2017) The emergence of artificial intelligence: how automation is changing auditing. J Emerg Technol Account 14(1):115–122

Kokina J, Gilleran R, Blanchette S, Stoddard D (2019) Accountant as digital innovator: roles and competencies in the age of automation. Available at: https://papers.ssrn.com/sol3/papers.cfm?abstract_id=3449720

Lacity MC, Willcocks LP (2017) Robotic process automation and risk mitigation. SB Publishing, London, UK

Lacity MC, Solomon S, Yan A, Willcocks LP (2011) Business process outsourcing studies: a critical review and research directions. J Inf Technol 26(4):221–258

Lacity MC, Willcocks LP, Craig A (2015). Robotic process automation at Telefónica 02. Available at: https://www.umsl.edu/~lacitym/TelefonicaOUWP022015FINAL.pdf

Langmann C, Turi D (2020) Robotic Process Automation (RPA) – Digitalisierung und Automatisierung von Prozessen. Springer, Wiesbaden, Germany

Lawson R (2019) New competencies for management accountants. CPA J 89(9):18–21

Libby R, Libby PA, Hodge F (2020) Financial accounting, 10th edn. McGraw–Hill Education, New York City, USA

Manita R, Elommal N, Baudier P, Hikkerova L (2020) The digital transformation of external audit and its impact on corporate governance. Technol Forecast Soc Change 150

Moffitt KC, Rozario AM, Vasarhelyi MA (2018) Robotic process automation for auditing. J Emerg Technol Account 15(1):1–10

Munoko I, Brown–Liburd HL, Vasarhelyi M (2019) The ethical implications of using artificial intelligence in auditing. J Bus Ethics

Needles BE, Powers M, Crosson SV (2013) Financial and managerial accounting, 10th edn. Cengage Learning, Boston, USA

Oesterreich TD, Teuteberg F, Bensberg F, Buscher G (2019) The controlling profession in the digital age: understanding the impact of digitization on the controller's job roles, skills and competences. Int J Account Inf Syst 35

Pellegrino M, Mega P (2020) Robotics Process Automation @ Merck. ReThinking Finance 3:33–42

Perrow C (1970) Organizational analysis – a sociological view. Brooks/Cole, Belmont, USA

Peters MD, Wieder B, Sutton SG, Wakefield J (2016) Business intelligence systems use in performance measurement capabilities: implications for enhanced competitive advantage. Int J Account Inf Syst 21:1–17

Pietrzak Ż, Wnuk-Pel T (2015) The roles and qualities of management accountants in organizations – evidence from the field. In: Presented at the 20th international scientific conference economics and management – 2015 (ICEM–2015), pp 281–285

PWC (2013) Financial shared service center on the rise toward valuable business partners – 2nd generation FSSCs. Available at: https://www.pwc.de/de/finanzdienstleistungen/assets/pwc_studie_financial_shared_service_centers.pdf

PWC (2018) Digitalisierung im Finanz– und Rechnungswesen und was sie für die Abschlussprüfung bedeutet. Available at: https://www.pwc.de/de/im-fokus/digitale-abschlusspruefung/pwc-digitale-abschlusspruefung-2018.pdf

PwC (2020) Robotic Process Automation (RPA) in der DACH–Region. Analyse mit blick auf finance & accounting. Available at: https://www.pwc.de/de/rechnungslegung/robotic-process-automation-rpa-in-der-dach-region.pdf

Reimann A, Möller K (2013). Shared Services für Controlling–Prozesse. Available at: https://assets.kpmg/content/dam/kpmg/pdf/2013/09/shared-services-controllingprozesse-neu-2013-kpmg.pdf

Rieg R (2018) Tasks, interaction and role perception of management accountants: evidence from Germany. J Manag Control 29(2):183–220

Sánchez–Rodríguez C, Spraakman G (2012) ERP systems and management accounting: a multiple case study. Qual Res Account Manag 9(4):398–414

Schäffer U, Brückner L (2019) Rollenspezifische Kompetenzprofile für das Controlling der Zukunft. Control Manag Rev 63(7):14–30

Schäffer U, Weber J (2018) Digitalisierung ante portas – Die Veränderung des Controllings im Spiegel der dritten WHU– Zukunftsstudie. Controlling 30(1):42–48

Seufert A, Kruk K (2016) Digitale Transformation und Controlling – Herausforderungen und Implikationen dargestellt am Beispiel der BASF. In: Leyk J, Kirchmann M, Grönke K, Gleich R (eds) Konzerncontrolling 2020. Haufe, Munich, Germany, pp 141–164

Sicotte H, Langley A (2000) Integration mechanisms and R&A project performance. J Eng Technol Manag 17(1):1–37

Siegel G, Sorensen J, Richtermeyer S (2003) Are you a business partner? Strateg Fin 85(3):38–43

Stewart C, Donnellan M, Read C (2004) CFO insights: achieving high performance through finance business process outsourcing. Wiley, Chichester

Taulli T (2020) The robotic process automation handbook. Springer, New York, USA

Tiberius C, Hirth S (2019) Impacts of digitization on auditing: a Delphi study for Germany. J Int Account Audit Tax 37

University of Washington (2019) The future of accounting: robotic process automation. Available at: https://blog.foster.uw.edu/rpa-future/

Vasarhelyi MA (2013) Formalization of standards, automation, robots, and IT governance. J Inf Syst 27(1):1–11

Vasarhelyi MA, Alles MG, Williams KT (2010) Continuous assurance for the now economy. Institute of Chartered Accountants of Australia, Sydney, Australia

Verstegen BH, De Loo I, Mol P, Slagter K, Geerkens H (2007) Classifying controllers by activities: an exploratory study. J Appl Manag Account Res 5(2):9–32

Wenning A, Przytulla G (2020) Robotic process automation im controlling. ReThinking Finance 3:9–16

Wenzel S (2020) RPA – das Altsystem von morgen oder doch Beschleuniger digitaler Transformation? ReThinking Finance 3:43–48

Williams JJ, Seaman AE (2002) Management accounting systems change and departmental performance: the influence of managerial information and task uncertainty. Manag Account Res 13(4):419–445

Ylinen M, Gullkvist B (2011) The effects of tolerance for ambiguity and task uncertainty on the balanced and combined use of project controls. Eur Account Rev 21(2):395–415

Zhang C (2019) Intelligent process automation in audit. J Emerg Technol Account 16(2):69–88

Mario Richard Smeets, Ralf Jürgen Ostendorf, and
Peter Gordon Rötzel

14 RPA for the financial industry

Particular challenges and outstanding suitability combined

Abstract: Like many service industries, the financial industry is largely characterized
by administrative and back-office processes and distinguished by a broad systems
landscape with a high proportion of legacy systems. Missing interfaces between information systems, user interfaces, or web applications often require many manual
activities. As banks are often functionally organized into traditional departments, a
process-oriented organizational structure is rarely in place. The financial industry
therefore offers enormous potential for the use of robotic process automation (RPA)
and the raising of potential benefits such as process-related cost savings, time reductions, and quality improvements.

The aim of this chapter is to describe the tremendous opportunities that the use of
RPA technology offers to the financial industry and to explain how these opportunities
can be realized. Therefore, we start by explaining the challenges that progressive digitalization poses to the industry and how RPA, but also more advanced technologies
(that work not only rule-based but also define own rules), such as artificial intelligence, can help to overcome them. As well as providing an overview of the various
applications of RPA in the financial industry, we also provide a comprehensive case
study of a relevant practical application.

Keywords: Robotic process automation, RPA applications, process automation, financial industry

14.1 Introduction

In financial institutions, they are on the daily agenda of many employees: time consuming processes that are completely rule-based and that follow rigid patterns. These
processes keep them away from other, often more important activities. Maintaining
data, checking, and entering systems using long lists and bridging non-existent technical interfaces by manual transfer work: in financial institutions, these activities are
mostly found in the back office, but also in IT or controlling (management accounting) and financial accounting. Automating such activities creates opportunities for
other, more complex tasks. But automation – here, the execution of repetitive tasks
by software robots (Ivancic et al., 2019) – is not always done as easily and quickly as
is sometimes propagated. Often, the costs of automation by creating interfaces and
(re)programming the applications exceed their possible benefits or are simply technically not feasible. There is an alternative: robotic process automation (RPA) – the use

https://doi.org/10.1515/9783110676693-014

of software for automated handling of digital processes. RPA is still a quite emerging technology, and it is currently receiving enormous attention, especially in the financial sector (e. g., Kumar, 2018 and Smeets et al., 2019).

The following part of the chapter places RPA in the sector focus of the financial industry. The chapter begins by briefly explaining the individual challenges that the digitization of the financial industry involves. It then shows to what extent RPA can make a valuable contribution to overcoming possible hurdles on the way to becoming a digital financial institution. The potential contribution of RPA is illustrated in more detail using three different categories of use cases. These are those in which RPA supports employees, replaces them, or enables completely new processes or even new business models. A final, comprehensive example clearly illustrates how RPA can help to overcome departmental boundaries and digitize service processes end-to-end.

The example used is a case study from 2019/2020, which describes the end-to-end digitalization and automation of a customer-oriented process in a German securities institution. The case study is supplemented by numerous experiences of the authors from several years of strategic and operational consulting of financial institutions in their application of RPA and similar technologies.

14.2 Digitalization: a challenge for the financial industry

The term digitalization can mean two things (Alt and Puschmann, 2016): First, digitalization refers to a technical transformation of originally analogue data (text, image, sound, etc.) into a form that can be processed by IT. Secondly, digitalization can mean a social transformation. This refers to the increasing integration of IT in all areas of life and the resulting changes in habits or processes of daily life. Both aspects have an impact on the financial industry. In the following, the latter understanding of digitalization is relevant. In the further course of the chapter, however, when it comes to analyzing the transformation of analogue to digital data, the former understanding becomes relevant.

Digitalization creates major challenges for the financial sector.[1] Customers demand digital information exchange, communication, and product deals. Banks and financial service providers are therefore required to provide their products and services digitally. This leads to a transformation of such processes from analogue to digital, the "digital transformation." But it often lacks an actual transformation. Rather,

---

1 Alt and Puschmann (2016) provide a good overview of the potential, but also the challenges of digitalization for the financial industry.

business processes that have been tried and tested in the field are reproduced digitally, without considering the differences between a digital and an analogue process (more on this in the further course). This regularly leads to unclear and inefficient processes. They are often only partially digitalized and are provided with media breaks. An actual end-to-end digitalization – a process that starts and ends with digital input without analogue interruptions – is missing, as the following example shows.

> A bank enables its customers to take out a liability insurance policy online – all digital – a typical commission business with which banks generate commission earnings outside the asset and liability business. For this purpose, the bank places advertisements on its own homepage. A direct link to the product offer is missing in the advertisement. Instead, it refers to the menu item to be selected. Once there, customers will find a wide variety of insurance packages, some with modular components that can be selected. As soon as the customers have made their decision, they enter their own data in an online mask and finally receive a confirmation that the data have been saved and forwarded. These data are now initially stored temporarily until a clerk in the bank's back office retrieves and prints them – after information by e-mail. With the help of the printout, he or she records the data in various systems. If individual data do not match, he or she creates a letter to the respective customer to request the remaining data or data that need to be corrected. If he or she receives the data a few days to weeks later, he or she creates the insurance policy in the system and sends all documents to the new customers (Smeets et al., 2019).

The example can be transferred to other areas and products, for example consumer credits or savings accounts. It shows the weak points of this digitalization attempt:
-   The process is not planned from the customer's side, otherwise a direct jump to product completion would be possible.
-   The variety of possible product variations makes it almost impossible to close a deal without prior comprehensive consultation – an example of digitalizing a stationary process without redesigning and adapting it accordingly – in other words, transforming it.
-   The subsequent steps and the printing and recapture of data show the break between digital and no longer digital process flow. There is no end-to-end digitalization.

However, a digitalization according to our understanding would be possible with some adjustments, as the following continuation of the example shows.

> The bank first revises the process by replanning it from the customer's side and eliminating obstacles and detours. The online product offering is reduced signifi-

cantly after analyses show that more than 80 % of customers who take out policies online choose a certain basic variant of liability insurance. All other combinations are chosen only very rarely. In the future, only two basic variants can be taken out online. For more specific variants, in the future there will again be stationary (or even media) advice from bank employees. Once customers have entered their data online, these could ideally be transferred directly into the legal database of all the necessary systems (Smeets et al., 2019).

From the customer's perspective, the process is fundamentally changed. The customer now finds a digital process that is so simple that they can find their way around on their own. However, a complete digitalization of the process has still not been achieved. As before, customer data are still processed by bank employees – manually – which still leads to unnecessary effort and costs. So, we must distinguish: digitalization of a process from the customer's point of view differs from digitalization from the point of view of the institute. While the former is achieved primarily through process adjustments, the latter requires technological adjustments. One technological alternative for taking the second step is RPA.

14.3 RPA in the financial industry

14.3.1 Our definition of RPA

In a first step, we need a suitable definition of RPA. We define it as follows (Smeets et al., 2019): RPA or the term "robot" does not mean a physical machine, but rather installable software. It supports people in carrying out their digitally executed activities and processes as a kind of virtual assistant. In most cases, processes can be automated with RPA when they are rule-based and structured. RPA communicates with other applications and systems, controls them, and transfers or manipulates data. This requires little or no intervention in existing IT architectures since RPA usually uses the user interface to operate the automated applications. There is no need for interfering with program code or for using interfaces to the automated applications. The software robots can work both on the desktops of employees and in a kind of dark processing – on servers, for example.

Unlike other authors (e. g., Ranerup and Henriksen, 2019), we explicitly distinguish RPA from artificial intelligence (AI), since RPA does not use any independent learning or the like, which in turn is key part of the definition of AI (see, e. g., Jarrahi, 2018, Kolbjørnsrud et al., 2017 or Mahroof, 2019). This precise differentiation enables us to regard AI as a complementary technology to process automation, which in our opinion promotes a clear distinction between those technologies in the automation environment that often require extensive explanation.

14.3.2 Goals of RPA

In a second step, it is useful to examine the different objectives that a financial institution can pursue with the use of the technology. There are at least four categories of potential that RPA has in store for the financial industry: cost savings, quality improvements, time reduction, and the other potentials that can often be derived from the first three (Smeets et al., 2019).

Cost savings

One of the most relevant arguments for process automation is the cost savings that can be achieved. These are often possible because employees can use their capacities for other activities if robots take over repetitive processes or process parts from them. This results in a reduction of the bound full-time equivalents (FTE) for the respective process. It should be noted that automation by RPA does not necessarily mean that the staff previously involved in process execution are released and no costs are incurred for them. Rather, the purpose of RPA is to free them from repetitive, time consuming processes, so that there is then more capacity available for value adding activities. The magnitude of the potential cost savings of RPA varies and depends on the process (its complexity and many other factors), the application area, and the industry. Cost savings range from 25 % (e. g., Ostrowicz, 2018 and Watson and Wright, 2017) up to 90 % (Smeets et al., 2019). The focus is in the range of approximately 30 % and 60–70 % (e. g., Willcocks and Lacity, 2016; Willcocks et al., 2017 and Tucci, 2015). The orders of magnitude also differ depending on the cost factors included. License costs, maintenance costs, and more should be considered, which unfortunately is not always the case. Based on the authors' many years of practical experience with RPAs, an order of magnitude of approximately 25 % cost saving compared to the current process using RPA technology appears to be a realistic value for financial industry.

Quality

Of course, the basic principle is always that the quality of a work result should be as high as possible. However, the quality objective is not always explicitly stated as a strategic goal and is often assumed to be more of a given. Nevertheless, such an increase in quality in process handling can also be a strategic goal for an RPA application. Human process handling, especially with frequent, repetitive activities, is prone to errors. However, process handling by RPA bots is not – if correctly developed and tested. Unsystematic errors – errors that occur randomly, for example caused by humans – are excluded by RPA. The only risk that remains is that of systematic errors, which should not be neglected. Incorrect programming that is not noticed until the RPA rollout can quickly lead to large volumes of false process results. This can be counteracted with appropriate tests, which are also required by supervisory authorities in the financial industry for software development (in Germany, e. g., BaFin, 2018).

Time reduction

Time reduction can be the third explicit goal of automation with RPA. It goes hand in hand with cost savings, as the following usually applies: Process costs are reduced through shorter processing times. Nevertheless, time savings can also be an advantage and can be considered an independent strategic goal. Especially in processes in which the (external) customer is directly or indirectly involved, an increase in speed can generate competitive advantages and improve customer satisfaction. This does not only apply to external customers, for example customers of the organization. Internal areas involved in or triggering processes are also considered customers and, as recipients of the services of another area, also often have the expectation of a high process speed.[2] Here, RPA contributes significantly to an increase in process speed (Willcocks and Lacity, 2016).

If the objective is "time reduction," the following things are important and should be considered: The speed of the robot depends largely on the underlying process. If this was prepared and optimized accordingly before automation ("process streamlining"), a bot can usually work faster. In the same way, the quality of the process development (i. e., the RPA code) influences its speed. Reaction times of automated systems cannot be influenced. Since the robot works on the surface (the graphical user interface [GUI]), it is completely dependent on the speed of these applications.

Further potentials

In addition to the above-mentioned potential benefits, RPA offers the financial industry further exciting opportunities. One is to use the technology to reduce compliance and similar risks. Two options are conceivable here. First, once an RPA artifact has been developed in accordance with the specifications and protected against modification, it cannot be modified unintentionally or unnoticed. Misuse is thus significantly restricted. In addition, every step and every system input by the bot is documented, both within the target applications and in RPA's own documentation. This means that all actions are fully verifiable by third parties, for example auditors (Willcocks and Lacity, 2016). The same applies to operational risks, for example those that lie outside the actual business activity. These are, for example, human errors, system errors, or errors within internal processes. Operational risks are a significant risk category, especially in the financial sector (Kaiser and Köhne, 2007). The discussed significant increase in process quality when using RPA reduces potential operational risks. Second, it is possible to carry out significantly more testing with RPA than with humans. Standardized test routines or even preparatory activities such as the gathering of information, which is particularly necessary in the audit areas, can be automated quickly and easily with RPA.

---

2 This is not always given. It depends on the customers' targets. If a customer outweighs quality over time, this statement might not be sufficient.

In practice, a high level of workload for the IT department can regularly be observed. In particular, this is the case when the bank has a heterogeneous system landscape with many applications and legacy systems. RPA can also provide support here by offering an alternative to build interfaces between these applications and systems.

RPA provides further potential for the financial industry by reducing the time-to-market for placing new products or setting up new processes, by standardized collection and evaluation of information, and much more.

14.3.3 Main areas for the application of RPA in the financial industry

Experience shows that processes suitable for RPA can be found in almost all areas of a financial institution. Regarding the above definition, however, those areas appear to be most suitable in which processes can be found that are exclusively digital and rule-based. These are the following (Smeets et al., 2019):
–   Back-office: The department of a bank in which customer data are managed and contracts are created or maintained. Here, many employees regularly carry out structured, rule-based processes.
–   Finance (for example accounting): The department usually prepares a variety of reports and analyses, checks invoices, makes transfers, etc., not always, but in many cases, rule-based and recurring work steps.
–   IT: In IT, structured processes (and thus RPA use cases) are found primarily around user and authorization management or incident handling – in other words, wherever a standardized approach is taken.
–   Human resources: The department also takes care of many issues where human interaction is necessary and useful, but especially in payroll accounting, high-volume and standardized work processes can be found repeatedly.

The individual assessments vary. For example, a study by the Information Services Group (ISG) assumes that IT will be the area most affected by automation in the coming years (Otto and Longo, 2017). Other studies differ, for example one conducted by PWC in 2017 among several dozen professionals in the United States. According to this study, the highest potential is offered by the back-office areas, with well over 80 % agreement. This is followed by the areas of finance and IT. In the areas of compliance, legal, risk control, and human resources, only minor potential for RPAs is assumed (approximately 5 % agreement). The same applies to sales. Ostrowicz (2018) also confirms the applicability in back-office, risk management, accounting, and HR.

Why are especially these units suitable? Wherever data are available in a digital format and are processed digitally, the use of RPAs is a viable option. If the degree of standardization of a process area is now added as a criterion, it becomes clear why the process areas of the back office and, for example, accounting are particularly suitable for RPA. It is precisely here that most of the processes are standardized, rule-based, and based on digitalized data. The typical sales areas, on the other hand, are less suitable for automation (which can be implemented at least with little effort) according to the understanding of RPA used here. Here, existing processes often must be sub-divided into individual sub-processes, some of which can then be automated. In the sales area, the use of desktop RPA is also quite conceivable (Almato, 2020).

14.3.4 RPA as a first step towards overcoming some of the obstacles to digitalization

We follow the example from Section 14.2. For the customer, the process shown in the example appears completely digital, since the interaction occurs completely online. The customer selects his favorite product from a digital offer. He or she then concludes the contract online. He or she does not need to interact with an employee or perform any other manual activities. This is different from the bank's point of view. Although the offer is made available in a digital format, it is far from certain that the customer's order to conclude the product can be processed digitally without media and process breaks. Up to now, this is still processed manually, for example in the core banking system. For the true end-to-end digitalization of the process, the technical process view must therefore also be considered, in particular, the transfer of online input masks to the legally leading systems.

Usually, this requires technical interfaces that enable data transfer from system A to system B. However, this would require an enormous amount of IT implementation work, as new interfaces would have to be developed, tested, provided, and maintained. RPA offers an alternative, as the continued example shows.

> Back to the online process with still existing system breaks and manual activities: In the future, a bot will take over the data entered by the customer and transfer them to all necessary systems – without paper printouts, without errors, and much faster than before. Instead of letters to customers, e-mails will be sent. Since the entry mask for customers was previously optimized and now contains mandatory fields and plausibility checks, the number of queries is reduced to a minimum. Only the final dispatch of the insurance policy is still done by a dispatch service provider. RPA thus manages to process a large proportion of cases automatically in the future. Human interaction will only be necessary in exceptional cases (Smeets et al., 2019).

The example shows how an end-to-end digitalization and thus digital (partial) transformation can be achieved with few changes. RPA enables an enormous reduction of effort compared to large IT-technical changes. The adaptations can be implemented much faster so that a short time-to-market is ensured, and increasingly shorter change cycles can be calmly faced. Murdoch (2018) even calls RPA a digital disruptor. This means that RPA can modify existing processes in such a way that they are not returned to their original state over time.

14.3.5 RPA, related technologies, and their interaction regarding the financial industry

RPA can now often be the method of choice for digitalizing processes. The condition for this is that the respective process or activity fulfils certain basic requirements. For example, an RPA bot can only start working when digital data input is available in a structured format (e. g., Willcocks and Lacity, 2016). In the above example, this is the case when the data entered by the customer are made in a structured online input mask and then transferred to the RPA bot. If, on the other hand, the customer writes an e-mail with an order for product completion, this is unstructured digital input. RPA – in our definition, thus, not able to deal with unstructured data – cannot handle this. In such cases, complementary technologies can augment. In the case outlined, for example, an AI component is conceivable. With the help of a correspondingly large amount of training data (which can be seen as a major obstacle towards implementing such a component), the AI component generates a kind of own experiential knowledge. After some time, it is able to recognize and derive rules and thus structure unstructured data (Davenport, 2019).

It becomes even more challenging when customer orders are not only received unstructured, but also non-digital, for example, when orders are sent by letter. This can also be remedied, for example by using optical character recognition (OCR) technology. OCR allows scanned documents to be converted into a machine-readable format. The common RPA software already has interfaces to OCR applications or has integrated them.

When it comes to digitalization, such a process line should be ruled out from the outset and, ideally, should not occur nowadays. But there are still examples in practice where exactly such data flows exist. In banks this is regularly the case when for example garnishments and alike are received. These are often still sent by mail, so they must first be digitalized.[3] Since not all forms look the same, there are also unstructured data that must be structured as in the example above. Figure 1 shows a process line combining RPA with OCR and AI. We are also going to discuss this interplay in the case example in Section 14.5.

---

3 At this point digitalization means the technical transformation of analogue data.

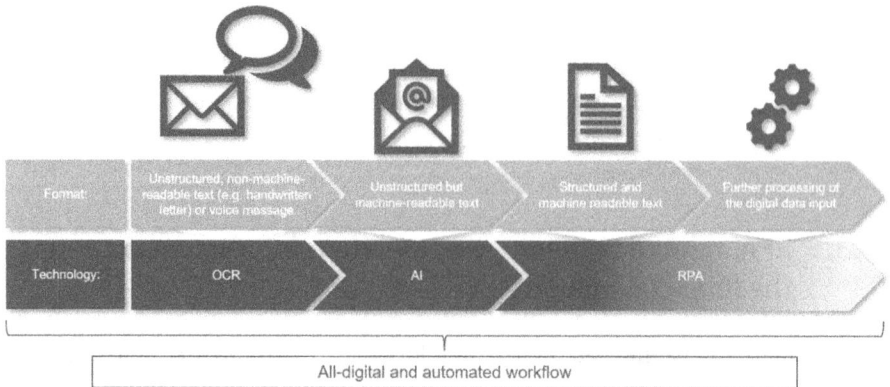

Figure 1: Digitalized and automated workflow (Smeets et al., 2019).

14.4 A selection of sector-specific RPA use cases in the financial industry

14.4.1 Possible roles of RPA

The roles that RPA can play are of great relevance for the classification of different use cases of the technology. Therefore, the following section explains different roles of RPA in the financial industry. The classical role of RPA is that of a digital assistant. It is assumed that the software robot supports humans in carrying out their tasks. The easiest way to imagine this is a desktop RPA that can be started by the employee on demand and takes care of delivery tasks.

Another role of RPA is that of a substitute for humans. Here, RPA carries out certain activities or individual tasks autonomously and independently of humans. The main difference to the first case is the independent starting of the robot. While in the first case the human triggers the robot, for example, it gives it a start and end signal, in the second case the robot is started by technical triggers. Alternatively, flow charts or similar can be stored to control the robot.

In both cases above it is assumed that RPA is used to automate existing processes. This is usually the case, especially at the beginning of an organization's RPA journey. Here, simple and rule-based processes are used and automated in a first step. But RPA can do more. Once RPA has been established in the in-house process management toolbox, it offers opportunities to set up new processes at a high speed and in some-times new ways. If new market demands are placed on products or the legal frame-work changes, new processes may often be necessary or give sense from a sales and business perspective. Up to now, these could often only be put together from many manual activities, as technical adjustments were relatively too expensive or took too long. RPA now offers the possibility to set up new processes quickly and flexibly – even if technical interfaces and other tools are not available.

In summary, RPA can therefore play three roles:
1. RPA as a support to humans in the execution of existing processes;
2. RPA as a replacement for humans in the execution of existing processes;
3. RPA as an opportunity to establish new business models or processes.

The following sections provide use cases for all three roles. Some of the examples can be found in Smeets et al. (2019). Importantly, all examples shown below refer to the exclusive use of RPA. If the above-mentioned complementary technologies like OCR and AI could be used, this is explicitly mentioned.

14.4.2 RPA applications to support humans in performing existing tasks

Provision of rule reporting

A bank's controlling department, which is organizationally assigned to overall bank management, creates daily and weekly reports for which various sources of information are used. In addition to in-house databases, the content of various web sites to which no interfaces can be created is also accessed, for example, statistical data or balance sheet data of other companies. All contents and data are condensed in a structured form and made available to the management of the bank in a layout that is always the same. In order to relieve the employees of these routine activities, an automation with RPA is introduced. The bots merge the information as far as possible and make it available to the employees of the controlling department. They then perform quality assurance, carry out final steps, and provide the final report: an example of the largely smooth interaction between man and machine. Due to the later inspection by humans, this is a cooperation. If the RPA results are of sufficient quality, it is even conceivable that humans could be completely replaced by robots in expansion stages.

Trading

Traders continuously monitor price thresholds to make changes to stop or limit prices or to execute buy and sell orders when the threshold is breached. To relieve them of the ongoing observation of prices and relevant market information, bots provide support for some of the activities. The bots monitor the prices in the institute's trading system as well as information on relevant web sites and send e-mails to the traders based on pre-defined patterns and when certain events occur. Once again, the advantage of RPA lies in the integration of different data sources. While trading systems today already have a wide range of functions, the integration of additional sources can generate a competitive advantage.

14.4.3 RPA applications to substitute human activities

Processing large amounts of data

A large securities institution regularly receives large amounts of data, which often have to be entered manually into further systems, for example, large volumes of securities orders for retail customers. The data are received as a CSV file and transferred manually to the core banking system. Direct processing is not yet possible. RPA can help here and transfer the data in each case – an RPA task that can be implemented with little effort.

Customization of customer data

A securities institution manages a high number of customer securities accounts. Using a variety of interfaces – digital and analogue – the institute receives up to several thousand change orders for customer data every day. After minor process adjustments, the digitally incoming data are further processed by bots, validated, and imported into various applications or databases – including the adjustment of the legally leading data sets. Even if the process does not achieve complete automation, a large proportion of all incoming orders can still be processed automatically. The additional use of an upstream OCR component could be considered, so that RPA can also process analogous incoming orders on forms.

Auditing of securities settlements and other book entries

In the same institute, several employees work daily on the reconciliation of securities transactions across different applications. Individual transactions are entered in in-house applications and transferred to spreadsheet programs for reconciliation. Visual checks and comparisons are carried out at the same time. This work can be fully automated. In particular, the transfer of data between systems and checking data for consistency or pre-defined values and thresholds are among the core capabilities of RPA.

Authorization management and IT

Every time an employee is hired, changes department, changes competence, or leaves the company, the IT department of an institute is required to grant, change, or delete various authorizations. In many cases, these are similar "authorization packages," especially in the case of new hires or employees leaving the company. In all other cases, too, the steps to be taken are largely identical. An ideal application for RPA. With the help of RPA, all authorizations can be processed in all necessary applications, so that human intervention is only required for basic specifications such as the master data or the areas of competence to be assigned. Everything else, the "hard work" that is often perceived as annoying, is carried out by bots.

Resetting of passwords
Another example from the area of authorization management is the resetting of pass-words, a use case that occurs daily in large quantities. Sometimes only small changes are required to make such processes automatable – for example, the implementation of a simple ticket system instead of a password hotline. Resetting passwords is just one example of the potential of RPA in IT. In principle, RPA can automate entire ticket systems and, in some cases, even answer first-level support queries independently (Beardmore, 2017). RPA is also suitable for monitoring servers or complex job chains, which is highly relevant for the IT areas of the financial industry.

Invoice processing
As a rule, incoming invoices are not posted immediately. Before the invoice amount is transferred, the correctness and legality of the invoice is usually checked. If all data are available in digital form, the entire process can be automated. If the data are avail-able in an (as yet) unstructured form, an OCR component must also be connected up-stream to make the data editable by RPA. Alternatively, initial cognitive components are already being used here, for example to recognize relevant information in unstruc-tured texts. AIMultiple (2019) represents such a process by integrating cognitive com-ponents. The savings achieved here – without further explanation of the reference value used – are estimated at 67 FTE and thus at about $4 million. At the same time, the processing time decreases from 6–8 minutes to about 30 seconds.

RPA in one-time scenarios
In most cases, the use of RPAs is aimed at the permanent automation of processes, i. e. the use of the technology in daily business. This need not always be the case. RPA can also be an attractive option for one-off applications. Let us give an example of data migration. A large bank transfers the accounts of a smaller subsidiary to its own core banking system. For various reasons, the migration cannot be carried out using technical interfaces. An alternative is the manual entry of hundreds of thousands of data records. This would take a long time and manual entry errors could not be ruled out, if not expected. Therefore, RPA was chosen as an alternative solution. Here, too, an interface description is first created, and a mapping is carried out. This is followed by extensive tests and a smooth data migration with robots.

14.4.4 RPA for innovation of new processes or even business models

Digital product terminations
In the future, a bank would like to offer its customers the possibility of concluding individual products and services online, such as an online current account. The data recorded digitally by the customer could be transferred to a service provider, which

– after a plausibility check – transfers the data by manual entry into the bank's core banking system. This solution already exists for some other activities. For a new product or process, however, it does not seem to make sense. The alternative creation of an interface that would enable a direct transfer of the data entered by the customer into the core banking system is not possible in the short term, and initially not desired. Instead, however, an RPA solution can be developed that enables both plausibility checks and data transfer. In this way, an actual end-to-end digitalization of the process is achieved. Furthermore, the processing time and thus the costs of the individual process are low.

Compliance

The compliance unit monitors and checks various processes and other activities, just like other controlling bodies of the institutions. It can only carry out the control activities to the extent that it has resources – for example employees. The use of RPA can create additional capacity here. This enables the establishment of additional test routines. The bots are particularly suitable for routines that would mean repetitive and non-complex activities for the employees, where the susceptibility to errors in the control is particularly high.

14.5 Case study from the financial industry: how RPA helps to overcome departmental boundaries and to digitalize a service process end-to-end

14.5.1 Status quo: one organization, three departments, three separated processes

The following case study analyzes a process automated in 2020.[4] Actually, it is initially about three processes, which have been combined into one at the end. The example shows impressively the possibilities for increasing efficiency that RPA can offer and how the technology can interact with other, related, but still advanced technologies. At the same time, it also becomes clear that it is rarely sensible to automate an existing process without first carrying out a thorough process analysis and subsequent reengineering. The scope of the latter varies from process to process and can, in extreme cases, lead to a completely new process being set up.

---

4 The case study is largely taken from practice. It is mostly a process that was automated in the year 2020. In some parts, necessary adjustments were made for didactic reasons.

The three processes considered here take place in a German securities institution. One of its core tasks is the management of securities accounts for retail customers. The securities institute has already been using the RPA technology for about 3 years. Around 60 processes have so far been automated and controlled by robots. The institute is supported in the implementation of new RPA processes by an external consulting firm that performs process analysis and RPA development. The processes discussed here were identified as automatable in an investigation to exploit efficiency improvement potentials around customer support. The original process flow is as follows.

A large proportion of the customers contact the bank during the year and ask it to prepare duplicates for statements of securities accounts, tax certificates, and the like. There are various ways for the customer to do this. Firstly, the customers call the call center and order the documents in a personal conversation with employees. Secondly, customers send letters, faxes, or e-mails which are read by employees and processed accordingly. Thirdly, the customers forward the order to the securities institution via their house banks. The latter orders also reach the bank via e-mail. In all three ways, employees are in contact with the customers or at least process the customer enquiry. Processing in the call center involves entering customer data and enquiries in an Excel list.

After the customer enquiry has been received by an employee in the first process, a second employee in the back-office creates the customer documents manually in the subsequent, second process. In doing so, he or she follows a kind of batch processing. The larger the batch, the longer the processing takes – no concrete deadlines have been agreed. An order is entered in the relevant system for this purpose. This is followed by an archiving process. In addition, documentation is made in another Excel list. This Excel list is passed on to a third employee.

This third employee, again in a different department, debits the fees corresponding to the respective customer order from the customer's securities account. Subsequently, archiving takes place here as well. The documents themselves have already been printed by an external service provider after the second process has been completed and sent to the customer centrally. Figure 2 shows the processes.

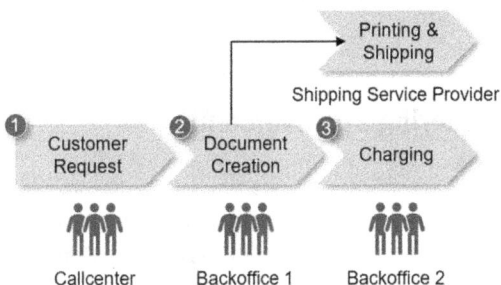

Figure 2: Initial process.

The processes and their interaction in their current state show numerous problems and – derived from them – potential for improvement:

1. Input channels:
   a. There are too many different input channels.
   b. Not all input channels are suitable for modern processes, for example, the input channel fax; here, non-digital and unstructured data are delivered. The processing can either be done by humans or – with enormous effort – by machines.
2. Process flow:
   a. With at least three employees involved, the number of process participants is too high.
   b. Waiting times result in long process throughput times. All in all, the process therefore takes too long – on the one hand from a business management point of view and on the other hand from the customer's perspective.
   c. Not all process steps appear relevant and necessary. For example, the necessity of documentation in an Excel list for statistical purposes must be strongly questioned.
3. Systems used:
   a. In addition to the input systems, data are recorded in Excel tables, a CRM system, portfolio management, a booking system, and archiving software. There are also other systems on the printing and dispatch side. All in all, there are clearly too many systems.
   b. There are almost no interfaces between the systems used. The only exceptions are securities account management and the archiving system. Work steps cannot therefore be automated or parallelized.
4. General: A long process duration results from the interaction of the above factors. This has a negative effect on process costs and employee and customer satisfaction.

Perhaps even more problem areas can be listed, but these are already numerous and offer extensive potential for improvement. All in all, the initial situation offers a non-digital process. This is of great relevance in terms of costs and in terms of external impact on the institute's customers.

14.5.2 Stage 1: Process reengineering and overcoming departmental boundaries

Digitalization and automation seem to be possible in principle. In a first step, however, an intensive process improvement is necessary. This is done in four steps, along the points listed above. Importantly, in contrast to classical process optimization projects, it must be considered that digitalization should be carried out with automation software, namely, RPA. The characteristics and requirements of such a technology should therefore ideally be considered in the process redesign right from the start. A further requirement for process optimization in this case is to overcome the department-specific "silos." Up to now, there have been three individual processes, each of which is specific to a department. The objective is to develop a cross-departmental end-to-end process.

Step 1: Reduction of the number of input channels and digitalization
The number of input channels is reduced. Faxes and letters will no longer be accepted. It is now only possible to place an order via e-mail, call the call center, or use the online input mask. This is a first important success. There is no longer any analogue input data; all data are received digitally – even if still unstructured. It can justifiably be argued here that the restriction of input channels could be perceived by customers as a restriction rather than an added value. However, a trade-off must be made between customer satisfaction and technical feasibility/efficiency. Here, the latter prevails, as it can be assumed that customer satisfaction will not suffer significantly from this limitation.

Step 2: Optimization of the process flow
All unnecessary process steps are eliminated, e. g., the collection of "statistical" data in an Excel spreadsheet. For this purpose, it is checked which process steps or information stores are necessary from a business point of view and which are not. In addition to banking requirements, the financial industry has many other complex requirements. These are, for example, high demands on data protection and confidentiality of data. Auditing and compliance monitor data storage and use, especially in the case of the sensitive handling of customer tax data. In addition, process responsibility is shifted to the first of the three departments involved – the call center. Although further processing is carried out in one step, which is to be assigned to the back-office, this is to be automated in the future. A back-office employee is therefore no longer necessary in the target picture. The full process responsibility is therefore transferred to the call center or the respective employees there. Time savings are already achieved by shifting the work steps forward and executing them from one source.

Step 3: Adding interfaces and removing systems
Wherever possible and feasible with little effort, system-side interfaces are created. Systems that are not necessary are eliminated from the process flow, such as the Excel application from step 2.[5] In some cases, information that must be entered in the individual systems can also be reduced.

---

5 We hereby assume that all process links are known and the procedure of eliminating systems does not lead to risks.

Step 4: Prepared process

Taken together, the changes achieved so far already result in a significant reduction of the process throughput time. Long waiting times – especially noticed by customers – are eliminated and the requested documents are made available more quickly than before. The process is now prepared and optimized for automation regarding business and technical requirements. Thus, an optimized, but still manual process is available.

14.5.3 Stage 2: Adding RPA bots

The next step is to use RPA technology. In the case study considered here, the bank is already a user of the technology. The software is available and installed, and the architecture – consisting of a central control unit, design components for the RPA engineers, and executing bots – is set up. In addition, sufficient resources are available to develop and test the future RPA process. The project team's approach follows a standardized procedure, which is shown in Figure 3.

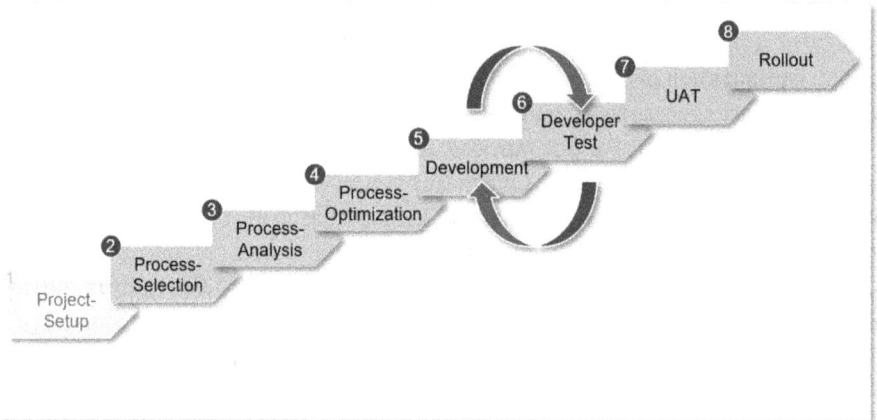

Figure 3: RPA implementation approach.

After selecting the process, the process analysis was carried out. The process was then optimized so that the development of the RPA process can now begin. The development follows an agile approach and takes place in so-called sprints. As soon as the required quality of the software development has been achieved and the developer tests have been completed, the user acceptance test (UAT) by the department follows. If this is successful, the RPA process can be transferred to productive operation.

Special requirements for the development process must be observed regularly when using a replication server in banks. In the financial industry in Germany, for example, BAIT (BaFin, 2018) makes demands on the software development process. Separation of functions and separate system environments must be considered. Many banks use standardized software development procedures and documentation, which should also be taken into account by RPA. At this point, it can be critically discussed whether RPA development can be counted as software development in the classical sense or whether it is rather a pure configuration of already developed software. This discussion will not be held here; in case of doubt, the treatment as classical software is the more secure variant (regarding audits and the like).

Figure 4 shows where RPA is used in the known process. The sales order is still received by call center employees. This is because although the orders are largely placed digitally – if not by telephone – the data are still unstructured. However, RPA needs structured data as input to be able to work with it. The call center employees therefore enter all customer orders in a prepared table. This table is located on a central drive. The corresponding customer names with securities account number and concrete order, for example, the creation of a new tax return, are collected here throughout the day. At the end of the day, an RPA bot automatically starts reading the data entered during the day. It transfers these data to all relevant systems, searches for the necessary documents, and issues the corresponding shipping orders to the shipping service provider. The robot then opens the booking system and debits the customer accounts with the corresponding charges. A receipt is then produced and subsequently archived. In the example, RPA replaces the human being. Human processing is therefore only necessary at the beginning of the process, to create the two necessary prerequisites for processing with RPA: digital and structured data.

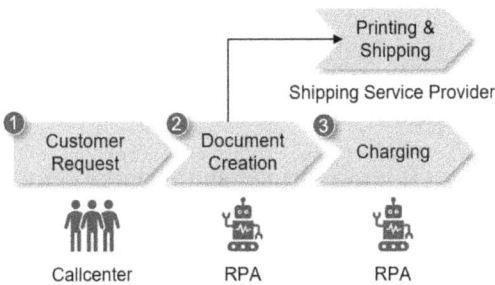

Figure 4: Process with integration of RPA.

14.5.4 Stage 3: Integration of machine learning

Much has already been achieved so far. Most of the process is automated with RPA and takes place in a dark processing environment. What is still missing is the automated processing of customer inquiries. Telephone orders are excluded at this point; these will continue to be received and answered by "real" employees. Since faxes and letters are no longer accepted, the e-mail channel remains. As already mentioned, e-mails are digital, but unstructured input. RPA cannot deal with this as there are no clear rules.

AI can provide a solution. In the meantime, approaches around machine learning have been developed which, after sufficient "training," can recognize specific patterns in unstructured data (Davenport, 2019). Using these patterns, the data or incoming orders can be classified and – metaphorically speaking – fed into a respective input channel. The RPA bot is developed in such a way that it receives a concrete rule for each input channel and can process the data accordingly. Hereby complete process automation is achieved. However, this is opposed by a rather high preparation effort. The machine learning component, or better, the machine learning algorithm, usually requires several thousand data sets to "learn." In this case, people must evaluate the classification of the algorithm – for example deciding whether the algorithm was right or wrong. A correspondingly large amount of time is required for this. The interaction of AI (machine learning) and RPA is shown in Figure 5.

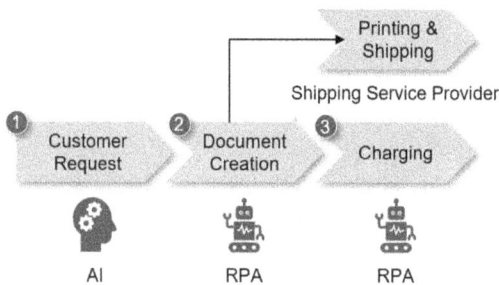

Figure 5: Process with integration of RPA and AI.

14.5.5 Interim summary and outlook

The case study shows three essential triggers to turn a complex and analogue process into a lean, digital, and automated one:

1. For successful automation with RPA, a preparatory process analysis and adaptation is almost always useful – especially if not only individual tasks but "real" processes are automated.
2. Even minor process adjustments sometimes have a big lever. With just a few changes, data input can often be made available digitally and in a structured form, making it editable with RPA.
3. Machine learning can be a useful supplement to turn a partially automated process into a fully automated one. However, this requires a great deal of preparation, so cost and benefit must be carefully weighed against each other.

The process offers further potential. For example, the input channel could become more standardized in the next step. If an online input mask were to be made available for customers and affiliated banks, structured data input would be available right at the start of the process, not unstructured (e-mail) as is currently the case. This would also make the machine learning component obsolete. If technical interfaces can be created between the data entry mask and the processing system, the need for an RPA solution could even be eliminated for part of the process.

14.6 Summary

Although a broad study is lacking, various minor studies and surveys indicate that there is a gap between existing and used potential of RPAs in the global financial industry. In the financial industry, but also in other industries, RPA can play different roles. It can facilitate the work for human employees, it can completely take over their tasks, or the technology can be used to develop new business opportunities. RPA processes can be found in all areas of banks and insurers, with the focus on the back-office, finance, and IT. As the case example shows, the transition to a digital process is not always difficult and can sometimes be done with little effort. It becomes understandable that AI can be a useful addition to RPA and can lift the process from partial to full automation.

What is still missing is a more in-depth scientific investigation of the most diverse open questions concerning RPA. Which processes are actually best suited? What are relevant success factors? How does RPA interact with other, related technologies? What influences the acceptance of RPA by employees? And there are many more questions. Individual case studies are available, but comprehensive studies based on scientific principles are not known to us so far and, therefore, offer great potential for further research.

Bibliography

AIMultiple (2019) RPA use cases. Accessed January 20, 2019. https://blog.aimultiple.com/robotic-process-automation-use-cases/#banking

Almato (2020). https://www.almato.com/automation/. Accessed May 22, 2020

Alt R, Puschmann T (2016) Digitalisierung der Finanzindustrie – Grundlagen der Fintech-Evolution. Springer, Berlin Heidelberg

Beardmore L (2017) Robotic process automation. https://www.capgemini.com/service/business-services/enabling-technologies/robotics-process-automation/. Accessed January 20, 2019

Bundesanstalt für Finanzdienstleistungsaufsicht (BaFin) (2018) Rundschreiben 10/2017 (BA) in der Fassung vom 14.09.2018, Bankaufsichtliche Anforderungen an die IT (BAIT). Accessed December 23, 2018. https://www.bafin.de/SharedDocs/Downloads/DE/Rundschreiben/dl_rs_1710_ba_BAIT.html

Davenport TH (2019) The AI advantage. How to put the artificial intelligence revolution to work. The MIT Press, Cambridge Massachusetts, London, England

Ivancic L, Susa Vugec D, Bosilj Vuksic V (2019) Robotic process automation: systematic literature review. In: Di Ciccio G et al (eds) Business process management, vol 361, pp 280–295

Jarrahi MH (2018) Artificial intelligence and the future of work: human-AI symbiosis in organizational decision making. Bus Horiz 61(4):577–586

Kaiser T, Köhne MF (2007) Operationelle Risiken in Finanzinstituten. Eine praxisorientierte Einführung, 2nd edn. Gabler, Wiesbaden

Kolbjørnsrud V, Amico R, Thomas RJ (2017) Partnering with AI: how organizations can win over skeptical managers. Strategy Leadersh 45(1):37–43

Kumar KN (2018) Robotic process automation – a study of the impact on customer experience in retail banking industry. J Int Bank Commer. http://www.icommercecentral.com/open-access/robotic-process-automation-a-study-of-the-impact-on-customer-experience-in-retail-banking-industry.php?aid=87176. Accessed May 16, 2020

Mahroof K (2019) A human-centric perspective exploring the readiness towards smart warehousing: the case of a large retail distribution warehouse. Int J Inf Manag 45:176–190

Murdoch R (2018) Robotic process automation. Guide to building software robots, automate repetitive tasks & become an RPA consultant. Self-published

Ostrowicz S (2018) Next Generation Process Automation: Integrierte Prozessautomation im Zeitalter der Digitalisierung. Ergebnisbericht Studie 2018. Horváth & Partners, Frankfurt a. M.

Otto S, Longo M (2017) ISG-Studie: Robotic Process Automation (RPA) sorgt für mehr Produktivität und nicht für Jobverluste. https://www.isg-one.com/docs/default-source/default-document-library/isg-automation-index-de_final_form.pdf?sfvrsn=15defe31_0. Accessed January 20, 2019

PWC (2017) What PwC's 2017 survey tells us about RPA in financial services today. https://www.pwc.com/us/en/financial-services/publications/assets/pwc-fsi-whitepaper-2017-rpa-survey.pdf. Accessed January 10, 2019

Ranerup A, Henriksen HZ (2019) Value positions viewed through the lens of automated decision-making: the case of social services. Gov Inf Q 36:101377

Smeets M, Erhard R, Kaussler T (2019) Robotic Process Automation (RPA) in der Finanzwirtschaft. Springer, Wiesbaden

Tucci L (2015) KPMG: death of BPO at the hands of RPA. https://searchcio.techtarget.com/blog/TotalCIO/KPMG-Death-of-BPO-at-the-hands-of-RPA. Accessed December 30, 2018

Watson J, Wright D (2017) The robots are ready. Are you? https://www.google.com/url?sa=t&rct=j&q=&esrc=s&source=web&cd=1&ved=2ahUKEwjizofA5MnfAhURYlAKHWHaBqoQFjAAegQIChAC&url=https%3A%2F%2Fwww2.deloitte.com%2Fcontent%2Fdam%2Fdeloitte%2Ftr%2FDocuments%2Ftechnology%2Fdeloitte-robots-are-ready.pdf&usg=AOvVaw2luiVlNhzNclPK70Ac7_zc. Accessed December 31, 2018

Willcocks L, Lacity M (2016) Service automation. Robots and the future of work. Steve Brooks Publishing, Warwickshire

Willcocks L, Lacity M, Craig A (2017) Robotic process automation: strategic transformation lever for global business services? J Inf Technol Teaching Cases 7:17–28

Oliver Gutermuth, Constantin Houy, and Peter Fettke

15 RPA for public administration enhancement

Abstract: Complex IT system landscapes are straining the digital transformation of public administration. Even sophisticated IT modernization actions can barely comply with the increased requirements regarding integrity, interoperability, and compatibility due to various dependencies. Robotic process automation (RPA) allows for cross-system automation of work processes. The integration of artificial intelligence into RPA tools supports the realization of the existing potential and the development of new fields of application. Flexible RPA tools can support the automation of a wide variety of processes quickly, consistently, and with reduced error-proneness. This chapter introduces fundamentals of RPA and discusses its relevance for enhancing public administration processes based on selected application examples as well as use cases in a governmental organization in Germany.

Keywords: Robotic process automation, public administration, public sector, artificial intelligence, cognitive services, case example

15.1 Motivation

15.1.1 Initial situation of public administrations in Germany

Digital transformation is a major challenge for public administration, especially in Germany. The process of digital transformation is accompanied by various modernization priorities and comprehensive changes in order to be able to develop and tap the existing potential and synergies using digital technologies. Against this background, public administration must also meet the increased demands of citizens and companies concerning new communication channels, operate economically, and implement a suitable human resources strategy. The introduction of new information technologies (IT) to support administrative processes can relieve activities and release a certain amount of capacity. However, this cannot always fully compensate the personnel requirements in other areas due to differing qualifications. A current lack of skilled employees and demographic factors exacerbate this problem.

A modern public administration requires integrated IT systems that use consistent standards and match the individual requirements of different public administration authorities. However, in public administrations in Germany there are highly diverse

Acknowledgement: The chapter is based on content and results taken from a study published in German (Gutermuth et al., 2020), which was funded by the *Nationales E-Government Kompetenzzentrum* (NEGZ e. V.), Berlin, Germany.

https://doi.org/10.1515/9783110676693-015

IT system landscapes with limited interconnection and limited interoperability due to their historic growth. Reasons for this can be found in the organizational structure, legal restrictions, and the development of IT landscapes over the last decades. Efforts to introduce common solutions are hampered by the autonomy of organizational units, the question of cost distribution, different requirement profiles, and the subjective assessment of alternative solutions.

These problems of public administration in Germany indicate which objectives should be pursued towards a digital future. The focus is on IT strategies that provide features to increase efficiency and enhance interoperability between IT systems. However, further selective developments by the providers and the costly change of individual IT systems hardly have any effect. Therefore, there is a need for innovative IT tools to improve the functionality and interoperability of all IT components regardless of their stand-alone automation potential. A promising approach that offers these possibilities is the use of robotic process automation (RPA).

RPA allows the development and implementation of automation concepts for individual processes by using special programs that automatically execute operations on existing IT systems according to certain specifications. Depending on the type of task, different methods are available for analyzing facts, decision making, and controlling the process flow. The complexity of processed information is a crucial aspect in this context. Depending on the type of task, artificial intelligence (AI) techniques can be involved and offer a wide range of new opportunities.

The market for RPA products is emerging, with sales of almost 850 million USD and a 63 % growth in 2018 (Gartner Research, 2019). According to Gartner, currently leading RPA providers are UIPath, Blue Prism, and Automation Anywhere. Their products provide flexible automation solutions that can be applied with comparatively little effort. As the market matures, the functionality of these products will probably increase. Recent advances in AI research will likely support this trend. Meanwhile, RPA already covers attractive solutions that offer advantages for many organizations. The following content investigates central RPA concepts in the domain of public administration and examines the related potential.

15.1.2 Objective, method, and structure

This chapter aims at providing an insight into the current and future features of RPA and existing RPA concepts for public administration. Therefore, we have studied available literature sources and developed relevant application scenarios in the governmental context. Furthermore, we describe several use cases in order to explain the potential of RPA in this field. The remainder of this chapter is as follows: Section 15.2 presents the conceptual foundations and terminology regarding essential aspects of RPA, related approaches from the field of AI, and the concept of *cognitive services*. Based on a selection of typical application areas in public administration,

Sections 15.3, 15.4, and 15.5 explain different application examples with varying scopes and technological focuses. In these scenarios, we differentiate between simple RPA approaches and *cognitive services*. In more detail, Section 15.3 deals with automation concepts that could already be realized today with available RPA solutions, and that can achieve success rather quickly with comparatively little effort. Section 15.4 describes application examples in which the performance of RPA can be significantly enhanced using AI and cognitive services. Section 15.5 illustrates a more comprehensive exemplary application scenario that combines different approaches and presents the flexibility in designing automation concepts with RPA. Section 15.6 explains RPA use cases in practice, especially RPA applications already used in a federal state of Germany. The potential, as well as the opportunities and risks of the technology, are discussed in the concluding Section 15.7.

15.2 Conceptual foundations and terminology

The concept of RPA is becoming increasingly well known and is more and more often used in numerous industries. However, it is implemented in quite different ways. In order to explain the underlying understanding of RPA in the addressed application domain, essential basics, fundamental terms, and concepts are covered in the following.

15.2.1 Robotic process automation

Increasing the efficiency of work processes is an important objective for many organizations. However, to automate manual operations or the manual usage of IT systems, further developments were previously required from software product providers. RPA helps organizations to overcome this limitation by allowing the RPA technology to identify, understand, and imitate manual operating steps that a user performs when working on business processes. The use of RPA's software robots has three crucial advantages:

- With software robots, automation concepts can be designed and implemented independently. Especially for IT components where desirable automation functionalities would be possible in principle but have not been implemented by the developers, a software robot can be assigned to carry out the manual steps and thus provide this functionality for the user.
- RPA can overcome missing interfaces between IT systems as the software robot can gather information from one system and transfer it to the other. If the required operations are not possible by accessing files, a software robot can also initiate the information output by controlling the user interfaces of related application

software. The output data can be read (*screen scraping*) and transferred to a target system.

– Individual solutions with software robots can be designed and introduced comparatively fast. Most available RPA solutions aim at providing good usability, especially concerning the control concept for software robots. Appropriate RPA solutions can "learn" business processes by recording and analyzing manually executed process instances. They try to understand the actions of humans, copy the execution, and, if the process is varied, identify or ask for relevant influencing factors.

In addition to the apparent interaction possibilities with operating systems or application software such as specialized business applications, office programs, or an Internet browser, database operations, complex algorithms, or AI techniques can also be included, which significantly expands the application spectrum of RPA (vom Brocke et al., 2018). An RPA-supported process is not necessarily a completely automated process. Software robots can also integrate human users in selected situations, depending on the specified mode of operation, trigger their participation, and then resume the automatic continuation of the process ("human-in-the-loop").

RPA systems can be described and distinguished by certain features. These include, in particular, the characteristic of whether the process control follows clear rules (*simple RPA*) or uses AI techniques (*cognitive services*). Also, some software robots can adjust their behavior according to the analysis of process instances generated by themselves (*self-learning RPA*) (Houy et al., 2019). Besides, a distinction is made between *attended bots* and *unattended bots*. While *unattended bots* independently initiate the automation of processes based on triggering events, *attended bots* are rather assisting, as they are executed and "instructed" selectively by humans to carry out a process (Smeets et al., 2019).

15.2.2 Artificial intelligence[1]

AI can be considered a key technology of the twenty-first century. The term AI was defined as early as 1956 in the context of the "Dartmouth Summer Research Project on Artificial Intelligence." In general, AI research pursues the goal of developing technical systems that are capable of solving problems for which a human being requires intelligence. However, this definition is not generally accepted. Hence, a number of AI sub-areas have emerged which pursue different sub-goals. A systematic classification of sub-areas can, e. g., be developed based on existing fields of application. Generally,

---

[1] The following section is based on Fettke (2019) and Fettke (2018) and was slightly adjusted.

a distinction can be made between applications in the economy, such as manufacturing, trade, services, or finance. Also, there are applications in science, which in turn can be further distinguished into applications in the natural sciences, social sciences, humanities, and technical sciences.

A different classification approach is based on central concepts, methods, and techniques that are considered a part of AI. Established AI sub-areas include those listed below. Especially the first four mentioned sub-areas play a significant role in the presented context.

- *Machine learning*: Systems are supposed to increasingly solve problems better by taking into account experience over time.
- *Knowledge representation and automated reasoning*: Knowledge is supposed to be represented in such a way that it can be used by machines and, in particular, that it is accessible to automated mechanical reasoning.
- *Pattern recognition*: Machines are supposed to recognize patterns or correlations in data, which were previously unknown, and which are of interest, relevance, and benefit.
- *Natural language processing (NLP) and natural language generation (NLG)*: Spoken and written language can be automatically analyzed, recognized, understood, translated, and synthesized by machines.
- *Automated planning and acting*: Actions and activities can automatically be analyzed and planned in advance to achieve specific goals and fulfill complex tasks.
- *Robotics*: Machines are equipped with various sensors and actuators so that they can move more or less autonomously and perform tasks.

A third classification approach can be based on the distinction of AI systems regarding the requirements and capabilities to be developed:

- *Narrow AI*: A very specific, clearly defined task which necessitates a human being and its intelligence to be carried out, shall be processed automatically. Typical examples are playing chess, planning a journey, or the recognition and classification of a tumor.
- *Universal AI*: The development goal in the context of creating a universal AI would be to create a technical system that has a problem-solving capability comparable to that of humans.
- *Super AI*: In contrast to a universal AI, the development goal in the creation of a super AI would be the creation of a technical system whose capabilities far exceed human intelligence.

Even though there are now plenty of technical systems available that fulfill the characteristics of a *narrow* AI and also exceed human capabilities in this particular task, no systems are available which have any rudimentary *universal* or even *super* AI capability. While some researchers predict the existence of *universal* or *super* AI in the future, other experts declare this claim pure speculation or even science fiction.

However, there have been some recent breakthroughs in machine learning, in particular in deep learning. The importance of this achievement is demonstrated by the fact that the Association for Computing Machinery (ACM) has awarded the renowned Turing Award 2019 to the three deep learning pioneers Bengio, Hinton, and LeCun. Table 1 presents typical applications that can now be processed very successfully using machine learning approaches with deep neural networks.

Table 1: Applications of machine learning with deep neural networks (Ng, 2016).

Input	Output	Application context
Picture	Answer to the question: "What or who is in the picture?"	Annotation of images
Credit application	Answer to the question: "Will the borrower be able to repay the loan?"	Credit application
Audio file	Text transcript of the audio file	Voice recognition
Sentence in English language	Sentence in German language	Natural language translation
Sensor data from machines, turbines, etc.	Answer to the question: "Will there be a breakdown this week?"	Predictive maintenance
Car camera and other sensors	Position of other cars	Autonomous driving

These applications technically work more or less according to the same principle: While the classical way of programming is to describe explicit rules and characteristics of human faces, machine parameters, credit agreements, etc., in the form of explicit algorithms, in machine learning no rules are programmed *a priori*. Instead, concrete examples of human faces, machine parameters, problematic credit agreements, etc., are collected. During a training phase, the machine tries to extract characteristic features from these example data on its own, which can then be used for the classification and prediction of unknown situations. Machine learning has led to performance improvements in certain areas. However, it should be noted that in other application areas, the necessary data or the amount of data for machine learning is not available. In addition, there are areas of application in which the use of machine learning does not make a lot of sense. This is, e. g., valid for applications in which known physical laws or normative specifications of a legislator must be considered. Why should (physical) laws be learned from data to be able to process them by a machine? Here, it is better to use classical methods of knowledge representation. In other words, machine learning is only one of the numerous sub-themes of AI research. Furthermore, it is interesting that several typical problems are only perceived as an application area of AI as long as they have not yet been solved. This shifting of the boundaries of what is considered AI is clearly illustrated by the examples of chess, route planning, or optical character recognition (OCR). Such systems are achievements of AI but are no longer necessarily perceived as AI by the public.

15.2.3 Cognitive services[2]

AI techniques can also be usefully applied to extend the range of services offered by RPA. While simple RPA approaches are strongly rule-based and mostly used for pure data manipulation in practice, there are recent efforts to combine RPA and AI. As a result, *cognitive services* can be added to RPA applications. But the terms *simple RPA* and *cognitive services* just mark two poles of a broad continuum of possible RPA solutions (Table 2).

Table 2: Simple vs. cognitive RPA (Houy et al., 2019).

	Simple RPA	Cognitive services
Task	routine	complex
Robot capability	follows rules	draws conclusions
Focus	broad	narrow
Marketability	ready	to be developed
Cost of implementation and operations	low	higher
Time needed for implementation	weeks	months

Besides the operational capabilities of cognitive services, AI can also support the preparation of an automation concept or the monitoring of RPA processes. A central challenge in the preparation and design of automation is the analysis of the conventional process execution and the transfer of this information into the control concept of the software robot. If there are several variants of a process, the identification and consolidated evaluation of factors leading to these variants are important for an appropriate design realizing the automation potential. If these factors are not fully known or very complex, AI can support both the identification and their weighting by analyzing relevant patterns (Veit et al., 2017). This procedure can be done, e. g., by using process mining methods for the analysis of recorded process data. AI can also support the recording of process execution data, e. g., by performing analyses of graphical user interfaces to identify interaction elements.

Furthermore, AI can provide useful services even after an RPA-supported process has been set up and gone live. Since automated execution can be critical, there are numerous measures for monitoring software robot activities. Among other things, AI can check the execution of a process instance against the entirety of past process instances for deviations from reference patterns. If significant abnormalities are detected, the

---

2 The following section is based on Fettke (2019) and Fettke (2018) and was slightly adjusted.

process can be interrupted or subjected to subsequent investigations. One cause of possible malfunctions of a software robot is regular updates of the underlying application software which the robot accesses. Here, e. g., changes to the design of the user interface can quickly lead to faulty execution. In these cases, AI can help to analyze the causes and eliminate them automatically ("self-healing"). For this purpose, modified interaction elements of the user interface must be identified and reassigned to the correct activities in the control concept of the software robot.

15.3 Simple RPA applications

Simple RPA applications are usually routine processes that contain a mainly rule-based flow and that are comparatively easy to implement. Now, Section 15.3 presents three examples of simple RPA applications. They are based on process knowledge from practice and were conceptually developed involving RPA potential.

15.3.1 Frequent controlling procedures

It is quite common for public administrations to use several systems for the audit and regular control of specific data. Since suitable interfaces between legacy systems are sometimes missing, many controlling processes must be carried out manually. A frequently required control process, which has a significant influence on a wide range of tasks in many public authorities in Germany, is the determination of the authority's *local responsibility*, which regulates the process governance for the specific concern of a citizen. Usually, the local responsibility is largely dependent on the habitual residence of the citizen. Especially when public authorities provide regular payments, e. g., aid money, there is an increased need for control. Risks arise from the fact that a change of residence is often only known to the new local *registration office*. These changes are not automatically synchronized with the data stocks of other public authorities. As the change of the *local responsibility* includes the obligation to provide, e. g., aid money, the dropping administration wants to know about such cases quickly. Due to resource constraints, however, local responsibility is only irregularly checked and sometimes at long time intervals.

With RPA, a fully automated check of relevant information can be set up. For this purpose, the relevant data stored in the application's software system is collected and compared with the residents' registration data via online access to the registration offices' data bases. A software robot could work like an employee using a specific user ID, call up all active cases in the application software in a systematic way (e. g., alphabetically), read the required data fields from the master data, e. g., by *screen scraping*, and transfer them to the query mask for accessing the according *registration office's* online portal. The query is carried out with a virtual mouse click. Results can then also be automatically read by identifying the relevant fields on the response web page. To log the procedure, the software robot can transfer the data to a database or an electronic list in which the addresses are compared with the data queried from the *registration office*. As soon as all cases have been processed, the report data can be evaluated (e. g., marking of cases with deviations), and the responsible employee can be notified (e. g., automatic e-mail in case of deviations). Theoretically, many further steps can be imagined, such as the automated creation of a letter to clarify the facts of the case. RPA can significantly increase the frequency of such control processes and thus prevent unintended payment provision. Since, within this process, only a manageable amount of data is transferred, it could even be carried out daily, ideally overnight, for a large number of active cases.

15.3.2 Data maintenance

Public authorities often use several application systems for different purposes. Certain processes require identical data entries or even a similar data processing in more than one of these systems. Without a central database, redundant operations can be necessary. In addition to the increased effort involved, this constellation poses a high risk of inconsistent data sets. Particularly in the administration of natural persons, multiple data records ("data duplicates") can occur, which must be identified and merged with great effort. A software robot can take over various tasks here. Within one system, it can read data records and first check them separately for completeness and plausibility. Missing data could, for example, be automatically requested by the software robot.

By specifying maintenance rules, the robot can also find data records that are either very similar or contradictory looking at all data records of one or more parallelly used application systems. The RPA-supported analysis of data sets can, thus, identify incorrect and inconsistent data records and in some cases also potential fraud attempts. However, the primary goal is to create and guarantee error-free data sets in the often heterogeneous landscape of (legacy) systems of public administrations.

15.3.3 Payment monitoring

Numerous processes in public administration entail posting to accounts. While internal postings and those where the administration is liable to pay can easily be documented and assigned to business processes, incoming payments from external process participants can cause problems and effort. For fee-based procedures, a payer can often choose between several payment alternatives. In addition to cash or debit card payment on site, payment by bank transfer is quite a popular method. The administration's problem in such processes results from the fact that the receipt of payment must be ensured and assigned to continue or finish the process. However, since the time of payment depends on the actions of the payer, there is a constant need to monitor certain accounts. Some systems already contain an adequate interface or integrate payment data that incoming payments can be identified and assigned automatically. In many areas, however, this can only be done with manual effort, as incoming payments from various sources are recorded with sometimes incorrect or incomplete payment data. Since transfer data for allocation purposes only contain the name, bank details, and the purpose – which is quite error-prone due to the high degree of freedom of design – the addressed procedure and the concrete case often have to be determined manually.

The analysis of postings data to identify specific payments can be automated with a software robot. This robot scans accounts at adjustable intervals and identifies relevant data records. In the case of unique postings, the robot can document the receipt directly in the respective systems and, if necessary, also generate a note to the responsible clerk. If the data show certain inadequacies, the software robot can still suggest an assignment within certain tolerance limits. Hence, it can determine an acceptable degree of deviation based on rules and then either assign, report, or mark the transaction for cancelation based on individual specifications. An RPA-supported monitoring of incoming payments has advantages for both the receiving public authority and the citizen or company liable to pay. The manual effort is reduced, and relevant data can be transferred directly to the target system. On the other hand, the external stakeholders liable to pay benefit from the increased processing speed as less time passes between receipt of money and its assignment to continue or complete the process.

15.4 Cognitive service applications

This section presents three RPA use cases in which cognitive services are used. Each case shows a typical work procedure in public administrations. To develop the automation concepts, AI techniques have been added. The assessment of these concepts is based on experiences with comparable AI tasks that could be transferred.

15.4.1 Natural language processing

In the context of content management activities in public authorities, *natural language processing* (NLP) techniques can be used to analyze documents. The range of possible applications is very extensive, and the potential of using them in work processes must be assessed in each individual case with regard to possible RPA support. Therefore, the degree of difficulty, the effort required for setup, and the susceptibility to errors have to be considered. In the following, we will illustrate this based on two related use cases with similar technological requirements but different consequences.

In the first example, e-mails (e. g., those collected by a pool address) are analyzed using NLP techniques. The objective is to identify the request and to determine a suitable addressee for forwarding. This information results either from a given reference (case number, etc.) or from the natural language context. If an unambiguous reference is identified, it is possible to assign it directly to the addressee in charge. If this is not successful, a software robot can try to analyze the content of the message using NLP and weight identified indications. As an example, the information in the e-mail's subject containing a reference to an addressed organizational unit can be processed with higher relevance than contradictory notes in the body of the text. Likewise, a name used as a form of address can be classified as particularly promising for the assignment. In addition, sentence constructions can be semantically analyzed by identifying parts of speech, grammatical structure, and meaningful keywords (e. g., "complaint" or "grievance") as well as their synonyms, if necessary, to derive the context of a message. Based on the information obtained, RPA can use NLP techniques to design the automated distribution for many incoming e-mails.

Another use case for processing natural language data is the examination of document content. These documents could, e. g., be certificates in an application procedure, such as medical findings or legal judgments. In principle, RPA can automatically evaluate such documents using NLP techniques. Key terms and their synonyms can be identified, which often allow interpretation and, e. g., summarize diagnoses based on medical terms. NLP techniques can be used to determine whether a described state of health has been confirmed or disproved. Whether RPA can already be used in practice for such process types must be assessed based on the reliability of the method and the consequences of possible errors.

In both scenarios, natural language data are processed. For e-mail content analysis, a faulty interpretation and the resulting choice of a wrong addressee usually is not critical. However, drawing the wrong conclusions in the automated analysis of certificates is comparatively severe. Nevertheless, the reliability of NLP procedures is continuously developing and thus, the growing potential of using it in combination with RPA is obvious. At present, however, it seems advisable to always consider the given risk of misinterpreted documents in this context and to only choose work processes with no high impact if such misinterpretations occur. Such NLP services should currently preferably be used in a process assistance manner and support public administration staff in their daily work processes.

15.4.2 Decision support and automation

The term *predictive process monitoring* describes and subsumes interesting concepts aiming at an anticipatory process monitoring and the provision of predictions about potential future processes. Therefore, decisions can be based on historically observed process instances and hence become automated. Such approaches are currently gaining relevance. Important objectives are the prediction of further process steps, the expected throughput times, and forecasts on process outcome (Fettke, 2019). Predictive process monitoring can also be used in the context of process automation with RPA in public administrations. If many different factors determine a process execution, grasping all influences, their dependencies, and individual relevance can be challenging. Predictive approaches in combination with RPA can support process-related decision making and automated process execution based on experiences gained from past process instances.

Business processes in public administrations, such as the handling of tax audits, often require a consolidated review of a large amount of data. This information is usually digitally available and can be easily processed by a software robot. Neural networks can be trained with data from such scenarios – i. e., data from similarly completed tax cases. This method includes, in particular, transmitted data on the tax situation, logged checks, and their results. New tax cases could now be classified by a software robot based on such neural networks so that a processing strategy could be derived from similar cases. At the same time, based on the classification, a forecast of result and processing time is also possible.

15.4.3 Dialogue systems

The development of AI-supported dialogue systems aims at providing human-like communication between a human and a machine. For this purpose, systems are developed that recognize and analyze natural language, initiate appropriate actions, and interact with users (Fettke, 2019). In public administration, there are useful voice-controlled applications, e. g., for information, electronic applications, or making appointments.

In the future, numerous application processes in public administrations shall be able to be carried out online. As a result, there is a need to meet emerging requests for information appropriately. In some cases, some systems already contain directly written dialogue ("live chat") between applicants and public administration staff. Under certain circumstances, such services can be automated with RPA. For this purpose, a specific type of software robot is used, which has to understand and generate natural language ("chat bot"). Simple dialogues can be controlled by keywords based on rules. In these cases, the software robot refers to a repertoire of information that is addressed depending on the dialogue input by a human. For example, such information could be specific explanations or definitions of technical terms used in an application. One superior ability of automated dialogue systems arises from the possibility to ask questions. Through particular questions, it is possible to concretize the user's concern successively and improve the prerequisites for appropriate interaction.

Along with a form, a chat bot can offer mostly rule-based assistance by providing examples for form fields or explaining dependencies. At any time, users can call up additional details, which should be easily provided by the chat bot as the content is related to a specific part of the form. The chat bot can also save dialogue history. Collected data can then be evaluated and used, for example, to enrich the chat bot's "knowledge" on frequently addressed topics. A further feature of chat bots is the ability to get feedback from the user. This is usually initiated by a question in which chat bots ask to evaluate the interaction retrospectively. Based on this feedback, the chat bot can learn and accumulate knowledge about which information was useful for a specific request. Chat bots can support processes between external stakeholders and public administrations to reduce the amount of consultation. At the same time, RPA can provide new services in this context that would not be possible without the technology. For example, the dialogue with a chat bot can be processed in almost any language because its digital character as a translation service can be integrated easily.

15.5 Comprehensive application example: application form document processing

One important focus of modernizing public administrations in Germany is the processing of documents and forms. In connection with RPA, there is a multitude of tasks regarding the automated recognition and distribution of information as well as automated information extraction and processing. AI techniques can be used to process not only well-structured texts and forms, but also weakly structured tables or unstructured text documents (Fettke, 2018). Due to the wide variety of document types used in public administrations such as applications, proofs, notices, invoices, etc., there are several different starting points for realizing automation potential in this context. The following section presents an automation concept with RPA processing application forms. It illustrates the interaction of different techniques and capabilities of the technology. The generalized concept was developed based on the knowledge about application processing gathered in several dialogues with public administration employees.

15.5.1 Application example description

The conventional processing of filed applications involves various activities and often several organizational units. This becomes obvious when looking at a simplified manual process for handling applications in Figure 1, which shows typical events and activities represented by a so-called event-driven process chain (EPC).

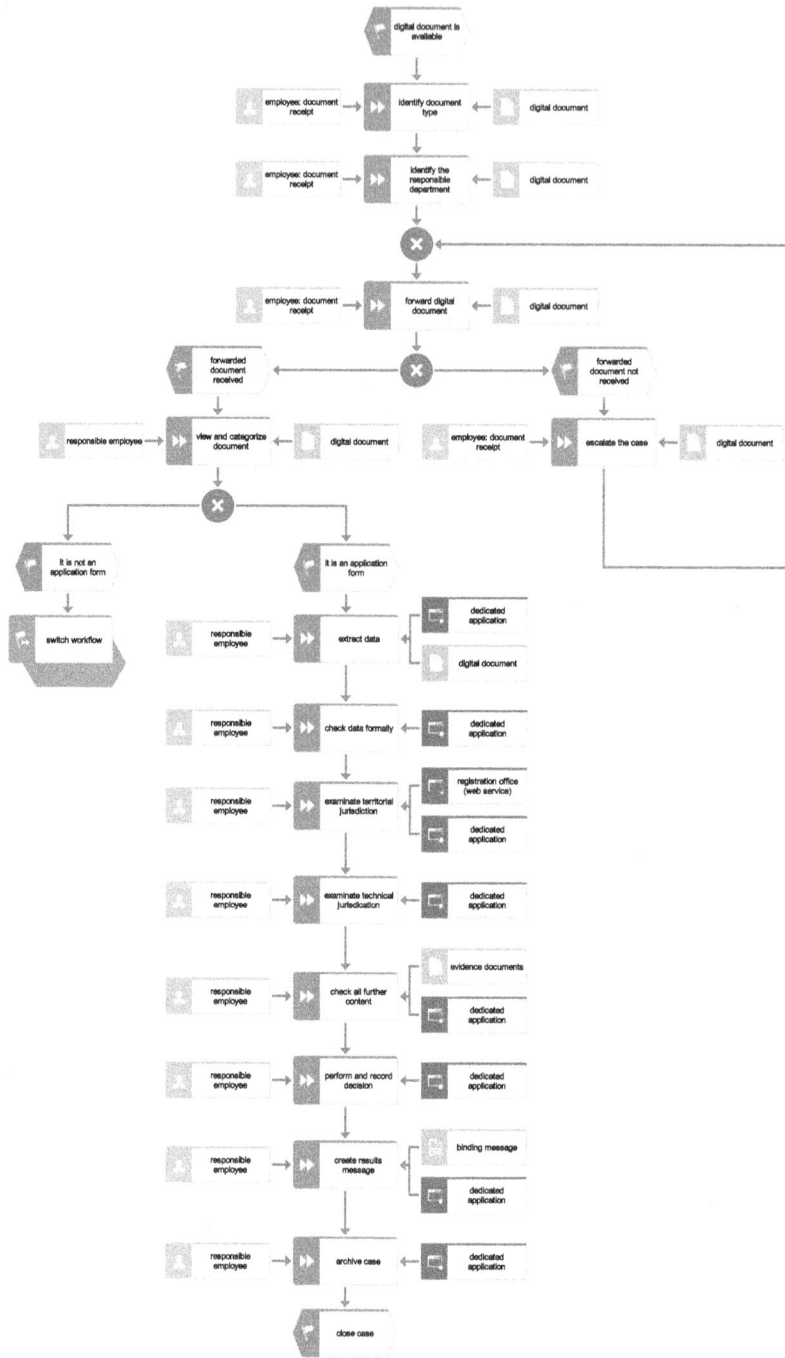

Figure 1: Generic process model "manual application handling."

The automation of such a process often requires the usage of different application systems that should be interlinked. They can be implemented by a single software robot performing some tasks based on rules and some based on cognitive services. For the selected process, three major tasks can be identified for automation, which are explained in more detail in the following sections.

15.5.2 Classification

A software robot can monitor storage media for incoming digital documents. If a corresponding file is stored or created in a target directory, its content can be analyzed immediately, e. g., classified. Artificial neural networks, which classify documents on the basis of their appearance and with the help of image data, can be used for this purpose (Houy et al., 2019). Such neural networks must be trained with a large number of document instances available in the public administration. Similarities within a document type are automatically learned based on external characteristics such as layout, etc. An application form, e. g., is characterized by its distinctive field structures and can be easily distinguished from other document types such as invoices or letters.

In order to distinguish between application forms and other documents, it would be sufficient for RPA to classify documents into two categories based on a neural network. However, a comprehensively trained neural network allows much more detailed differentiation (Houy et al., 2019). For recognizing different application forms, other document classes should be identifiable, e. g., for each particular application procedure. Successful recognition then also allows for the derivation of the organizational units and systems involved in further processing. In connection with neural networks, RPA can support a proper automated assignment of incoming application documents and initiate automated processing.

15.5.3 Data extraction

In addition to the classification of documents, neural networks can also help to identify information relevant to each document class and to find corresponding fields within the document. Once relevant fields in scanned documents have been identified, relevant information can be extracted and further processed using *optical character recognition* (OCR) methods (Houy et al., 2019).

Files that represent a completed application form may be suitable for automated recording of information contained in different ways, e. g., extraction from paper-based applications but also electronically filed applications. If characters can be reliably recognized using OCR, data extraction can also be performed automatically from paper-based and scanned or photographed applications. If the readability or error probability is critical, data extraction could still be performed, but the software robot should then support the subsequent manual entry by suggesting the characters which are probably correct. Finally, the suggested data entries should be corrected and completed by an employee if necessary. Given that the form type has been identified and the field contents have been correctly extracted, the RPA-supported transfer to all necessary systems (application software, databases, etc.) and the control of further case processing can take place.

15.5.4 Processing

The processing of application forms' content is highly dependent on the respective administrative procedure. Nevertheless, there are some generic process steps relevant in most cases. For example, a software robot can perform formal checks, which ensures the completeness and plausibility of the information contained in the application. In case of deficiencies, an automated dialogue with the applicant can be performed to obtain the necessary information. Ideally, this dialogue should also be designed in a digital form and manner so that a reply from the applicant can be processed automatically. Such a procedure could largely be implemented in a rule-based way.

Once all the data in the application form have been entered, the content can be checked. Content checks could comprise checking the current jurisdiction or determining the basis of alleged claims. Appropriate procedures have to be chosen individually. In-depth content checks usually require the inclusion of further information that is difficult to process in a rule-based manner. The success of such operations mostly depends on the degree of complexity and the quality of relevant information sources. If, for example, certificates or records have to be analyzed, a software robot can apply advanced NLP methods. However, the usage of NLP techniques brings the risk of misinterpretations and ambiguities. Thus, monitoring and checking the automatically created results by a human actor is of importance. Whether an AI-supported software robot can and should carry out content-related tasks automatically depends on the reliability with which it recognizes and interprets relevant aspects and uses them for decision-making. This is technically linked to whether it correctly recognizes the relevant data by identifying known patterns and judging them appropriately. At the moment, developing and using techniques that assist humans with well-founded recommendations seem to be the best choice for public administrations until those methods have matured.

Once the content processing steps in the business process have been completed, application procedures are usually followed by activities such as the preparation of a decision, accounting processes, and archiving. Here, many activities can be automated in a rule-based manner. This also applies to the creation of notifications. Finally, the software robot can document the executed steps with all relevant information and save them to the documents in the electronic file.

15.5.5 Overview of RPA potential in the process

Compared to Sections 15.3 and 15.4, which explained RPA support for rather brief tasks, Section 15.5 presented a more comprehensive end-to-end process. This application example is well suited for the general analysis of RPA potential because the process comprises different perspectives on the topic and various organizational units performing several tasks. In such an environment, RPA can demonstrate its versatility. The identified automation potential described before can be examined in the process model in Figure 2 on the next page. Besides a short description of the potential, two symbols are used to indicate whether a rule-based (🛠) or cognitive (🌐) RPA approach is primarily used. The fact that a major part of the process could be successfully supported by RPA stresses the versatile application possibilities of this technology.

15.6 RPA projects in practice – an example case from Germany

The following section presents the example case of a governmental organization (GO) in Germany. First, we describe the case context, and then we describe the challenges addressed in several different RPA projects in this authority, before a solution approach is described and discussed and an outlook on potential future activities is given.

15.6.1 Case context

Some GOs in Germany are currently pioneering the use of RPA. They are often responsible for proper IT operations of various public authorities and organize broad modernization activities. Some of them currently investigate RPA in pilot projects focusing on the technology's potential and aim at spreading successful digitalization concepts. We have been discussing current RPA-related project activities with one specific GO in Germany. The following case example relates to this GO and presents findings and experiences from their current RPA activities.

    The GO that we are referring to is a service unit for all IT and digitalization activities of one of the German federal state governments, which has been established in 2015. In total, this GO has more than 100 employees working on IT and digitalization topics. Its topics of interest regarding digitalization and digital transformation are (1) Urban Life and Smart City, (2) Mobility and Energy, (3) Health and Social Life, (4) Culture and Sports, (5) Economy and Work, (6) Knowledge and Education, and (7) Security and Judiciaries. In these fields of interest, several different dig-

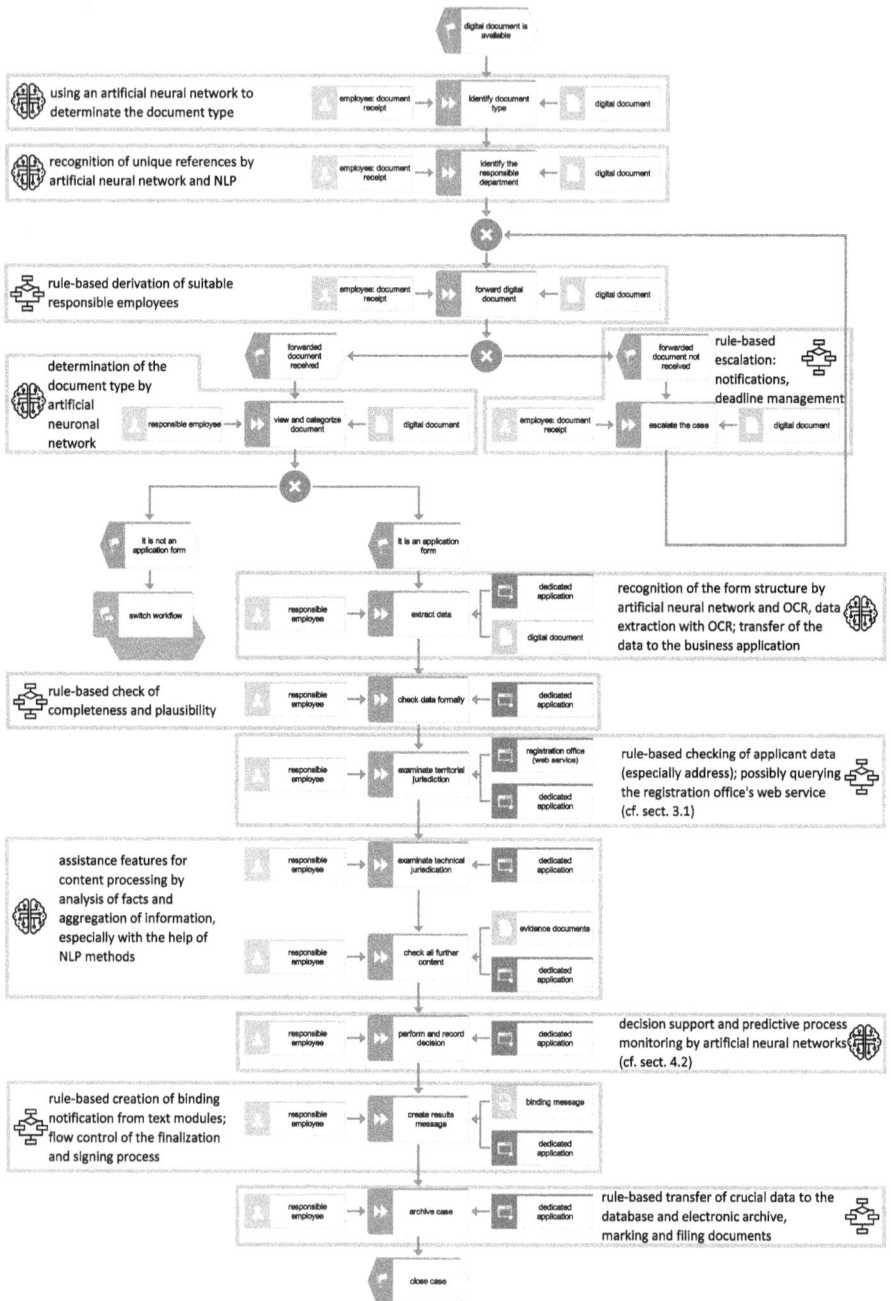

Figure 2: Overview of RPA potential in the above presented process "manual application handling."

ital transformation projects have been and are currently conducted, e. g., the development and setup of digital demonstration labs, innovation workshops, urban data hubs, platforms, etc. Their primary goal is to support public authorities (as a consultant or project partner) in tapping the full potential of innovative technology to provide the best possible service to their citizens.

The project group working on RPA projects within this GO consists of about 15 people treating different topics like RPA, business process management, and the potential of machine learning in this context. Some of them belong to private external service providers, and some of them are employees of the federal state's government.

15.6.2 Problem

The main problem for the RPA project group is the current lack of RPA experience in public authorities. It is aware that the automation of processes can significantly reduce the workload. Furthermore, only flexible RPA tools seem to be appropriate to meet the different requirements in its area of responsibility. Hence, the GO has identified RPA as an essential topic for the digital transformation of public authorities. They need a strategy to provide RPA to all associated public authorities and support its implementation in selected processes. While they are still in the early stages, it is their strategic goal to provide RPA solutions to most public authorities in the federal state as long as the technology can offer proper support. The main problem that RPA is supposed to solve is the growing workload of public administration employees while the budget for according personnel is not developing similarly. The GO identified challenges (described in more detail) along the way from the idea to the dissemination of a mature RPA concept and the related IT platform. Primary challenges are the following:

1. *Lack of technical knowledge*: This includes a lack of process knowledge, which already complicates the selection of potential process candidates and leads to additional effort during the implementation. If an administrative procedure appears suitable for RPA, the involved organizational units must be convinced by the potential benefits and the feasibility of a technical realization.
2. *Critical attitude*: Employees whose activities are directly affected by automation projects might have personal concerns. Hence, in such a scenario, there is a particular risk of retained information and neglected collaboration.
3. *Governance*: In addition to the operational challenges of RPA projects, other aspects need to be clarified. These include organizational details on the acquisition, supervision, and maintenance of an RPA system. Especially the selection of an RPA provider and the design of governance structures for operation, monitoring, data management, etc., is essential. By facing these challenges, a general strategy to introduce RPA in various cases must be created.

15.6.3 Solution approach

The solution approach taken by the RPA project group of the GO describes two different perspectives. First, a long-term strategy was designed to bring RPA to several public authorities and to spread it throughout the federal state. Second, they created a general procedure to support a single process with RPA. The long-term strategy consists of three stages:

1. *Proof-of-concept*: For the development of an RPA introduction concept, the roadmap and the vision have to be designed. In a broad survey, the potential shall be collected on a large scale, and a selection of suitable providers has to be made considering identified requirements. Based on this information, a proof-of-concept (PoC) can be created.

2. *Implementation*: By introducing and establishing an increasing number of RPA processes, additional experience can be gathered to apply and improve change management activities, appropriate training, and solutions for operating with RPA components.

3. *RPA platform*: The last stage is the permanent deployment of an RPR platform, where proven concepts are available and can quickly be adopted by interested public authorities. New approaches can also be designed, implemented, and disseminated using existing architectures, know-how, and concepts.

As a part of this strategy, individual projects are executed to automate selected processes. Now, the RPA project group of the GO is piloting some single approaches to gather RPA knowledge and to demonstrate the technology's strengths. Therefore, it follows three steps:

1. The first step is to collect ideas for promising projects, analyze the specific potential, and discuss the possibilities for implementation.

2. In the second step, automation approaches are designed and piloted. Subsequently, change management, staff training, and other related organizational actions shall be based on the concepts' characteristics.

3. In a third step, it is their goal to create an overarching platform providing RPA functionality that contains the required software and operational data.

In detail, the supervising RPA project group of the GO collects information on the entire process sets in selected areas. The initiative can be inspired either by a central authority, by the respective authority operating the processes recommended for RPA support, or by third party knowledge like other public authorities, private organizations, or consultants. This information is analyzed regarding the expected benefits and feasibility. Based on the resulting pre-selection ("long-list"), there are discussions with experts from the respective area to decide whether an RPA concept should be designed or discarded. In the case of promising processes, the analysis is intensified, and reengineering of relevant activity structures is considered. The goal is to ensure that a process is first improved and then automated, if necessary. Then, the automation concept is finally designed, implemented, and tested. If the tests are successful and all prerequisites for a changeover have been met, the live operation will be started. From this point on, operation, monitoring, and the necessary maintenance tasks are handed over to the responsible organizational unit.

15.6.4 Results

The GO already implemented RPA in selected administrative procedures. We have gathered information regarding two PoCs of RPA applications, which are currently under construction. One example process is the classification of document types to prepare their forwarding. Here, arriving paper documents are digitalized by an external service provider. The files are sent to the authority and must be forwarded to the responsible organizational unit. Without RPA, employees had to open the data on a screen, check the content, find out who is accountable, and forward every single document manually. Now that RPA is introduced, the employees' workload is reduced as several document types can be identified and sent automatically. Therefore, an RPA system is trained to identify numerous incoming document classes that have common characteristics. For example, application forms for public services, which are approximately 50 % of the incoming documents in this authority, can be easily identified by their headlines and layout. This fact is used for classification by localizing the headline on the document, extracting this part of the image, improving the image quality to read the letters, and applying OCR. Based on the recognized letters, a match to familiar document types is calculated and decided by using the Levenshtein distance approach.

This procedure is currently being extended to include other types of documents. It is planned for the technique to go beyond the consideration of headlines but also analyze additional text and layout characteristics for classification. For this purpose, a *support vector machine* (SVM) is trained so that a universal classification component is created, which allows adaption and extension. As a second PoC, the GO is working on the setup of a similar procedure to forward incoming e-mails. This case does not need to convert image data into text. To access the content of text messages, NLP techniques receive significant attention. They can be used, e. g., to identify relevant entities (e. g., *named entity recognition*), essential information based on term frequencies (e. g., *term frequency/inverse document frequency* [TF-IDF]), and important phrases using *n-gram analysis*. In general, this case also targets the objective to locate responsible organizational units quickly and to carry out forwarding.

The tasks for which the GO has already developed an RPA support are entirely independent of the piloting organizational unit and could also be easily transferred to other departments and agencies. The current state of their projects demonstrates that RPA can perform a useful administrative task and conveys a general impression of how successful concepts can be leveraged in many different areas. Thus, the two objectives of supporting individual processes with RPA on the one hand and gathering experience for further projects on the other hand were fulfilled.

15.6.5 Case outlook

Plans for the future focus on the achievement of a long-term strategy. Therefore, it is crucial to find solutions for the described key challenges and to implement successful RPA pilot processes. While change management tasks must be performed primarily by appropriate communication, the lack of process knowledge and the identification of suitable processes for automation can be supported by technologies. Amongst other methods, *process mining* shall be used to analyze logs representing the current execution of business processes using IT systems. Thus, findings on processes can be gathered where not enough or no information is available. Furthermore, this technique can be used to generate process metrics that help to identify weaknesses in process organization. Another focus is on the investigation of *cognitive services*. The progress in the application of AI already shows great potential. However, the performance and reliability in practical use must be ensured. In addition, such procedures must also be justified to external parties involved in the process and supervisory authorities. Thus, the explainability and transparency of applied algorithms are further focal points of their research and development in projects. With the gained experience and the introduced automation concepts, supra-regional knowledge exchange with other public authorities could also be established, providing benefits for all participating actors.

15.7 Conclusions

15.7.1 Summary of application potential

In the above sections, we have developed and illustrated exemplary automation concepts and explained use cases from practice with technical reference to typical public administration processes. Table 3 summarizes the application examples, presents the focus of automation, and lists the most important techniques offered in each application example viz. use case.

15.7.2 Discussion

In general, the chapter has investigated and presented RPA as a versatile technology for the automation of processes in public administrations. The described examples differentiate between simple RPA concepts and cognitive services. These two categories

Table 3: Results of the case studies.

	Application case	Focus of automation	Central techniques
Application examples for simple RPA	Frequent controlling procedures	• data transfer from databases or application systems into web forms • comparison of web queries with data sets • creation of a report in case of deviations	• rule-based processing
	Data maintenance	• checking individual data sets for completeness and plausibility • comparison of the data stocks of different systems • finding duplicates, contradictions, or potential fraud	• rule-based processing
	Payment monitoring	• monitoring and analysis of sales data • attempt to allocate to open operations • registration of the receipt or delivery for manual processing or cancelation	• rule-based processing
Application examples for cognitive services	Natural language processing	• interpretation of texts in natural language • identification of relevant areas and text passages • identification and weighting of mail areas • classification of competence	• rule-based processing • NLP • OCR
	Decision support and automation	• recording of tax data • classification with neural network • recommendation of an audit strategy • automated execution/preparation/support of validation steps	• rule-based processing • neural networks
	Dialogue systems	• interpretation of texts in natural language • context analysis • generation of information using available knowledge sources • control of queries (specialization of content, feedback, etc.)	• rule-based processing • NLP • learning algorithms
Comprehensive application example	Application form document processing	• classification of documents • identification of relevant form fields • data extraction • preparation of communication with the applicant • content examination/content preparation • document creation • archiving	• rule-based processing • neural networks • OCR • NLP

Table 3: (continued)

	Application case	Focus of automation	Central techniques
Case study from practice	Paper document classification	• identification of relevant areas and text passages • image improvement • text extraction • keyword comparison	• rule-based processing • image pre-processing • OCR
	E-mail forwarding	• interpretation of texts in natural language • identification and weighting of mail areas • classification of competence	• rule-based processing • NLP

mark two poles of a broad range of possible RPA concepts. Considering these two different concepts was useful to investigate the current practicability of available techniques and estimate the future potential of AI-based RPA technology. The following discussion continues this distinction because it is particularly useful when considering opportunities and risks. First, however, the basic idea of RPAs is discussed in general.

Generally, the main incentive for using RPA arises from the advantages of automated process execution, which can lead to reduced costs for personnel or create an increased process execution performance without putting additional strain on the existing personnel. Opportunities also arise from the high operating speed of software robots so that process run-times can be significantly reduced. At the same time, RPA can log the details of the automated execution of each individual process instance, thus increasing the traceability of processes to internal and external parties with regard to their status. RPA can also be introduced in a very targeted manner, exactly where there is an acute need or where a particularly high benefit is expected from process automation. Compared to many other IT strategies (e. g., integrating a new IT system), parallel processes that are not affected by this technology do not change at all. Hence, comprehensive change management is often not necessary.

The primary challenge for successful RPA is the adequate setup of process control. If the process design is inadequate, a process that has significant shortcomings may be automated. The faulty execution and the resulting damage, as well as possible correction efforts, can then multiply within a short time Kirchmer (2017). To avoid such shortcomings, the careful development of each individual concept is necessary. However, this requires sufficient process knowledge, which is still under development in many areas of public administration and therefore requires process surveys to be carried out first. If RPA concepts are successfully introduced, the released human work capacities can and should be reorganized in a meaningful way. Accordingly, people could take care of new functions and tasks, which increase motivation. In the medium and long term, RPA could entail the risk of neglecting the further development of existing IT systems because certain deficiencies are circumvented but not remedied by RPA. Table 4 summarizes the opportunities and risks of general RPA concepts.

Table 4: Generic opportunities and risks of RPA.

	Opportunities	Risks
RPA (generic)	• increase of economic efficiency	• consideration of all possible process variants is difficult
	• reduction of processing times	• automation of faulty processes multiplies negative consequences
	• higher process and data consistency	• "blind faith" in automatic execution
	• comprehensive logging of the process details	• extensive process knowledge in administrations is not always available
	• process transparency can increase service quality for external parties	• released personnel capacities must be reorganized in a meaningful way
	• implementations often do not require comprehensive change management	• potential neglect of the further development of central IT components

Simple RPA concepts are characterized by comparatively little variation in the automated process. In the simplest case, the process does not vary at all. Here, a software robot would execute a sequence of operating steps as often as required. If the course of the process depends on certain influences, these can be clearly identified in simple RPA concepts and follow defined rules. This creates consistent process executions and can reduce the susceptibility to errors. In most cases, routine processes are addressed that occur frequently but are not complex. This means that implementation is relatively quick, and the RPA potential can be tapped quickly. At the same time, the procedure executed by software robots remains easily comprehensible, so that a high level of acceptance can be achieved among both employees and external process participants. Simple RPA is currently already used in various industries to increase the execution frequency of monotonous procedures and to relieve employees. There are numerous suitable applications for such approaches in public administration, which could easily be implemented from a technical point of view.

However, the versatility of RPA also entails some risks. Especially in public administration, the number of processes that can be automated with simple RPA concepts could quickly become confusing due to the high diversity of (legacy) systems and processes. This already complicates the identification and selection of potential process candidates. After the comprehensive implementation of simple RPA concepts, the system diversity would continue to pose a risk because changes to individual IT components (e. g., updating application software) could then possibly result in a need for maintenance of various RPA-supported processes that use that component. In addition to the acute expense, processes could also come to a complete standstill in this way if no more personnel is scheduled for alternative processing. Table 5 summarizes the opportunities and risks of simple RPA concepts.

Table 5: Opportunities and risks of simple RPA concepts.

	Opportunities	Risks
Simple RPA	• simple and fast implementation • lower susceptibility to errors • consistent operation • working methods are well comprehensible • broad acceptance	• uncertain procedure for process selection and prioritization • need for adaptation in case of changes to IT components that are integrated • acute workload in case of malfunction of automated process execution

Cognitive services are targeting tasks for which humans need intelligence. In many cases, they are very efficient because they can process complex information quickly. The application focus is narrower compared to simple RPA concepts, and commercial solutions are currently only just emerging. In terms of process automation, public administration will see particular opportunities in the handling of image data such as electronic documents or the processing of texts in natural language. These techniques also enable the introduction of new approaches such as chat bots, which can expand the existing range of services offered by the public administration. In addition, cognitive services can also use the knowledge implicitly contained in recorded process data to control process instances or to evaluate the decisions made by employees in a process.

In the case of cognitive services, risks result primarily from the requirements for included data. In public administrations in Germany, the necessary data needed for proper machine learning are often not or only insufficiently available. For generic tasks such as recognizing characters utilizing OCR, many RPA products offer pretrained solutions that can achieve good results. Other applications, such as the extraction of data from invoice documents with unknown layouts, are currently under development and becoming increasingly reliable. Here, public administrations can benefit from the private sector, as there are overlaps in several areas of activity. However, RPA solutions for highly administration-specific procedures can only be created with the involvement of public authorities and require the inclusion of their data. Depending on the process, these data might first be created or comprehensively processed. A significant challenge is the requirement to combine technically relevant aspects and process information so that essential interrelationships are reflected in the data. If the administration succeeds in providing suitable data, the implementation of the necessary machine learning steps is still extensive and does not necessarily lead to a feasible solution with the required reliability.

Furthermore, the methods provided by AI techniques are sometimes difficult to understand, which can impact the acceptance of *cognitive services*. This aspect is particularly important for public administrations in order not to jeopardize trust in objectivity and performance. Regardless of how a cognitive service works, the effort required to maintain an individual service is comparatively high. Adaptations to new conditions in the process can require new learning phases, especially in machine learning processes, and thus cause increased effort. Furthermore, only little experience has been gained in dealing with cognitive services so far, so that extensive tests would first be required before operational introduction in public administrations. Table 6 summarizes the opportunities and risks of cognitive services.

Table 6: Opportunities and risks of cognitive services.

	Opportunities	Risks
Cognitive services	• fast acquisition and processing of complex data • interpretation of image data and natural language, especially for document processing • new services such as multilingual dialogue systems • process decisions can be based on implicit knowledge in data • control of the degree of automation from process-related decision support to full automation	• dependency on data in terms of quantity and quality • initial setup effort with uncertain prospects of success • acceptance problems due to a lack of explanation • extensive testing required

15.7.3 Outlook

The automation of processes is a crucial endeavor to meet the requirements of a modern digital public administration. RPA provides a technology that creates new possibilities. The opportunities and risks of the technology are emphasized. The contribution's focus concentrates on a broad range of possible applications and the description of the identified potential. While other IT strategies are often limited to a specific field, RPA offers the opportunity to develop tailored solutions for multiple problems.

RPA supports the development of individual digitalization strategies for public administrations. This feature also enables an adjusted agenda of priorities. Probably public administrations will mainly limit RPA concepts to established techniques and pick up methods used in the private economy with some delay. Thus, for now, the focus would be primarily on processes that can be automated with simple RPA concepts. The primary objectives pursued would be to relieve the workload on personnel, cut costs, raise consistency, and reduce errors and processing times.

However, RPA is being presented as a "tool" for public administrations for a good reason. The technology requires an active deployment and maintenance. Even the identification and selection of processes suitable for automation concepts is a severe challenge due to the diversity of activities in the administration. However, this preparation can be supported by techniques such as the analysis of recorded process data (Geyer-Klingeberg et al., 2018). If necessary, the general process flow should also be reconsidered to prevent a transformation from *flawed processes* into *automated flawed processes*. Taking these aspects into account, the administration should pragmatically develop and test RPA concepts for individual non-critical processes with suitable conditions. Experiences can thus be made, and an expansion of the usage can be prepared based on such pilot automation projects.

Conversely, the diversity in the administration, which makes it difficult to overview and select processes for RPA concepts, also marks an environment with excellent pre-conditions to benefit from the technology. In particular, the transport of information through heterogenous system landscapes can be made considerably faster and highly consistent with RPA. Many organizational units facing similar challenges can exchange experiences, develop common automation concepts, and often share the technical infrastructure for an RPA system.

Cognitive services already indicate the performance of the next generation of RPA product solutions. Soon, they will create and support automated processes that can handle complex tasks that would either take a lot of time or even could not be performed at all without AI. When these products mature, cognitive services should be tested and evaluated in non-critical processes first. They could support employees, assist the process execution, and operate "under observation" until reliability is ensured.

The presented concepts focus on the requirements and conditions of public administrations in Germany. Accordingly, the organizational structures, the diversity of IT systems, and the need for interfaces to overcome borders between responsible units are quite specific and can differ from other countries. Nevertheless, it can be assumed that even countries with low organizational fragmentation and intense system integration will have to handle a great diversity of processes with a wide range of properties. Therefore, the automation of processes may have a different focus compared to Germany but still shows appropriate potential to benefit from RPA knowledge, the proposed application examples, and gathered results.

If public administrations consider introducing RPA-supported processes, the communication of the measures must be a focal aspect of the strategy. The technology will lead to a shift of manual tasks from repetitive routine operations to more individualized activities. The staff must sufficiently accept this change. Thus, it is crucial to create appropriate perspectives for those employees whose activity profile has a high potential for automation. Similarly, the use of RPA must not compromise the confidence of citizens and companies in the efficiency and objectivity of public administration. RPA procedures should only be introduced if they are highly reliable and should be permanently controlled under strict conditions.

While our chapter focuses on technical and organizational aspects, it has not included some other important aspects such as legal and ethical details. Especially the collection of legal requirements can reveal further challenges for an RPA strategy in public administrations. Also, the need for ethical discussions can be expected mainly due to the field of AI applications creating decisions for process flows. From a scientific point of view, these aspects indicate additional research gaps and further challenges for assessing the applicability of RPA in public administrations.

Bibliography

Fettke P (2018) Umsatzsteuer, Zoll und Künstliche Intelligenz - Eine Einführung. Mehrwertsteuerrecht 11:457–496

Fettke P (2019) Künstliche Intelligenz für die Digitalisierung der Steuerfunktion. Rethinking Tax 1:12–22

Gartner Research (2019) Magic quadrant for robotic process automation software. 08 07 2019. [Online]. Available: https://www.gartner.com/en/documents/3947184/magic-quadrant-for-robotic-process-automation-software

Geyer-Klingeberg J, Nekladal J, Baldauf F, Veit F (2018) Process mining and robotic process automation: a perfect match. In: 16th international conference on business process management, Sydney

Gutermuth O, Houy C, Fettke P (2020) Robotergestützte Prozessautomatisierung für die Digitale Verwaltung. Nationales E-Government Kompetenzzentrum (NEGZ) e. V., Berichte des NEGZ Nr 10

Houy C, Hamberg M, Fettke P (2019) Robotic process automation in public administrations. In: Digitalisierung von Staat und Verwaltung. Gesellschaft für Informatik e. V., Bonn, pp 62–74

Kirchmer M (2017) Robotic process automation – pragmatic solution or dangerous illusion? BTOES Insights (Business Transformation and Operational Excellence Summit Insights), 06 2017

Ng A (2016) What artificial intelligence can and can't do right now. Harvard Business Review Digital Articles, 9 11 2016

Smeets M, Erhard R, Kaußler T (2019) Robotic Process Automation (RPA) in der Finanzwirtschaft. Springer, Wiesbaden

Veit F, Geyer-Klingeberg J, Madrzak J, Haug M, Thomson J (2017) The proactive insights engine: process mining meets machine learning and artificial intelligence. In: 15th international conference on business process management, 2017, Barcelona

vom Brocke J, Maaß W, Buxmann P, Maedche A, Leimeister J, Pecht G (2018) Future work and enterprise systems. Bus Inf Syst Eng 60(4):357–366

Peter Pfeiffer and Peter Fettke

16 Applications of RPA in manufacturing

Abstract: Robotic process automation (RPA) tools are nowadays frequently used in sectors with primarily office work like services, telecommunications, administration, finance, and insurance. However, industrial domains like manufacturing also have huge potential for RPA to automate a large variety of tasks. As in office work, there are a lot of more or less complex activities and workflows that are repetitive and error-prone. In this chapter, we will introduce potential use cases for RPA in manufacturing along the Y-CIM model and show one practical application of cognitive RPA in this domain for retrieving a computer-aided design (CAD) model from a query image. The digitalization of the industrial sector offers a lot of possibilities for automation. Many processes are supported by computer-aided machines and information is stored and shared using a unified database. During product development and production, CAD is frequently used nowadays to design and modify a workpiece realistically on a computer before going into production. During manufacturing, CAD data are available and can be used in computer-aided machines to automate certain parts of the manufacturing process. A new artificial intelligence application will be introduced which is able to propose a list of CAD models from a database given a photo of a workpiece. An operator can check this list and select the correct CAD model. This is not only a new method to retrieve CAD models from images but also one of the first approaches to enable the use of RPA in the industrial domain.

Keywords: Industrial RPA, CAD retrieval, computer-integrated manufacturing, few-shot learning

16.1 Introduction

Robotic process automation (RPA) and cognitive RPA have shown great applications in domains where a lot of office work is being done. They are used to automate front- and back-office tasks like payroll processes, customer interactions via chatbots, or other administrative processes like transferring customer data from one system to another. In some domains, e. g., public administration, a large variety of tasks can be automated using RPA and cognitive RPA as shown in Houy et al. (2019). In the industrial domain, concepts like Industry 4.0 require new technologies to exploit the automation potential and increase the efficiency (Lasi et al., 2014). However, RPA in the industrial sector has not been investigated in literature so far. In this domain, a lot of repetitive

Acknowledgement: The chapter is based on content and results of the Software Campus Project "R2TRIEV3," which was funded by the German Federal Ministry of Education and Research (BMBF) [01IS17043].

https://doi.org/10.1515/9783110676693-016

and error-prone tasks – just like in office work – are performed, which are great candidates for automation. Examples are transferring and transforming production sensory data into a structured database, retrieving relevant requirements from a document, or scheduling new orders into the production. Digitalization of the industrial sector has a huge impact on workflows and systems but also offers possibilities to enhance processes.

With more digitalization in industrial sites, more information is collected which allows more collaboration between machines, employees, and robots. Computer-aided manufacturing (CAM) and computer-integrated manufacturing (CIM), introduced by Scheer (2012), are widely used nowadays and serve as a great foundation to implement RPA solutions in industrial sites. As an important part of digitalization, automation helps people to work more efficiently and effectively by executing certain activities without the need for human action. With more machines being computer-aided, more information is available while more automation can be implemented at the same time. The information can be stored and shared between machines and humans in several workflows. Information and data created during the product development can be used during manufacturing. In the same way, information created during manufacturing can be used while monitoring, in quality control, or in controlling. Intelligent services use this information, e. g., to automatically identify workpieces and present related order information, order spare parts, or show the individual components of the workpiece. Furthermore, reports from information gained during production can be created automatically.

As an example of RPA in manufacturing, a cognitive RPA service has been implemented and will be presented in more detail in this chapter. It helps to automate several tasks in manufacturing processes by retrieving similar computer-aided design (CAD) models to a workpiece in a photo or image. The application makes use of CAD data, which are frequently used in product development, design, and production. Before being produced, a workpiece is nowadays realistically designed on the computer as a CAD model. In some production steps, information linked to the physical workpiece like the material or its delivery date must be known. Once the workpiece and its related CAD model are identified, this information can be accessed. Finding the correct CAD model to a physical workpiece is a demanding task that requires expert knowledge. Moreover, the person inspecting the real object might not be the same as the one who designed the workpiece as CAD model. Finding the corresponding CAD model usually involves searching though the set of all CAD models that have ever been designed or produced. With several hundreds or thousands of different CAD models in the database of an average manufacturer, searching for the correct one can be time-consuming. Usually there are at least as many CAD models as products, or even more. Apart from the high number of objects in the database, there are more problems and challenges one has to deal with. Three-dimensional representations can be difficult for humans to understand, especially for persons who do not often deal with 3D models. Small deviations of similar looking CAD models (e. g., in product families) are hard to detect and may cause the wrong model to be selected.

In this chapter, new opportunities for RPA in the industrial sector will be outlined. Therefore, automation candidate tasks along the Y-CIM model are investigated and the use of RPA for these tasks is explained. In the next section, conceptual foundation will be given. Section 16.3 introduces the RPA applications along the Y-CIM model. For each task, a scenario explains the technical problem domain and outlines how the task can be automated. The RPA solution to retrieve CAD models from a photo is explained, implemented, and evaluated in Section 16.4 as an example for the use of cognitive RPA in the manufacturing sector. Section 16.5 outlines related work while Section 16.6 concludes the chapter.

16.2 Foundations

16.2.1 RPA and cognitive RPA

RPA is a term used for services that perform instructions on computer programs as humans would do (van der Aalst et al., 2018) using (graphical) user interfaces, e. g., HTML, a lower-level interface like APIs, or the command line interface (Fettke and Loos, 2019). The term is used in the academic world and by practitioners. However, there is no established definition of the term. RPA is especially used for programs or tools, so-called software bots or services, that automate processes or routines; usually repetitive, error-prone, rule-based ones humans perform. RPA, as a technology, usually describes the software being used (Ansari et al., 2019). However, additional hardware may be required sometimes to enable the use of RPA.

Different to workflow technology software, the information system the RPA service operates on remains unchanged (van der Aalst et al., 2018). RPA does not require the system or workflows to be changed to its needs. Only small changes in workflows or information systems need to be made. Most tasks which are automated by RPA are driven by simple rules and logic, for example, to transfer structured data from one information system to another.

RPA tools often use technology from data analytics or process mining (van der Aalst et al., 2018). Simple RPA services using rule-based approaches are often limited to simple and repetitive tasks on structured data and simple interfaces. However, there are many of these tasks that have a huge automation potential. Artificial intelligence and machine learning techniques enable RPA services to operate on unstructured data and non-static interfaces (van der Aalst et al., 2018) solving knowledge-intensive tasks that can bring more value (Ivančić et al., 2019). Such applications are called cognitive or intelligent RPA services and are one possibility of broadening the scope of RPA as it is conceptually not limited to simple tasks (Fettke and Loos, 2019). Cognitive RPA service tools support humans in coming to conclusions (Fettke and Loos, 2019), e. g., by aggregating data into useful charts using intelligent data processing. In contrast to simple RPA, cognitive RPA can take over a wider range of tasks. Rather than setting up rules, scripts, or click-path, they can be trained on data from previous executions by humans and act autonomously afterwards. Techniques from natural language processing (NLP) or computer vision can be used in cognitive RPA, e. g., to implement an intelligent chat bot that answers customers' questions or a document scanner that transfers data from a paper invoice into the ERP system. Such applications can bring huge benefit in automating repetitive and time-consuming tasks. They increase efficiency, reduce errors, and allow humans to work on more valuable tasks.

16.2.2 Computer-integrated manufacturing (CIM)

CIM describes the integration of economic and technical information of an industrial company in a single database (Scheer, 2012). Figure 1 (reprint from Vareille et al., 2016) shows the Y-CIM model. The left part shows the preliminary business and planning processes of an industrial company like production planning and control, while the right part is more concerned with technical processes like product development, production control, and quality control (Scheer et al., 2007). The upper parts of each leg describe the planning activities while the lower parts are concerned with manufacturing and implementation. Around the Y shape are the business activities like management, coordination, and accounting. All tasks and activities are conceptualized as business processes.

Information is made available in a central CIM system and shared between all processes of a manufacturer. For example, production planning uses information from logistics such as bills of material. The data are centralized in one IT infrastructure. Another case where CIM helps is in engineering. During the production planning process, required tools like drills are noted in the construction plan (CAD model). In the production process, this information can be used to automatically equip machines with the correct drills, which reduces manual work and speeds up the production.

16.2.2.1 Computer-aided manufacturing (CAM)

CAM describes the use of computers to control machines in production, e. g., for logistics, transport, or manufacturing. It is sometimes also used for computer-aided production planning and control(CAP). In CAM, computerized numerical control

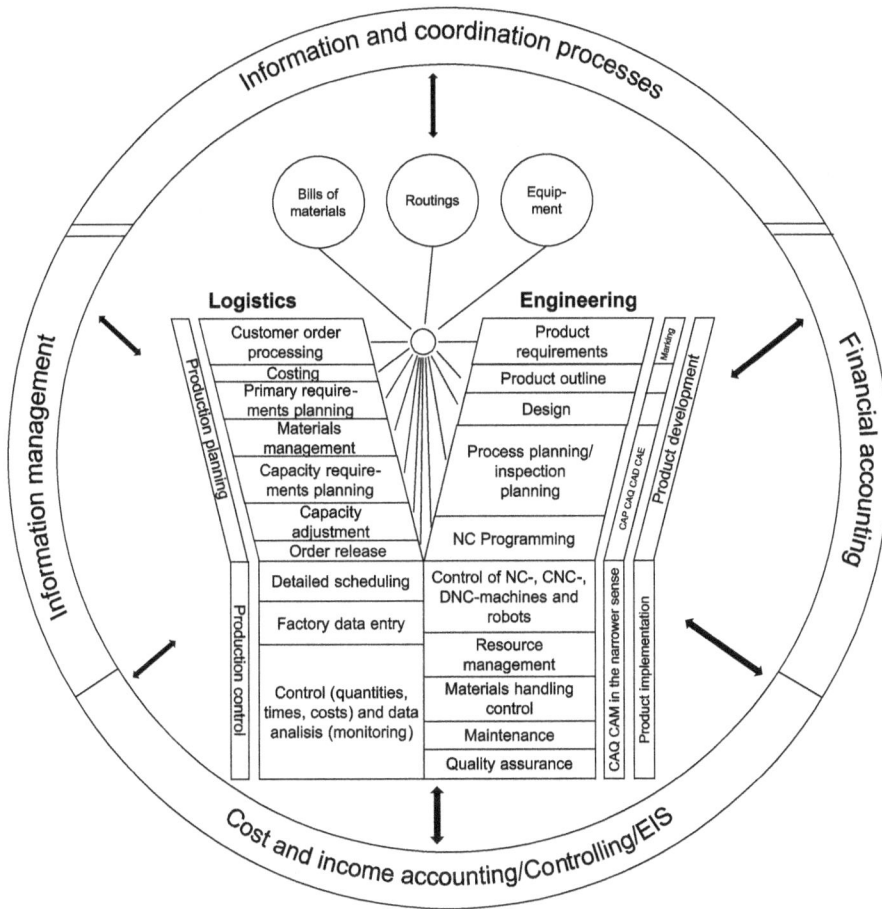

Figure 1: Y-CIM model.

machines are used instead of non-computerized ones. Furthermore, robots with sensors, automated warehouse systems, and driverless transport systems are used. Using computer-aided systems in production also requires new forms of organization, for example, machining centers where machines automatically change tools and do several manufacturing steps like drilling and milling in one place (Scheer, 1990).

16.2.2.2 Computer-aided design (CAD)

CAD describes the use of computer (both hardware and software) during design, development, analysis, and modification of an engineering or construction design (Groover and Zimmers, 1983; Sarcar et al., 2008) and is a part of the Y-CIM model. It is used in many industrial areas for the mechanical design of automotives, aircrafts, prosthetics, electronic circuits, and much more. Modern CAD software uses vector-based graphics to draw objects of any geometrical shape or raster graphics to show the overall appearance of an object. CAD models can be curves and figures in 2D or surfaces and solids in 3D. Three-dimensional objects are constructed using wireframe, surface, or volume models (Scheer, 2012). Standardized 2D and 3D elements for design are available through a database. Using Boolean operators such as union or subtraction, complex structures can be created from standardized elements. Figure 2 shows an example of a cylinder block as a 3D wireframe model.

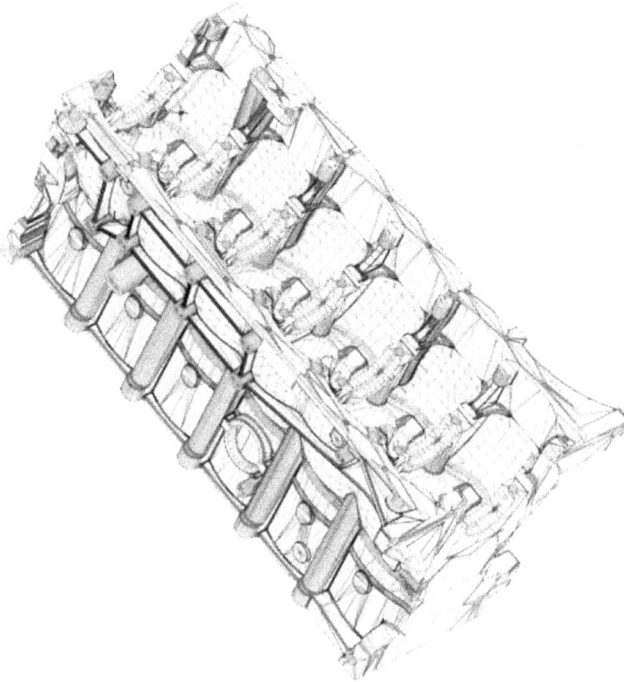

Figure 2: Wireframe visualization of a cylinder block.

Beside the mathematical or geometrical description of an object, CAD models can also be described using physical attributes like density or optical, mechanical, and thermal properties. Some CAD software allows to simulate forces and find weaknesses of the design that may cause fractions. Usually, the output is an electronic file in a format like *DXF*, *STEP*, or *SLT*. Beside drawing objects using shapes, CAD files often contain information about the material, surface, dimensions, and tolerances. CAD software allows to manipulate objects and enables to view them from any angle. Furthermore, objects can be visualized in different materials.

16.2.3 Few-shot learning

Few-shot learning is a machine learning task that is about learning from only a few examples. For many machine learning tasks, deep neural networks with several layers are used. Due to their architecture, they require intensive training with several thousands to millions of training examples and perform badly when generalizing from only a few examples or from unbalanced data. Unfortunately, for most real-life tasks it is hard or impossible to collect that many data or labels for the problem to solve, e. g., in changing environments where the objects to classify vary from time to time or in cases where only a few examples are available for certain classes. Imagine a manufacturer for customer-specific workpieces. From order to order, the workpieces vary. A state-of-the-art deep neural network image classification model would have difficulties to correctly identify the individual objects in the images. Furthermore, if the number of samples per object is imbalanced, deep learning often fails to correctly classify the underrepresented classes. Human brains on the other hand, from which neural networks are inspired, are able to learn from a single example. A child for example can recognize giraffes after seeing a single image (Vinyals et al., 2016). Most machine learning algorithms that are per definition intended to learn from experience struggle to incorporate prior knowledge in such tasks (Wang et al., 2020).

The few-shot learning task was proposed to test techniques that are intended to work with limited data, e. g., techniques such as data augmentation, transfer learning, active or meta-learning, triplet loss, or Siamese networks. It is used as a test suite for how well an algorithm works on little supervised information. If only a single training instance is available, as in the example of the child and the giraffe, the task is called one-shot learning. Zero-shot learning is learning from no sample data by building prior knowledge on unlabeled data, e. g., a dictionary with semantic information (Xian et al., 2018).

In few-shot learning, the K-way N-shot task is usually used to measure the performance of a classification algorithm given a limited data set consisting of K classes and N samples per class, split into a support set S and a separate query set Q. From the $K * N$ samples in S, the model has to find a parameterization to classify the samples in the query set Q (Vinyals et al., 2016). Usually, the support set is small, e. g., consisting of 10 different samples in the 5-way, 2-shot tasks. During testing, the classes in the support and query set can but do not need to be the same. Sometimes only the shots (samples) are different. Note that the K-way N-shot task does not prevent models from being pre-trained on different data. It just defines the type of task the model solves. As for object detection, special data sets exist in order to benchmark and compare different few-shot approaches. One example is the Omniglot (Lake et al., 2015) data set that consists of handwritten characters from 50 alphabets, each drawn 20 times by different people. There are a lot of special neural network types designed for few-shot learning which are able to solve the K-way N-shot task. A survey on these approaches can be found in Wang et al. (2020).

16.3 Use cases for RPA in manufacturing

The systematic literature review of RPA conducted by Ivančić et al. (2019) in 2019 has shown that most of the scientific work on RPA concerns the use in services, telecommunications, finance and insurance, and healthcare management. The authors did not find any work applying RPA in producing industries, e. g., in manufacturing or production processes. Most use cases for RPA are in sectors that do a lot of office work, such as in service, telecommunications, and administration. However, there are a need and opportunities for RPA in other sectors (e. g., manufacturing), as these become more and more digitalized. In the following, we will give some examples where RPA could be used in the mentioned domain. As in current applications, RPA is not intended to replace humans completely but to rationalize simple tasks by still asking a human for approval. The applications are oriented on the Y-CIM model and therefore split into the four main tasks production planning, product development, production control, and product implementation. Other applications not matching one of the four tasks are introduced as well. Production planning and product development build the upper parts in the Y-CIM model concerned with planning tasks, while production control and product implementation are the lower parts in the model concerned with manufacturing tasks. For each of the four main tasks, scenarios how to apply RPA are given. The outer tasks (Information and Coordination Processes) around the Y-shape are typical office work tasks for which RPA tools have already been discussed, e. g., by Houy et al. (2019) or Fettke and Loos (2019). Similar to the use of RPA in office work, it can be used in industrial settings for automatic data transfer, reading and writing into databases, extracting data, creating reports, operating ERP/CIM programs, integrating data from different systems, executing simple if-else rules, and doing calculations (Houy et al., 2019; Nederland, 2019). In the following, manufacturing-focused RPA scenarios will be explained. All applications are intended to work with existing information systems like CIM using CAM, CAP, and CAD or ERP software.

16.3.1 Production planning

During production planning, the production order is planned and scheduled, and required materials are noted.
– Automated deviation of requirements from customer orders:
  During product development, certain specifications must be considered. They are usually described in a specification sheet that comes with a request and differs

in detail from order to order. Companies translate these specifications into a fact sheet when creating an offer, which usually has the same structure and contains the same information for all products of a certain product family. Searching and transferring this information from the requirements to the fact sheet can be automated using an RPA tool that automatically identifies, tags, and transfers relevant information from the requirement sheet into the fact sheet. For this task, several techniques from NLP are used. First, relevant words are localized in the requirement sheet and tagged with an identifier, indicating what kind of information the phrase contains. In NLP, this is a typical named entity recognition (NER) task. In the next step, the tagged information is transferred to the fact sheet as a key-value matching. Even if this algorithm can only transfer half of the relevant data, the benefit is still significant, as some companies have to analyze more than 100 specification sheets per month. Furthermore, there is a benefit by automatically highlighting the relevant parts of the requirement sheet and tagging it. Afterwards, a human employee double checks the transferred facts and validates that no relevant information is missing. The highlighted section can guide them through this step.

– (Semi-)automated offer creation:
 After a fact sheet is available, an offer can be created. An RPA service can (semi-)automatically calculate the total costs using the facts in the fact sheet and the cost rates. Furthermore, CAD models that are similar to the fact sheet and have similar requirements can be retrieved from recent offers for comparison. Therefore, the requirements as well as the facts can be embedded in a multi-dimensional space together with the CAD models using techniques from NLP (Le and Mikolov, 2014) and computer vision (see Su et al., 2015). Similar CAD models for a request can be retrieved in this multi-dimensional space. Afterwards, employees can be supported in the process by proposing similar CAD models, cost rates, calculations, and more.

– Requirements and material planning:
 Using the fact sheet and the information from the order as well as access to the currently and previously scheduled orders and the ERP system, the material planning can be optimized using special optimization software. As an example, the optimization target can be a faster or more cost-efficient production. Afterwards, an RPA service can propose the optimization result and support employees in taking these decisions.

16.3.2 Product development

Similar to production planning, the product is constructed and the production environment is created and defined during product development.

– Automated retrieval of a previously created CAD model:
Similar to the service for (semi-)automated offer creation, similar CAD models in the database of previously created CAD models can be retrieved using the information in the fact sheet and the requirements in the customer request. For this service, a model can be trained that embeds the textual information in a high-dimensional vector. An RPA service can propose the user a list of previously created CAD models that had similar requirements and facts by searching for similar entries in the vector space. These models can be used as a starting point for further product development.

16.3.3 Production control

During production control, the order is scheduled in detail and the progress is reported.
– Detailed scheduling:
During production planning, the order has to be scheduled, which is a highly complex and demanding task. Many factors like the availability of goods and setup, waiting, and shipping times as well as employee working hours must be considered. However, previous schedules with similar circumstances might exist that give a good starting point for the scheduling at hand. An RPA service can help and suggest an initial scheduling plan by searching recent schedules and proposing the employee a set of schedules. For this task, data and process mining methods have been used in literature to find matching schedules (Rehse et al., 2018).
– Factory data entry and monitoring:
Automatically transfer, process, and transform machine sensory data streams and other data like images, videos, or audio into a structured data which can be stored in a database. These data can be used to monitor production using NLP, computer vision, and other data mining and machine learning techniques. The monitored values can automatically be compared with their target values or analyzed for outliers to detect deviations and give a notification in such circumstances (Fahim and Sillitti, 2019).

16.3.4 Product implementation

During product implementation, the defined product environment is actually used to realize the order.
– Image-to-CAD system:
Retrieving CAD models for a workpiece in a given image. This will be explained in detail in the next section.

- Predictive maintenance:
  Defect machines can put a whole production line out of action. Maintaining machines in advance, before a defect happens, can keep the factory running, prevent unexpected defects, and reduce the total downtime. Predictive maintenance can be used to monitor machines by analyzing sensory streams, audio streams, videos, or images for unwanted behavior (Fahim and Sillitti, 2019).

16.3.5 Others

Other tasks that are not directly concerned with the four mentioned main tasks can also be automated.
- Taking simple or routine decisions:
  Based on manufacturing data and information like the schedule, manufacturing speed, etc., propose or take simple decisions. Rule mining and machine learning can be used to derive these rules. If a rule can be applied, an RPA service can propose the decision, predict the effects, and implement the decision (and ask a human for verification if requested).
- Digitalize and automate older or analog machines:
  Companies use their machines for many years. However, in order to integrate them into automated production processes, they sometimes lack software or hardware equipment, for example, older, non-computer-aided machines that use mechanical buttons/keys that cannot be digitalized, machines where the software is not maintainable or changeable anymore, or machines that lack connectivity. RPA can help in those scenarios to integrate such machines into a fully digitalized factory. Therefore, hardware robots that press mechanical or display buttons, operate levers, or collect and send sensory data from added sensors to the CIM system can be installed. They replace a human worker required to operate such machines. Instead of one employee per machine, one employee can operate and monitor several machines at once.
- Automated creation of bill of material (BOM):
  As proposed by Madakam et al. (2019), an RPA service can be used to automatically create the BOM for a product given the CAD model or other information.

16.3.6 PEAS description

In Table 1, the PEAS description of the RPA service will be given for each scenario. All services use software based on CIM or similar systems. However, each service requires access and works on a subset of information available in these systems.

Table 1: Overview of the RPA services as PEAS descriptions.

Agent type	Performance	Environment	Actuators	Sensors
Requirement deviation from customer orders	Number of extracted facts	Requirement database	Write fact to fact sheet	Read requirement from customer orders
Customer offer creation	Number of created offers	Offer and requirement database	Write offer	Read requirements and offers
Requirement and material planning	Production efficiency, downtimes in hours	scheduling database, resource database (e. g., ERP system)	Write scheduling plan	Read fact sheet, orders, and available resources
CAD-based CAD model retrieval	Number of correctly retrieved CAD models	CAD model, requirement and fact sheet database	Write and display proposed CAD models	Read CAD models, requirements, and fact sheets
Scheduling	Manufacturing efficiency	Resource and scheduling database	Write scheduling plan	Read schedules and supplier status
Monitoring	Number of transferred data entries, detected deviations	Manufacturing machines, manufacturing database	Write to database, raise notification	Read machine data streams and target values
Predictive maintenance	Detected deviations/ prevented defects	Manufacturing machines or database	Raise notification	Read machine data streams and default values
Taking routine decisions	Number of proposed and valid decisions	Manufacturing database	Display decision, implement decision	Read manufacturing data, process human feedback
Digitalize analog machines	Number of digitally carried out tasks, error-free operating hours	Analog machine or devices	Devices to operate and collect data from machines (i. e., attachments to press buttons or sensors to collect information), write collected data into database	Received operations, feedback from attachments, sensor data
Automated BOM creation	Number of created BOMs	Workpiece database	Write BOM	Read workpiece data

16.4 Image-based CAD retrieval

Apart from the scenarios in the previous section, there are various other scenarios in manufacturing (and apart from it) where the CAD model for a specific physically available object at hand, e. g., a workpiece in production, is required. Therefore, an algorithm will be presented that can be embedded into RPA services dealing with this scenario. The algorithm takes a query image containing the object as input and has access to a database with CAD models (e. g., through a CIM system). The algorithm can be used to solve the following tasks during manufacturing:

- identifying the CAD model for the object in the image (image-based CAD model identification);
- retrieving CAD models similar to the object in the image (image-based CAD model retrieval);
- retrieving CAD models similar to a given CAD model (CAD-based CAD model retrieval).

Industrial companies usually have a large set of CAD models ranging from some hundred to some thousand. Some manufacturers produce workpieces in product families that have only very little variation from piece to piece. Furthermore, CAD models are 3D, which makes it more difficult to view them on a screen. Therefore, finding the correct CAD model to a workpiece is a demanding task that requires expert knowledge and is very hard to solve for a non-expert. By using the algorithm, the following applications can be realized:

- CAD Retrieval: During the manufacturing process of a workpiece, information about the order must be known at certain points in the process. As the order contains information about the workpiece as a CAD model, the order and other information can be retrieved when the CAD model of the workpiece at hand is known. Using the algorithm, the CAD model and corresponding information (e. g., measurement plan for quality check, other parts in this order, etc.) can be retrieved using only an image of the workpiece.
- Retrieving the individual parts: Workpieces often consist of individual components. By taking an image of the object, the RPA service can show the operator the parts the workpiece consists of.
- Ordering of spare parts: Before ordering spare parts, the part and its name/ID must be known. By using the system, the algorithm could order a spare part by just taking an image of the broken object (assuming the object is still identifiable).
- Finding 3D-printable templates: For a given object (CAD model or image), the algorithm can propose a set of similar 3D-printable objects, e. g., to replace a broken or lost part.

In Figure 3, one can see a workflow as BPMN in which the CAD model for a workpiece is required for the three following sample tasks. The left side of Figure 4 shows the

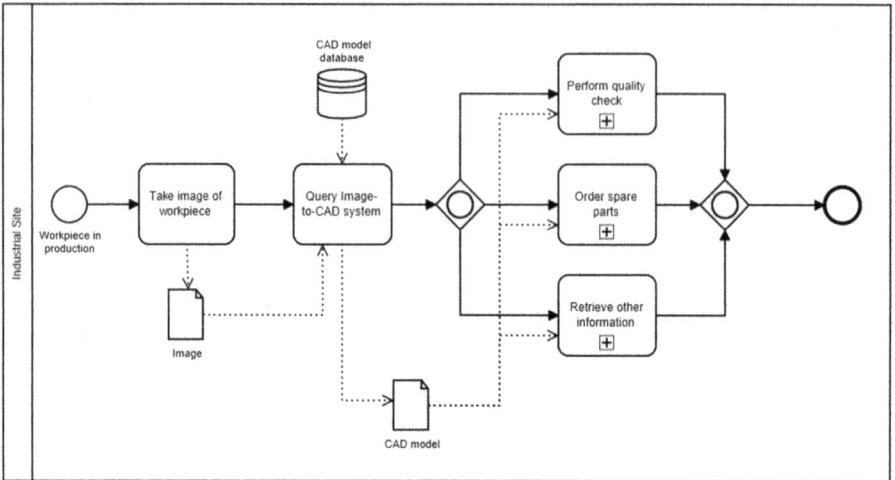

Figure 3: BPMN of the workflow involving a CAD retrieval task.

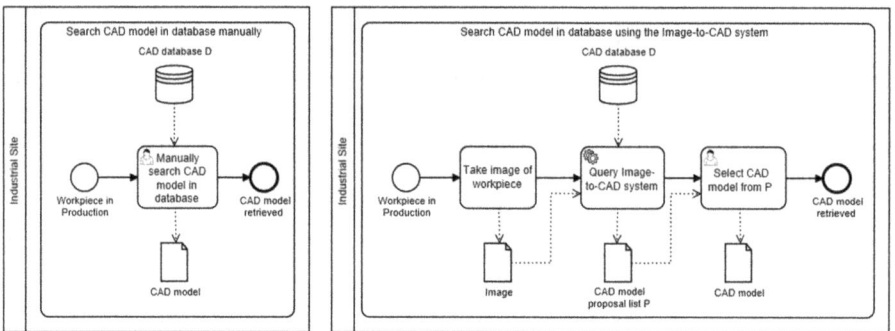

Figure 4: Left: BPMN without the Image-to-CAD system. Right: Workflow using the Image-to-CAD system.

workflow retrieving the CAD model manually by searching the whole database before being able to execute the sample tasks. On the right side, the retrieval process using the Image-to-CAD system is shown. Technical details of the Image-to-CAD system will be explained in the following. Instead of searching the whole database manually the process changes slightly. First, an image must be taken (manually or automatically), the Image-to-CAD system queried, and the correct model selected from the generated proposal list of CAD models P. Instead of one manual task, the process now consists of three steps. The first two steps can be automated. Selecting the correct CAD model from the proposals in P should be done or at least validated by humans to avoid errors. However, depending on the accuracy of the system, this task can also be automated.

In the following, the Image-to-CAD system is conceptualized, implemented, and tested. It is especially intended to be used in industrial settings with a low number of sample images per CAD object and changing workpieces.

16.4.1 Technical concept of the Image-to-CAD system

16.4.1.1 Solution architecture

The algorithm is split into two stages solving different tasks and two phases – one for online operation and one for offline training. Figure 5 shows the architecture of the algorithm as one system, called Image-to-CAD system, that can be used to solve the given tasks. The first stage's (stage 1) task is to classify the object in the image while in the second stage (stage 2), similar CADs for a given CAD model are found using the database D of CAD models. As a result, the Image-to-CAD system proposes a list P consisting of the top j CAD models from database D that are most similar to the object in the query image. Note that the system is intended to propose a list P from which an operator has to select the correct CAD model. Following the top j CAD models, other CAD models in the database are concatenated. This has different reasons. As mentioned before, selecting the correct CAD model from a list to an object at hand already is a challenging task. The task becomes harder the more CAD models are in database D and the bigger the product families become. If only one sample image is available, the task is very complicated as only one perspective is shown, and details might be hidden (e. g., if characteristics that identify the workpiece are on the not captured side of the object). Therefore, the algorithm always proposes a list of j CAD models to show the operator the most similar objects. The list and the following models can be ordered based on the similarity proposed by the algorithm. If the operator has physical access to the workpiece or more information available, he can go through the list and select the correct one. Furthermore, by letting the operator pick the correct model from the list P or the following models, ground truth annotations are generated which can be used for further training. That is, during operation (online phase) the user takes an image of a workpiece, lets the system propose a list of CAD models, and picks the correct one from this list (Case A). If the correct model is not in the top j proposals of P, the operator can search the other models in the whole database D (Case B) for the correct one by going through the other entries following P. Thereby, the image becomes annotated with its correct label and can be used as another training example in the offline phase.

As the workpieces and CAD models are individual from operator[1] to operator, stage 1 must be able to adapt to new workpieces and to work precisely with only a

---

[1] Operator denotes the company or person (user) who uses the machine. However, in the same company different persons can operate one machine but share the same set of CAD models.

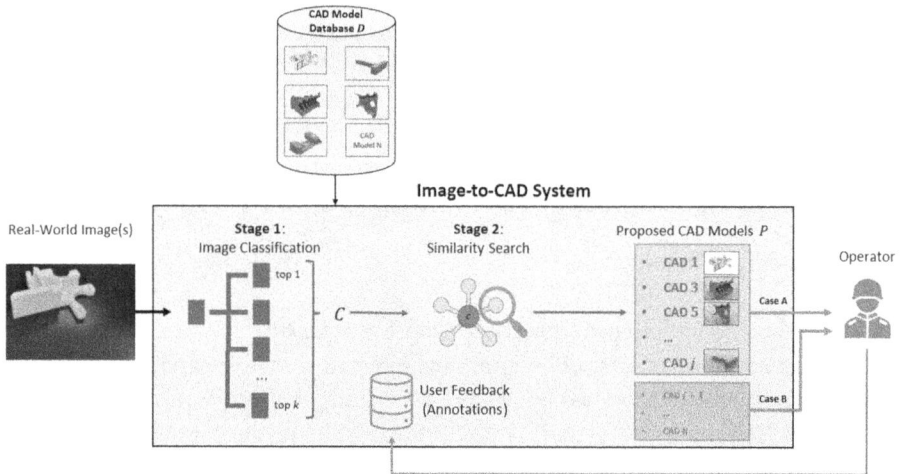

Figure 5: Technical architecture of the Image-to-CAD system in the online phase.

few examples available. Therefore, a neural network designed to solve the few-shot learning task will be used. The annotations generated during operation are used as new samples for the few-shot approach. In each query, the model solves the K-way N-shot classification task with varying number of samples per class. Stage 2 searches for similar CAD models in database D given the classification result from stage 1. Furthermore, the operator's picks during operation together with the corresponding images are saved and will be used as new training examples to improve the whole system accuracy. For stage 2, two different approaches using different representations of CAD models are used. Different to stage 1, they can be pre-trained on large-scale data sets and to rely on images and annotations from the operator's individual workpieces. However, feedback can be used to further fine-tune the similarity search on the operator-specific objects.

During operation, both stages work collaboratively to propose similar objects to the queried one. When the system is not in operation, e. g., during nighttime or breaks, the collected feedback from the operator serve as annotations to train on new objects and improve the accuracy on existing ones. As feedback is actively used to optimize the system, its performance in terms of accuracy will likely improve over time. The gradually increasing availability of training data makes the system an online learning or incremental learning model.

The Image-to-CAD systems approach splits the complex CAD retrieval problem into two distinct tasks and makes use of approaches specifically developed to solve each subtask. In literature, 3D object retrieval is often done in one algorithm. However, such approaches do somehow need to bridge the domain gap between 2D images and 3D data to work in the setting in this work. Furthermore, the low number of sample images per object class makes the task even harder. The approach at hand solves the object identification task using 2D information rather than information from 3D and retrieves similar objects in 3D based on the 2D image classification result. Although 3D object detection has made great progress in recent time, object classification in 2D is better understood and archives higher accuracies, especially when it comes to cases with very few samples per class. This two-stage approach is not only the first known algorithm able to retrieve 3D objects from 2D images in an industrial setting with very few training examples, both stages might also be able to increase the performance if used together over the performance of each stage individually. Depending on the use case, stage 1 and stage 2 can be used as a stand-alone version, e. g., to find similar CAD models to a query 3D CAD model (CAD-based CAD retrieval) using stage 2. If only the CAD model identification is required (Image-based CAD model identification), stage 1 can be used stand-alone.

16.4.1.2 Stage 1

Stage 1 identifies the object in the image by solving a classification problem. Additionally, only a few training examples per object are available and the objects are changing from time to time. As input, one real-world image showing the query object is given (the algorithm can be changed to use multiple input images) and a classification result C of the top k classes c^2 is returned. Stage 1 has access to all the recently queried images together with their annotations. From the operator picks, stage 1 also recognizes if a new object was added to the database. If no sample image with annotation is available for a workpiece in D, stage 1 cannot classify it. Stage 1 can only classify a workpiece once an image has been taken and annotated by the operator. The more images with annotations are available for one workpiece, the better the accuracy in identifying this workpiece becomes. For example, an individual product for a customer that is produced only once will be seen by the algorithm only a few times. We assume that the average number of sample images per class is around 5. Therefore, the task is considered a few-shot problem. Each time an image of an object is queried and an annotation is made by the operator, the image is used as a new shot ($N + 1$). In the case it is the first image of a new object, it is added as a new class ($K + 1$) in the K-way N-shot task. At a certain point in time, e. g., after 5 newly added images from known objects, a new class got added or when the algorithm is not in use, stage 1 has to be retrained in order to be able to classify newly added objects or optimize the performance using recently added shots.

For solving stage 1's task, the matching network (MN) as introduced by Vinyals et al. (2016) will be used. MNs, a combination of neural network architecture and training method, are designed to solve the K-way N-shot task with few examples. In the pro-

---

2 The number k for the top k classification results is not related to the K in the K-way N-shot task.

posed work, a convolutional neural network (CNN) is used as feature extractor which is also able to adapt to difficult lightning scenes, illuminations, or object appearances. Different to "classical" image classification network architectures with stacked convolutional and a final fully connected layer with SoftMax activation function, MNs use stacked convolutional layers together with an attention kernel and a full context embedding (FCE) layer. The attention kernel acts as a trainable discriminator with which nearest neighbors can be found using a distance metric. The FCE embeds the previously seen examples in a contextual vector.

16.4.1.3 Stage 2

Stage 2 uses the classification result C as input and produces a list P of the top j CAD models as output. P contains the most similar objects as CAD models to the ones in C. Therefore, the model is doing a similarity search in D based on the classification results C. As CAD models of all objects are available in database D, 3D information can be obtained from it. The similarity is therefore measured on this information rather than the input images of stage 1. To compare the CAD objects against each other, some features or characteristics must be found and compared. In literature, this is often done by constructing a feature vector from the CAD model data. An image-based and a point cloud-based approach will be used in stage 2 as feature extractors. Both are neural networks – one is using 2D images for the view-based and the other one sets of 3D coordinates for the point cloud-based approach – to produce a feature vector while learning to solve a classification task. After being trained, the classification layer is removed and the penultimate layer is used to produce the feature vector. These are compared using the L2 or cosine distance metric. The view-based approach uses multiple 2D renders from the same 3D object in different perspectives. To this end, the multi-view CNN (MVCNN) introduced by Su et al. (2015) is implemented. The second method processes 3D information directly. Point clouds are unordered sets of 3D coordinates (x, y, z) in a Euclidean space. PointNet++ (Qi et al., 2017) is used to process the 3D information and extract features from it in a metric space. Like CNNs, PointNet++ processes the point clouds in hierarchically ordered layers and abstracts local features along its hierarchy.

16.4.1.4 Online and offline phases

In the operational mode (online phase), the Image-to-CAD system is applied on a query image, proposes the list P of similar objects, and saves the feedback generated by the operator's picks. This is done using both stages: stage 1 takes the image as input, produces a list C of the top k classes, and hands it over to stage 2. Stage 2 then searches for the most similar objects for each or a subset of the elements in C and proposes the list P containing j objects. Afterwards, the operator can check P and select the correct CAD model, either from P (Case A) or other models in D concatenated to P after the top j results (Case B). Searching the whole database is the fallback case for the algorithm where searching and selecting the correct CAD model takes as much time as without the help of the algorithm (plus the time to propose P).

The training mode (offline phase) is run whenever the machine is not in use or the requirements for retraining are given. This can for example be the case if a certain number of new images with the operator's feedback has been recorded or an initial image of a new object has been added. Other reasons for retraining are possible, too. For example, if the user is unsatisfied with the current accuracy or unused objects have been deleted.

Retraining stage 1 involves training the model on the K-way N-shot classification task on all images and classes available so far. All recently added and all historical feedback is used. K is the number of different workpieces while N is the number of images per workpiece.[3] As stage 2 is intended to be trained on large-scale data sets, retraining stage 2 should only be done if the accuracy is bad or the results of the similarity search are not satisfying.

To speed up the total processing time required in the online phase to find the most similar objects to a given one, stage 2 computes the feature vectors of all objects and finds the most similar objects using the distance metric. This information is stored as the search index. The search index allows to access the most similar objects immediately without searching through the whole database D in the online phase. This speeds up the total computation time in the online phase drastically.

16.4.2 Evaluation

16.4.2.1 Data sets

For the evaluation we used two different data sets. Unfortunately, there is a lack of large image data sets containing objects whose CAD models are known and where the images are annotated with the CAD model in the image. The first data set is Model-Net40 (Wu et al., 2015), which consists of 12,114 CAD models from 40 different classes. For this data set, no images are available. Therefore, renders were created that are used as query input for evaluation and pre-training the MVCNN in stage 2. The MVTec ITODD (Drost et al., 2017) data set consists of real-world images with annotations and CAD models. There are more than 3,500 scenes with three different images from different perspectives each, showing 28 different industrial workpieces. For each scene, the CAD model in the image can be retrieved from another file in the data set. We had to

---

3 As N must be the same for all K object classes, random images of a workpiece are copied for all classes with less than N images.

clean the images manually from scenes where different CAD models are in one image. We kept images with multiple instances of the same workpiece.

16.4.2.2 Stage 1

We used the pytorch-based implementation of MN[4] and verified the implementation using the Omniglot data set. The implementation reaches very similar accuracies as stated by the authors using the L2 instead of the cosine distance in the attention kernel – 99.10 % in the 5-way 5-shot task and 97.40 % in the 20-way 5-shot task. Due to conceptual differences between the querying strategy in the few-shot learning task and the querying strategy given by the use cases of the Image-to-CAD system, we had to change the training and testing strategy in the following. In few-shot learning, the classifier is tested on the K-way N-shot task – which is a discriminative instead of a single image classification task. When training the MN, the model therefore randomly queries N samples from K random classes changing from the samples and classes from training interval to training interval. During testing, the model is queried on N samples from K classes each. However, neither the classes nor the numbers K or N need to be the same between training and testing. On Omniglot, the MN was trained on a set of 1,200 different classes (characters) and tested on the remaining classes. Training and testing classes and shots were disjoint. During training, the model was trained on K out of 1,200 classes and N out of 20 samples, each with varying classes and shots from step to step. Therefore, the model got queried on all 1,200 classes during the training phase with the training objective to solve the K-way N-shot discriminative classification task in each step. In most practical use cases addressed in our scenarios, the training and test sets will have the same K classes while K is the number of different classes in D for which images exist. Furthermore, MNs have to be queried with a query set Q consisting of K different classes and N different samples per class. However, in the practical use cases it is very uncommon to have exactly N query images from all K classes at once. As the authors of MN suggested to train and test on the same conditions as faced when querying, we further modified the querying strategy to account for single sample queries which stage 1 will face in the Image-to-CAD approach in the online phase. All N available images per class in the offline phase will be split into a training and a test set. The training set will have $N-1$ samples while the test set features have a single sample per class – which is exactly the condition in the online phase. As N must be the same for all classes, the training set is populated with training images until the number of images per class is balanced. If there are 20 CAD models in D and 5 samples are available for each model, the model would be trained as a 20-way 4-shot model and queried as a 20-way 1-shot task in the offline phase. In

---

4 https://github.com/oscarknagg/few-shot

the online phase, Q is also a 20-way 1-shot task which consists only of the query image copied 20 times. Note that it is not possible to populate Q with 20 different classes as the query image class is unknown. All training images are used as the support set in the online phase. We furthermore increased the image size when using the MVTec data set from 28×28 pixels in the original implementation to 64×64 and used rotations as image augmentation which increased the accuracy consistently across all tasks. Using other rotations like flipping, cropping, or resizing decreases the accuracy when using MN. The prediction that occurs most often when querying with Q is used as the top 1 result, the second most often as top 2, and so on. This version of MN with fixed classes and modified querying method is used in the Image-to-CAD system. In the following, we will evaluate the accuracy of stage 1 if used to identify the CAD model in an image.

As baseline (Baseline CNN) method, we used a fully supervised ResNet18 with SoftMax classification layer finetuned on the data sets in the specific task. We first evaluated the effect of having fixed classes (MN fixed) and later the effect when modifying the querying method (MN fixed & query). We trained each model in each setting 5 times and averaged the accuracies. The results on the Omniglot data set are shown in Table 2 comparing the original MN implementation with the fixed class training and the baseline method. In Table 3, results on the industrial MVTec data set are shown comparing the accuracies of the MN with fixed classes and the modified querying method against the baseline model. Note that the number of different classes is much lower on MVTec but the images are very challenging and match the real use case much more.

Table 2: Accuracies on the Omniglot data set.

Method	5-way 1-shot	5-way 5-shot	20-way 1-shot	20-way 5-shot	100-way 1-shot	100-way 5-shot	200-way 1-shot	200-way 5-shot
Baseline CNN	52.00%	52.80%	22.50%	24.00%	6.80%	7.84%	3.55%	5.06%
MN (original)	90.32%	95.92%	90.54%	95.48%	86.33%	94.75%	83.77%	93.04%
MN (fixed)	74.44%	92.44%	48.39%	82.34%	36.68%	73.59%	27.94%	–

Table 3: Accuracies on the MVTec data set.

Method	5-way 1-shot	5-way 5-shot	10-way 1-shot	10-way 5-shot	20-way 1-shot	20-way 5-shot	28-way 1-shot	28-way 5-shot
Baseline CNN	66.00%	71.20%	44.00%	50.00%	28.50%	45.00%	22.50%	36.50%
MN (fixed)	85.20%	96.32%	81.60%	93.12%	75.92%	89.30%	73.58%	91.31%
MN (fixed & query)	53.20%	91.00%	45.89%	73.00%	38.60%	75.80%	34.80%	72.70%

On Omniglot, the classification accuracy dropped from 87.17% on average to 76.82% when fixing the classes. The drop is bigger in the 1-shot tasks than in the 5-shot tasks.

However, the results are still significantly higher than for the baseline model, which reached 27.66 % on average on the same tasks. On MVTec, MN performs better than the baseline model but the drop in accuracy when using the modified querying method is very high. However, MN's accuracy benefits significantly when using 5 shots in comparison to the baseline model. We further noted that training the MN on a higher number of classes than being tested on later increases the accuracy across all tasks. On MVTec, the MN (fixed) trained as a 28-way 5-shot model reached 91.92 % when queried on a 20-way 5-shot task in comparison to 89.30 % reached by the model trained on this task. All these findings have been validated on the ModelNet40 data set where renders of all model were used. Due to the larger number of models in ModelNet40, we tested with up to 500 classes (500-way 5-shot).

We also investigated how much the number of shots influences the accuracy using MN with fixed classes and modified querying method. Doubling the number of shots (N) from 1 to 2 increased the accuracy on MVTec by 31.60 % on average while on ModelNet40, the accuracy increased by 701.59 % on average. The higher the number of classes (K), the higher the increase. Going from 2-shot to 3-shot increases the accuracy by 15.44 % on MVTec and by 31.21 % on ModelNet40, while doubling from 5 to 10 shots increases the accuracy only by 13.20 % and 3.79 %, respectively.

16.4.2.3 Stage 2

Both approaches, the view-based MVCNN[5] and point cloud-based PointNet++,[6] are available as pytorch implementation. We trained both approaches on the ModelNet40 shape classification task on the standard training and test split for which we created renders and point clouds from each model. Therefore, we built our own pipelines for rendering and point cloud sampling in order to ensure that the resulting data are consistent across both data sets – ModelNet40 and MVTec. Figure 6 shows a render of a CAD model from MVTec and a render of the point cloud with the coordinates rendered as white spheres. Note that PointNet++ consumes the set of coordinates and not the render of the point cloud. While MVCNN reached a classification accuracy of 85 % on ModelNet40, PointNet++ with multi-scale grouping reached 86 %. Figure 7 shows the confusion matrices of both approaches where one can see that both made the same mistake at times. The flowerpot was frequently classified as a plant by both approaches (upper right greenish quarter) or a vase (blueish quarter further right). On the other side, MVCNN misclassified a stool as a chair while PointNet often misclassified the curtain as a keyboard.

---

5 https://github.com/jongchyisu/mvcnn_pytorch
6 https://github.com/charlesq34/pointnet2

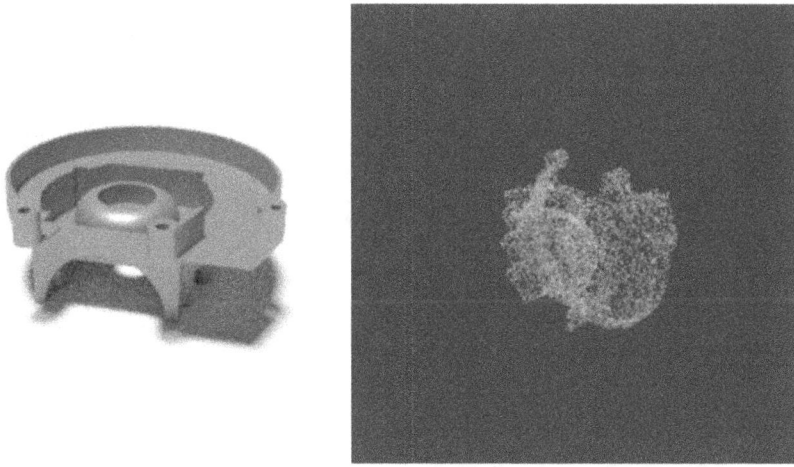

Figure 6: The same CAD model as render (left) and point-cloud (rendered visualization).

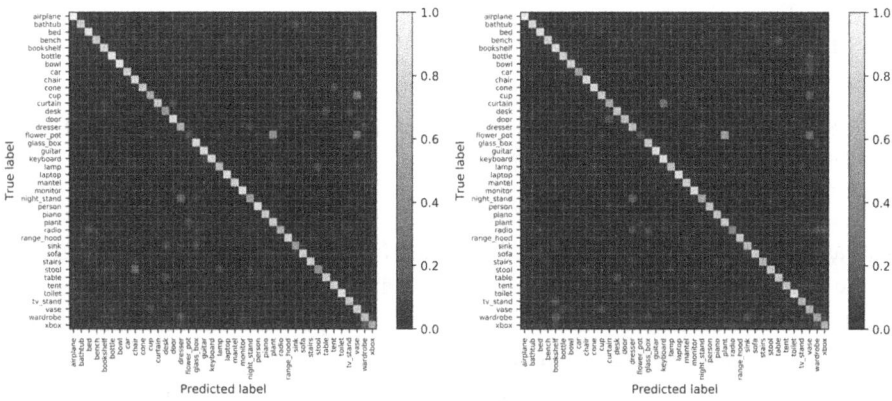

Figure 7: Confusion matrices (accuracy) of the MVCNN (left) and PointNet++ (right).

In the online phase of stage 2, the classification layer is removed and the output of the penultimate layer used as the feature vector on which the similarity is computed using the L2 distance. Retrieving similar CAD models using a query CAD model works very well with both approaches on ModelNet40 and MVTec likewise. In almost all queries, the results are very reasonable. However, both approaches have some tendencies that could be noted. While the view-based approaches only propose objects where the renders are similar, the point cloud-based approach proposes models that are structurally similar. In some examples, objects with similar structure have been rendered once in a horizontal position and once in a vertical position – e. g., in Figure 8. While MVCNN did not propose the horizontally rendered objects when querying the vertically rendered ones, PointNet++ ignores such rotations and proposes differently oriented ob-

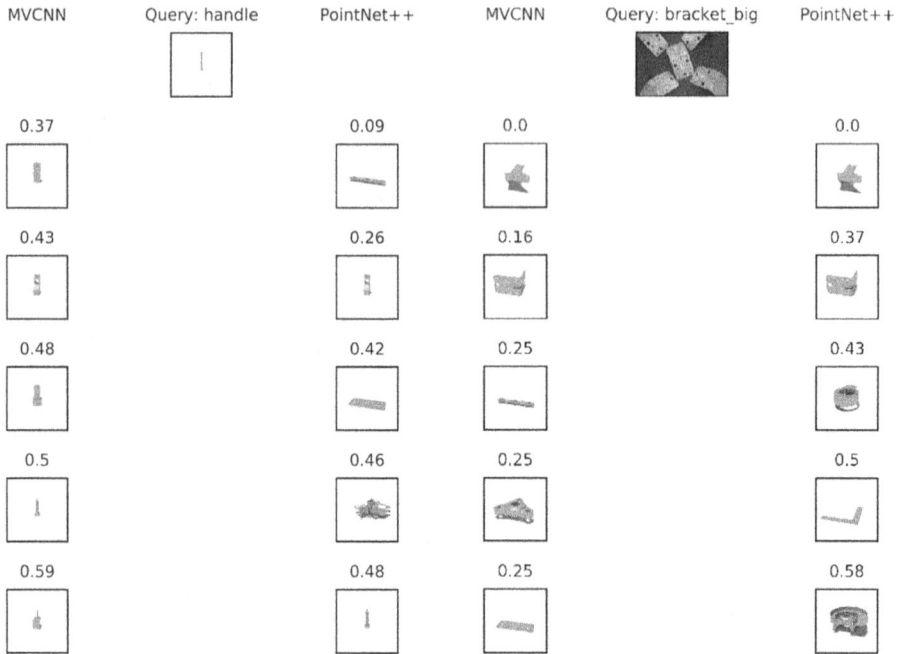

Figure 8: Two examples of *P* for the view-based approach (left from query) and the point-cloud-based approach (right).

jects as well. However, MVCNN is more sensitive to fine structures but fails in samples where the renders are faulty. The sensitivity to fine structures could be increased in PointNet++ when using more than 1,024 coordinates per point cloud. However, this further increases the computation time required.

It is also possible to train both approaches on MVTec only. However, due to the lower number of samples and the fact that only one model per class is available, instead of several thousands in ModelNet40, the retrieval results are better when trained on ModelNet40.

16.4.2.4 Image-to-CAD proposals

Figure 8 shows two queries (render from a handle in the left and a real image of a bracket from MVTec data set in the right), resulting in four proposals *P* of the top 5 results using the Image-to-CAD system in the Image-based CAD model retrieval task. Both approaches in stage 2 used the same classification result *C* from stage 1. The first row shows the top 1 proposal of stage 2, the second row the top 2 proposals, and so on. The top 1 proposal is also the top 1 classification result from stage 1 (*C*). The cosine similarity distance, noted on top of each proposed CAD render, is therefore 0 in this case. On the right, the query image contains multiple instances of a bracket. The top 1 proposal when querying the bracket is not the correct CAD model. Both proposed the correct model as the top 2 proposal. However, both are similar components. Note that this error is caused by stage 1 as stage 2 only proposes the top 1 classification result of C as its top 1 proposal.

In the following, the top 5 accuracy of the Image-to-CAD system will be tested, i. e., the accuracy when using the top 1 classification result from C generated by stage 1 and finding the top j similar CAD models using stage 2 based on the top 1 result of stage 1. This reflects the performance of the model in the image-based CAD model retrieval task. The top 5 accuracy denotes how often the correct CAD model is in the top 5 results of P divided by the number of queries. As the system is not in operation now, user feedback cannot be obtained and processed. In all experiments, both approaches in stage 2 were pre-trained on all CAD models in the ModelNet40 data set. This gave the best results across all tasks. Stage 1 is trained 5 times on random classes and shots. After each training phase, the whole system will be queried on 200 random samples (or the maximum number of samples available in settings with a lower number of classes) using MVCNN or PointNet++ in stage 2 and the top 5 accuracies will be noted and averaged across all runs. For evaluating the Image-to-CAD system in a productive environment, an iterative algorithm simulating the real use case is implemented.

16.4.2.5 *K*-way *N*-shot accuracy

Table 4 shows the top 5 accuracies on the MVTec and ModelNet40 data sets. On MVTec and the 1-shot setting, the PointNet++ approach reaches higher accuracies, while MVCNN performs slightly better in the 5-shot setting. On ModelNet40, the PointNet++ approach is better except for the 200-way 1-shot setting. The standard deviation of the Image-to-CAD system is 1.93 and 1.78 in the 28-way 5-shot on the MVTec data set using MVCNN and PointNet++, and 1.28 and 3.58 on ModelNet40, respectively.

The top 1 accuracy of the Image-to-CAD system is by design bounded by the accuracy of stage 1. If the top 1 result of C is not correct, the top 1 result of P is also not correct, as stage 2 proposed its query object top 1 result. The accuracies of the Image-to-CAD system are increasing if the top 5 accuracy is used. This implies that stage 2 is able to retrieve similar objects and enhance the top j performance. On all data sets and on both approaches for stage 2, the top 5 accuracies reached by the Image-to-CAD system are consistently lower than the top 5 accuracy of stage 1 alone, i. e., the classification result C. It was also tested if combining the proposals P from the top 1 and top 2 results of C can increase the top 5 accuracy of the Image-to-CAD system. Therefore, stage 2 was queried on the top 1 and top 2 results from C and both proposals combined, ordered by their distance and the first top j entries proposed as the final P. Unfortunately, this did not increase the accuracy.

Table 4: Top 5 accuracies on the ModelNet40 and MVTec data set.

		MVCNN		PointNet++	
		1-shot	5-shot	1-shot	5-shot
ModelNet40					
K-way training	5-way	100.00 %	100.00 %	100.00 %	100.00 %
	20-way	24.80 %	87.00 %	25.40 %	87.30 %
	100-way	2.00 %	82.00 %	2.00 %	84.30 %
	200-way	2.60 %	81.90 %	1.10 %	84.50 %
MVTec					
K-way training	5-way	100.00 %	100.00 %	100.00 %	100.00 %
	10-way	64.60 %	80.10 %	67.00 %	71.10 %
	20-way	44.50 %	79.20 %	45.80 %	77.10 %
	28-way	43.40 %	83.20 %	45.40 %	83.30 %

16.4.2.6 Iterative training

Beside the static test on fixed K-way N-shot settings, the system will now be tested on constantly increasing numbers of classes and samples. Therefore, a script was written that iteratively either adds a new class (way) or new sample (shot), trains stage 1 on the new setting, and tests its accuracy. Adding a new class (way) represents the initial run when the operator queries the Image-to-CAD algorithm and picks a certain CAD model from the database. Adding a new sample (shot) represents the case where an already known workpiece is used in the Image-to-CAD system once more. Each time a new sample is added, a random shot for a random class is selected and added to the training set. Therefore, the number of samples the model is trained on increases only for one class each time – not for all classes. For all other classes, the available shots are used once more to balance the number of shots across all object classes. The number of samples per class is therefore not balanced, which means, for example, there might be classes for which 3 different samples (shots) exist, while for others, the same sample (shot) is used 3 times. This script is intended to simulate the real use case where new classes and samples are added from time to time but the utilization is different from workpiece to workpiece – i. e. the number of times the workpiece is queried with the Image-to-CAD system. It is run 5 times for MVCNN and PointNet++ each.

Figure 9 shows the top 5 accuracies and number of samples for one simulation run using MVCNN. Starting with 1 class and 1 sample, a new random shot (sample) was added to one random class every third iteration, while in each other iteration a new class (way) was added. The K line shows the number of classes (ways) while its color indicates the maximum number of samples (shots) available. As one can see, with increasing use of the system, the number of classes and shots increases as well. The accuracy is decreasing after the 7th iteration but tends to flatten (on average) from

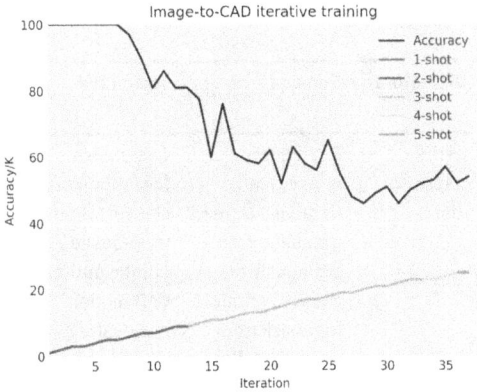

Figure 9: Top 5 accuracies in one iterative training run on the MVTec data set using MVCNN.

the 27th iteration on. The reached accuracies in the last iteration between all simulation runs are similar on average (standard deviation of 2.04 and 4.28). The averaged final top 5 accuracies reached in all 5 runs are 51.55 % using MVCNN and 46.83 % using PointNet++. Due to the imbalanced number of samples per class, the accuracies are lower than the 28-way 5-shot accuracies reached in the previous, static experiments. Note that the accuracies between each run and between MVCNN and PointNet++ cannot be compared directly as the number of samples and shots is different from run to run due to the random adding of samples.

16.5 Related work

In this section, related work using RPA in manufacturing and for the CAD model retrieval problem will be presented. To the best of our knowledge, there is only one work that applies RPA in manufacturing – Lin et al. (2018) apply RPA to automatically remote control equipment in a semiconductor factory. Nederland (2019) introduced six best-practice examples on how to integrate RPA in manufacturing using SAP S/4HANA on a very abstract level without technical details. Krupka and Becker (2020) recently presented two scenarios where artificial intelligence is used in production automation without using the term RPA. Apart from that, RPA is often coined together with manufacturing and terms like smart manufacturing and Industry 4.0 (Feld et al., 2017). Other works on RPA either mention the potential of RPA in manufacturing without giving examples – like Madakam et al. (2019) – or show RPA potential for back-office processes in manufacturing (Atos, 2020).

Most of the existing work on retrieving 3D CAD models from 2D images is limited to a certain set of objects, e. g., chairs, or requires extensive alignment computations. There is a lot of work using depth information like 2.5D sensors or RGB-D im-

Table 5: PEAS description of the methods used in related work.

Related work	Performance	Environment	Actuators	Sensors	Technique
Image-to-CAD system	Top j retrieval accuracy	Database D with previously taken images and their annotations	Write proposal list	Read query image, read database D, read database with previously taken images, obtain feedback from operators' choice	Two stages, few-shot image classification, view-based and point cloud-based CAD model retrieval
Filaliansary et al. (2005)	Recall and precision of the N relevant models in the top A retrievals	CAD model database	Write proposals	Read query image and CAD model database with characteristic views	Characteristic 2D view creation using Zernike moments, indexing using Bayesian probabilistic approach
Gao et al. (2010)	Average recall and precision	CAD model database	Write proposals	Read query image, CAD model database, and CAD model views	2D view creation and probabilistic graph model
Gao et al. (2014)	Discounted cumulative gain (DCG) and average normalized modified retrieval rank (ANMRR)	CAD model database	Write proposals	Read query image, CAD model database, and relevant feedback	2D view matching using Hausdorff distance learning
Leng et al. (2015)	Precision-recall-curve, first tier and second tier, F-measure, nearest neighbor, DCG, ANMRR	CAD model database	Write proposals	Read query image and CAD model database	Stacked local convolutional autoencoder for feature descriptor generation of 3D objects
Grabner et al. (2018)	Top 1 accuracy	CAD model database	Write proposals	Read query image, CAD model database, and render database	CNN for 3D pose prediction, second CNN for matching between render and query image

Table 5: (continued)

Related work	Performance	Environment	Actuators	Sensors	Technique
Sarkar and Stricker (2019), Sarkar et al. (2017)	Object recognition recall	CAD model database	Write recognition	Ready query image, CAD model database, and synthetic images	Domain adaption by placing renders in real environments and fine-tuning CNNs
Li et al. (2015)	Area under curve (AUC)	CAD model database	Write proposals	Ready query image, CAD model database, and real image database	Training a CNN to map images and 3D shapes into a shared embedding, retrieving similar 3D objects by nearest neighbor search in the embedding space

ages (Bosche and Haas, 2008; Chang et al., 2015; Wang et al., 2014; Wu et al., 2015). As these put another restriction on the use of the approach, they will not be discussed. All of the presented methods have in common that they need to bridge the domain gap between 2D images and 3D CAD model representation. Filaliansary et al. (2005) presented a probabilistic approach to retrieve a CAD model given a 2D image. In a first step, they selected characteristic views of a CAD model that represent the model best by capturing it from many different perspectives and generating descriptors of it. Three different descriptors were used – curvatures histogram, Zernike moments, and curvature scale space – but only Zernike moments were applicable in their setting. When querying an image, the approach computes the probability that the object in the image belongs to one characteristic view – for all objects and views. They demonstrated that the approach works with synthetic and real images on a set of mechanical parts. The presented idea is widely used in CAD model retrieval literature, but the implementation uses outdated feature descriptors and has a very high complexity. Different methods use similar retrieval approaches with 2D views, e. g., graph models in Gao et al. (2010) or Hausdorff distance learning in Gao et al. (2014). In order to get better feature descriptors, Leng et al. (2015) used a stacked local convolutional autoencoder on the characteristic views. Grabner et al. (2018) proposed a method that renders a variety of views of a CAD model offline from different perspectives. When querying an image, the pose is estimated first and the candidate CAD model is found using a trainable matching between images and renders in a certain pose. Sarkar and Stricker (2019) and Sarkar et al. (2017) proposed and improved a method that extracts features from snapshots of CAD models – renders of CAD models in varying poses in real-world images used as background. Different to these methods, Li et al. (2015) proposed a method that created a joint embedding between renders and real-world images of CAD models.

16.6 Conclusion

In this chapter, new applications of RPA for industrial manufacturing were introduced alongside the well-known Y-CIM model. We have shown that there is a large variety of tasks in manufacturing that can be automated and supported by RPA services. Beside simple applications from office domains that can be adopted to the industrial domain, there are also simple tasks in the industrial domain, e. g., manufacturing data entry or simple decision-making where RPA can bring similar benefits. Furthermore, there is a large number of complex and cognitive demanding tasks where cognitive services can be applied. CAM, CAP, and CIM build the ideal foundation to implemented RPA solutions in the industrial domain. The presented Image-to-CAD system is one example of a cognitive RPA service in manufacturing that was implemented and evaluated with very realistic and challenging data. It is able to automate a variety of tasks in the manufacturing process, e. g., help employees in retrieving the correct CAD model of the workpiece at hand. In assembly line production, the Image-to-CAD system can save a lot of time when many products must be investigated. It automates a repetitive, error-prone, and cognitive demanding task that is usually done by humans. It uses a lower-level interface (database D) and runs as a software tool on existing information systems. Changes to existing workflows and information systems are minimal. The accuracy of the Image-to-CAD system depends on the number of shots in comparison to the number of different classes. If 5 samples of each workpiece are available, the accuracy is very high. If the number is imbalanced, the accuracy decreases. Furthermore, MN accuracy diminishes a lot when modifying the querying strategy to single image queries. On the other side, using more than one shot increases the accuracy tremendously. For stage 2, both approaches obtain very reasonable results in retrieving similar CAD models. The system shows that few-shot learning and view-based as well as point-cloud-based methods have great potential to support employees in their daily tasks.

Bibliography

Ansari WA, Ali W, Diya P, Patil S, Patil S (2019) A review on robotic process automation – the future of business organizations. SSRN Electron J
Atos (2020) Robotic Process Automation (RPA) for Manufacturing. Digital Transformation

Bosche F, Haas CT (2008) Automated retrieval of 3D CAD model objects in construction range images. Autom Constr 17(4)

Chang AX, Funkhouser T, Guibas L, Hanrahan P, Huang Q, Li Z, Savarese S, Savva M, Song S, Su H, Xiao J, Yi L, Yu F (2015) ShapeNet: an information-rich 3D model repository. Stanford University, Princeton University, Toyota Technological Institute at Chicago

Drost B, Ulrich M, Bergmann P, Härtinger P, Steger C (2017) Introducing MVTec ITODD — a dataset for 3D object recognition in industry. In: 2017 IEEE international conference on computer vision workshops (ICCVW)

Fahim M, Sillitti A (2019) Anomaly detection, analysis and prediction techniques in IoT environment: a systematic literature review. IEEE Access 7:81664–81681

Feld T, Hilt B, Homburg O, Konz A, Lehmann H, Linn C, Storck U, Werth D, Scheer AW, Wittenburg G, Ziewer P (2017) Wie Unternehmen von Robotic Process Automation profitieren - Automate, Predict, Inspect, Assist, Optimize. In: Scheer AW, Feld T (eds) Working paper scheer holding 2017. Scheer Holding

Fettke P, Loos P (2019) "Strukturieren, Strukturieren, Strukturieren" in the era of robotic process automation. In: The art of structuring: bridging the gap between information systems research and practice. Springer, Berlin

Filaliansary T, Vandeborre J-P, Daoudi M (2005) A framework for 3D CAD models retrieval from 2D images. Ann Télécommun 60(11)

Gao Y, Tang J, Li H, Dai Q, Zhang N (2010) View-based 3D model retrieval with probabilistic graph model. Neurocomputing 73(10)

Gao Y, Wang M, Ji R, Wu X, Dai Q (2014) 3-D object retrieval with Hausdorff distance learning. IEEE Trans Ind Inform 61(4)

Grabner A, Roth PM, Lepetit V (2018) 3D Pose Estimation and 3D Model Retrieval for Objects in the Wild. CoRR

Groover M, Zimmers EWJR (1983) CAD/CAM: computer-aided design and manufacturing. Pearson Education, Upper Saddle River

Houy C, Hamberg M, Fettke P (2019) Robotic process automation in public administrations. In: Digitalisierung von Staat und Verwaltung

Ivančić L, Suša Vugec D, Vukšić VB (2019) Robotic process automation: systematic literature review. Springer, Berlin

Krupka D, Becker N (2020) Anwendungsszenarien KI-Systeme in der Produktionsautomatisierung. Gesellschaft für Informatik e. V. (GI)

Lake BM, Salakhutdinov R, Tenenbaum JB (2015) Human-level concept learning through probabilistic program induction. Science 350

Lasi H, Fettke P, Kemper H-G, Feld T, Hoffmann M (2014) Industry 4.0. Bus Inf Syst Eng 6(4):239–242

Le Q, Mikolov T (2014) Distributed representations of sentences and documents. In: International conference on machine learning

Leng B, Guo S, Zhang X, Xiong Z (2015) 3D object retrieval with stacked local convolutional autoencoder. Signal Process 112

Li Y, Su H, Qi CR, Fish N, Cohen-Or D, Guibas LJ (2015) Joint embeddings of shapes and images via CNN image purification. ACM Trans Graph 34

Lin SC, Shih LH, Yang D, Lin J, Kung JF (2018) Apply RPA (robotic process automation) in semiconductor smart manufacturing. In: 2018 e-manufacturing & design collaboration symposium (eMDC)

Madakam S, Holmukhe RM, Durgesh Kumar J (2019) The future digital work force: robotic process automation (RPA). J Inf Syst Technol Manag 16

Nederland, Knowledgebase Scheer (2019) Manufacturing and RPA. Robotic Process Automation – Industry Best Practices Manufacturing

Qi CR, Yi L, Su H, Guibas LJ (2017) PointNet++: Deep Hierarchical Feature Learning on Point Sets in a Metric Space. CoRR

Rehse J-R, Dadashnia S, Fettke P (2018) Business process management for industry 4.0 – three application cases in the DFKI-smart-lego-factory. IT, Inf Technol 60(3):133–141

Sarcar MMM, Rao KM, Narayan KL (2008) Computer aided design and manufacturing. PHI Learning Pvt. Ltd.

Sarkar K, Stricker D (2019) Simple domain adaptation for CAD based object recognition. In: International conference on pattern recognition applications and methods (ICPRAM-2019)

Sarkar K, Varanasi K, Stricker D (2017) Trained 3D models for CNN based object recognition

Scheer AW (1990) CIM computer integrated manufacturing. Springer Verlag, Berlin Heidelberg

Scheer A-W (2012) CIM computer integrated manufacturing: towards the factory of the future. Springer Science & Business Media

Scheer A-W, Jost W, Gungoz Ö (2007) A reference model for industrial enterprises. Reference modeling for business systems analysis. IGI Global, pp 167–181

Su H, Maji S, Kalogerakis E, Learned-Miller E (2015) Multi-view convolutional neural networks for 3D shape recognition. In: 2015 IEEE international conference on computer vision (ICCV)

van der Aalst W, Bichler M, Heinzl A (2018) Robotic process automation. Bus Inf Syst Eng 60(4)

Vareille J, Espes D, Autret Y, Le Parc P (2016) Low-cost high-tech robotics for ambient assisted living: from experiments to a methodology. J Intell Syst 25(4):455

Vinyals O, Blundell C, Lillicrap TP, Kavukcuoglu K, Wierstra D (2016) Matching networks for one shot learning. CoRR

Wang Y, Feng J, Wu Z, Wang J, Chang S-F (2014) From low-cost depth sensors to CAD: cross-domain 3D shape retrieval via regression tree fields. In: Fleet D, Pajdla Bernt Schiele T, Tuytelaars T (eds) Computer vision – ECCV 2014. Springer International Publishing

Wang Y, Yao Q, Kwok J, Ni L (2020) Generalizing from a few examples: a survey on few-shot learning. ACM Comput Surv 53:1–34

Wu Z, Song S, Khosla A, Yu F, Zhang L, Tang X, Xiao J (2015) 3D ShapeNets: a deep representation for volumetric shapes. In: 2015 IEEE conference on computer vision and pattern recognition (CVPR)

Xian Y, Lampert CH, Schiele B, Akata Z (2018) Zero-shot learning—a comprehensive evaluation of the good, the bad and the ugly. IEEE Trans Pattern Anal Mach Intell 41(9)

Part V: **RPA practice**

Eldar Sultanow, Alina Chircu, René Plath, Daniel Friedmann,
Tim Merscheid, and Kalpesh Sharma

17 AI evolves IA

A practitioner view on artificial intelligence information architecture

Abstract: In this chapter we develop an information architecture (IA) model for artificial intelligence (AI) technologies organized in four domains: human–computer interaction, robotic process automation (RPA), cognitive Internet of Things (Cognitive IoT), and customer service automation. The model showcases the business capabilities afforded by the AI technology in a variety of industry sectors such as automotive, pharma, hospitality, energy, public, logistics, entertainment, aviation, finance and insurance, and E-commerce. The methodology used in this chapter is based on well-established processes of developing an IA, informed by an analysis of AI use cases published in academic and practitioner literature. The model can help companies integrate these technologies into a structural design within a shared information environment, and offers a blueprint for understanding their benefits. In addition, the model can serve as a source for innovation by showcasing applications in different sectors. Individual employees and educators can also benefit from the model by understanding the impact of AI on current jobs and identifying upskilling and reskilling needs and strategies.

Keywords: Artificial intelligence, intelligent automation, robotic process automation, machine learning, business capability, use case

17.1 Introduction

Artificial intelligence (AI), an academic and practitioner field focused on building systems that exhibit intelligent behavior (Asensio et al., 2014; Laird et al., 2017), was once only science fiction. AI was first popularized in movies in which intelligent machines sometimes helped humans, but more often overtook and enslaved mankind, terrifying moviegoers and leaving them with mixed feelings about AI's potential impact on society. Today, however, AI has become a reality in many areas of the economy and society. As AI technologies become more powerful, they are more and more able to solve complex problems in an expanding number of settings, such as banking and finance, healthcare, manufacturing, and government – just to name a few. AI's benefits for businesses include creating efficiencies, improving and standardizing processes, discovering previously invisible patterns, learning from experience, and providing predictions.

https://doi.org/10.1515/9783110676693-017

As AI technologies evolve exponentially, and so do their complexity and potential impacts. And a new AI-related fear is becoming a reality – not the old fear of being ruled by machines, but the fear of being replaced by machines and losing one's job. The AI technology at the source of these concerns is robotic process automation (RPA) – the autonomous execution of business processes by software programs based on pre-defined business rules (Hofmann et al., 2020). But while RPA does automate repetitive, tedious human tasks, it is not intended to replace humans, but instead to enhance existing jobs, facilitate better human–machine interaction (HCI), and allow employees to leverage complementary skills and technologies for value-added tasks such as process improvement, exception handling, and advanced analysis (van der Aalst et al., 2018; Hofmann et al., 2020). RPA can also be viewed as "one step on the way to more intelligent and cognitive automation" (Hofmann et al., 2020) – i.e., it can learn from humans and can be enhanced with AI technologies in order to handle more complex and less defined tasks (van der Aalst et al., 2018). Thus, understanding its potential requires adopting a strategic view on AI technologies and analyzing their implications in detail before implementation (Hofmann et al., 2020).

Because the full impact of AI on both businesses and their employees is not yet fully understood, it is important to document the major technologies in the market and the extent to which different industries can benefit from them. For businesses to use the full potential of AI technologies, they need to understand how to integrate these technologies into a structural design within a shared information environment. In this chapter, we develop a model which shows the potential of AI technologies, including RPA, and how these can be put in a context of an information architecture (IA). Furthermore, this research seeks to find business capabilities for a selection of industry sectors, and shows how these sectors can benefit from the identified technologies.

17.2 Theoretical underpinnings

17.2.1 Artificial intelligence

Based on the Gartner IT Glossary, AI is a technology that is supposed to emulate human performance, especially human cognitive performance. More concretely, this includes learning, drawing conclusions and executing complex tasks, and in some cases holding end-to-end conversations in a natural way (Gartner, 2018a). AI research views minds – the functional entities "that can think, and thus support intelligent behavior" as "computational entities of a special sort. These entities, known as cognitive systems, can be implemented through a diversity of physical devices [...] whether natural brains, traditional general purpose computers, or other sufficiently functional forms of hardware or wetware" (Laird et al., 2017). Two approaches can be used – building and training AI systems based on data obtained from human behavior or designing the AI systems based on models of human cognition (Asensio et al., 2014; Laird et al.,

2017). To evaluate the results, AI researchers use tests based on the "imitation game" originally proposed by Turing in which judges observe behavior (such as providing answers to questions or playing a video game) and try to determine if it is generated by a human or not (Asensio et al., 2014).

Many AI researchers agree that in order to have human-like capabilities and emulate human minds, an AI-based system must incorporate several different components – perception and motor, working memory, declarative long-term memory, and procedural long-term memory, as well as processing algorithms for each capability and for interaction and information exchanges among the components (Laird et al., 2017). The memory components store, maintain, and retrieve content – both domain data about symbols and their relationships, and metadata such as frequency, recency, etc. The perception component converts external signals (vision, audition, etc.) into memory content, while the motor component converts the memory content into external action (Laird et al., 2017). The processing algorithms enable the system to operate by performing cognitive cycles and learning – i. e., automatically creating new symbol structures, adjusting the metadata, and allowing the adaptation of the perception and motor systems (Laird et al., 2017). A machine that interacts with its environment, for example, needs to identify objects in this environment. The technology behind this capability is called computer (or machine) vision. The input data generated with video sensors are converted and processed using machine learning (ML) algorithms that mimic what happens in a human brain with visual processing, automatically discover patterns in huge amounts of data, and learn from experience. The resulting AI-supported system can thus continuously improve its abilities for decision-making and predictions. With the help of natural language processing (NLP) the machine can also communicate its decisions and predictions to a human using natural language (Laurent et al., 2015).

AI technologies will affect every department as well as most processes and employees of a company. Those who want to keep up with the rapid advances in AI technology face the challenge of drastically reshaping their entire organization. Existing products and even whole business models will be changed by AI-based technologies (Reeves, 2018). Companies that can rapidly adopt and effectively embed AI in their operations are likely to enjoy long-term competitive advantage, as the technology–process combination and AI's ability to learn from the past will create dynamic capabilities and path dependencies that will be difficult to imitate by others (Schoemaker et al., 2018).

17.2.2 Information architecture

IA is an interdisciplinary field focused on "the structural design of shared information environments" (Information Architecture Institute, 2013). The term IA is also used to describe "the art and science of organizing and labeling web sites, intranets, online communities and software to support usability and findability," and the "emerging community of practice focused on bringing principles of design and architecture to the digital landscape" (Information Architecture Institute, 2013). An architecture is useful "whenever we want to define a high-level overview of interrelated components and when the relationships among them are complex and difficult to understand. [...] The common theme is that architecture is used to organize information about a topic in order to manage it in a structured way" (Evernden and Evernden, 2003). First-generation IAs (1970s and 1980s) were focused on stand-alone applications described through simple 2D diagrams, second-generation IAs (1990s) were focused on enterprise-wide systems and more complex 2D models and industry reference models, and third-generation IAs (late 1990s to 2000s) are focused on organizational use of information, rather than technology, and employ multi-dimensional models that capture different viewpoints (Evernden and Evernden, 2003).

The process of designing an IA includes specifying sources and destinations of the information flows as well as their path within the information system, in order to make things understandable (Information Architecture Institute, 2013). Due to the often-high complexity of the shared information environments, the development of IA models is a commonly used tool in this field. Models further show the information units, their functions, their accessibility, and how a user of the information can interact with these units (Gartner, 2018b). One common way of organizing the information is by identifying different dimensions for classifying the information and generating 2D matrices or multi-dimensional diagrams to illustrate the relevant features of the information environment (Evernden and Evernden, 2003). By fulfilling these requirements, the model can be used as a blueprint for the creation of an information environment that, once established, allows the potential user to have the best possible access to the information and a highly efficient utilization of it.

17.3 Methodology

The methodology used in this chapter is based on the well-established processes of developing an IA (Evernden and Evernden, 2003; Gartner, 2018a; Information Architecture Institute, 2013), informed by the design science approach (Vaishnavi et al., 2017). The methodology for developing the IA included deciding which information is needed and which dimensions will be used to organize it, creating diagrams based on the chosen dimensions (such as table or grid structures comparing one architectural dimension against another), and providing related descriptions, definitions, and examples of how the information is or could be used (Evernden and Evernden, 2003). To facilitate this process, we conducted a review of both academic and practitioner literature, we used experiences from real-world projects conducted by several of the chapter authors, and we sought feedback on the model content from industry experts, who commented on its usefulness.

Because our focus was on developing an IA for AI technologies, we analyzed a variety of AI technology use cases to distill the information at the focus of the IA – AI business capabilities – and the dimensions that can be used to organize this information. To this end, we reviewed academic literature on AI applications and practitioner resources related to AI (such as online practitioner reports and white papers from business consulting companies and companies that use AI technologies for their products and services), which we identified through Internet searches of relevant keywords. We had to rely on both academic and practitioner sources because, due to the rapid evolution of AI technologies, academic literature sources (which go through a lengthy review process) are less complete in their coverage of AI topics than practitioner sources (which reflect the most recent technology developments).

The academic literature sources were used for basic definitions of topics, for identifying frameworks for classification of AI topics, and for discovering clusters based on what the academic community identifies as enabling technologies for the unlimited and fast evolving applications of AI. This supported the identification of the first dimension of the model – the technology domains. To clearly define the domains and further divide them into sub-domains, we reduced the wide variety of technologies to several high-level clusters of technologies. We further validated the resulting domains through an iterative process as described later in this paragraph. The academic and practitioner literature, taken together, supported the identification of the second dimension of the model – industry sectors that were most commonly investigated by academic researchers and business representatives alike. For the purpose of this chapter, we focused on the most commonly mentioned sectors, rather than attempting to compile a complete list of sectors. In general, we found that the number of business capabilities increases with the number of investigated sectors. As we investigated new sectors, we used the newly identified business capabilities to validate the domain dimensions. The rule we followed was that if a high number of business capabilities that do not fit into one of the existing domains are found, this is an indicator that the existing domains are either not abstract enough or incomplete, and need further refinement. Additionally, to have a wide-angle view of real-world processes and data flows, our methodology considered AI and automation, spanning across multiple industries and sectors. The potential of AI/ML can very well be exploited when relationships and connections between events or trends are discovered and data across the industries or sectors are analyzed, correlated, and regressed. This process resulted in the final list of technology domains, industry sectors, and business capabilities, which were organized in the 2D IA model explained in the next sections.

17.4 The IA model structure

The IA model for AI business capabilities developed based on the methodology described in the previous section is shown as a high-level diagram in Figure 1 and as a

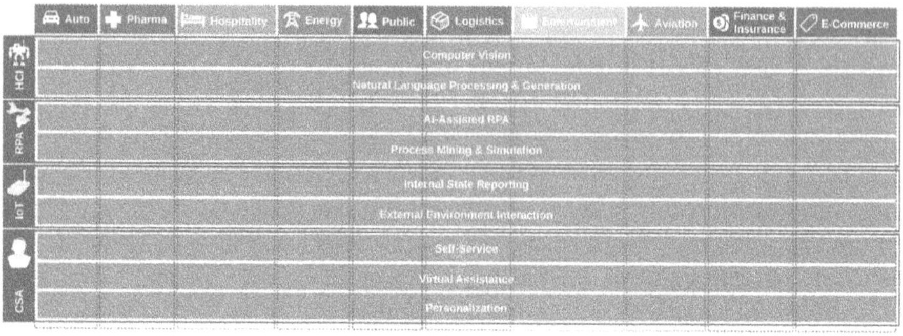

Figure 1: Overall IA for AI: AI technologies, industry sectors, and business capabilities.

detailed diagram in Figure 2a and b. The elements of the model are explained in detail in the next sections. The model reduces the complexity of the AI information environment to only two dimensions: the technology domains and relevant sub-domains (shown on the *y*-axis) and the industry sectors (shown on the *x*-axis). The intersections between domains and sectors show AI business capabilities and concrete use cases of AI within the sectors. To meet the requirement of simplicity the model can only show a selection out of the wide range of possible sectors. However, because of the methodology we followed, the model has the advantage that all dimensions that can be extended as new AI technologies are developed and applied in different sectors.

17.5 Technology domains and sub-domains

The AI technology domains are one of the dimensions of the IA developed in this chapter. The domains can be thought of as generic technology areas, such as HCI, that can be infused with AI. Identifying relevant domains and sub-domains is a challenging task in a complex and rapidly evolving field. Ideally, the domains need to be clearly delineated from each other. In reality, the many technologies available in practice have many overlaps, as well as many use cases in different areas. The following definitions of the technology domains are based on an aggregation of different academic and practitioner sources that use the terms related to each domain. They are also based on the result of validation based on the identified business capabilities, as explained in the methodology section.

17.5.1 Human–computer interaction

AI drastically changes the way that humans interact with machines. Unlike traditional input/output devices, the AI-based technologies for HCI move the interaction between machines and humans closer to a natural, human-to-human-like form of interaction. This enables closer collaboration between the two (Dickson, 2017). We identify several relevant sub-domains of HCI as follows.

17.5.1.1 Computer vision

Computer vision, also known as machine vision, acts like the eye of a machine. The impressions the machine gets from its video sensors are interpreted by ML algorithms. To accomplish this, training of the algorithms requires evaluating a huge amount of image data in order to increase the ability to recognize or even interpret complex images (Marr, 2018).

17.5.1.2 Natural language processing and natural language generation

NLP and natural language generation (NLG) enable communication between computers (or machines in general) and humans in a natural language. While NLP means the ability of a machine to understand natural language, NLG has the aim to enable machines to answer in a natural language (Paris et al., 1991).

17.5.2 Robotic process automation

RPA involves the use of software bots that replicate organizational processes and workflows originally performed by a human – like the manipulation of application software such as ERP or CRM. This way RPA software is able to move information through and between different systems in a much faster way and with a smaller error rate than humans. In addition, RPA digitalizes manual processes and thus generates useful data that otherwise would not be recorded (Kroll et al., 2016). We identify several relevant sub-domains of RPA as follows.

17.5.2.1 AI-assisted robotics process automation

In general, the actions performed by RPA software bots are rule-based. A new approach is adding AI technologies to make the software bots "smart." This way data that are collected while running the processes as well as further data input can be used to fulfill more complex tasks using ML techniques (Kroll et al., 2016).

17.5.2.2 Process mining and simulation

Manual process mining to discover, document, and manage organizational processes is a demanding task. Recorded processes are too often the result of subjective human opinions. With the new possibilities AI offers, enterprise transactions and event logs can be automatically analyzed, and underlying processes can be documented fully and objectively. Furthermore, processes can be simulated, and the results can be used to optimize processes in a more cost-effective way (Tian, 2017).

17.5.3 Cognitive Internet of Things

Internet of Things (IoT) is a term used to describe a network of uniquely identified physical objects that communicate with each other and with the Internet. IoT has two main characteristics. On the one hand, the things in the network are able to record data about their internal states and report them. On the other hand, the things in the network are able to interact with their external environment. These characteristics each lead to different business capabilities (Gartner, 2018c). Cognitive IoT is a term used to describe IoT paired with AI technologies. Cognition in this context means collecting the large volume of structured and unstructured IoT data, deducing meaning from it, and using these learnings to solve problems (Matthews, 2016). We identify several relevant sub-domains of cognitive IoT as follows.

17.5.3.1 Internal state reporting

By performing internal state reporting, IoT-enabled smart physical things support real-time monitoring and predictive maintenance. The data generated can be processed using advanced analytics and identifying operational adjustments that in turn lead to more efficiency, lower costs, and prevention of major problems. This has positive effects on productivity and the overall customer experience, among others (Marr, 2017).

17.5.3.2 External environment interaction

IoT-enabled smart physical things are equipped with sensors that capture and share a large amount of data about and with their environment in real-time. This data is uploaded into the cloud, making it accessible from everywhere, and enabling advanced analytics to be performed as needed. The ability of IoT-enabled things to communicate with each other and interact with their external environment is the basis for automations in every sector (Rajguru et al., 2015).

17.5.4 Customer service automation

Customer service automation covers all AI-supported automation technologies that help improve the customer experience along the customer journey. The automation speeds up the issue resolution for the customer while the involved systems constantly learn from the input and thus provide a better understanding of the customer. Additionally, the company saves resources that can be used elsewhere (Schneider, 2017).

17.5.4.1 Self-service

Self-service follows the trend of customers trying to help themselves without interaction with another human. Kiosks with touchscreens and displays enable the customer to virtually try out products or place orders. Thus, the customer can inform him- or herself about a product or service, customize it based on his preferences, and manage the whole purchase process on his own. However, the ways in which self-service technologies are used differ from industry to industry (Salas, 2017).

17.5.4.2 Virtual assistance

Virtual assistance is a technology based on ML, speech recognition, and NLP that interacts with a user and is able to hold an end-to-end conversation with him or her (written or spoken) to help him or her with his specific request. Virtual assistance applications attempt to understand commands, as well as the intent and context of the request, even with lots of background noise. Virtual assistance applications also attempt to personalize responses based on the identified voice of the interacting user.

This technology can appear in the form of chatbots – which are rule-based software bots that can help the user with simple repetitive tasks. Chatbots are text-based dialogue systems that replace classic and inflexible FAQ pages. There are two different types of chatbots: retrieval-based and generative bots. In the first approach, after evaluating the request, the chatbot accesses a response repository. In the generative approach, a chatbot learns from past conversations and their answers. These can be conversations from person to person. Typical requests to a chatbot in the area of E-commerce are the requests for the dispatch status of an order or help with the commissioning of newly purchased devices. If the system can no longer answer a question independently, it can then be forwarded to a human support employee. Chatbots can reduce the costs of customer service support up to 30 % (Techlabs, 2017).

When virtual assistance is combined with AI technology, the term "virtual agent" is used. A virtual agent is able to guide the customer through complex processes. It can hold an end-to-end conversation, it can understand what the customer wants to achieve, and it learns and uncovers patterns. Connected to other systems, it provides insights that help meet the customer's needs and improve the customer service (Backhshi et al., 2018).

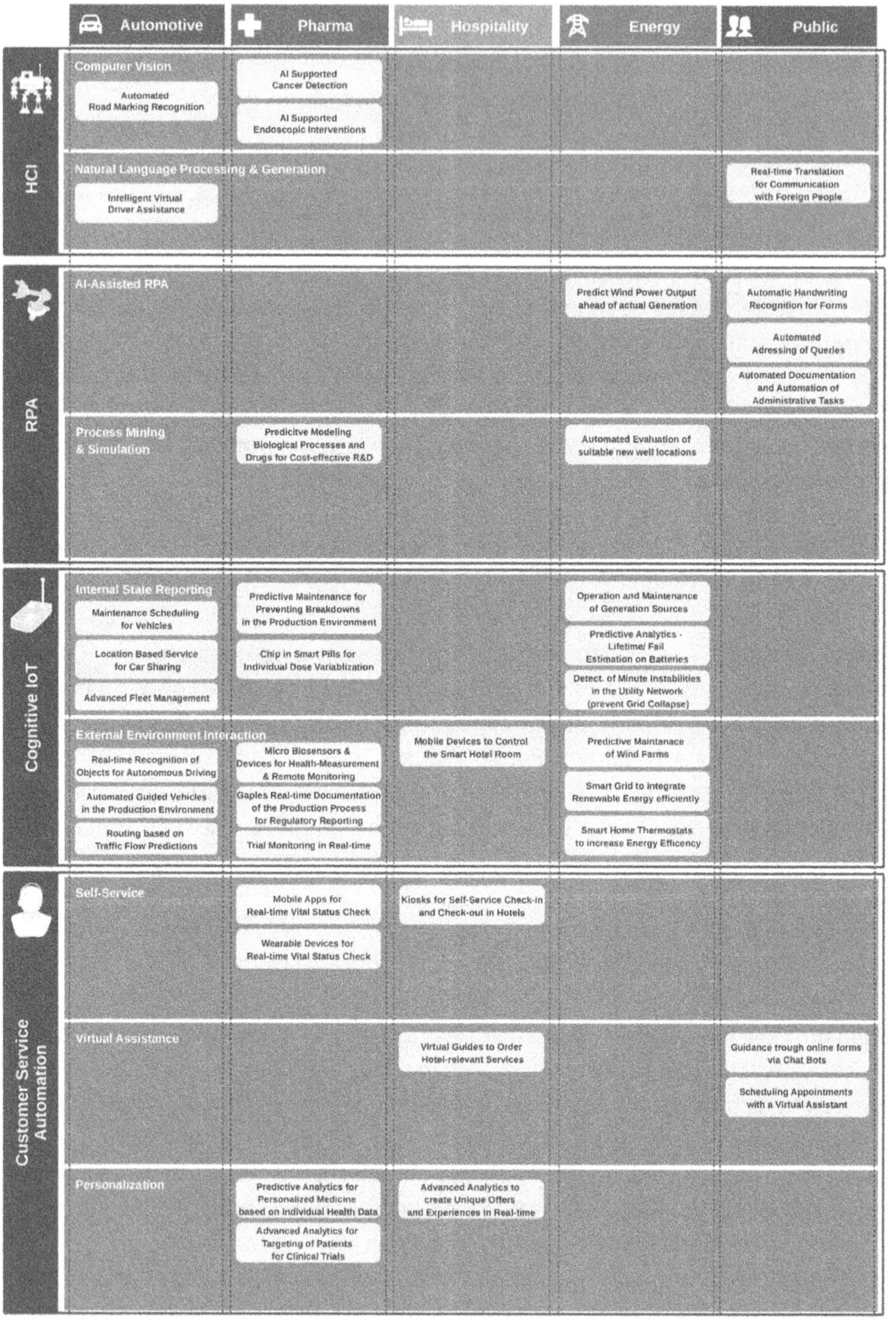

Figure 2: Detailed model showing AI-based capabilities (Part 1 – automotive, pharma, hospitality, energy, and public industry sectors).

		Logistics	Entertainment	Aviation	Finance & Insurance	E-Commerce
HCI	Computer Vision	Unloading and receipt of a trailer of inventory	Facial Recognition for Editing and Automated Content Creation	Facial Recognition for Customer Identity Verification; Baggage Screening and Threat Detection		
	Natural Language Processing & Generation		Navigation through the Content Menu via Voice Commands			
RPA	AI-Assisted RPA	Decoding Handwritten Text on Packages	Machine-driven Indexing, Metadata-tagging and Cataloging of Content; Anomaly Detection to Monitor and Flag Inappropriate Content; Content Fingerprinting for Effective Media Search		Analytics of Financial Data to Enhance Descisions; Automated Pattern Recognition for Fraud Detection; Automated Intelligent Reporting	Automated Product Inventory Updates; Automated Categorization and Tagging of Products; Automated Customer Return Processing
	Process Mining & Simulation					Prediction of Customer Behavior
Cognitive IoT	Internal State Reporting	Real-time Logistics Visibility for Tracking; Real-time Parameter Reporting				
	External Environment Interaction	Last Minute delivery by Autonomous Drones; Smart Warehousing for Supply Chain Automation		Autonomous Loaders to Transport Bags between the Terminal and Aircraft; Real-time Tracking of Baggage to provide Information to Passenger		
Customer Service Automation	Self-Service	Digitization handwritten artifacts (e.g. proof of delivery)	Kiosks as Ticketing and Gaming Sales Platform	Voice Commands for Domestic Airline Flight Info; Kiosks for Matching Passengers to their Luggage; Kiosks for Determining Luggage Sizes before Proceeding to Gate	Financial ATMs and Bill-pay Kiosks; Automated Insurance Claim Processing via Mobile App	Real-time Order Status Updates
	Virtual Assistance			Advanced Analytics to Predict which Costumers face Flight Cancellations	Guiding the Customer trough Complex Financial Transitions	Guiding the Customer trough the Payment Process
	Personalization		Identification and Tracking of Consumer Viewing Behaviour; Personalized Content Recommendations			Personalized Offers and Advertising

Figure 2: (continued). (Part 2 – logistics, entertainment, aviation, finance and insurance, and E-commerce industry sectors).

17.5.4.3 Personalization

The idea behind personalization is to customize the products, services, and every touchpoint in the customer journey for each individual customer. The spectrum of interactions that can be personalized is large – from simple product recommendations to real-time redesign of websites. Based on a wide variety of data sources and ML algorithms, personalization is the key to a positive customer experience and to generating new business by cross-selling and up-selling (Schneider, 2017).

17.6 Sectors and business capabilities

The IA model resulting from this research shows AI use cases for relevant sectors. For this chapter, we highlight sectors that have a high number of use cases with significant advantages for the involved players, and highlight the resulting business capabilities for each technology domain and sector.

17.6.1 Automotive

The automotive industry is facing new trends such as autonomous driving, connectivity, electric cars, and car sharing. For all of these trends, AI is either the basic technology or is playing a major role. The domain of cognitive IoT in particular contains many use cases starting from the manufacturing of a car as a physical product to the maintenance of the car and the services that require a car that is able to interact with its environment (Kässer et al., 2018). Autonomous driving alone has a great demand for technologies from almost every domain in our model. Enabling a car to drive by its own requires an interface with its surroundings. This is where specified IoT sensors come into play. These sensors collect huge amounts of complex data during test rides, which are processed by ML algorithms (Ravindra, 2017). Furthermore, we identify applications of AI-based technologies – smart factories – that are not limited to the usage in the automotive sector. Nevertheless, the automotive sector is the one that puts the most effort in the realization of smart factories (Gill et al., 2017). Cognitive IoT is the most relevant domain in this context. A smart factory contains a high number of items that are equipped with sensors and are connected in a network. The coordination and effective communication of the participants within this network requires advanced AI technologies. A smart factory, however, is more than just the interaction among physical items. The integration of enterprise resource planning (ERP) systems or manufacturing execution systems (MESs) is a necessary prerequisite for the realization of an autonomous operating smart factory. This involves the RPA domain in our model as well (Radziwon et al., 2013).

Another application of AI technology is advanced driving assistance. These systems interact with the driver and can therefore be an interface between the driver and the car. With the help of ML algorithms, the services of the systems can be personalized, and this way meet the expectations of the driver to an increasing level (Joshi, 2017). Related to the HCI computer vision domain, automated road marking recognition is an important part of AI in the automotive sector, contributing to the goal of a self-contained vehicle. Nowadays, assistance systems are already able to recognize the road (based on lane markers, arrows, and other indicators) and prevent getting off the track by autonomous intervention. Computer vision, coupled with ML, enables real-time lane detection by constantly analyzing images of the road ahead. Researchers have demonstrated an approach using a support vector machine with the aim of minimizing the impacts of the external environment such as the viewing angle, the brightness, and the background. The accuracy of the road detection was over 97 %, with a processing time of 0.26 s (Gang et al., 2017). Related to the HCI domain and the NLP/NLG sub-domain, some automotive manufacturers such as BMW are introducing intelligent virtual assistants that can recognize the driver's spoken commands, learn driver preferences, provide advice on using car features, and assist with navigation (BMW Group, 2018).

17.6.2 Pharma

Like in the automotive industry, the pharmaceutical industry is affected by major developments in AI technology. Cognitive IoT is one of the most relevant AI technologies regarding use cases with a high benefit potential. IoT can help collect data that the industry is depending on. Because of the high complexity of the supply chain within the pharma industry, real-time decision-making is very difficult. The advantages of IoT equipment are the way to face these challenges. Based on the data that is recorded by sensors, all along the supply chain and the processing of these data with help of ML and RPA, decisions can be made much more efficiently and the error rate that is caused by the big variety of different systems can be significantly reduced (Behner and Ehrhardt, 2016). In addition to this, the pharma industry operates in a regulatory environment which requires extensive monitoring. IoT can help companies document the production processes in order to meet strict regulations.

Disease identification and diagnosis of ailments are primary topics of the pharma industry. ML has a high potential to advance these fields (Faggella, 2018). Pharma product development can benefit from collecting large amounts of data from individuals in order to improve treatment and prevent adverse effects in patients. The efficiency of drug discovery increases significantly by the data which the patients collect and provide. Further, the performance of new drugs can be monitored to a much higher extent than before. With the analysis of such data, the effectiveness of medical treatments can be understood and improved in a significant way. The data collection can be outsourced in part to the patient him- or herself, who uses smart devices to record health and body vitals data. The process includes use cases that fall under the domain self-service and its sub-domain personalization especially through the use of wearable devices. In 2017 around 140 million wearable devices were sold, and around 453 million sales are expected in 2022 (Gartner, 2019). The number of features and functions are increasing, and more wearables now include health-related functions, such as monitoring one's heart rate or even recording an electrocardiogram (ECG) to be sent to a doctor, as in the case of the Apple Watch. It is likely that in years to come, patients will collect comprehensive data on their health conditions themselves. This information can be precious for diagnosis, especially if the wearable device is a daily companion of a patient. ML can help to process these data and detect abnormalities – which can lead to scheduling doctor or emergency room visits, starting or changing treatment, and a more targeted process overall. In addition to the sensors in wearables worn by the patients, there are sensors that can be taken as a pill. These smart pills are able to record data about the condition of the patients and the performance of a treatment that wearables could not access. This can be valuable not only for research and development purposes but also as a lifesaver in cases where the smart pill in collaboration with a smartwatch or a similar device can remind the patient to take the medicine or consult a doctor (Champagne et al., 2015).

Many interesting use cases exist in the HCI and computer vision sub-domain in the area of disease detection. For example, researchers have developed artificial neuronal networks (ANNs) which compute the likelihood of breast cancer based on the interaction of genes, nutrients, and demographic indicators, with an accuracy of about 94 %. In addition, systems designed for the detection of cancer metastases showed an error rate of 7.5 % for AI systems, an error rate of 3.5 % for human pathologists, and an error rate of only 0.5 % for human pathologists supported by AI (National Science and Technology Council, 2016), showing the potential for collaboration between doctors and AI to significantly improve detection. AI can also support endoscopic interventions for diagnosis or treatment. While these minimal interventions allow wounds to heal faster and minimize the risk of infection, they need to be performed at very early disease stages in order to be successful. ML can help to process sensor data and to draw further conclusions with the goal of detecting malignant changes earlier so that therapy is still possible (Magoulas and Prentza, 2001). By analyzing data with ML, multiple interventions can be avoided. This is especially valuable for elderly patients, as each additional surgery is a burden on their overall state of health.

17.6.3 Hospitality

The hospitality sector puts a lot of effort in the automation of the customer service. Via self-service applications, the customer can perform time-intensive procedures like check-ins and check-outs on his or her own. In an interaction with the devices and applications, the customer generates data that can be used to personalize offers and help improve customer satisfaction (Taylor, 2017). In general, hotels have the problem that their staff spends too much time with tasks that are monotonous and repetitive – a problem that can easily be solved with current AI technologies. The key term here is "intelligent hotel" – which relies on almost every technology domain we investigate in this paper. Voice-activated services are already a common application of NLP techniques. These techniques also form the basis for the interaction between hotel guests and physical concierge robots. Self-service in the form of digital assistance helps reduce monotonous and repetitive tasks that otherwise would burden resources. These resources now can be used to enhance the travel experience of the customer. The interaction between the guests and the AI applications, in turn, are a source of data that in a second step will be processed by ML algorithms. This leads to an increasing understanding of customer needs. During the planning of the travel, AI can be used by providers to submit a personalized offer (Phillips, 2018). When it comes to dining out, customer can book a restaurant table in interaction with a virtual assistant, and kiosks can be used to speed up the order process. Based on AI, kiosks can recommend meals to the customer based on his or her eating preferences or demographic data (Sennaar, 2018). During their whole journey, travelers benefit from personalized offers and from saving time, which can lead to increased customer satisfaction, resulting in competitive advantage for the providers using AI technologies.

17.6.4 Energy

The energy sector is characterized by two dominating topics: first, the prevention of breakdowns and the maintenance of the grid, and second, the improvement of energy efficiency. The cognitive IoT domain of the model is the most relevant one in this context. The concept of a smart grid is to interconnect all participants in a power grid – including areas of generation, storage, and consumption. The energy system, therefore, supplies not only the actual electricity but also a large number of metrics. The smart grid gives feedback about its internal state, and this way helps prevent breakdowns. If an incident occurs nonetheless, the field workforce can fix damages much faster due to the real-time information provided by the smart grid. AI can be used for grid reliability and resilience, including rapid damage assessment and information sharing for power restoration (SEAB, 2020). Two companies in this area are Brain4Drones LLC and Elintrix. Brain4Drones (Brains4Drones, 2020) seeks to reduce outage durations, improve the resilience of the energy sector, and keep linemen and first responders safe by developing an accessory for drones that would enable them to rapidly assess the condition of overhead distribution lines and transmitting those data back to the utility. Elintrix (Elintrix, 2020) seeks to inform protective relaying operation and reduce incidents of failure-to-trip misoperation by utilizing AI to extract and analyze previously unavailable impulse responses.

A smart grid also leads to better utilization of the conventional grid infrastructure, which reduces the need for expansion and improves grid stability at the same capacity utilization (Bundesnetzagentur, 2011). The integration of small, localized, and decentralized power generation enables private, business, and industrial customers to generate their electricity on their own and sell it to the grid with minimal technical or regulatory barriers (Wei et al., 2009). There are many projects in this area: Tesla, for instance, presented the Solar Roofs project, a solution for integrating solar cells into roof tiles. By expanding into a smart grid and decentralizing the power grid, the electricity can be used locally where it is generated. Renewable energies can thus be used more efficiently. The data from this smart grid need processing in order to monitor the grid constantly. Integrating ML ensures the reliability of the power grid. The digitalization of the power grid also makes it more vulnerable to cyber attacks. ML can also help in this case by monitoring the network for possible attacks or even predicting them.

Smart grid sensors also give information about their environmental conditions – and the collected data can ensure that only as much energy as actually needed will be produced or spent (Dawate, 2018). Qualitative data plus ML algorithms allow energy providers to benefit from advanced analytics. The energy providers do not only use the data that are created by the smart grid but also general data like weather data or data of upcoming events that lead to deviations of the average energy demand (Powal, 2018). Based on large amounts of data, decision-making can be much more effective (Booth et al., 2016). Like in every sector, repetitive and monotonous tasks can be automated with RPA technologies and this way relieve the back-office. In addition, the already mentioned weather data have a high relevance in the energy sector, especially regarding the rise of renewable energy, since a reliable weather forecast is a key factor for the efficient management of the electricity network (Wettengel 2016).

All these developments leave more room for the energy supplier to create personalized products that meet the expectations of their customers to a higher extent. This can generate critical competitive advantage within a highly regulated market. To improve the customer experience, insights must be gathered from a growing variety of sales channels. The online and mobile channels are especially valuable data sources since the customer creates and combines the products according to his or her personal needs with the help of self-service applications. Furthermore, the energy sector benefits indirectly from the AI-driven trends in society. IoT, smart homes, and the concepts of smart cities offer opportunities for new business fields and partnerships, and for governments to actively promote the further development of related technologies (Booth et al., 2016).

ML can boost the value of renewable energy (Elkin and Witherspoon, 2019). For example, the variable nature of wind itself makes it an unpredictable energy source

– less useful than one that can reliably deliver power at a set time. In search of a solution to this problem, DeepMind and Google started applying ML algorithms to 700 megawatts of wind power capacity in the central United States. These wind farms – part of Google's global fleet of renewable energy projects (Katz, 2020) – collectively generate as much electricity as is needed by a medium-sized city. Using a neural network trained on widely available weather forecasts and historical turbine data, the DeepMind system has been configured to predict wind power output 36 hours ahead of actual generation. Based on these predictions, an ML model recommends how to make optimal hourly delivery commitments to the power grid a full day in advance. This is important, because energy sources that can be scheduled (i. e., can deliver a set amount of electricity at a set time) are often more valuable to the grid (Elkin and Witherspoon, 2019; Katz, 2020). ML and related techniques can also support investment optimization (Mahendra, 2019) – as in the case of BP using AI to enabling them to analyze seismic images and geological models to increase the chances of success when drilling wells (BP, 2017).

17.6.5 Public sector

The main pain point in the public sector that can be solved by AI technology is that employees spend most of their work time for documenting and administrative tasks paired with backlogs and paperwork burdens. These tasks can already easily be performed by using state-of-the-art AI technologies. By implementing such technologies, governments can cut costs and public employees can focus on more critical tasks (Eggers et al., 2017). RPA is the technology to relieve employees from repetitive rule-based tasks. Those tasks that do not require human judgment can be left to software robots. This not only saves time and resources, it also reduces the error rate.

In addition, a lot of tasks can be outsourced to the citizen via intelligent self-services. The public sector has many processes in which the identity of the citizen must be determined without any doubt. ML algorithms fed with image data allow a constant improvement in this field. Answering questions from citizens, providing the right documents for a specific case, and helping with filling them out correctly are the most frequent tasks that use a lot of resources but that at the same time can relatively easily be performed using AI technologies. Many questions regarding documents are quite similar. Virtual agents and chatbots can instantly respond to these questions, which also increases the consistency of the information provided for each request. This reduces the necessity of in-person visits and long phone calls. Even complex cases with legal relevance can be processed this way.

The big amount of data that governmental institutions have to handle should not be underestimated. This circumstance is one decisive reason that processes take longer than expected. RPA definitely can improve these processes already to a high extent but even beyond that, AI allows predicting scenarios. This way time-consuming tasks can be organized in a way that the response time can be further reduced (Mehr, 2017). Less obvious is the fact that even the cognitive IoT domain has significant benefits for the public sector. There is for example the public transportation system that, equipped with sensors, provides the citizens with real-time information about the buses or trains they are waiting for. Another transportation-related use case for cognitive IoT technology is the possibility of real-time analytics of traffic to prevent traffic congestions (Maissin et al., 2016).

17.6.6 Logistics

Tractica Research estimates that the worldwide sales of warehousing and logistics robots will reach 22.4 billion USD (Tractica, 2020) by the end of 2021. Robots are locating, tracking, and moving inventory inside warehouses, and they are conveying and sorting oversized packages (Williams, 2010) at ground distribution hubs. The logistics sector continuously stands under high pressure as transportation costs depend a lot on fuel prices. To manage the risk of rising fuel prices, regulations, or other external impacts which the logistics sector has no control over, the logistic managers must optimize all processes as a whole. Logistics has always been dealing with many sources of information. IoT technologies now generate even more data that must be managed because it is essential to overcome challenges (Taylor, 2017). ML algorithms can process the data and use them to predict demand and improve capacity planning, routing, and pricing. AI-generated insights can improve many facets of the supply chain like route optimization and supply chain transparency. For example, UPS was able to save 10 million gallons of fuel annually (Kendall, 2017) by optimizing driver routes, and companies are getting smarter with last-mile deliveries (Lebied, 2017). Predictive analyses are further used for better risk management, which is a condition to ensure supply chain continuity. Platforms can integrate several players along the supply chain and allow them to have access to the data and analytics. This is useful because of the dependency between the players (Gesing et al., 2018). Because of the dependencies within the supply chain, the breakdown of involved machines, transport vehicles, or other technical equipment of the chain can lead to serious consequences. This risk can significantly be lowered by IoT sensors that continuously give status updates as a basis for predictive analytics and predictive maintenance (Riedl, 2018). By offering IoT-enabled condition monitoring, spare parts, and equipment repair services, original equipment manufacturers can remotely monitor asset health in their customers' plants, anticipate failures, order the parts, and often execute repairs before the failure occurs.

AI analysis can also be used to safeguard against other risks. Another good example from DHL (Gesing et al., 2018) is their platform which monitors more than 8 million online and social media posts to identify potential supply chain problems. Through advanced ML and NLP the system can understand the sentiment of online conversations and identify potential material shortages, access issues, and supplier status.

Innovations in the field of HCI have the potential to save work steps. Equipping warehouse workers with sensors integrated into their uniforms or in wearables is a possibility to eliminate repetitive tasks like scanning each picked item. Also, the documentation of the movement of the items is made more time-effective and the error rate is reduced at the same time.

As already mentioned, the logistics sector not only has to deal with a huge amount of heterogeneous data but also with the interplay of many independent systems. Nevertheless, RPA can solve problems and increase efficiency. The advancement of image recognition technologies that were once used to decode handwritten addresses on packages can now, empowered by AI, recognize movements of items. Warehouse workers can pick items and machines will automatically recognize them and transfer this information into the ERP system. In addition, the movement of goods along the different stages of the supply chain from the manufacturer to the end customer can be recorded into the systems and be further processed with the help of RPA (Eschberger, 2017), which can automatically digitize handwritten artifacts (invoices, bills, payment, proof of deliveries, etc.) directly to the document repository and automatically initiate workflows.

17.6.7 Entertainment

The potential AI technologies has to offer for the entertainment industry is outstanding. The entertainment sector is represented in every domain shown in the model. Multimedia devices interact with the consumer via gestures and voice commands, and ML algorithms help to categorize content which makes a high level of personalization possible (Narang, 2017).

The availability and the high number of data sources are advantages the entertainment sector has – but the available data are generally unstructured. With the development of AI technologies, it becomes easier to process these data and use them to significantly improve the services of the industry. Improving service in this context could mean a high level of personalization which requires insights about which content the customers want and other information in regard to their media consumption behavior. Publishers and broadcasters in the entertainment sector benefit from the fact that more and more customers consume the content via mobile apps. These apps create data of high value for a better personalization (eMarketer, 2016). The diverse social media channels are an important and extensive source of data in the form of direct consumer feedback. People share their impressions for example about the latest episode of their favorite series. AI with ML algorithms make it possible for the content producer and other stakeholders to evaluate the data and turn them into valuable insights for future productions (Newman, 2017).

AI also comes into play at the stage of content creation. It drastically changes the way moviemakers bring their films to commercial success. Instead of spending increasingly high amounts of money for special effects, AI helps to meet the consumers' expectations more precisely and this way avoids spending for more and more special effects that only bring limited value (Lourie, 2017).

As it is now possible to get these insights about what the ideal content could look like, the industry already tries to get one step further and integrates machines into the creative process of developing stories. Based on the knowledge gained from data, AI is able to deliver optimized story frames which can then be filled with the ideas of human authors. AI in this way becomes a co-author of movies (Newman, 2017), although platforms that provide third-party content need to make sure that the foreign content is not inappropriate (Narang, 2017).

17.6.8 Aviation

The applications of AI in the field of aviation span many different areas such customer service, baggage screening, self-check-in, and the overall flight process. Using AI-supported biometric recognition systems, passengers can perform a self-check-in while their baggage is scanned for unauthorized items and its size and weight are determined (Akcay et al., 2016). Moreover, AI can assist in the process of threat detection during surveillance (Scylla, 2020). Using camera systems, for instance, suspicious behavior or harmful items can be detected. The images are transmitted in real-time to an AI system for evaluation. With the support of AI image processing, security guards may react faster and in a more effective way, which increases the overall security at the airport. Furthermore, the surveillance also enables the measure of passengers flowing in different areas throughout the airport, thus allowing for optimizing internal workflows.

However, the use of AI is not only limited to the area of security, as these technology can also enhance the flight process. Using forecasting models, possible delays can be predicted ahead of time (Chakrabarty, 2019). This allows passengers to plan their journeys more precisely and react to delays at an early stage. In addition, necessary ground operations like loading and unloading the plane can also be scheduled in a more proactive manner.

By using AI-assisted real-time processing, it is also possible to inform passengers about the processing status of their baggage at any time. In case the baggage is lost, it can be found more easily, which leads to higher customer satisfaction and lower costs due to otherwise necessary time-consuming search processes.

17.6.9 Finance and insurance

The finance and insurance sector presents many opportunities for combining RPA with AI, resulting in multiple benefits for industry players as well as end customers. RPA-based reporting capabilities that incorporate AI functionalities form the most interesting and promising areas of process automation. Currently, financial agents manually compile reports on business figures, expected sales forecasts, or claims to support decision-making. In these cases, RPA mechanisms can be used to support and accelerate the process in a reactive manner. The addition of AI enables a shift from reactive report generation to a proactive approach – for example by using ML techniques for the prediction of stock prices and stock price developments (Moukalled et al., 2019).

Other capabilities include enterprise fraud management for suspicious transaction detection and intelligent input management which enables insurance customers to use mobile apps to photograph damages and upload documents to submit insurance claims (Scanbot, 2019). An AI-based text recognition system can then analyze, classify, and prepare the documents for the insurance company in such a way that rapid automated processing is possible. The forecasting of costs is also a relevant part in the field of insurance (Burri et al., 2019).

17.6.10 E-commerce

The E-commerce sector is typically one that synergistically combines RPA with AI. The automation and real-time access of the product inventory information is an essential factor for a successful online shop. If a customer is not informed in time that a desired product is no longer in stock, the customer will likely order from a competitor in the future. A reliable system for automatically updating the current product inventory is therefore crucial. The use of AI technology can further improve the system by analyzing customer purchase data and forecasting demand. This enables the creation of intelligent reports, which, in turn, can be used to make management decisions (Lingam, 2018), e. g., increasing the capacity in a certain product category.

The process of adding new products to an online store includes aspects such as uploading the product photo, including manufacturer documents, and providing meaningful keywords. This is where RPA helps speed up the repetitive upload tasks. In addition, AI systems can help with keyword research or assigning products directly to the suitable categories based on their properties. Furthermore, products which are often purchased together can be collectively presented to the customers (Kronberger and Affenzeller, 2012).

The automation of customer returns can save valuable time, especially since returns are not revenue-generating activities and need to be performed as efficiently as possible. With the assistance of AI systems, it is possible to analyze these cases more precisely and identify the most common reasons why a return is made, which in turn can provide suggestions for improving products and order processes to minimize the likelihood of returns.

For the E-commerce sector, certain times, such as the time before major holidays such as Christmas, are always a challenge. In addition, unpredictable events such as a natural disaster or a pandemic can also lead to increased demand in certain product categories. In these cases, companies need to react fast in order to ensure increased inventory levels and adequate delivery capabilities, which in turn will result in satisfied customers and increased profits. By predicting the purchasing behavior of customers, AI systems can provide important early warnings for these situations (Valecha et al., 2018).

Informing customers automatically about the status of their order is a service that can be found in a variety of online shops. In addition, AI systems can help to forecast the arrival of an order based on past experience data as well as current events.

Different payment systems lead to increased complexity in the ordering process. A guided process can help to maintain customer satisfaction during a checkout process. For this purpose, the use of AI technologies, which can evaluate data collected during the purchase process, is useful. This enables, for instance, the automated and intelligent sorting of payment providers according to their popularity.

Personalized offers and promotions contribute to customer satisfaction by providing them with faster access to what they are looking for (Earley, 2016). In this case, time is indeed money. If a customer fails to find what they are looking for on time, it is likely that they leave the site without making a purchase. Using AI technology, search results can be optimized, product rankings can be adjusted, and customized categories can be generated, thus enhancing the customer experience.

17.7 Conclusions and future work

In this chapter, we developed an IA model for AI technology by deriving two important dimensions for organizing AI applications – technology domains and industry sectors. We further populated the model with business capabilities at each domain/sector intersection. Each one of the AI technology domains – HCI, RPA, cognitive IoT, and customer service automation – creates multiple capabilities in a variety of industry sectors – automotive, pharma, hospitality, energy, public, logistics, entertainment, aviation, finance and insurance, and E-commerce. We also note that some industry sectors have yet to take advantage of promising technologies – for example, there seems to be a need to develop use cases for HCI in hospitality, energy, finance and insurance, and E-commerce, or RPA in automotive, hospitality, and aviation. We hope that our model can provide a blueprint for businesses to understand how they can benefit from AI technologies, and offer them a tool for deriving new applications by borrowing lessons from a different sector, combining technology domains to support a complex application area, or combining the existing capabilities into new ones. Employees can use the model to understand the impact of AI on their current jobs and identify opportunities for upskilling (when their job can be enhanced by using AI, but new skills are needed to understand the nuances of using the new technology) or reskilling (when their job is replaced by AI but creates opportunities for engaging in different value-added work). Similarly, educators can use this model to develop curricula that support the reskilling and upskilling needs of the existing workforce and equip the workforce of tomorrow with AI-ready skills.

This work has several limitations. The model reflects the perspectives available in the academic and practitioner literature at a given point in time and based on a critical mass of use cases. However, as AI is evolving rapidly, additional technology sub-domains and their interdependencies may need to be considered. In addition, the model captures many but not all possible industries where AI can be applied. While we received positive feedback regarding the model – in terms of both comprehensiveness of content and usefulness – from practitioners involved with AI and IA, we were not able to fully test the model in a real project setting. Thus, the current model only reflects one development cycle and does not incorporate feedback from multiple development and testing iterations.

The business capabilities included in our model can be understood as examples of the current state of AI technology development in particular industry sectors. Other researchers may be able to evolve the model by extending its dimensions or finding new capabilities. Future research can also investigate additional dimensions for the IA model in order to capture multiple perspectives or generate industry-specific reference models. As more academic papers on AI applications are published, a systematic literature review may help provide a more comprehensive picture of business capabilities by technology and industry. Last, but not least, real-world evaluation of the model – such as investigating expert opinions about its usefulness or the benefits from using it in different organizational settings – would be valuable.

Bibliography

Akcay S, Kundegorski ME, Devereux M, Breckon TP (2016) Transfer learning using convolutional neural networks for object classification within X-ray baggage security imagery. In: 2016 IEEE international conference on image processing (ICIP), proceedings, Phoenix, Arizona, USA, September 25–28, 2016 IEEE, Piscataway, NJ, pp 1057–1061

Asensio JML, Peralta J, Arrabales R, Bedia MG, Cortez P, Peña AL (2014) Artificial intelligence approaches for the generation and assessment of believable human-like behaviour in virtual characters. Expert Syst Appl 41(16):7281–7290

Backhshi N, Berg H, Broersen S (2018) Chatbots point of view. Available at: https://www.forbes.com/sites/forbescommunicationscouncil/2017/08/09/how-self-service-can-become-more-h. Accessed December 5, 2018

Behner P, Ehrhardt M (2016) Digitization in pharma – gaining an edge in operations. Available at: https://www.strategyand.pwc.com/media/file/Digitization-in-pharma.pdf. Accessed March 6, 2018

BMW Group (2018) Hey BMW, now we're talking!. Available at: https://www.press.bmwgroup.com/global/article/detail/T0284429EN/%E2%80%9Chey-bmw-now-we%E2%80%99re-talking-bmws-are-about-to-get-a-personality-with-the-company%E2%80%99s-intelligent-personal-assistant?language=en. Accessed June 6, 2020

Booth A, Peters P, Mohr N (2016) The digital utility: new opportunities and challenges. Available at: https://www.mckinsey.com/industries/electric-power-and-natural-gas/our-insights/the-digital-utility-new-opportunities-and-challenges. Accessed March 6, 2018

BP (2017) Caltech startup, beyond limits secures investment of $20 million from BP ventures. Available at: https://www.bp.com/en/global/corporate/news-and-insights/press-releases/caltech-startup-beyond-limits-secures-investment-of-20-million-from-bp-ventures.html Accessed June 6, 2020

Brains4Drones (2020) Available at: https://brains4drones.com/. Accessed June 6, 2020

Bundesnetzagentur (2011) "Smart Grid" und "Smart Market": Eckpunktepapier der Bundes-netzagentur zu den Aspekten des sich verändern-den Energieversorgungssystems. Available at: https://www.bundesnetzagentur.de/SharedDocs/Downloads/DE/Sachgebiete/Energie/Unternehmen_Institutionen/NetzzugangUndMesswesen/SmartGridEckpunktepapier/SmartGridPapierpdf.pdf?__blob=publicationFile&v=2. Accessed November 29, 2019

Burri RD, Burri R, Bojja RR, Buruga SR (2019) Insurance claim analysis using machine learning algorithms. Available at: https://www.ijitee.org/wp-content/uploads/papers/v8i6s4/F11180486S419.pdf. Accessed June 19, 2020

Chakrabarty N (2019) A data mining approach to flight arrival delay prediction for American Airlines. Available at: https://arxiv.org/abs/1903.06740. Accessed June 19, 2020

Champagne D, Hung A, Leclerc O (2015) The road to digital success in pharma. Available at: https://www.mckinsey.com/industries/pharmaceuticals-and-medical-products/our-insights/the-road-to-digital-success-in-pharma. Accessed December 5, 2018

Dawate R (2018) Artificial intelligence adoption in energy sector. Available at: https://www.linkedin.com/pulse/artificial-intelligence-adoption-energy-sector-ramesh-dawate/. Accessed December 5, 2018

Dickson B (2017) How artificial intelligence is revolutionizing human-computer interaction. Available at: https://thenextweb.com/artificial-intelligence/2017/05/10/artificial-intelligence-revolutionizing-human-computer-interaction/. Accessed December 5, 2018

Earley S (2016) There is no AI without IA. IT Prof 18(3):58–64

Eggers WD, Schatsky D, Viechnicki P (2017) AI-augmented Government. Available at: https://www2.deloitte.com/insights/us/en/focus/cognitive-technologies/artificial-intelligence-government.html. Accessed March 20, 2018

Elintrix (2020) Smartgrid. Available at: http://www.elintrix.com/sectors/smart-grid/. Accessed June 06, 2020

Elkin K, Witherspoon S (2019) Machine learning can boost the value of wind energy. Available at: https://deepmind.com/blog/article/machine-learning-can-boost-value-wind-energy. Accessed June 06, 2020

eMarketer (2016) Internet of Things is changing how media and entertainment companies operate. Available at: https://www.emarketer.com/Article/Internet-of-Things-Changing-How-Media-Entertainment-Companies-Operate/1013545. Accessed March 20, 2018

Eschberger T (2017) Human machine interaction: how people and machines will complement each other at a workplace in the future. Available at: http://www.lead-innovation.com/english-blog/human-machine-interaction. Accessed December 5, 2018

Evernden R, Evernden E (2003) Third-generation information architecture. Commun ACM 46(3):95–98

Faggella D (2018) 7 applications of machine learning in pharma and medicine. Available at: https://www.techemergence.com/machine-learning-in-pharma-medicine/. Accessed December 5, 2018

Gang L, Zhang M, Zhang L, Hu J (2017) Automatic road marking recognition for intelligent vehicle systems application. In: Advances in mechanical engineering, vol 9

Gartner IT Glossary (2018a) Artificial intelligence (AI). Available at: https://www.gartner.com/it-glossary/artificial-intelligence/. Accessed December 5, 2018

Gartner IT Glossary (2018b) Information architecture. Available at: https://www.gartner.com/it-glossary/information-architecture/. Accessed December 5, 2018

Gartner IT Glossary (2018c) Internet of Things (IoT). Available at: https://www.gartner.com/it-glossary/Internet-of-things/. Accessed December 5, 2018

Gartner (2019) Gartner says worldwide wearable device sales to grow 26 percent in 2019. Available at: https://www.gartner.com/en/newsroom/press-releases/2018-11-29-gartner-says-worldwide-wearable-device-sales-to-grow-. Accessed November 23, 2019

Gesing B, Peterson S, Michelsen D (2018) Artificial intelligence in logistics – a collaborative report by DHL and IBM on implications and use cases for the logistics industry. Available at: https://www.logistics.dhl/content/dam/dhl/global/core/documents/pdf/glo-ai-in-logistics-white-paper.pdf. Accessed March 6, 2018

Gill N, Schneider-Maul R, Buvat J (2017) Putting automotive manufacturers in the digital industrial revolution driving seat. Available at: https://www.capgemini.com/wp-content/uploads/2018/04/automotive-smart-factories-putting-auto-manufacturers-in-the-digital-industrial-revolution-driving-seat.pdf. Accessed May 26, 2018

Hofmann P, Samp C, Urbach N (2020) Robotic process automation. EM 30(1):99–106

Information Architecture Institute (2013) What is IA. Available at: https://www.iainstitute.org/sites/default/files/what_is_ia.pdf. Accessed May 12, 2018

Joshi N (2017) Machine learning in the automotive industry. Available at: https://www.allerin.com/blog/machine-learning-in-the-automotive-industry. Accessed May 26, 2018

Kässer M, Padhi A, Tschiesner A (2018) Artificial intelligence – automotive's new value-creating engine. Available at: https://www.mckinsey.com/industries/automotive-and-assembly/our-insights/artificial-intelligence-as-auto-companies-new-engine-of-value. Accessed May 12, 2018

Katz J (2020) Building a new industry: a visit to three places where a push for renewable energy is boosting the local economy. Available at: https://about.google/intl/en-GB/stories/renewable-energy-is-boosting-economies/. Accessed June 6, 2020

Kendall G (2017) Why UPS drivers don't turn left and you probably shouldn't either. The conversation. Available at: https://theconversation.com/why-ups-drivers-dont-turn-left-and-you-probably-shouldnt-either-71432. Accessed June 6, 2020

Kroll C, Bujak A, Darius V (2016) Robotic process automation – robots conquer business processes in back offices. Available at: https://www.capgemini.com/consulting-de/wp-content/uploads/sites/32/2017/08/robotic-process-automation-study.pdf. Accessed May 12, 2018

Kronberger G, Affenzeller M (2012) Market basket analysis of retail data: supervised learning approach. In: Computer aided systems theory (EUROCAST 2011). Springer, Berlin, Heidelberg, pp 464–471

Laird JE, Lebiere C, Rosenbloom PS (2017) A standard model of the mind: toward a common computational framework across artificial intelligence, cognitive science, neuroscience, and robotics. AI Mag 38(4):13–26

Laurent P, Chollet T, Herzberg E (2015) Intelligent automation entering the business world. Available at: https://www2.deloitte.com/content/dam/Deloitte/lu/Documents/operations/lu-intelligent-automation-business-world.pdf. Accessed May 12, 2018

Lebied M (2017) 5 examples of how Big Data in logistics can transform the supply chain. Available at: https://www.datapine.com/blog/how-big-data-logistics-transform-supply-chain/. Accessed June 6, 2020

Lingam YK (2018) The role of artificial intelligence (AI) in making accurate stock decisions in E-commerce industry. Int J Adv Res Ideas Innov Technol 4(3):2281–2286

Lourie G (2017) How AI is changing the entertainment industry. Available at: https://techfinancials.co.za/2017/08/24/ai-changing-entertainment-industry/. Accessed May 12, 2018

Magoulas D, Prentza A (2001) Machine learning in medical applications. In: Paliouras G, Karkaletsis V, Spyropoulos CD (eds) Machine learning and its applications: advanced lectures. Lecture notes in computer science, vol 2049. Springer, Berlin, Heidelberg, pp 300–307

Mahendra R (2019) AI is the new electricity. Smart Energy International. Available at: https://www.smart-energy.com/industry-sectors/new-technology/ai-is-the-new-electricity/. Accessed June 6, 2020

Maissin J, Elst R, Colin F (2016) How will IoT improve public sector services? Available at: https://www2.deloitte.com/content/dam/Deloitte/lu/Documents/public-sector/lu_en_how-will-iot-improve-public-sector-services_122015.pdf. Accessed May 12, 2018

Marr B (2017) Internet of Things and predictive maintenance transform the service industry. Available at: https://www.forbes.com/sites/bernardmarr/2017/05/05/Internet-of-things-and-predictive-maintenance-transform-the-service-industry/#4afe904aeaf4. Accessed May 12, 2018

Marr B (2018) The amazing ways Google uses artificial intelligence and satellite data to prevent illegal fishing. Available at: https://www.forbes.com/sites/bernardmarr/2018/04/09/the-amazing-ways-google-uses-artificial-intelligence-and-satellite-data-to-prevent-illegal-fishing/#564ba2e21c14. Accessed May 12, 2018

Matthews S (2016) What is cognitive IoT? Available at: http://www.ibmbigdatahub.com/blog/what-cognitive-iot. Accessed May 12, 2018

Mehr H (2017) Artificial intelligence for citizen services and government. Available at: https://ash.harvard.edu/files/ash/files/artificial_intelligence_for_citizen_services.pdf. Accessed June 3, 2018

Moukalled M, El-Hajj W, Jaber M (2019) Automated stock price prediction using machine learning. Available at: https://ep.liu.se/ecp/165/003/ecp19165003.pdf. Accessed June 19, 2020

Narang N (2017) Top 10 areas artificial intelligence is leading automation in media industry. Available at: http://www.mediaentertainmentinfo.com/2017/09/top-10-areas-artificial-intelligence-is-leading-automation-in-media-industry.html/. Accessed May 12, 2018

National Science and Technology Council (NSTC) (2016) Preparing for the future of artificial intelligence. Available at: https://obamawhitehouse.archives.gov/sites/default/files/whitehouse_files/microsites/ostp/NSTC/preparing_for_the_future_of_ai.pdf. Accessed November 26, 2019

Newman D (2017) Top six digital transformation trends in media and entertainment. Available at: https://www.forbes.com/sites/danielnewman/2017/04/25/top-six-digital-transformation-trends-in-media-and-entertainment/#4138a4166729. Accessed May 12, 2018

Paris C, Swartout W, Mann W (1991) Natural language generation in artificial intelligence and computational linguistics. Springer Science & Business Media

Phillips C (2018) How hotels are using artificial intelligence to provide an awesome user experience. Available at: https://www.kdnuggets.com/2017/06/machine-learning-algorithms-used-self-driving-cars.html. Accessed June 3, 2018

Powal AS (2018) Implementing machine learning – what are the benefits for the energy sector? Available at: https://www.powel.com/news/implementing-machine-learning--what-are-the-benefits-for-the-energy-sector/. Accessed June 3, 2018

Radziwon A, Bilberg AS, Bogers M (2013) The smart factory: exploring adaptive and flexible manufacturing solutions: analysis of Internet of Things in a smart environment. Available at: https://ac.els-cdn.com/S1877705814003543/1-s2.0-S1877705814003543-main.pdf?_tid=1e3f105d-8d9b-4af4-b93f-e6aff870fc95&acdnat=1527338193_6078a0b8963b00a76d6818ad788d6a9c. Accessed May 26, 2018

Rajguru S, Kinhekar S, Pati S (2015) Analysis of Internet of Things in a smart environment. Available at: https://pdfs.semanticscholar.org/35fe/c9f1837928c482ed3ad344fa639736bd2506.pdf. Accessed May 12, 2018

Ravindra S (2017) The machine learning algorithms used in self-driving cars. Available at: https://www.kdnuggets.com/2017/06/machine-learning-algorithms-used-self-driving-cars.html. Accessed May 26, 2018

Reeves M (2018) How AI will reshape companies, industries and nations. Available at: https://www.bcg.com/de-de/publications/2018/artificial-intelligence-will-reshape-companies-industries-nations-interview-kai-fu-lee.aspx. Accessed May 12, 2018

Riedl J (2018) Digital transformation in the logistics industry. Available at: https://www.bcg.com/de-de/industries/transportation-travel-tourism/center-digital-transportation/logistics.aspx. Accessed May 12, 2018

Salas D (2017) How self-service can become more human. Available at: https://www.forbes.com/sites/forbescommunicationscouncil/2017/08/09/how-self-service-can-become-more-human/#8631d7559129. Accessed May 12, 2018

Scanbot SDK (2019) A Scanner SDK for the insurance sector. Available at: https://scanbot.io/en/sdk/industries/insurance-scanner-sdk. Accessed June 19, 2020

Schneider C (2017) 10 reasons why AI-powered, automated customer service is the future. Available at: https://www.ibm.com/blogs/watson/2017/10/10-reasons-ai-powered-automated-customer-service-future/. Accessed May 12, 2018

Schoemaker PJH, Heaton S, Teece D (2018) Innovation, dynamic capabilities, and leadership. Calif Manag Rev 61(1):15–42

Scylla Artificial Intelligence (2020) Available at: https://www.scylla.ai/. Accessed June 19, 2020

SEAB (2020) Preliminary Findings, SEAB AIML Working Group. Available at: https://www.energy.gov/sites/prod/files/2020/04/f73/SEAB%20AI%20WG%20PRELIMINARY%20FINDINGS_0.pdf. Accessed June 6, 2020

Sennaar K (2018) Examples of AI in restaurants and food services. Available at: https://www.techemergence.com/ai-in-restaurants-food-services/. Accessed June 3, 2018

Taylor C (2017) Artificial intelligence and logistics is transforming business. Available at: https://www.datamation.com/big-data/artificial-intelligence-and-logistics-is-transforming-business.html. Accessed June 3, 2018

Techlabs M (2017) Can chatbots help reduce customer service costs by 30 %?. Available at: https://chatbotsmagazine.com/how-with-the-help-of-chatbots-customer-service-costs-could-be-reduced-up-to-30-b9266a369945. Accessed November 30, 2019

Tian Z (2017) Robotic process automation – robots conquer business processes in back offices. Available at: http://digital.pwc.ch/de/blog-detail/rpa-data-analytics-diesel-fuer-die-digitale-transformation.html. Accessed May 12, 2018

Tractica (2020) Warehousing and logistics robots. Available at: https://www.tractica.com/research/warehousing-and-logistics-robots/. Accessed June 6, 2020

Vaishnavi V, Kuechler W, Petter S (2017) Design Science Research in Information Systems. DESRIST.org (created in 2004 and updated until 2015 by Vaishnavi, V. and Kuechler, W.; last updated by Vaishnavi, V. and Petter, S. on 2017/12/20). Accessed June 20, 2020

Valecha H, Varma A, Khare I, Sachdeva A, Goyal M (2018) Prediction of consumer behaviour using random forest algorithm. In: 5th IEEE Uttar Pradesh section international conference on electrical, electronics and computer engineering (UPCON), Gorakhpur, pp 1–6

van der Aalst WMP, Bichler M, Heinzl A (2018) Robotic process automation. Bus Inf Syst Eng 60:269–272

Wei X, Yu-hui Z, Jie-lin Z (2009) Energy-efficient distribution in smart grid. In: 2009 international conference on sustainable power generation and supply. IEEE, pp 1–6

Wettengel J (2016) Volatile but predictable: Forecasting renewable power generation. Available at: https://www.cleanenergywire.org/factsheets/volatile-predictable-forecasting-renewable-power-generation. Accessed June 6, 2020.

Williams A (2010) How Autonomous Mobile Robots Are Changing the Logistics Landscape. Robotics Business Review. Available at: https://www.roboticsbusinessreview.com/supply-chain/autonomous-mobile-robots-changing-logistics-landscape/. Accessed June 6, 2020

Adina Stenzel, Konstantin Ritschel, and Christoph Stummer

18 The broad use of RPA based on three practical cases

Abstract: In this chapter the IT and management consultancy Detecon describes three real-world RPA cases, including determining the need for automation, implementation and challenges, and client benefits. It provides lessons learned for assessing business processes and using RPA-based solutions to optimize manual, outdated, or insufficient processes.

The first case deals with an efficiency increase in the daily business of the public sector. A monthly database extraction is performed automatically to validate personal data entries with an external database. The clients focus was an increase of efficiency in the business process using RPA, which also resulted in higher motivation of the employees.

The second case demonstrates the temporary use of RPA to achieve a business-critical project goal in the telecommunications industry. The goal was to migrate ISDN products to IP technology for large corporate clients in a short period of time. The challenge was to manage and transfer a great amount of data to shut down expensive legacy systems. Thus, the project goal was efficiently achieved with the use of RPA.

The third case illustrates security measures in the daily business of the telecommunications industry by demonstrating the enabling capabilities of RPA towards business processes. It supports the management of firewalls to protect a sensitive technical customer base from external interferences. The robot creates transparency about the network load and reports events, e. g., network attacks to an employee. Therefore, RPA supports optimal network utilization and improved security settings.

The reader shall receive practical insight from the three cases presented. The chapter shows in which scenarios RPA can be used, how RPA can be implemented, and the lessons learned. The reader can take these recommendations into account in a future RPA project to avoid common mistakes in practice.

Keywords: Robotic process automation, business process, practical cases, RPA applications, project approach, telecommunication industry, public sector

18.1 Introduction

According to Gartner, global spending on robotic process automation (RPA) totaled 680 million USD in 2018, an increase of 57 % over the previous year (Gartner, 2018). By 2022 RPA software spending is expected to reach a total of 2.4 billion USD (Statista, 2020). Experts believe the biggest adopters of RPA are organizations running outdated and failing legacy systems. Those organizations include banks, insurance companies,

https://doi.org/10.1515/9783110676693-018

utilities, telecommunications companies, and others (Koch and Fedtke, 2020). Every-day processes often depend on existing legacy systems, and introducing a smarter, more efficient, up-to-date option is often high-priced. RPA is particularly helpful in these situations because it works without changing the existing IT systems. However, there may be circumstances where other automation solutions are a better fit, for example, processes with a frequently changing user interface. RPA would require continuous adjustment due to its dependency on the user interface (AI Multiple, 2020).

The IT and management consultancy Detecon explains the use of RPA based on three real-world examples. This chapter considers cases where Detecon has accompanied clients in increasing their efficiency by applying automation to selected parts of the businesses' internal activities. Detecon shares practical insight and lessons learned to reflect and define an RPA project approach based on experience. Our consulting portfolio includes services to help clients understand RPA at an early stage and support the implementation of RPA. For each of the practical cases we will describe the manual process, how we implemented RPA, and finally the findings of each project. The three cases selected provide insights into the practical usage of RPA, with which we aim to support the decision making process when implementing RPA. The reader shall receive insights into the multitude of motivations for the usage of RPA, and the resulting forms of implementation.

18.2 First practical case: efficiency increase in the public sector

18.2.1 Context and problem description

The first case deals with an efficiency increase in the daily business of an organization within the *public sector*. The clients focus was to reduce the amount of manual work performed by the employees to increase efficiency, sustainability, and general motivation of the employees.

From our perspective, automation can be highly effective for the public sector, as many employees often still perform mundane and repetitive tasks. Digital transformation initiatives have tried to digitalize the public sector for quite some time now. Even to this day, many processes are still paper-driven (Mergel et al., 2019). Public service employees often perform repetitive and time consuming tasks, rather than tasks that take advantage of their analytical and strategic decision making skills (Smeets et al., 2019). Processes that are most suitable for automation in the public sector are processes of high volume, low in variability, rule-based, and with common data types. A few examples are human resource processes, public record inquiries, document management, supplier intake and management, financial and accounting processes, child maintenance, and pension management (Dumitru and Stănculescu, 2020).

The employees of the client in our first case were simply overloaded with paper-driven tasks. One of the client's biggest goals was to help relieve their employees' workload and motivate them to do more engaging and higher-quality tasks. The employees generally welcomed the idea of automating parts of their work but the fear of becoming obsolete was noticeable.

18.2.2 Process before automation

The IT department of the organization performs a monthly data extraction to validate personal, insurance-relevant data entries. The monthly data extraction is then compared with an external web portal, which contains the latest personal information. To do that, the IT department sends an e-mail to the team leader containing the extracted data in an Excel spreadsheet. The team leader then saves the Excel spreadsheet on the team's file share. Before the employees are able to work, the team leader converts and cleanses the data. The team leader prints the Excel file in batches and distributes the lists to the employees.

Each month the employees need to match the spreadsheet with the external database via the web portal, which holds all insurance-relevant changes that might have occurred throughout the month. Now the manual comparison and categorization of each individual data entry begins. After comparing the values cell by cell, the employees make a manual note on the printed list depending on the categorization. If entries in the external database match the information in the Excel spreadsheet, no additional processing is required. If a change of personal data occurs, additional processing is required, and the employee transfers this change of information directly into another internal system.

Most time consuming for the employees is the categorization itself, which is a highly repetitive task and therefore prone to human error. After comparing the information on the paper list with the one in the system, all results of the entries are printed out. As soon as all cases in the printed Excel list have been processed and noted for statistics, the monthly comparison is complete. The documents are kept for one year until they are automatically deleted by the system. A simplified visualization of the manual process is shown in Figure 1.

18.2.3 Automation implementation and challenges

After thoroughly analyzing, documenting, and visualizing the manual process in close consultation with our client, we noticed that the most significant challenge were security restrictions applied to the personal and therefore highly sensitive data. Despite this challenge, we identified the following aspects that could be streamlined through automation without compromising the security of the data.

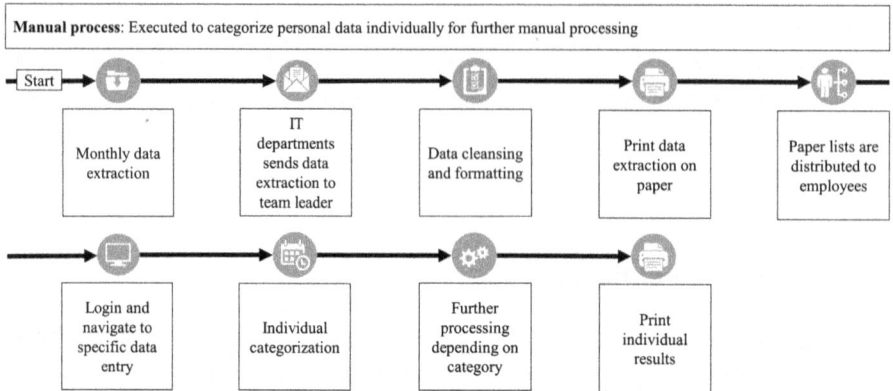

Figure 1: First practical case – manual process.

In the manual process, employees individually categorize each data entry. While designing an optimized process flow, the option to upload one list with all the data entries in the web portal was included, so the employees did not have to categorize each entry individually. The external web portal offered two options through which the data could be compared. One method was the individual comparison (manual process), and the other was a bulk comparison where one list with approximately 20,000 data entries could be uploaded at once. The second option has not been used by the client and follows a certain template with specific file and formatting restrictions for uploading.

In the manual process, the IT department delivered an unfiltered monthly extraction that holds information beyond what is needed. This was why the team leader had to cleanse the data in the manual process. As part of the automation project we decided together with the IT department that the monthly data extraction would follow the required template for the bulk upload, with no additional information. Most of the highly sensitive data were kept where they were and only relevant data for the online query were extracted by the IT department. Therefore, the data cleansing by the team leader was no longer necessary.

As the monthly extracted data still contained personal data, it was important for the client to have a trusted employee manually upload the list with all the entries. To address this requirement, we divided the automated process in three steps.

In the first step of the automated process the robot was programmed to notify the employee monthly when the data are available and ready for upload. The robot is triggered once the IT department provides the data in the required template on the teams file share. Unnecessary e-mail transactions to transfer sensitive data are eliminated. From there, the employee could access the file directly and upload it to the web portal.

After the employee uploaded the file manually and transferred the returned file to the team share, the robot is once again triggered and begins the third automated step. The robot converts the returned file into the required format and begins the comparison of the two files. The robot checks the original file with the received file by examining each entry of the two files to compare and categorize the data. The aim in the initial conception of the RPA script was to divide the data into two categories, one category for unchanged data entries and one for changed data entries. The employees then manually processed the category with changed data entries and updated the changed values in the application.

As an added benefit, the robot created an overview of the categorization for statistical purposes. One employee needed approximately five minutes to categorize each data entry. For 20,000 data entries to categorize, the employee needed 1667 hours. After automation, the robot needs only seven minutes to compare the two files. A visualization of the automated process is shown in Figure 2.

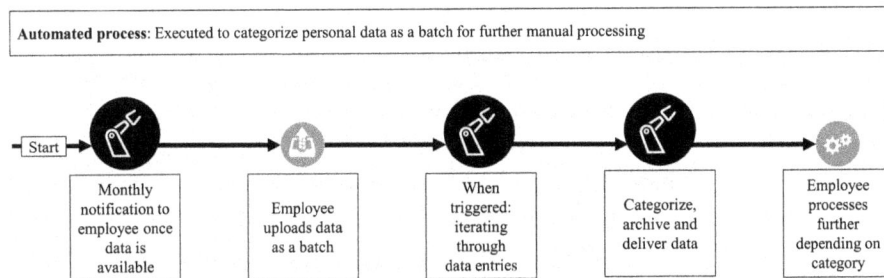

Figure 2: First practical case – automated process.

18.2.4 Findings

In the case presented above, employees not only perform redundant, manual tasks, but they convert already digitalized data into paper lists, only to digitalize them again after updating them. This fact combined with the high transactional volume made it a suitable case to demonstrate how much automation potential lies in the public sector.

Together with the employees, we looked at every step very critically and evaluated whether there was potential to increase efficiency. We advise that the RPA developers work closely together with the employees. It might seem time consuming at first, but in our experience the employees' process knowledge and their work experience must be considered during implementation. In this case, the IT department was asked to format the desired Excel spreadsheet when providing it to the team. This meant that the IT department changed their monthly routine to support the overall efficiency of the business process, even though it was less efficient for the IT department itself. If many different departments depend on each other, it is challenging to organize such a change.

The public service employees still have manual work, but the categorization was outsourced to the robot, which was their most time consuming task. Often tasks are performed a certain way because "it has always been done this way" – no matter how inefficient or outdated the process is. After automating this process, the client's goal of better supporting their employees and freeing up their time for more meaningful tasks was achieved. This case also shows that it is not always necessary to automate an entire process, but it may be sufficient to automate specific time consuming sections of the process.

18.3 Second practical case: RPA to achieve a business-critical project goal

18.3.1 Context and problem description

The second case demonstrates the temporary use of RPA to achieve a business-critical project goal in the *telecommunications industry*. In the context of a network transformation project, ISDN-based connections were migrated to IP technology for large corporate clients. The overall goal was to migrate to IP technology to shut down expensive legacy systems. The challenge was to manage many corporate client migrations in a short period of time.

To migrate the complex corporate client networks, individual target product portfolios had to be determined. Information had to be extracted from multiple systems to prioritize different connection scenarios and work packages.

18.3.2 Process before automation

Within the scope of the IP-based network transformation, individual client connections were converted from ISDN to IP technology. To select the connections to be considered for the conversion, it was necessary to determine the infrastructure conditions at the location of each individual client. To retrieve the relevant information the employee logs on to an application system, navigates to the desired function, and uses an Excel list with the necessary parameters as input.

The first step is to enter the location data. Then the system validates the address. The data fields for the address needed to be separated from a combined string into street, building number, building number suffix, city, and postal code, which was time consuming. In the next step, the employee configured the necessary parameters for choosing the right target product.

The employee then checked the feasibility at the client's location by selecting a connection line for transmission and starting validation. The system then delivered a confirmation of the results for the feasibility of the location. The employee saved these results into the information sheet for the location by manually copy-pasting them. This data extraction was highly standardized and regimented. Visualized in Figure 3 is the manual process for only one of the tasks in the overall process. In the day-to-day business, this step takes several hours due to the number of times it is performed.

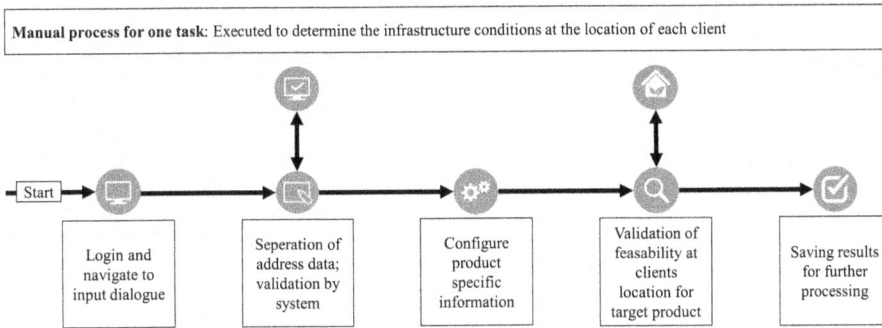

Figure 3: Second practical case – manual process for one of the employees' tasks.

18.3.3 Automation implementation and challenges

For the automated process, it is important to mention that the process itself did not deviate from the manual process. The visualization above for one of the tasks in the overall process would be equal to the automated process of this task. What did change however was the way the data could be accessed by the employee for client consultations. The best possible option to gain the relevant information as a basis for consultation would have been via a database interface.

Unfortunately, it was not possible to query the information on a database level, since the system compiled the feedback from various interfaces, and therefore multiple different databases. However, in this case the web application sends requests to these databases allowing to access the information. Access via web application is a helpful option if information is not accessible via one database alone.

Since the lack of information transparency prevented meaningful prioritization and overall project planning, we programmed the robot to handle the web application and retrieve the data. This was an added benefit for the employee as it performed the highly standardized and rule-based tasks that were most time consuming.

In the further course of the project, the described concept for the use of RPA could be used on a scaled basis. An initiative of the project aimed to improve the project processes by collecting and preparing data. All conventionally available data, accessible via database extracts, was collected. However, required information beyond the available data remained missing. These data were essential for consulting purposes but failed to be obtained conventionally due to their distributed storage in multiple databases. To fix this problem, we provided RPA solutions to access and extract the data. The processes for collecting the data were chosen, because they did not have a dynamic trigger and could be processed as a batch, resulting in a lean robot operation.

The aim was to ensure that the data required for the consultation were available centrally before the consultation and not collected by the consultant during the process itself. This way, the client's consultations were more effective, and the employee was able to focus more on answering the clients open technical question.

18.3.4 Findings

By introducing RPA, an optimized process flow was created that is less time consuming for the employee and more controllable and transparent for management. The employees now interact with fewer systems during the consulting process and thus have increased information transparency for their tasks.

As a result, not only was the process itself optimized, but the process structure was changed as well. Combining RPA with a central data management system provides a transparent overview and helps the employee to access the order placement forms with all the relevant information to successfully migrate the client's connection.

Figure 4 shows the two main benefits for the overall client consultation process for the migration of their network connections: The transparency of data and the creation of relevant order forms replace time consuming manual tasks across multiple research systems.

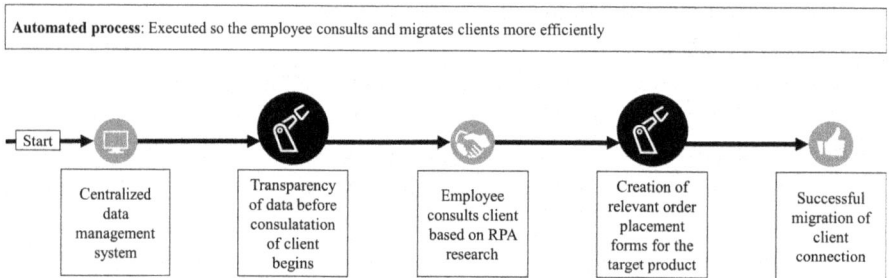

Figure 4: Second practical case – benefits of automation during the overall client consultation process.

An adaptation of the project procedure based on the RPA technology led to the development of further cases in the context of data collection and creation for the migrations of the network connections. This demonstrates a high scalability of RPA applications within projects.

Ultimately, whereas the employee needed approximately three hours to perform the tasks manually, the task after automation was performed in approximately one hour by the employee combined with a robot run-time of three minutes involved. To put this into perspective, this optimized and automated process helped employees to consult 16,000 client locations for research and migrated approximately 34,000 voice connections a lot faster. RPA reduced the end-to-end process run-time by approximately 70 %. The project goal was efficiently achieved by the use of RPA, showing not only that RPA is limited to long-term business process optimization, but also that it can support temporary business-critical project goals in a short period of time.

18.4 Third practical case: security measures in the telecommunications industry

18.4.1 Context and problem description

The third case shows how to design a new use case with RPA to improve the service quality in the daily business of the *telecommunications industry*. The client in this case had no previous experience with RPA. We analyzed potentially interesting cases and checked whether RPA could benefit the client.

The goal was to first gain knowledge and experience with the technology, before any business-critical processes were addressed. The client was only willing to automate processes that did not directly impact core business functions, as they feared potential errors in implementation. After getting to know the technology, the client's aim was to implement RPA solutions to help support everyday business life and improve existing business processes.

18.4.2 Process before automation

In this case, a manual process did not exist because no employee had time to perform the task. This caused a drop in service quality and customer dissatisfaction since errors could only be fixed reactively. The goal was to correct these deficits by using a more proactive approach.

Before the use of RPA, users approached the operational IT support regarding errors that occurred during daily work, including for example "connection errors" or notifications that "application performance is poor." The user created a ticket for the IT department. During the ticket resolution process, the firewall was identified as the cause of the error. IT incident management, together with the firewall administration team, then resolved the error. The problem was that errors were only discovered when they directly affected a user. Other problems remained and reduced the performance of the systems.

18.4.3 Automation implementation and challenges

To identify possible use cases, workshops were held with multiple business units. Methodologically, the workshop was structured with questions directed towards the employees. We deliberately sought out activities that were not being performed due to a lack of employee resources. In the end, after comparing several potential use cases, one was selected that stood out due to its time intensity.

To reduce problems and ensure better performance of the systems, a proactive maintenance of the firewall seemed necessary. Through an assessment of the firewall logs it would be possible to prevent errors from occurring. A preventive approach to addressing misconfigurations in the firewall would, if executed manually, proceed as follows. The employee would log into several virtual desktop connections on the system, where the firewall monitoring is executed. The employee would copy the relevant data into a file and move the file from the virtual desktop to a fully featured desktop environment for troubleshooting. Due to the nested virtual desktop environments, where the user must authenticate themselves several times, the process is error-prone.

The extraction of data from the system needed to be performed via copy and paste actions, as the application offered no interface for data extraction. Depending on the report volume, hundreds of copy and paste actions needed to be performed, a very time consuming task. For these reasons, preventive maintenance of the firewall had not been established. It was not economical to extract the information. However, the use of RPA changes the type of processes that can be performed in the daily business. For example, thousands of copy and paste actions are possible, as required in this case. Tasks like this would be uneconomical for an employee but are well suited for a robot.

The process automated by RPA is executed once a day. The robot replicates the behavior of the employee by logging into the systems, collecting relevant information for potential hazards and creating the report. The report is generated and then sent to the recipient by e-mail. The employee receives the report at the beginning of the working day and is then able to proactively see and react to potential issues, as seen in Figure 5. This creates transparency about the network load and events such as network attacks.

18.4.4 Findings

This case shows how RPA can not only optimize existing processes or help an existing process by performing sub-processes, but also establish new processes to further im-

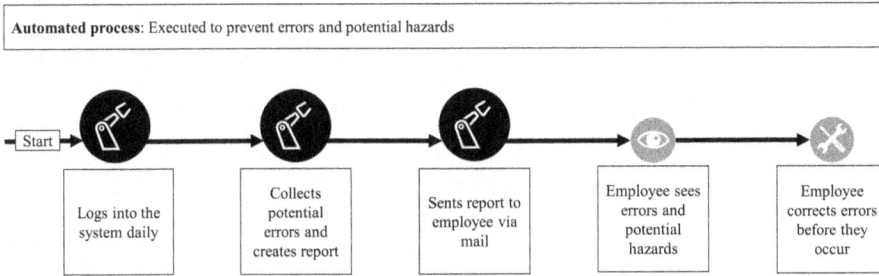

Automated process: Executed to prevent errors and potential hazards

Start
- Logs into the system daily
- Collects potential errors and creates report
- Sents report to employee via mail
- Employee sees errors and potential hazards
- Employee corrects errors before they occur

Figure 5: Third practical case – automated process.

prove business processes. In this case specifically, overall work performance was significantly improved as a result of identifying potential hazards before they occurred. Therefore, RPA supports optimal network utilization and improved security settings. Similar preventive methods can be useful in various domains and industries.

To identify this type of RPA use case, a different approach is needed. Rather than mapping existing processes, you observe ongoing challenges to design new business processes performed by robots. Typically, these processes are not executed due to a high time commitment, high error rates when executed by a person, or a lack of personnel. Since no existing business processes were automated in this example, the effects in the event of errors are minor. This type of RPA application is therefore a good introduction to the topic to gain experience and realize first economic successes.

18.5 Recapitulation of the practical cases

The three cases show that existing processes can be improved, RPA can be beneficial in projects, and new business processes performed by robots can be designed. In Table 1, we summarize the relevant criteria of the three cases presented. The distinguishing criteria are impact, industry, periodicity, added value, and quantity.

While there are many possibilities to determine whether the usage of RPA is senseful or not, we added five parameters based on our project experience that can be considered as guidance:
1. If you have strict, rules-based, high-volume transactions in your organization.
2. If you have internal processes that interact with multiple different applications or systems. Since RPA does not need to change existing systems, it can help transfer information faster than any employee.
3. If you are part of an industry or department with a high workload outside the regular office hours, as RPA can be operated 24/7.
4. If gaps in digitization can be cushioned by so-called "swivel chair activities," where data are entered into one system and then the same data are entered into another system.

5. If your employees cannot focus on higher-quality activities due to a high volume of administrative, repetitive tasks, you can relief your employees of those tasks through the usage of RPA.

Table 1: Distinctive criteria of the practical cases.

Distinctive criteria	Case 1	Case 2	Case 3
Impact	Optimizing existing process	Temporary support to achieve the project goal	New process
Industry	Public industry	Telecommunication industry	Telecommunication industry
Periodicity	Monthly	Once	Daily
Added value	Increase of performance and employee satisfaction	Time saving and higher customer satisfaction	Increase of quality and performance; preventive method to handle errors
Quantity	>20,000 data entries per month	Support of consulting 16,000 client locations for research and 34,000 voice connections	Approximately 10 error notifications a day

The cases have shown us that, in addition to the correct selection of the use of RPA, based on process analysis, the early involvement of the employees and decision makers concerned is also essential. One of the most common challenges is that it is not clear who is responsible for developing and operating RPA projects. A possible reason may be that once the RPA script is developed, the operational implementation is unsuccessful because the business or IT department does not have the time or resources to align with each other. For RPA to be effective, there must be clear responsibility or a central RPA team that has the time and skills to analyze potential processes and align IT and business departments (Langmann and Turi, 2020).

RPA is a lean technology, but in spite of that, or perhaps because of it, you need a solid strategy or governance behind it. We often experience that RPA is perceived as a trend technology to quickly close automation gaps. Nevertheless, the basis for successful implementation and operation must be created in advance to achieve the desired effects in the long term (Jovanović et al., 2018).

18.6 Our RPA approach

Based on the three practical cases and lessons learned within RPA projects similar to the ones described, we designed an initial approach towards RPA, visualized in Figure 6. As part of the initial implementation, we advise considering the topic of setting up a center of excellence. For subsequent implementation, the approach can be used in an adapted form, based on the knowledge and circumstances in the company.

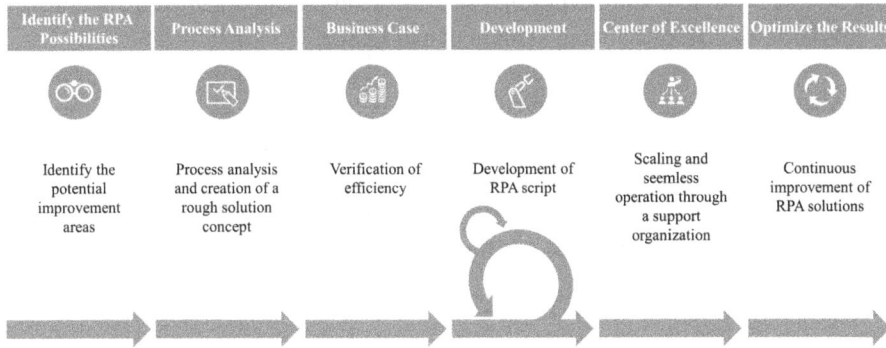

Figure 6: Our RPA project approach.

In the first step of our approach, RPA possibilities are identified. We recommend testing RPA optimization possibilities in various process areas through short sprints. Furthermore, we advise any organization considering automation to first thoroughly analyze the manual business processes before performing any automation work. This way any unnecessary or outdated steps can be eliminated and the process itself can be optimized before any automation work begins. Automating outdated steps is just as inefficient as performing them manually. When choosing a process, it is advised to consider a large number of different processes. If a high number of cases are considered, the comparison of the individual processes makes it easier to determine where RPA is most useful and has the most impact.

In the second step, all possible potential areas for improvement are analyzed through the creation of a brief solution concept. Then, we conduct and document a detailed process analysis of the status quo. This step includes how the process can be optimized and defining the success factors to be achieved with the use of RPA. On this basis, we are able to determine the applicability of RPA and transfer the process to a prioritized RPA backlog.

In the third step, the feasibility of the chosen RPA possibility is analyzed by creating a business case for each of the processes under consideration. If the business case shows that the selected use case is feasible for the client, the development of an RPA script begins. Within the software of the RPA supplier the process flow is reconstructed and thus the RPA script is developed.

As part of the fourth step, a first minimum viable product (MVP) should be developed and tested to show technical feasibility. The different interfaces to the business units, triggers, and input and output parameters for the robot should be clarified at an early stage. After the MVP is developed, the solution is transferred to operations and documentation is handed over to the client. During the first few weeks of implementation our team provides a service for dedicated monitoring of the process operation.

Step five is to work on setting up a support organization for RPA solutions. The goal is to promote RPA within the company and establish an organizational support for RPA solutions by introducing a center of excellence.

In the final and sixth phase, the existing RPA processes will be further optimized and enriched with additional technologies. They will be considered as part of the next wave of RPA improvement and will therefore be continuously developed. We mentioned to carefully analyze, document, and visualize the manual process before performing any automation work before. The truth is the optimization should never stop. For RPA to be as effective as it can be, it needs continuous improvement.

18.7 Conclusion

To explain RPA and achieve employee buy-in for automation projects is one of the most challenging aspects of automating business processes. Fear of automation making our jobs obsolete is common. However, the possibility that automation creates new, more engaging, and challenging tasks for employees that require decision making skills is often overlooked. If an employee must perform many redundant tasks, it might seem that the employee's whole job is redundant – and therefore the fear of not being needed or the fear of being easily replaced arises. No employee wants to be redundant. But the underlying message is that only redundant tasks should be eliminated so the employee can evolve and move on to more digital and challenging tasks and therefore grow professionally. Employees should not see RPA as a threat but as a support, especially when it comes to relieving mundane and repetitive tasks. This way, employees are encouraged to actively participate in digitization initiatives. The following guidelines summarize our experience from RPA projects. In our opinion, the application of these guidelines provides for a higher efficiency in the topic RPA:
- Expertise should be built up in the company to implement RPA solutions and operate the infrastructure.
- Processes should be identified and checked for RPA relevance.
- Optimization before automating business processes should be considered.
- Stakeholders and affected persons should be involved in RPA projects at an early stage.
- Change management and communication measures should ensure that employees and RPA are aligned.
- Responsibility between RPA owner, IT department, and business side should be determined.
- Synchronization between legacy systems and RPA should be ensured.

– Agile development and project management should be paired with RPA.
– The governance and operation for RPA projects should be centrally defined.

These guidelines demonstrate the criticality of change management and governance in any RPA approach. In the long term, these two core dimensions are essential to the success of RPA projects within your company.

Bibliography

AI Multiple (2020) 70 process automation tools of 2020: a comprehensive guide. Massachusetts, United States

Dumitru VF, Stănculescu SM (2020) In: 6th BASIQ international conference on new trends in sustainable business and consumption Editura ASE, Messina, Italy, pp 105–112

Gartner, Inc. (2018) Press releases. Goa, India

Jovanović SZ, Durić JS, Šibalija TV (2018) Robotic process automation: overview and opportunities. Int J Adv Qual 6

Koch C, Fedtke S (2020) Der Rollout – wie führe ich RPA flächendeckend im Unternehmen ein? Springer Vieweg, Berlin, Heidelberg

Langmann C, Turi D (2020) Robotic Process Automation (RPA)-Digitalisierung und Automatisierung von Prozessen. Springer Books, Germany

Mergel IE Edelmann N Haug N (2019) Defining digital transformation: Results from expert interviews. Germany and Austria: Government Information Quarterly

Smeets ME, Erhard R, Kaußler T (2019) Robotic Process Automation (RPA) in der Finanzwirtschaft. Springer Books, Germany

Statista (2020) Robotic process automation software market revenue worldwide 2017–2022. Worldwide

Andreas Kronz and Thomas Thiel

19 Digitization applied to automate freight paper processing

How EgeTrans Internationale Spedition GmbH achieves end-to-end automation by an integrated application of RPA and OCR

Abstract: Until today, paper-based tasks are part of a large part of the executed business processes. The successful management of the resulting media discontinuities consists not only of automated data extraction from unavoidable paper documents, but also of automated further processing, which can be successfully realized with robotic process automation (RPA) in many cases. This article outlines a real-life project in the German logistics industry. EgeTrans Internationale Spedition GmbH makes use of a combination of optic character recognition and RPA to extract information from freight papers and transfer it to their legacy transport management system. Detailed information about challenges, objectives, and solutions is provided to help the reader understand the journey which EgeTrans and their advisors from Scheer Group have been going through in the course of the project.

Keywords: Process automation, logistics, robotic process automation, manual task, OCR, freight papers

19.1 Status quo

Over the past years, talks about digital transformation and disruptive business models have become omni-present. Decision makers are confused by the large number of differing views on what these buzz words actually mean. Consequently, they do not know how to tackle the resulting challenges in their companies. As a matter of fact, digital technologies have changed the way we communicate, consume, and live both our private and our professional lives. But what does this development imply for daily operations in an ordinary company? Digitization has not only created entirely new lines of business, it has also both changed customer expectations and increased cost pressure. Consequently, businesses not keeping up with the rapidly proceeding technical developments will lose competitiveness in the future. The only way out is to take action.

This case study aims at making the topic more tangible for practitioners by outlining one stage of the digital transformation journey of EgeTrans Internationale Spedition GmbH (EgeTrans), an innovative and internationally oriented logistics company based near Stuttgart, Germany. During the project, EgeTrans enjoyed the support of Scheer's consulting practice. The project's objective was to automate one of the firm's core business processes, i. e., the transfer of data from incoming freight papers to their transportation management system (TMS).

https://doi.org/10.1515/9783110676693-019

19.2 Companies involved

19.2.1 EgeTrans Internationale Spedition GmbH

In today's dynamic and highly globalized world economy, fast and efficient movement of goods across all borders has become indispensable for the success of internationally operating industrial companies. The logistics required for this must be able to flexibly adapt to these needs. The globally active medium-sized logistics firm EgeTrans headquartered in Marbach am Neckar, together with its two subsidiaries based in the US and Mexico, has set itself the goal to fulfill this need. The group specializes primarily in the two large and globally relevant markets of Europe and North America.

EgeTrans acts as a professional and competent partner of industry in logistics management as well as procurement logistics and offers its clients tailor-made solutions in these areas. The locations in Europe and North and Central America control the entire goods process, from on-time transport to the seamless supply of parts to numerous international industrial companies. The company has its main fields of activity in the following areas:

- worldwide air and sea transport from and to Europe;
- European and North American overland transport;
- supply chain and logistics management (warehousing, customs, logistics services);
- full-service freight handling through door-to-door services;
- value-added services.

Being an owner-managed family business with lean structures, fast decision making, clear responsibilities, and fast communication gives EgeTrans a high level of agility and creates room for smart solutions – allowing to go off the beaten track and to constantly deliver great impact.

The success of EgeTrans is based on two factors: clients and employees. They form the basis on which the business can be further expanded. EgeTrans as a brand is synonymous with an exceptional level of service quality. This is reflected in seamless customer care, a constant flow of information, very fast response times, a clearly defined personal contact for each client, and the support of the entire team. The firm's dogma to grow through and with both its customers and its employees is reflected in its rigorous innovation approach. EgeTrans constantly invests in its human capital by offering an extensive training portfolio and by fostering international staff exchange. Likewise, technological developments are followed closely. Given a positive outcome of the following detailed analysis, new developments which add value are absorbed quickly, but always at a controlled speed to ensure a sustainable long-term development.

19.2.2 Scheer GmbH

Scheer GmbH is the flagship company of Scheer Group, which operates in various European countries as well as in the US, Singapore, and Australia. Dr. August-Wilhelm Scheer, being professor of business informatics, inventor of the ARIS concept, and successful entrepreneur, founded Scheer Group as a network of strong-growing IT companies. Close cooperation with science and research enhances the innovative strength of the different companies and opens up new markets. As a consulting and software house with proven process expertise, Scheer GmbH supports companies in the development of new business models, with the optimization and implementation of efficient business processes as well as with the dependable operation of their IT systems. Scheer is the partner of choice for many well-known companies working towards the useful and efficient implementation of SAP and SAP S/4 HANA. Furthermore, consulting in the context of the current development of business process management, process mining, and robotic process automation (RPA) support the quality of innovative business model processes.

19.2.3 Automation subject: the business process

In a nutshell, the core function of a logistics company is to plan, carry out, and control the movement of goods within a supply chain, i. e., between the points of origin and consumption. On an operational level, goods received on a daily basis are redistributed and shipped in the optimal way considering various factors such as speed and cost-efficiency. The necessary planning is complex and performed with the help of a TMS. The objective of the project outlined in the present case study was to optimize the process of capturing and transferring the data needed by the TMS. Prior to the automation, the process was performed manually, i. e., an employee read the freight papers and manually input the data into the TMS.

Issues faced by EgeTrans due to the manual processing of data are both obvious and typical for business processes being considered for automation through RPA. Working with big amounts of data or repeating the same task again and again, it is very human to make mistakes. The reason behind this is very simple. Humans are excellent in using creativity to solve complex problems and in reacting to changing circumstances. This is how evolution brought us to the top of the food chain. Being trapped in tedious tasks, however, our brains lose focus and we make clerical mistakes. Of course, you can apply the four-eyes principle to enhance data quality, but this approach is intensive in both time and cost. And this is where RPA comes in. Being computer programs, software robots are resistant to the type of error described before. And moreover, they are much faster in performing repetitive tasks and easy to duplicate or retrain for other purposes if not needed anymore. All in all, these reasons made EgeTrans decide for an automation of the process, which is outlined in Figure 1.

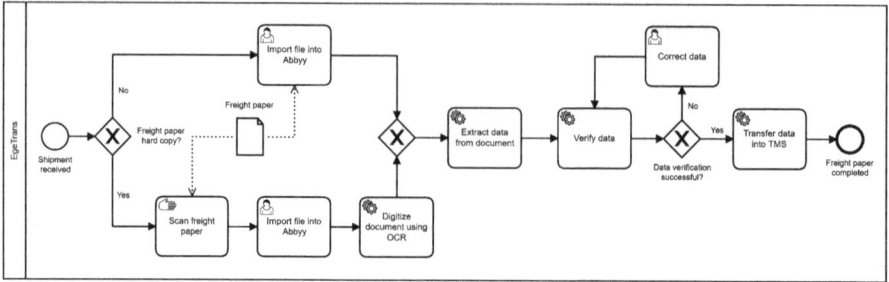

Figure 1: Automated business process.

The aforementioned criteria of processing speed and error reduction are among the top arguments in the majority of RPA projects. The actual impact on the business process however depends on various factors and differs from project to project. In the application case at hand, EgeTrans managed to decrease average processing time by 72%. Simultaneously, data quality increased significantly, with 15% of documents being marked for manual review by the system.

19.3 Technical components

19.3.1 RPA and the idea of hyper-automation

Even though a standard definition does not exist, a software robot can be defined as a configurable computer program with the ability to emulate human interaction with a computer. In their early days, software robots were mainly running on remote computers to perform repetitive and tedious tasks. Their ability to control computer programs with both graphical and command line interfaces made them the method of choice to automate labor-intensive standard processes for early adopters like the financial industry (Feld et al., 2020). With an increasing automation level of these straightforward processes, there have been calls for advanced ways to automate more complex routines. This development paved the way for the next stage of robotic process automation (Scheer, 2017). Figure 2 shows the contemporary approach of hyper-automation, whereas the technologies displayed are only an extract of the full list. Hyper-automation describes the idea of combining advanced technologies to automate complex processes (Gartner, 2019).

Hyper-automation is the next level of robotic process automation. RPA shown in the middle does not mean it is more important than the other technologies. It rather underlines the fact that RPA often acts as the link in between. To make an example, imagine a customer service process where a client interacts with a chat bot. The chat bot finds out about the client's need and asks for all the necessary details before hav-

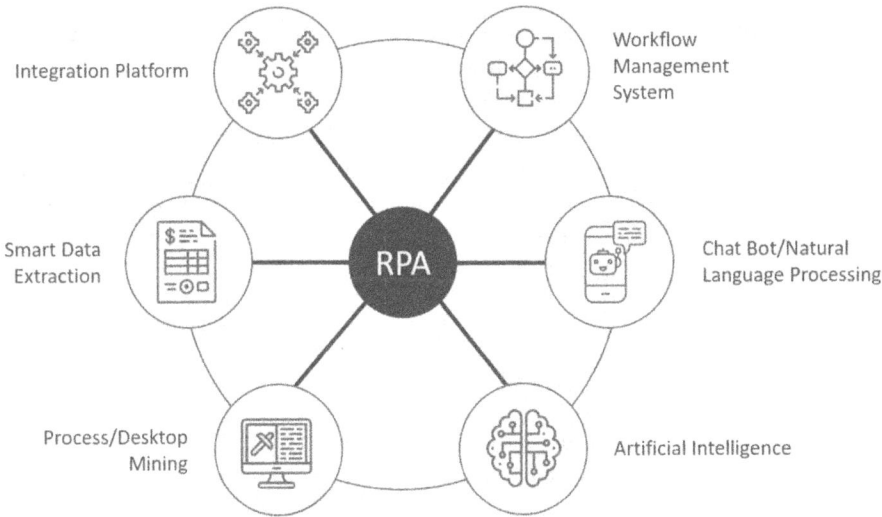

Figure 2: Hyper-automation approach.

ing a software robot perform a value adding process, e. g., looking up data in some system or creating a document for the customer. Having received the deliverable back from the software robot, the chat bot hands it over to the customer and finishes the conversation. In this scenario, the robot does not only create the deliverable, but also acts as an interface. To sum up, hyper-automation is the idea of automating processes end-to-end, making use of a variety of technologies. RPA, utilizing its unrivaled flexibility, often acts as a bridge in this context. Having this in mind, the project at hand also falls in the category of hyper-automation. The freight paper processing was automated from end to end, from reading data out of a document to entering them into the TMS. The technologies used to reach this goal were RPA and optical character recognition (OCR).

19.3.2 OCR

The described freight paper processing demands a feature which goes beyond the core RPA functionality: extracting data from documents. A special need of EgeTrans in this context was that the process had to be able to process both digital and analogue (originally paper-based) documents. Digital documents, usually present in the form of native PDFs, contain both an image layer which humans read and an invisible text layer which can be used by a computer to understand what is written in the document. On the contrary, analogue documents, usually present in the form of scanned PDFs, only contain an image layer which cannot be directly interpreted by a machine. To make analogue documents machine-readable, they must run through a procedure called

OCR. Having machine-readable documents is only the first step, though. The business need was to specifically extract data from them. This step is called document understanding. Like freight papers, many other business documents like invoices contain tables which need to be extracted. The challenge here is that even native PDF files often do not contain real tables, but the table is just a visual feature. As a simplification in the course of this text, the totality of technologies used to extract data from business documents is referred to as OCR. Even though offered by some RPA vendors from one source, RPA and OCR should always be considered separately.

19.3.3 Solution design

As mentioned before, hyper-automation aims at automating processes from end to end. Eliminating potential disruptions of the digital process flow is hence a top priority. It is acceptable – and in many cases even explicitly desired – to have selected steps performed by human employees. To not sabotage your own digitization progress, it is however crucial that the execution of these human tasks stays inside the digital ecosystem. To make an example, if a process includes a decision which shall be made by a human, each of them can be represented by a distinct task in a workflow management system. This approach guarantees the necessary levels of transparency and integration. Even though not relevant to the described project, it shall be mentioned that the in this way generated digital records about human decision behavior are highly valuable for possible usage as input for machine learning and a subsequent application of artificial intelligence (AI) to support humans in decision making. With regard to the EgeTrans process, a stringent end-to-end automation has been achieved by applying the setup shown in Figure 3.

Figure 3: Solution design.

Freight papers arrive at EgeTrans via e-mail. This has not changed compared to the pre-automation process. Naturally, digitization is change. Nevertheless, modifications should not be forced where not indispensable. Man is a creature of habit. It is very common to refuse change if it comes too fast. Where possible, it is always a good idea to leave anchor points unchanged when digitizing a business process. An end-to-end automated process has the advantage that it can be performed independently of any human interaction. That is why it is not an employee watching the e-mail inbox. Instead, EgeTrans has a software robot do this job around the clock. After classifying an incoming e-mail as relevant to the process and performing some initial checks, the robot imports the attachment into the OCR suite which afterwards performs all the necessary steps to extract the desired data from the document. If the software faces any issues, e. g., part of the data cannot be found or reliably extracted, a task is created in a dedicated part of the suite. Subsequently, an employee needs to look into the issue and fix it before the process can continue. This is a typical example of human–robot collaboration, which is another characteristic of hyper-automation. Following the verification step, the process is resumed by the software robot. Finally, it enters the extracted data into the TMS. In the case of EgeTrans, the TMS is a command line-based software which makes the automation of the process an even greater relief for the employees.

19.4 Recommendations

An old saying is that mistakes are the best teachers. In times of agile project methodologies, this wisdom is all the more true. But even if there is nothing worth to be called a mistake, the underlying principle of continuous learning is vital to corporate project management. In that sense, of course there are lessons to be learned from EgeTrans' freight paper processing automation. With this case study, the authors hope to give readers seeking to get into or deepen their knowledge in the topic some helpful guidance by making recommendations for mastering the complex task of digitizing their companies.

Get started. Now
Digitization has been a buzzword in politics and boardrooms for years. The degree of implementation however is lagging behind. There are a lot of reasons why companies should finally enter the digital age. Two of them however are compelling. First, there is efficiency. Increasing efficiency through automation is particularly important for established companies seeing themselves confronted with a growing number of customer attracting startups in their industries. These firms do not struggle with making themselves fit for the future, they did rather never ever have any outdated processes. This gives them the decisive competitive advantage of lower cost for producing products and services. Second, there is access to clients and employees. Whereas long established for physical products, convenience or ease of use has made it to particular importance also for services. In the age of apps, it is fatal to not keep up with contemporary ways of client communication. Both product placement and scaling become exceptionally difficult when not matching the customer favorite. Whereas the described problem seems obvious for client access, the same is true for attracting and retaining workforce. It is becoming increasingly difficult to find staff proficient in operating legacy systems or willing to work with antiquated analogue processes that do

not match their digital life styles. The crux of the matter here is: If you have not taken the first step of your digitization journey, get started. Now.

Define a clear strategy

"A vision without a strategy remains an illusion" (Forbes, 2018). In practice, many companies start small. Their first step is to experiment with new technologies like RPA or AI. The concept proven, the next stage is a pilot. Again successful, they say they enter the scaling phase. Scaling can however not succeed if it consists of the consecutive implementation of detached projects. With regard to digitization, the whole being more than the sum of its parts means that its full potential can only be realized if all parts are well connected. Thinking of digitization as a puzzle, it is not sufficient to collect all the pieces; they also need to be put together. End-to-end automation is not just a dictum for single processes, the principle rather also applies on a company level. It is perfectly acceptable – often even the method of choice – to have an innovation approach relying on try and error, intentionally failing on a small scale to trigger insights and consequently succeed on a large scale. Make sure however to have a clear strategy. It is the key to the successful transition from exploration to exploitation.

Apply the principles of hyper-automation

This rule goes alongside with having a well-defined digitization strategy. As this case study is about automation, it shall however be particularly highlighted. Hyper-automation is the path to creating the automated, intelligent enterprise of tomorrow. When developing your automation plan, make sure to incorporate the dogma's major principles. The robotization of single processes to boost efficiency is not the ultimate goal. You rather want to perform a transformation towards a fully automated and integrated process landscape meeting today's requirements, but also being flexible enough to react to future changes at any time. This first objective of hyper-automation can only be reached by an integrating application of the entire spectrum of state-of-the-art technologies, part of which are displayed in Figure 2. The second principle of hyper-automation is the democratization of technology. Technology democratization means to grant everybody, i. e., also the average business users outside of specialized functions and the internal IT department, access to technology tools. By doing so, the approach underlines the idea of a decentralized IT organization. In practice though, having citizen developers implement technical solutions quickly runs up against its limitations. Oftentimes, fostering the collaboration between business users and professional developers is the more promising concept. Possible actions include installing a center of excellence being in charge of both strategy definition and execution. The team should maintain an extended network in the entire organization and enable employees to file automation ideas through a standardized and easy-to-use process. The third doctrine worth to be mentioned in this context is the promotion of human–robot collaboration. Whereas the success of RPA during its early days was mainly due to unattended robots, the current trend is towards attended automation, i. e., processes which intendedly need human attention (Thiel and Kronz, 2020). The authors are of the opinion that in the future, companies will provide more and more employees with their own software robots of various kinds for individual assistance. Without elaborating on the widespread alarmism that RPA will cause mass unemployment, the goal of digitization is not to create deserted offices (Abolhassan, 2017). Humans will keep playing a key role in the value creation of the economy. Just like humankind has always used tools to accomplish things that are impossible with bare hands, digitization is just the application of this principle to business processes. Supported by a combination of software robots and complementary technologies, human employees are relieved of stupid and at the same time error-prone work and can concentrate on activities that really add value.

Change is pain

It lies in the nature of the human being to be skeptical about change at first. It is important to respect your employees' fears. To overcome their concerns, take everybody by their hands and make your firm's digitization a joint journey (Thiel and Kronz, 2020). As a side mark, this phenomenon does not depend on the kind of change which is about to be induced. Change management is a wide-ranging and independent topic, but should not go unmentioned as a decisive success factor in the course of this case study. Many digitization projects have failed because they were set up and carried out as pure technology projects, but ignored the organizational change aspect. In practice, a distinct change manager role has proven to be a promising approach.

Bibliography

Abolhassan F (2017) Robotic Process Automation macht Unternehmen produktiver – wenn sie die Mannschaft mitnehmen. IM+io Fachmag 3. https://www.im-io.de/digitalisierung/robotic-process-automation-macht-unternehmen-produktiver-wenn-sie-die-mannschaft-mitnehmen/

Feld T, Kronz A, Scheer A-W (2020) Wie Unternehmen von Robotic Process Automation profitieren. Scheer Group. https://www.scheer-group.com/workingpaper-rpa/

Forbes (2018) Why do strategies fail? https://www.forbesindia.com/blog/business-strategy/why-do-strategies-fail/

Gartner (2019) Gartner Top 10 Strategic Technology Trends for 2020. https://www.gartner.com/smarterwithgartner/gartner-top-10-strategic-technology-trends-for-2020/

Scheer A-W (2017) Robotic Process Automation: Revolution der Unternehmenssoftware. IM+io Fachmag 3:30–41. https://www.im-io.de/mdocs-posts/imio-art-07-scheer/

Thiel T, Kronz A (2020) 7 Fakten über Robotic Process Automation. Process 3:38–42

Index

www.ingramcontent.com/pod-product-compliance
Lightning Source LLC
Chambersburg PA
CBHW080139220326
41598CB00032B/5118